Dreamweaver™
Bible

Dreamweaver™ Bible

Joseph W. Lowery

IDG Books Worldwide, Inc.
An International Data Group Company

Foster City, CA ✦ Chicago, IL ✦ Indianapolis, IN ✦ New York, NY

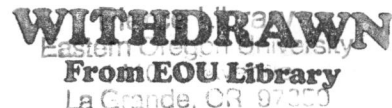

Dreamweaver™ Bible

Published by
IDG Books Worldwide, Inc.
An International Data Group Company
919 E. Hillsdale Blvd., Suite 400
Foster City, CA 94404
www.idgbooks.com (IDG Books Worldwide Web site)

Library of Congress Catalog Card Number: 98-071856

ISBN: 0-7645-3225-1

Printed in the United States of America

10 9 8 7 6 5 4 3 2 1

XX/RR/QY/ZY/FC

Distributed in the United States by IDG Books Worldwide, Inc.

Distributed by Macmillan Canada for Canada; by Transworld Publishers Limited in the United Kingdom; by IDG Norge Books for Norway; by IDG Sweden Books for Sweden; by Woodslane Pty. Ltd. for Australia; by Woodslane (NZ) Ltd. for New Zealand; by Addison Wesley Longman Singapore Pte Ltd. for Singapore, Malaysia, Thailand, Indonesia, and Korea; by Norma Comunicaciones S.A. for Colombia; by Intersoft for South Africa; by International Thomson Publishing for Germany, Austria, and Switzerland; by Toppan Company Ltd. for Japan; by Distribuidora Cuspide for Argentina; by Livraria Cultura for Brazil; by Ediciencia S.A. for Ecuador; by Ediciones ZETA S.C.R. Ltda. for Peru; by WS Computer Publishing Corporation, Inc., for the Philippines; by Unalis Corporation for Taiwan; by Contemporanea de Ediciones for Venezuela; by Computer Book & Magazine Store for Puerto Rico; by Express Computer Distributors for the Caribbean and West Indies. Authorized Sales Agent: Anthony Rudkin Associates for the Middle East and North Africa.

For general information on IDG Books Worldwide's books in the U.S., please call our Consumer Customer Service department at 800-762-2974. For reseller information, including discounts and premium sales, please call our Reseller Customer Service department at 800-434-3422.

For information on where to purchase IDG Books Worldwide's books outside the U.S., please contact our International Sales department at 650-655-3200 or fax 650-655-3297.

For information on foreign language translations, please contact our Foreign & Subsidiary Rights department at 650-655-3021 or fax 650-655-3281.

For sales inquiries and special prices for bulk quantities, please contact our Sales department at 650-655-3200 or write to the address above.

For information on using IDG Books Worldwide's books in the classroom or for ordering examination copies, please contact our Educational Sales department at 800-434-2086 or fax 317-596-5499.

For press review copies, author interviews, or other publicity information, please contact our Public Relations department at 650-655-3000 or fax 650-655-3299.

For authorization to photocopy items for corporate, personal, or educational use, please contact Copyright Clearance Center, 222 Rosewood Drive, Danvers, MA 01923, or fax 978-750-4470.

is a trademark under exclusive license to IDG Books Worldwide, Inc., from International Data Group, Inc.

ABOUT IDG BOOKS WORLDWIDE

Welcome to the world of IDG Books Worldwide.

IDG Books Worldwide, Inc., is a subsidiary of International Data Group, the world's largest publisher of computer-related information and the leading global provider of information services on information technology. IDG was founded more than 25 years ago and now employs more than 8,500 people worldwide. IDG publishes more than 275 computer publications in over 75 countries (see listing below). More than 90 million people read one or more IDG publications each month.

Launched in 1990, IDG Books Worldwide is today the #1 publisher of best-selling computer books in the United States. We are proud to have received eight awards from the Computer Press Association in recognition of editorial excellence and three from *Computer Currents'* First Annual Readers' Choice Awards. Our best-selling *...For Dummies*® series has more than 50 million copies in print with translations in 38 languages. IDG Books Worldwide, through a joint venture with IDG's Hi-Tech Beijing, became the first U.S. publisher to publish a computer book in the People's Republic of China. In record time, IDG Books Worldwide has become the first choice for millions of readers around the world who want to learn how to better manage their businesses.

Our mission is simple: Every one of our books is designed to bring extra value and skill-building instructions to the reader. Our books are written by experts who understand and care about our readers. The knowledge base of our editorial staff comes from years of experience in publishing, education, and journalism — experience we use to produce books for the '90s. In short, we care about books, so we attract the best people. We devote special attention to details such as audience, interior design, use of icons, and illustrations. And because we use an efficient process of authoring, editing, and desktop publishing our books electronically, we can spend more time ensuring superior content and spend less time on the technicalities of making books.

You can count on our commitment to deliver high-quality books at competitive prices on topics you want to read about. At IDG Books Worldwide, we continue in the IDG tradition of delivering quality for more than 25 years. You'll find no better book on a subject than one from IDG Books Worldwide.

John Kilcullen
CEO
IDG Books Worldwide, Inc.

Steven Berkowitz
President and Publisher
IDG Books Worldwide, Inc.

*Eighth Annual
Computer Press
Awards ≥1992*

*Ninth Annual
Computer Press
Awards ≥1993*

*Tenth Annual
Computer Press
Awards ≥1994*

*Eleventh Annual
Computer Press
Awards ≥1995*

IDG Books Worldwide, Inc., is a subsidiary of International Data Group, the world's largest publisher of computer-related information and the leading global provider of information services on information technology. International Data Group publishes over 275 computer publications in over 75 countries. More than 90 million people read one or more International Data Group publications each month. International Data Group's publications include: **ARGENTINA:** Buyer's Guide, Computerworld Argentina, PC World Argentina; **AUSTRALIA:** Australian Macworld, Australian PC World, Australian Reseller News, Computerworld, IT Casebook, Network World, Publish, Webmaster; **AUSTRIA:** Computerwelt Osterreich, Networks Austria, PC Tip Austria; **BANGLADESH:** PC World Bangladesh; **BELARUS:** PC World Belarus; **BELGIUM:** Data News; **BRAZIL:** Annuário de Informática, Computerworld, Connections, Macworld, PC Player, PC World, Publish, Reseller News, Supergamepower; **BULGARIA:** Computerworld Bulgaria, Network World Bulgaria, PC & MacWorld Bulgaria; **CANADA:** CIO Canada, Client/Server World, ComputerWorld Canada, InfoWorld Canada, NetworkWorld Canada, WebWorld; **CHILE:** Computerworld Chile, PC World Chile; **COLOMBIA:** Computerworld Colombia, PC World Colombia; **COSTA RICA:** PC World Centro America; **THE CZECH AND SLOVAK REPUBLICS:** Computerworld Czechoslovakia, Macworld Czech Republic, PC World Czechoslovakia; **DENMARK:** Communications World Danmark, Computerworld Danmark, Macworld Danmark, PC World Danmark, Techworld Denmark; **DOMINICAN REPUBLIC:** PC World Republica Dominicana; **ECUADOR:** PC World Ecuador; **EGYPT:** Computerworld Middle East, PC World Middle East; **EL SALVADOR:** PC World Centro America; **FINLAND:** MikroPC, Tietoverkko, Tietoviikko; **FRANCE:** Distributique, Hebdo, Info PC, Le Monde Informatique, Macworld, Reseaux & Telecoms, WebMaster France; **GERMANY:** Computer Partner, Computerwoche, Computerwoche Extra, Computerwoche FOCUS, Global Online, Macwelt, PC Welt; **GREECE:** Amiga Computing, GamePro Greece, Multimedia World; **GUATEMALA:** PC World Centro America; **HONDURAS:** PC World Centro America; **HONG KONG:** Computerworld Hong Kong, PC World Hong Kong, Publish in Asia; **HUNGARY:** ABCD CD-ROM, Computerworld Szamitastechnika, Internetto online Magazine, PC World Hungary, PC-X Magazin Hungary; **ICELAND:** Tolvuheimur PC World Island; **INDIA:** Information Communications World, Information Systems Computerworld, PC World India, Publish in Asia; **INDONESIA:** InfoKomputer PC World, Komputek Computerworld, Publish in Asia; **IRELAND:** ComputerScope, PC Live!; **ISRAEL:** Macworld Israel, People & Computers/Computerworld; **ITALY:** Computerworld Italia, Macworld Italia, Networking Italia, PC World Italia; **JAPAN:** DTP World, Macworld Japan, Nikkei Personal Computing, OS/2 World Japan, SunWorld Japan, Windows NT World, Windows World Japan; **KENYA:** PC World East African; **KOREA:** Hi-Tech Information, Macworld Korea, PC World Korea; **MACEDONIA:** PC World Macedonia; **MALAYSIA:** Computerworld Malaysia, PC World Malaysia, Publish in Asia; **MALTA:** PC World Malta; **MEXICO:** Computerworld Mexico, PC World Mexico; **MYANMAR:** PC World Myanmar; **NETHERLANDS:** Computer! Totaal, LAN Internetworking Magazine, LAN World Buyers Guide, Macworld Netherlands, Net, WebWereld; **NEW ZEALAND:** Absolute Beginners Guide and Plain & Simple Series, Computer Buyer, Computer Industry Directory, Computerworld New Zealand, MTB, Network World, PC World New Zealand; **NICARAGUA:** PC World Centro America; **NORWAY:** Computerworld Norge, CW Rapport, Datamagasinet, Financial Rapport, Kursguide Norge, Macworld Norge, Multimediaworld Norge, PC World Ekspress Norge, PC World Nettverk, PC World Norge, PC World ProduktGuide Norge; **PAKISTAN:** Computerworld Pakistan; **PANAMA:** PC World Panama; **PEOPLE'S REPUBLIC OF CHINA:** China Computer Users, China Computerworld, China InfoWorld, China Telecom World Weekly, Computer & Communication, Electronic Design China, Electronics Today, Electronics Weekly, Game Software, PC World China, Popular Computer Week, Software Weekly, Software World, Telecom World; **PERU:** Computerworld Peru, PC World Professional Peru, PC World SoHo Peru; **PHILIPPINES:** Click!, Computerworld Philippines, PC World Philippines, Publish in Asia; **POLAND:** Computerworld Poland, Computerworld Special Report Poland, Cyber, Macworld Poland, Networld Poland, PC World Komputer; **PORTUGAL:** Cerebro/PC World, Computerworld/Correio Informático, Dealer World Portugal, Mac*In/PC*In Portugal, Multimedia World; **PUERTO RICO:** PC World Puerto Rico; **ROMANIA:** Computerworld Romania, PC World Romania, Telecom Romania; **RUSSIA:** Computerworld Russia, Mir PK, Publish, Seti; **SINGAPORE:** Computerworld Singapore, PC World Singapore, Publish in Asia; **SLOVENIA:** Monitor; **SOUTH AFRICA:** Computing SA, Network World SA, Software World SA; **SPAIN:** Communicaciones World España, Computerworld España, Dealer World España, Macworld España, PC World España, PC World España; **SRI LANKA:** Infolink PC World; **SWEDEN:** CAP&Design, Computer Sweden, Corporate Computing Sweden, Internetworld Sweden, it.branschen, Macworld Sweden, MaxiData Sweden, MikroDatorn, Natverk & Kommunikation, PC World Sweden, PCaktiv, Windows World Sweden; **SWITZERLAND:** Computerworld Schweiz, Macworld Schweiz, PCtip; **TAIWAN:** Computerworld Taiwan, Macworld Taiwan, NEW ViSiON/Publish, PC World Taiwan, Windows World Taiwan; **THAILAND:** Publish in Asia, Thai Computerworld; **TURKEY:** Computerworld Turkiye, Macworld Turkiye, Network World Turkiye, PC World Turkiye; **UKRAINE:** Computerworld Kiev, Multimedia World Ukraine, PC World Ukraine; **UNITED KINGDOM:** Acorn User UK, Amiga Action UK, Amiga Computing UK, Apple Talk UK, Computing, Macworld, Parents and Computers UK, PC Advisor, PC Home, PSX Pro, The WEB; **UNITED STATES:** Cable in the Classroom, CIO Magazine, Computerworld, DOS World, Federal Computer Week, GamePro Magazine, InfoWorld, I-Way, Macworld, Network World, PC Games, PC World, Publish, Video Event, THE WEB Magazine, and WebMaster; online webzines: JavaWorld, NetscapeWorld, and SunWorld Online; **URUGUAY:** InfoWorld Uruguay; **VENEZUELA:** Computerworld Venezuela, PC World Venezuela; and **VIETNAM:** PC World Vietnam.   5/7/98

Credits

Acquisitions Editor
Juliana Aldous

Development Editors
Carol Henry
Susannah Pfalzer

Technical Editor
Stephen Jacobs

Copy Editors
Michael D. Welch
Eric Hahn
Tracy Brown

Project Coordinator
Ritchie Durdin

Graphics and Production Specialists
Linda Marousek
Hector Mendoza
Dina F Quan
Mark Yim

Quality Control Specialists
Mark Schumann
Mick Arellano

Cover Design
Murder by Design

Proofreader
Annie Sheldon

Indexer
Richard T. Evans

About the Author

Joseph W. Lowery has been writing about computers and new technology since 1981. He is the author of *Buying Online For Dummies* (IDG Books Worldwide). He has also written books on Internet Explorer and HTML, and has contributed to several books on Microsoft Office.

Joseph is currently Webmaster for a variety of sites, including the MCP Office 97 Resource Center, a managed health care organization, an international public relations school, and a bar. Joseph and his wife, dancer/choreographer Debra Wanner, have a daughter, Margot.

For my daughter, Margot—may your dreams be as free as your smile and as full as your heart. And may you get your own computer someday. Soon.

Foreword

I have received lots of e-mails thanking me for designing Dreamweaver. Well, I didn't design Dreamweaver — in fact, neither did our engineers. Dreamweaver is the first visual Web page authoring tool designed by you. The most important process during product development was to sit back and listen to customers. Web site developers are one of the most impassioned groups of people I've ever met. Thanks to your ideas and enthusiasm, Dreamweaver has become the best-selling professional Web design tool on the planet.

Let me take a step back and examine how and why we created Dreamweaver. At Macromedia, we have a long-standing relationship with creative professionals. Macromedia Director and FreeHand are two of the most popular design tools for multimedia and graphics, and just about every creative professional with a computer has one or both of those products. As our customer base began moving into Web site development, we were amazed that the so-called WYSIWYG HTML editors were simply not catching on. Everyone was still editing entirely with text editors — most commonly, Bare Bones Software's BBEdit or Allaire's HomeSite. Though these text-based tools are great and continue to be essential, we sensed an opportunity to make people more productive.

In late 1996, the Dreamweaver team began a series of customer meetings. We focused our meetings on high-end developers and contractors — people who take pride in their work. Top Web developers like Vivid Studios, C|Net, CKS Interactive, and HotWired told us about their challenges and ideas. In addition, they told us why they couldn't use the visual HTML editors on the market. Virtually without exception, every developer made it clear that they required one element from their HTML editor: complete and absolute control over the HTML source code. Whenever they would try a new editor, they found that it rearranged, reformatted, and rewrote the HTML code they had developed in another editor. These developers wanted a visual tool to help them work faster, but not at the expense of control.

So, we set out to create the first (and still the only) visual HTML editor that leaves you in complete control over all aspects of your HTML code. In fact, we came up with a special name, Roundtrip HTML, to describe our commitment to control. Roundtrip HTML simply means you can switch back and forth ("make round-trips") between any text editor and Dreamweaver without fear of alterations to your code. You can also open and edit any existing Web page without fear of unexpected changes.

Great! Now we had a mission: Roundtrip HTML. At this point, Kevin Lynch, Macromedia's Vice President of Internet Authoring, set out to write the "19 Dreams." The dreams were a series of scenarios about optimal customer experiences. Our goal was to make the dreams into reality. These dreams served as the basis for Dreamweaver.

Our next step was to create an advisory council of top Web developers and designers to keep us honest as we developed Dreamweaver. Again, we recruited from the top Web site development houses, carefully picking individuals who were not easy to please. On a regular basis, we presented our plans and progress to this group and listened to their feedback — but feedback doesn't accurately describe the spirit of those discussions. On several occasions, entire feature categories were tossed aside as we bounced back to the drawing board.

Early in the process, a new technology called Dynamic HTML (DHTML) arrived on the scene. DHTML encompasses a basket of new features in Netscape Navigator 4 and Microsoft Internet Explorer 4 that allows developers to add more multimedia and interactivity to Web pages. Everyone on the Dreamweaver team saw the potential for DHTML, but our customers weren't asking for it yet. So we set out to learn about the technology and build relationships with early adopters. As a vehicle, we created a Web site called DHTML Zone (`http://www.DHTMLZone.com`), the first browser-independent resource for developers who wanted to use DHTML. The Web site was and still is a hit, serving as a gathering place for people who use DHTML to create compelling sites. Best of all, we learned about the challenges for DHTML and JavaScript developers, and used those experiences to build a set of DHTML features that has become the industry standard.

After over a year of development, we released the first incarnation of Dreamweaver at the December 1997 Internet World in New York. The reception was fabulous, and we garnered the show's award for best Web site authoring tool. For the first time, professional Web developers around the world are taking advantage of visual tools as they discover the productivity of Roundtrip HTML and the power of Dynamic HTML with Dreamweaver.

We still believe that the crux of our success lies in constant and thorough communication with our customers. If you have any ideas, criticisms, problems, or praise for Dreamweaver, please let us know. The Dreamweaver engineers, the quality assurance staff, technical support, and marketing staff participate in our lively discussion forum at `news://forums.macromedia.com/ macromedia.dreamweaver`. You can also send new feature ideas via e-mail to `wish-dreamweaver@macromedia.com`. Please join us and help create the next generation of the best professional Web site design tool.

Steve Shannon
Senior Product Manager
Macromedia

Preface

Among other accolades, Macromedia's Dreamweaver has one of the most appropriate product names in recent memory. Web page design is a blend of art and craft — whether you're a deadline-driven professional or a vision-filled amateur, Dreamweaver is the perfect tool for many Web designers. Dreamweaver is not only the first Web authoring tool to bring the ease of visual editing to an HTML code-oriented world; it also brings a point-and-click interface to complex JavaScript coding.

To use this book, you only need two items: the Dreamweaver software and a desire to make cutting-edge Web pages. (Actually, you don't even need Dreamweaver to begin; the CD-ROM contains a fully functional demo.) From quick design prototyping to ongoing Web site management, Dreamweaver automates and simplifies much of a Webmaster's workload. Unfortunately, even Dynamic HTML, which Dreamweaver handles elegantly, cannot accomplish all the tasks of a modern Web page. As a result, this book contains step-by-step instructions on how to handle every Web design task — through Dreamweaver's visual interface or its integrated HTML code editors.

Underneath its simple, intuitive interface, Dreamweaver is a complex program that makes high-end Web concepts (Dynamic HTML, Cascading Style Sheets, and JavaScript Behaviors) accessible for the first time. *Dreamweaver Bible* is designed to help you master every nuance of the program. Are you creating a straight-forward layout with the visual editor? Do you need to extend Dreamweaver's capabilities by building your own custom objects? With Dreamweaver and this book, you can weave your dreams into reality for the entire world to experience.

Who Should Read This Book?

Dreamweaver attracts a wide range of Web developers. Because it's the first Web authoring tool that doesn't rewrite original code, veteran designers are drawn to using Dreamweaver as their first visual editor. Because it also automates complicated effects, beginning Web designers are interested in Dreamweaver's power and performance. *Dreamweaver Bible* addresses the full spectrum of Web professionals, providing basic information on HTML if you're just starting, as well as advanced tips and tricks for seasoned pros. Moreover, this book is a complete reference for everyone working with Dreamweaver on a daily basis.

What Hardware and Software Do You Need?

Dreamweaver Bible includes coverage of Dreamweaver 1.2. If you don't own a copy of the program, the CD-ROM contains a demo version for your trial use. Written to be platform-independent, this book covers both Macintosh and Windows 95/NT versions of Dreamweaver 1.2.

Macromedia recommends the following minimum requirements for running Dreamweaver on a Macintosh:

+ Power Macintosh
+ MacOS 7.5 or later
+ 24MB of available RAM
+ 20MB of available disk space
+ Color monitor
+ CD-ROM drive

Macromedia recommends the following minimum requirements for running Dreamweaver on a Windows system:

+ Intel Pentium processor, 90 MHz or equivalent
+ Windows 95 or NT 4.0
+ 16MB of available RAM
+ 20MB of available disk space
+ Color monitor
+ CD-ROM drive

Please note that these are the minimum requirements. As with all graphics-based design tools, more capability is definitely better for Dreamweaver, especially in terms of memory and processor speed.

How This Book Is Organized

Dreamweaver Bible can take you from raw beginner to full-fledged professional if read cover-to-cover. However, you're more likely to read each section as needed, taking the necessary information and coming back later. To facilitate this approach, *Dreamweaver Bible* is divided into eight major task-oriented parts. Once you're familiar with Dreamweaver, feel free to skip around the book, using it as a reference guide as you build up your own knowledge base.

The early chapters present the basics, and all chapters contain clearly written steps for the tasks you need to perform. In later chapters, you encounter boxed sections labeled "Dreamweaver Techniques." Dreamweaver Techniques are step-by-step instructions on how to accomplish specific Web designer tasks: for example, building an image map that uses rollovers, or eliminating underlines from hyperlinks through Cascading Style Sheets. Naturally, you can also use the Dreamweaver Techniques as stepping stones for your own explorations into Web page creation.

If you're running Dreamweaver while reading this book, don't forget to use the CD-ROM. As an integral element of the book, the CD-ROM offers additional Dreamweaver Behaviors, Objects, Browser Profiles, Style Sheets, and Templates in addition to relevant code from the book.

Part I: Getting Started with Dreamweaver

Part I begins with an overview of Dreamweaver's philosophy and design. To get the most out of the program, you need to understand the key advantages it offers and the deficiencies it addresses. Part I takes you all the way to setting up your first site.

The opening chapters give you a full reference to the Dreamweaver interface and all of its customizable features. You also learn how you can access Dreamweaver's full-bodied online help and find additional resources on the Web. Chapter 5 takes you all the way from the consideration of various Web site design models to publishing your finished site on the Internet.

Part II: Basic HTML in Dreamweaver

Although Dreamweaver is partly a visual design tool, its roots derive from the language of the Web: HTML. Part II gives you a solid foundation in the basics of HTML, even if you've never seen code. Chapter 6 covers the theory of HTML, describing how a Web page is constructed and alerting you to some potential pitfalls to look out for.

The three fundamentals of Web pages are text, images, and links. You explore how to incorporate these elements to their fullest extent in Chapters 7, 8, and 9, respectively. Chapter 8, "Inserting Images," also includes a special section on using animated GIFs. Chapter 10 examines another fundamental HTML option: lists. You study the list in all of its forms: numbered lists, bulleted lists, definition lists, nested lists, and more.

Part III: Incorporating Advanced HTML

Part III begins to investigate some of the more advanced structural elements of HTML as implemented in Dreamweaver. Chapter 11 examines the various uses of tables — from a clear presentation of data to organizing entire Web pages. Here you learn how to use Dreamweaver's visual table editor to resize and reshape your HTML tables quickly.

Chapter 12 is devoted to image maps and shows how to use Dreamweaver's built-in Image Map Editor to create client-side image maps. The chapter also explains how you can build server-side image maps and demonstrates a technique for creating image map rollovers. Forms are the focus of Chapter 13, where you find all you need to know about gathering information from your Web page visitors. Chapter 14 investigates the somewhat complex world of frames — and shows how Dreamweaver has greatly simplified the task of building and managing these multifile creations. You also see how to handle more advanced design tasks like updated multiple frames with just one click.

Part IV: Extending HTML through Dreamweaver

HTML is a language with extensive capabilities for expanding its own power. Part IV begins with Chapter 15, which introduces you to the world of CGI programs, external plug-ins, Java applets, ActiveX controls, and scripting with JavaScript and VBScript. You also find techniques for ensuring a secure middle ground of cross-browser compatibility in the ongoing browser wars.

With its own set of objects and behaviors, Dreamweaver complements HTML's extensibility. Chapter 16 shows how you can use the built-in objects to accomplish most of your Web page-layout chores quickly and efficiently — and when you're ready for increased automation, the chapter explains how to build your own custom objects. Chapter 17 offers an in-depth look at the capabilities of Dreamweaver Behaviors. Each standard behavior is covered in detail with step-by-step instructions. If you're JavaScript-savvy, the second half of the chapter gives you the material you need to construct your own behaviors and reduce your day-to-day workload.

Part V: Adding Multimedia Elements

In recent years, the Web has moved from a relatively static display of text and simple images to a full-blown multimedia circus with streaming video, background music, and interactive animations. Part V contains the power tools for incorporating various media files into your Web site.

Chapter 18 covers digital video in its many forms: downloadable AVI files, streaming RealVideo displays, and panoramic QuickTime movies. Chapter 19 focuses on digital audio, with coverage of standard WAV and MIDI sound files as well as the newer streaming audio formats. A special section covers the exciting possibilities offered by Beatnik and the new Rich Music Format.

In addition to Dreamweaver, Macromedia is perhaps best known for one other contribution to Web multimedia: Shockwave. Chapter 20 explores the possibilities offered by incorporating Shockwave Director and Shockwave Flash movies into Dreamweaver-designed Web pages, and includes everything you need to know about configuring MIME types. You also find step-by-step instructions for building Shockwave inline controls and playing Shockwave movies in frame-based Web pages.

Part VI: Dynamic HTML and Dreamweaver

Dynamic HTML brought a new world of promises to Web designers — promises that went largely unfulfilled until Dreamweaver was released. Part VI of the *Dreamweaver Bible* examines this brave new world of pixel-perfect positioning, layers that fly in and then disappear as if by magic, and Web sites that can change their look-and-feel with the drop of a hat.

Chapter 21 provides an overview of Dynamic HTML and explores the different implementations by the major browsers. Chapter 22 takes a detailed look at the elegance of Cascading Style Sheets and gives techniques for accomplishing the most requested tasks, such as creating an external style sheet. Much of the advantages of Dynamic HTML come from the use of layers, which allow absolute positioning of page elements, visibility control, and a sense of depth. You discover how to handle all of these layer capabilities and more in Chapter 23. Chapter 24 focuses on timelines, which have the potential to take your Web page into the fourth dimension. The chapter concludes with a blow-by-blow description of how to create a multiscreen slide show, complete with layers that fly in and out on command.

Part VII: Web Site Management under Dreamweaver

Although Web page design gets all the glory, Web site management pays the bills. In Part VII you see how Dreamweaver makes this essential part of any Webmaster's day easier to handle. Chapter 25 describes Dreamweaver's built-in tools for maintaining cross- and backwards-browser compatibility. A Dreamweaver Technique demonstrates a browser-checking Web page that automatically directs users to the appropriate links.

Chapter 26 covers the Library, which can significantly reduce any Webmaster's workload. Chapter 27 explains all you need to know about managing your working Web site through Dreamweaver's primary management tool, Site FTP — including such innovative features as file checkin/checkout. Chapter 28 rounds out Part VII with a look at Dreamweaver Templates and how they can speed up production while ensuring a unified look and feel across your Web site.

Appendixes

Dreamweaver comes with a fully functional internal HTML editor, and the full version of the program is bundled with two industrial-strength external HTML editors: BBEdit for the Macintosh and HomeSite for Windows. Although both editors offer extensive online help, an abbreviated user's manual for both programs appears in Appendixes A and B. Each appendix also has detailed information on integrating the external editors with Dreamweaver.

No program as full-featured as Dreamweaver can be used without running into the occasional glitch. Appendix C offers a troubleshooting guide containing solutions to common problems. Appendix D describes the contents of this book's CD-ROM.

Conventions Used in This Book

The following conventions are used throughout this book.

Windows and Macintosh Conventions

Because *Dreamweaver Bible* is a cross-platform book, it gives instructions for both Windows and Macintosh users when keystrokes for a particular task differ. Throughout this book, the Windows keystrokes are given first and the Macintosh are given second in parentheses, as follows:

To undo an action, press Ctrl-Z (Command-Z).

The first instruction is for Windows users to press the Ctrl and *Z* keys in combination, and the second instruction in parentheses is for Macintosh users to press the Command and *Z* keys together.

Key-Combinations

When you are instructed to press two or more keys simultaneously, each key in the combination is separated by a hyphen. For example:

Ctrl-Alt-T (Command-Option-T)

The preceding tells you to press the three listed keys for your system at the same time. You can also hold down one or more keys and then press the final key. Release all the keys at the same time.

Mouse Instructions

When instructed to click an item, you must move the mouse pointer to the specified item and click the mouse button once. Windows users use the left mouse button unless otherwise instructed. Double-click means to click the mouse button twice in rapid succession.

When instructed to select an item, you may click it once as previously described. If you are selecting text or multiple objects, you must click the mouse button once, hold it down, and then move the mouse to a new location. The item or items selected invert color. To clear the selection, click once anywhere on the Web page.

Menu Commands

When instructed to select a command from a menu, you see the menu and the command separated by an arrow symbol. For example, when instructed to execute the Open command from the File menu, you see the notation File ⇨ Open. Some menus use submenus, in which case you see an arrow for each submenu, as follows: Insert ⇨ Form Object ⇨ Text Field.

Typographical Conventions

Italic type is used for new terms and for emphasis. **Boldface** type is used for text that you need to type directly from the computer keyboard.

Code

A special typeface indicates HTML or other code, as demonstrated in the following example:

```
<html>
<head>
<title>Untitled Document</title>
</head>
<body bgcolor="#FFFFFF">
</body>
</html>
```

This code font is also used within paragraphs to designate HTML tags, attributes, and values such as <body>, bgcolor, and #FFFFFF. All HTML tags are presented in lowercase, as written by Dreamweaver, although browsers are not generally case-sensitive in terms of HTML.

The (¬) character at the end of a code line means you should type the next line of code before pressing the Enter (Return) key.

Navigating Through This Book

Various signposts and icons are located throughout *Dreamweaver Bible* for your assistance.

Each chapter begins with an overview of its information, and ends with a quick summary.

Icons are placed in the text to indicate important or especially helpful items. Here's a list of the icons and their functions:

 Tips provide you with extra knowledge that separates the novice from the pro.

 Notes provide additional or critical information and technical data on the current topic.

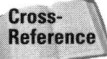 Look for the Cross-Reference icon to find more information on a particular topic.

 The Caution icon is your warning of a potential problem or pitfall.

 The CD icon indicates that the CD-ROM contains a related file in the given folder.

Further Information

You can find more help for specific problems and questions by investigating several Web sites. Macromedia's own Dreamweaver Web site is the best place to start:

    http://www.dreamweaver.com

I heartily recommend that you visit and participate in the official Dreamweaver newsgroup:

```
news://forums.macromedia.com/macromedia.dreamweaver
```

You're also invited to visit my Web site for book updates and new developments:

```
http://www.idest.com/dreamweaver
```

You can also e-mail me:

```
jlowery@idest.com
```

I can't promise instantaneous turnaround, but I'll answer all my mail to the best of my abilities.

Acknowledgments

I've always wished I'd said, "If I've seen farther, it's because I stood on the shoulders of giants" — but Sir Isaac Newton beat me to it. So I'll just have to settle for the following, "If you drop this book on your toe and it hurts, it's only because I got a lot of info and help from other folks." Here's hoping I can remember them all.

In a tie for first, I'd like to thank my agent, Laura Belt, for her countless hours of playing phone tag with editors and publishers across the country, and Juliana Aldous, Acquisitions Editor at IDG Books Worldwide for being one of the editors who answered those calls. You two are the top buttons on my speed-dial of life and I greatly appreciate the trust and encouragement you've offered with this project. Here's a warm, bicoastal hug for Carol Henry, Development Editor Extraordinaire for her 24-7 (is that all?) support. I hope we meet again on the editorial playing fields. My technical editor, Steve Jacobs, deserves a special nod for overseeing the dual-platform nature of this book, while juggling a full-fledged family and a professorship at a hot university. Steve also bore the brunt of all my bad jokes in place of the readers — although one or two Easter eggs are waiting for you to discover. Of course, I want to thank all the IDG Books personnel who've assisted with the book, led by Susannah Pfalzer and Michael Welch.

Then there are my new friends whom I met only through the happy accident of this book. A very special thanks goes to Matthew David, who came through in a crunch with vital material for the heart of this book. Thanks for all your hard work, and tell your wife the kidnapping is over — for the moment. I'm also grateful to Brett Skogen and David Welton for their work on the HTML editor appendixes that round out the book. The hordes of late-night programmers thank you as well. The book is also richer because of the material contributed by Andrew Woolridge, Michael Davis, and Richard Millward, who so graciously gave consent for their programming efforts to be distributed through the CD-ROM. I'd also like to thank George Olsen for his insights into the murkier reaches of browser compatibility. Special kudos go to the folks at Headspace, both for making the cool tool Beatnik and allowing its inclusion on the CD-ROM.

Macromedia has been extraordinarily supportive of this book, both corporately and through their individual representatives. As Dreamweaver Product Marketing Managers, Steve Shannon and Beth Davis greased the industrial wheels and made the ride as smooth as possible — as did Jon Brovitz, Leona Lapez, and Mary Leong. Needed technical assistance came from all quarters at Macromedia, but I'm especially indebted to Heidi Bauer, Derrick Brown, Ben Fuller, Dave George, and Lori Hylan for staring comprehensibly at my incomprehensible questions — and always coming back with the answers. A hearty "Whew!" goes out to self-styled curmudgeon Matt Brown, who has supported my efforts from day one.

Of course, the biggest thank-you goes to the Dreamweaver development team, led by Kevin Lynch, for putting this particular dream on the shelf.

Contents at a Glance

Contents

● ●

Part V: Adding Multimedia Elements   435

Chapter 18: Adding Video to Your Web Page 437

Chapter 19: Using Audio on Your Web Page............................453

Chapter 20: Inserting Shockwave Movies 475

Getting Started with Dreamweaver

What Is Dreamweaver?

Dreamweaver, by Macromedia, is a professional Web site development program. Among its many distinctions, Dreamweaver is the first Web development program to take advantage of the capabilities of the latest generation of browsers, making it easy for developers to use advanced features such as Cascading Style Sheets and Dynamic HTML.

Dreamweaver is truly a tool by Web developers, for Web developers. Designed from the ground up to work the way professional Web designers do, Dreamweaver speeds site construction and streamlines site maintenance. Throughout this chapter you'll see the philosophical underpinnings of the program and get a better sense of how Dreamweaver blends traditional HTML with cutting-edge techniques. You'll also learn some of the advanced features that Dreamweaver offers to help you manage a Web site.

The Real World of Dreamweaver

Dreamweaver is a program very much rooted in the real world. For example, Dreamweaver recognizes the problem of incompatible browser commands and addresses it by producing cross-browser compatible code. Dreamweaver even includes browser- specific HTML validation so you can see how your existing or new code works in a particular browser.

Integrated visual and text editors

In the early days of the World Wide Web, most developers "hand-coded" their Web pages using simple text editors such as Notepad and SimpleText. The second generation of Web authoring tools brought visual design or WYSIWYG ("what you see is what you get") editors to market. What these products furnished in ease of layout, they lacked in completeness of code. Professional Web developers found they still needed to hand-code their Web pages, even with the most sophisticated WYSIWYG editor.

Dreamweaver acknowledges this reality and has integrated a superb visual editor with a number of text editors. You can work with Dreamweaver's internal HTML Inspector or a dedicated external editor. Figure 1-1 shows Dreamweaver's visual editor and text editor working together. Any change made in the visual editor is instantly reflected into the text editor and vice versa. While Dreamweaver lets you work with any text editor you would like, it includes both BBEdit for Macintosh developers and HomeSite for Microsoft Windows developers. Dreamweaver enables a natural, dynamic flow between the visual and text editors.

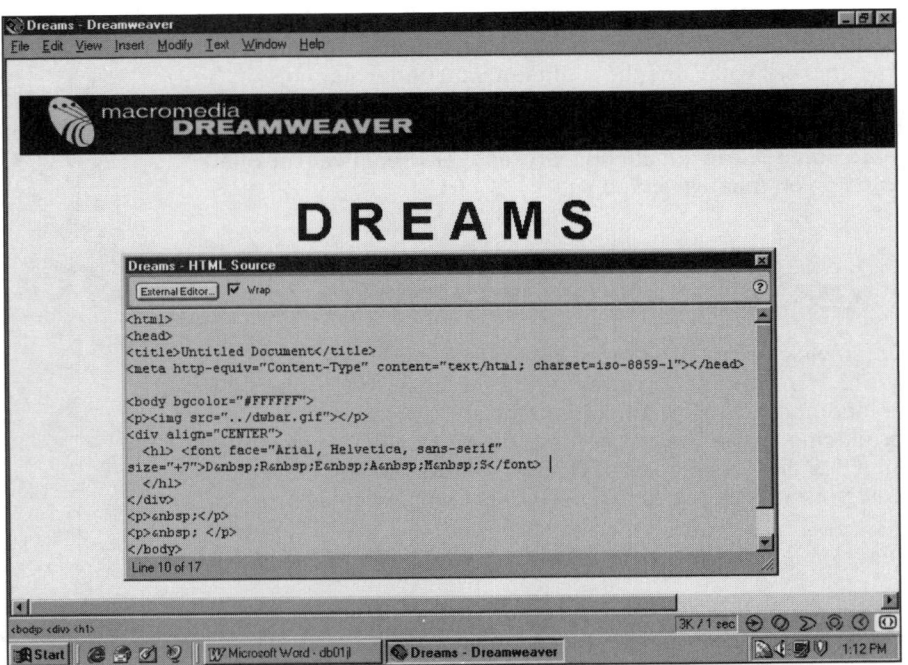

Figure 1-1: Dreamweaver lets you work with both a visual WYSIWYG editor and an HTML text editor simultaneously.

Roundtrip HTML

Most Web authoring programs modify any code that passes through its system —
inserting returns, removing indents, adding <meta> tags, uppercasing commands,
and so forth. Dreamweaver's programmers understand and respect that Web
developers all have their own particular coding styles. An underlying concept,
Roundtrip HTML, ensures that you can move back and forth between the visual
editor and any HTML text editor without your code being rewritten.

Web site maintenance tools

The Dreamweaver creators also understand that creating a site is only a part of
the Webmaster's job. Maintaining the Web site can be an ongoing, time-consuming
chore. Dreamweaver simplifies the job with a group of site management tools,
including a library of repeating elements and a file-locking capability for easy team
updates.

The Dreamweaver Interface

When creating a Web page, Webmasters do two things over and over: they insert an
element — whether text, image, or layer — and then they modify it. Dreamweaver
excels at such Web page creation. The Dreamweaver workspace combines a series
of windows, palettes, and inspectors to make the process as fluid as possible,
thereby speeding up the Webmaster's work.

Easy text entry

Although much of the World Wide Web's glitz comes from multimedia elements
such as images and sound, Web pages are primarily a text-based medium.
Dreamweaver recognizes this and makes the text cursor the default tool. To add
text, just click in Dreamweaver's main workspace — the document window — and
start typing. As shown in Figure 1-2, the Text Property Inspector lets you change
the characteristics of the text such as the size, font, position, or color.

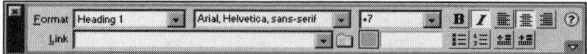

Figure 1-2: Use the Text Property Inspector to change
the format of the selected text.

One-stop object modification

You can select Web page elements other than text from the Object Palette. Adding a picture to a Web page is as easy as clicking the Insert Image button from the Object Palette. Dreamweaver asks you to select the file for the image, and a placeholder appears in your current cursor position. Once your graphic is on screen, double-clicking it brings up the appropriate Property Inspector to enable you to make modifications. The same technique holds true for any other inserted element — from horizontal rules to Shockwave Flash movies.

Complete custom environment

Dreamweaver lets you customize your workspace to suit you best. A handy Launcher opens and closes various windows, palettes, and inspectors, all of which are movable. Just drag them wherever you want them on screen. Want to see your page by itself? You can hide all windows at the touch of a function button; press it again and your controls are revealed.

Dreamweaver's customization capabilities extend even further. If you find that you are inserting something over and over, such as a QuickTime video or .wav sound file, you can add that element to your Object Palette. Dreamweaver even lets you add a specific element, a "Home" button for example, to the Object Palette. In fact, you can add entire categories of objects if you like.

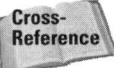

Cross-Reference   For more information on customizing your Object Palette, see Chapter 16, "Creating and Using Objects."

Simple selection process

As with most modern layout programs, in order to modify anything in Dreamweaver you must select it first. The usual process for this is to click an object to highlight it, or to click and drag over a block of text to select it. Dreamweaver streamlines this process through the Tag Selector feature. Click anywhere on a Web page under construction and then look at Dreamweaver's status bar. The applicable HTML tags appear on the left side of the status bar.

In the example shown in Figure 1-3, the Tag Selector shows

```
<body> <div> <table> <tr> <td> <p>
```

Click one of these tags and the corresponding elements are selected on your page, ready for modification. The Tag Selector is a terrific time-saver; throughout this book I'll point out how you can use it under various circumstances.

Selected text

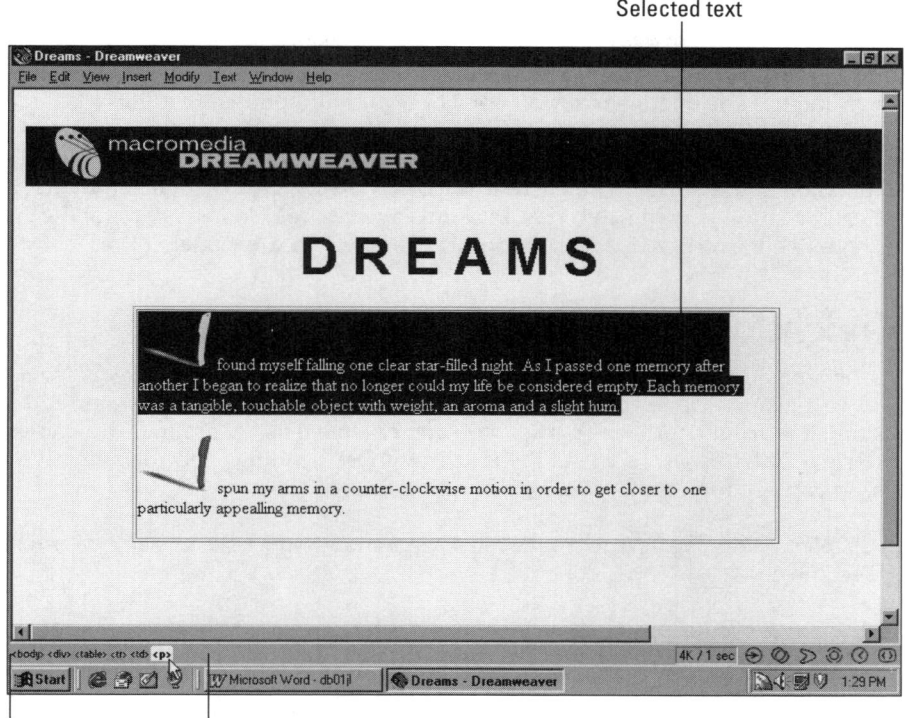

Tag selector   Status bar

Figure 1-3: Choosing the <p> tag in Dreamweaver's Tag Selector is a quick and easy way to highlight the current paragraph on your Web page.

Enhanced layout options

Dreamweaver works much more like a desktop publishing program than do other visual HTML editors. Today's browser capabilities permit images and text to be placed in specific locations on the Web page — a concept known as *absolute positioning*. To enable you to take full advantage of this new power, Dreamweaver includes both rulers and grids. You can specify the type of measurement to be used (inches, pixels, or centimeters), as well as the spacing and the appearance of the grid lines. You can even have objects snap to the grid for easy alignment.

Cross-Reference

To find out more about absolute positioning, see Chapter 23, "Working with Layers."

Up-to-Date HTML Standards

Most Web pages are created in HyperText Markup Language (HTML). This programming language — really a series of tags that modify a text file — is standardized by an organization known as the World Wide Web Consortium (http://www.w3.org). Each new release of HTML incorporates an enhanced set of commands and features. The current version, HTML 3.2, is recognized by the majority of browsers in use today. Dreamweaver writes clear, easy-to-follow HTML 3.2 code whenever you insert or modify an element in the visual editor.

Straightforward text and graphics support

Text is a basic building block of any Web page, and Dreamweaver makes formatting your text a snap. Once you've inserted your text, either by typing it in directly or pasting it in from another program, you can change its appearance. You can use the generic HTML formats, such as the H1 through H6 headings and their relative sizes, or you can use font families and exact point sizes.

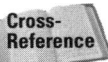

Chapter 7, "Adding Text to Your Web Page," shows you how to work with text in Dreamweaver.

Additional text support in Dreamweaver enables you to add both numbered and bulleted lists to your Web page. The Text Property Inspector gives you buttons for both kinds of lists as well as easy alignment control. Some elements, including lists, offer extended options. In Dreamweaver, clicking the Property Inspector's expander arrow opens a section where you can access additional controls.

Graphics are handled in much the same easy-to-use manner. Select the image or its placeholder to enable the Image Property Inspector. From there, you can modify any available attributes including the image's source, its width or height, and its alignment on the page. Need to touch up your image? Send it to your favorite graphics program with just a click of the Edit Image button.

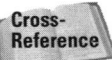

You'll learn all about adding and modifying Dreamweaver images in Chapter 8, "Inserting Images."

Enhanced table capabilities

Other features — standard, yet more advanced — are similarly straightforward in Dreamweaver. Tables are a key component in today's Web pages, and Dreamweaver gives you full control over all their functionality. Dreamweaver changes the work of resizing the column or row of a table, previously a tedious hand-coding task, into an easy click-and-drag motion. Likewise, you can delete all the width and height values from a table with the click of a button. Figure 1-4 shows the Table Column Properties dialog box, called from the Property Inspector.

Table Column Properties dialog box

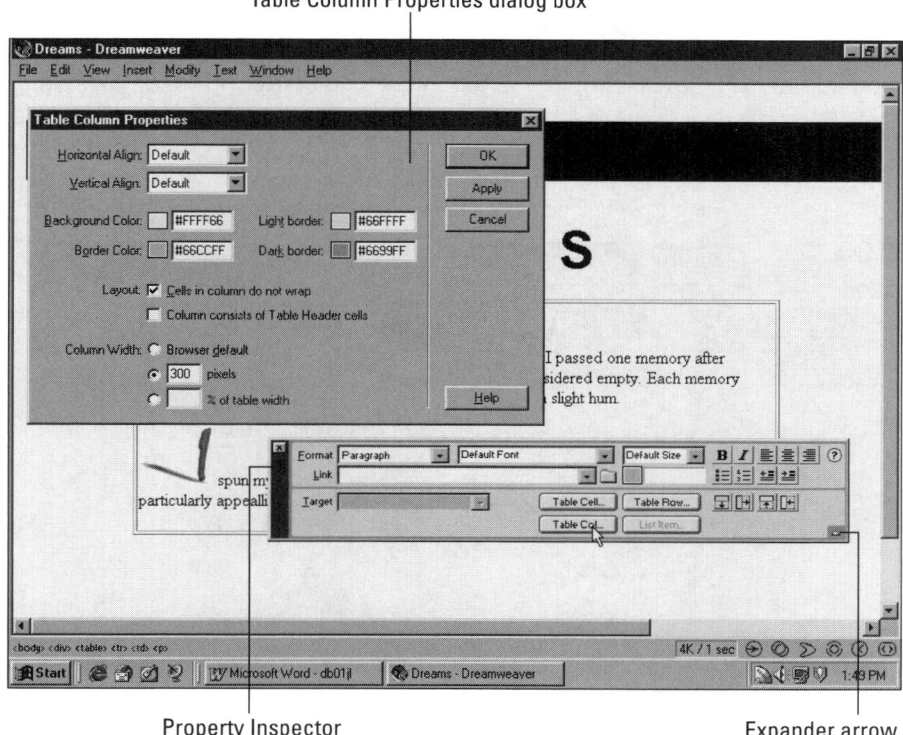

Property Inspector   Expander arrow

Figure 1-4: The Table Column Properties dialog box is just one of Dreamweaver's paths to a full range of control over the appearance of your table.

Easy form entry

Forms, the basic vehicle for Web page data exchange, are just as easy to implement as tables in Dreamweaver. Switch to the Forms panel of the Object Palette and insert any of the available elements: text boxes, radio buttons, check boxes, and even pop-up menus or scrolling lists. Dreamweaver even includes a sample CGI script to help you make the connection between client and server.

Click-and-drag frame setup

Frames, which enable separate Web pages to be viewed on a single screen, are often considered one of the most difficult HTML techniques to master. Dreamweaver employs a click-and-drag method for establishing your frame outlines. After you've set up your frame structure, open the Frame Inspector (see Figure 1-5) to select any frame and modify it with the Property Inspector. Dreamweaver writes the necessary code for linking all the HTML files in a frameset, no matter how many Web pages are used.

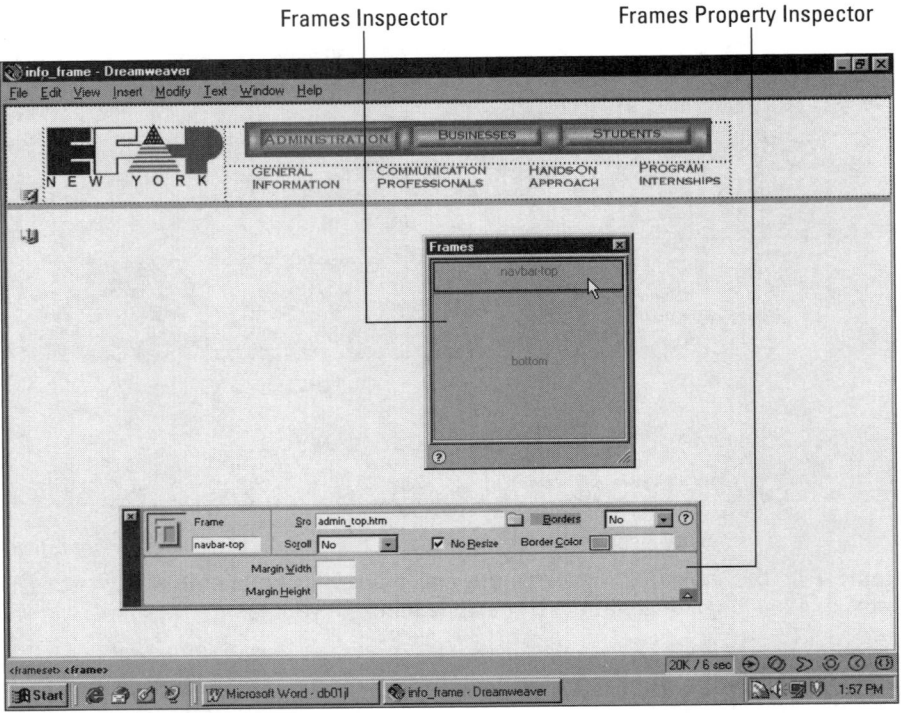

Figure 1-5: In Dreamweaver you use the Frame Inspector to choose which frame you want to modify through the Property Inspector.

Cross-Reference For more information on creating frame-based Web pages, see Chapter 14, "Using Frames and Framesets."

Multimedia enhancements

Dreamweaver enables you to drop in any number of multimedia extensions, plug-ins, applets, or controls. Just click the appropriate button on the Object Palette and modify with the Property Inspector. Two multimedia elements, Shockwave Director movies and Shockwave Flash movies — both from Macromedia — warrant special consideration in Macromedia's Dreamweaver. When you insert either of these objects, Dreamweaver automatically includes the necessary HTML code to ensure the widest browser acceptance, and you can edit all the respective properties.

Next-Generation Features

Dreamweaver is among the first Web authoring tools to work with the new capabilities brought in by the 4.0 generation of browsers. Both Netscape Communicator 4.0 and Microsoft Internet Explorer 4.0 include variations of Dynamic HTML (DHTML). Moreover, both of these latest browsers adhere to the Cascading Style Sheet (CSS) standards with support for absolute and relative positioning. Dreamweaver gives Web developers an interface that takes these advanced possibilities and makes them realities.

3D layers

One particular Dynamic HTML feature enables Dreamweaver to be called "the first 3D Web authoring tool." Until now, Web pages existed on a two-dimensional plane — images and text could only be placed side-by-side. Dreamweaver supports control of Dynamic HTML *layers,* meaning that objects can be placed in front of or behind other objects. Layers can contain text, graphics, links, controls — you can even nest one layer inside another.

You create a layer in Dreamweaver by clicking the Layer button on the Object Palette. Once created, layers can be positioned anywhere on the page by clicking and dragging the selection handle. As with other Dreamweaver objects, you can modify a layer through the Property Inspector.

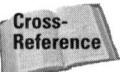

Detailed information on using Dynamic HTML in Dreamweaver starts in Chapter 21, "What's Dynamic HTML?"

Animated objects

Not only can objects in layers be positioned anywhere on the Web page during its creation, they can also be moved when the page is viewed. Dreamweaver takes this capability and, with the addition of its Timeline Inspector, becomes the first *4D* Web authoring tool! The Timeline Inspector, shown in Figure 1-6, is designed along the lines of Macromedia's world-class multimedia creation program, Director. With Timelines, you can control a layer's position, size, 3D placement, and even visibility on a frame-by-frame basis.

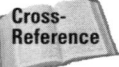

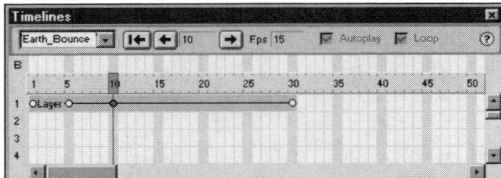

Figure 1-6: Use the Timeline Inspector to animate objects in layers using Dreamweaver's advanced Dynamic HTML features.

Dynamic style updates

Dreamweaver completely supports the Cascading Style Sheets (CSS) specification agreed upon by the World Wide Web Consortium. CSS gives Web designers more flexible control over almost every element on their Web pages. Dreamweaver applies CSS abilities as if they are styles in a word processor. For example, you could make all the 〈h1〉 tags blue, italic, and in small caps. If your site's color scheme changes, you could make all the 〈h1〉 tags red — and you can do this throughout your Web site, with one command. Dreamweaver gives you style control over type, background, blocks, boxes, borders, lists, and positioning.

Dreamweaver enables you to change styles online as well as offline. By linking a CSS change to a user-driven event such as moving the mouse, text can be highlighted or de-emphasized, screen areas can light up, and figures can even be animated. And it can all be done without repeated trips to the server or huge file downloads.

Cross-Reference   Details on using CSS begin in Chapter 22, "Building Style Sheet Web Pages."

JavaScript behaviors

Through the development of JavaScript behaviors, Dreamweaver combines the power of JavaScript with the ease of a drag-and-drop interface. A *behavior* is defined as a combination of an event and an action — whenever your Web page user does something and then something else happens, that's a behavior. What makes behaviors extremely useful is that they require no programming whatsoever.

JavaScript Behaviors

Behaviors are JavaScript-based, and this is significant because JavaScript is supported to varying degrees by existing browsers. Dreamweaver has simplified the task of identifying which JavaScript command works with a particular browser. You simply select the Web page element that you want to use to control the action, and open the Behavior Inspector from the Launcher. As shown in Figure 1-7, Dreamweaver lets you pick a JavaScript command that works with all browsers or a subset of browsers or one browser in particular. Next, you choose from a full list of available actions, such as go to a URL, play a sound, pop up a message, or start an animation. You can assign multiple actions and even determine when they occur.

Figure 1-7: Dreamweaver offers only the JavaScript commands that work with the browser you specify.

Cross-Reference For the complete details on JavaScript behaviors, see Chapter 17, "Creating and Using Behaviors."

Site Management Tools

Long after your killer Web site is launched, you'll find yourself continually updating and revising it. For this reason, site management tools are as important as site creation tools are to a Web authoring program. Dreamweaver delivers on both counts.

Object Libraries

In addition to site management functions that have become traditional, such as FTP publishing, Dreamweaver adds a whole new class of functionality called *Libraries*. One of the truisms of Web page development is that if you repeat an element across your site, you're sure to have to change it — on every page. Dreamweaver Libraries eliminate that drudgery.

You can define almost anything as a Library element: a paragraph of text, an image, a link, a table, a form, a Java applet, an ActiveX control, and so on. Just choose the item and open the Library palette (see Figure 1-8). Once you've created the Library entry, you can reuse it throughout your Web site. Each Web site can have its own Library, and you can copy entries from one Library to another.

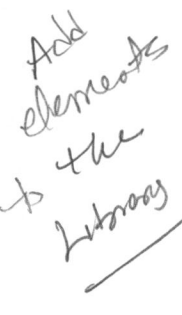

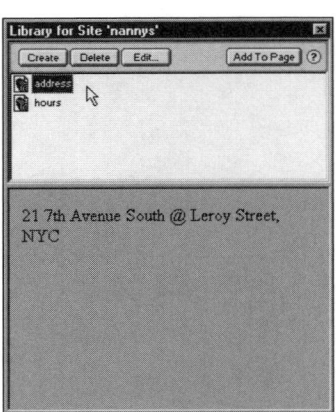

Figure 1-8: Use Dreamweaver's Library feature to simplify the task of updating elements repeated across many Web pages.

Being able to include "boilerplate" Web elements is one thing, being able to update them across the site simultaneously is quite another! You can easily change a Library entry through the Library Palette. Once the change is complete, Dreamweaver detects the modification and asks if you want to update your site. Imagine updating copyright information across a 400+ page Web site in the wink of an eye, and you'll start to understand the power of Dreamweaver Libraries.

To find out more about making sitewide changes, see Chapter 26, "Using the Repeating Elements Library."

Browser targeting

Browser targeting is another site management innovation from Dreamweaver. One of the major steps in any site development project is to test the Web pages in various browsers to look for inconsistencies and invalid code. Dreamweaver's Browser Targeting function lets you check your HTML against any existing browser's profile. Dreamweaver includes predefined profiles for several browsers and lets you create a profile for any browser you'd like to check.

To see how you can set up your own profile for Browser Targeting, see Chapter 25, "Maximizing Browser Targeting."

You can also preview your Web page in any number of browsers. Dreamweaver lets you specify primary and secondary browsers that can display your page at the press of a function key. You can install up to 18 other browsers for previewing your Web page. The entire list of browsers is available through the Preview in Browser command under the File menu.

Converting Web pages

Although Web site designers may have access to the latest HTML tools and browsers, much of the public uses older, more limited versions of browsers. Dreamweaver gives you the power to build Web pages with the high-end capabilities of fourth-generation browsers — and then convert those pages so that older browsers, too, can read what you've created. Moreover, you can take previously designed Web pages and "upgrade" them to take advantage of the latest HTML features. Dreamweaver goes a long way toward helping you bridge the gap between browser versions.

Verifying links

Web sites are ever-evolving entities. Maintaining valid connections and links amid all that diversity is a constant challenge. Dreamweaver includes a built-in link checker so you can verify the links on a page, in a directory, or across your entire site. The link checker quickly shows you which files have broken links, which files have links to external sites, and which files may have been "orphaned" (so that no other file connects with them).

FTP publishing

The final step in Web page creation is publishing your page to the Internet. As any Webmaster knows, this "final step" is one that happens over and over again, as the site is continually updated and maintained. Dreamweaver includes an FTP publisher that simplifies the work of posting your site (FTP stands for *file transfer protocol*).

You can work with sites originating from a local folder, such as one on your own hard drive. Or, in a collaborative team environment, you can work with sites being developed on a remote server. Dreamweaver lets you set up an unlimited number of sites to include the source and destination directories, FTP user names and passwords, and more.

The Dreamweaver FTP Site window, shown in Figure 1-9, is a visual interface in which you can click and drag files, or select a number of files and transfer them with the Get and Put buttons. You can even set the preferences so the system automatically disconnects after remaining idle for a user-definable period of time.

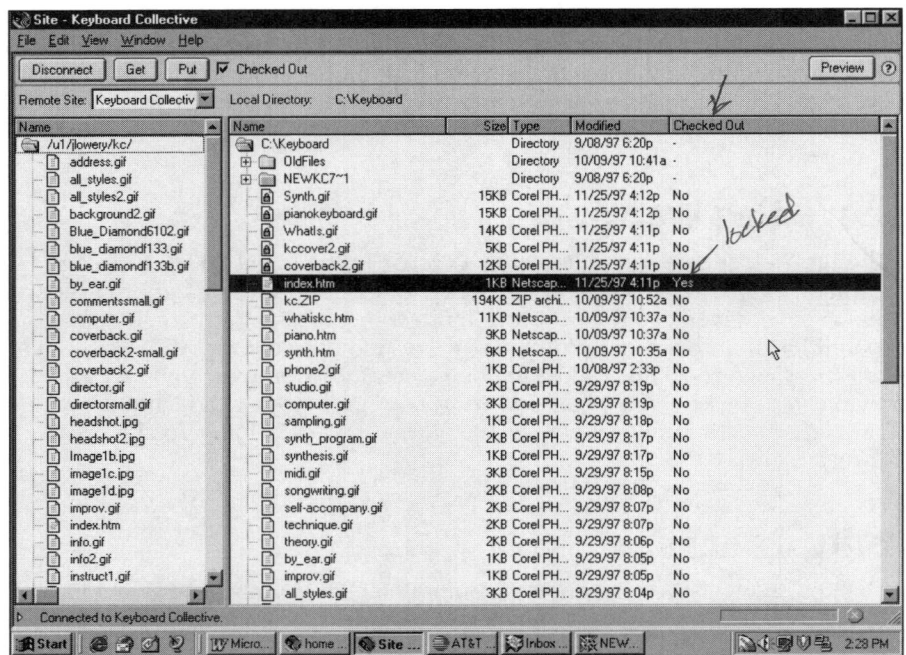

Figure 1-9: The FTP Site window lets you publish your Web site directly from within Dreamweaver.

File checkout/checkin

On larger Web projects, more than one person is usually responsible for creation and daily upkeep of the site. An editor may need to include the latest company press release, or a graphic artist may have to upload a photo of the newest product — all on the same page. To avoid conflicts with overlapping updates, Dreamweaver has devised a system under which Web pages can be marked as "checked out" and locked to prevent any other corrections until the file is once again "checked in."

Dreamweaver places a green check mark over a file's icon in the FTP Site window when it has been checked out by you, and a red mark if it has been checked out by another member of your team. And, so you won't have to guess who that team member is, Dreamweaver displays the name of the person next to the filename. You can also keep track of who last checked out a particular Web page (or image) — Dreamweaver keeps an ongoing log listing the file, person, and the date and time of the checkout.

 You can learn all about Dreamweaver's Web publishing capabilities in Chapter 27, "Publishing via Site FTP."

Templates and techniques

The more your Web site grows, the more you'll find yourself using the same basic format for different pages. Dreamweaver enables the use of Web page templates to standardize the look and feel of a Web site and to cut down on the repetitive work of creating new pages. A Dreamweaver template can hold the basic structure for the page — an image embedded in the background, a navigation bar along the left side, and a set-width table in the center for holding the main text, for example — with as many elements predefined as possible.

To give you a head start on the learning curve, Macromedia includes a number of sample templates for both regular pages and frame-based Web pages. You can access these by choosing Help ➪ Open Template. Naturally, Dreamweaver lets you save any template that you create in the same folder, so that your own templates, too, are accessible through the Open Template command.

sAmple templates

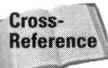 You'll find more about using and creating templates in Chapter 28, "Using Dreamweaver Templates."

In addition, Dreamweaver includes several fully developed techniques to help you master some of the more esoteric features of the program, such as Styles and Rollovers. Each technique is a combination of examples and heavily commented code, so you can see how the technique works and then take a look at the engine underneath. Just open the technique in Dreamweaver and press F12 to preview the example in your primary browser. From there, you can see either the code or a detailed step-by-step outline of how to apply the technique in Dreamweaver.

 This book's CD-ROM includes a number of additional templates, examples, and techniques. For more information on how to access these features, see Appendix D, "What's On the CD-ROM."

Summary

Building a Web site is half craft and half art, and Dreamweaver is the perfect tool for blending these often dueling disciplines. Dreamweaver's visual editor enables quick and artful page creation and, at the same time, its integrated text editors offer the detail-oriented focus required by programmers. Dreamweaver's key features include the following:

✦ Dreamweaver works the way professional Web developers do, with integrated visual and text editors. Dreamweaver won't convert your HTML code when it's used with pre-existing Web pages.

✦ Dreamweaver supports HTML standard commands with easy entry and editing of text, graphics, tables, and multimedia elements.

✦ Dreamweaver makes cutting-edge features, such as Dynamic HTML and Cascading Style Sheets, easy to use.

✦ Dreamweaver offers you a variety of reusable JavaScript behaviors, object libraries, techniques, and templates to streamline your Web page creation.

✦ Dreamweaver's wide range of site management tools include FTP Publishing with a file-locking capability that encourages team creation and maintenance as well as a built-in link checker.

In the next chapter, you'll receive a full tour of the Dreamweaver workspace.

✦   ✦   ✦

Touring Dreamweaver

Dreamweaver's user interface is very clean, very efficient, and very powerful. By offering streamlined tools and controls, Dreamweaver helps you focus on the most important area of the screen: your Web page design. This chapter provides a detailed overview of the Dreamweaver workspace so you'll know where all the tools are when you need to use them.

Viewing the Document Window

Dreamweaver's primary workspace is the Document Window. When you first start Dreamweaver, you'll see what is essentially an empty canvas, as shown in Figure 2-1. This is where you create your Web pages by typing in headlines and paragraphs, inserting images and links, and creating tables, forms, and other HTML elements.

The Web design process consists of creating your page in Dreamweaver and then previewing the results in one or more browsers. As your Web page begins to take shape, Dreamweaver shows you an approximate representation of how the page will look when viewed through a browser such as Netscape Communicator or Internet Explorer. You can do this as often as you like — Dreamweaver displays the page in your favorite browser with the press of a button.

Dreamweaver surrounds your "empty canvas" with all the tools you'll need to create your Web masterpiece. The first of these is known as the status bar.

Menus   Document Window   Object Palette

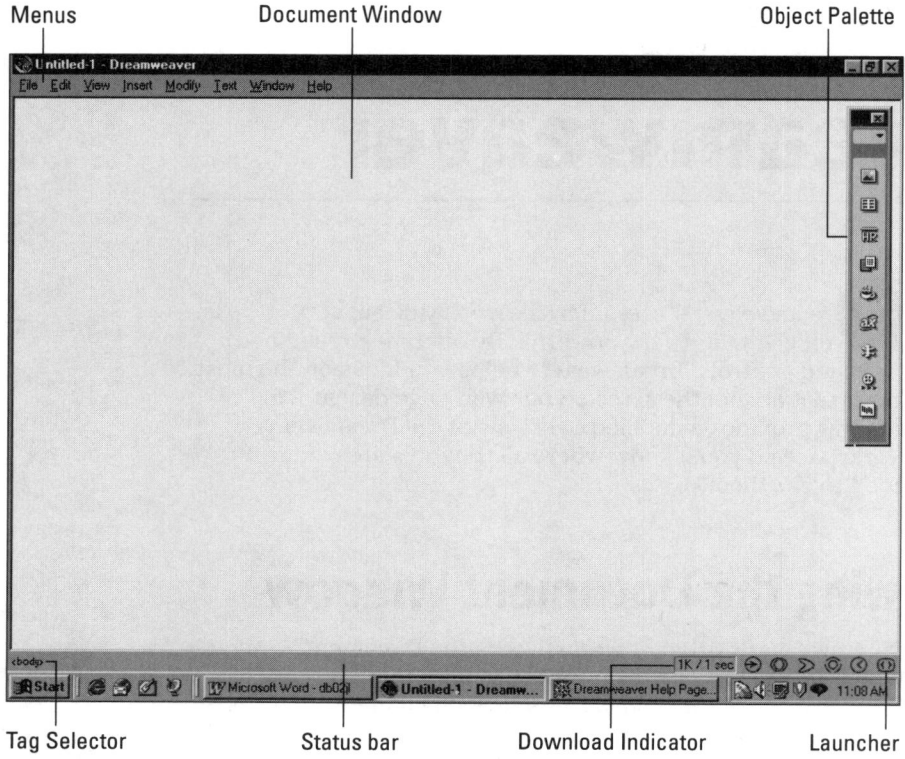

Tag Selector   Status bar   Download Indicator   Launcher

Figure 2-1: Dreamweaver's opening screen is designed to maximize your workspace with a minimum of distracting tools and windows.

Status bar

The status bar is found at the bottom of the Document Window. Embedded here are three important tools: the Tag Selector, the Download Indicator, and the Launcher. Beyond displaying useful information such as which windows are open, these status bar tools are extremely helpful and provide the Web designer with several time-saving utilities.

Tip

If you don't see the status bar at the bottom of your screen, check the View menu. Make sure there's a check mark next to the status bar item; if not, select it with your mouse to enable it.

Tag Selector

The Tag Selector is an excellent example of Dreamweaver's elegant design approach. On the left side of the status bar you'll see a listing of the current HTML tags. When you first open a blank page in Dreamweaver, you'll see only the <body> tag. If you type a line of text and then press Enter (Return), the paragraph tag <p> appears. Your cursor's position in the document determines which tags are displayed in the Tag Selector. The Tag Selector constantly keeps track of where you are in the HTML document by displaying the tags surrounding your current cursor position. This becomes especially important when you are building complex Web pages that use such features as nested tables.

As its name implies, the Tag Selector does more than just indicate a position in a document. Using the Tag Selector, you can quickly choose any of the elements surrounding your current cursor. Once an element is selected, you can quickly modify or delete it. If you have the Property Inspector (described later in this chapter) on screen, choosing a different code from the Tag Selector makes the corresponding options available in the Property Inspector.

Tip

If you want to quickly clear most of your HTML page, choose the <body> tag and press Delete. All graphics, text and other elements you have inserted through the Document Window will be erased. Left intact is any HTML code in the <head> section, including your title, meta tags, and any preliminary JavaScript.

In a more complex Web page section such as the one shown in Figure 2-2, the Tag Selector shows a wider variety of HTML tags. As you move your pointer over individual codes in the Tag Selector, they light up; click one and the code becomes bold while the tag remains highlighted. Tags are displayed from left to right in the Tag Selector, starting on the far left with the most inclusive (in this case the <body> tag) and proceeding to the narrowest selection (here, the underline <u> tag) on the far right.

As a Web page developer, you're constantly selecting elements in order to modify them. Rather than relying on the clicking-and-dragging method to highlight an area — which often grabs unwanted sections of your code — use the Tag Selector to unerringly pick just the code you want. Dreamweaver's Tag Selector is a subtle but extremely useful tool that can speed up your work significantly.

Download Indicator

So you've built your Web masterpiece and you've just finished uploading the HTML, along with the 23 JPEGs, eight audio files and three QuickTime movies that make up the page. You open the page over the Net and — surprise! — it takes forever to download. Okay, this example is a tad extreme, but every Web developer knows that opening a page from your hard drive and opening a page over the Internet are two vastly different experiences. Dreamweaver has taken the guesswork out of loading a page from the Web by providing the Download Indicator.

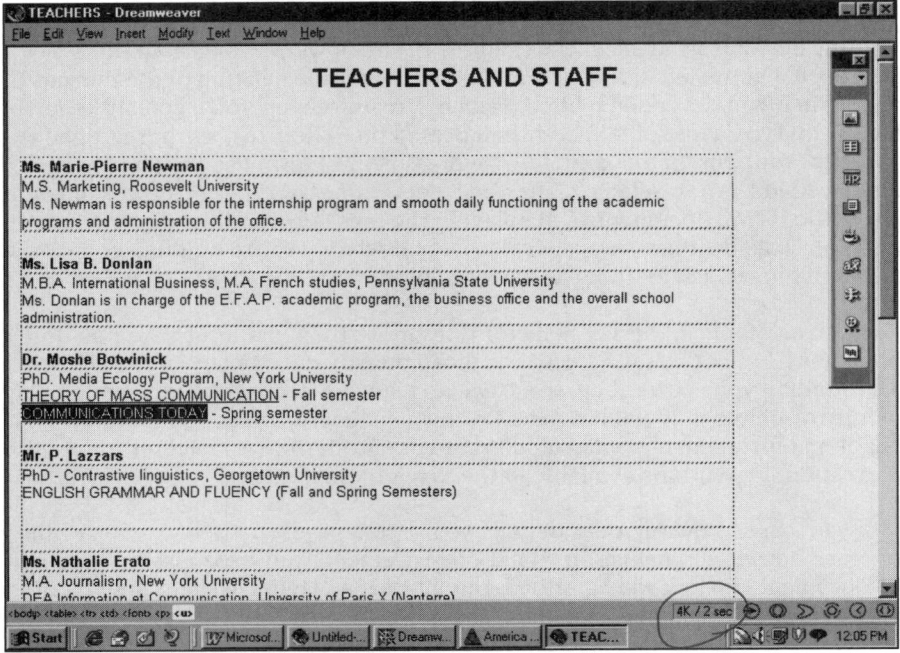

Figure 2-2: The Tag Selector lets you highlight just the code you want. Here, selecting the <u> tag chooses only the underlined portion of the text.

The Download Indicator is the located to the far right of the Tag Selector on the status bar. As illustrated in Figure 2-3, Dreamweaver gives you two sets of figures, separated by a slash character:

✦ The cumulative size of the page, including all the associated graphics, plug-ins, and multimedia files, measured in kilobytes (K).

✦ The time it takes to download at a particular modem connection speed, measured in seconds (sec).

The Download Indicator is a very handy real-world check. As you build your Web pages, it's a good practice to keep an eye on your file's download size — both in kilobytes and seconds. Ultimately, as a Web designer you have to decide what your audience will judge is worth the wait and what will have them reaching for that Stop button. For example, the graphic shown in Figure 2-3 is very pretty, but at 56K it's on the borderline of an acceptable size. The graphic should probably either be resized or the colors reduced to lower the overall "weight" of the page.

File size   Download Indicator   Download time

Figure 2-3: Take notice of the Download Indicator whenever you lay out a page with extensive graphics or other large multimedia files.

Cross-Reference

Not everybody has a standard 28.8 modem connection. If you are working with an intranet, you can set your connection speed far higher. Likewise, if your site gets a lot of traffic you can lower the connection speed. You change the anticipated download speed through the Dreamweaver Preferences, as explained in Chapter 3, "Setting Your Preferences."

Launcher

On the far right of the status bar, you'll find the Launcher — or, rather, one of the Launchers. In addition to this one on the status bar, Dreamweaver offers an independent, draggable palette with larger, named buttons that is also known as the Launcher. Both Launchers open and close the same windows: Site, Library, Styles, Behavior, Timeline, and HTML windows and Inspectors.

As with the Tag Selector, each one of the buttons in the status bar's Launcher lights up when the pointer passes over it and stays lit when selected. You can also use the Launcher to close the windows it has opened — just click the highlighted button. Dreamweaver lets you keep open any or all of the six different windows at the same time.

Tip

If you don't want to have the Launcher appear in the status bar, you can turn it off. Choose Edit ⇨ Preferences and then select the General category. Click Show Launcher in Status Bar to remove its check mark and then click OK. Naturally, you can turn the status bar Launcher back on by rechecking its box.

The features of the various windows controlled through the status bar Launcher are discussed in the "Using the Launcher" section later in this chapter.

Selecting from the Object Palette

The Object Palette holds the items most often used — the primary colors, as it were — when designing Web pages. Everything from images, to ActiveX plug-ins, to HTML comments can be selected from the Object Palette. Moreover, the Object Palette is completely customizable — you can add your own favorite items and even set up how the Palette is organized.

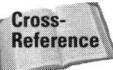

Cross-Reference To see how you can build your own Dreamweaver objects and modify the Object Palette, turn to Chapter 20, "Creating and Using Objects."

The Object Palette is divided into three separate panels of objects: Common, Forms, and Invisibles. The initial view is of the Common panel. To switch from one panel to another, select the small expander arrow (see Figure 2-4) and then choose an option from the resulting pop-up menu. Each panel is described in detail in the following sections.

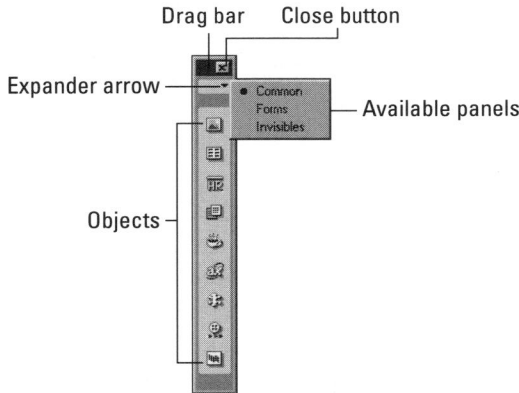

Figure 2-4: The Object Palette acts as a toolbox for holding your most commonly used Web page elements.

If the Object Palette is not available when you first start Dreamweaver, you can enable it by choosing Window ➪ Objects. Likewise, choosing Window ➪ Objects again deselects it and closes the Palette. You can also remove the Palette from your screen by clicking its Close button.

To reposition the Object Palette — or any of the Dreamweaver windows or floating toolbars — just position your cursor over the drag bar at the top of the window and drag it to a new place. The Object Palette can be placed anywhere on the screen, not just inside the Document Window. Some Web designers like to size their Document Window to a standard width that renders well across a variety of platforms and resolutions, and then place the Object Palette outside of that window so they will have a clear canvas with which to work.

Tip You can reshape the Object Palette by positioning your pointer over the Palette's border so that a double-headed arrow appears. Click and drag the rectangle into a new size or shape, and the icons within the Palette will rearrange themselves to fit. If your resized Palette is too small to fit all the objects, a small scroll arrow is displayed. Select the arrow, and the Palette scrolls to show additional objects; at the same time, another arrow appears at the opposite side of the window to indicate more hidden objects.

Common Objects panel

The most often-used HTML elements, aside from text, are accessible through the Common Objects panel of the Object Palette. Table 2-1 explains what each of icons represent.

<table>
<tr><td colspan="4" align="center">Table 2-1
Object Palette</td></tr>
<tr><td>*Icon*</td><td>*Name*</td><td>*Description*</td><td>*For Detailed Information*</td></tr>
<tr><td></td><td>Insert Image</td><td>Use for including any graphic or picture, including animated GIFs, at the cursor position</td><td>Chapter 8, "Inserting Images"</td></tr>
<tr><td></td><td>Insert Table</td><td>Opens a dialog box for creating a table at the cursor position</td><td>Chapter 11, "Setting Up Tables"</td></tr>
<tr><td></td><td>Insert Horizontal Rule</td><td>Draws a line across the page at the cursor position</td><td>See "Dividing the Web Page with Horizontal Rules" in Chapter 8</td></tr>
<tr><td></td><td>Marquee Layer</td><td>Enables you to drag out a layer of specific size and shape at a specific location</td><td>Chapter 23, "Working with Layers"</td></tr>
<tr><td></td><td>Insert Applet</td><td>Includes a Java applet at the cursor position</td><td>See "Adding Java Applets" in Chapter 15</td></tr>
<tr><td></td><td>Insert ActiveX</td><td>Puts a placeholder for an ActiveX control at the cursor position, using the `<object>` tag</td><td>See "Working with ActiveX Components" in Chapter 15</td></tr>
</table>

(continued)

		Table 2-1 *(continued)*	
Icon	**Name**	**Description**	**For Detailed Information**
	Insert Plug-in	Inserts a placeholder for a plug-in at the cursor position, using the `<embed>` tag	See "Incorporating Plug-ins" in Chapter 15
	Insert Flash Movie	Use to include a Shockwave Flash movie	Chapter 20, "Inserting Shockwave Elements"
	Insert Director Movie	Use to include a Shockwave Director movie	Chapter 20, "Inserting Shockwave Elements"

All of the Common objects except for Insert Horizontal Rule and Marquee Layer open a dialog box that enables you to specify or browse for a file.

Tip

If you'd prefer to enter all your information, including the necessary filenames, through the Property Inspector, you can turn off the automatic appearance of the file requester when you insert any object through the Object Palette or the menus. Choose Edit ➪ Preferences and, from the General Category, select Show Dialog When Inserting Objects to uncheck it.

Form objects

The form is the primary method for implementing HTML interactivity. The Forms panel of the Object Palette gives you nine basic building blocks for creating your Web-based form. Table 2-2 describes each of the elements found in the Forms panel.

		Table 2-2 **Forms Palette**	
Icon	**Name**	**Description**	**For Detailed Information**
	Insert Form	Creates the overall HTML form structure at the cursor position	Chapter 13, "Interactive Forms"
	Insert Text Field	Places a text box or a text area at the cursor position	See "Using Text Boxes" in Chapter 13
	Insert Button	Inserts a Submit, Reset or user-definable button at the cursor position	See "Activating Your Form with Buttons" in Chapter 13

Icon	Name	Description	For Detailed Information
	Insert Check Box	Inserts a check box for selecting any number of options at the cursor position	See "Providing Check Boxes and Radio Buttons" in Chapter 13
	Insert Radio Button	Puts a radio button for making a single choice from a set of options at the cursor position	See "Providing Check Boxes and Radio Buttons" in Chapter 13
	Insert List/Menu	Enables either a pop-up menu or a scrolling list at the cursor position	See "Creating Form Lists and Menus" in Chapter 13
	Insert File Field	Inserts a text box and Browse button for selecting a file to submit	See "Additional Form Fields" in Chapter 13
	Insert Image Field	Includes an image that can be used as a button	See "Additional Form Fields" in Chapter 13
	Insert Hidden Field	Inserts an invisible field used for passing variables to a CGI program	See "Additional Form Fields" in Chapter 13

As you can see demonstrated in Figure 2-5, you can use a table inside a form to get objects to line up properly. All forms return user input via either a CGI or JavaScript program. See Chapter 13, "Interactive Forms," for more detailed information.

Invisible objects

As any experienced Web designer knows, what you see on screen is, increasingly, a small part of the code necessary for the page's generation. Often you need to include an element that Dreamweaver categorizes as an Invisible. The third panel of the Objects Palette gives you quick access to the most commonly inserted behind-the-scenes tags, as described in Table 2-3.

Form outline   Text box   Radio button

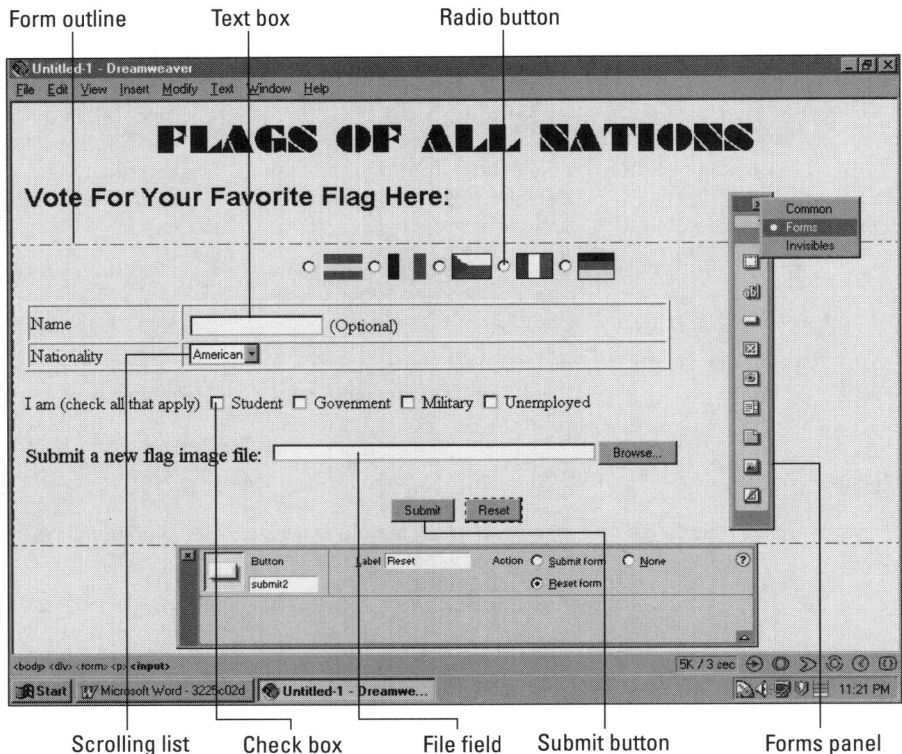

Scrolling list   Check box   File field   Submit button   Forms panel

Figure 2-5: Dreamweaver puts a distinctive dashed line around any form.

Table 2-3
Invisible Objects

Icon	Name	Description	For Detailed Information
	Insert Named Anchor	Use to put a hyperlink at a particular place on a Web page	See "Navigating with Anchors" in Chapter 9
	Insert Comment	Places HTML comment tags inside your script; these comments are ignored by the browser	See "Commenting Your Code" in Chapter 7

Icon	Name	Description	For Detailed Information
	Insert Script	Inserts JavaScript or VBScript either directly or from a file	See "Adding JavaScript and VBScript" in Chapter 15
	Insert Line Break	Puts in a tag which causes the line to wrap at the cursor position	See "Working with Paragraphs" in Chapter 7

Tip

Other invisible elements can be turned on or off through the Preferences dialog box. Choose Edit ➪ Preferences and then select the Invisible Elements category. You'll see a list of 12 options (including the four listed in the Invisibles panel). To turn off an option, click once to remove the check mark from the option's check box. For a complete description of all the Invisible elements and other preferences, see Chapter 3, "Setting Your Preferences."

Getting the Most Out of the Property Inspector

Dreamweaver's Property Inspector is your primary tool for specifying an object's particulars. What exactly those particulars are — in HTML, these are known as *attributes* — depends on the object itself. The contents of the Property Inspector change depending on which object is selected. For example, click anywhere on a blank Web page and the Property Inspector shows text attributes for format, font name and size, and so on. If you click an image, the Property Inspector displays a small thumbnail of the picture, and the image's attributes for height and width, image source, link, and alternative text. Figure 2-6 shows a Property Inspector for a line of text with an attached hyperlink.

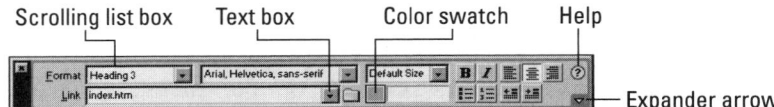

Figure 2-6: The Property Inspector takes many forms, depending on which HTML element you select.

Manipulating the Property Inspector

The Property Inspector is enabled by choosing Window ➪ Properties. As with the Object Palette, the Property Inspector can be closed by either selecting the Close button or unchecking Window ➪ Properties.

You can reposition the Property Inspector in one of two ways. You can click and drag the title bar of the window and move it to a new location, or — unlike the Object Palette — you can click and drag any open gray area in the Inspector itself. This is very handy for quickly moving the Inspector aside, out of your way.

The Property Inspector initially displays the most typical attributes for a given element. To see additional properties, click the expander arrow in the lower-right corner of the Property Inspector. Virtually all the inserted objects have additional parameters that can be modified. Unless you're tight on screen real estate, it's a good idea to keep the Property Inspector expanded so you can see all your options.

Tip   In addition to using the expander arrow, you can reveal (or hide) the expanded attributes by double-clicking any open gray area of the Property Inspector.

Property Inspector elements

Many of the attributes in the Property Inspector are text boxes; just click in any one and enter the desired value. If a value already appears in the text box, whether number or name, double-click it (or click and drag over it) to highlight the information and then enter your new data — the old value is immediately replaced. You can see the effect your modification has had by pressing the Tab key to move to the next attribute or by clicking outside of the Property Inspector.

The Property Inspector also uses scrolling list boxes for several attributes that provide a limited number of responses for you to choose. To open the drop-down list of available options, click the arrow button to the right of the list box. Then choose an option by highlighting it.

If you see a folder icon next to a text box (see the List item in the Inspector shown in Figure 2-6), you have the option of browsing for a filename on your local or networked drive, or manually inputting a name. Clicking the folder opens a standard Open File dialog box; after you've chosen your file and clicked Open, Dreamweaver inputs the name and any necessary path information in the correct attribute.

Cross-Reference   Dreamweaver can handle all forms of absolute and relative addressing. For more information on specifying HTML pages, be sure to see "Understanding Relative and Absolute Paths" in Chapter 5.

Certain objects such as text, layers and tables enable you to specify a color attribute. The Property Inspector alerts you to these options with a small color swatch next to the text box. You can type in a color's name (such as "blue"), or its six-figure hexadecimal value ("#3366FF"), or select the color swatch. Choosing the color swatch displays a color table with the 216 colors common to both the Netscape and Microsoft browsers — the so-called browser-safe colors. You can go outside of this range by clicking the small painter's palette in the lower-right corner of the color table. This opens a full-range Color dialog box in which you can choose a color visually or enter its red, green, and blue values or its hue, saturation, and luminance values.

One final aspect of the Property Inspector is worth noting: The encircled question mark in the upper-right corner of the Property Inspector is the Help button. Selecting this button invokes online help and displays specific information about the particular Property Inspector you're using.

The Help button is also available throughout all of the windows opened by the Launcher as described in the next section.

Using the Launcher

Dreamweaver's third main control panel, along with the Object Palette and the Property Inspector, is called the Launcher, shown in Figure 2-7.

Close button   Drag bar

Horizontal/vertical orientation

Figure 2-7: The Launcher gives you access to six different Dreamweaver functions.

The Launcher opens and closes six windows, each of which handles a different aspect of the program:

✦ **The Site Window** handles all elements of publishing to the Web, as well as basic file maintenance such as moving and deleting folders.

✦ **The Library Palette** is used to manage the repeating elements feature, which enables Dreamweaver to simultaneously update any number of Web pages on a site.

✦ **The Styles Palette** coordinates the Cascading Style Sheet modifications on each Web page and, if used in conjunction with an external style sheet, throughout your entire Web site.

✦ **The Behavior Inspector** assigns one or more JavaScript actions to a JavaScript event selected from a browser-targeted list.

✦ **The Timeline Inspector** controls the animations of images or layers over time.

✦ **The HTML Inspector** is Dreamweaver's internal HTML editor, integrated with the Document Window's visual editor.

Similarly to the other control panels, the Launcher can be started by choosing Window ➪ Launcher and closed by either selecting the Close button or choosing Window ➪ Launcher again. A standard title bar is available on the Launcher for dragging the palette into a new position. The Launcher also includes a small button in the lower-right corner (see Figure 2-7) that serves to change the panel's orientation from a horizontal shape to a vertical one, and vice versa.

The free-floating Launcher Palette functions identically to the status bar Launcher. Each one of the Launcher buttons highlights when the pointer passes over it and, when chosen, remains highlighted. As noted, the Launcher can be used to close the windows as well as open them — just click the highlighted button. Any or all of the windows can be "launched" simultaneously.

Site window

The Site Window is your gateway to the Web. Through it, you can transfer files from the development folder on your local drive to your online Web server. Any member of your development team can check out a file to work on it with no fear that another member is making changes at the same time. The team leader can even check Dreamweaver's log to see who is working on what.

Open the Site Window by choosing the Site button, on either the Launcher Palette or the status bar Launcher, by selecting Window ➪ Sites or by pressing F5. As you can see in Figure 2-8, the Site Window is two-paned: Local files are shown on the right side and remote files are displayed on the left. The headings across the top of each pane and the panes themselves can be resized. Position your pointer over a border until a double-headed arrow appears and then click and drag the border to a new position.

Remote pane   Local pane

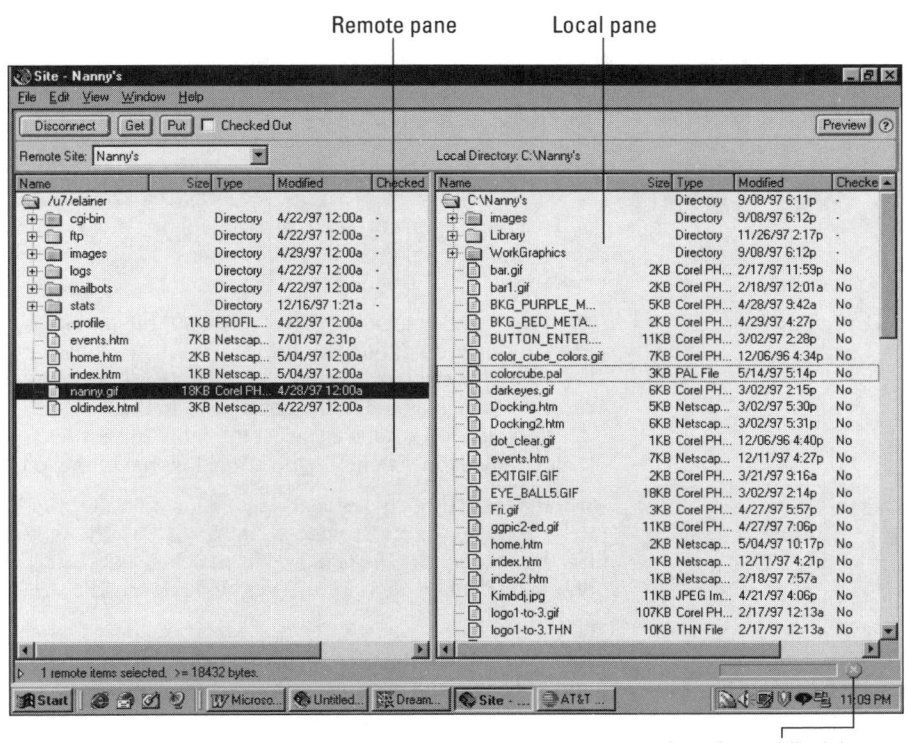

Stop Current Task button

Figure 2-8: Dreamweaver's Site Window handles the Webmaster's site management chores.

Tip

The files of both the local and remote folders can be sorted by name, file size, file type, date modified, or checkout status — all the options corresponding to the headings across each pane. For example, to display your files in A-to-Z alphabetical order, click the Name button once. To show them in descending (Z-to-A) order, click the Name button again. If you're constantly updating your site, it's good practice to have your folders sorted in descending date order so that your most recently modified files appear at the top of each pane.

The major operations performed in the Site Window (see Figure 2-8) include the following:

Site Window Function	Site Window Actions
Connecting to the site	When your site is properly configured, the Connect button automatically calls your remote site and uses whatever log-in and password is necessary to get you online. After the connection is confirmed the button changes into a Disconnect button.
Transferring files	To move files between your local drive and the remote server, use the Get and Put buttons. Get copies whatever files are highlighted in the Remote pane to the local folder, and Put copies files highlighted in the Local pane to the remote directory. To stop a transfer, select the Stop Current Task button — the stop sign in the lower-right corner of the window.
Locking files	When a team of Web designers is working on a site, you have to be able to prevent two people from working on the same file simultaneously. The Checked In/Checked Out indicator not only shows that a file is in use, but who has the file.
Previewing files	As a site grows in complexity, it is often necessary to make sure you are working with the correct file. The Preview button displays any highlighted file in your primary browser.

Cross-Reference

Maintaining a Web site is a major portion of a Webmaster's responsibility. To learn more about Dreamweaver's site management features, see Part 7, "Web Site Management Under Dreamweaver."

Library Palette

The Library Palette manages Dreamweaver's repeating element feature. Through the Library Palette you can turn any item on your Web page — or series of items — into a kind of "linked boilerplate." Not only can you drop your "boilerplate" text or images into any page of your site, but you can update them all by just modifying one item. The Library feature can save a Web development team many, many work-hours in both the creation and maintenance phases.

You can open the Library Palette by selecting the Library button from the Launcher, by choosing Window ➪ Library, or by pressing F6. As you can see from Figure 2-9, the Library Palette is a draggable, resizable window divided horizontally into two panes. The upper portion of the window displays the list of Library items for the current Web site. When one of these items is selected, the lower portion of the

Library Palette, the Preview pane, illustrates the item. You can resize the two panes by positioning your pointer over the separating border and then clicking and dragging the border to a new place.

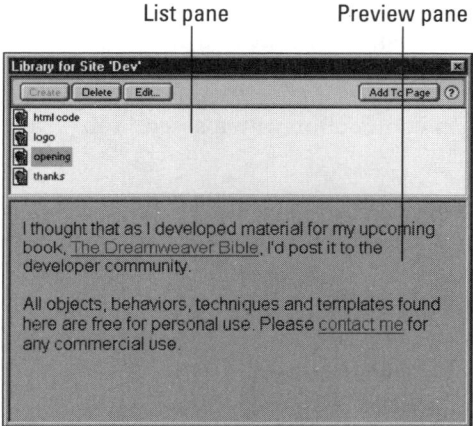

Figure 2-9: The Library Palette manages the repeating elements throughout your Web site.

The primary features of the Library Palette are listed in the following table:

Library Palette Function	Site Window Actions
Creating new entries	You define a Library item by first selecting it, either in the Document Window or the HTML Inspector, and then clicking the Create button.
Deleting old entries	Remove an item from the Library by selecting the Delete button.
Editing entries	To alter a defined Library item, select it and press the Edit button. This opens another Dreamweaver window containing your Library item. After you've made your modifications, closing the window alerts Dreamweaver to your changes, and the item is updated.
Inserting entries	After you've built and defined your Library items, use the Add to Page button to insert it into your pages at the current cursor position.

Cross-Reference To find out more about the powerful Library feature, turn to Chapter 26, "Using the Repeating Elements Library."

Styles Palette

Through the Styles Palette, Dreamweaver makes creating and applying Cascading Style Sheets (CSS) easy. CSSs give the Web designer a terrific degree of control over the appearance of text and other elements, throughout the creation stage and when the Web site is live. Styles can be used in conjunction with a single Web page or an entire site.

The Styles Palette, shown in Figure 2-10, is accessed by clicking the Styles button from either the Launcher Palette or the status bar Launcher. You can also open the Styles Palette by choosing Window ⇨ Styles or by pressing F7. You can drag or resize the Styles Palette with the mouse.

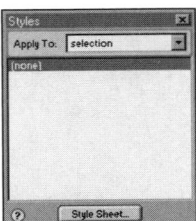

Figure 2-10: The Styles Palette displays custom styles and gives you access to Dreamweaver's point-and-click CSS editing capabilities.

The Styles Palette has three key uses:

Styles Palette Function	Site Window Actions
Defining styles	Through the Style Sheet button on the Styles Palette you can create, modify, and remove CSS formats. CSSs either redefine existing HTML tags or create new user-defined classes.
Selecting tags	With styles, like most editing functions, you have to select the item you want to affect. The Apply To: button lets you quickly choose any available tag, depending on your current cursor position.
Applying styles	Once your styles are defined, you can easily apply them to any selected text throughout your Web page. Just click the desired style in the Styles Palette list.

For more detailed information on how to use the Styles Palette, see Chapter 22, "Building Style Sheet Web Pages."

Behavior Inspector

The Behavior Inspector enables nonprogrammers to build cutting-edge Web pages through prebuilt JavaScript actions. Moreover, the Behavior Inspector is browser-savvy and won't let you assign a JavaScript event that only works on 4.0 browsers when you need 3.0 compatibility. With the Behavior Inspector, not only can you link several actions to a single event, but you can also specify the order of the actions.

Use the Behavior button on either Launcher (palette or status bar) to open the Behavior Inspector. You can also press F8 or choose Window ⇨ Behaviors. Like the other windows, you can resize or reposition the Behavior Inspector with the mouse using the click-and-drag technique. As shown in Figure 2-11, the Behavior Inspector is made up of two main parts: the Events pane and the Actions pane.

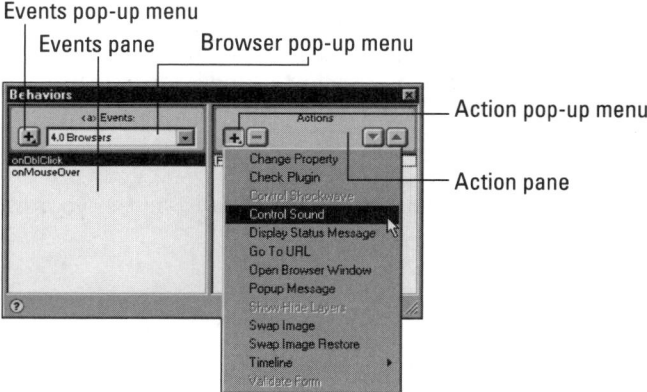

Figure 2-11: Linking an action to an event creates a JavaScript behavior in the Behavior Inspector.

Use the Behavior Inspector to perform the functions outlined in the following table.

Behavior Inspector Function	Site Window Actions
Specifying a browser	The various browsers and browser versions understand specific JavaScript commands. You can target individual browsers by manufacturer or version number, or a combination of the two, by using the Browser pop-up menu.
Picking an event	Events are linked to specific HTML tags; not all HTML tags have events associated with them. The events listed under the Events pop-up menu (the + button in the Events pane) are determined by what's selected in the Browser pop-up menu.
Naming an action	Once an event is chosen, selecting the Action pop-up menu (the + button in the Actions pane) displays a list of available actions. Remove an action by highlighting it and clicking the – button.
Order the actions	Because you can assign more than one action to an event, Dreamweaver enables you to rearrange the order of the actions. Use the Up/Down arrows to rearrange the order of your action list.

On the CD-ROM

Be sure to check out the Behaviors section of the CD-ROM to add to your list of Dreamweaver action capabilities.

Cross-Reference

Behaviors are user-definable. In Chapter 17, "Creating and Using Behaviors," you'll see how to create your own actions.

Timeline Inspector

Dreamweaver controls the potential of built-in Dynamic HTML animation through its Timeline Inspector. The Timeline Inspector plots the position of a selected image or layer on a frame-by-frame basis. In your new role as animator in addition to Web designer, you select one keyframe after another; then Dreamweaver interpolates — or, as animators say, *tweens* — the frames in between. The Timeline Inspector can handle any number of objects on the Timeline for any length of time, limited only by system resources such as memory and processing power.

Open the Timeline Inspector through one of the usual methods: Select its button from either Launcher, press F9, or choose Window ➪ Timelines. As shown in Figure 2-12, the Timeline Inspector is grid-based — the numbers running horizontally denote frames, and the vertical numbers indicate the object in the timeline.

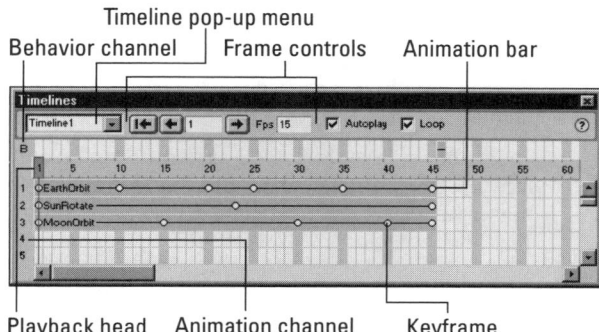

Figure 2-12: The Timeline Inspector can animate layers or images, which can be previewed in Dreamweaver or in any 4.0 browser.

Use the Timeline Inspector for the functions in the following table.

Timeline Inspector Function	Site Window Actions
Drag and drop objects	To link an object to a timeline, just drag and drop it onto the Timeline Inspector's next available Animation Channel. At present, only layers and images can be animated.
Set the run length	The Animation Bar determines how many frames each object plays. You can extend the length of the animation by dragging out the Animation Bar's endpoint.
Make the keyframes	Keyframes indicate moments of change — in position, size, or visibility. You can set a keyframe on the Timeline Inspector in a number of ways, including choosing Modify ➪ Timeline ➪ Add Keyframe.

(continued)

Timeline Inspector Function	Site Window Actions
Add a behavior	The simplest way to add a behavior to a Timeline is by selecting the Loop option. This creates an event in the Behavior Channel that causes the timeline to run itself again at the end of the animation. You can add numerous actions to specific frames.
View the frames	By dragging the Playback Head or selecting one of the Frame Controls, you can view any frame of your animation.
Use multiple timelines	Your Dreamweaver-built Web page can employ multiple timelines for your animation. Use the Timeline pop-up menu to choose which timeline is displayed in the Timeline Inspector.

Cross-Reference To better understand how you can manipulate timelines, see Chapter 24, "Working with Timelines."

HTML Inspector

The final window controlled by the Launcher is the HTML Inspector (shown in Figure 2-13) — the internal editor designed to complement Dreamweaver's visual layout facility. Although you can opt to use an external editor such as the bundled BBEdit or HomeSite for extensive coding, the HTML Inspector is great for making spot edits or quickly checking your code. The tight integration between the Dreamweaver's text and visual editors allows for simultaneous input and instant updating.

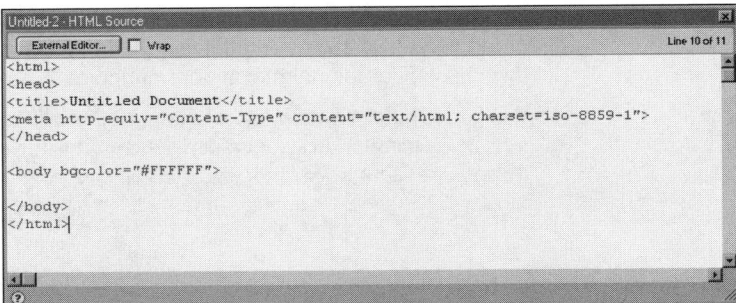

Figure 2-13: The HTML Inspector gives you instant access for tweaking your code — or adding entirely new elements by hand.

Clicking the HTML button on either Launcher opens and closes the HTML Inspector, as does choosing Window ➪ HTML or pressing F10. Once the HTML Inspector is open, changes made in the Document Window are incorporated in real-time. However, in order to properly check the code, any changes made in the HTML Inspector are not updated in the Document Window until the Document Window is activated. You can alternate between the two windows by pressing Ctrl-Tab (Command-Tab).

Note

Note to MS Office for Mac 4 users: The Command-Tab hot switch in Dreamweaver conflicts with Office's QuickSwitch feature. To turn off the QuickSwitch in MS Office, go to the Office Manager drop-down menu, select Customize, and then deselect the QuickSwitch check box.

Tip

You can see the tight integration between the visual editor and the HTML Inspector when you have both windows open and you select an object in the Document Window. The corresponding code is instantly displayed in the HTML Inspector. This feature is very useful for quickly finding a specific HTML element for alteration.

By design, the HTML Inspector's layout is simple, to give maximum emphasis to your code. There are really only two buttons, aside from Help and Close, in the HTML Inspector. First you can turn on or off the line wrap function by selecting the Wrap button. This is useful if you encounter an error message that displays a line number; temporarily turn off the wrap feature to locate the line. Second, if you decide you need to do more extensive coding, you can select the External Editor button to open your full-featured editor.

Accessing the Menus

Like many programs, Dreamweaver's menus duplicate most of the features that are accessible through windows and palettes. Certain features, however, are only available through the menus or through a corresponding keyboard shortcut. This section offers a reference guide to the menus when you need a particular feature or command.

Tip

In Tables 2-4 through 2-10, if a keyboard shortcut is not available for a particular option, you'll see the abbreviation "n/a."

The File menu

The File menu contains commands for file handling and overall site management. Table 2-4 describes the commands and their keyboard shortcuts.

Table 2-4
File Menu Commands

Command	Description	Windows	Macintosh
New Window	Adds a new Document Window	Ctrl-N	n/a
New	Replaces the current document with a blank document	Ctrl-Shift-N	Command-N
Open	Displays the Open dialog box to open an existing file	Ctrl-O	Command-O
Open in Frame	Opens an existing file in the selected frame	Ctrl-Shift-O	Command-Shift-O
Open Site ⇨ Your Site List	Displays user-definable list of sites; when one is selected, the Site Window opens pointing to the selected site	n/a	n/a
Open Site ⇨ Edit Sites	Displays the Site Information dialog box for setting up a new site, or for modifying or deleting an existing site	n/a	n/a
Close	Closes the current window	Ctrl-W	Command-W
Save	Saves the current document, or displays the Save As dialog box for an unnamed document	Ctrl-S	Command-S
Save As	Displays the Save As dialog box before saving the document	n/a	n/a
Save Frameset	Saves a file describing the current frameset, or displays the Save As dialog box for an unnamed document	n/a	n/a
Save Frameset As	Displays the Save As Frameset before saving the current frameset	n/a	n/a
Save All	Saves all open documents (including framesets, if applicable)	Ctrl-Shift-S	Command-Shift-S
Convert ⇨ 3.0 Browser Compatible	Creates a new Web page, converting all layers to tables	Ctrl-F6	Command-F6
Convert ⇨ Tables to Layers	Creates a new Web page, converting all tables to layers	Ctrl-Shift-F6	Command-Shift-F6

Command	Description	Windows	Macintosh
Preview in Browser ➪ Your Browser List	Displays list of browsers established in Preferences; choose one to preview the current page using that browser	F12 (Primary) Shift-F12 (Secondary)	F12 (Primary) Shift-F12 (Secondary)
Preview in Browser ➪ Edit Browser List	Displays the Preview in Browser category of Preferences, where the user can add, edit, or delete additional preview browsers	n/a	n/a
Check Links ➪ This Document	Verifies hypertext links for the current document	Ctrl-F7	Command-F7
Check Links ➪ Entire Site	Verifies hypertext links for the current site	Ctrl-F8	Command-F8
Check Target Browsers	Displays the Check Target Browsers dialog box, where the user can validate the current file against installed browser profiles	n/a	n/a
Your Last Opened Files	Displays the last four opened files; select any name to reopen the file	n/a	n/a
Exit	Closes all open files and quits Dreamweaver	Ctrl-Q	Command-Q

The Edit menu

The Edit menu gives you the commands necessary to quickly modify your page — or recover from a devastating accident. Many of the commands (Cut, Copy, and Paste) are standard on other programs; others, such as Paste as Text, are unique to Dreamweaver. Table 2-5 details all of the features to be found under the Edit menu.

Table 2-5 Edit Menu Commands			
Command	Description	Windows	Macintosh
Undo	Reverses the last action; the number of times you can Undo is determined by system resources	Ctrl-Z	Command-Z

(continued)

Table 2-5 *(continued)*

Command	Description	Windows	Macintosh
Redo	Reverses the last Undo; the number of times you can Redo is determined by system resources	Ctrl-Y	Command-Y
Cut	Places a copy of the current selection on the clipboard and removes the selection from the current document	Ctrl-X	Command-X
Copy	Places a copy of the current selection on the clipboard and leaves the selection in the current document	Ctrl-C	Command-C
Paste	Copies the clipboard to the current cursor position	Ctrl-V	Command-V
Clear	Removes the current selection from the document	Delete	Delete
Select All	Highlights all the elements in the current document or frame	Ctrl-A	Command-A
Copy As Text	Copies the current selection onto the clipboard with all HTML codes rendered as text	Ctrl-Shift-C	Command-Shift-C
Paste As Text	Pastes the current selection from the clipboard with all HTML codes rendered as text	Ctrl-Shift-V	Command-Shift-V
Find	Displays the Find dialog box for searching the current document	Ctrl-F	Command-F
Find Next	Repeats the previous Find operation	F3	F3
Replace	Displays the Replace dialog box	Ctrl-H	Command-H
Launch External Editor	Opens the External HTML Editor as defined in Preferences ⇨ General ⇨ External Editor Path	Ctrl-E	Command-E
Preferences	Displays the Preferences dialog box	Ctrl-U	Command-U

The View menu

As you build your Web pages, you'll find that it's helpful to be able to turn certain features on and off. The View menu centralizes all these commands. Certain capabilities, such as rulers and grids, are only useful when used with layers. Table 2-6 describes each command under the View menu.

	Table 2-6 View Menu Commands		
Command	*Description*	*Windows*	*Macintosh*
Invisible Elements	Controls whether the symbols for certain HTML tags are shown	Ctrl-Shift-I	Command-Shift-I
Rulers ⇨ Show	Displays the horizontal and vertical rulers	Ctrl-Alt-Shift-R	Command-Option-Shift-R
Rulers ⇨ Reset Origin	Resets the ruler's 0,0 coordinates to the upper-left corner of the window	n/a	n/a
Rulers ⇨ Pixels / Inches / Centimeters	Sets the rulers to a selected measurement system	n/a	n/a
Grid ⇨ Show	Displays a background grid using the current settings	Ctrl-Alt-Shift-G	Command-Option-Shift-G
Grid ⇨ Snap To	Forces inserted objects to align with the nearest snap setting	Ctrl-Alt-G	Command-Option-G
Grid ⇨ Settings	Displays the Grid Settings dialog box	n/a	n/a
Status Bar	Enables the status bar to be shown	n/a	n/a
Layer Borders	Makes a border visible outlining an unselected layer	n/a	n/a
Table Borders	Makes a border visible outlining an unselected table	n/a	n/a
Frame Borders	Enables borders necessary for drag-and-drop frame creation	n/a	n/a

The Insert menu

The Insert menu contains the same items available through the Object Palette. In fact, if you add additional objects (as discussed in Chapter 20, "Creating and Using Dreamweaver Objects") the next time you start Dreamweaver you'll see your objects listed on the Insert menu. All objects are inserted at the current cursor position.

Table 2-7 details the items available to be inserted in the standard Dreamweaver.

Table 2-7 Insert Menu Commands			
Command	**Description**	**Windows**	**Macintosh**
Image	Opens the Insert Image dialog box that lets you input or browse for a graphics file	Ctrl-Alt-I	Command-Option-I
Table	Opens the Insert Table dialog box for establishing a table layout	Ctrl-Alt-T	Command-Option-T
Horizontal Rule	Inserts a horizontal line the width of the current window	n/a	n/a
Layer	Inserts a layer of a preset size	n/a	n/a
Applet	Opens the Insert Applet dialog box that permits you to input or browse for a Java Class source	n/a	n/a
ActiveX	Inserts an ActiveX placeholder	n/a	n/a
Plug-in	Opens the Insert Plug-in dialog box so you can either input or browse for a plug-in	n/a	n/a
Flash Movie	Opens the Insert Flash Movie dialog box so you can either type in or browse for a movie file	Ctrl-Alt-F	Command-Option-F
Shockwave Director	Opens the Insert Shockwave Director dialog box for you to input or browse for a Director file	Ctrl-Alt-D	Command-Option-D
Form	Creates the form structure on your Web page	n/a	n/a

Command	Description	Windows	Macintosh
Form Object ⇨ Text Field / Button / Check Box / Radio Button / List/Menu	Inserts the selected form object at the current cursor position	n/a	n/a
Named Anchor	Displays the Insert Named Anchor dialog box	Ctrl-Alt-A	Command-Option-A
Comment	Displays the Insert Comment dialog box	n/a	n/a
Script	Displays the Insert Script dialog box	n/a	n/a
Line Break	Inserts a line break tag	n/a	n/a

The Modify menu

Inserting objects is less than half the battle of creating a Web page. Most Web designers spend most of their time adjusting, experimenting, and tweaking the various elements. The Modify menu lists all the commands for altering existing selections. Table 2-8 details all the Modify options.

Table 2-8 Modify Menu Commands			
Command	**Description**	**Windows**	**Macintosh**
Page Properties	Opens the Page Properties dialog box	Ctrl-J	Command-J
Selection Properties	Displays and hides the Property Inspector	n/a	n/a
Table ⇨ Cell Properties / Row Properties / Column Properties	Opens the Cell, Row, or Column Properties dialog box	n/a	n/a

(continued)

— Modify menu —

Table 2-8 *(continued)*

Command	Description	Windows	Macintosh
Table ⇨ Select Table	Highlights the entire table surrounding the current cursor position	n/a	n/a
Table ⇨ Insert Rows	Opens the Insert Rows dialog box, which enables multiple rows to be inserted above or below the current row	n/a	n/a
Table ⇨ Insert Row	Adds a new row below the current row	Ctrl-M	Command-M
Table ⇨ Delete Row	Removes the current row	Ctrl-Shift-M	Command-Shift-M
Table ⇨ Increase Row Span / Decrease Row Span	Increases or decreases by one row the span of the current cell	n/a	n/a
Table ⇨ Clear Row Heights	Removes specified row height values for the entire selected table	n/a	n/a
Table ⇨ Insert Columns	Opens the Insert Columns dialog box that enables multiple columns to be inserted to the left or right of the current column	n/a	n/a
Table ⇨ Delete Column	Removes the current column	n/a	n/a
Table ⇨ Increase Column Span / Decrease Column Span	Increases or decreases the column span of the current cell by one column	n/a	n/a
Table ⇨ Clear Column Widths	Removes specified column width values for the entire selected table	n/a	n/a
Table ⇨ Convert Widths to Pixels	Changes column widths from percents to pixels for the entire selected table	n/a	n/a
Table ⇨ Convert Widths to Percent	Changes column widths from pixels to percents for the entire selected table	n/a	n/a
Frameset ⇨ Edit No Frames Content	Opens a new window for content to be seen by browsers that do not support frames	n/a	n/a

Command	Description	Windows	Macintosh
Frameset ⇨ Split Frame Left / Split Frame Right / Split Frame Up / Split Frame Down	Moves the current frame in the specified direction and adds a new frame opposite	n/a	n/a
Alignment ⇨ Left	Aligns the selected object or the current line to the left	Ctrl-Alt-L	Command-Option-L
Alignment ⇨ Center	Centers the selected object or the current line on the page	Ctrl-Alt-C	Command-Option-C
Alignment ⇨ Right	Aligns the selected object or the current line to the right	Ctrl-Alt-R	Command-Option-R
Add Object to Library	Opens the Library Palette and adds the selected object	n/a	n/a
Library ⇨ Update Current Page / Update Entire Site	Replaces any modified Library items in the current page/current site	n/a	n/a
Add Object to Timeline	Opens the Timeline Inspector and inserts the current image or layer	n/a	n/a
Add Behavior to Timeline	Opens the Timeline Inspector and inserts an `onFrame` event using the current frame	n/a	n/a
Timeline ⇨ Add Keyframe	Inserts a keyframe at the current Playback Head position	Shift-F9	Shift-F9
Timeline ⇨ Remove Keyframe	Deletes the currently selected keyframe	Delete	Delete
Timeline ⇨ Remove Object / Remove Behavior	Deletes the currently selected Object or Behavior	n/a	n/a
Timeline ⇨ Add Frame / Remove Frame	Inserts or deletes a frame at the current Playback Head position	n/a	n/a
Timeline ⇨ Add Timeline / Remove Timeline / Rename Timeline	Inserts an additional timeline, deletes the current timeline, or renames the current timeline	n/a	n/a

The Text menu

The Internet was initially an all-text medium and, despite all the multimedia development, the World Wide Web hasn't traveled far from these beginnings. The Text menu, as described in Table 2-9, covers overall formatting as well as text-oriented functions such as spell-checking.

	Table 2-9 Text Menu Commands		
Command	**Description**	**Windows**	**Macintosh**
Indent	Marks the selected text or the current paragraph with the `<blockquote>` tag to indent it	Ctrl-]	Command-]
Outdent	Removes a `<dir>` surrounding the selected text or current paragraph	Ctrl-[	Command-[
Format ➪ None	Removes all HTML formatting tags surrounding the current selection	Ctrl-0 (zero)	Command-0 (zero)
Format ➪ Paragraph	Converts the selected text to paragraph format	Ctrl-T	Command-T
Format ➪ Heading 1–6	Changes the selected text to the specified heading format	Ctrl-1–6	Command-1–6
Format ➪ Preformatted Text	Formats the selected text with a monospaced font	n/a	n/a
Format ➪ Unordered List	Makes the selected text into a bulleted list	n/a	n/a
Format ➪ Ordered List	Makes the selected text into a numbered list	n/a	n/a
Format ➪ Definition List	Converts the selected text into alternating definition terms and items	n/a	n/a
Alignment ➪ Left	Aligns the selected text to the left of the page	Ctrl-Alt-L	Command-Option-L
Alignment ➪ Center	Aligns the selected text to the center of the current page	Ctrl-Alt-C	Command-Option-C
Alignment ➪ Right	Aligns the selected text to the right of the page	Ctrl-Alt-R	Command-Option-R
Font ➪ Your Font List	Displays fonts in your current font list	n/a	n/a

Command	Description	Windows	Macintosh
Font ➪ Edit Font List	Opens the Font List dialog box for adding or deleting fonts from the current list	n/a	n/a
Style ➪ Bold	Makes the selected text bold	Ctrl-B	Command-B
Style ➪ Italic	Makes the selected text italic	Ctrl-I	Command-I
Style ➪ Underline	Underlines the selected text	n/a	n/a
Style ➪ Strikethrough	Surrounds the selected text with the `<s>...</s>` tags for text with a line through it	n/a	n/a
Style ➪ Teletype	Surrounds the selected text with the `<tt>...</tt>` tags for a monospaced font	n/a	n/a
Style ➪ Emphasis	Surrounds the selected text with the `<emp>...</emp>` tags for slightly emphasized, usually italic, text	n/a	n/a
Style ➪ Strong Emphasis	Surrounds the selected text with the `<strong>...</strong>` tags for more emphasized, usually bold, text	n/a	n/a
Style ➪ Code	Surrounds the selected text with HTML code for depicting programming code	n/a	n/a
Style ➪ Variable	Surrounds the selected text with HTML code for depicting a variable in programming, typically as in italic	n/a	n/a
Style ➪ Sample ➪ Keyboard	Surrounds the selected text with HTML code for depicting monospaced fonts	n/a	n/a
Custom Style (selection) ➪ Your Style List	Applies a user-defined style to selected text	n/a	n/a
Custom Style (selection) ➪ Edit Style Sheet	Opens the Edit Style Sheet dialog box for adding, deleting, or modifying custom styles	Ctrl-Shift-E	Command-Shift-E

(continued)

— Text menu —

Table 2-9 *(continued)*

Command	Description	Windows	Macintosh
Size ⇨ Default ⇨ 1 – 7	Converts the selected text to the chosen font size	n/a	n/a
Size Increase ⇨ +1 – +7	Increases the size of the selected text relative to the defined basefont size (default is 3)	n/a	n/a
Size Decrease ⇨ –1 through –7	Decreases the size of the selected text relative to the defined basefont size (default is 3)	n/a	n/a
Color	Opens the Color dialog box to alter the color of selected or following text	n/a	n/a
Check Spelling	Opens the Spell Check dialog box	Shift-F7	Shift-F7

The Window menu

The Window menu manages both program and user-opened windows. Through this menu, detailed in Table 2-10, you can open, close, arrange, bring to the front, or hide all of the additional Dreamweaver screens. There's even a command to open one additional window — that of Dreamweaver.com.

Tip　　All the commands for Dreamweaver's various windows, palettes and inspectors are toggles. Select them once to open the window; select again to close.

Table 2-10
Window Menu Commands

Command	Description	Windows	Macintosh
Objects	Opens the Object Palette	n/a	n/a
Properties	Shows the Property Inspector for the currently selected item	n/a	n/a
Launcher	Opens the Launcher Palette	n/a	n/a
Sites	Displays the Sites Window	F5	F5
Library	Opens the Library Palette	F6	F6
Styles	Opens the Styles Inspector	F7	F7
Behaviors	Shows the Behaviors Inspector	F8	F8

Command	Description	Windows	Macintosh
Timelines	Shows the Timelines Inspector	F9	F9
HTML	Displays the HTML Inspector	F10	F10
Layers	Opens the Layers Inspector	F11	F11
Frames	Opens the Frames Inspector	n/a	n/a
Arrange Floating Windows	Moves all open windows to preset positions	n/a	n/a
Show/Hide Floating Windows	Displays/hides all open windows	F4	F4
Dreamweaver Online	Goes online to the Dreamweaver Developer's Center Support Web site	Ctrl-F1	Command-F1
Your Open Windows	Displays a list of the currently open Dreamweaver windows	n/a	n/a

The Help menu

The final menu, the Help menu, offers access to Dreamweaver's excellent online help as well as special examples and templates. Table 2-11 explains each of these useful options.

Table 2-11 Help Menu Commands			
Command	Description	Windows	Macintosh
Dreamweaver Help Topics	Opens the Dreamweaver online Help system in your primary browser	F1	n/a
Register Dreamweaver	Goes online to register your copy of Dreamweaver	n/a	n/a
Open Template	Displays an Open File dialog box pointing to the Template folder	n/a	n/a
Open Example	Displays an Open File dialog box pointing to the Example folder	n/a	n/a
About Dreamweaver	Shows the opening Dreamweaver splash screen with credits and version information	n/a	n/a

Summary

In this chapter, you've observed the power and had a look at the well-designed layout of Dreamweaver. From the Object Palette to the various tools controlled through the Launcher, Dreamweaver offers you an elegant, flexible workspace for creating next-generation Web sites.

✦ The Document Window is your main canvas for visually designing your Dreamweaver Web pages. This workspace includes simple, powerful tools such as the Tag Selector and the status bar Launcher.

✦ The Object Palette is Dreamweaver's toolbox. Completely customizable, the Object Palette holds the elements you'll need most often, in three initial categories: Common, Forms, and Invisibles.

✦ Dreamweaver's mechanism for assigning details and attributes to an HTML object is the Property Inspector. The Property Inspector is context-sensitive and varies its options according to the object selected.

✦ The Launcher is the control center for Dreamweaver's specialized functions: the Site Window, the Library Palette, the Styles Palette, the Behavior Inspector, the Timeline Inspector, and the HTML Inspector. You have two Launchers to choose from — one free-floating palette, and the one accessible through the status bar.

✦ Dreamweaver's full-featured menus offer complete file manipulation, a wide range of insertable objects, the tools to modify them, and extensive online — and on-the-Web — help. Many menu items can be invoked through keyboard shortcuts.

In the next chapter, you'll learn how to customize Dreamweaver to work the way you want to work by establishing your own preferences for the program and its interface.

✦   ✦   ✦

Setting Your Preferences

Everyone works differently. Whether you need to conform to a corporate style sheet handed down from the powers that be or you think "it just looks better that way," Dreamweaver offers you the flexibility to shape your Web page tools and your code output. This chapter describes the options available to you in Dreamweaver's Preferences and then details how you can tell Dreamweaver to format your source code in your way.

Customizing Your Environment

The vast majority of Dreamweaver's settings are controlled through the Preferences dialog box. You can open Preferences by choosing Edit ⇨ Preferences, or by using the keyboard shortcuts Control-U (Command-U). Within Preferences, you find thirteen different subjects listed on the left side of the screen. As you switch from one category to another by selecting its name in this Category list, the options available for that category appear in the main area of the dialog box. Although this chapter covers all the options available to you in each category, the categories are grouped by function rather than examined in the same order as in the Category list.

Most changes to Preferences take effect immediately after you close the window by clicking OK or the Close button. Only two preferences are not updated instantly:

✦ First, if you opt for the large fonts display, you have to restart Dreamweaver.

✦ Second, if you elect to modify the source format profile, as described in a following section, you should complete this modification outside of Dreamweaver (in a text editor), save your work, and then start the program.

General Preferences

Dreamweaver's General Preferences, as seen in Figure 3-1, cover program appearance, user operation, and external editor integration. The appearance of the program's interface may seem to be a trivial matter, but Dreamweaver is a program for designers — to whom appearance is extremely important. These user-operation choices are based purely on how you, the user, work best.

Screen color scheme   General options

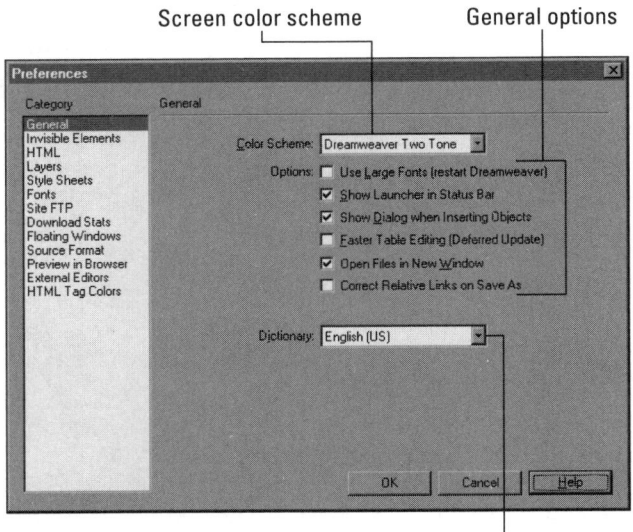

Spelling dictionary options

Figure 3-1: Dreamweaver's General Preferences enable you to change your program's appearance and certain overall operations.

Tip

In choosing all the preferences, including the General ones, you can work in two ways. If you are a seasoned Web designer, you'll probably want Dreamweaver to work in your established manner to minimize your learning curve. If you're just starting out as a Web page creator, work with the default options for a while, and then go back and try other options. You'll know right away which style works for you.

Color Scheme

The first choice is purely a cosmetic one: the color scheme of the screens presented to you as you work with the program. Dreamweaver offers three different color combinations. Click the arrow button next to Color Scheme to open the drop-down list and choose from the following options:

Color Scheme Options	Description
Dreamweaver Two Tone	The default color scheme; uses two shades of gray.
Desktop Two Tone	Picks up your desktop primary color and one contrasting color to define window borders and other areas.
Desktop Standard	Uses the system default colors for a monochromatic approach.

Tip

On the Launcher Palette, the icon text is anti-aliased to appear smooth against the default background, which is a light gray. If your desktop or system color is much darker in tone, you'll probably notice some distracting artifacts (miscolored pixels) around the letters. To fix this problem, switch to a lighter desktop color or choose the Dreamweaver Two Tone color scheme.

General options

The second section of the General Preferences screen consists of numerous checkbox options you can turn on or off. Overall, these choices fall into the user-interaction category or "What's good for you?" Take the Show Dialog When Inserting Objects choice, for example. Some Web creators prefer to enter all their attributes at one time through the Property Inspector and would rather not have the dialog boxes appear for every inserted object. Others want to get their file sources in immediately and modify the rest later. Your choice depends on how you want to work.

The listed options are described in the following paragraphs.

Use Large Fonts (Windows only)

When the Use Large Fonts option is enabled, all system text elements including menu commands, dialog box options, and palette titles are enlarged. You must restart Dreamweaver for this option to take effect.

Caution

If you're using Internet Explorer 4.0 and have turned on the Desktop Update mode, the Use Large Fonts option won't work. You need to disable Desktop Integration first, turn on Use Large Fonts, and then reactivate Desktop Integration.

Tip

If Dreamweaver's Use Large Fonts option doesn't achieve the desired effect, you can increase the overall size of your system fonts through the Desktop Properties dialog box. From the Windows 95 desktop, right-click in any open area and select Properties from the shortcut menu. Choose the Appearance tab and in the Scheme drop-down list select any color scheme that is followed by "(Large)." This setting increases all the system and menu fonts — including Dreamweaver's — to a more readable size.

Show Launcher in Status Bar

The default setting enables the status bar Launcher. When this option is disabled, you always have to access the Launcher by choosing Window ➪ Launcher from the menus.

Show Dialog When Inserting Objects

By default, almost all the objects that Dreamweaver inserts — via either the Object palette or the Insert menu — open an initial dialog box to gather needed information. In most cases, the dialog box enables you to input a URL or browse for a source file. When you turn off the Show Dialog option, it causes Dreamweaver to insert a default-sized object, or a placeholder, for the object. You must then enter all attributes through the Property Inspector.

Faster Table Editing (Deferred Updates)

When you enter text into a table, the current column width automatically expands while the other columns shrink correspondingly. If you're working with very large tables, this updating process can slow down your editing. Dreamweaver gives you the choice between faster input or instantaneous feedback.

When the Faster Table Editing preference is turned on, Dreamweaver updates the entire table only when you click outside the table, or if you press Ctrl-spacebar (Command-spacebar). If you prefer to see the table form as you type, turn this option off.

Open Files in New Window (Windows Only)

Select the Open Files in New Window option if you are working in a situation where you need to have several Web pages open simultaneously. Alternatively, if you want to free up some of your system resources (such as memory) and you only need one Dreamweaver window, you can deselect this option.

When the Open Files in New Window option is turned on, Dreamweaver opens a new window every time — even if your initial window is empty.

Correct Relative Links on Save As

For your Web page to locate any document-relative links correctly — for images, plug-ins, other Web pages, and so forth — Dreamweaver requires that you establish one root directory for each site. Should you save your Web page in a different directory, all of the corresponding links are broken, unless the Correct Relative Links on Save As option is selected. If this option is enabled, Dreamweaver automatically corrects every link.

You should set up your development Web site so that it mirrors your online site. For more information on this topic, see Chapter 5, "Setting Up Your First Site."

Preferences for Invisible Elements

By their nature, all HTML markup tags remain unseen to one degree or another when presented for viewing through the browser. You may want to see certain elements while designing a page, however. For example, adjusting line spacing is a common task, and turning on the visibility of the line break tag <BR> can help you understand the layout.

Dreamweaver enables you to control the visibility of 12 different codes — or rather their symbols, as shown in Figure 3-2. When, for example, a named anchor is inserted, Dreamweaver shows you a small gold shield with an anchor emblem. This shield not only indicates the anchor's position, but you can also manipulate the code with cut-and-paste or drag-and-drop techniques. Moreover, double-clicking the symbol opens the pertinent Property Inspector and allows quick changes to the tag's attributes.

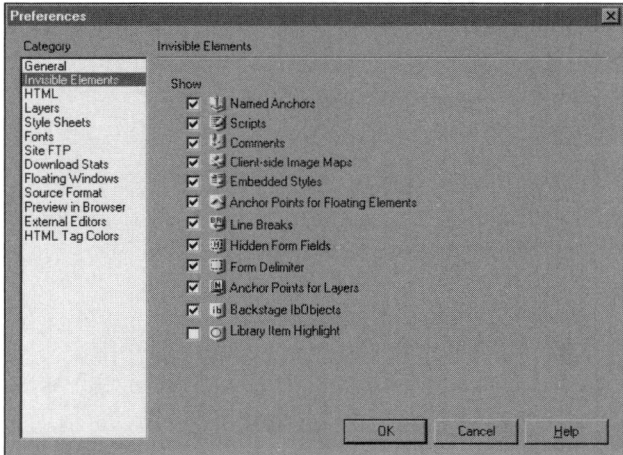

Figure 3-2: You can show or hide any or all of the 12 invisible elements listed in the Preferences dialog box.

The 12 items controlled through the Invisible Elements panel follow:

Named Anchors	Scripts
Comments	Client-Side Image Maps
Embedded Styles	Anchor Points for Floating Elements
Line Breaks	Hidden Form Fields
Form Delimiter	Anchor Points for Layers
Backstage lbObjects	Library Item Highlight

The vast majority of the Invisible Elements options display or hide small symbols in Dreamweaver's visual document window. Several options, however, show an outline or another type of highlight. Turning off Form Delimiter, for example, removes the dashed line that surrounds a form in the document window. Similarly, deselecting the Library Item Highlight removes the yellow highlight automatically applied to any portion of the page created from a library item.

HTML Preferences

The exception to Dreamweaver's policy of not altering imported code occurs when HTML is incorrectly structured. Dreamweaver automatically fixes tags that are nested in the wrong order or have additional, unnecessary closing tags — unless you tell Dreamweaver otherwise by setting up the HTML Preferences accordingly (see Figure 3-3).

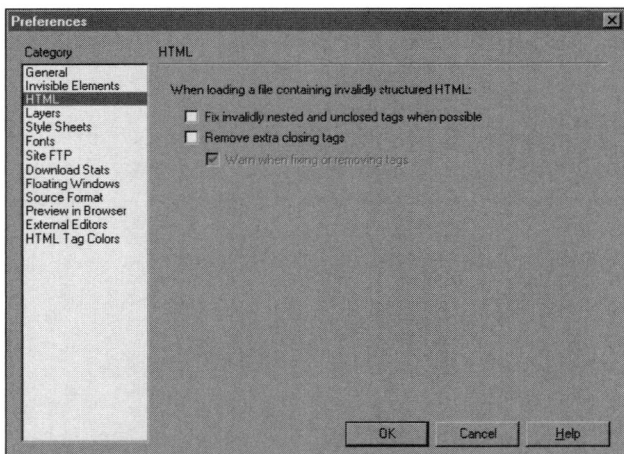

Figure 3-3: The HTML Preferences panel can be used to protect nonstandard HTML from being automatically changed by Dreamweaver.

Following are descriptions of the particular controls of the HTML Preferences.

Fix invalidly nesting and unclosed tags where possible

When enabled, this option repairs incorrectly placed HTML tags. For example, if a file contained the following line:

```
<h3><b>Welcome to the Monkey House!</h3></b>
```

Dreamweaver rewrites it as follows:

```
<h3><b>Welcome to the Monkey House!</b></h3>
```

Open that same file while the Fix option is turned off, and Dreamweaver highlights the misplaced code in the document window. Double-clicking the code brings up a window with a brief explanation.

Caution   If a browser encounters nonstandard HTML, the code will probably be ignored. Dreamweaver does not follow this protocol, however. Unless Dreamweaver is familiar with the type of code you are using, your code could be altered when the page is opened. If you are using specially formatted database tags or other nonstandard HTML programming, be sure to open a test page first.

✓ Remove extra closing tags

When you're editing your code by hand, it's fairly easy to miss a closing tag. Dreamweaver cleans up such code if you enable the Remove extra closing tags option. You may, for example, have the following line in a previously edited file:

```
<p>And now back to our show...</p></i>
```

Notice that the closing italic tag, $</i>$, has no matching opening partner. If you open this file into Dreamweaver with the Remove option enabled, Dreamweaver plucks out the offending $</i>$.

Tip   In some circumstances, you want to make sure your pages remain as originally formatted. If you edit pages in Dreamweaver that are preprocessed by a server — such as Allaire's Cold Fusion — prior to the display of the pages, make sure to disable both the Fix invalidly nesting and unclosed tags where possible and the Remove extra closing tags options.

Warn when fixing or removing tags

If you're editing a lot of Web pages created on another system, you should enable the Warn When Fixing or Removing Tags option. If this setting is turned on, Dreamweaver displays a list of changes that have been made to your code in the HTML Parser Results dialog box. As you can see from Figure 3-4, the changes can be quite extensive when Dreamweaver opens what it regards as a poorly formatted page.

Caution   Remember that once you've enabled these "Fix HTML" options, the fixes occur automatically. If this sequence happens to you by mistake, immediately close the file (without saving it!), disable the HTML Preference options, and reopen the document.

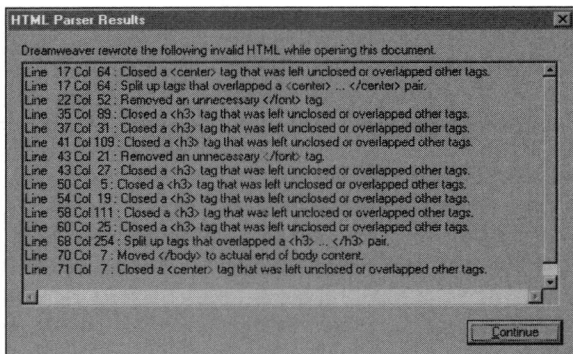

Figure 3-4: Dreamweaver can automatically catch and repair certain HTML errors. You can set Dreamweaver to send a report to the screen in the HTML Parser Results dialog box.

HTML Tag Color Preferences

HTML code is a combination of the tags that structure the language, and the text that provides the content. Often a Web page designer has difficulty distinguishing swiftly between the two — and finding the right code to modify. Version 1.2 of Dreamweaver enables you to set color preferences for the code as it appears in the HTML Inspector. Not only can you alter colors for the background, default tags, text and general comments, but you can also specify certain tags to get certain colors.

To modify any of the basic elements (Background, Text, Tag Default, or Comments), select the color swatch next to the corresponding name, as illustrated in Figure 3-5. Select a color from any of the 216 displayed in the color picker or choose the small palette icon to select from the full range of colors available to your system.

To select a different color for a specific tag, first select the tag from the list box. Then choose either the Default option (which assigns the same color as specified for the Tag Default) or a custom color by clicking the color swatch and choosing the color. If you want to set all of the code and text enclosed by the selected tag to the same color, choose the Include Contents option. This option is useful for setting off large blocks of code, such as the code included in the <script> section.

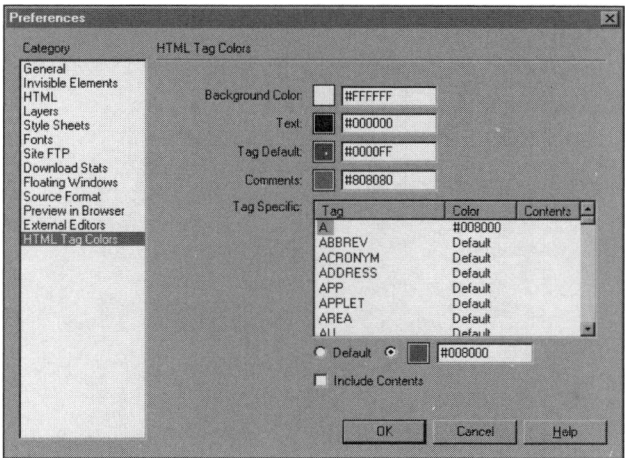

Figure 3-5: Use the HTML Tag Colors Preferences panel to custom color-code the HTML Inspector.

Font Preferences

Under the Fonts preference category, shown in Figure 3-6, you can control the fonts as seen by a user's browser and the fonts that you see when programming. The Encoding section lets you choose either Western style fonts for Web pages to be rendered in English and all Western European languages or one of the Asian languages: Japanese, Traditional Chinese, Simplified Chinese, or Korean. The Asian language options require what is known as a *double-byte* font. Double-byte fonts are necessary to convey the larger number of characters found in the many Eastern alphabets.

In the bottom portion of the Font Preferences panel, you can alter the default font and size for three different fonts:

✦ Proportional Font — This font option sets the default font used in Dreamweaver's Document Window to depict paragraphs, headings, and lists. Choose the arrow button to select from any font on your system.

✦ Fixed Font — In a fixed font, every character is allocated the same width. Dreamweaver uses your chosen fixed font to depict preformatted styled text.

✦ HTML Inspector Font — The HTML Inspector font is used by Dreamweaver's built-in text editor. You should probably use a monospaced font like Courier. A monospaced font makes it easy to count characters, which is often necessary when debugging your code.

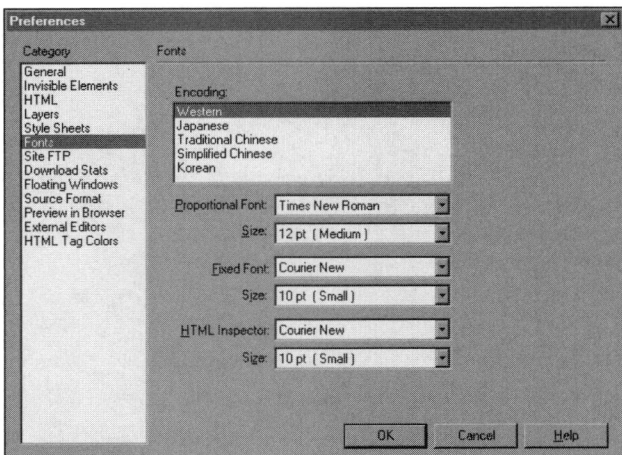

Figure 3-6: Set both the font encoding each Web page and the fonts you use when programming in the Fonts Preferences panel.

For all three font options, select your font by clicking the Font list and highlighting your choice of font. Change the font size by selecting the value in the Size text box or by typing in a new number.

Caution   Don't be misled into thinking that by changing your Proportional Font preference to Arial or another font, all of your Web pages are automatically viewed in that typeface. Changing these Font Preferences only affects the default fonts that you see when developing the Web page; the default font that the user sees is controlled by the user's browser. To ensure that a different font is used, you have to specify it for any selected text through the Text Properties Inspector.

Preferences for Download Stats

Dreamweaver provides a handy "speedometer" for Web page designers: the Download Indicator section of the status bar. By keeping an eye on the page's collective file size and approximate download time, you can avoid creating pages that take too long for the user to view. But once you've realized that a page is too "heavy," how do you know where to trim the fat? Dreamweaver also shows download statistics for individual images in the Property Inspector. The Download Stats panel of preferences (Figure 3-7) lets you specify whether you'd prefer to see the image file size expressed in kilobytes or seconds.

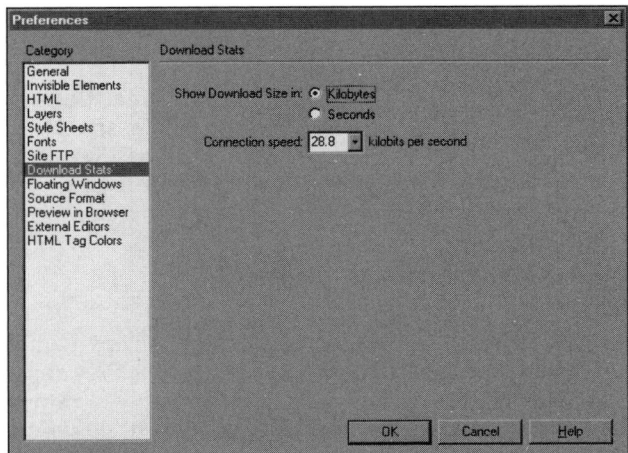

Figure 3-7: Use the Download Stats Preferences panel to evaluate your real-world download times.

In addition, Dreamweaver understands that not all access speeds are created equal, so the Download Stats panel enables you to check the download time for your page (or the individual images) at a variety of rates.

Let's take a closer look at the two options on the Download Stats Preferences panel.

Show Download Size

You can elect to display the download size on the left side of the Property Inspector either by file size or time. To show the full size of your file, select Kilobytes. To display the anticipated download time for your page at a predetermined connection speed, select Seconds. If the Property Inspector is on screen when you change from Kilobytes to Seconds or vice versa, you must close and reopen the Inspector for your change to take effect.

Connection Speed

The Connection Speed setting evaluates the download statistics in both the status bar and, if you opt to show the download size in seconds, the Property Inspector. You can choose from six preset connection speeds, all in kilobytes per second: 14.4, 28, 33, 56, 128, and 1500. The lower speeds (14.4 through 33) represent common dial-up modem connection rates — if you are building a page for the mass market, you should select one of these slower rates. Although 56K modems are on the market, they are not commonly used except in special intranet installations. Use the 128 setting if your audience connects through an ISDN line. If everyone will be viewing your page through a direct LAN connection, change the connection speed to 1500.

You are not limited to these preset settings. You can type any desired speed directly into the Connection Speed text box. You could, for example, specify a connection speed more often experienced in the real world, such as 23.3. If you find yourself designing for an audience using cable modems in the near future, you could change the Connection Speed to 500.

Floating Windows

Although the various windows, palettes, and inspectors are convenient, sometimes you just want a clear view of your document. The Floating Windows Preferences panel enables you to choose which of Dreamweaver's accessory screens stay on top of the document window. As shown in Figure 3-8, you can adjust ten different elements. By default, they are all set to float above the document window.

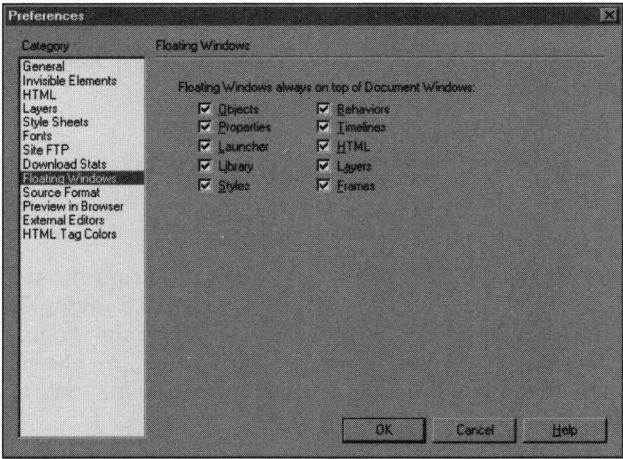

Figure 3-8: If you deselect any of the Floating Windows screens, they move behind the document window.

If you use the HTML Inspector often, you might consider taking it off the "always on top" list. Then, after you've made your HTML code edits, click in the document window. This sequence updates the visual document, incorporating any changes, and simultaneously pushes the HTML Inspector behind the document window. You can switch between the two views of your Web page by using the Ctrl-Tab (Command-Tab) key combination.

Tip

You can use the Show/Hide Floating Windows key to bring back any screen element that has gone behind the document window. Just press F4 twice.

External Editor Preferences

Refinement is often the name of the game in Web design, and giving you quick access to your favorite modification tools — whether you're modifying code or graphics — is one of Dreamweaver's key features. The External Editors Preferences panel, shown in Figure 3-9, is where you specify the program you want Dreamweaver to call for you.

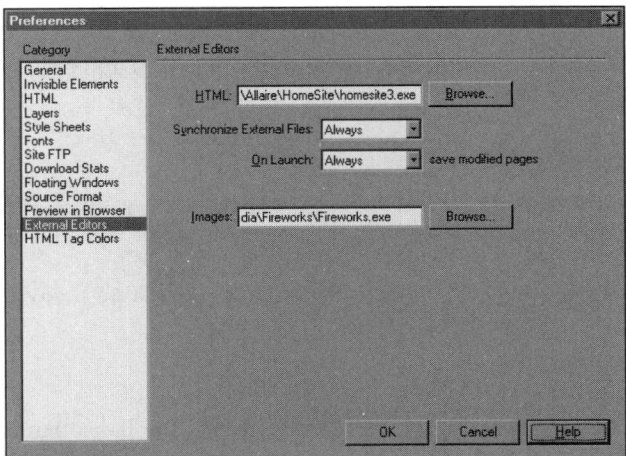

Figure 3-9: Assign your favorite HTML and graphic editors and their associated options through the External Editors Preferences panel.

Dreamweaver recognizes the importance of your choice of a text editor. Although Dreamweaver ships with two extremely robust HTML editors, you can opt to use any other program. To select your editor, enter the path in the HTML text box, or select the Browse button to choose the appropriate executable file.

The two included editors, BBEdit for Macintosh and HomeSite for Windows, are integrated with Dreamweaver to varying degrees. Both of the editors can be called from within Dreamweaver and both have "Dreamweaver" buttons for returning to the main program — switching between the editor and Dreamweaver automatically updates the page. Like Dreamweaver's internal HTML editor, BBEdit highlights the corresponding code to a selection made in Dreamweaver; this property does not, however, extend to HomeSite.

You specify and control your external editor selection with the following options.

Enable BBEdit Integration (Macintosh only)

Dreamweaver for Macintosh ships with this option activated. If you prefer to use another editor or an older version of BBEdit that lacks the integration capabilities, deselect this option.

Synchronize External Files

The drop-down list for this setting offers three selections you can make from the option box for working with an external editor:

✦ Prompt — detects when files are updated by another program and enables you to decide whether to update them within Dreamweaver.

✦ Always — updates the file in Dreamweaver automatically when the file is changed in an outside program.

✦ Never — assumes that you want to make all updates from within Dreamweaver yourself.

Personally, I prefer to have Dreamweaver always update my files. I find it saves a couple of mouse clicks — not to mention time.

On Launch

Any external HTML editor — even the integrated HomeSite or BBEdit — opens and reads a previously saved file. Therefore, if you make any changes in Dreamweaver's visual editor and switch to your editor without saving, the editor will only show the most recently saved version. To control this function, you have three choices:

✦ Prompt — determines that unsaved changes have been made and asks you to save the file. If you do not, the external editor reverts to the last saved version.

✦ Always — saves the file automatically before opening it in the external editor.

✦ Never — disregards any changes made since the last save, and the external editor opens the previously saved file.

Here again, as with Synchronize External Files, I prefer to always save my files when switching back and forth. If I don't like the changes, I take advantage of Dreamweaver's unlimited Undo capability.

Tip   If you try to open a file that has never been saved in an external editor, Dreamweaver prompts you to save it regardless of your preference settings. If you opt not to save the file, the external editor is not opened because it has no saved file to display.

Image editor preferences

In Version 1.2, Dreamweaver gives you the ability to call an image editor at the touch of a button. When you import a graphic, you often need to modify its color, size, shape, transparency, or another feature to make it work correctly on the Web page. Rather than force you to start your graphics program independently, load the image, make the changes, and resave the image, Dreamweaver lets you send any selected image directly to your editor. After you've made your modifications and saved the file, the altered image appears automatically in Dreamweaver.

Select your favorite graphics program as your Dreamweaver image editor by entering the program's path and filename in the Images text box. You can also use the Browse button to locate and select the executable file.

Tip   Be sure that your graphics program is adept at handling the three graphic formats used on the Web: GIFs, JPEGs, and PNG images. Macromedia has just released Fireworks, a graphics editor designed for the Web that integrates nicely with Dreamweaver.

Adjusting Advanced Features

Evolution of the Web and its language, HTML, never ends. New features emerge often from leading browser developers. A competing developer can introduce a similar feature that works in a slightly different way. The HTML standards organization — the World Wide Web Consortium, also known as the W3C — can then endorse one approach or introduce an entirely new method of reaching a similar goal. Eventually, one method usually wins the approval of the marketplace and becomes the accepted coding technique.

To permit the widest range of features, Dreamweaver enables you to designate how your code is written to accommodate the latest HTML features, layers and style sheets. The default preferences for these elements offer the highest degree of cross-browser and backwards compatibility. If your Web pages are intended for a more specific audience, such as a Netscape Navigator-only intranet, Dreamweaver lets you take advantage of a more specific feature set.

Layers Preferences

Aside from helping you control the underlying coding method for producing layers, Dreamweaver lets you define the default layer. This capability is especially useful during a major production effort in which the Web development team must produce hundreds of layers spread over a Web site. Being able to specify in advance the initial size, color, background, and visibility saves numerous steps — each of which would have to be repeated for every layer. Figure 3-10 shows the layout of the Layers Preference panel.

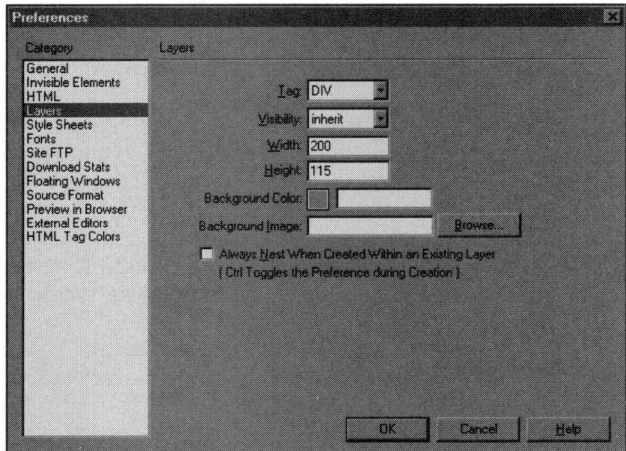

Figure 3-10: In Layers Preferences, you can predetermine the structure of the default Dreamweaver layer.

The controls accessible through the Layers Preference panel include the following.

Tag

Select the arrow button to see the tags for the four HTML code methods for implementing layers: <div>, <span>, <layer>, and <ilayer>. The first two, <div> and <span>, were developed by the W3C as part of their Cascading Style Sheets recommendation and are supported by both the Netscape and Microsoft 4.0 browsers. Netscape developed the latter two HTML commands, <layer> and <ilayer>; currently only Communicator 4.0 supports these tags.

Dreamweaver uses the <div> tag for its default. Supported by both major 4.0 browsers, the <div> element offers the widest cross-browser compatibility. You should only use one of the other Tag options if you are building a Web site intended for a specific browser.

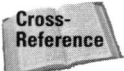

To learn more about the uses of the various tags, see Chapter 23, "Working with Layers."

Visibility

Layers can be either visible or hidden when the Web page is first loaded. A layer created using the Default visibility preference is always displayed initially; however, no specific information is written into the code. Selecting Visible forces Dreamweaver to include a `visibility:visible` line in your layer code. Likewise, if you select Hidden from the Visibility options, the layer is initially hidden.

The Inherit option is used when creating nested layers. Creating one layer inside another makes the outer layer the parent, and the inner layer the child. If the parent layer is visible and the child layer is set to `visibility:inherit`, then the child is also visible. This option makes it possible to affect the visibility of many layers with one command — hide the parent layer, and all the inheriting child layers disappear as well.

Width and Height

When you choose Marquee Layer from the Object Palette, you drag out the size and shape of your layer. Choosing Insert ⇨ Layer puts a layer of a default size and shape at your current cursor position. The Width and Height options enable you to set these defaults. Select the text boxes and type your new values. Dreamweaver's default is a layer 200 pixels wide by 115 pixels high.

Background Color ✓ (Layers)

Layers can have their own background color independent of the Web page's overall background color (which is set as a `<body>` attribute). You can define the default background color of any layer inserted either through the Insert menu or the Object Palette. For this preference setting, type a color, either by its standard name or as a hexadecimal triplet, directly into the text box. You can also click on the color swatch to display the Dreamweaver browser-safe color picker.

Note that while you can specify a different background color for the layer, you can't alter the layer's default text and link colors (except on a layer-by-layer basis) as you can with a page. If your page and layer background colors are highly contrasting, be sure your text and links are readable in both environments. A similar caveat applies to the use of a layer's background image, as explained in the next section.

Background Image ✓ (Layers)

Just as you can pick a specific background color for layers, you can select a different background image for layers. You can type a file source directly into the Background Image text box or select your file from a dialog box by choosing the Browse button. The layer's background image supersedes the layer background color, just as it does with the HTML page. Also, just as the page's background image tiles to fill the page, so does the layer's background image.

Caution

Internet Explorer 4.0 has a more substantial implementation of the `<div>` tag for layers and allows both background color and images to be set. To view either attribute in Netscape Communicator 4.0, use the `<layer>` or `<ilayer>` tags.

Always Nest When Created Within an Existing Layer

One of the two best features about layers seem to be directly opposed: overlapping and nesting layers. You can design layers to appear one on top of another, and you can code layers so that they are within one another. Both techniques are valuable options, and Dreamweaver lets you decide which one should be the overriding method.

If you are working primarily with nested layers and plan on using the inheritance facility, check the Always Nest When Created Within an Existing Layer option. If your design entails a number of overlapping but independent layers, make sure this option is turned off. Regardless of your preference, you can reverse it on a individual basis by pressing the Ctrl (or Command) key when drawing out your layers.

Style Sheets Preferences

The Style Sheets Preferences panel (Figure 3-11) is entirely devoted to how your code is written. As specified by the W3C, Cascading Style Sheets (CSS) declarations — the specifications of a style — can be written in several ways. One method displays a series of items, separated by semicolons, presented all in one line like the following:

```
H1 { font-family: helvetica; font-size: 12pt; line-height:
14pt; font-weight: bold;}
```

Certain properties (such as font) have their own grouping shorthand, developed to be more readable to designers coming from a traditional print background. A second, "shorthand" method of rendering the preceding declaration follows:

```
H1 { font: helvetica 12pt/14pt bold  }
```

The Style Sheet Preferences panel lets you enable the shorthand method for any or all of the five different properties that permit it. Select any of the check boxes under Use Shorthand For to have Dreamweaver write your style code in this fashion.

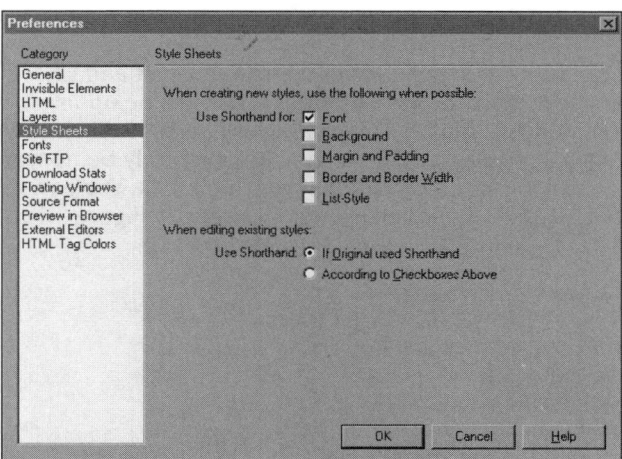

Figure 3-11: The Style Sheet Preferences panel lets you code the style sheet sections of your Web pages in a graphics designer-friendly manner.

The second option on the Style Sheets panel determines how Dreamweaver edits styles in previously coded pages. If you want to retain the format of the original page, click Use Shorthand If Original used Shorthand. If you want Dreamweaver to write new code in the manner that you decide, select Use Shorthand According to Checkboxes Above.

Caution

Although the leading varieties of the 4.0 browsers can read the style's shorthand with no difficulty, Internet Explorer 3.0 does not have this capability. IE3 is the only other mainstream browser that can claim support for Cascading Style Sheets, but it doesn't understand the shorthand form. If you want to maintain browser backwards-compatibility, don't enable any of the shorthand options.

Making Online Connections

Dreamweaver's visual layout editor offers an approximation of your Web page's appearance in the real world of browsers — offline or online. After you've created the initial draft of your Web page, you should preview it through one or more browsers. When your project nears completion, you should transfer the files to a server for online, real-time viewing and further testing. Dreamweaver gives you control over all these stages of Web page development, through the Site FTP and Preview in Browser Preferences panels.

Site FTP Preferences

The Site FTP Preferences focuses on Dreamweaver's file Check Out and Check In features. The ever-changing nature of the Web dictates that sites be updated frequently and that files be modified offline. Dreamweaver can keep track of which files — including HTML pages, graphics, and sounds — are currently being worked on. Dreamweaver even keeps a log of which users have which files. You can set these elements through the Site FTP Preferences panel as seen in Figure 3-12.

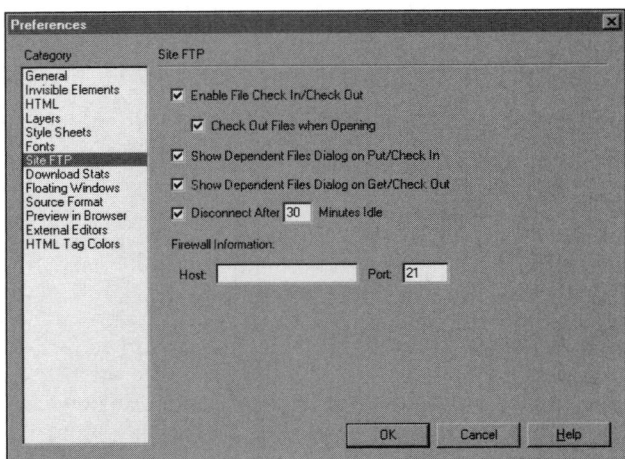

Figure 3-12: Options for Dreamweaver's File Check In/ Check Out capabilities are handled through the Site FTP Preferences panel.

The available Site FTP Preferences are described in the following paragraphs.

Enable File Check In/Check Out

File Check In/Check Out is especially useful when the Web site is being developed or maintained by a team of designers and programmers. Dreamweaver not only places a check mark next to the file in the remote directory pane of the Site Window, but it also makes the local version of a checked-in file read-only. This capability prevents accidental editing of a file that's already on the site. If you are solely creating or maintaining a site, however, you may find it easier to disable the File Check In/Check Out feature.

Check Out Files When Opening

To mark your open files as checked out automatically, enable the Check Out Files When Opening option. This feature works when opening files from either the remote or the local directories of the Site Window.

Show Dependent Files Dialog on Put/Check In and Get/Check Out

Web pages are very seldom just single HTML files. Any graphic — whether it's in the background, part of your main logo, or used on a navigational button — is uploaded as a separate file. The same is true for any additional multimedia add-ons such as audio or video files. If you've enabled File Check In/Check Out, Dreamweaver can also track these so-called dependent files.

Enabling the Show Dependent Files Dialog causes Dreamweaver to ask you if you'd like to transfer the dependent files when you check out an HTML file. You can opt to show the dialog box for checking files in, checking them out, or both.

Disconnect After __ Minutes Idle

You can easily forget you're online when you are busy modifying a page. You can set Dreamweaver to automatically disconnect you from an FTP site after a specified interval. The default is 30 minutes; if you want to set a different interval, you can select the value in the Disconnect After text box. Dreamweaver now asks if you want to continue to wait or to disconnect when the time limit is reached, but you can maintain your online connection regardless by deselecting this option.

Firewall Information

A new feature in Dreamweaver 1.2 enables users to access remote FTP servers outside their network firewall. A *firewall* is a security component that protects the internal network from unauthorized outsiders, while allowing Internet access. To enable firewall access, enter the Host and Port Number in the appropriate text boxes; if you do not know these values, contact your network administrator.

Caution Before you can transfer files via FTP through the firewall, you also need to choose File ➪ Open Site ➪ Edit Site, and in the Site Information dialog box enable the option to Use Firewall (in Preferences).

Preview in Browser Preferences

Browser testing is an essential stage of Web page development. Previewing your Web page within the environment of a particular browser gives you a more exact representation of how it looks when viewed online. Because each browser renders the HTML slightly differently, you should preview your work in several browsers. Dreamweaver lets you select both a primary and secondary browser, which can both be called by pressing a function key. You can name up to 18 additional browsers through the Preview in Browser Preferences pane shown in Figure 3-13. This list of preferences is also called when you choose File ➪ Preview in Browser ➪ Edit Browser List.

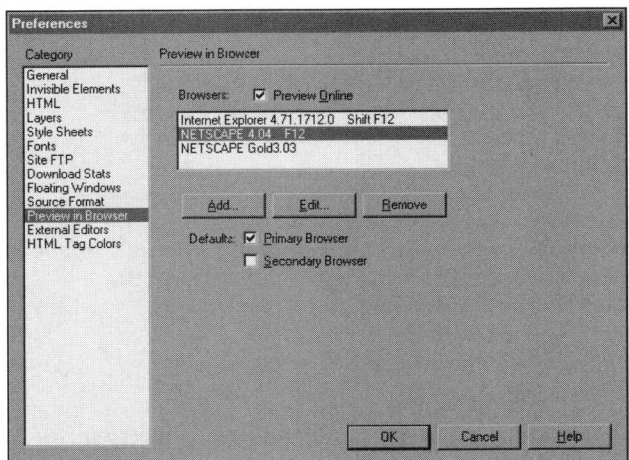

Figure 3-13: The Preview in Browser Preference pane lists browsers currently available for preview and lets you modify the list.

If you are developing for Windows, your Web page is using site root relative paths for links, and you have a local server setup, enable the Preview Online option. This capability ensures that your previews link correctly. The other method to preview sites using site root relative paths places the files on a remote server.

Adding a browser to the preview list

To add a browser to your preview list, follow these steps:

1. Choose Edit ➪ Preferences or press the keyboard shortcut: Ctrl-U (Command-U).

2. Select the Preview in Browser category.

3. Select the Add button.

4. In the Add Browser dialog box, type the browser name you want listed into the Name text box.

5. Enter the path to the browser file in the Path text box, or click the Browse button to pick the file from the Select Browser dialog box.

6. If you want to designate this browser as your Primary or Secondary browser, select one of those check boxes in the Default section.

7. Click OK when you have finished.

8. You can continue to add browsers (up to a total of 20) by following steps 3 through 7. Click OK when you have finished.

Once you've added a browser to your list, you can modify your selection by following these steps:

1. Open the Preview in Browser Preferences and highlight the browser you want to alter.

2. Select the Edit button to get the Edit Browser dialog box.

3. After you've made your modifications, click OK to close the dialog box.

 **Tip**

You can quickly make a browser your Primary or Secondary previewing choice without going through the Edit screen. From the Preview in Browser Preferences panel, select the desired browser and click either Primary Browser or Secondary Browser. Note that if you already have a primary or secondary browser defined, this action overrides your previous choice.

You can also easily remove a browser from your Preview list:

1. Open the Preview in Browser Preferences and choose the browser you want to delete from the list.

2. Select the Remove button, and click OK.

Customizing Your Code

For all its multimedia flash and visual interactivity, the Web is based on code. The more you code, the more particular about your code you are likely to become. Achieving a consistent look-and-feel to your code enhances its readability and, thus, your productivity. In Dreamweaver, you can even design the HTML code that underlies a Web page's structure.

Dreamweaver includes two tools for customizing your HTML. The first is an easy-to-use, point-and-click preferences panel. The second is a text file called the Source Format Profile (SourceFormat.profile), which must be modified by hand and controls the output of every HTML tag. You can modify your HTML using either or both techniques. All of the options controlled by the Source Format Preferences panel are written out to the text file.

Source Format Preferences

Most of your HTML code parameters can be controlled through the Source Format Preferences panel. The only reason to alter the SourceFormat.profile text file by hand is if you want to control the appearance of your HTML code at the tag level.

In the Preferences panel, you can decide whether to use indentations — if so, whether to use spaces or tabs and how many of each — or to turn off indents for major elements such as tables and frames. You can also globally control the case of your HTML tags and their attributes. As you can see in Figure 3-14, the Source Format Preferences panel is full-featured.

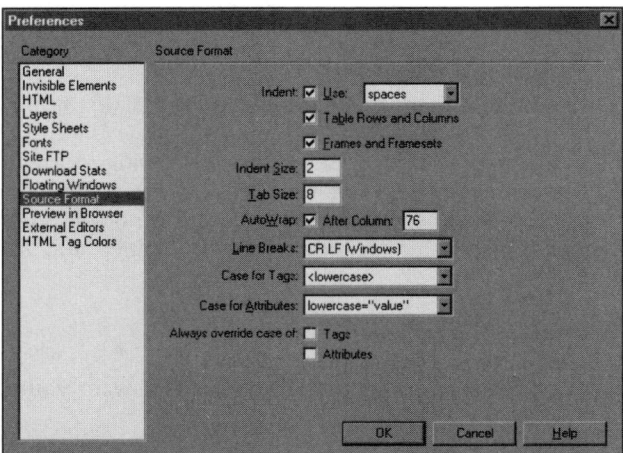

Figure 3-14: The Source Format Preferences panel enables you to shape your HTML to your own specifications.

To examine the available options in the Source Format Preferences panel, let's separate them into three areas: indent control, line control, and case control.

Indent control

Indenting your code generally makes it more readable. Dreamweaver defaults to indenting most HTML tags with two spaces, and giving extra indentation grouping to tables and frames. All of these parameters can be altered through the Source Format Preferences panel.

The first Indent option enables indenting and enables you to switch from spaces to tabs. To permit indenting, make sure a check mark is displayed in Indent check box. Of the 52 separate HTML tags Dreamweaver identifies in its Source Format Profile, 30 tags are designed to be indented. If you prefer your code to be displayed flush left, turn off the Indent option altogether.

To use Tabs instead of the default Spaces, click on the Use arrow button and select Tabs from the drop-down list. If you anticipate transferring your code to a word-processing program for formatting and print out, you should use tabs; otherwise, stay with the default spaces.

Dreamweaver formats both tables and frames as special indentation groups. Within each of these structural elements, the related tags are indented (or nested) more than the initial two spaces. As you can see in Listing 3-1, each table row (<tr>) is indented within the table tag, and the table data tags (<td>) are nested within the table row.

Listing 3-1: **An indented code sample**

```
<table border="1" width="75%">
  <tr>
    <td>Row 1, Column 1</td>
    <td>Row 1, Column 2</td>
    <td>Row 1, Column 3</td>
  </tr>
  <tr>
    <td>Row 2, Column 1</td>
    <td>Row 2, Column 2 </td>
    <td>Row 2, Column 3</td>
  </tr>
</table>
```

If you want to disable the special indentation grouping for tables, deselect Table Rows and Columns in the Source Format Preferences panel. Turn off frame indenting by unchecking Frames and Framesets (this option is selected by default).

The other two items in the indent control section of Source Format Preferences are Indent Size and Tab Size. Change the value in Indent Size to establish the size of indents using spaces. To alter the size of tab indents, change the Tab Size number.

Line control

The browser is responsible for ultimately formatting an HTML page for viewing. This formatting includes wrapping text according to each user's screen size and the placement of the paragraph (<p>...</p>) tags. Therefore, you control how your code wraps in your HTML editor. You can both turn off the automatic wrapping feature or set it for a particular column through the line control options of the Source Format Preferences panel.

To turn off the automatic word-wrapping capability, deselect AutoWrap. When you are trying to debug your code and looking for specific line numbers and character positions, enable this option. You can also set the specific column for the word wrap to take effect. Be sure AutoWrap is enabled, and then type your new value in the After Column text box.

Tip   If you're using the HTML Inspector, selecting its Wrap option overrides the AutoWrap setting in Source Format preferences.

The Line Breaks setting determines which line break character is appended to each line of the page. Each of the major operating systems employs a different ending character: Macintosh uses a carriage return (CR), UNIX uses a line feed (LF), and Windows uses both (CR LF). If you know the operating system for your remote server, choosing the corresponding line break character helps the file to appear correctly when viewed online. Click the arrow button next to Line Breaks and select your system.

Caution   The operating system for your local development machine may be different from the operating system of your remote server. If so, using the Line Breaks option may cause your HTML to appear incorrectly when viewed through a simple text editor (like Notepad or vi). The Dreamweaver HTML Inspector, however, does render the code correctly.

Case control

Whether an HTML tag or attribute is in uppercase or lowercase doesn't matter to most browsers — the command is rendered regardless of case. Case is only a personal preference among Web designers. That said, some Webmasters take case consideration as a serious preference and insist on their codes being all uppercase, all lowercase, or a combination. Dreamweaver gives you control over the tags and attributes it creates, as well as over case conversion for files that Dreamweaver imports.

The Dreamweaver default for both tags and attributes is lowercase. Click on the arrow button next to Case for Tags and/or Case for Attributes to alter the selection. After you have selected OK from the Source Format Preferences panel, Dreamweaver changes all the tags in any currently open file. Choose File ➪ Save to write the changes to disk.

You can also use Dreamweaver to standardize the letter case in tags of previously saved files. To alter imported files, select the Always override case of Tags and/or the Always override case of Attributes options. When enabled, these options enforce your choices made in the Case for Tags and Case for Attributes option boxes in any file Dreamweaver loads. Again, be sure to save your file to keep the changes.

Understanding the Source Format Profile

As noted earlier, Dreamweaver pulls its code configuration guidelines from a text file named SourceFormat.profile. When Dreamweaver is installed, this file is put in the Dreamweaver\Configuration folder along with one other file, SourceFormat.original. When you make a modification to the Source Format Preferences panel, the initial profile is renamed as SourceFormat.backup and then Dreamweaver writes a new SourceFormat.profile.

Tip

You can restore the default Source Profile settings at any time. When Dreamweaver is closed, delete SourceFormat.profile and then make a copy of the SourceFormat.original file. Finally, rename the copy as SourceFormat.profile.

Dreamweaver uses a specialized HTML format to create a SourceFormat.profile that can be viewed and edited in any text editor. Three main sections exist, each denoted with a <?keyword> format: <?options>, <?elements>, and <?attributes>. Prior to each section, Dreamweaver uses the HTML comment tags to describe them. The file closes with the <?end> keyword.

The Source Format Profile (Listing 3-2) starts with two HTML comments. The first describes the overall document ("Dreamweaver Source Format Profile"), followed by the option section.

> **Listing 3-2: The Source Format Profile, edited in any text editor, lets you fine-tune Dreamweaver's HTML output**

```
<!-- Dreamweaver source formatting profile -->

<!-- options

   INDENTION  : indention options
      ENABLE   - allows indention
      INDENT   - columns per indention
      TABS     - columns per tab character
      USE      - TABS or SPACES for indention
      ACTIVE   - active indention groups (IGROUP)

   LINES      : end-of-line options
      AUTOWRAP - enable automatic line wrapping
      BREAK    - CRLF, CR, LF
      COLUMN   - auto wrap lines after column

   OMIT  : element omission options
      OPTIONS  - options

   ELEMENT    : element options
      CASE   - "UPPER" or "lower" case
      ALWAYS - always use preferred element case
               (instead of original case)
```

Option syntax

(continued)

Listing 3-2 *(continued)*

```
ATTRIBUTE  : attribute options
   CASE    - "UPPER" or "lower" case
   ALWAYS  - always use preferred attribute case
             (instead of original case)

-->
<?options>
<indention enable indent="2" tabs="8" use="spaces"
active="1,2">
<lines autowrap column="76">
<omit options="0">
<element case="lower">
<attribute case="lower">
<colors text="0x00000000" tag="0x00000000"
unknowntag="0x00000000" comment="0x00000000"
invalid="0x00000000" object="0x00000000">

<!-- element information
   line breaks          : BREAK  = "before,inside start,
                                    inside end, after"
   indent contents      : INDENT
   indent group         : IGROUP = "indention group number"
                                   (1 through 8)
   specific name case   : NAMECASE = "CustomName"
   prevent formatting   : NOFORMAT
-->
<?elements>
<address break="1,0,0,1">
<applet break="0,1,1,0" indent>
<area break="1,0,0,1">
<base break="1,0,0,1">
<blockquote break="1,0,0,1" indent>
<body break="1,1,1,1">
<br break="0,0,0,1">
<caption break="1,0,0,1">
<center break="1,1,1,1" indent>
<dd break="1,0,0,1" indent>
<dir break="1,0,0,1" indent>
<div break="1,0,0,1" indent>
<dl break="1,0,0,1" indent>
<dt break="1,0,0,1" indent>
<embed break="1,0,0,1" indent>
<form break="1,1,1,1" indent>
<frame break="1,0,0,1">
<frameset break="1,0,0,1" indent igroup="2">
<h1 break="1,0,0,1" indent>
<h2 break="1,0,0,1" indent>
```

Option syntax

Selected options

Element syntax

Beginning of detailed elements

```
<h3 break="1,0,0,1" indent>
<h4 break="1,0,0,1" indent>
<h5 break="1,0,0,1" indent>
<h6 break="1,0,0,1" indent>
<head break="1,1,1,1" indent>
<hr break="1,0,0,1">
<html break="1,1,1,1">
<ilayer break="1,0,0,1">
<input break="1,0,0,1">
<isindex break="1,0,0,1">
<layer break="1,0,0,1">
<li break="1,0,0,1" indent>
<link break="1,0,0,1">
<map break="0,1,1,0" indent>
<menu break="1,0,0,1" indent>
<meta break="1,0,0,1">
<object break="0,1,1,0" indent>
<ol break="1,1,1,1" indent>
<option break="1,0,0,1">
<p break="1,0,0,1" indent>
<param break="1,0,0,1">
<pre break="1,0,0,1" noformat>
<script break="1,0,0,1" noformat>
<select break="1,1,1,1" indent>
<style break="1,0,0,1" noformat>
<table break="1,1,1,1" indent igroup="1">
<td break="1,0,0,1" indent igroup="1">
<textarea break="1,0,0,1" noformat>
<th break="1,0,0,1" indent igroup="1">
<title break="1,0,0,1">
<tr break="1,0,0,1" indent igroup="1">
<ul break="1,1,1,1" indent>

<!-- attribute information
  specific name case      : NAMECASE = "CustomName"
  values follow attr case  : SAMECASE
-->
<?attributes>
<align samecase>
<checked samecase>
<codetype samecase>
<compact samecase>
<ismap samecase>
<frame samecase>
<method samecase>
<multiple samecase>
```

(continued)

Listing 3-2 *(continued)*

```
<noresize samecase>
<noshade samecase>
<nowrap samecase>
<selected samecase>
<shape samecase>
<target samecase>
<type samecase>
<valign samecase>
<visibility samecase>
<?end>
```

Options

The Options section parallels the choices set in the Source Format Preferences panel. You can either use Dreamweaver's point-and-click interface by choosing Edit ⇨ Preferences and then selecting the Source Format category; or you can edit the <?options> section of the SourceFormat.profile file. In the Options description, five parameters are outlined: indention, lines, omit, element, and attribute.

The indention item denotes the indent options:

```
ENABLE - allows indention
INDENT - columns per indention
TABS   - columns per tab character
USE    - TABS or SPACES for indention

ACTIVE - active indention groups (IGROUP)
```

The final Indention option, ACTIVE, relates to the special grouping function that Dreamweaver calls IGROUPS. By default, Dreamweaver assigns IGROUP #1 to Table Rows and Columns and IGROUP #2 to Frames and Framesets.

The line options are detailed as follows:

```
AUTOWRAP - enable automatic line wrapping
BREAK  - CRLF, CR, LF
COLUMN - auto wrap lines after column
```

As mentioned earlier, the BREAK options are used to insert the type of line break character recognized by your Web server's operating system. Use CRLF for Windows, CR for Macintosh, and LF for Unix.

The next Option section, `OMIT`, is reserved by Dreamweaver for further expansion and is not currently used.

The Element and Attribute sections control the case of HTML elements (or tags) and attributes:

```
CASE   - "UPPER" or "lower" case
ALWAYS - always use preferred element case (instead of original
case)
```

If the `ALWAYS` keyword is used, Dreamweaver alters the case of tags and/or attributes when you import a previously saved file.

The Colors section lists values for six different aspects of the HTML Inspector. As of this writing, these values have no effect on the program.

The following section of the Source Format Profile that starts with `<?options>` contains the actual options read by Dreamweaver at startup. This listing shows the default options from the SourceFormat.original file for Dreamweaver 1.2:

```
<?options>
<indention enable indent="2" tabs="8" use="spaces"
active="1,2">
<lines autowrap column="76">
<omit options="0">
<element case="lower">
<attribute case="lower">
<colors text="0x00000000" tag="0x00000000"
unknowntag="0x00000000" comment="0x00000000"
invalid="0x00000000" object="0x00000000">
```

Elements

The Element information in the next section of the Source Format Profile describes the syntax and options for individually controlling each HTML tag.

```
line breaks      : BREAK  = "before, inside start, inside end,
after"
indent contents  : INDENT
indent group     : IGROUP = "indention group number" (1 through
8)
specific name case  : NAMECASE = "CustomName"
prevent formatting  : NOFORMAT
```

break

The syntax for break refers to the number of line breaks surrounding the opening and closing HTML tags. For example, the default syntax for the <h1> tag follows:

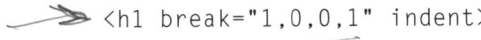

```
<h1 break="1,0,0,1" indent>
```

The preceding produces code that looks like the following:

```
<h1>Welcome!</h1>
```

If you want to display the opening and closing tags on their own lines, you could change the break value as follows:

```
<h1 break="1,1,1,1" indent>
```

The preceding gives you the following result:

```
<h1>
 Welcome!
</h1>
```

Use zero in the "before" and "after" positions when you want a tag to appear in line with the other code, as in this map tag:

```
<map break="0,1,1,0" indent>
```

Note   ✓The Elements list only contains tags that have opening and closing elements, which are also known as *container tags.* Any single-element tags, such as the image tag, <img>, are presented in line with other elements.

You're not restricted to using 1 and 0 values for break. If you want to isolate a tag so that it really stands out, use 2 in the "before" and "after" positions. For example:

```
<p break="2,1,1,2" indent>
```

The preceding produces completely separated paragraphs like the following:

```
<p>
Synapse Advertising is your first choice for the best in
subliminal advertising.
</p>

<p>
Call Synapse when you want your clients to come a-knockin' at
your door -- and have no idea why!
</p>
```

indent

The indent keyword ensures that the text contained between the opening and closing tags wraps to the same text column as the tag rather than appearing flush left. The difference is apparent when you compare almost any text format tag, from paragraph <p>, to any heading <h1> through <h6> tag, to the preformatted tag <pre>.

```
<p>Four score and seven years ago our fathers brought forth
on this continent, a new nation, conceived in liberty, and
dedicated to the proposition that all men are created
equal.</p>
<pre>The above speech was offered by President Abraham Lincoln
and is known as the Gettysburg Address. Now recognized by many
as the leading speech of the Lincoln presidency, the Gettysburg
Address was initially received to mixed reviews...</pre>
```

igroup

The igroup keyword is used only when applied to special indentation groups such as tables and frames. For example, all the elements contained in a table have igroup="1" as part of their source profile, as shown in the following:

```
<table break="1,1,1,1" indent igroup="1">
<td break="1,0,0,1" indent igroup="1">
<th break="1,0,0,1" indent igroup="1">
<tr break="1,0,0,1" indent igroup="1">
```

The igroup attribute in the indention option activates the indentation set for all the tags in that group. For example, if the indention option read as follows:

```
<indention enable indent="2" tabs="8" use="spaces" active="2">
```

then indenting would be turned off for igroup number 1, tables.

The active igroup causes each element to use the indentation level of the outermost group member as its left margin — and indent from there. Thus, with the indented <table>...</table> pair as the outer igroup member, the <tr>...</tr> pair is indented two more spaces and the <td>...</td> pair is indented another two spaces, so it looks like the following:

```
<table border="2" width="50%">
  <tr>
    <td>Symbol</td>
    <td>Element</td>
  </tr>
  <tr>
    <td>H</td>
    <td>Hydrogen</td>
  </tr>
</table>
```

You can currently define up to six `igroups`, in addition to the preset tables and frames.

namecase

You can override the general case conventions for any element with the `namecase` keyword. If you want to use a title case or mixed case for certain tags, you would define them in the following way:

```
<applet break="0,1,1,0" indent namecase="Applet">
<blockquote break="1,0,0,1" indent namecase="BlockQuote">
```

You may also use the `namecase` keyword when defining a custom tag for use in conjunction with a new object. Let's say you've created a series of objects for use with Cold Fusion and you want them to stand out in the code. To accentuate your new tag pair, `<cfif>...</cfif>`, you could add the following line to your Source Format Profile:

```
<cfif break="1,1,1,1" indent namecase="CFIF">
```

This line ensures that a Cold Fusion "if" tag is always inserted in uppercase.

noformat

As the name implies, the `noformat` keyword presents the tag-surrounded text without any additional formatting. This keyword is primarily used when the tag is used to reproduce verbatim information, such as when using the preformatted tag `<pre>`. The `noformat` keyword is also used when the element requires attributes and values in a specific format, such as with `<style>` or `<script>`.

color

The `color` keyword is an addition to Dreamweaver 1.2 and will eventually be used to specify the text colors used in the HTML Inspector. As of this writing, no correlation exists between the options specified in the Source Format Profile and the program itself. To change the colors of the HTML Inspector text, choose Edit ⇨ Preferences, select the HTML Tag Color category, and select the various color swatches to make your modifications.

Attributes

The Attributes section has only two options, `namecase`, which works as previously described for the Elements section, and `samecase`. The `samecase` option ensures that an attribute and its value uses the same case as its tag. If the `<input>` tag is uppercase, then the named attribute and the value will be uppercase. Dreamweaver 1.2 lists 17 different attributes with the `samecase` option enabled.

Caution

Never use the `samecase` option with any attribute that that requires a case-sensitive value. The most common instance of this situation is an attribute like `src` that takes a file name as its value—which in most cases is case-sensitive.

No individual attributes are defined with independent `namecase` values in the shipping version of Dreamweaver. Case is determined for all attributes by the following line found in the Objects section:

```
<attribute case="lower">
```

As with the Elements, you can alter the case of attributes individually by specifying them in this section. For example, if you always want the source attribute of the image tag to be uppercase, you can include the following line in the Attribute section:

```
<src namecase="SRC">
```

The preceding produces code like the following:

```
<img SRC="logo.gif>
```

This capability is handy when you are scanning your code and quickly want to find all the source files.

Modifying the Source Format Profile

Because you have to restart Dreamweaver for any Source Format Profile modifications to take effect, you should edit the file with Dreamweaver closed. You can use any editor capable of saving an ASCII or regular text file. If you want to preserve the previous profile, you can use the Save As feature of your editor to save the file under a different name, such as SourceFormat.backup, prior to making any changes. Then, after you complete your alterations, use Save As again and name it SourceFormat.profile.

Make your changes only to those sections marked with the `<?keyword>`, such as `<?options>` or `<?elements>`. Remember that Dreamweaver is not case-sensitive when it comes to changing commands—other than with the namecase keyword—so you can write lines like the following:

```
<element case="LOWER">
```

In the preceding, all of your tags are still created, as specified, in lowercase.

Dreamweaver is fairly protective of its Source Format Profile. If you accidentally misspell a keyword (for example, "ident" instead of "indent"), Dreamweaver ignores and then deletes the misspelled keyword. Likewise, misplaced keywords — for instance, using the `enable` keyword when defining an element instead of an option — are removed from the file when Dreamweaver loads.

The Source Format Profile is an HTML tinker's paradise. You can shape your code as precisely as necessary and Dreamweaver outputs it for you. Feel free to experiment and try different code arrangements. Just be sure to have a copy of the original Source Format Profile available as a reference.

Summary

Creating Web pages, like any design job, is easier when the tools fit your hands. Through Preferences and the Source Format Profile, you can make Dreamweaver work the way you want to work.

✦ Dreamweaver lets you customize your Web page design and HTML coding environment through a series of easy-to-use point-and-click panels.

✦ You can decide how best to use cutting-edge features, such as layers and style sheets, depending on the degree of cross-browser and backwards compatibility you need.

✦ Dreamweaver gives you plenty of elbow room for previewing and testing by providing for 20 selections on your browser list.

✦ The Source Format Profile can be modified. You can make alterations, from across-the-board case changes to tag-by-tag presentation, to define the way Dreamweaver writes your HTML code.

In the next chapter, you'll learn how to get online and offline help from Dreamweaver.

✦   ✦   ✦

Using the Help System

Dreamweaver includes a multifaceted help system that you can rely on in any number of situations:

✦ To provide quick context-sensitive answers to questions on how to use specific Dreamweaver features.

✦ To learn the program using step-by-step instructions presented in a tutorial format.

✦ To explain various concepts and capabilities through the hyperlinked Help Pages and their embedded Show Me movies.

✦ To seek specific programming assistance from the peer-to-peer network of the online newsgroups or the Dreamweaver technical support team at Macromedia.

Navigating the Help Screen

To assist your understanding of Dreamweaver — in both the short term and the long term — Macromedia includes a full electronic manual with the program.

✦ For Windows system users, choose Help ⇨ Help Contents or press the keyboard shortcut, F1, to open the Dreamweaver HTML Help Pages.

✦ To access Dreamweaver Help on the Macintosh, select Help ⇨ Dreamweaver Help Topics.

If you have defined a primary browser in Dreamweaver through the Preferences, or with File ⇨ Preview in Browser ⇨ Edit Browser List, that browser opens and the Help Pages are loaded. Otherwise, Dreamweaver uses your system's default browser to display the Help Pages.

The Dreamweaver Help Pages are presented within an HTML frameset as shown in Figure 4-1. Navigational buttons — Back, Forward, Previous, Next and What's New — are positioned along the top frame. At the top of the frame on the left side of the screen, you'll find the main control buttons for switching between the Help Contents, Index, and Search facilities. The main portion of the frame is reserved for showing the Help Pages themselves.

Subjects

Controls

Navigational buttons

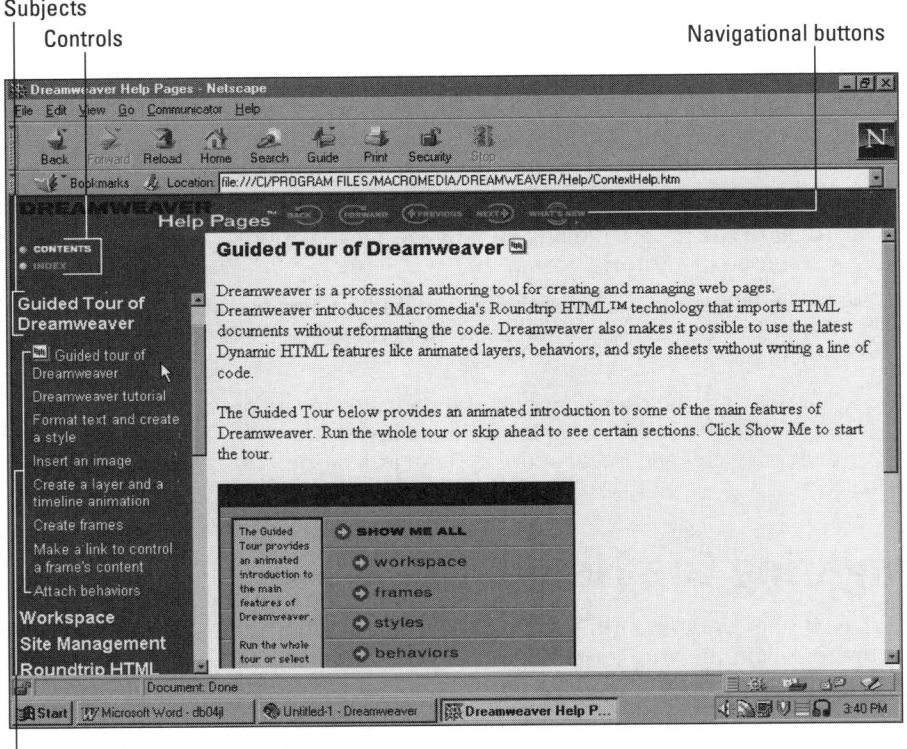

Subtopics

Figure 4-1: The Dreamweaver Help Pages comprise a hyperlinked, multimedia manual that is displayed in your primary or default browser.

Browsing the Help Contents

To get the most benefit from the Help Pages, maximize your browser window. You can alternate between the Contents and Index by selecting one or the other control button. When you choose Contents, the frame immediately below the control buttons provides a list of Dreamweaver main subjects and a handy scroll bar for moving through the list.

Selecting any main topic in the Help Contents reveals another list of subtopics. You can collapse the main topic by selecting it again or by choosing another main topic. Note that you must click a subtopic to load the information into the main viewing frame. If there is too much information to be displayed on a single screen, another scroll bar appears on the far-right side of the frame. To see the additional text, you can drag the scroll bar or select the frame and use your Page Up and Page Down keys.

Note

Dreamweaver takes advantage of your browser's HTML capabilities, and many Help Pages contain hyperlinks to other help screens. However, if you follow a hyperlink from the main screen, the Contents listing does not update to reflect your new position.

Using the navigational controls

As you browse through the Help Pages, you'll find you can use your browser's Back and Forward buttons to revisit pages you have already viewed. You can also use the Help Pages' own navigational system to move back and forth or from topic to topic. The Help Pages navigational controls are described in Table 4-1.

	Table 4-1	
	Help Pages Navigational Buttons	
Button	**Name**	**Purpose**
BACK	Back	Moves to the last page viewed.
FORWARD	Forward	Returns to the most recent page viewed, if you have clicked the Back button.
PREVIOUS	Previous	Displays the prior subtopic in the current subject.
NEXT	Next	Shows the subtopic following the current one in the present subject.
WHAT'S NEW	What's New	Goes online to visit the Dreamweaver Developers Center.

The Help Pages' Back and Forward buttons function identically to those of your browser's — although without some of the functionality of the 4.0 browser's buttons. The Next and Previous buttons, however, are somewhat different. Next and

Previous are tied to the Help Pages' content structure and only display current subtopics within each major subject. If you reach the last subtopic and attempt to use the Next button, you'll get a JavaScript alert telling you you are at the end of a section. A similar event occurs when you are looking at the first subtopic and try to view the Previous one. To go on to another major subject, you have to select it from the Contents listing and then select one of the subtopics.

The final navigational button, What's New, is a direct link to the Dreamweaver Web site. This button takes you to a special section of the Dreamweaver Developers Center, also called What's New. There you'll find the most recently published articles for beginners, which will be helpful as well to advanced users interested in getting the most out of Dreamweaver. The What's New page opens within the Help Pages frameset, so you still have access to your listing of contents or the Index. For a complete description of the What's New page, see "Getting Help Online" later in this chapter.

Playing the Show Me movies

 Dreamweaver incorporates a number of multimedia feature demonstrations called Show Me movies. Each Show Me movie is a separate Shockwave animation that graphically illustrates the workings of the interface or one of the more advanced Dreamweaver capabilities. You can see which topics include Show Me movies by looking for the Shockwave icon (shown here in the margin) displayed next to the subtopic in the Contents listing.

 To run the Show Me movies, you must have the Shockwave plug-in for your browser installed. If you installed Dreamweaver through its CD-ROM, the appropriate plug-in was included in the installation. If you downloaded Dreamweaver from the Macromedia or another Web site, you can get the plug-in by visiting

```
www.macromedia.com/shockwave/download/
```

The Guided Tour of Dreamweaver (see Figure 4-1) contains a Show Me movie that plays all of the animations in sequence, or you can pick and choose your topic. You start the entire tour by clicking the Show Me All button. This loads the first movie, an introduction to the Dreamweaver workspace.

There are a few simple controls for viewing any of the Show Me movies:

1. When you are ready to view the movie, select the flashing Show Me button.

2. At the end of each screen's presentation, the Next button begins to flash. Click the Next button to proceed.

3. To review a step previously shown, select the Back button, shown in Figure 4-2.

Exit button   Back button   Next button

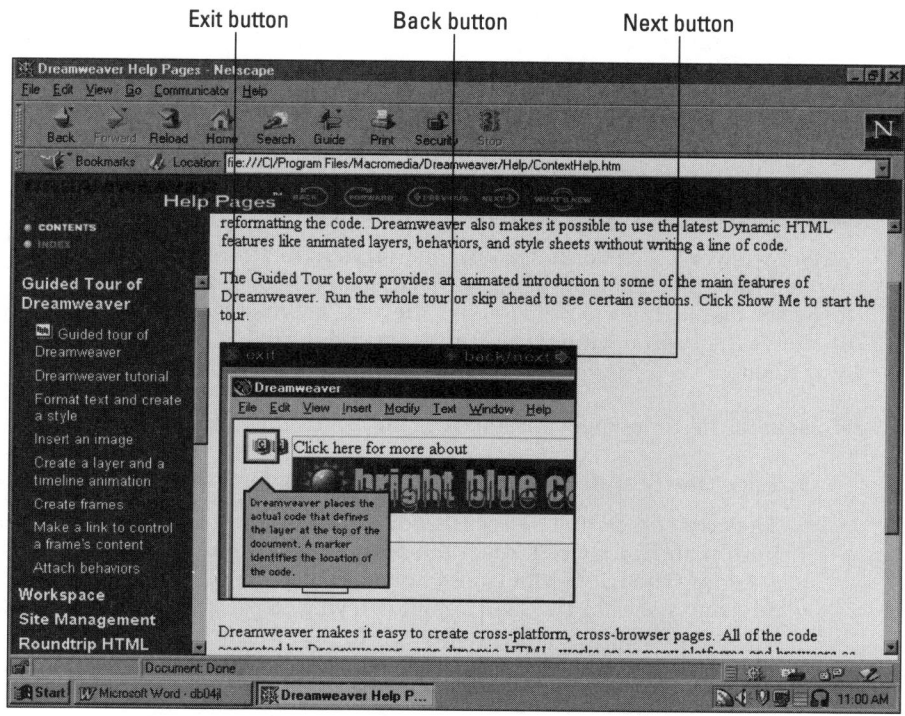

Figure 4-2: All the Show Me movies, like this one about working with layers, provide excellent introductions to the subjects.

4. When you have finished viewing the movie, select the Exit button.

5. If you are taking the Guided Tour, the next movie starts immediately after you exit from the previous one. To stop the Guided Tour completely, press the Exit button from the Guided Tour main screen.

Tip

Be sure the sound is turned up on your system when running the Show Me movies. All the movies punctuate their actions with sound, and audio is especially integral to the Show Me movie on Behaviors.

Using the Help Index

Selecting the Index control button loads an alphabetical listing of topics covered in the Dreamweaver Help Pages. To find the subject you need, scroll down the list by dragging the scroll bar at the near-right. You can also click anywhere in the frame and use your system's Page Up and Page Down keys to navigate through the Index.

When you find your subject, select it from the list. The corresponding Help Page appears in the main frame. Note that in situations where an index listing is divided into a topic and related subtopics, you must choose one of the subtopics to get the related Help Page. In this case, the topics themselves are not linked to any specific Help Page.

Search the Help Files

Dreamweaver 1.2 has added a new search function to the Help Pages. As designed by Macromedia, the search engine is actually a Java applet that runs within your browser displaying the Help Pages. There is one major advantage to this approach: it allows the search window to stay open and available as you look for the material you need.

To search the Help Pages for a particular topic, follow these steps:

1. Select the Search button found on the left side of the Help Pages frame.

   The contents listing below the command buttons are replaced by a Launch button and a note regarding the search applet. As the note states, after selecting the Launch button, you may receive a warning from your system advising you that the Java applet is trying to read the files on your hard drive. If you receive the warning, click OK to permit the search engine to proceed. The message further states that nothing is written to the hard drive and only the Dreamweaver Help Pages are searched.

2. Select the Launch button to start the Java applet.

3. In the Search window, shown in Figure 4-3, enter keywords in the upper text box.

   - To search for a phrase, enter the words as you would normally, for example, "shockwave director" (without the quotes).

   - To search for several related keywords that do not have to appear next to each other, enter the words with a plus sign between them, like this:

     ```
     shockwave + director
     ```

   - By default the search is case sensitive. To turn off this feature, deselect the Case sensitive checkbox.

4. After you've entered your search criteria, select the List Topics button.

   As each page is searched, pages matching your search criteria are displayed in the results window.

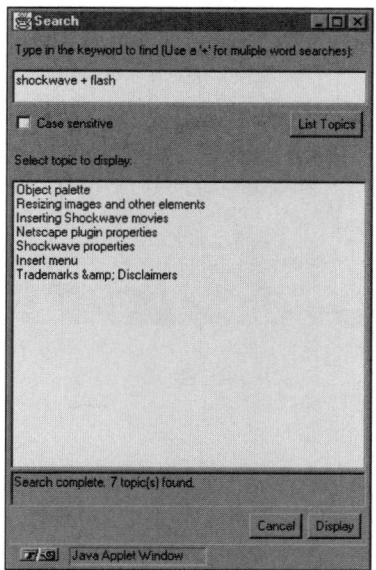

Figure 4-3: Quickly find the topics you're looking for with Dreamweaver's new Help Pages search engine.

5. To see an individual page, double-click its title in the results window. You can also select the title of the page and click the Display button.

    The page linked to the title is displayed in the main frame of the Help Pages.

6. Repeat Steps 3–5 to continue searching.

7. Click the Cancel button to close the Search window.

To return to either the Contents or the Index listing select the Contents or Index command buttons, respectively.

Stepping Through the Tutorial

The Dreamweaver Help Pages include a step-by-step tutorial that demonstrates how to use the latest Dynamic HTML features to create a Web page. To access the tutorial, first select the Index control button and then scroll down to choose Tutorial.

Tip

Macromedia recommends that you familiarize yourself with Dreamweaver by first taking the Guided Tour (mentioned earlier in the section on Show Me movies). When you are ready to try your hand at the tutorial, click the Show Me All in the Show Me movie to see the first tutorial topic, "Format text and create a style."

There are six tutorial topics in all, including: "Insert an Image," "Create a layer and a timeline animation," "Create frames," "Make a link to control a frame's content," and "Attach Behaviors." Figure 4-4 illustrates the beginning of the tutorial section on how to insert a graphic in your Web page.

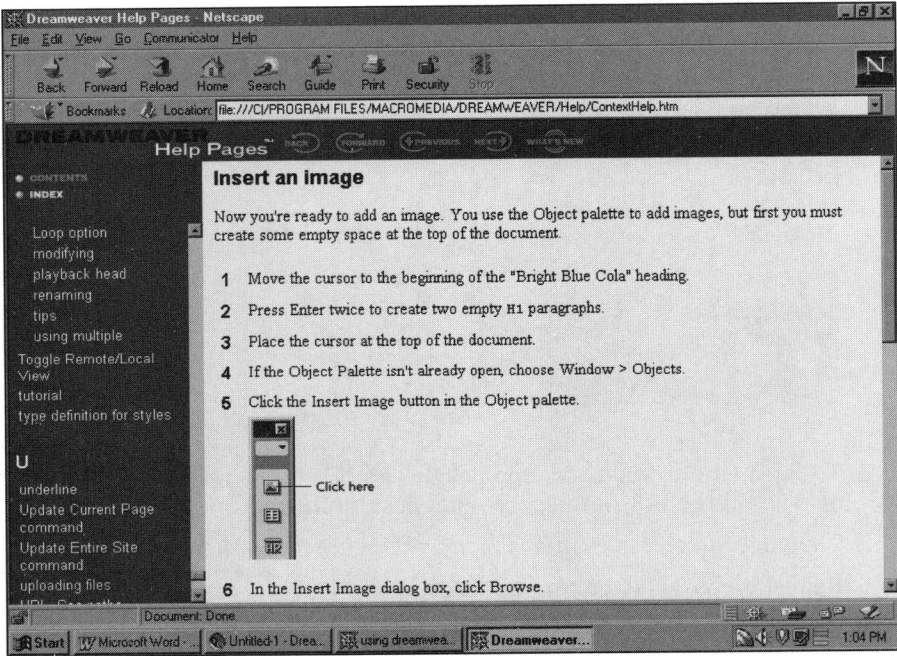

Figure 4-4: Dreamweaver includes a tutorial that demonstrates how to use the program to build an advanced Web page, step by step.

After you've completed the tutorial, you can compare the page you've created with the official version, by opening SiteFrameSet.htm located in Dreamweaver's Tutorial Folder.

Mastering the Techniques

The Help Pages contain several specialized tutorials called Dreamweaver Techniques. Techniques show how to perform certain common Web page design functions, or achieve particular HTML effects by combining step-by-step instructions, the final results and an examination of the HTML code.

You can access the Dreamweaver Techniques by first selecting the Contents control button from the Help Pages. Next, scroll down until you see Dreamweaver Techniques and select it. A brief explanation of the Techniques appears in the main frame, and the available Techniques are listed in the expanded Contents listing. Click any one of the Techniques to open it.

Unlike other information from the Dreamweaver Help Pages, the Techniques open in a separate browser window, independent of the Help Pages system. Figure 4-5 shows the Technique on Using Style Sheets, which demonstrates one the Web's latest innovations. All Techniques have an identifying header with two hyperlink buttons: See the Code and Do It in Dreamweaver. The remainder of the page is the final, working result of the chosen Technique.

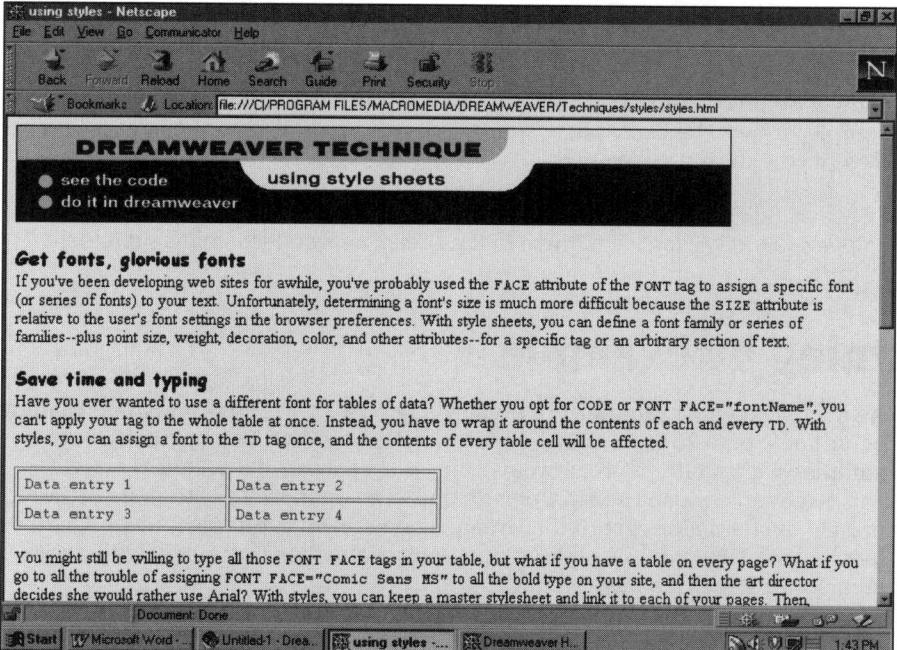

Figure 4-5: Dreamweaver Techniques give you a completed Web page, with links to step-by-step instructions on how to create the page in Dreamweaver, as well as the underlying HTML code.

After you've taken a moment to examine the working Web page, click the Do It in Dreamweaver button. This action opens another HTML document in your browser that describes precisely how to accomplish the final result. You can switch back and forth between Dreamweaver and these instructions as you learn to use the current Technique — or you might want to just print out the instructions. When you're finished, click the Back button of your browser or the header on top of the instructions page. Either action takes you back to the selected Techniques page.

Bear in mind that the HTML code presented in the Techniques is different from what Dreamweaver creates for you, even if you follow each Technique step exactly. The Techniques' HTML was coded by hand for a particular situation and is not as cross-browser compatible as the code that is produced by Dreamweaver. You'll also notice, primarily because of the extensive error-checking built into Dreamweaver, that the Dreamweaver code tends to be fairly long, while the Techniques' code is relatively compact.

To view the Techniques' code, choose the See the Code button in the Techniques' header. This opens a third Web page filled with heavily commented HTML, line-numbered for easy reference. Within the comments — on the Techniques' Code as well as the Instructions pages — you'll find links (coded in red) to other documents that will help your understanding of the method being discussed. Figure 4-6, for example, shows the Code page from the Style Sheets Technique, along with a referenced external style sheet.

Several additional Dreamweaver Techniques are included on the *Dreamweaver Bible*'s CD-ROM. You'll find them in the Dreamweaver\Techniques subfolders.

Learning by Example

The Dreamweaver Examples are presented in a less structured fashion than the Techniques, but are extremely helpful nonetheless. You can open any of the Examples within either Dreamweaver or your browser. To access them via Dreamweaver, choose Help ➪ Open Example; to open them with your browser, point your Open File dialog box to the Dreamweaver\Help\Examples folder. Once you have located the Examples folder, open any of the files that begin with an _example extension, such as frames_example.html.

If you are working on a Web page that uses frames, such as the Frames Example, and you attempt to open any nonframed HTML document in Dreamweaver, the page loads into your currently selected frame rather than establishing its own frameset. You can work around this by making sure to select the frameset first, by clicking the frame borders themselves. Another solution is to open a new Dreamweaver window (File ➪ New Window) prior to opening your nonframed page.

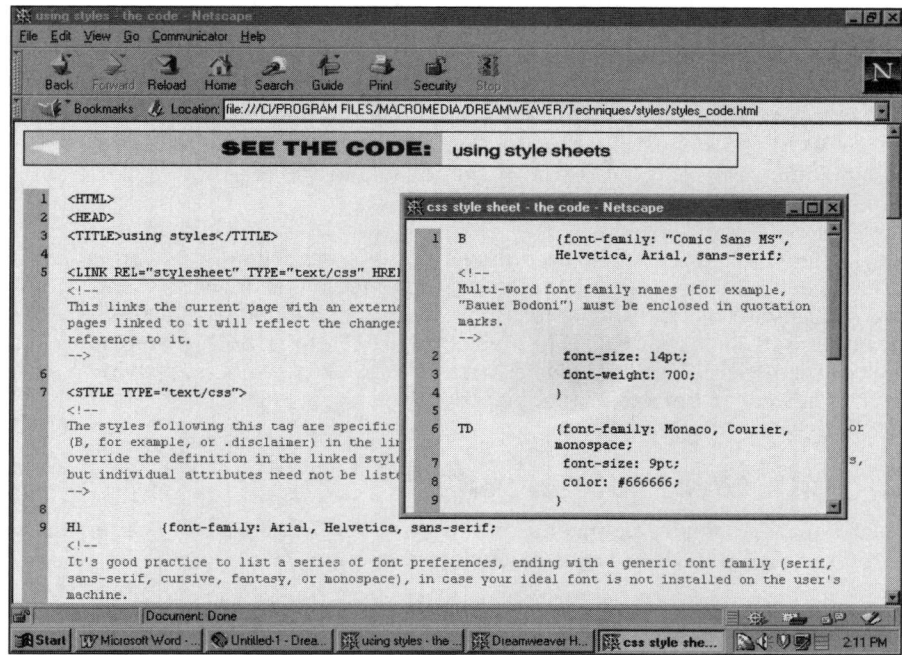

Figure 4-6: If you opt to See the Code in a Dreamweaver Technique, you'll also get in-depth comments explaining your options and the other suggestions.

Because there is no See the Code button to reveal the code in the Examples, as there is in the Techniques, you must open the HTML Inspector or invoke your external editor to take a look at the HTML. You will find the code produced in the Examples is far more similar, if not identical, to the HTML that Dreamweaver outputs. In some instances, this makes it easier to follow along and experiment.

Tip

One of the most useful methods I've found for learning how to code Web pages is to take an existing page and make changes, one at a time, to see what new effects — or mistakes — are possible. The Examples provide an excellent environment for learning with this method.

On the CD-ROM

You'll find extra Examples on the Dreamweaver Bible CD-ROM, in the Dreamweaver\Help\Examples folder. To have them appear when you select Help ➪ Open Example, copy the CD-ROM files into your local Dreamweaver Examples folder.

Getting Help Online

I think one of the factors helping the Web to grow so rapidly is the fact that it is largely self-documenting. Want to learn more about developing Web pages? Find out on the Web! The same holds true for Dreamweaver. There is already an extensive array of information about Dreamweaver available online — and more coming every day.

Macromedia has done — and continues to do — an excellent job of supporting Dreamweaver on the Web. To that end, Macromedia has developed and sponsored two Web sites. One, the Dynamic HTML Zone, is dedicated to an extensive discussion of issues related to implementing DHTML. The other Web source is a part of the general Macromedia site and focuses exclusively on providing support for Dreamweaver. Let's take a look at this one first.

Dreamweaver support site

Macromedia's primary help center on the Web for Dreamweaver is a terrific resource. Visit the Dreamweaver Developers Support Center at:

```
www.macromedia.com/support/dreamweaver/
```

to find the latest technical data, free downloads, and peer-to-peer connections — and it's all specific to Dreamweaver, naturally. One of the most impressive aspects of the site is its multilevel approach; there's material here for everyone, from rank beginner to the savviest code jockey.

When you visit the Dreamweaver Developers Support Center, you'll find six separate categories of help (discussed in the following paragraphs) as well as a search facility. Macromedia has plans to update the site, shown in Figure 4-7, on at least a monthly basis. It's definitely worth bookmarking in your browser and visiting often.

What's New

As mentioned earlier in the chapter, the What's New page is a launching point for the latest in Dreamweaver technology. Each of the different areas of the Dreamweaver Support Center contributes an article or two that is listed on the What's New page each month. Here, you'll find links to

✦ Articles in the Dreamweaver for Beginners series.

✦ Tutorials on intermediate techniques such as creating a slideshow with layers.

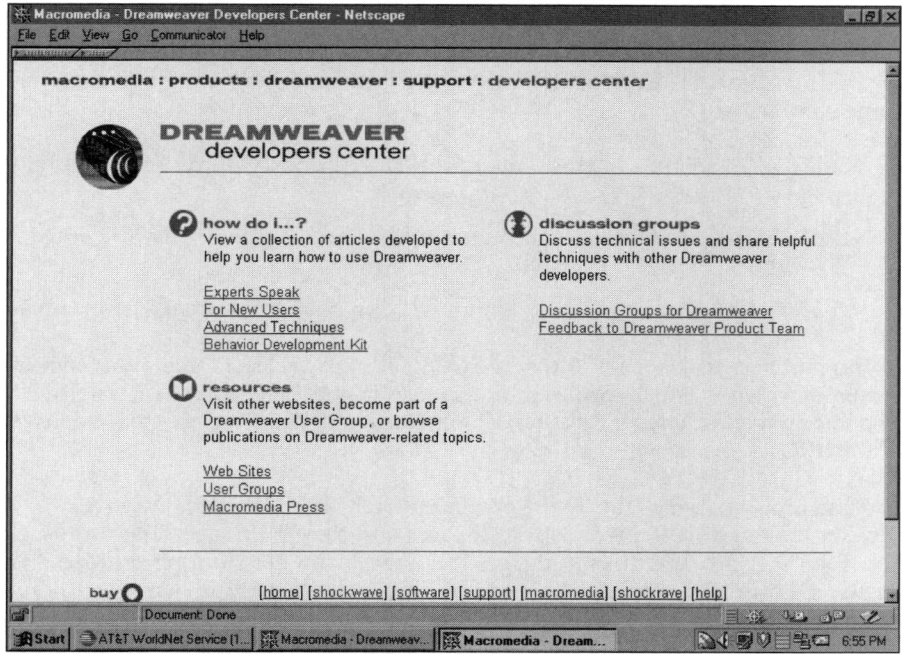

Figure 4-7: The Dreamweaver Developers Support Center Web site is a central resource for gathering the newest information and software related to Dreamweaver.

✦ Interviews with Webmasters, focusing on how they work their magic with Dreamweaver.

✦ Expert-level information such as the Behavior Development Kit and Tutorial.

Select any of the links to reach the desired article. If you click on the Next button at the bottom of the page, What's New goes to the top level of the Dreamweaver Developers Support Center.

How Do I?

You can directly access the skill area you're most interested in through the How Do I? sections. Each section — Dreamweaver for Beginners, Intermediate & Advanced Techniques, The Experts Speak — contain all the articles posted to date to the Dreamweaver Developers Support Center. Use the How Do I? section to quickly find just the expertise you want.

TechNotes

TechNotes are straightforward answers from the Dreamweaver development team, to specific questions from users. Each TechNote addresses a single issue. Here are some samples:

✦ **12761** How can I edit the name of the Title property of the Frameset HTML page without using the HTML Inspector?

✦ **12787** How can I use Dreamweaver to Create Documents in non-Latin Encoding?

✦ **12786** Why aren't my WAVE audios playing back from Navigator on my MAC?

Tip The numbers that appear at the beginning of each TechNote title are identification numbers. Often you'll encounter a response in the Dreamweaver newsgroup to a question that includes a TechNote ID number — and it's a lot easier to jot down than the URL.

You can jump to two of the TechNotes areas right from the Dreamweaver Developers Support Center: Top TechNotes and New & Updated TechNotes. Go to Top TechNotes to find links to the most common troubleshooting problems and answers. From there you can also search the TechNotes by keyword or ID number, or you can gain access to the full list of Dreamweaver TechNotes. New & Updated TechNotes brings you to a list of the TechNotes added or revised in the last month.

Updates and downloads

Being able to extend Dreamweaver's power with additional objects and behaviors offers great creative potential. But where do you find such new tools? The Object & Behaviors Exchange is the online center for Dreamweaver developers to submit and download program extensions. Anyone can enter an object or behavior action for posting. Once an item is accepted by the Dreamweaver development team, it is free to download and freely distributable.

After you enter the Object & Behaviors Exchange area, select either the Download Objects Or Behavior Actions link or the Submit Objects Or Behavior Actions link. Both selections take you to a Macromedia licensing agreement, to which you must agree before proceeding. Be sure to read the agreement carefully. Select the Accept button if you wish to continue.

The Download area is divided into two areas: objects and behavior actions. If you find an item that provides you with a new, needed functionality, select the correct file for your platform (Windows or Macintosh). The Save As dialog box appears; enter the appropriate path and file name and press the Save button. After the file has downloaded to your computer, decompress it and move the expanded files to their proper folder. New objects consist of two files — an HTML file and a GIF file —

and are stored in the Dreamweaver\Configuration\Objects*panel* folder (where *panel* represents either the Common, Forms, or Invisibles folder). New behaviors are contained in a single HTML file and should be moved to the Dreamweaver\Configuration\Behaviors\Actions folder. Dreamweaver must be restarted before it will recognize new behavior actions or objects.

If you wish to upload a new object or behavior action, you'll be asked to submit your Dreamweaver tool via e-mail. Follow the instructions from the Submit page; they ask you to include your personal information as well as information about the item you are submitting. Attach the necessary files to the e-mail and send it to the posted address. If approved, the object or behavior action is posted within a month. (The item might not be approved because it duplicates an already existing element or doesn't meet Macromedia's quality standards.)

Interact Area

To pose a technical question or to offer the Dreamweaver Development Team some feedback, visit the Interact area of the support site. There you find links to newsgroups hosted by Macromedia, including the Dreamweaver and Dynamic.HTML forums. Newsgroups are extraordinarily useful for getting help from other users or the Dreamweaver support team. It's likely that, quite often, other users will have encountered the same or similar problems to the ones you are facing. Or you may have unearthed a unique situation that reveals an undiscovered bug in the program — which the Dreamweaver staff needs to know about. Either way, participating in the newsgroup is an especially rewarding way to broaden your connection to the Dreamweaver community.

If you'd like to make some program suggestions to the Dreamweaver Development Team, select the Feedback link in the Interact area. You'll be lead to a page explaining your options for communicating with Macromedia. If you don't find a suitable resource, click the Feedback link at the bottom of the page. The next page displays a full list of e-mail addresses for sending feedback directly to the various areas at Macromedia. The Dreamweaver address is:

```
wish-dreamweaver@macromedia.com
```

Feel free to send the Dreamweaver Team a list of the items on your wish list.

Resources

The final area in the Dreamweaver Developers Support Center is a disparate but valuable collection of resources for the Web designer. The Resources area includes links to the following:

> ✦ **User Groups.** Macromedia currently has a list of 45 official user groups around the world. These grassroots organizations provide excellent

connections to other developers, business contacts and Macromedia itself. Check the list for the group nearest you.

✦ **Web Sites.** On this page, you'll find links to specific technical resources such as the W3C's Positioning HTML Elements with Cascading Style Sheets spec, as well as general resources such as the DHTML Zone (covered in the next section).

✦ **Events.** Keep in touch with Macromedia on the road by visiting this Events page. Highlights of past events and dates for upcoming shows and seminars are listed.

✦ **Made with Macromedia Program.** If you wish to distribute your applications made with Director or Authorware, visit this page to learn how to participate in Macromedia's royalty-free licensing program.

Dynamic HTML Zone

The Dynamic HTML Zone, at

```
www.dhtmlzone.com
```

is another extremely valuable online resource center. This site is also hosted by Macromedia, but here the focus is less on Dreamweaver than on implementing Dynamic HTML features in your Web pages. The Dynamic HTML Zone, shown in Figure 4-8, is a great jumping off place for learning about DHTML through a variety of methods. Here's just some of what you'll find at "the Dzone:"

Articles

The Dynamic HTML Zone contains a collection of some of the finest technical papers about creating DHTML pages on the Web. Both browser-specific and cross-browser features are explained by experts in the field. Sample articles include "Creating Multimedia with Dynamic HTML: An Overview," "Cross-Browser Dynamic HTML," and "Techniques for Building Backward Compatible DHTML."

Tutorials

Learning from tutorials can be dry and tedious — but not at the DZone! Visit SuperFly Fashions and learn helpful general techniques, such as working with CSS layers and Initializations. You also find more advanced methods, such as pull-down menus and scrolling text. The tutorials come with an overview as well as a line-by-line analysis of the JavaScript subroutines and other needed HTML code.

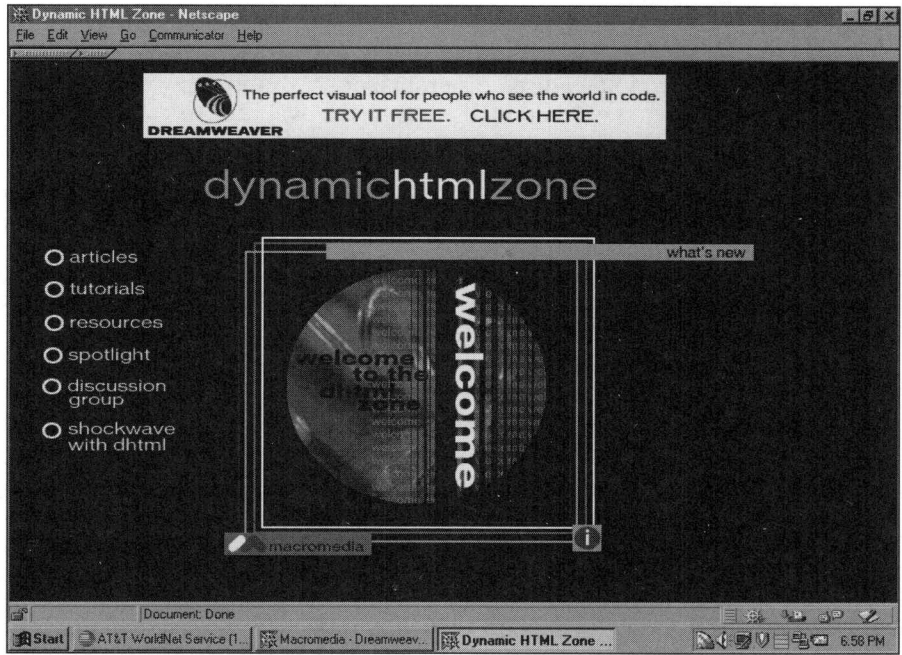

Figure 4-8: Visit the Dynamic HTML Zone for the latest information on building your Web pages with cutting-edge DHTML capabilities.

Resources

The Resources area is a collection of links to articles, reference guides, demos, various tutorials, and browser data—all related to DHTML. Pulling equally from the Microsoft and Netscape camps, as well as independent organizations such as C I Net and the W3C, these links are a great jumping-off place for all things DHTML.

Spotlight

Want to see what else is being accomplished with Dynamic HTML? Check out the Spotlight area. In addition to the site that's currently "in the Spotlight," this page maintains an archive of past sites so honored.

Shockwave in DHTML

Combining the interactivity of Shockwave with the flexibility of Dynamic HTML is an exciting concept, and this area of the DZone gives you all the tools you need to make this marriage happen. You'll find both technical white papers and full-featured demos you can learn from.

Summary

Dreamweaver is a very full-featured program incorporating many new technologies. This chapter describes the substantial alternatives available to you for shortening your learning curve. The key methods are:

✦ The expansive electronic manual, Dreamweaver Help Pages, which explains how to accomplish specific Web page building tasks through hyperlinked text and embedded multimedia.

✦ Built-in tutorials for learning how to get started with Dreamweaver, by making a Web page with some of the latest effects.

✦ Dreamweaver Techniques — specially designed lessons that offer you a working page, with step-by-step instructions for creating that page, and heavily commented HTML explaining how the experts did it.

✦ Examples of the most popular HTML features as created in Dreamweaver. You can also use the Examples as templates, by substituting your own objects and text for Macromedia's.

✦ A wealth of information, online. Constantly updated, always available, Dreamweaver's online resources are a tremendous benefit to any Web designer or developer, no matter what your level of skills.

In the next chapter, you'll see how to set up your first Dreamweaver site, step by step.

✦   ✦   ✦

Setting Up Your First Site

Web sites are far more than collections of HTML documents. Every image — from the smallest navigation button to the largest imagemap — is a separate file that must be uploaded with your HTML page. And if you add any additional elements, such as a background sound, digital video or Java applet, their files must be transferred as well. To preview the Web site locally and view in properly on the Internet, you have to organize your material in a specific manner.

Each time you begin developing a new site, you can follow the straightforward procedure described in this chapter. These steps lay the groundwork for Dreamweaver to properly link your local development site with your remote online site. For those who are just starting to create Web sites, this chapter begins with a brief discussion of approaches to online design. The remainder of the chapter is devoted to the mechanics of setting up your site — which type of Internet addressing to use, file management in Dreamweaver, and publishing to the Web with Dreamweaver's Site FTP facility.

Planning Your Site

Planning in Web design, just as in any other design process, is essential. Not only will careful planning cut your development time considerably, but it makes it far easier to achieve a uniform look-and-feel for your Web site — and thus make it friendlier and easier to use. This first section briefly covers some of the basics of Web site design: what to focus on, what options to consider, and what pitfalls to avoid. If you are an established Web site developer who has covered this ground before, feel free to skip this section.

Primary considerations

Even before you choose from various models to design your site, you'll need to address the all-important issues of message, audience, and budget.

What do you want to say?

If I had to pick one overriding concern for Web site design, it would be to answer the question: "What are you trying to say?" The clearer your idea of your message, the more focused your Web site will be. To this end, I find it useful to try and state the purpose of a Web site in one sentence. And "to create the coolest Web site on the planet" doesn't count. Though it could be regarded as a goal, it's so open-ended that it's almost no concept at all.

Here are some examples of clearly stated Web site concepts:

✦ "To provide the best small-business resource center focused on Microsoft's Office 97 software."

✦ "To chronicle the world's first voyage around the world by hot air balloon."

✦ "To advertise music lessons offered by a collective of keyboard teachers in New York City."

Who is your audience?

Right behind a site's concept — some would say neck-and-neck with it — is the site's audience. Who are you trying to reach? Quite often a site's style is heavily influenced by a clear vision of the site's intended audience. Take, for example, Macromedia's Dynamic HTML Zone (www.dhtmlzone.com) discussed in Chapter 4, "Using the Help System." This is a really good example of a site that is perfectly pitched toward its target; in this case, the intended audience is composed of professional developers and designers. Hence, you'll find the site snazzy but informative and filled with exciting examples of cutting-edge programming techniques.

In contrast, a site that is devoted to mass-market e-commerce must work with a very different group in mind: shoppers. Everyone at one time or another falls into this category, so we're really talking about a state of mind rather than a profession. Many shopping sites use a very straightforward page design, easily maneuverable, and comforting in its repetition, where visitors can quickly find what they are looking for and — with as few impediments as possible — buy it.

What are your resources?

Unfortunately, Web sites aren't created in a vacuum. Virtually all development work happens under real-world constraints of some kind or other. A professional Web designer is accustomed to working within a budget. In fact, the term *budget* can apply to several concepts.

First, you have a monetary budget — how much is the client willing to spend? This translates into a combination of development time (for designers and programmers), materials (custom graphics, stock photos, and the like), and ongoing maintenance. You can build a large site with many pages that pulls dynamically from an internal database and requires very little hands-on upkeep. Or you can construct a small, graphics-intensive site that must be updated by hand on a weekly basis. Yet it's entirely possible that both sites will end up costing the same.

Budget also applies to the amount of time you can afford to spend on any given project. The professional Web designer is quick to realize that time is an essential commodity. The resources needed when undertaking a showcase for yourself with no deadline are very different from contracting on June 30th for a job that must be ready to launch on July 4th.

The final real-world budgetary item to consider is bandwidth. The Web, with faster modems and an improved infrastructure, is slowly shedding its image as the "World Wide Wait." That means today's Webmaster must keep a steady eye on a page's *weight* — how long it takes to download under the most typical modem rates. Of course, you can always decide to include that animated video masterpiece that takes 33 minutes to download on a 28.8 modem — you just can't expect anyone to see it.

In conclusion, when you are trying to define your Web page, filter it through these three ideas: message, audience, and the various faces of the budget. The time spent visualizing your Web page in these terms will be time decidedly well spent.

Design options

Many Web professionals borrow a technique used extensively in developing other mass-marketing forms: storyboarding. *Storyboarding* for the Web entails first diagramming the various pages in your site — much like the more traditional storyboarding in videos or filmmaking — and then detailing connections for the separate pages to form the overall site. How you connect the disparate pages determines how your visitors will navigate the completed Web site.

There are several basic navigational models; the modern Web designer should be familiar with them all because each one serves a different purpose and they can be mixed and matched as needed.

The linear approach

Prior to the World Wide Web, most media formats were linear — that is, one image or page following another in an unalterable sequence. In contrast, the Web and its interactive personality allow the user to jump from topic to topic. Nevertheless, you can still use a linear approach to a Web site and have one page appear after another, like a multimedia book.

The linear navigational model, shown in Figure 5-1, works well for computer-based training applications and other expository scenarios in which you want to tightly control the viewer's experience. Some Web designers use a linear-style entrance or exit from their main site, connected to a multilevel navigational model. One advantage that Dynamic HTML brings is that you can achieve the effects of moving through several pages in a single page through layering.

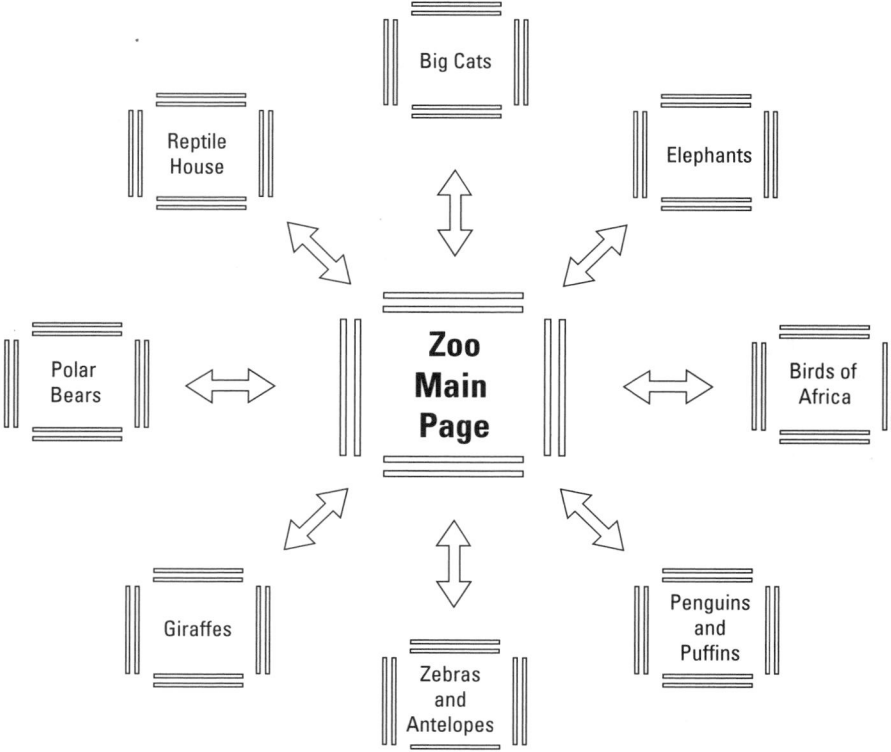

Figure 5-1: The linear navigational model takes the visitor through a series of Web pages.

Caution   Keep in mind that Web search engines can index the content of every page of your site separately. Each page of your site — not just your home page — then becomes a potential independent entrance point. So be sure to include, on every page, navigation buttons back to your home page, especially if you use a linear navigation style.

The hierarchical model

Hierarchical navigational models emerge from top-down designs. Start with one key concept which becomes your home page. From the home page, branch off to several main pages; if needed, these main pages can, in turn, branch off into many separate pages. Everything flows from the home page; it's very much like a company's organization chart, with the CEO on top followed by the various company divisions.

The hierarchical Web site, shown in Figure 5-2, is best known for maintaining a visitor's sense of place in the site. Some Web designers even depict the treelike structure as a navigation device and include each branch traveled as a link. This allows visitors to quickly retrace their steps, branch by branch, to investigate different routes.

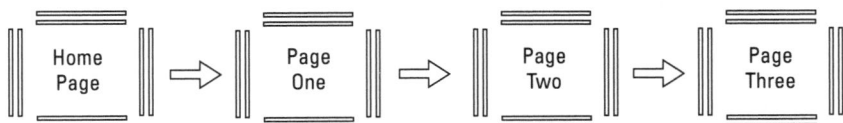

Figure 5-2: A hierarchical Web layout allows the main topics to branch into their own subtopics.

The spoke-and-hub model

Given the Web's flexible hyperlink structure, the spoke-and-hub navigational model works extremely well. The hub is, naturally, the site's home page. The spokes projecting out from the center connect to all the major pages in the site. This layout permits fairly immediate access to any key page in just two jumps — one jump always leading back to the hub/home page and one jump leading off to a new direction. Figure 5-3 shows a typical spoke-and-hub structure for a Web site.

The main drawback to the spoke-and-hub structure is the constant return to the home page. Many Web designers get around this limitation by making the first jump off the hub into a Web page using frames, in which the navigation bars are always available. This design also allows for visitors using non-frames-capable browsers to take a different path.

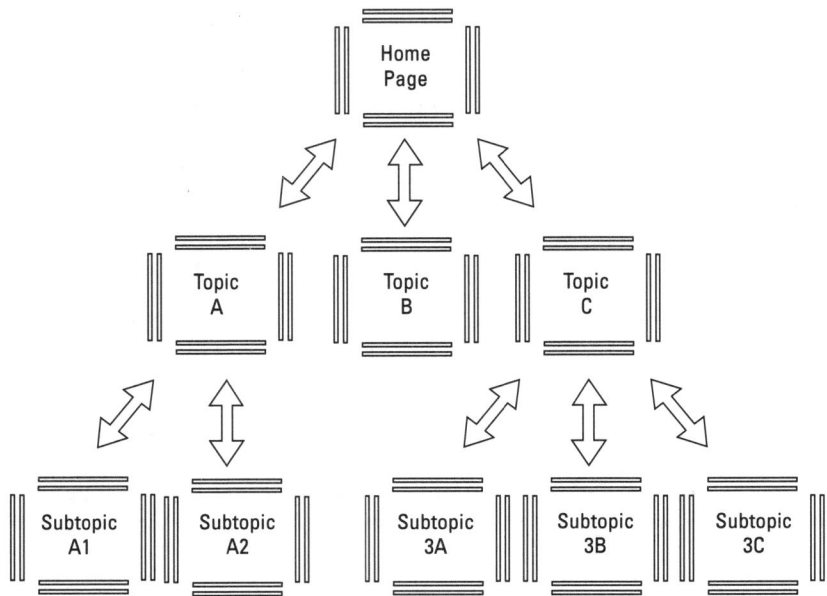

Figure 5-3: This storyboard diagram for a Zoo's Web site shows how a Spoke-and-Hub model might work.

The full Web design

The seemingly least structured approach for a Web site — FullWeb — takes the most advantage of the Web's hyperlink capabilities. This design allows virtually every page to connect to every other page. The full Web design, shown in Figure 5-4, works well for sites that are explorations of a particular topic, because the approach encourages visitors to experience the site according to their own needs, not based on the notions of any one designer. The danger in using full Web for your site design is that the visitor can literally get lost. As an escape hatch, many Web designers include a link to a clickable site map, especially for large-scale sites of this design.

> **Tip**
>
> A common rule of thumb for Web-site navigation is to make sure that none of your content is more than three jumps away from the home page. You want to avoid making it difficult for your visitors to find the material they want on your site; otherwise, they'll look elsewhere.

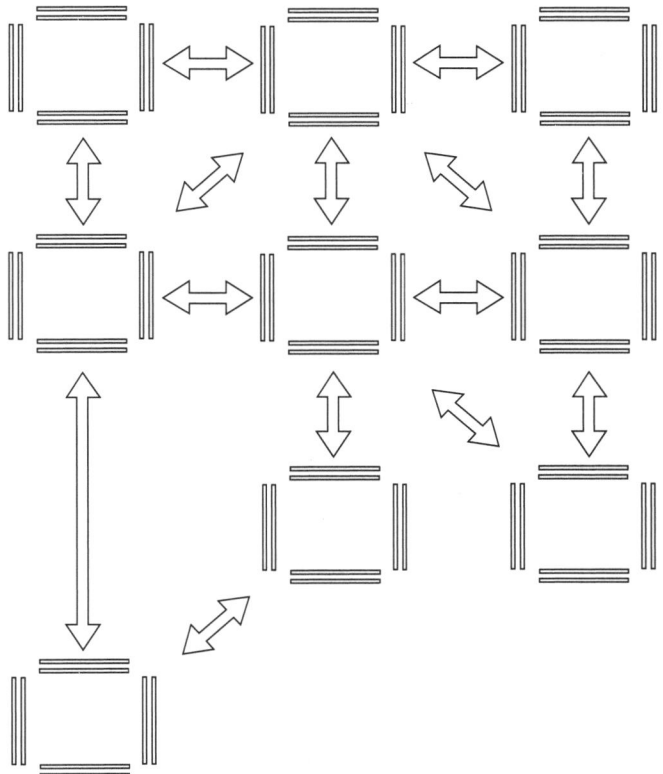

Figure 5-4: In a full Web design, each page can have multiple links to other pages.

Defining a Local Site

Now that you've decided on a design and mapped your site, you're ready to set it up in Dreamweaver. Once your site is on your Web server and fully operational, it consists of many files—HTML, graphics, and others—that make up the individual Web pages. All of these associated files are kept on the server in one main folder, which may use one or more subfolders. This main folder is called the *remote site root.* In order for Dreamweaver to properly display your linked pages and embedded images—just as they are displayed online—the program creates a mirror of your remote site on your local development system. This primary mirror folder on your system is known as the *local site root.*

Although you can establish the local site root at any time, it's best to do it at the beginning of a project. This ensures that Dreamweaver duplicates the complete structure of the Web development site when it comes time to publish your pages to the Web. One of Dreamweaver's key site-management features enables you to select just the HTML pages for publication, and Dreamweaver then automatically transfers all the associated files, creating any needed folders in the process. The mirror images of your local and remote site roots are critical to Dreamweaver's ability to expedite your workload in this way.

Tip   If you do decide to transfer an existing Web site to a new Dreamweaver local site root, run Dreamweaver's Link Checker after you've consolidated all your files. Choose File ➪ Check Links ➪ Entire Site or press the keyboard shortcut, Ctrl-F8 (Command-F8). The Link Checker tells you of broken links and orphan files as well. For more information on the Link Checker, see Chapter 27, "Publishing via Site FTP."

To set up a local site root folder in Dreamweaver, follow these steps:

1. Select File ➪ Open Site ➪ Edit Sites.

   The Site Window opens, followed shortly by the Site Information dialog box, as shown in Figure 5-5. (If you have previously created any sites in Dreamweaver, they will be listed in the Sites list box, and their information can be displayed in the fields of the dialog box.)

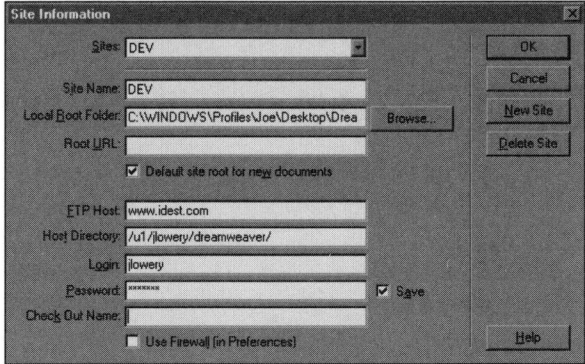

Figure 5-5: Set up your local site root through the Site Information dialog box.

2. Click the New Site button.

   The term "untitled" appears in the Sites list box and, highlighted, in the Site Name text box.

3. Type the name for your Site in the Site Name text box.

This name is reflected in the Sites list box just above. (It is also the name that appears in the user-defined site list displayed when you select File ⇨ Open Site.)

4. Specify the folder to serve as the local site root, by either typing the path name directly into Site Root Folder text box or clicking the Browse button. The Browse button opens the Choose Local Directory dialog box. When you've made your choice there, click the Select button.

5. If you want Dreamweaver to store all your new documents in the selected local site root folder, select the Default site root for new documents check box.

6. If you know the FTP information for your site, you can enter in the corresponding fields (see the following table). If you do not yet know it or don't want to enter it at this time, click OK to exit the dialog box.

Site Information Field	Contents
FTP Host	The host name of your Web server, usually in the form `www.sitename.com`. Do *not* include the full URL, such as `http://www.sitename.com/index.html`.
Host Directory	The directory in which publicly accessible documents are stored on the server. Your remote site root folder will be a subfolder of the Host Directory. Check with your Web server administrator for the proper directory path.
Login	The login name you have been assigned for access to the Web server.
Password	The password necessary for you to gain access to the Web server. Many servers are case-sensitive when it comes to logins and passwords.
Save	Check this box if you are the only one accessing the server from the current system and want to have the password entered automatically when you log in to the server.
Check Out Name	The name listed when you check out a file from the server for editing.
Firewall	Check this option if your system is behind a firewall and you've set the Preferences with the correct host and port information.

7. You can continue to enter new sites by following steps 2–6 or you can click the OK button to exit the dialog box.

Tip   Once you have established your local site root, you can begin to save your HTML files in the folder. If you're working primarily on one major site, I recommend selecting the Default site root for new documents check box in the Site Information dialog box. Dreamweaver then automatically points to your chosen folder whenever you save new Web pages.

You can change any of the information associated with your local site roots by selecting File ➪ Open Site ➪ Edit Sites from either the main Dreamweaver menu or from the Site Window menu. Choose the site you want to modify from the Site list box at the top of the Site Information dialog box, and you'll see the corresponding information for you to edit.

After your participation in a project has ended, you can remove the site from your list. Select File ➪ Open Site ➪ Edit Sites to open the Site Information dialog box, choose the site you want to remove in the Site list box, and click the Delete Site button. Note that this action removes the site only from Dreamweaver's internal list; it does not delete any files or folders from your hard drive.

With the local site root folder established, Dreamweaver can properly manage links no matter which address format is used. The various address formats are explained in the following section.

Relative and Absolute Addresses

In Dreamweaver, you can specify the type of link as well as the link itself. There are three formats for HTML links or URLs: absolute addresses, document relative addresses, and site root relative addresses.

Before you begin coding your Web pages with one form of addressing or another, it's best to understand the differences between them so that you can pick the best format for your Web site. Otherwise, you might find that you have to recode most if not all of the links on your site—a time-consuming, tedious task.

Absolute addresses

An *absolute address* is the full *uniform resource locator* (URL), specifying the type of protocol, the domain name or ID, the path, and the filename. Most often, the absolute address takes a form similar to this one:

```
http://www.idest.com/dreamweaver/index.htm
```

Absolute addresses are generally used when you are linking to a Web page on another server. Although you could code all the links on your Dreamweaver pages with absolute addresses, this approach has two drawbacks. First, it takes a lot more typing than using relative addresses; second — and much more significantly — you have to redo every single link if your linked files get moved.

As an example of a worst-case scenario, let's assume the Dreamweaver site listed just above (currently in a subfolder on my own domain) becomes so popular that I decide to move it to its own domain. With absolute addressing in effect, I will have to go and change every link that points to my home page, to something like this:

```
http://www.dreamweaver-etc/index.html
```

The best policy is to avoid using an absolute address except when you have no other choice — specifically, when the file is on another server out of your control.

Tip Should you ever need to rename every link in your Web site, Dreamweaver does offer some automated help through its included HTML editors. Both BBEdit and HomeSite have extensive search-and-replace features that allow you to establish substitutes for multiple files in one operation. For more information on these features, see Appendix B or Appendix C.

Document relative addresses

Whereas an absolute address includes every part of the URL, a relative address omits one or more elements. As its name implies, a *document relative address* assumes that the current HTML page is the point of departure, and all elements leading up to the document name are left out of the address. For example, if I were using absolute addresses to establish a link between a button on my home page (index.html), and another page (say, objects.html) stored in the same folder, I would set the link to:

```
http://www.idest.com/dreamweaver/objects.html
```

However, because they are in the same folder, I could use document relative addressing and shorten the link to:

```
objects.html
```

This is possible because the linked page is, relative to the current document (index.html), in the same location. More importantly, if the site changes servers or domains, all the links will still be valid.

Caution   To use document relative addresses in Dreamweaver you must first save your file, preferably in an established local site root. If you attempt to link anything on the current page without first saving it, Dreamweaver suggests that you save it first. If you don't save the file, the link will be inserted with a "file://*path*" prefix, where path is the location of the object on your local drive. For example:

```
file://C|/Dreamweaver/Dev/images/button04.gif
```

The "file://" references will not work properly if posted to a remote server.

You can specify a link to a subfolder using document relative addressing. It's a relatively common practice for Web designers to store their graphics in a separate folder from their HTML pages. To insert a logo kept in a subfolder called images, for instance, you would use this syntax in the link:

```
images/logo.gif
```

The slash character indicates a subfolder contained in the same directory as the current document. You can also nest folders, like this:

```
images/flags/states/ny/cities/nyc.gif
```

which would link to a graphic located five subfolders deep, relative to the current page.

It is also possible to use relative document addressing to link to an object located in a folder above the current one in the directory structure. The symbol indicating a higher folder is two dots and a slash (../) and looks like this:

```
../../resume.html
```

Such a link would move up the directory tree two folders from the current document, and then call a document found there.

Document relative addressing is a good all-around solution for small-to-medium Web sites. If you are working on a large-scale Web site that employs multiple servers, site root relative addresses (explained next) are a better choice.

Site root relative addresses

Just as a document relative address omits the protocol, server and path portion of a URL, a *site root relative address* leaves off the protocol and server segments, but retains the path. Why is this difference important? The answer lies in the capability of Web servers to host more than one site at a time — or to allow one site to be spread across multiple servers.

All Web site folders are stored on a Web server in a special directory that has been designated as being publicly accessible — unlike other, administrator-only areas of the system. This special directory is known as the *Host Directory*; you'll recall that it is noted in one of the fields of Dreamweaver's Site Information dialog box when the local root folder is established. A site root relative address uses the Host Directory as its base, much as a document relative address uses the current HTML page.

The format for a site root relative address calls for the link to start with a slash, followed by the folder name. Let's again use my Dreamweaver site as an example: suppose I'm keeping it in the root directory of my domain. I could use this form of site root relative addressing:

```
/dreamweaver-etc/objects.html
```

Building Placeholder Pages

One technique that I've found helpful over the years — and especially so with the use of document relative addressing in Dreamweaver Web projects — is what I call *placeholder pages*. These placeholder pages can fill the need to include links *as you create each Web page,* in as effortless a manner as possible.

Let's say, for example, you've just finished laying out most of the text and graphics for your home page and you want to put in some navigational buttons. You drop in your button images and align them just so. All that's missing is the link. If you're using document relative addressing, the best way to handle assigning the link would be to click the Browse for File button in the Property Inspector and select your file. But what do you do if you haven't created any other pages yet and there aren't any files to select? That's when you can put placeholder pages to work.

After you've designed the basics of your site and created your local site root, as described elsewhere in this chapter, start with a blank Dreamweaver page. Type a single identifying word on the page and save it in the local site root. Do this for all the Web pages in your plan. When it comes time to make your links, all you have to do is point and click to the appropriate placeholder page. This arrangement also gives you an immediate framework for link testing.

When it comes time to work on the next page, just open up the correct placeholder page and start to work. You can even add Dreamweaver's template feature (as described in Chapter 28, "Utilizing Dreamweaver Templates") to define a default page and get your work done even faster!

Note the beginning forward-slash character in the preceding line of code. Site root relative addressing is used on larger sites that require multiple servers to handle the substantial number of hits received. The same material can be mirrored onto several Web servers that the system administrator has set up as aliases of one another. Site root relative addressing also allows a site to be easily moved from one server to another.

The primary drawback to using site root relative addressing is that browsers cannot recognize a site root when it is used locally. In other words, if you attempted to call a graphic with a link such as this:

```
/dreamweaver-etc/images/logo.gif
```

when previewed it on your system with your primary or alternate browsers, the image would not display, although you can still see it within the Dreamweaver Document Window. To preview content that is site root relative addressed, you must make one of the following arrangements:

✦ (Windows only) Set up a local server and enable the Preview Online option found in the Preview in Browser panel of Preferences.

✦ Move the file to a remote server to view the page in your browser.

For these reasons, you'll want to use the site root relative addressing format only when you are working on a large-scale Web site and your in-process pages are stored on a local (or remote) server.

Creating and Saving New Pages

You've considered message, audience, and budget issues. You've chosen a design. You've set up your site and its address. All the preliminary planning is completed, and now you're ready to really rev up Dreamweaver and begin creating pages. This section covers the basic mechanics of opening and saving Web pages in development.

Starting Dreamweaver

Start Dreamweaver as you would any other program. Double-click the Dreamweaver program icon, or single-click if you are using Internet Explorer 4.0's Desktop Integration feature.

After the splash screen, Dreamweaver opens with a new blank page. This page is created from the Default.html file found in the Dreamweaver/Configuration/ Templates folder. Of course, it's likely that you'll want to replace the original Default.html file with one of your own — perhaps with your copyright information. All of your blank pages will then be created from a template that you've created.

Tip If you do decide to create your own Default template, it's probably a good idea to rename the Dreamweaver Default template — as Original-Default.html or something similar — prior to creating your new, personalized Default template.

Opening an existing file

If you're looking to work on a Web page in Dreamweaver that was created in another application, choose File ➪ Open, or the keyboard shortcut Control-O (Command-O). From the standard Open File dialog box, you can browse to your file's location and select it.

If you have just started Dreamweaver or if your current document is blank, your selected file will load into the current window. If, however, you have another Web page open or have begun creating a new one, Dreamweaver opens your file in a new window.

Opening Other Types of Files

Dreamweaver defaults to searching for HTML files with an extension of either .html or .htm. To look for other types of files, select the Files of Type arrow button. Dreamweaver 1.2 allows several other file types, including server-side includes (.shtml or .shtm), Active server pages (.asp) and Cold Fusion (.cfm or .cfml). If you need to load a valid HTML file with a different extension, select the All Files option.

If you are working consistently with a different file format, you can add your own extensions and file types to the Dreamweaver Open File dialog box. In the Configuration folder, there is an editable text file called Extensions.txt. Open this file in your favorite text editor to make any additions. If you use Dreamweaver, be sure to edit the file in the HTML Inspector to see the correct format.

The syntax must follow this format:

```
HTM,HTML:HTML Documents
SHTM,SHTML:Server Includes
LBI:Library Files
CSS:Style Sheets
ASP:Active Server Pages
CFM,CFML:Cold Fusion Templates
TXT:Text Files
```

To add an entry, place your cursor at the end of the line *above* where you want your new file format to be placed, and press Enter (Return). Type in your file extension(s) in capital letters, followed by a colon and then the text description. Save the Extensions.txt file and restart Dreamweaver to see your modifications.

When you first open an existing Web page, Dreamweaver checks the HTML syntax. If it finds any errors, Dreamweaver corrects them and then informs you of the corrections through the HTML Parser Results dialog box. As discussed in Chapter 3, "Setting Your Preferences," you can turn off this HTML syntax checking feature. Select Edit ➪ Preferences and then, from the HTML pane of the Preferences dialog box, deselect one or more of the check box options for HTML syntax checking.

Opening a new window

You can work on as many Dreamweaver documents as your system memory can sustain. When you choose File ➪ New Window or one of the keyboard shortcuts (Control-N or Command-N), Dreamweaver opens a new blank page in a separate window. Once the window is open, you can switch among the various windows. To do this in Windows 95/NT, you select the appropriate icon in the taskbar or use the Alt-Tab method. To switch between Dreamweaver windows on a Macintosh, click on the individual window or use the Window menu.

Opening a new page

After working for a while on a design, you sometimes need just to start over or switch entirely to a new project. In either case, choose File ➪ New or one of the keyboard shortcuts, Control-Shift-N (Command-Shift-N). This closes the current document and opens a new blank page in the same window.

If you've made any modifications to your page, Dreamweaver asks if you would like to save the page. Click the Yes button to save the file or the No button to continue without saving it. To abort the new page opening, click Cancel.

Each time you open a new page, whether in the existing window or in a new window, Dreamweaver temporarily names the file "Untitled-n," where n is the next number in sequence. This prevents you from accidentally overwriting a new file opened in the same session.

Saving your page

Saving your work is very important in any computer-related task, and Dreamweaver is no exception. To initially save the current page, choose File ➪ Save or the keyboard shortcut Control-S (Command-S). The Save dialog box opens; you can enter a filename and, if desired, a different path.

By default, all files are saved with an .htm filename extension. To save your file with another extension, such as .shtml, change the Files of Type option to the specific file type and then enter your full filename, without the extension.

Tip

It seems kind of backward in this day and age of long filenames, but it's still a good idea to choose names for your files without spaces or punctuation other than an underscore or hyphen. Otherwise, not all servers will read the file name correctly and you'll have problems linking your pages.

Closing the page

When you're finished with a page — or if your system is running low on resources — you can close a file without quitting Dreamweaver. To close a page, select File ⇨ Close or one of the keyboard shortcuts, Control-W (Command-W). If you have made any modifications to the page since you saved it last, Dreamweaver prompts you to save it.

If you only have one Dreamweaver window open and you close the current page, Dreamweaver presents you with a new, blank page.

Quitting the program

Once you're done for the day — or, more often, the late, late night — you can close Dreamweaver by choosing File ⇨ Exit or one of the standard keyboard shortcuts, Control-Q (Command-Q).

Previewing Your Web Pages

When using Dreamweaver or any other Web authoring tool, it's important to constantly check your progress in one or more browsers. Dreamweaver's Document Window offers a near-browser view of your Web page, but because of the variations among the different browsers, it's imperative that you preview your page early and often. Dreamweaver offers you easy access to a maximum of 20 browsers — and they're just a function key away.

You add a browser to your preview list by selecting File ⇨ Preview in Browser ⇨ Edit Browser List or by choosing the Preview in Browser category from the Preferences dialog box. Both actions open the Preview in Browser Preferences panel. The steps for editing your browser list are described in detail in Chapter 3, "Setting Your Preferences." Here's a brief recap:

1. Select File ⇨ Preview in Browser ⇨ Edit Browser List.
2. To add a browser (up to 20), click the Add button and fill out the following fields:

Name	How you want the browser listed.
Path	Type it in or click the Browse button to locate the browser .EXE file.
Primary/Secondary	If desired, check one of these to designate the current browser as such.

3. After you've added a browser to your list, you can easily edit or delete it. Choose File ➪ Preview in Browser ➪ Edit Browser List as before, and highlight the browser you want to modify or delete.

4. To alter your selection, click the Edit button. To delete your selection, click the Remove button.

5. After you've completed your modifications, click OK to close the dialog box.

Caution

Whenever you preview your Web page in Internet Explorer 4.0, Dreamweaver opens a new browser window rather than posting the update to the currently open window. As a workaround, you can either close your current browser each time you've finished previewing it, or save the file in Dreamweaver and then open it by file name in Internet Explorer 4.0, and use the Refresh button after you've saved any changes.

Once you've added one or more browsers to your list, you can preview the current page in these browsers. Select File ➪ Preview in Browser ➪ *BrowserName* where *BrowserName* indicates the particular program. Dreamweaver saves the page to a temporary file, starts the browser and loads the page.

Note that, in order to view any changes you've made to your Web page under construction, you must select the Preview in Browser menu option again (or press one of the function keys for primary/secondary browser previewing, described just below). Clicking the Refresh/Reload button in your browser will not load in any modifications. The temporary preview files are deleted when you quit Dreamweaver.

You can also use keyboard shortcuts to preview two different browsers, by pressing a function key: Press F12 to preview the current Dreamweaver page in your primary browser, and Shift-F12 to preview the same page in your secondary browser. These are the Primary and Secondary Browser settings you establish in the Preferences/Preview in Browser dialog box, explained in Chapter 3, "Setting Your Preferences."

In fact, with Dreamweaver's Preview in Browser Preferences you can so easily switch the designations of Primary and Secondary browser that you can use that setup for "debugging" a Web page in any browser, simply by changing the preferences. Go to the Preview in Browser Preferences pane, select the browser you want to use for debugging, and check the appropriate check box to designate the browser as Primary or Secondary. In the list of browsers in this Preferences pane, you'll see the indicator of F12 or Shift-F12 appear next to the browser's name.

Tip   In addition to checking your Web page output on a variety of browsers on your system, it's also a good idea to preview the page on other platforms. If you're designing on a Macintosh, try to view your pages on a Windows system, and vice versa. Watch out for some not-so-subtle differences between the two environments, in terms of color rendering (colors in Macs tend to be brighter than in PCs) and screen resolution.

Putting Your Pages Online

The final phase of setting up your Dreamweaver site is publishing your pages to the Web. When you begin this publishing process is up to you. Some Web designers wait until everything is absolutely perfect on the local development site and then upload everything at once. Others like to establish an early connection to the remote site and extend the transfer of files over a longer period of time.

I fall into the latter camp. When I start transferring files at the beginning of the process, I find that I catch my mistakes earlier and avoid having to effect massive changes to the site after everything is up. For example, in developing one large site I started out using filenames with mixed case, as in ELFhome.html. After publishing some early drafts of a few Web pages, however, I discovered that the host had switched servers; on the new server, filenames had to be all lowercase. Had I waited until the last moment to upload everything, I would have been faced with an unexpected and gigantic search-and-replace job.

Once you've established your local site root — and you've included your remote site's FTP information in the setup — the actual publishing of your files to the Web is a very straightforward process. To transfer your local Web pages to an online site, follow these steps:

1. Choose File ➪ Open Site ➪ *Site Name* where *Site Name* is the current site.

    The Site Window opens, displaying the current site.

2. From the Site Window, click the Connect button. (You may need to complete your connection to the Internet prior to choosing the Connect button.)

    Dreamweaver displays a message box showing the progress of the connection.

3. If you didn't enter a Password in the Site Information dialog box, or if you entered a password but didn't opt to Save it, Dreamweaver asks you to type in your Password.

4. Once the connection is complete, the directory listing of the remote site appears in the Remote (left-hand) pane of the Site Window.

5. In the Local (right-hand) pane, highlight the HTML files you would like to transfer.

6. Click the Put button at the top of the Site Window.

7. Dreamweaver asks if you would like to move the dependent files as well. Select Yes to transfer all embedded graphics and other objects, or No if you'd prefer to move these yourself. You can also select the Don't Ask Me Again box to make transfers of dependent files automatic in the future.

   Dreamweaver displays the progress of the file transfer in the Site Window's status bar.

8. When each file transfer is finished, Dreamweaver places a green check mark next to each file (if File Check In/Out has been enabled in the Site FTP Preferences pane).

9. When you've finished transferring your files, click the Disconnect button.

Remember, the only files you have to highlight for transfer to the remote site are the HTML files. As noted above, Dreamweaver automatically transfers any dependent file (if you allow it) which means that you'll never forget to move a GIF again! (Nor will you ever move an unnecessary file, such as an earlier version of an image, by mistake.) Moreover, Dreamweaver automatically creates any subfolders necessary to maintain the site's integrity. These two features combined will save you substantial time and worry.

Some files, especially CGI programs, require that you set the file permissions before they can be used. For information about setting file permissions from within Dreamweaver, see Chapter 15, "Accessing External Programs."

So now your site has been prepped from the planning stages, through the local site root and onto the Web. Congratulations — all that's left is to fill those pages with insightful content, amazing graphics, and wondrous code. Let's get to it!

Summary

In this chapter, you studied some options for planning your Web site and what you need to do in Dreamweaver to initialize the site. This planning and initialization process is not a detailed one, but there are particular steps to take that can greatly smooth your development path down the road.

✦ Put as much time into planning your site as possible. The more clearly conceived the site, the cleaner the execution.

✦ Set up your local site root in Dreamweaver right away. The local site root is essential for Dreamweaver to properly publish your files to the remote site later.

✦ Decide on the type of addressing to use in your links. Document relative addressing is good for most small-to-medium Web sites, and site root relative addressing is best for most large sites. Use absolute addressing only when linking to an outside server.

✦ Preview early, often, and with various browsers. Dreamweaver gives you quick function-key access to a Primary and Secondary browser. Check your pages frequently in these browsers, and then spend some time checking your pages against other available browsers and browser versions.

✦ Establish an early connection to the Web and use it frequently. You can begin publishing your local site through Dreamweaver's Site Window almost immediately.

In the next chapter, you'll see how to use Dreamweaver to begin coding your Web pages.

✦   ✦   ✦

Using Basic HTML in Dreamweaver

P A R T

II

◆ ◆ ◆ ◆

In This Part

Chapter 6
How HTML Works

Chapter 7
Adding Text to Your
Web Page

Chapter 8
Inserting Images

Chapter 9
Establishing Web
Links

Chapter 10
Creating Lists

◆ ◆ ◆ ◆

How HTML Works

In a perfect world, you could lay out the most complex Web site with a visual authoring tool and never have to see the HTML, much less code in it. Dreamweaver takes you a long way toward this goal — in fact, you can create many types of Web pages using only Dreamweaver's Document Window. As your pages become more complex, however, you will probably need to tweak your HTML just a tad.

This chapter gives you a basic understanding of how HTML works in general, and the specific building blocks you need to begin creating Web pages. The Dreamweaver-specific material in this chapter — primarily describing how Dreamweaver sets and modifies a page's properties — is suitable for even the most accomplished Web designers. Armed with these fundamentals, you'll be ready to begin your exploration of Web page creation.

The Structure of an HTML Page

The simplest explanation of how HTML works derives from the full expansion of its acronym: HyperText Markup Language. *HyperText* refers to one of the World Wide Web's main properties — the capability to jump from one page to another, no matter where the pages are located on the Web. *Markup Language* means that a Web page is really just a heavily annotated text file. The basic building blocks of HTML, such as `<strong>` and `<p>`, are known as *markup elements* or *tags*. The terms *element* and *tag* are used interchangeably.

An HTML page, then, is a set of instructions (the tags) suggesting to your browser how to display the enclosed text and images. The browser knows what kind of page it is handling based on the tag that opens the page, `<html>`, and the tag that closes the page, `</html>`. The great majority of HTML tags come in such pairs, in which the closing tag always has a forward slash before the keyword. Two examples of tag pairs are: `<p>`...`</p>` and `<title>`...`</title>`. A few important tags are represented by a single element; the image tag `<img>`, for example.

The HTML page is divided into two primary sections: the `<head>` and the `<body>`. Information relating to the entire document goes in the `<head>` section: the title, description, keywords, and any language subroutines that may be called from within the `<body>`. The content of the Web page is found in the `<body>` section. All the text, graphics, embedded animations, Java applets, and other elements of the page are found between the opening `<body>` and the closing `</body>` tags.

When you start a new document in Dreamweaver, the basic format is already laid out for you. Listing 6-1 shows the code from a Dreamweaver blank Web page.

Listing 6-1: **The HTML for a new Dreamweaver page**

```
<html>
<head>
<title>Untitled Document</title>
<meta http-equiv= Content-Type  content= text/html;
charset=iso-8859-1 >
</head>

<body bgcolor= #FFFFFF >

</body>
</html>
```

Notice how the `<head>`...`</head>` pair is separate from the `<body>`...`</body>` pair, and that both are contained within the `<html>`...`</html>` tags.

Also notice that the `<body>` tag has an additional element:

```
bgcolor= #FFFFFF
```

This type of element is known as an attribute. *Attributes* modify the basic tag and can either be equal to a value or can stand alone; in this example, the attribute, `bgcolor`, is set to a hexadecimal number that represents the color white. Thus, this attribute sets the background color of the body — the page — to white. Not every tag has attributes, but when it does, the attributes are specific.

Tip
If you're using the PC version of Dreamweaver, you have access to an excellent HTML guide through the HomeSite editor. From the HomeSite window, select Help ⇨ Help Topics and then open the HTML Reference from the Help pane.

One last note about an HTML page: You are free to use carriage returns, spaces, and tabs as needed to make your code more readable. The interpreting browser ignores all but the included tags and text to create your page. There are some minor, browser-specific differences in interpretation of these elements that will be pointed out through the book, but by and large, you can indent or space your code as you desire.

Defining <head> Elements

Information pertaining to the Web page overall is contained in the <head> section of an HTML page. Browsers read the <head> to find out how to render the page — for example, is the page to be displayed using the Western, Chinese or some other character set? This section is also read by search engine spiders to glean a summary of the page quickly.

When you begin inserting JavaScript (or code from another scripting language) into your Web page, all of the subroutines and document-wide declarations go into the <head> area. Dreamweaver uses this format by default when you insert a JavaScript behavior.

Tip
Currently, you can only set a few of the elements/tags that are part of the <head> section — the ones relating to the page's properties — through Dreamweaver's visual interface. Others, such as most <meta> elements, need to be hand-coded.

Establishing page properties

When you first start Dreamweaver, your default Web page is untitled and uncolored, with no background image. You can change all of these properties and more through Dreamweaver's Page Properties dialog box.

As usual, Dreamweaver gives you more than one method for accessing the Page Properties dialog box. You can select Modify ⇨ Page Properties, or you can use the keyboard shortcut — Ctrl-J (Command-J).

Tip
Here's the other way to open the Page Properties. Right-click (Ctrl-click) any open area in the document window — that is, any part of the screen not occupied by an image or other object (text is okay to click, however). From the Shortcut menu, select Page Properties.

The Page Properties dialog box, shown in Figure 6-1, enables you easy control of your HTML page's overall look and feel.

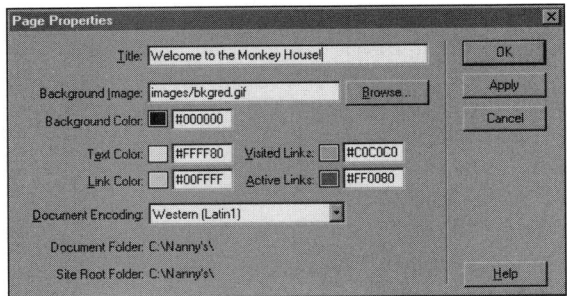

Figure 6-1: Change your Web page's overall appearance through the Page Properties dialog box.

Note   Technically, some of the values you assign through the Page Properties dialog box are applied to the `<body>` tag; because they affect the overall appearance of a page, however, they are covered in this `<head>` section.

The key areas of the Page Properties dialog box are explained in the following table.

Page Property	*Description*
Title	The title of your Web page. The name you enter here appears in the browser's title bar when your page is viewed and is also regarded as one of the important indexing clues by search engine spiders.
Background Image	The filename of the graphic you want in the page background. Either type in the path directly or pick a file by clicking the Browse button. You can embed any graphic of your choice in the background of your page; if the image is smaller than your content requires, the browser tiles the image to fill out the page. Specifying a background image overrides any selection in the Background Color field.
Background Color	Click on this color swatch to change the background color of the Web page. Select one of the browser-safe colors from the pop-up menu, or enter its name or hexadecimal representation (for example, "#FFFFFF") directly into the text box.

Page Property	Description
Text Color	Click on this color swatch to control the color of default text.
Link Color	Click this color swatch to modify the color of any text designated as a link, or the border around an image link.
Visited Links	Click this color swatch to select the color to which linked text will change after a visitor to your Web page has selected that link and then returns to the page.
Active Links	Click this color swatch to choose the color to which linked text changes briefly when a user selects the link.
Document Encoding	The character set in which you want your Web page to be displayed. Choose one from the drop-down list. The default is Western (Latin 1).

The Page Properties dialog box also displays the current site root folder if one has been selected, and the document folder if the page has been saved.

Using <meta> tags

Summary information about the content of a page — and a lot more — is conveyed through <meta> tags used within the <head> section. The <meta> tag can be read by the server to create a header file, which makes it easier for indexing software used by search engines to catalog sites. Numerous different types of <meta> tags exist. At this time, all but one type of <meta> tag must be entered by hand.

The Document Encoding option of the Page Properties dialog box determines the character set used by the current Web page and is displayed in the <head> section as follows:

```
<meta http-equiv= Content-Type  content= text/html;
charset=iso-8859-1 >
```

The preceding <meta> tag tells the browser that this page is, in fact, an HTML page and that the page should be rendered using the specified character set (the charset attribute). The key attribute here is "http-equiv"; this attribute is responsible for generating a *server response header.*

Tip

Once you've determined your <meta> tags for a Web site, the same basic <meta> information can go on every Web page. Dreamweaver gives you two ways to avoid typing (or even cutting-and-pasting) the same lines again and again. One way makes the necessary <meta> tags a Library Element, and drops that Library Element in for every page — which enables you to update all the pages at once, if necessary. You can also add the `<meta>` code to a Dreamweaver template or to the default page. In fact, you could have the best of both worlds by adding a `<meta>` tag Library Element to a template!

For more on Library Elements, see Chapter 26, "Using the Repeating Elements Library." For more on templates, turn to Chapter 28, "Utilizing Dreamweaver Templates."

Indexing with <meta> tags

Let's take a closer look at the `<meta>` tag's important role of conveying indexing and descriptive information to search engine spiders. If, for example, you want to categorize your Web page as a homage to the music of the early seventies, you can use the following `<meta>` tag:

```
<meta http-equiv= keywords  content= music, 70s, 70 s, eagles,
ronstadt, bee gees, pop, rock >
```

In the preceding, the `content` list is composed of words or phrases, separated by commas, and all enclosed in quotes. The same syntax holds true for inserting a `<meta>` tag describing the page:

```
<meta http-equiv= description  content= The definitive look
back to the power pop rock stylings of early 1970s music with
special sections devoted to The Eagles, Linda Ronstadt and the
Bee Gees. >
```

Keep in mind that the `<meta>` tag description should complement and extend both the keywords and the Web page title. You have more room in `<meta>` tags — really, an unlimited amount — than in the page title, which should be on the short side in order to fit into the browser's title bar.

Caution

When using `<meta>` tags with the keywords or description attributes, don't stuff the `<meta>` tags with the same word repeated over and over again. The search engines are engineered to reject multiple words and your description will not get the attention it deserves.

Changing bases

Through the `<base>` element, the `<head>` section enables you to exert fundamental control over the basic HTML element: the link. The `<base>` tag specifies the base URL for the current page. If you use relative addressing (covered in Chapter 5), you can switch all of your links to another directory — even another Web site — with one command. The `<base>` tag takes one attribute, `href`, which redirects all the other relative links on your page.

Let's say you define one link as follows:

```
images/backgnd.gif
```

Normally, the browser looks in the same folder as the current page for a subfolder named images. A different sequence occurs, however, if you set the `<base>` tag to another URL in the following way:

```
<base href= http://www.testsite.com/client-demo01/ >
```

With this `<base>` tag, when the same `images/backgnd.gif` link is activated, the browser looks for its file in the following location:

```
http://www.testsite.com/client-demo01/images/backgnd.gif
```

Caution   Because of the all-or-nothing capability of `<base>` tags, many Webmasters use them cautiously, if at all.

Adding to the <body>

The content of a Web page — the text, images, links, and plug-ins — is all contained in the `<body>` section of an HTML document. The great majority of `<body>` tags can be inserted through Dreamweaver's visual layout interface.

To use the `<body>` tags efficiently, you need to understand the distinction between *logical styles* and *physical styles* used in HTML. An underlying philosophy of HTML is to keep the Web as universally accessible as possible. Web content is not only intended to be platform- and resolution-independent, but the content itself is designed to be styled by its intent, as well. This philosophy is supported by the existence of logical `<body>` tags (such as `<code>` and `<cite>`), with which a block of text can be rendered according to its meaning, as well as physical style tags for directly italicizing or underlining text. HTML lets you choose between logical styles, which are relative to the text, or physical styles, which can be regarded as absolute.

Logical styles

Logical styles are contextual rather than explicit. Choose a logical style when you want to ensure that the meaning, rather than a specific look, is conveyed. Table 6-1 shows a listing of logical style tags and their most common usage. Tags not supported through Dreamweaver's visual interface are noted.

Table 6-1
HTML Logical Style Tags

Tag	Usage
`<big>`	Increases the size of the selected text relative to the surrounding text. Not currently supported by Dreamweaver.
`<cite>`	Citations, titles, and references; usually shown in italic.
`<code>`	Code; for showing programming code, usually displayed in a monospaced font.
`<dfn>`	Defining instance; used to mark the introduction of a new term.
`<em>`	Emphasis; depicted usually as underlined or italicized text.
`<kbd>`	Keyboard; used to render text to be entered exactly.
`<s>`	Strikethrough text; used for showing text that has been deleted.
`<samp>`	Sample; a sequence of literal characters.
`<small>`	Decreases the size of the selected text relative to the surrounding text. Not currently supported by Dreamweaver.
`<strong>`	Strong emphasis; usually rendered as bold text.
`<sub>`	Subscript; the text is shown slightly lowered below the baseline. Not currently supported by Dreamweaver.
`<sup>`	Superscript; the text is shown slightly raised above the baseline. Not currently supported by Dreamweaver.
`<tt>`	Teletype; displayed with a monospaced font such as Courier.
`<var>`	Variable; used to distinguish variables from other programming code.

Logical styles are going to become increasingly important as more browsers accept Cascading Style Sheets. Style sheets make it possible to combine the best elements of both logical and physical styles. With style sheets, you can easily make the text within your `<code>` tags blue, and the variables, denoted with the `<var>` tag, green.

Caution   If a tag is not currently supported by Dreamweaver, you must enter the tag by hand and preview the result in a browser. For example, you can use the `<sub>` tag to create a formula for water (H_2O), but you don't see the subscripted 2 in the formula until you view the page through a browser.

Physical styles

HTML picked up the use of physical styles from modern typography and word-processing programs. Use a physical style when you want something to be bold, italic, or underline (or, as we say in HTML, `<b>`, `<i>`, and `<u>`, respectively) absolutely. You can apply the bold and the italic tags to selected text through the Property Inspector or by selecting Text ➪ Style; the underline style is only available through the Text menu.

With HTML Version 3.2, a fourth physical style tag was added: `<font>`. Most browsers recognize the `size` attribute, which enables you to make the selected text larger or smaller, relatively or directly. To change a font size absolutely, select your text and then select Text ➪ Size; Dreamweaver inserts a

```
<font size=n>
```

tag, where *n* is a number from 1 to 7. To make text larger than the default text, select Text ➪ Size Increase and then choose the value you want. Here Dreamweaver inserts the

```
<font size=+n>
```

The plus sign indicates the relative nature of the font. Make text smaller than the default text by selecting Text ➪ Size Decrease; Dreamweaver inserts a

```
<font size=-n>
```

You can also expressly change the type of font used and its color through the `face` and `color` attributes. Because you can't be sure what fonts will be on a user's system, common practice and good form dictates that you should list alternatives for a selected font. For instance, rather than just specifying Arial — a sans serif font common on PCs but relatively unknown on the Mac — you could insert a tag like the following:

```
<font face= Arial, Helvetica, sans-serif >
```

In the preceding case, if the browser doesn't find the first font, it looks for the second one (and so forth, as specified). Dreamweaver handles the font face attribute through its Font List dialog box, which is explained fully in Chapter 7.

Inserting Symbols and Special Characters

When working with Dreamweaver, you're usually entering text directly from your keyboard, one keystroke at a time, with each representing a letter, number, or other keyboard character. Some situations, however, require special letters that have diacritics or common symbols such as the copyright mark, which are outside of the regular, standard character set represented on your keyboard. HTML enables you to insert a full range of such *character entities* through two systems. The more familiar special characters have been assigned a mnemonic code-name to make them easy to remember; these are called *named characters*. Less typical characters must be inserted by entering a numeric code; these are known as *decimal characters*. For the sake of completeness, named characters also have a corresponding decimal character code.

Both named and decimal characters codes begin with an ampersand (&) symbol and end with a semicolon. For example, the HTML code for a copyright symbol follows:

&

Its decimal character equivalent follows:

&

If, during the browser-testing phase of your Web page, you suddenly see an HTML code on screen rather than a symbol, double-check your HTML. The code could be just a typo; you may have left off the closing semicolon, for instance. If the code is correct and you're using a named character, however, switch to its decimal equivalent. Some of the earlier browser versions are not perfect in rendering named characters.

Named characters

HTML coding conventions require that certain characters, including the angle brackets that surround tags, be entered as character entities. Table 6-2 lists the most common named characters.

Table 6-2
Common Named Characters

Named Entity	Symbol	Description
&lt;	<	A left-hand angle bracket or the less-than symbol.
&gt;	>	A right-hand angle bracket or the greater-than symbol.
&amp;	&	An ampersand.

Named Entity	Symbol	Description
&quot;	"	A double quotation mark.
		A nonbreaking space.
&copy;	©	A copyright symbol.
&reg;	®	A registered mark.
&trade;	™	A trademark symbol. Cannot be previewed in Dreamweaver, but is supported in Internet Explorer.

Those characters that you can type directly into Dreamweaver's document window, including the brackets and the ampersand, are automatically translated into the correct named characters in HTML. Try this with the HTML Inspector open. You can enter a nonbreaking space in Dreamweaver by typing Shift-Ctrl-Spacebar (Shift-Command-Spacebar).

Decimal characters

To enter almost any character that has a diacritic — such as á, ñ, or â — in Dreamweaver, you must explicitly enter the corresponding decimal character into your HTML page. As mentioned in the preceding section, decimal characters take the form of *&#number*, where the *number* can range from 00 to 255. Not all *numbers* have matching symbols; the range from 14 through 31 is currently unused, while the range &#127 through &#159 is currently supported only by Internet Explorer.

To make your life — or at least the part concerned with decimal characters — a little simpler, the CD-ROM includes a Characters object. Copy both the char_entities.htm and char_entities.gif files into one of your Object folders (Common, Invisibles, or Forms) and then start Dreamweaver. You'll find a new item, Character Entities, on the Object Palette. Position your cursor where you want to insert the decimal character, and select the Character Entities Object. Choose your symbol from the table that opens on the screen and click OK. If you have the HTML Inspector open, you see the decimal character inserted into your code. With the Character Entities Object, you can enter a single decimal character or a series of them at one time.

To enter a decimal code by hand, look up the symbol in Table 6-3 and type its code on your page in the HTML Inspector. Dreamweaver previews the code correctly in its document window.

Special
Characters

Table 6-3
Decimal Character Codes

Decimal Code	Character Produced	Description
&#00; – &#08;		Unused
&#09;		Horizontal tab
&#10;		Line feed
&#13;		Carriage return
&#11; – 		Unused
&#32;		Space
&#33;	!	Exclamation mark
&#34;		Quotation mark
&#35;	#	Number sign
&#36;	$	Dollar sign
&#37;	%	Percent sign
&#38;	&	Ampersand
&#39;		Apostrophe
&#40;	(	Left parenthesis
&#41;	)	Right parenthesis
&#42;	*	Asterisk
&#43;	+	Plus sign
&#44;	,	Comma
&#14; – &#31;		Unused
&#45;	-	Hyphen
&#46;	.	Period (full stop)
&#47;	/	Solidus
0 – 9	0 – 9	Decimal digits
&#58;	:	Colon
&#59;	;	Semicolon
&#60;	<	Less than
&#61;	=	Equals sign

Decimal Code	Character Produced	Description
&#62;	>	Greater than
&#63;	?	Question mark
&#64;	@	Commercial at
A – Z	A – Z	Uppercase letters
&#91;	[	Left square bracket
&#92;	\	Reverse solidus (backslash)
&#93;	]	Right square bracket
&#94;	^	Caret
&#95;	_	Horizontal bar
&#96;	`	Grave accent
a – z	a – z	Lowercase letters
&#123;	{	Left curly brace
|	|	Vertical bar
&#125;	}	Right curly brace
&#126;	~	Tilde
&#127; – 		Unused
&#130;	,	Comma (IE Only)
&#131;	ƒ	Mathematical function f (IE Only)
&#132;	„	Low quotation mark (IE Only)
&#133;	…	Triple dots (ellipsis) (IE Only)
&#134;	†	Footnote mark (IE Only)
&#135;	‡	Double footnote mark (IE Only)
&#136;	ˆ	Circumflex accent (IE Only)
&#137;	‰	Per thousandth (IE Only)
&#138;	Š	Capital S, inverted circumflex (IE Only)
&#139;	‹	Small less than (IE Only)
&#140;	Œ	Capital OE dipthong (IE Only)
 – 		Unused
&#145;	'	Single quote, opening (IE Only)

(continued)

Table 6-3 (continued)

Decimal Code	Character Produced	Description
&#146;	'	Single quote, closing (IE Only)
&#147;	"	Double quote, opening (IE Only)
&#148;	"	Double quote, closing (IE Only)
&#149;	•	Large middle dot (IE Only)
&#150;	–	Middle dash (IE Only)
&#151;	—	Double middle dash (IE Only)
&#152;	~	Tilde (IE Only)
&#153;	™	Trademark (IE and NS 4 Only)
&#154;	š	Small s, inverted circumflex (IE Only)
&#155;	›	Small greater than (IE Only)
&#156;	œ	Small oe dipthong (IE Only)
 – ž		Unused
&#159;	Ÿ	Capital Y with umlaut (IE Only)
		Nonbreaking space
&#161;	¡	Inverted exclamation
&#162;	¢	Cent sign
&#163;	£	Pound sterling
&#164;	¤	General currency sign
&#165;	¥	Yen sign
&#166;	¦	Broken vertical bar
&#167;	§	Section sign
&#168;	¨	Umlaut
&#169;	©	Copyright
&#170;	ª	Feminine ordinal
&#171;	«	Left angle quote
&#172;	¬	Not sign
&#173;	-	Soft hyphen
&#174;	®	Registered trademark
&#175;	¯	Macron accent

Decimal Code	Character Produced	Description
&#176;	°	Degree sign
&#177;	±	Plus or minus
&#178;	2	Superscript 2
&#179;	3	Superscript 3
&#180;	´	Acute accent
&#181;	µ	Micro sign
&#182;	¶	Paragraph sign
&#183;	·	Middle dot
&#184;	¸	Cedilla
&#185;	1	Superscript 1
&#186;	º	Masculine ordinal
&#187;	»	Right angle quote
&#188;	¼	Fraction one-fourth
&#189;	½	Fraction one-half
&#190;	¾	Fraction three-fourths
&#191;	¿	Inverted question mark
&#192;	À	Capital A, grave accent
&#193;	Á	Capital A, acute accent
&#194;	Â	Capital A, circumflex accent
&#195;	Ã	Capital A, tilde
&#196;	Ä	Capital A, dieresis or umlaut mark
&#197;	Å	Capital A, ring
&#198;	Æ	Capital AE dipthong (ligature)
&#199;	Ç	Capital C, cedilla
&#200;	È	Capital E, grave accent
&#201;	É	Capital E, acute accent
&#202;	Ê	Capital E, circumflex accent
&#203;	Ë	Capital E, dieresis or umlaut mark
&#204;	Ì	Capital I, grave accent

(continued)

Table 6-3 *(continued)*

Decimal Code	Character Produced	Description
&#205;	Í	Capital I, acute accent
&#206;	Î	Capital I, circumflex accent
&#207;	Ï	Capital I, dieresis or umlaut mark
&#208;	Ð	Capital Eth, Icelandic
&#209;	Ñ	Capital N, tilde
&#210;	Ò	Capital O, grave accent
&#211;	Ó	Capital O, acute accent
&#212;	Ô	Capital O, circumflex accent
&#213;	Õ	Capital O, tilde
&#214;	Ö	Capital O, dieresis or umlaut mark
&#215;	×	Multiplication sign
&#216;	Ø	Capital O, slash
&#217;	Ù	Capital U, grave accent
&#218;	Ú	Capital U, acute accent
&#219;	Û	Capital U, circumflex accent
&#220;	Ü	Capital U, dieresis or umlaut mark
&#221;	Ý	Capital Y, acute accent
&#222;	Þ	Capital THORN, Icelandic
&#223;	ß	Small sharp s, German (sz ligature)
&#224;	à	Small a, grave accent
&#225;	á	Small a, acute accent
&#226;	â	Small a, circumflex accent
&#227;	ã	Small a, tilde
&#228;	ä	Small a, dieresis or umlaut mark
&#229;	å	Small a, ring
&#230;	æ	Small ae dipthong (ligature)
&#231;	ç	Small c, cedilla
&#232;	è	Small e, grave accent
&#233;	é	Small e, acute accent

Decimal Code	Character Produced	Description
&#234;	ê	Small e, circumflex accent
&#235;	ë	Small e, dieresis or umlaut mark
&#236;	ì	Small i, grave accent
&#237;	í	Small i, acute accent
&#238;	î	Small i, circumflex accent
&#239;	ï	Small i, dieresis or umlaut mark
&#240;	ð	Small eth, Icelandic
&#241;	ñ	Small n, tilde
&#242;	ò	Small o, grave accent
&#243;	ó	Small o, acute accent
&#244;	ô	Small o, circumflex accent
&#245;	õ	Small o, tilde
&#246;	ö	Small o, dieresis or umlaut mark
&#247;	÷	Division sign
&#248;	ø	Small o, slash
&#249;	ù	Small u, grave accent
&#250;	ú	Small u, acute accent
&#251;	û	Small u, circumflex accent
&#252;	ü	Small u, dieresis or umlaut mark
&#253;	ý	Small y, acute accent
&#254;	þ	Small thorn, Icelandic
&#255;	ÿ	Small y, dieresis or umlaut mark

Summary

Creating Web pages with Dreamweaver is a special blend of using visual layout tools and HTML coding. Regardless, you need to understand the basics of HTML so that you'll have the knowledge and the tools to modify your code when necessary. This chapter covers these key areas:

✦ An HTML page is divided into two main sections: the `<head>` and the `<body>`. Information pertaining to the entire page is kept in the `<head>` section; all the actual content of the Web page goes in the `<body>` section.

✦ You can change the color and background of your entire page, as well as set its title, through the Page Properties dialog box.

✦ Use `<meta>` tags to summarize your Web page so that search engines can properly catalog it.

✦ When possible, use logical style tags, such as `<strong>` and `<cite>`, rather than hard-coding your page with physical style tags. Style sheets bring a great deal of control and flexibility to logical style tags.

✦ Special extended characters such as symbols and accented letters require the use of HTML character entities, which can either be named (as in ") or in decimal format (as in ").

In the next chapter, you'll see how to insert and format text in Dreamweaver.

✦   ✦   ✦

Adding Text to Your Web Page

If content is king on the Web, then certainly style is queen —together they rule hand in hand. Entering, editing, and formatting text on a Web page is a major part of a Webmaster's job. Dreamweaver gives you the tools to make the task as clear-cut as possible. From headlines to comments, this chapter covers all the essentials of working with basic text.

Until relatively recently, Web designers didn't have many options for manipulating text. The majority of browsers can now understand a limited number of text-related commands, and the designer can specify the font as well as its color and size. These topics are covered in this chapter, along with an important discussion of manipulating whitespace in the Web page.

Starting with Headings

Text in HTML is primarily composed of headings and paragraphs. Headings separate and introduce major sections of the document, just as a newspaper uses headlines to announce a story and subheads to provide essential details. HTML has six levels of headings; the syntax for the heading tags is <hn> where *n* is a number from 1 to 6. The largest heading is <h1> and the smallest is <h6>.

Remember that HTML headings are not linked to any specific point size, unlike type produced in a page layout or word-processing program. Headings in an HTML document are sized relative to each other, and their final exact size depends on the browser used. The sample headlines in Figure 7-1 depict the basic headings as rendered through Internet Explorer 4.0, and as compared to the default paragraph font size. As you can see, some headings are rendered in type smaller than that used for the default paragraph. Headings are usually displayed with a boldface attribute.

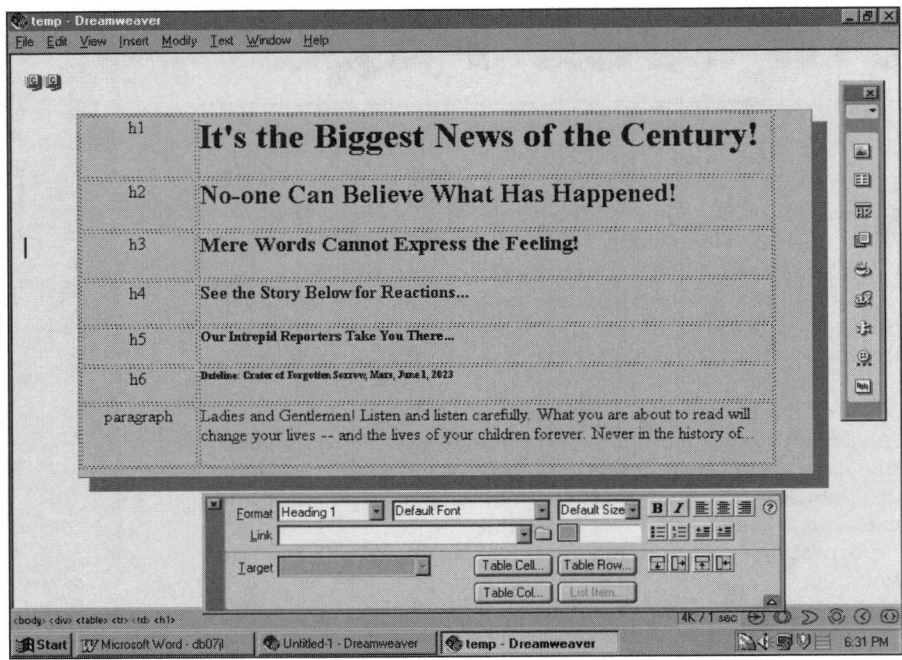

Figure 7-1: You can use up to six different sizes of headings in your HTML page.

Two methods set text as a particular heading size in Dreamweaver. In both cases, you first need to select the text you want to affect. If you are styling a single line or paragraph as a heading, just position the cursor anywhere in the paragraph to select it. If you want to convert more than one paragraph, click and drag out your selection.

Tip

You can't mix heading levels in a single paragraph. That is, you can't have a word with an <h1> heading in a line next to a word styled with an <h4> heading. Furthermore, headings belong to a group of HTML text tags called *block elements.* All block elements are rendered with a paragraph return both above and below, which isolates ("blocks") the text. To work around both of these restrictions, you can use <font size=n> tags to achieve the effect of varying sizes for words within the same line, or for lines of different sizes close to one another. The <font size=n> tag is covered later in this chapter in the "Styling Your Text" section.

Once the text for the heading is selected, you can choose your heading level by selecting Text ⇨ Format and then one of the Headings 1 through 6 from the submenu. Alternatively, you can make your selection from the Text Property Inspector. (If it's not already open, display the Property Inspector by selecting Window ⇨ Properties.) In the Text Property Inspector, open the Format drop-down list (see Figure 7-2) and choose one of the six headings.

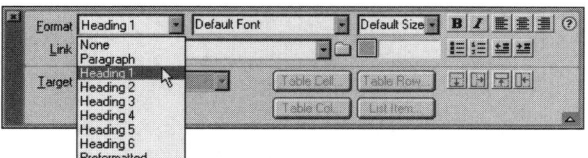

Figure 7-2: You can convert any paragraph or line into a heading through the Format options in the Text Property Inspector.

Headings are often used in a hierarchical fashion, largest to smallest — but you don't have to do it that way. You can have an <h4> line followed by an <h1> paragraph, if that's what your design needs. Be careful using the smallest heading, <h6>; it's likely to be difficult to read on any resolution higher than 800x600.

Working with Paragraphs

Usually the bulk of text on any Web page is composed of *paragraphs*. Paragraphs in HTML are denoted by the <p> and </p> pair of tags. When your Web page is processed, the browser formats everything between those two tags as one paragraph and renders it to fit the user's screen, word wrapping as needed at the margins. Any additional line breaks and unnecessary white space (beyond one space between words and between sentences) in the HTML code are ignored.

Tip

In the early version of HTML, paragraphs used just the opening <p> tag, and browsers rendered everything between <p> tags as one paragraph; the closing tag was optional. As of HTML 3.2, however, an optional closing </p> tag was added. Because so many Web pages have been created with just the opening paragraph tag, most browsers still recognize the single-tag format. To be on the safe side in terms of future compatibility, you should enclose your paragraphs with both the opening and closing tags, as Dreamweaver does.

Dreamweaver starts a new paragraph every time you press Enter (Return) when composing text in the document window. If you have the HTML Inspector open when you work, you can see that Dreamweaver inserts the following code with each new paragraph:

```
<p> </p>
```

The code between the tags creates a nonbreaking space that allows the new line to be visible. You won't see the new line if you have just the paragraph tags with nothing (neither a character or a character entity, such as) in between, as follows:

```
<p></p>
```

When you continue typing, Dreamweaver replaces the nonbreaking space with your input, unless you press Enter (Return) again. Figure 7-3 illustrates two paragraphs with text and a third paragraph where the nonbreaking space is still in place.

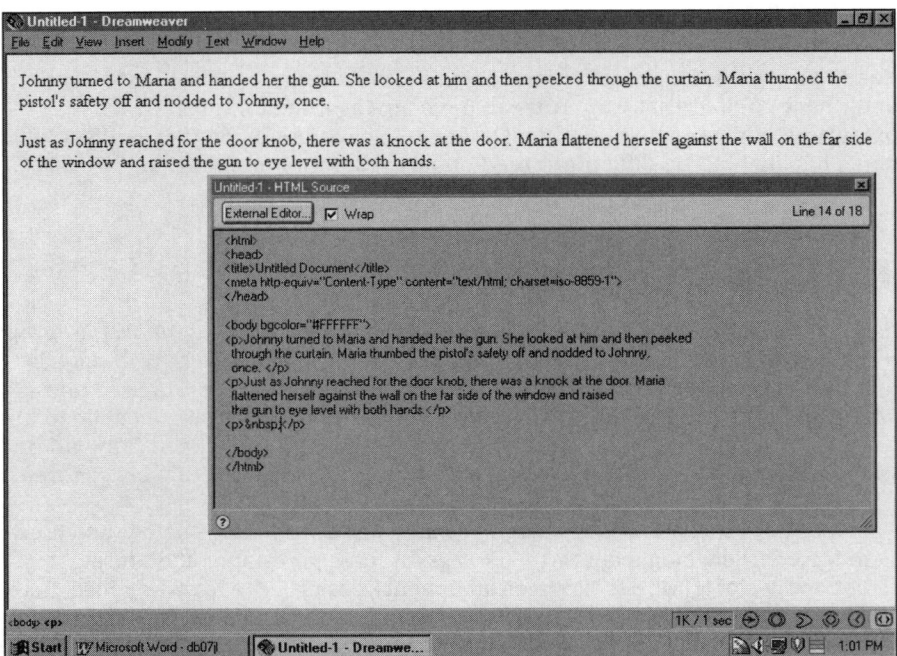

Figure 7-3: Dreamweaver automatically wraps any text inserted into the document window. If you press Enter (Return) without entering text, Dreamweaver enters paragraph tags surrounding a nonbreaking space.

You can easily change text from most other formats, such as a heading, to paragraph format. First, select the text you want to alter. Then in the Property Inspector open the Format options drop-down list and choose Paragraph. You can also choose Text ⇨ Format ⇨ Paragraph from the menu or use the keyboard shortcut, Ctrl-T (Command-T). Hint: Think *T* for *t*ext.

All paragraphs are initially rendered on the page in the default font at the default size. The user can designate these defaults through the browser preferences, although most people don't bother to alter them.

If you want to change the font name or the font size for selected paragraphs explicitly, use the techniques described in the upcoming section, "Styling Your Text."

Tip   Remember, you can always use the Tag Selector on the status bar to select and highlight any tag surrounding your current cursor position. This method makes it easy to see what exactly is being affected by a particular tag.

Editing paragraphs

By and large, the editing features of Dreamweaver are similar to other modern word-processing programs — with one or two Web-oriented twists. Dreamweaver has cut, copy, and paste options, as well as Undo and Redo commands. You can search for and replace any text on your Web page under construction and even check its spelling.

The "twists" come from the relationship between the document window and HTML Inspector. Dreamweaver has some special functionality for copying and pasting text. Let's see how that works.

Inserting text

You've already seen how you can position the cursor on the page and directly enter text. In this sense, Dreamweaver acts like a word-processing program rather than a page layout program. On a blank page, the cursor starts at the top-left corner of the page. Words automatically wrap to the next line when the text exceeds the right margin. Press Enter (Return) to end the current paragraph and start the next one.

Indenting text

In Dreamweaver, you cannot indent text as in a word processor. Tabs normally have no effect in HTML. To indent a paragraph's first line, one method uses nonbreaking spaces, which can be inserted with the keyboard shortcut: Ctrl-Shift-Space (Command-Shift-Space). Nonbreaking spaces are an essential part of any Web designer's palette because they provide single character spacing — often necessary to nudge an image or other object into alignment. You've already seen the code for a nonbreaking space: the   that Dreamweaver inserts between the <p>...</p> tag pair to make the line visible.

Aside from the keyboard shortcut, two other methods insert nonbreaking spaces. You can enter its character code —   — directly into the HTML code. You can also style your text as preformatted; this technique is discussed later in this chapter.

> **Tip**
>
> Another method exists for indenting the first line of a paragraph: Cascading Style Sheets. You can set an existing HTML tag, such as <p>, to any indent amount using the Text Indent option found on the Box panel of the Style Sheet dialog box. Be aware, however, that style sheets have only recently been fully implemented in browsers. In fact, text indent won't appear in Dreamweaver; you have to use Internet Explorer 3.0 or either primary 4.0 browser. You'll find a full discussion of text indent and other style sheet controls in Chapter 22, "Building Style Sheet Web Pages."

Cutting, copying, and pasting

Text can be moved from one place to another — or from one Web document to another — by using the standard cut-and-paste techniques. No surprises here: before you can cut or copy anything, you must select it. Select by clicking the mouse at the beginning of the text you want to cut or copy, drag the highlight to the end of your selection, and then release the mouse button.

Here are some other selection methods:

✦ Double-click a word to select it.

✦ Move the pointer to the left margin of the text until the pointer changes to an arrow. Click once to highlight a single line. Click and drag down the margin to select a group of lines.

✦ Position the cursor at the beginning of your selection. Hold down the Shift key and then click once at the end of the selection.

✦ You can select everything in the body of your document by using Edit ➪ Select All or the keyboard shortcut Ctrl-A (Command-A).

✦ Use the Tag Selector to select text or other objects contained within specific tags.

When you want to move a block of text, first select it and then use Edit ➪ Cut or the keyboard shortcut, Ctrl-X (Command-X). This sequence places the text on your system's Clipboard. To paste the text, move the pointer to the new location and click once to place the cursor. Then select Edit ➪ Paste or the keyboard shortcut, Ctrl-V (Command-V). The text is copied from the Clipboard to its new location. You can continue pasting this same text from the Clipboard until another block of text is copied or cut.

To copy text, the procedure is much the same. Select the text using one of the preceding methods, and then use Edit ⇨ Copy or Ctrl-C (Command-C). The selected text is copied to the Clipboard and the original text is left in place. Then position the cursor in a new location and select Edit ⇨ Paste (or use the keyboard shortcut).

Using Drag-and-Drop: The other, quicker method for moving or copying text is the drag-and-drop technique. Once you've selected your text, release the mouse button and move the cursor over the highlighted area. The cursor changes from an I-beam to an arrow. To move the text, click the selected area with the arrow cursor and drag your mouse to a new location. The arrow cursor now has a small box attached to it, indicating that it is carrying something. As you move your cursor, a bar (the insertion point) moves with you, indicating where the text will be positioned. Release the mouse button to drop the text. You can copy text in the same manner by holding down the Ctrl (Command) key as you drag-and-drop your selected text. When copying in this manner, the box attached to the cursor is marked with a plus sign.

To completely remove text, select it and then choose Edit ⇨ Clear or press Delete. The only way to recover deleted text is to use the Undo feature described in the following section.

Inserting Text from Other Applications

The Paste command can also insert text from another program into Dreamweaver. If you cut or copy text from a file in any other program — whether it is a word processor, spreadsheet, or a database program — Dreamweaver inserts it at the cursor position. The results of this paste operation vary, however.

Dreamweaver can only paste plain, unformatted text. In addition, all the text on the Clipboard is inserted as a single paragraph, no matter how many returns are in the original text if you use the regular Paste command. To retain text in separate paragraphs coming from a file in another program, you must copy and then paste them into Dreamweaver using the Paste as Text command, covered in detail later in this chapter.

If you need to import a great deal of text and want to retain as much formatting as possible, you can use another application, such as the latest version of Microsoft Word, to save your text as an HTML file. Then open that file in Dreamweaver.

Undo and Redo

The Undo command has to be one of the greatest inventions of the twentieth century. Make a mistake? Undo! Want to experiment with two different choices? Undo! Change your mind again? Redo! The Undo command reverses your last action, whether you changed a link, added a graphic, or deleted the entire page. The Redo command lets you reverse your Undo actions.

Dreamweaver's implementation of the Undo command enables you to back up as many steps as your system's memory allows. To use the Undo command, simply choose Edit ➪ Undo or press the keyboard shortcut Ctrl-Z (Command-Z).

The complement to Undo is the Redo command. To reverse an Undo command, choose Edit ➪ Redo or Ctrl-Y (Command-Y). Like Undo, the number of Redo steps available to you is limited only by memory.

The best use I've found for the Redo command is in concert with Undo. When I'm try-ing to decide between two alternatives, such as two different images, I'll replace one choice with another and then use the Undo/Redo combination to go back and forth between them. Because Dreamweaver replaces any selected object with the current object from the Clipboard — even if one is a block of text and the other is a layer — you can easily view two separate options with this trick.

The Undo and Redo "memories" are maintained until you save your file, at which point the memories are cleared. You can't undo or redo an operation after you've saved your file. If this approach seems limiting to you, remember that saving your file also has the effect of speeding up an increasingly sluggish system by releasing what-ever amount of memory has been set aside for the Undo/Redo commands. You should save your file after every major change.

 ### Copy and Paste As Text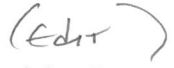

A preceding section mentioned that Dreamweaver includes a couple of "twists" to the standard cut, copy, and paste options. You've seen how regular text entered into the document window is immediately converted to text marked up by HTML tags, visible in the HTML Inspector. Dreamweaver includes two functions that let you translate text and corresponding codes back and forth from one form to the other.

To understand these two features, Copy As Text and Paste As Text (both on the Edit menu), let's examine exactly how they are used. Table 7-1 explains each command.

Table 7-1 Results of Copy/Paste Compared to Copy/Paste as Text Commands				
Selected Text	**Copy From**	**Command Used**	**Paste To**	**Result**
Example Text	Document window	Copy	Other program	`<b>Example Text</b>`
Example Text	Document window	Copy As Text	Other program	Example Text
`<b>Example Text</b>`	HTML Inspector or other program	Paste	Document window	**Example Text**
`<b>Example Text</b>`	HTML Inspector or other program	Paste As Text	Document window	`<b>Example Text</b>`
Example Text	Document window	Paste As Text	HTML Inspector	`&lt;b&gt; Example Text&lt; /b&gt;`

Notice that in the final row of Table 7-1, if you copy formatted text like the boldface "Example Text" sample and use the Paste As Text command to insert it in the HTML Inspector, you get the following:

```
&lt;b&gt;Example Text&lt;/b&gt;
```

If you remember the section on named character entities in Chapter 6, you may recognize `&lt;` as the code for the less-than symbol (<) and `&gt;` as the one for the greater-than symbol (>). These symbols are used to represent tags such as `<b>` and `</b>` to prevent a browser from interpreting them as tag delimiters.

So what possible real-life uses could there be for the Copy/Paste As Text command and Dreamweaver's implementation of the regular Copy/Paste commands? First, these commands are a major benefit for programmers, teachers, and writers who constantly have to communicate in both HTML code and regular text. If an instructor is attempting to demonstrate a coding technique on a Web page, for example, she can just copy the code in the HTML Inspector (or the document window) and use Paste As Text to put it into the document window — instantly transforming the code into something readable online. Previously, this task required a tedious hand-coding process to convert the angle brackets to character entities.

Another use of this approach transfers code from another text editor directly into the Dreamweaver document window. You copy the code in the other window normally, position the cursor in Dreamweaver, and then Paste in the document window. No need to open the HTML Inspector and hunt for the right place in the code — another troublesome task eliminated.

I find these commands to be a major boost to my productivity and an excellent example of how Dreamweaver is firmly rooted in the real world of the Webmaster.

Using Find and Replace

Dreamweaver's Find and Replace features are both timesaving and lifesaving (well, almost). You can use Find and Replace to cut your input time substantially by searching for abbreviations and expanding them to their full state. You can also Find a client's name that's incorrect and replace it with the correctly spelled version — that's a lifesaver!

Three commands make up the Find and Replace "set": Find, Find Next, and Replace. All three commands are used in Dreamweaver's document window. You can use Find independently of or in conjunction with Replace.

To find some text on your Web page, follow these steps:

1. Choose Edit ⇨ Find or press the keyboard shortcut, Ctrl-F (Command-F).

2. In the Find dialog box, type the word or phrase for which you want to search in the Find what text box. Alternatively, you can select and copy a phrase from the text and then paste it into the text box using the keyboard shortcut, Ctrl-V (Command-V).

3. If you want to find an exact replica of the word as you entered it, select the Match Case check box; otherwise, Dreamweaver searches for all variations of your text, regardless of case.

4. Select the Find Next button to begin the search from the cursor's current position.

   • If Dreamweaver finds the desired text, it highlights the text in the document window.

   • If Dreamweaver doesn't find the text in the remaining portion of the document, it asks if you want to continue searching from the beginning. Select Yes to continue or No to exit.

5. If you want to look for the next occurrence of your selected text, click the Find Next button again.

6. After searching the page, Dreamweaver tells you how many occurrences of your selection, if any, were found.

7. You can enter other text for which to search, or exit the Find dialog box by clicking the Cancel button.

The text you enter in the Find dialog box is kept in memory until it's replaced by your next usage of the Find feature. After you have executed the Find command once, you can continue to search for your text without redisplaying the Find dialog box, by selecting Edit ⇨ Find Next or the keyboard shortcut, F3. If Dreamweaver finds your text, it is highlighted — in fact, Dreamweaver acts exactly the same as with the Find dialog box open. The Find Next command — especially when you put the F3 key to work — gives you a quick way to search through a long document.

When you add the Replace command to a Find operation, you can search your text for a word or phrase and, if it's found, replace it with a word or phrase of your choice. As mentioned earlier, the Replace feature is a handy way to correct mistakes and expand abbreviations. Figure 7-4 shows an example of the latter operation. This example intentionally uses the abbreviation *DW* throughout the input text of a Web page article. Then the example uses the Replace All function to expand all the *DW*s to *Dreamweaver* — in one fell swoop. This technique is much faster than typing *Dreamweaver* 14 times.

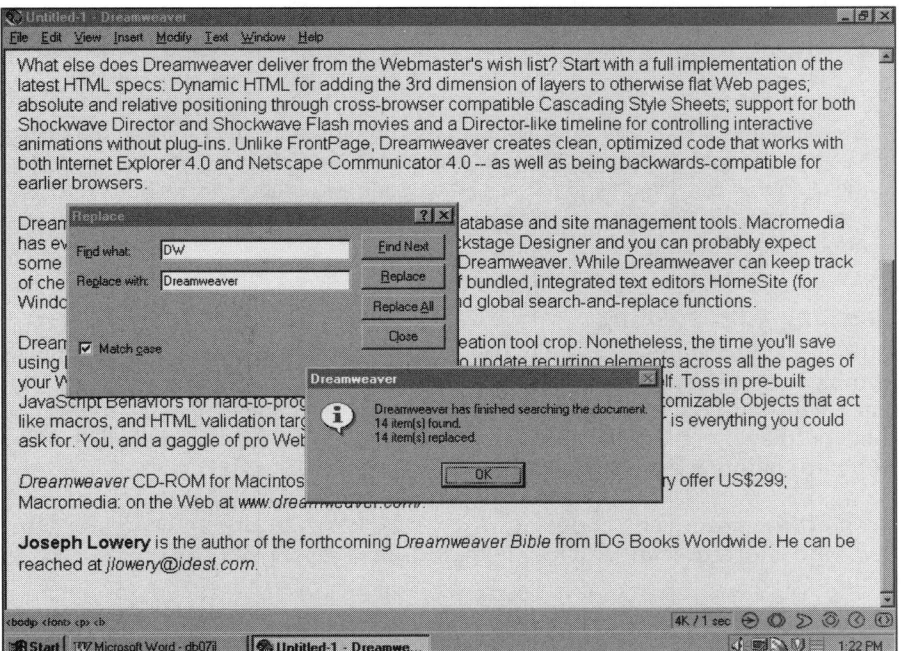

Figure 7-4: Use the Edit ⇨ Replace command to correct your text, one item at a time or all at once.

Follow these steps to use Dreamweaver's Replace feature:

1. Choose Edit ➪ Replace or the keyboard shortcut, Ctrl-H (Command-H) to open the Replace dialog box.

2. In the Find what text box, type the word or phrase for which you want to search in the document window.

3. In the Replace with text box, type the substitute word.

4. Click the Find Next button. Dreamweaver begins searching from the current cursor position. If Dreamweaver finds the text, it is highlighted.

   If the text is not found, Dreamweaver asks if you want to continue searching from the top of the document. Select Yes to continue or No to exit.

5. To replace the highlighted occurrence of your text, select the Replace button. Dreamweaver replaces the found text with the substitute text and then automatically searches for the next occurrence.

6. If you want to replace all instances of the Find text, select the Replace All button.

7. When Dreamweaver has found all the occurrences of your Find text, it displays the number of replacement operations.

8. When you've finished using the Replace dialog box, click the Cancel button to exit.

Tip

Dreamweaver's Find and Replace functions are limited to text for one file at a time, but both HomeSite and BBEdit have enhanced Find and Replace features. Both of these editors can search and replace HTML code within a single file or within multiple files in a folder. For more information on how to use BBEdit and HomeSite, refer to Appendixes A and B.

Checking your spelling

Although a typo is the smallest of items, it can make a significant impression. Nothing is more embarrassing than showing a new Web site to a client and having that client point out a spelling error. Dreamweaver includes an easy-to-use spell checker to avoid such awkward moments. I make it a practice to spell-check every Web page before it's posted online.

You start the process by choosing Text ➪ Check Spelling, or you can press the keyboard shortcut Shift-F7. This sequence opens the Spell Check dialog box as seen in Figure 7-5.

Once you've opened the Spell Check dialog box, Dreamweaver begins searching your text for errors. As a general practice, position your cursor at the top of the Web page before you begin spell-checking. When you reach the bottom of the page,

Dreamweaver asks if you want to continue checking from the top of the document. By beginning at the top, you know that you've already checked the full document.

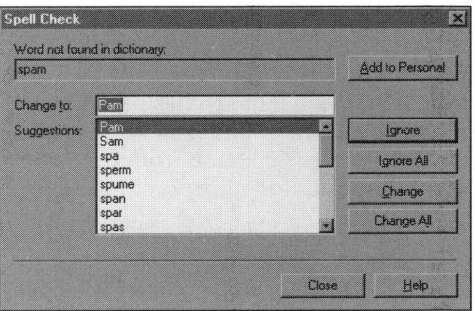

Figure 7-5: Dreamweaver's spell checker double-checks your spelling and can find the typos on any Web page.

Dreamweaver checks your Web page text against two dictionaries: a standard English dictionary and a personal dictionary to which you can add words. If the spell checker finds any text not in either of the program's dictionaries, the text is highlighted in the document window and appears in the Word Not Found In Dictionary field of the dialog box. A list of suggested corrections appears in the Suggestions list box, with the topmost one highlighted and also displayed in the Change to box. If Dreamweaver cannot find any suggestions, the Change to box is left blank. At this point, you have the following options:

✦ **Add to Personal**. Select this button to include the highlighted word in your personal dictionary and prevent Dreamweaver from tagging it as an error in the future.

✦ **Ignore**. Choose this button when you want Dreamweaver to leave the currently highlighted word alone and continue searching the text.

✦ **Ignore All**. Select this button when you want Dreamweaver to disregard all occurrences of this word in the current document.

✦ **Change**. If you see the correct replacement among the list of suggestions, highlight it and select the Change button. If no suggestion is appropriate, you can type the correct word into the Change to text box and then select this button.

✦ **Change All**. Choosing this button causes all instances of the current word to be replaced with the word in the Change to text box.

Tip

Have you ever accidentally added a misspelled word to your personal dictionary and then been stuck with the error for all eternity? Dreamweaver lets you recover from your mistake by giving you access to the dictionary itself. The personal dictionary, stored in the Dreamweaver/Configuration/Dictionary/personal.dat file, can be opened and modified in any text editor.

The <br> tag

The paragraph tag falls among the class of HTML objects called block elements, just like headings. As such, any text marked with the <p></p> tag pair is always rendered with an extra line above and below the text. To have a series of blank lines appear one after the other, use the break tag <br>.

Break tags are used within block elements, such as headings and paragraphs, to provide a line break where the <br> is inserted. Dreamweaver provides two ways to insert a <br> tag: you can choose the Enter Line Break button from the Invisibles panel of the Object Palette, or you can use the keyboard shortcut Shift-Enter (Shift-Return).

Figure 7-6 clearly demonstrates the effect of the <br> tag. The menu items in Column A on the left are the result of using the <br> tag within a paragraph. In Column B on the right, paragraph tags alone are used. The <h1> heading is also split at the top (modified through style sheet selections) with a break tag to avoid the insertion of an unwanted line.

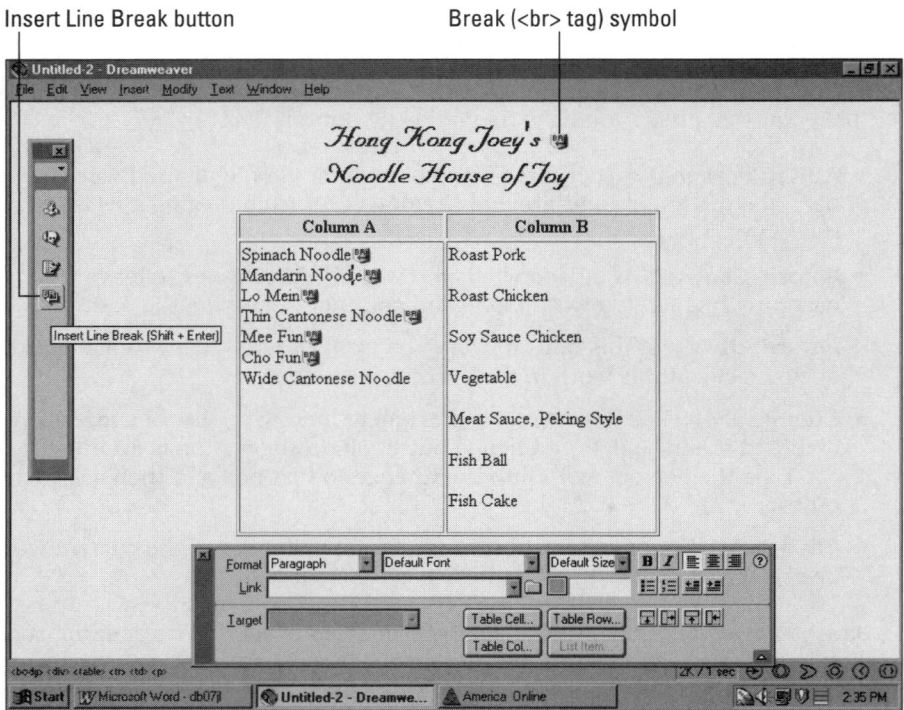

Figure 7-6: Use break tags to have your lines wrap without the additional line spacing brought about by <p> tags.

Overcoming Line-Spacing Difficulties

Line spacing is a major issue and a common problem for Web designers. Often a design calls for lines to be tightly spaced, but also of various sizes. If you use the break tag to separate your lines, you'll get the tight spacing required, but you won't be able to make each line a different heading size. As far as HTML and your browser are concerned, the text is still one block element, no matter how many line breaks are inserted. If, on the other hand, you make each line a separate paragraph or heading, the line spacing will be unattractively "open."

You can use one of several workarounds for this problem. First, if you're using line breaks, you can alter the size of each line by selecting it and choosing a different font size, either from the Property Inspector or the Text ➪ Size menu. The only drawback to this approach is that the attribute you insert with this action — `<font size=n>` — is not recognized by older browsers.

A second option renders all the text as a graphics object and inserts it as an image. This gives you total control over the font's appearance and line spacing, as well as across-the-board browser compliance at the cost of added download time.

For a third possible solution, take a look at the section on preformatted text later in this chapter. Because you can apply styles to a preformatted text block (which can include line breaks and extra white space), you can alter the size, color, and font of each line, if necessary.

By default, Dreamweaver marks `<br>` tags with a symbol: a gold shield with the letters BR and the standard Enter/Return symbol. You can turn off this display feature by choosing Preferences ➪ Invisible Elements and deselecting the Line Breaks check box.

Other white space tags

If you can't get the alignment effect you want through the regular text options available in Dreamweaver, two other HTML tags can affect whitespace: `<nobr>` and `<wbr>`. Although a tad on the obscure side, these tags can be just the ticket in a particular circumstance. Let's see how they work.

The <nobr> Tag

Most of the time, you want the user's browser to handle the word-wrapping chores automatically. Occasionally, however, you may need to make sure that a particular string of text is rendered in one piece. For these situations, you can use the no break tag `<nobr>`. Any text that comes in between the opening and closing tag pair — `<nobr>...</nobr>` — is displayed in one continuous line. If the line of text is wider than the current browser window, a horizontal scroll bar automatically appears along the bottom of the browser.

The <nobr> tag is only supported through the Netscape and Microsoft browsers and must be entered by hand into your HTML code. The <nobr> is a tag to be used under very special circumstances.

The <wbr> Tag

The companion to the <nobr> tag is the word break tag <wbr>. Similar to a soft hyphen in a word-processing program, the <wbr> tag tells the browser where to break a word, if necessary. When used within <nobr> tags, <wbr> is the equivalent of telling a browser, "Keep all this text in one line, but if you *have* to break it, break it here."

Like the <nobr> tag, <wbr> is only supported by Netscape and Microsoft browsers and must be entered by hand in either the HTML Inspector or your external editor.

Styling Your Text

When the Internet was founded, its intended focus was to make scientific data widely accessible. Soon it became apparent that even raw data could benefit from being styled contextually without detracting from the Internet's openness and universality. Over the short history of HTML, text styles have become increasingly important and the W3C has sought to keep a balance between substance and style.

Dreamweaver enables the Web designer to apply the most popular HTML styles directly through the program's menus and Property Inspector. Less prevalent styles can be inserted through the integrated text editors or by hand.

Working with preformatted text

Browsers ignore the formatting niceties considered irrelevant to the page content: tabs, extra line-feeds, indents, and added white space. You can force browsers to read all the text, including the white space, exactly as you have entered it. By applying the preformatted tag, <pre>, you tell the browser that it should keep any additional white space encountered within the text. By default, the <pre> tag also renders its content with a monospace font such as Courier. For these reasons, in the early days of HTML the <pre> tag was used to lay out text in columns, before tables were widely available.

You can apply the preformatted tag either through the Property Inspector or the menus. Before you use either technique, however, be sure to select the text or position the cursor where you want the preformatted text to begin. To use the Property Inspector, open the Format list box and choose Preformatted. To use the menus, choose Text ➪ Format ➪ Preformatted.

The `<pre>` tag is a block element format, like the paragraph or the headings tags, rather than a style. This designation as a block element format has two important implications: First, you can't apply the `<pre>` tag to part of a line; when you use this tag, the entire paragraph is altered. Second, you can apply styles to preformatted text — this lets you increase the size or alter the font but at the same time maintain the white space feature made possible with the `<pre>` tag. All text in Figure 7-7 uses the `<pre>` tag; the column on the left is the standard output with monospaced font; the column on the right uses a different font in a larger size.

Figure 7-7: Preformatted text gives you full control over the line breaks, tabs, and other white space in your Web page.

Depicting various styles

As explained in Chapter 6, HTML's logical styles are used to mark text relatively or within a particular context, rather than with a specific look. The eventual displayed appearance of logical styles is completely up to the viewer's browser. This technique is very useful when you are working with documents from different sources — reports from different research laboratories around the country, for instance — and you want a certain conformity of style. Logical styles are very utilitarian; physical styles like boldface and italic are decorative. Both types of styles have their uses in material published on today's Web.

All of Dreamweaver's styles are accessed by choosing Text ⇨ Style and selecting from the 13 available style name options. A check mark appears next to the selected tags. Style tags can be nested (put inside one another), and you can mix logical and physical tags within a word, line, or document. You can have a bold, strikethrough, *variable* style; or you can have an underlined *cited* style. (Both *variable* and *cite* are particular logical styles covered later in this section.) If, however, you are trying to achieve a particular look using logical styles, you should probably use the Cascading Style Sheets feature.

Cross-Reference   The styles that can be applied through regular HTML are just the tip of the iceberg compared to the possibilities with Cascading Style Sheets. For details on using this feature, see Chapter 22, "Building Style Sheet Web Pages."

Take a look at Figure 7-8 for a comparison of how the styles are rendered in Dreamweaver, Internet Explorer 4.0, and Netscape Communicator 4.0. While the various renderings are mostly the same, notice the browser differences in the Definition styles, and the difference in how the Keyboard style is rendered in Dreamweaver and either browser.

Two of the three physical style tags — bold and italic — are both available from the Text Property Inspector and through keyboard shortcuts (Ctrl-B or Command-B, and Ctrl-I or Command-I, respectively). The Underline tag, <u>, is only available through the Text ⇨ Style menu. Underlining text on a Web page is generally discouraged to avoid confusion with links, which are typically displayed underlined.

Both physical and logical style tags are described, with example uses, in Table 7-2.

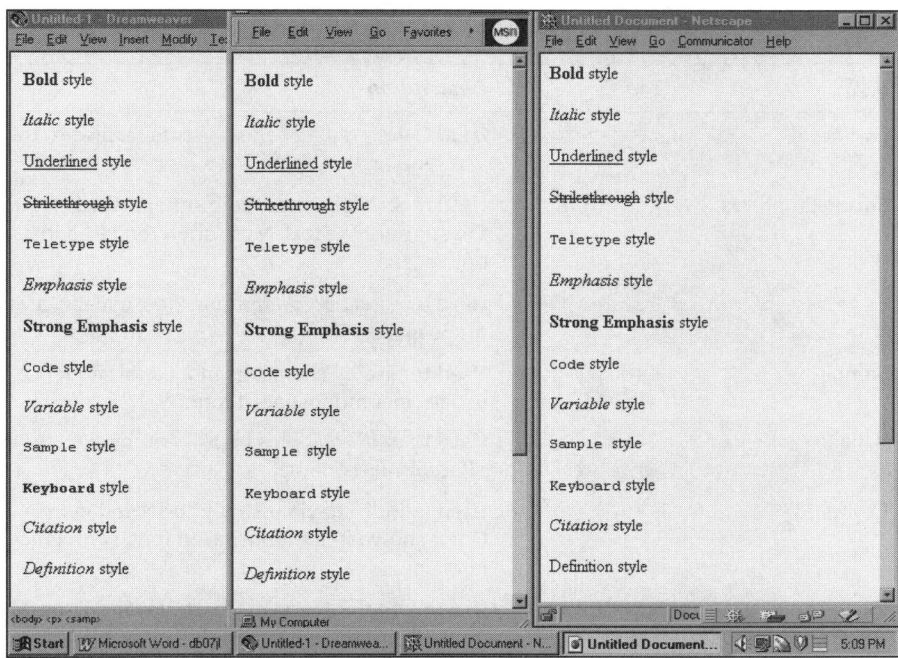

Figure 7-8: In this comparison chart, the various renderings of Dreamweaver style tags are, from left to right, from Dreamweaver, Internet Explorer 4.0, and Netscape Communicator 4.0.

	Table 7-2
	Dreamweaver Style Tags

Style	Tag	Description
Bold	`<b>`	Text is rendered with a bold face.
Italic	`<i>`	Text is rendered with an italic face.
Underline	`<u>`	Text is rendered underlined.
Strikethrough	`<s>`	Used primarily in edited documents to depict edited text. Usually rendered with a line through the text.
Teletype	`<tt>`	Used to represent an old-style typewriter. Rendered in a monospace font such as Courier.

(continued)

Style	Tag	Description
		Table 7-2 *(continued)*
Emphasis	`<em>`	Used to accentuate certain words relative to the surrounding text. Most often rendered in italic.
Strong Emphasis	`<strong>`	Used to strongly accentuate certain words relative to the surrounding text. Most often rendered in boldface.
Code	`<code>`	Used to depict programming code, usually in a monospaced font.
Sample	`<samp>`	Used to display characters in a literal sequence, usually in a monospaced font.
Variable	`<var>`	Used to mark variables in programming code. Most often displayed in italics.
Keyboard	`<kbd>`	Used to indicate what should be typed in by a user. Often shown in a monospaced font, sometimes in boldface.
Citation	`<cite>`	Used to mark citations, references, and titles. Most often displayed in italic.
Definition	`<dfn>`	Used to denote the first, defining instance of a term. Usually displayed in italic.

Using the <address> tag

One useful logical style tag is not currently supported by Dreamweaver: the `<address>` tag. Typically rendered as italic text by browsers, the `<address>`... `</address>` tag pair often marks the signature and e-mail address of a Web page's creator. The `<address>` tags should go around a paragraph tag pair; otherwise, Dreamweaver flags the closing `</p>` as invalid. Also, you should use `<br>` tags to form line breaks. The following is an example of proper use of the `<address>` tags:

```
<address><p>The President<br>
   1600 Pennsylvania Avenue<br>
   Washington, DC 20001</p></address>
```

This preceding code will be shown on a Web browser as follows:

The President
1600 Pennsylvania Avenue
Washington, DC 20001

Tip

To remove a style, highlight the styled text, choose Text ➪ Style, and select the name of the style you want to remove. The check mark disappears from the style name.

Modifying the Text Format

As a Web designer, you easily spend at least as much time adjusting your text as you do getting it into your Web pages. Luckily, Dreamweaver puts most of the tools you need for this task right at your fingertips. All the text-formatting options are available through the Text Property Inspector. Instead of hand-coding `<font>`, `<blockquote>`, and alignment tags, just select your text and click a button.

Note

The general move in HTML text formatting today is toward using Cascading Style Sheets and away from hard-coding text with `<font>` and other tags. Both 4.0 versions of the major Web browsers are supporting Cascading Style Sheets more than ever, and Internet Explorer has had some support since the 3.0 version. The current realities of browser competition, however, dictate that to take advantage of the widest support range, Web designers must continue to use the character-specific tags for now. Even after Cascading Style Sheets gain widespread acceptance, you'll probably still need to apply tags on the "local level" occasionally.

Adjusting font size

The six HTML heading types enable you to assign relative sizes to a line or to an entire paragraph. In addition, HTML gives you a finer degree of control through the size attribute of the font tag. In contrast to publishing environments, both traditional and desktop, font size is not specified in HTML with points. Rather, the `<font>` tag enables you to choose one of seven different explicit sizes that the browser can render (absolute sizing), or you can select one relative to the page's basic font. Figure 7-9 shows the default absolute and relative sizes, compared to a more page-designer-friendly point chart (accomplished with Dreamweaver's Cascading Style Sheets features).

Which way should you go — absolute or relative? Some designers think that relative sizing gives them more options. As you can see by the chart in Figure 7-9, browsers are limited to displaying 7 different sizes no matter what — unless you're using Cascading Style Sheets. Relative sizing does give you additional flexibility, though, because you can resize all the fonts in an entire Web page with one command. Absolute sizes, on the other hand, are more straightforward to use and can be coded in Dreamweaver without any additional HTML programming. Once again, it's the designer's choice.

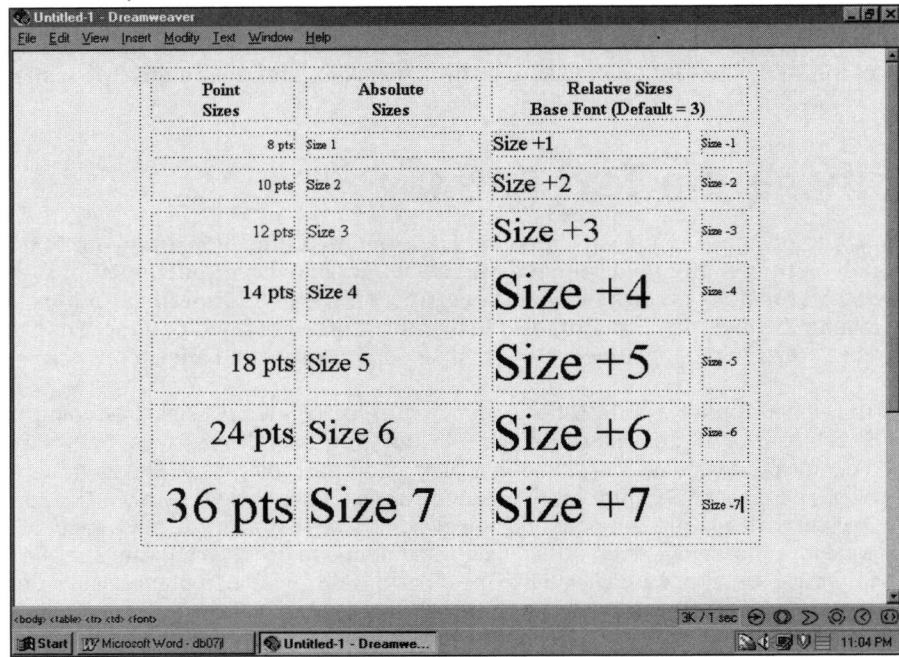

Figure 7-9: In this chart, you can see the relationships between the various font sizes in an HTML browser and as compared to "real-world" point sizes.

Absolute size

You can assign an absolute font size either through the Property Inspector or through the menus. In both cases you choose a value, 1 through 7, to which you want to resize your text. The font sizes go from 1 to 7, smallest to largest; you may note that this order is the reverse of the heading sizes, which range from H1 to H6, largest to smallest.

To use the Property Inspector to pick an absolute font size, follow these steps:

1. Select your text.

2. In the Property Inspector, open the Font Size drop-down list of choices.

3. Choose a value from 1 to 7.

To pick an absolute font size from the menu, follow these steps:

1. Select your text.

2. Choose Text ➪ Size and pick a value from 1 to 7, or Default (which is 3).

Tip

You can also use the keyboard shortcuts for changing absolute font sizes. Headings 1 through 6 correspond to Ctrl-1 through Ctrl-6 (Command-1 through Command-6). The Paragraph option is rendered with a Ctrl-T (Command-T); you can remove all formatting with a Ctrl-0 (Command-0).

Relative size

To what exactly are relative font sizes relative? The default font size, of course. The advantage of relative font sizes is that you can alter a Web page's default font size with one command, the `<basefont>` tag. The tag takes the following form:

```
<basefont size=value>
```

where *value* is a number from 1 to 7. The `<basefont>` tag is usually placed immediately following the opening `<body>` tag. Dreamweaver does not support the previewing of the results of altering the `<basefont>` tag, and the tag has to be entered by hand or through the external editor.

You can distinguish a relative from an absolute font size by the plus or minus sign that precedes the value. The relative sizes are plus or minus the current `<basefont>` size. Thus a `<font size=+1>` is normally rendered with a size 4 font, because the default `<basefont>` is 3. If you include the following line in your Web page:

```
<basefont size=5>
```

text marked with a `<font size=+1>` is displayed with a size 6 font. Because browsers only display seven different size fonts with a `<basefont size=5>` setting — unless you're using Cascading Style Sheets — any relative size over <font size=+2> won't display differently when previewed in a browser.

Relative font sizes can also be selected from either the Property Inspector or the menus. To use the Property Inspector to pick an absolute font size, follow these steps:

1. Select your text or position the cursor where you want the new text size to begin.

2. In the Property Inspector, open the Font Size drop-down list of choices.

3. To increase the size of your text, choose a value from +1 through +7.

   To decrease the size of your text, choose a value from −1 to −7.

To pick an absolute font size from the menus, follow these steps:

1. Select your text or position the cursor where you want the new text size to begin.

2. To reduce the size of your text, choose Text ⇨ Size Increase and pick a value from +1 to +7.

   To reduce the size of your text, choose Text ⇨ Size Decrease and pick a value from –1 to –7.

Adding font color

Unless you assign a color to text on your Web page, the browser uses its own default, typically black. As noted in "Establishing Page Properties" in Chapter 6, you can change the font color for the entire page by choosing Modify ⇨ Page Properties and selecting a new color from the Text Color swatch. You can also color any specific headings, words, or paragraphs that you have selected in Dreamweaver.

The `<font>` tag goes to work again when you add color to selected elements of the page — this time, with the color attribute set to a particular value. HTML color is expressed in either a hexadecimal color number or a color name. The hexadecimal color number is based on the color's red-green-blue value and is written like as follows:

```
#FFFFFF
```

The preceding represents the color white. You can also use standard color names instead of the hexadecimal color numbers. A sample color code line follows:

```
I m <font color= green >GREEN</font> with envy.
```

Dreamweaver understands both color names and hexadecimal color numbers, but its HTML code output is in hexadecimal color numbers only.

Dreamweaver's Color Pickers

Dreamweaver includes a color picker that includes the 216 colors common to the Macintosh and Windows palette — you already know these as the browser-safe colors. If you choose a color outside of this "safe" range, you have no assurances of how the color is rendered on a viewer's browser. Some systems select the closest color in RGB values; some use dithering (positioning two or more colors next to each other to simulate another color) to try and overcome the limitations of the current screen color depth. So be forewarned: if at all possible, stick with the browser-safe colors, especially when coloring text.

Mac Users: The Color Picker for Macintosh systems is far more elaborate than the one provided for Window users. The Mac version has several color schemes to use: CMYK (for print-related colors), RGB (for screen-based colors), and HTML (for Web-based colors). The CMYK, HTML, and RGB systems offer you color swatches and three or four sliders with text entry boxes, and accept percentage values for RGB and CMYK and hex values for HTML. Both RGB and HTML also have a "snap-to-Web color" option for matching your chosen color to the closest browser-safe color. The Hue, Saturation, and Value (or Lightness) sliders also have color wheels.

Again, there are two ways you can add color to your text in Dreamweaver. The Property Inspector displays a drop-down list of the browser-safe colors, and also gives you an option to choose from a full-spectrum Color dialog box. If you approach your coloring task via the menus, the Text ⇨ Color command takes you immediately to the Color dialog box.

To use the Property Inspector to color a range of text in Dreamweaver, follow these steps:

1. Select the text you want to color, or position the cursor where you want the new text color to begin.

2. From the Property Inspector, you can:

   • Type a hexadecimal color number directly into the Font Color text box.

   • Type a color name directly into the Font Color text box.

   • Select the Font Color swatch to open the browser-safe color picker.

3. If you chose to type a color name or number directly into Font Color text box, press Tab or click on the document window to see the color applied.

4. If you clicked the Font Color swatch, select your color from the 216 browser-safe colors available. As you move your pointer over the color swatches, Dreamweaver displays the color in the corner and the color's hexadecimal number below.

5. For a wider color selection from the Color dialog box, select the Palette icon in the lower-right corner of the Color Swatch.

To access the full-spectrum color picker immediately, follow these steps:

1. Select your text or position your cursor where you want the new text color to begin.

2. Choose Text ⇨ Color to open the Color dialog box as shown in Figure 7-10.

Standard colors   Hue/Saturation pointer

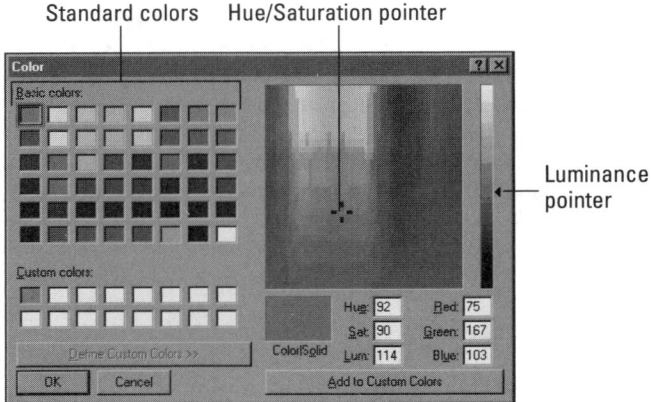

Luminance
pointer

Figure 7-10: The Color dialog box can be used
for choosing a color for your font outside of the
browser-safe palette.

3. Select one of the 48 preset standard colors from the color swatches on the left
   of the Color dialog box, or use either of the following methods:

   • Select a color by moving the Hue/Saturation pointer and the Luminance
     pointer.

   • Enter decimal values directly into either the Red, Green and Blue boxes
     or the Hue, Saturation, and Luminance boxes.

4. If you create a custom color, you can add it to your palette by selecting Add to
   Custom Colors. You can add up to 16 custom colors.

5. Click OK when you are finished.

When you add a Custom Color to your palette, the new color swatch goes into the
currently selected swatch or, if no swatch is selected, the next available swatch. Make
sure you have selected an empty or replaceable swatch before selecting the Add to
Custom Color button. To clear the Custom Colors, first set the palette to white by
bringing the Luminance slider all the way to the top. Then, select the Add to Custom
Color button until all the color swatches text boxes are empty.

Assigning a specific font

Along with size and color, you can also specify the typeface in which you want
particular text to be rendered. Dreamweaver uses a special method for choosing
font names for a range of selected text due to HTML's unique way of handling fonts.
Before you learn how to change a typeface in Dreamweaver, let's further examine
how fonts in HTML work.

About HTML fonts

Page layout designers can incorporate as many different fonts as available to their own systems. Web layout designers, on the other hand, can only use those fonts on their viewers' systems. If you designate a paragraph to be in Bodoni Bold Condensed, for instance, and put it on the Web, the paragraph will be displayed with that font only if that exact font name is on the user's system. Otherwise, the browser uses the default system fault, which is often Times or Times New Roman.

Fonts are specified with the `<font>` tag, aided by the `name` attribute. Because a designer can never be certain of which fonts are on visitors' computers, HTML enables you to offer a number of options to the browser, as follows:

```
<font name= Arial, Helvetica, sans-serif >Swiss Maid
Foundry</font>
```

The browser encountering the preceding tag first looks for the Arial font to render the enclosed text. If Arial isn't there, the browser looks for the next font in the list, which in this case is Helvetica. Failing to find any of the specified fonts listed, the browser uses whichever font has been assigned to the category for the font — sans-serif in this case.

Five main categories of fonts are recognized by the W3C and some Web browsers: serif, sans-serif, monospace, cursive, and fantasy. Internet Explorer has a higher compliance rating on this issue than Netscape Communicator.

Selecting a font

The process for assigning a font name to a range of text is similar to that of assigning a font size or color. Instead of selecting one font *name*, however, you're usually selecting one font *series*. That series could contain three or more fonts, as previously explained. Font series are chosen from the Property Inspector or through a menu item.

Tip   Dreamweaver lets you assign any font on your system — or even any font you can name — to a font series, as covered in the following "Editing the font list" section in this chapter.

To assign a specific font series to your text, follow these steps:

1. Select the text or position your cursor where you want the new text font to begin.

2. From the Property Inspector, open the drop-down list of font names. You can also choose Text ⇨ Font from the menu bar. Your Font List is displayed.

3. Select a font from the Font List. To return to the system font, choose Default Font from the list.

Tip

Font peculiarities are one of the key reasons for always testing your Web pages on several platforms. Not only do Macintosh and Windows have different names for the same basic fonts (Arial in Windows is almost identical to Helvetica in Macintosh, for instance), but even the standard font sizes vary between the platforms. Overall, PC fonts are larger than fonts on a Macintosh. Be sure to check out your page on as many systems as possible before finalizing your design.

Editing the font list

With the Font List dialog box, Dreamweaver gives you a point-and-click interface for building your font lists. Once the Font List dialog box is open, you can delete an existing font series, add a new one, or change the order of the list so your favorite ones are on top. Take a look at Figure 7-11 to see the sections of the Font List dialog box: the current Font List, the Available Fonts on your system, and the Chosen Fonts. The Chosen Fonts are the individual fonts that you've selected to be incorporated into a font series.

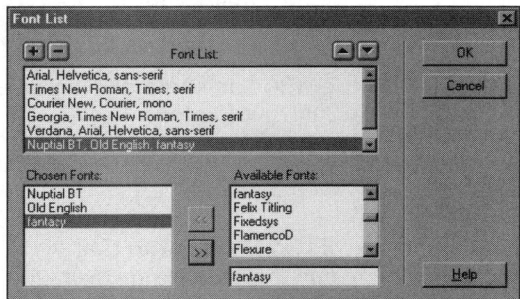

Figure 7-11: Dreamweaver's Font List dialog box gives you considerable control over the fonts that you can add to your Web page.

Let's step through the process of constructing a new font series and adding it to the Font List:

1. To open the Font List dialog box, either choose Edit Font List through the Font Name option arrow in the Property Inspector, or select Text ⇨ Font ⇨ Edit Font List.

2. Clear the Chosen Font box by selecting the plus (+) button at the top of the dialog box. You can also scroll down to the bottom of the current Font List and select (Add fonts in list below).

3. Select a font from the Available Fonts list.

4. Click the << button to transfer the selected font to the Chosen Fonts list.

5. To remove a font you no longer want or have chosen in error, highlight it in the Chosen Fonts list and select the >> button.

6. Repeat steps 3 through 5 until the Chosen Fonts list contains the alternative fonts desired.

7. If you want to add another, separate font series, repeat steps 2 through 5.

8. Click OK when you are finished adding fonts.

To change the order in which font series are listed in the Font List, follow these steps:

1. In the Font List dialog box, select the font series that you want to move.

2. If you want to move the series higher up the list, select the up-arrow button at the top-right of the Font List. If you want to move the series lower down the list, select the down-arrow button.

To remove a font series from the current Font List, highlight it and select the minus (–) button at the top-left of the list.

Remember, you need to have the fonts on your system to make them a part of your font list. To add a font unavailable on your computer, type the name of the font into the text box below the Available Fonts list and press Enter (Return).

Aligning text

You can easily align text in Dreamweaver as in a traditional word-processing program. HTML supports the alignment of text to the left or right margin, or in the center of the browser window. Like a word-processing program, Dreamweaver aligns text one paragraph at a time. You can't left-align one word, center the next, and then right-align the third word in the same paragraph.

To align text, you can use one of three methods: a menu command, the Property Inspector, or a keyboard shortcut. To use the menus, choose Text ➪ Alignment and then pick the alignment you prefer (Left, Right or Center). Table 7-3 explains the Text Property Inspector's Alignment buttons and the associated keyboard shortcuts.

Table 7-3
Text Alignment Options in the Property Inspector

Button	Alignment	Keyboard Shortcut
	Left	Ctrl-Alt-L (Command-Option-L)
	Center	Ctrl-Alt-C (Command-Option-C)
	Right	Ctrl-Alt-R (Command-Option-R)

Cross-
Reference   Traditional HTML alignment options are limited. For a finer degree of control, be sure
to investigate precise positioning with layers in Chapter 23, "Working with Layers."

Indenting entire paragraphs

HTML offers one tag that enables you to indent whole paragraphs, such as inset
quotations or name-and-address blocks. Not too surprisingly, the tag used is called
the `<blockquote>` tag. Dreamweaver gives you instant access to the
`<blockquote>` tag through the Indent and Outdent buttons located on the Text
Property Inspector, as shown in Figure 7-12.

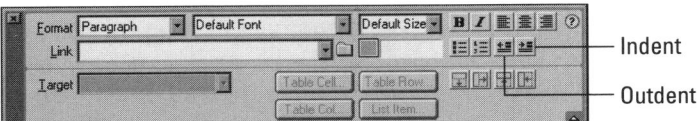

Figure 7-12: Indent paragraphs and blocks of text with
the Indent and the Outdent buttons.

To indent one or more paragraphs, select them and click the Indent button in the
Property Inspector. Paragraphs can be indented multiple times; each time you click
the Indent button, another `<blockquote>`...`</blockquote>` tag pair is added.

Note that you can't control how much space by which a single `<blockquote>`
indents a paragraph — that characteristic is determined by the browser.

If you find that you have over-indented, you can use the Outdent button, which is
also located also on the Property Inspector. The Outdent button has no effect if
your text is already at the left edge.

You also have the option of indenting your paragraphs through the menus; choose Text ⇨ Indent or Text ⇨ Outdent.

Tip
You can tell how many `<blockquote>` tags are being used to create a particular look by placing your cursor in the text and looking at the Tag Selector.

Commenting Your Code

When will you know to start inserting comments into your HTML code? The first time you go back to an earlier Web page, look at the code and say, "What on earth was I thinking?" You should plan ahead and develop the habit of commenting your code now.

Browsers run just fine without your comments, but for any continued development — of the Web page or of yourself as a Webmaster — commenting your code is extremely beneficial. Sometimes, as in a corporate setting, Web pages are codeveloped by teams of designers and programmers. In this situation, commenting your code may not just be a good idea; it may be required.

An HTML comment looks like the following:

```
<!-- Created by Hummer Associates, Inc. -->
```

You're not restricted to any particular line length or number of lines for comments. The text included between the opening of the comment, `<!--`, and the closing, `-->`, can span regular paragraphs or HTML code. In fact, one of the most common uses for comments during the testing and debugging phase of page design is to "comment out" sections of code as a means of tracking down an elusive bug.

To insert a comment in Dreamweaver, first place your cursor in either the document window or the HTML Inspector where you want the comment to appear. Then select the Insert Comment button from the Invisibles panel of the Object Palette. This sequence opens the Comment dialog box where you can insert the desired text; click OK when you've finished. Figure 7-13 shows the Comment dialog box, with the corresponding completed comment in the HTML Inspector.

By default, Dreamweaver inserts a Comment symbol in the document window. As with the other Invisibles, you can hide the Comment symbol by choosing Edit ⇨ Preferences and then deselecting the Comments check box in the Invisible Elements panel. You can also hide the any displayed Invisibles by selecting View ⇨ Invisible Elements or using the keyboard shortcut Ctrl-Shift-I (Command-Shift-I).

Insert Comment button   Comment symbol   HTML comment   Comment dialog box

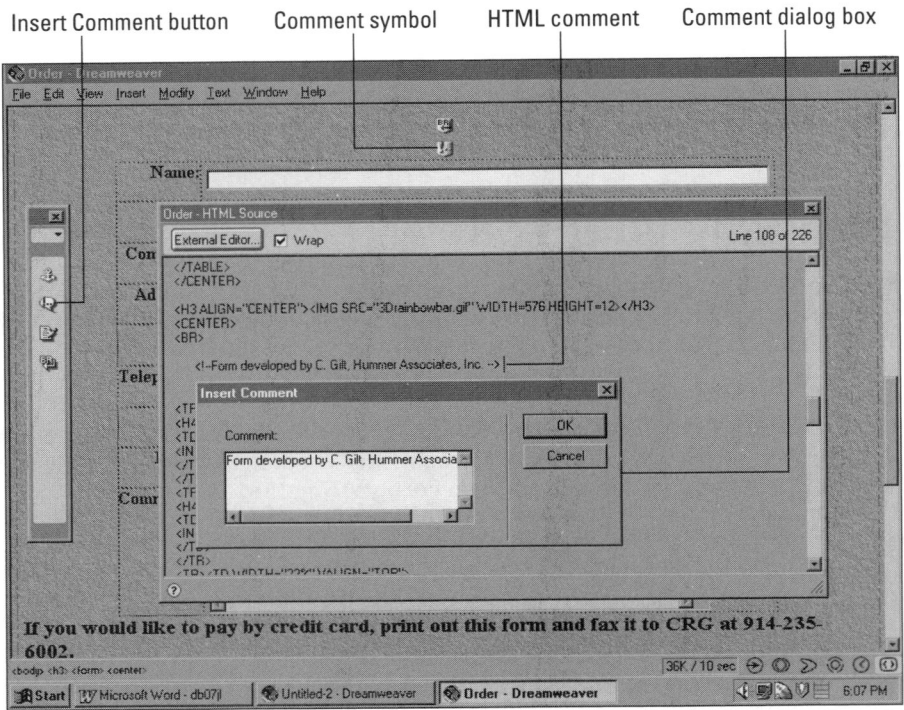

Figure 7-13: Comments are extremely useful for inserting information in the code not visible on the rendered Web page.

When you need to edit a comment, double-click on the Comment symbol to display the current comment in an editable window. After you've finished making your changes to the comment, select the Close button of the Comment window. A comment can be moved or duplicated by selecting its symbol and using the Cut, Copy, and Paste commands under the Edit menu. You can also right-click (Control-click) the Comment symbol to bring up the shortcut menu. Finally, you can click and drag Comment symbols to move the corresponding comment to a new location.

Summary

Learning to manipulate text is an essential design skill for creating Web pages. Dreamweaver gives you the tools to insert and modify the full range of HTML text quickly and easily.

✦ HTML headings are available in six different sizes: <h1> through <h6>. Headings are used primarily as headlines and subheads to separate divisions of the Web page.

✦ Blocks of text are formatted with the paragraph tag, <p>. Each paragraph is separated from the other paragraphs by a line of white space above and below. Use the line break tag, <br>, to make lines appear directly above or below one another.

✦ Dreamweaver offers a full complement of text-editing tools — everything from cut-and-paste to find-and-replace. Two commands, Copy as Text and Paste As Text, are unique to Dreamweaver and make short work of switching between text and commands.

✦ Where possible, text in HTML is formatted according to its meaning. Dreamweaver applies the styles selected through the Text ⇨ Style menu. For most styles, the browser determines what the user views.

✦ You can format Web page text much as you can text in a word processing program. Within certain limitations, you can select a font's size and color, as well as the font itself.

✦ HTML comments are a useful (and often requisite) vehicle for embedding information into a Web page that remains unseen by the casual viewer. Comments can annotate program code or insert copyright information.

In the next chapter, you'll learn how to insert and work with graphics.

✦   ✦   ✦

Inserting Images

The Internet started as a text-based medium primarily used for sharing data among research scientists and the U.S. military organization. Today, the Web is as visually appealing as any mass medium. Dreamweaver's power becomes even more apparent as you use its visual layout tools to incorporate background and foreground images into your Web page designs.

Completely baffled by all the various image formats out there? This chapter opens with a discussion of the key Web-oriented graphics formats, including the new PNG. Also, this chapter discusses techniques for incorporating both background and foreground images — and modifying them using new methods available in Dreamweaver 1.2. The final part of the chapter takes a look at animation graphics and how you can use them in your Web pages.

Web Graphic Formats

If you've worked in the computer graphics field, you know that virtually every platform — as well as every paint and graphics program — has its own proprietary file format for images. One of the critical factors in the Web's rapid, expansive growth is the use of cross-platform graphics. Regardless of the system you use to create your images, these versatile files ensure that the graphics can be viewed by all platforms.

The trade-off for universal acceptance of image files is a restricted field: just two file formats, with a possible third just coming into view. Currently, only GIF and JPEG formats are fully supported by browsers. A third alternative, the PNG graphics format, is experiencing a limited but growing acceptance.

You need to understand the uses and limitations of each of the formats so you can apply them successfully in Dreamweaver. Let's look at the fundamentals.

GIF

GIF, the Graphics Interchange Format, was developed by CompuServe in the late 1980s to address the problem of cross-platform compatibility. With GIF viewers available for every system from PC and Macintosh to Amiga and NeXT, the format became a natural choice for an inline (adjacent to text) image graphic. GIFs are *bitmapped* images, which means that each pixel is given or *mapped to* a specific color. You can have up to 256 colors for a GIF graphic. These images are generally used for illustrations, logos, or cartoons — anything that doesn't require thousands of colors for a smooth color blend, such as a photograph. With a proper graphics tool, you can reduce the number of colors in a GIF image to a minimum, thereby compressing the file and reducing download time.

The GIF format has two varieties: "regular" (technically, GIF87a) and an enhanced version known as GIF89a. This improved GIF file brings three important attributes to the format. First, GIF89a supports transparency, where one or more of the colors can become invisible. This property is necessary for creating nonrectangular-appearing images. Whenever you see a round or irregularly-shaped logo or illustration on the Web, a rectangular frame is displayed as the image is loading — this is the actual size and shape of the graphic. The colors surrounding the irregularly-shaped central image are set to transparent in a graphics editing program (such as Adobe Photoshop), before the image is saved in GIF89a format.

Although the outer area of a graphic seems to disappear with GIF89a, you won't be able to overlap your Web images using this format without using layers. Figure 8-1 demonstrates this situation. In this figure, the same image is presented twice — one lacks the transparency and one has transparency applied. The image on the left is saved as a standard GIF without transparency, and you can plainly see the shape of the full image. The image on the right was saved with the white background color made transparent, so the central figure seems to float on the background.

Tip
You may also notice a bit of a problem in Figure 8-1. In the transparent image on the right, the man's shadow doesn't blend well with the contrasting background. This image was constructed to work with an off-white background. Any images using blends or drop shadows should use a background close to the final Web page background. Otherwise, you get artifacting similar to this image.

The second valuable attribute contributed by GIF89a format is interlacing. One of the most common complaints about graphics on the Web regards lengthy download times. Interlacing won't speed up your GIF downloads, but it gives your Web page visitors something to view other than an blank screen. A graphic saved with the interlace turned on gives the appearance of "developing," like an instant picture, as the file is downloading. Use of this design option is up to you and your clients. Some folks swear by it; others can't abide it.

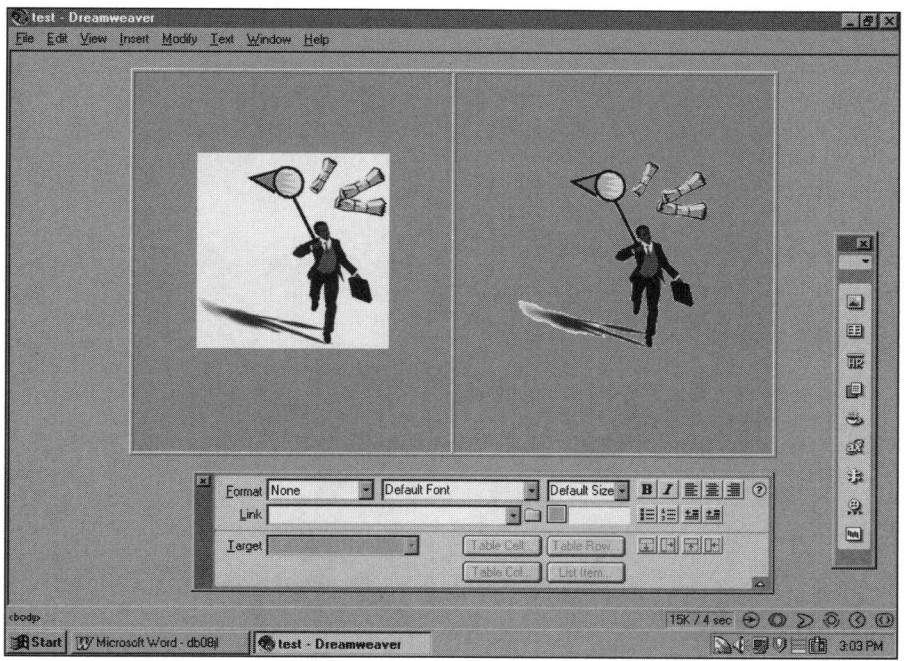

Figure 8-1: The same picture, saved without GIF transparency (left) and with GIF transparency (right).

Animation is the final advantage offered by the GIF89a format. Certain software programs enable you to group your GIF files together into one large, page-flipping file. With this capability, you can bring simple animation to your page without additional plug-ins or helper applications. Unfortunately, the trade-off is that the files get very big, very fast.

Cross-Reference   For more on animated GIFs in Dreamweaver, see "Applying Simple Web Animation," later in this chapter.

JPEG

The JPEG format was developed by the Joint Photographic Experts Groups specifically to handle photographic images. JPEGs offer millions of colors at 24 bits of color information available per pixel, as opposed to the GIF format's 8-bit and 256 colors. To make JPEGs usable, the large amount of color information must be compressed, which is accomplished by removing what the algorithm considers redundant information.

The more compressed your JPEG file, the more degraded the image. When you first save a JPEG image, your graphics program asks you for the desired level of compression. As an example, take a look at the three pictures in Figure 8-2. Here you can compare the effects of JPEG compression ratios and resulting file sizes to the original image itself. As you can probably tell, JPEG does an excellent job of compression, with even the highest degree of compression having only a little visible impact. Keep in mind that each picture has its own reaction to compression.

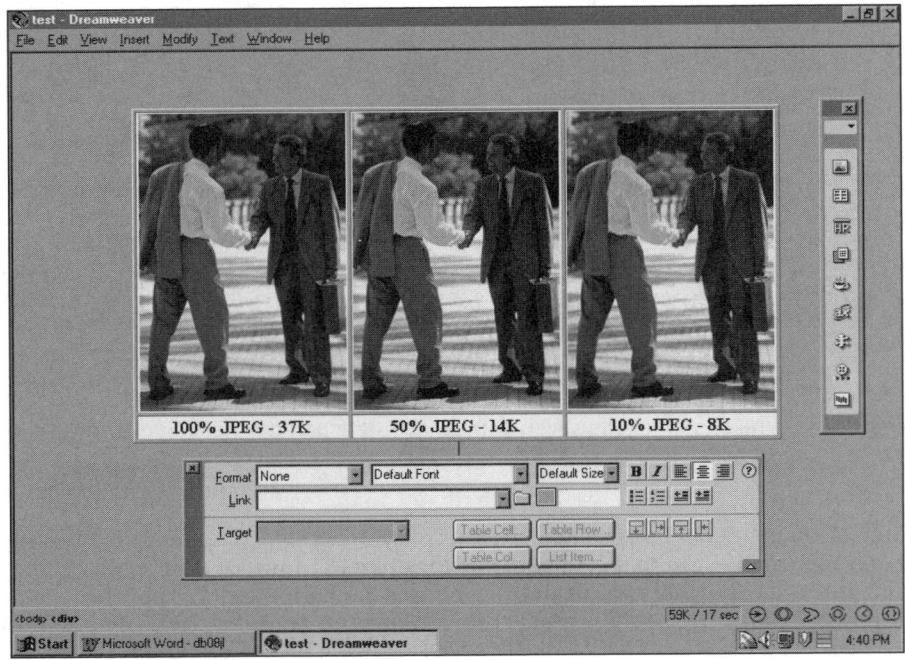

Figure 8-2: JPEG compression can save your Web visitors substantial download time, with little loss of image quality.

Tip   With the JPEG image-compression algorithm, the initial elements of an image "compressed away" are least noticeable. Subtle variations in brightness and hue are the first to disappear. When possible, preview your image in your graphics program while adjusting the compression level to observe the changes. With additional compression, the image grows darker and less varied in its color range.

With JPEGs, what is compressed to store must be decompressed to view. When a JPEG picture on your Web page is accessed by a visitor's browser, the image must first be downloaded to the browser and then decompressed before it can be viewed. This dual process adds additional time to the Web browsing process, but this time is well-spent for photographic images.

JPEGs, unlike GIFs, have neither transparency nor animation features. A new strand of JPEG called Progressive JPEG gives you the interlace option of the GIF format, however. Although all browsers do not support the interlace feature of Progressive JPEG, they render the image regardless.

PNG

The latest entry into the Web graphics arena is the Portable Network Graphics format or PNG. Combining the best of both worlds, PNG has lossless compression, like GIF, and is capable of millions of colors, like JPEG. Moreover, PNG offers an interlace scheme that appears much more quickly than either GIF or JPEG, as well as transparency support that is far superior to both the other formats.

One valuable aspect of the PNG format allows the display of PNG pictures to appear more uniform across various computer platforms. Generally, graphics made on a PC look brighter on a Macintosh, and Mac-made images seem darker on a PC. PNG includes gamma correction capabilities that alter the image depending on the computer used by the viewer.

Until recently, the various browsers supported PNG only through plug-ins. After PNG was endorsed as a new Web graphic format by the W3C, both 4.0 versions of Netscape and Microsoft browsers added native, inline support of the new format. Perhaps most importantly, however, Dreamweaver is among the first Web authoring tools to offer native PNG support. Inserted PNG images preview in the document window just like GIFs and JPEGs. Browser support is currently not widespread enough to warrant a total switch-over to the PNG format, but its growing acceptance certainly bears watching.

An excellent resource for more on the PNG format is the PNG home page at:

```
http://www.cdrom.com/pub/png
```

Using Inline Images

An *inline image* can appear directly next to text — literally in the same line. The ability to render inline images is one of the major innovations of the World Wide Web's transition from the Internet. This section covers all the basics of inserting inline images into Dreamweaver and modifying the attributes.

Inserting images

Dreamweaver can open and preview any graphic in a GIF, JPEG, or PNG format. Three methods can place a graphic on your Web page. No matter which method you choose, you first must position the cursor at the point where you want the image to appear on the page. Then pick one of the following:

✦ From the Object Palette, select the Insert Image button.

✦ From the menu bar, choose Insert ➪ Image.

✦ From the keyboard, press Control-Alt-I (Command-Option-I).

Tip   Dreamweaver 1.2 adds a new method of inserting graphics into your Web page: drag-and-drop. Now you can drag the icon from your file manager or desktop and drop it directly into Dreamweaver. The image appears at the current location of the insertion point. One key advantage to using drag-and-drop to open images is that you can insert multiple images at the same time. Just select two or more images in your file manager or desktop and then drag them into Dreamweaver. When inserted, they appear one after the other and can be moved to a new position, if necessary.

After you've used one of the preceding methods, Dreamweaver opens the Insert Image dialog box (Figure 8-3) and asks you for the path or *address* to your image file. Remember that in HTML, all graphics are stored in separate files linked from your Web page. The image's address can be just a filename, a directory path and filename on your system, a directory path and filename on your remote system, or a full URL to a graphic on a completely separate Web server. You don't have to have the file immediately available to insert the code into your HTML. If Dreamweaver can't find the file to display, it inserts a placeholder depicting a broken image.

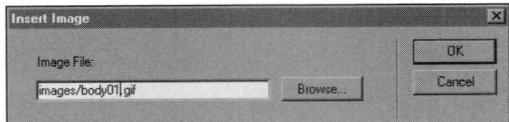

Figure 8-3: You can explicitly input the path to your image, or select the Browse button to pick your file.

Tip   When you first insert an image in Dreamweaver, the graphic appears to be covered with a gray screen. This screen indicates the image is still selected; click elsewhere on the page to deselect the image and restore the colors to normal.

Most often, you'll be laying out the Web page on your development system, which also contains your stored graphics. The simplest way to get the correct filename for the image you want to insert is to select the Browse button, which opens a customized Select File dialog box.

From the Select File dialog box, Figure 8-4, you can browse to the folder to select your images. In the lower portion of the dialog box, the URL text box displays the format of the address Dreamweaver inserts into your code. Below the URL text box is the Relative To option list box. Here you can choose to declare an image to be relative to the document you're working on (the default), or relative to the Site Root. (After you've saved your document, you'll see its name beside the Relative To box.)

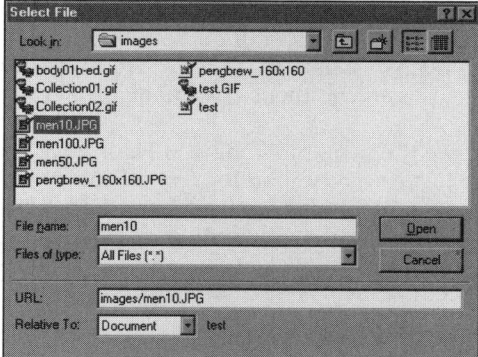

Figure 8-4: In this Select File dialog box you can keep track of your image's location relative to your current Web page.

Cross-Reference

To take full advantage of Dreamweaver's site management features, you must open a site, establish a local site root, and save the current Web page before beginning to insert images. For more on how to begin a Dreamweaver project, and about document-relative and site root-relative addressing, see Chapter 5, "Setting Up Your First Site."

Relative to Document: Once you've saved your Web page and have chosen Relative to Document, Dreamweaver displays the address in the URL text box. If the image is located in a folder on the same level as or within your current site root folder, the address is formatted with just a path and filename. For instance, let's say you're inserting a graphic from the subfolder named images. Dreamweaver inserts an address like the following:

```
images/men10.jpg
```

If you try to insert an image currently stored outside of the local site root folder, Dreamweaver temporarily appends a prefix that tells the browser to look on your local system for the file. For instance:

```
file:///C|/Dreamweaver/Figs/men10.jpg
```

Caution

Dreamweaver also appends the `file:///C|` prefix if you haven't yet saved your document. It is strongly recommended that you save your file before you begin developing the Web page. You can easily upload Web pages with this `file:///C|` prefix in place — and miss the error completely. Because your local browser can find the referenced image on your system, even when you are browsing the remote site, the Web page appears perfect. However, anyone else browsing your Web site only sees placeholders for broken links. Saving your page before you begin allows Dreamweaver to help you avoid these errors. To this end, do not check the Don't show me this message again box that appears when you're reminded to save your file the first time. This message will save you an enormous amount of grief!

After you select your image file, you'll see the prompt window in Figure 8-5. Dreamweaver asks if you want to copy this image to your local site root folder. Whenever possible, keep all of your images within the local site root folder so that Dreamweaver can handle the site management most efficiently. Click OK, and you next see a Save As dialog box, which points to the local site root folder. If you select Cancel, you're brought back to the preceding Insert File dialog box.

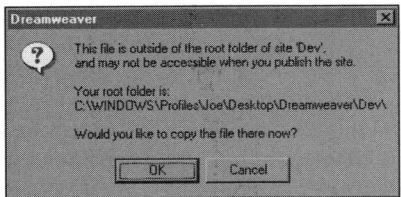

Figure 8-5: Dreamweaver reminds you to keep all of your graphics in the local site root folder for easy site management.

Relative to Site Root: Should you select Site Root in the Relative To field of the Select File dialog, and you are within your site root folder, Dreamweaver appends a leading forward slash to the directory in the path so the browser can correctly read the address. Thus, the same `men10.jpg` file appears in both the URL box and the HTML code as follows:

```
/images/men10.jpg
```

When you use site-root relative addressing and you select a file outside of the site root, you get the same reminder from Dreamweaver about copying the file into your local site root folder — just as with document relative addressing.

Modifying images

When you insert an image in Dreamweaver, the image tag, `<img>`, is inserted into your HTML code. The `<img>` tag takes several attributes, all of which can be entered through the Property Inspector. Code for a basic image looks like the following:

```
<img src= images/Collection01.gif  width= 172  height= 180 >
```

Dreamweaver centralizes all of its image functions in the Property Inspector. The Image Property Inspector, shown in Figure 8-6, displays a small thumbnail of the image as well as its file size. Dreamweaver automatically inserts the image filename in the Src text box (as the `src` attribute). To replace a currently selected image with another, click the folder icon next to the Src text box, or double-click the image itself. This sequence opens the Insert Image dialog box. When you've selected the desired file, Dreamweaver automatically refreshes the page and corrects the code.

Figure 8-6: The Image Property Inspector gives you total control over the HTML code for every image.

With the Property Inspector open when you insert your image, you can begin to modify it immediately.

Editing the image

Dreamweaver is a terrific Web authoring tool, but it's not a graphics editor. Quite often, after you've inserted an image into your Web page, you'll find that the picture needs to be altered in some way. Perhaps you need to crop part of the image or make the background transparent. Dreamweaver 1.2 lets you specify your primary graphics editor in the External Editors panel of Preferences.

Note   Dreamweaver seamlessly refreshed the images being edited in all the image editors I tested. However, there have been reports of images not reappearing in their modified form. If this happens, click the Refresh button in the Property inspector after you select your image.

Once you've picked an image editor, clicking the Edit Image button in the Property Inspector opens the application with the current image. After you've made the modifications, just save the file in your image editor and switch back to Dreamweaver. You'll see that the new, modified graphic has already been included in the Web page.

Note   In all the image editors tested for this book, Dreamweaver seamlessly refreshed the images being edited. There have been reports, however, of images not reappearing in their modified form. If this happens, select the H and/or W buttons to refresh the image.

Adjusting the height and width

The width and height attributes are important: browsers build Web pages faster when they know the size and shape of the included images. These attributes are read by Dreamweaver when the image is first loaded. The width and height values are initially expressed in pixels and are automatically inserted as attributes in the HTML code.

Browsers can dynamically resize an image if the height and width are different from the original. For example, you can load your primary logo on the home page and then use a smaller version of it on subsequent pages by inserting the same image with reduced height and width values. Because you're only loading the image once and letting the browser resize it, download time for your Web page can be significantly reduced.

You don't have to use pixels to enter your resizing measurements. You can also use inches ("in"), picas ("pc"), points ("pt"), millimeters ("mm"), or centimeters ("cm"). The values must be entered without spaces between the number and the measurement abbreviation, as follows:

72pt

You can also combine measurement systems. Suppose, for example, you want to resize a picture's height to 2 inches and 5 centimeters. In the Property Inspector, you enter the following value in the H text box:

```
2in+5cm
```

When you use values with a combined measurement system, you can only add values — you can't subtract them.

When you press the Tab key or click outside of height and width boxes, Dreamweaver converts your value to pixels.

Tip   With Dreamweaver 1.2, you can visually resize your graphics by using the click-and-drag method. A selected image has three sizing handles located on the right, bottom, and lower-right corners of its bounding box. Click any of these handles and drag it out to a new location — when you release the mouse, Dreamweaver resizes the image. You can hold down the Shift key while dragging the corner sizing handle, and Dreamweaver maintains the current height/width aspect ratio.

If you alter either the height or the width of an image in the Property Inspector, Dreamweaver displays the values in bold in their respective fields. You can restore an image's default measurements by selecting either the H or the V text box independently.

Caution   If you elect to allow your viewer's browser to resize your image on-the-fly using the height/width values you specify, keep in mind that the browser is not a graphics editing program and that the browser's resizing algorithms are not sophisticated. View your resized images through several browsers to make sure that the results are acceptable.

Using margins

You can offset images with surrounding white space by using the margin attributes. The amount of white space around your image can be designated both vertically and horizontally through the vspace and hspace attributes, respectively. These margin values are entered, in pixels, into the V Space and H Space text boxes in the Image Property Inspector.

The V Space value adds the same amount of white space along the top and bottom of your image; the H Space value increases the white space along the left and right sides of the image. These values must be positive; HTML doesn't allow images to overlap text or other images (outside of layers); unlike in page layout, "negative white space" does not exist.

Naming your image

When you first insert a graphic into the page, the Image Property Inspector displays a blank text box next to the thumbnail and file size. Fill in this box with a unique name for the image to be called in JavaScript and other applications.

As a page is loading over the Web, the image is first displayed as an empty rectangle if the <img> tag contains the width and height information. Sometimes these rectangles include a brief title to describe the coming image. You can enter this alternative text in the Alt text box of the Image Property Inspector.

Good coding practice associates an Alt title with all of your graphics. Aside from giving the user some clue as to what's coming, these minititles are also used to display the screen tips that pop up when the user's pointer passes over the graphic. The real benefit of minititles, however, provides input for browsers not displaying graphics. Text-only browsers are still in use and some users, interested only in content, turn off the graphics to speed up the text display. Moreover, the W3C is working toward standards for browsers for the visually impaired, and the Alt text can be used to describe the page.

Specifying a LowSRC

Another option for loading Web page images, the lowsrc attribute, displays a smaller version of a large graphic file while the larger file is loading. The lowsrc file can be a grayscale version of the original, or a version that is physically smaller or reduced in color or resolution. This option is designed to reduce the file size significantly for quick loading.

Select your lowsrc file by choosing the file icon next to the Low text box in the Image Property Inspector. The same criteria that applies to inserting your original image also applies to the lowsrc picture.

One handy lowsrc technique first proportionally scales down a large file in a graphic processing program. This file becomes your lowsrc file. Because browsers use the final image's height and width information for both the lowsrc and the final image, your visitors immediately see a "blocky" version of your graphic, which will be replaced by the final version when the picture is fully loaded.

Working with alignment options

Images can be aligned to the left, right, or center just like text. In fact, images have much more flexibility than text in terms of alignment. In addition to the same horizontal alignment options, you can align your images vertically in nine different ways. You can even turn a picture into a floating image type, allowing text to wrap around it.

Horizontal alignment

When you change the horizontal alignment of a line — from left to center or from center to right — the entire paragraph moves. Any inline images that are part of that paragraph also move. Likewise, selecting one of a series of inline images in a row and realigning it horizontally causes all the images in the row to shift.

In Dreamweaver, the horizontal alignment of an inline image is changed in exactly the same way you realign text. Select Text ⇨ Alignment and then choose your option: Left, Right, or Center. You can also click the Left, Center, and Right buttons from the Text Property Inspector or use the following keyboard shortcuts:

- ✦ Ctrl-Alt-L (Command-Option-L) for Left
- ✦ Ctrl-Alt-C (Command-Option-C) for Center
- ✦ Ctrl-Alt-R (Command-Option-R) for Right

Vertical alignment

Because you can place text next to an image — and images vary so greatly in size — HTML includes a variety of options for specifying just how image and text line up. As you can see from the chart in Figure 8-7, a wide range of possibilities are available.

To change the vertical alignment of any graphic in Dreamweaver, open the Align drop-down list in the Image Property Inspector and choose one of the options. Dreamweaver writes your choice into the `align` attribute of the `<img>` tag.

The various vertical alignment options are listed in the following table, and you can see examples of each type of alignment in Figure 8-7.

Vertical Alignment Option	Results
Browser Default	No alignment attribute is included in the `<img>` tag. Most browsers use the baseline as an alignment default.
Baseline	The bottom of the image is aligned with the baseline of the surrounding text.
Top	The top of the image is aligned with the top of the tallest object in the current line.
Middle	The middle of the image is aligned with the baseline of the current line.
Texttop	The top of the image is aligned with the tallest letter in the current line.

(continued)

Vertical Alignment Option	Results
Absolute Middle	The middle of the image is aligned with the middle of the text or object in the current line.
Absolute Bottom	The bottom of the image is aligned with the descenders (i.e., y, g, p, and so forth) that fall below the current line.
Left	The image is aligned to the left-edge of the browser or table cell and all text in the current line flows around the right-hand side of the image.
Right	The image is aligned to the right-edge of the browser or table cell and all text in the current line flows around the left-hand side of the image.

The final two alignment options, Left and Right, are special cases; details on how to use their features are covered in the following section.

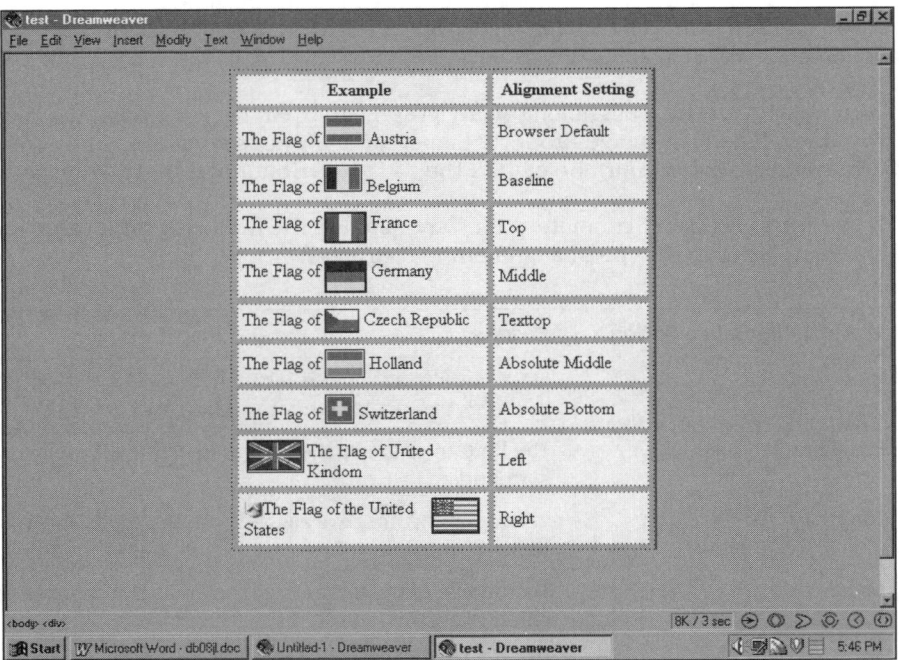

Figure 8-7: You can align text and images in one of nine different ways using the Align option box on the Image Property Inspector.

Wrapping text

Long a popular design option in conventional publishing, wrapping text around an image on a Web page is also supported by most, but not all, browsers. As noted in the preceding section, the Left and Right alignment options turn a picture into a *floating image type*, so called because the image can move depending on the amount of text and the size of the browser window.

Tip

Using both floating image types (Left and Right) in combination, you can actually position images flush-left and flush-right, with text in the middle. Insert both images side-by-side, and then set the leftmost image to align left and the rightmost one to align right. Insert your text immediately following the second image. Unless you place a `<p>` or `<br>` at the top, this arrangement does not render correctly in Dreamweaver (the first line overlaps the left image); but it does display as expected in most browsers.

Your text wraps around the image depending on where the floating image is placed (or anchored). If you have the feature enabled in the Invisibles pane of Preferences, Dreamweaver inserts a Floating Image Anchor symbol to mark the floating image's place. Figure 8-8 shows two examples of text wrapping. In the uppermost section, the Floating Image Anchor symbol is placed at the front of the second paragraph, which causes the three paragraphs to flow around the right-aligned image. In the lower section, you can't see the Floating Image Anchor because the left-aligned image overlaps the anchor, which is placed at the front of the first paragraph.

The Floating Image Anchor is not just a static symbol. You can click and drag the anchor to a new location and cause the paragraph to wrap in a different fashion. Be careful though — if you delete the Anchor, you also delete the image it represents.

You can also wrap a portion of the text around your left- or right-aligned picture and then force the remaining text to appear below the floating image. However, the HTML necessary to do this task cannot currently be inserted by Dreamweaver, and must be coded by hand. You have to force an opening to appear by inserting a break tag, with a special `clear` attribute, where you want the text to break. This special `<br>` tag has three forms:

`<br clear=left>`	Causes the line to break, and the following text moves down vertically until there are no floating images on the left.
`<br clear=right>`	Causes the line to break, and the following text moves down vertically until there are no floating images on the right.
`<br clear=all>`	Moves the text following the image down until there are no floating images on either the left or the right.

Floating Image Anchor

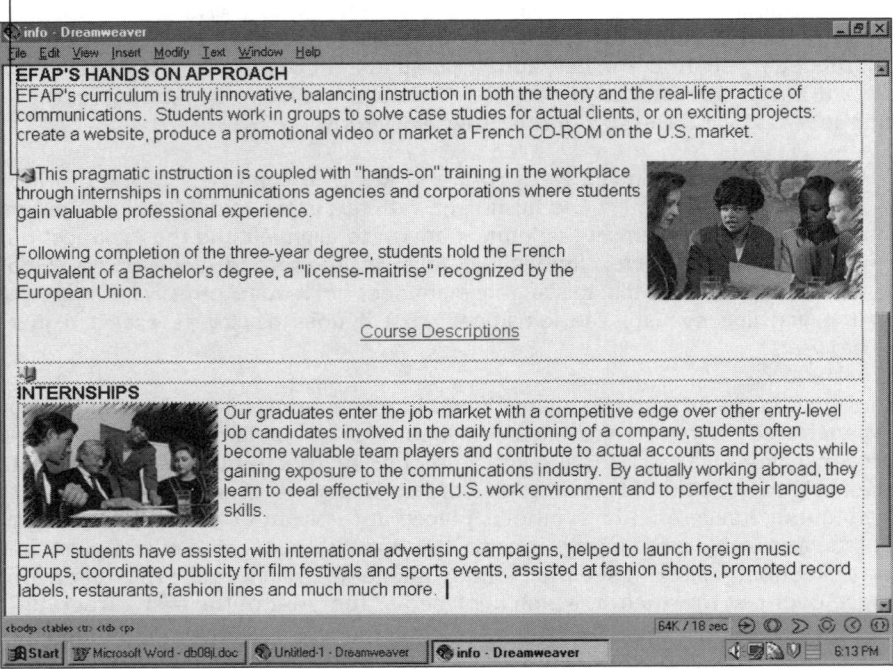

Figure 8-8: Aligning an image left or right allows text to wrap around your images.

One of the Dreamweaver objects included on the CD-ROM is an enhanced break tag that enables you to include any version of the `clear` attribute. To access these objects, copy the two files, new_break.htm and new_break.gif, from the Dreamweaver/Configuration/Objects/Invisibles folder into the same folder on your system; then restart Dreamweaver.

Putting Pictures in the Background

In this chapter, you've learned only about working with the surface graphics on a Web page. As seen in Chapter 6, you can also have an image in the background of an HTML page. This section covers some of the basic techniques for incorporating a background image in your Dreamweaver page.

Note

Remember, you add an image to your background in Dreamweaver by modifying the Page Properties. Either choose Modify ⇨ Page Properties, or select Page Properties from the shortcut menu that pops up when you right-click (Ctrl-click) any open area on the Web page. In the Page Properties dialog box, select a graphic by choosing the Browse button next to the Background Image text box. You can use any file format supported by Dreamweaver—GIF, JPEG, or PNG—although the PNG format is currently not supported in enough browsers to permit widespread distribution.

Two key differences exist between background images and the foreground, inline images discussed in the preceding sections of this chapter. First and most obvious: all other text and graphics on the Web page are superimposed over your chosen background image. This capability can bring extra depth and texture to your work; unfortunately, you have to make sure the foreground text and images work well with the background.

Basically, you want to ascertain that there is enough contrast between foreground and background. You can set the default text and the various link colors through the Page Properties dialog box. When trying out a new background pattern, you should set up some dummy text and links. Then use the Apply button on the Page Properties dialog box to test different color combinations. See Figure 8-9 for an example of this test at work.

The second distinguishing feature of background images is that the viewing browser completely fills either the browser window or the area behind the content of your Web page, whichever is larger. So, if you've created a splash page with only a 200×200 foreground logo, and you've incorporated an amazing 1024×768 background that took you weeks to compose, no one sees the fruits of your labor in the background — unless they resize their browser window to 1024×768. On the other hand, if your background image is smaller than either the browser window or what the Web page content needs to display, the browser and Dreamweaver repeat (or tile) your image to make up the difference. Let's see how that works.

Tiling images

Web designers use the tiling property of background images to create a variety of effects with very low file-size overhead. Columns typically found on one side of Web pages are a good example of tiling. Columns are popular because they allow the designer to place navigational buttons in a visual context. An easy way to create a column that runs the full length of your Web page uses a long, narrow background image.

Take a look at Figure 8-10. The background image is 45 pixels high, 800 pixels wide, and only 6K in size. When the browser window is set at 640×480 or 800×600, the image is tiled down the page to create the vertical column effect. You could just as easily create an image 1000 pixels high by 40 pixels wide to create a horizontal column.

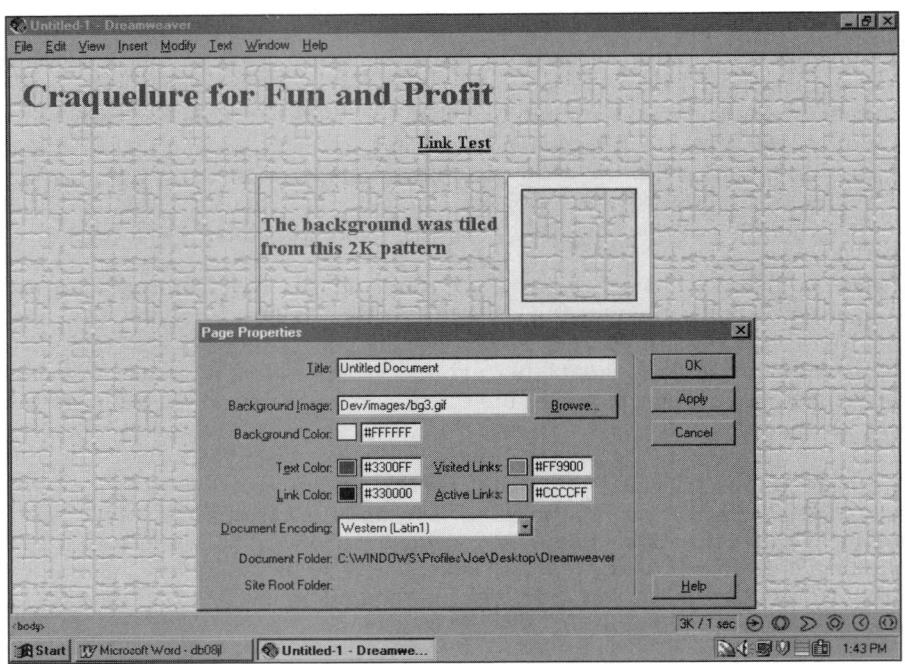

Figure 8-9: If you're using a background image, be sure to check the default colors for text and links to make sure there is enough contrast between background and foreground.

Dividing the Web Page with Horizontal Rules

HTML includes a standard horizontal line that can divide your Web page into specific sections. The horizontal rule tag, `<hr>`, is a good tool for adding a little diversion to your page without adding download time. You can control the width (either absolutely or relative to the browser window), the height, the alignment, and the shading property of the rule. These horizontal rules appear on a line by themselves; you cannot place text or images on the same line as a horizontal rule.

To insert a horizontal rule in your Web page in Dreamweaver, follow these steps:

1. Place your cursor where you want the horizontal rule to appear.

2. From the Common pane of the Object Palette, select the Insert Horizontal Rule button or choose the Insert ➪ Horizontal Rule command.

   Dreamweaver inserts the horizontal rule and opens the Horizontal Rule Property Inspector as shown in Figure 8-11.

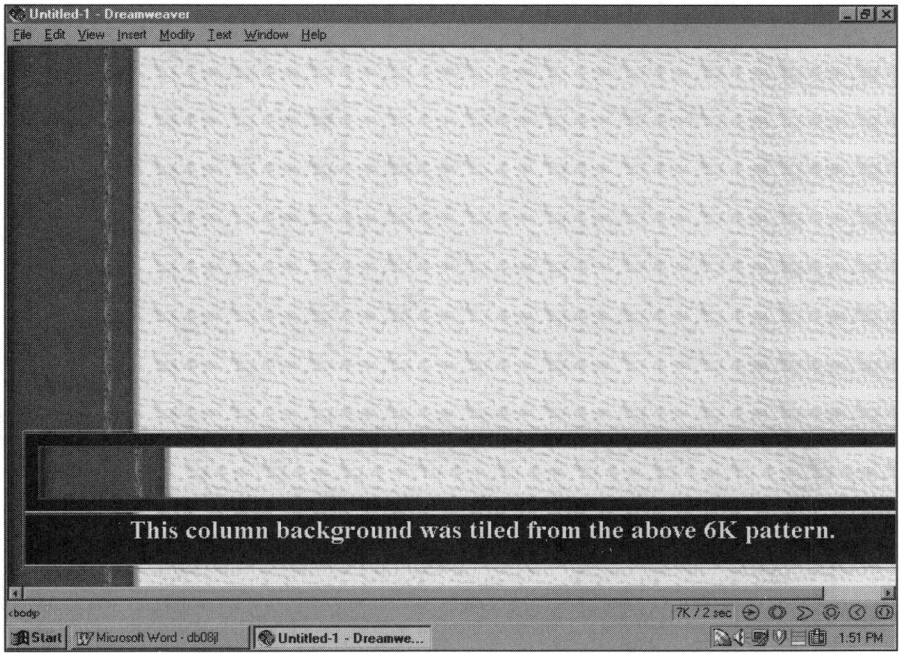

Figure 8-10: You can use a browser's tiling property to create vertical or horizontal column effects.

3. To change the width of the line, enter a value in the width (W) text box. You can either insert an absolute width in pixels or a relative value as a percentage of the screen.

   • To set a horizontal rule to an exact width, enter the measurement in pixels in the width (W) text box and press the Tab key. Then select pixels in the drop-down list.

   • To set a horizontal rule to a width relative to the browser window, enter the percentage amount in the width (W) text box and press Tab. Then select the percent sign (%) in the drop-down list.

4. To change the height of the horizontal rule, type a pixel measurement in the height (H) text box.

   For both the width and height values, you can also enter a value in inches (in), picas (pc), points (pt), millimeters (mm), or centimeters (cm), just as with images. When you press Tab to leave the text box, Dreamweaver converts your entry to pixels.

Figure 8-11: The Horizontal Rule Property Inspector controls the width, height, and alignment for these HTML lines.

5. To change the alignment from the default (centered), open the Align drop-down list and choose another alignment.

6. To disable the default "embossed" look for the rule, deselect the Shading check box.

7. If you intend to address (call) your horizontal rule in a JavaScript or another application, you can give it a unique name. Type it into the unlabeled name text box located directly left of the H text box.

To modify any inserted horizontal rule, simply click it. (If the Property Inspector is not already open, you have to double-click the rule.) As a general practice, size horizontal rules using the percentage option if they are being used to separate items on a full screen. If the horizontal rules are being used to divide items in a specifically sized table column or cell, use the pixel method.

Tip

To use the Shading property of the horizontal rule properly, your background should be a shade of gray. The default shading is black along the top and left, and white along the bottom and right. The center line is generally transparent (although Internet

Explorer enables you to assign a color attribute). If you use a different background color or image, be sure to check the appearance of your horizontal rules in that context.

Many designers prefer to create more elaborate horizontal rules; in fact, these rules are an active area of clip-art design. These types of horizontal rules are regular graphics and are inserted and modified as such.

Applying Simple Web Animation

Why include a section on animation in the chapter on inline images? On the Web, animations are, for the most part, inline images that move. Outside of the possibilities offered by Dynamic HTML (covered in Part VI, "Dynamic HTML and Dreamweaver"), Web animations are either animated GIF files or created with a program such as Flash that requires a plug-in. This section takes a brief look at the capabilities and use of GIF animations.

A GIF animation is a series of still GIF images flipped rapidly to create the illusion of motion. Because animation creation programs compress all the frames of your animation into one file, a GIF animation is placed on a Web page in the same manner as a still graphic.

In Dreamweaver, click the Insert Image button in the Object Palette or choose Insert ➪ Image and then select the file. Dreamweaver shows the first frame of your animation in the document window. To play the animation, preview your Web page in any graphics-capable browser.

As you can imagine, GIF animations can quickly grow to be very large. The key to controlling file size is to think small: keep your images as small as possible with a low bit-depth (number of colors), and use as few frames as possible.

To create your animation, use any graphics program to produce the separate frames. One excellent technique uses an image-processing program such as Adobe Photoshop and progressively applies a filter to the same image over a series of frames. Figure 8-12 shows the individual frames created with Photoshop's Lighting Effects filter. When animated, a spotlight appears to move across the word.

You need an animation program to compress the separate frames and build your animated GIF file. GIF Construction Set on the Windows platform and GIFBuilder on the Mac are extremely popular. Both of these programs are shareware; there are also many commercial programs that can handle GIF animation, including Macromedia's new Fireworks. Most animation programs enable you to control the number of times an animation loops, the delay between frames, and how transparency is handled within each frame.

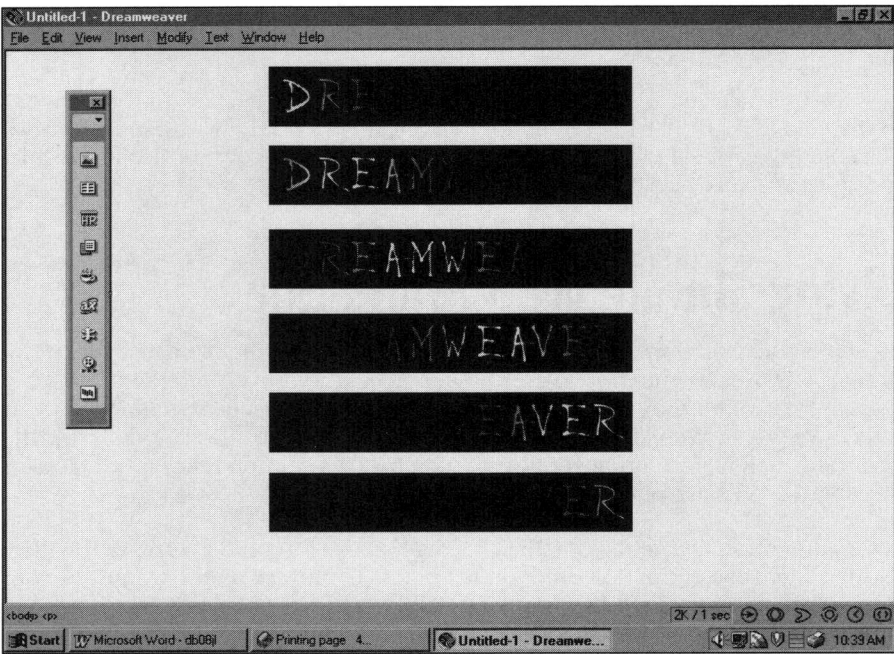

Figure 8-12: Six of twelve frames that are compressed into one animated file.

Cross-Reference   If you want to use an advanced animation tool, but still have full backward-compatibility, check out Flash and the Aftershock utility, both from Macromedia. Flash outputs small vector-based animations that require a plug-in to view, and Aftershock can convert vector animation to GIF animation. Both programs are discussed in Chapter 20, "Inserting Shockwave Elements."

Summary

In this chapter you explored how to include both foreground and background images in Dreamweaver. Understanding how images are handled in HTML is an absolute necessity for the Web designer. Some of the key points follow:

✦ Web pages are restricted to using specific graphic formats. Virtually all browsers support GIF and JPEG files. A new format, PNG, is rapidly gaining acceptance. Dreamweaver can preview all three image types.

✦ Images are inserted in the foreground in Dreamweaver through the Insert Image command of the Object Palette. Once the graphic is inserted, almost all modifications can be handled through the Property Inspector.

✦ You can use HTML's background image function to lay a full-frame picture or a tiled series of the same image underneath your text and graphics. Tiled images can be employed to create columns and other designs with small files.

✦ The simplest HTML graphic is the built-in horizontal rule. Useful for dividing your Web page into separate sections, the horizontal rule can be sized either absolutely or relatively.

✦ Animated images can be inserted alongside and in the same manner as still graphics. The individual frames of a GIF animation must be created in a graphics program and then combined in an animation program.

In the next chapter, you'll learn about how to use hyperlinks in Dreamweaver.

✦   ✦   ✦

Establishing Web Links

◆   ◆   ◆   ◆

In This Chapter

All about Internet
addresses

Linking Web pages

Creating anchors
within Web pages

URL targeting

◆   ◆   ◆   ◆

To me, links *are* the Web. Everything else about the medium can be replicated in another form, but without links there would be no World Wide Web. As your Web design work becomes more sophisticated, you'll find more enhanced uses for links: sending mail, connecting to an FTP site — even downloading software. In this chapter, you see how Dreamweaver helps you manage the various types of links, set anchors within documents to get smooth and accurate navigation, and establish targets for your URLs. But first, let's begin with an overview on Internet addresses to give you the full picture of the possibilities.

Understanding URLs

URL stands for Uniform Resource Locator. An awkward phrase, it nonetheless describes itself well — the URL's function is to provide a standard method for finding anything on the Internet. From Web pages to newsgroups to the smallest graphic on the most esoteric of pages, everything can be referenced through the URL system.

The URL can use up to six different parts, although all parts are not necessary for the URL to be read. Each part is separated by some combination of a slash, colon, and hash mark delimiter. The entire URL is generally enclosed within quotes to ensure that the address is read as one unit. A generic URL using all the parts looks like the following:

```
method://server:port/path/file#anchor
```

Here's a real-world example that also uses every section:

```
http://www.idest.com:80/dreamweaver/index.htm#
bible
```

In order of appearance in the body of an Internet address, left to right, the parts denote the following:

✦ **The method used to access the resource.** The method to address Web servers is the HyperText Transport Protocol (HTTP). Other methods are discussed later in this section.

✦ **The name of the server providing the resource.** The server can either be a domain name (with or without the "www" prefix) or an Internet Protocol (IP) address such as 199.227.52.143.

✦ **The port number to be used on the server.** Most URLs do not include a port number, which is analogous to a telephone extension number on the server, because most servers use the defaults.

✦ **The directory path to the resource.** Depending on where the resource (for example, the Web page) is located on the server, the following paths can be specified: no path (indicating that the resource is in the public root of the server), a single folder name, or a number of folders and subfolders.

✦ **The filename of the resource.** If the filename is omitted, the Web browser looks for a default page, often named `index.html` or `index.htm`. The browser reacts differently depending on the type of file. For example, GIFs and JPEGs are displayed by themselves; executable files are downloaded.

✦ **The named anchor in the HTML document.** This part is another optional section. The named anchor enables the Web designer to send the viewer to a particular section of an HTML page.

Additional access methods and protocols

Because it is used to communicate with servers, the HTTP access method is far and away the most prevalent method on today's World Wide Web. In addition to the HTTP access method, other methods connect with other types of servers. Table 9-1 discusses some of these options.

Table 9-1 **Various Internet Access Methods and Protocols**		
Name	*Syntax*	*Usage*
File Transfer Protocol	ftp://	Links to an FTP server that is generally used for the uploading and downloading of files. The server can be accessed anonymously, or it may require a user name and password.

Name	Syntax	Usage
Gopher	gopher://	Connects to a directory tree structure primarily used for disseminating all-text documents.
HyperText Transfer Protocol	http://	Used for connecting to a document available on a World Wide Web server.
Mailto	mailto:	Opens an e-mail form with the recipient's address already filled in. These links are useful when embedded in your Web pages to provide visitors with an easy feedback method.
News	news:	Connects to the specified Usenet newsgroup. Newsgroups are public theme-oriented message boards where anyone can post or reply to a message.
Telnet	telnet://	Enables users to log directly on to remote host computers and interact directly with the operating system software.

Part of the richness of today's Web browsers stems from their capability to connect with all the preceding (and additional) services.

Tip

Not only does the mailto: access method enable you to open up a preaddressed e-mail form, you can also specify the topic with a little extra work. For example, if Joe Lowery wants to include a link to his e-mail address with the subject heading, "Dreamweaver Bible," he can insert a link like the following:

```
mailto:jlowery@idest.com?subject=Bible Feedback
```

The question mark acts as a delimiter that allows a variable and a value to be passed to the browser. When you're trying to encourage feedback from your Web page visitors, every little bit helps. A note of caution: This method is not standardized HTML and, while it works with most browsers, you could get unexpected results with some systems.

Surfing the Web with Hypertext

Most often, you'll be assigning a link to a word or phrase on your page, an image such as a navigation button, or a section of graphic for an image map (a large graphic in which various parts are links). Once you have created the link, you have to preview it in a browser; links are not active in Dreamweaver's document window.

Designate links in HTML through the anchor tag pair: `<a>` and `</a>`. The anchor tag always takes one main attribute — the hypertext reference — which is written as follows:

```
href= link name
```

When you create a link in Dreamweaver, the anchor pair surrounds the text or object that is being linked. For example, if you link the phrase "Back to Home Page," it may look like the following:

```
<a href= index.html >Back to Home Page</a>
```

When you attach a link to an image, logo.gif, your code looks as follows:

```
<a href= home.html ><img src= images/logo.gif ></a>
```

Creating a basic link in Dreamweaver is easy. Simply follow these steps:

1. Select the text, image, or object you want to establish as a link.

2. In the Property Inspector, enter the URL in the Link text box as shown in Figure 9-1. You can either:

   • Type the URL directly into the Link text box.

   • Select the folder icon next to the Link text box to open the Select HTML File dialog box, where you can browse for the file.

Link folder icon

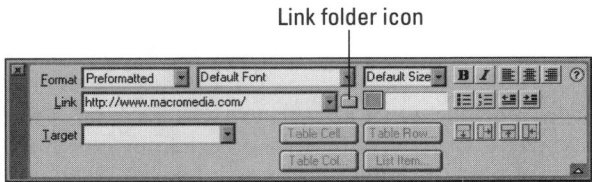

Figure 9-1: You can enter your link directly into the Link text box or select the folder icon to browse for a file.

Only a few restrictions exist for specifying linked URLs. Dreamweaver does not support any letters from the extended character set (also known as High ASCII), such as ¡, à, or ñ. Complete URLs must have fewer than a total of 255 characters. You should be cautious about using spaces in path names and, thus, URLs. Although most browsers can interpret the address, spaces are changed to a %20 symbol for proper UNIX usage, which can make your URLs difficult to read.

Links without Underscores

To remove the underlined aspect of a link, you can use one of two methods. The classic method — which works for all graphics-capable browsers — uses an image rather than text as the link. You must make sure the Border attribute of your image is set to 0, because a linked image displays a blue border if a Border attribute exists.

The second, newer method uses Cascading Style Sheets, bearing in mind that these can be read only by the more recent browser versions. Refer to the Dreamweaver technique for eliminating the underlines in links in Chapter 22, "Building Style Sheet Pages."

Note

White space in your HTML usually doesn't have an adverse effect. Netscape browsers are a tad sensitive to white space when assigning a link to an image, however. If you isolate your image tag like the following, for instance:

```
<a href= index.htm >
<img src= images/Austria.gif  width= 34  height= 24 >
</a>
```

Netscape attaches a small blue underscore — a tail, really — to your image. Because Dreamweaver codes the anchor tag properly, without any additional white space, this odd case only applies to hand-coded or previously coded HTML.

Text links are most often rendered with a blue color and underlined. You can alter the link color by choosing Modify ➪ Page Properties and selecting the Link Color swatch. In Page Properties, you can also alter the color to which the links change after being selected (the Visited Link Color) and the color flashed when the link is clicked (the Active Link Color).

Addressing types

As you learned in Chapter 5, three types of URLs are used as links: absolute addresses, document relative addresses, and site root relative addresses. Let's briefly recap these address types.

✦ Absolute addresses require the full URL, as follows:

```
http://www.macromedia.com/software/dreamweaver/
```

This type is most often used for referencing links on another Web server.

✦ Document relative addresses know the method, server, and path aspects of the URL. You only need to include additional path information if the link is outside of the current Web page's folder. Links in the current document's folder can be addressed with their filename only. To reference an item in a subfolder, just name the folder, enter a forward slash, and then enter the item's file name, as follows:

```
images/background.gif
```

✦ Site root relative addresses are indicated with a leading forward slash. For example:

```
/upndown.html
```

The preceding address links to a file named upndown.html stored in the primary directory of the current site. Links using site root relative addresses must be saved on a Web server to be previewed.

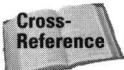

For a full discussion of the advantages and uses of the different URL addressing methods, see the section "Understanding Relative and Absolute Paths" in Chapter 5.

A Webmaster must often perform the tedious but necessary task of verifying the links on all the Web pages in a site. Because of the Web's fluid nature, links can work one day and then be broken the next. Although Dreamweaver doesn't currently offer any site-management tools for link verification, both of the included HTML text editors, HomeSite and BBEdit, provide this functionality. Refer to the Appendixes for more information on how to use these timesaving features.

Navigating with Anchors

Whenever you normally link to an HTML page, through absolute or relative addressing, the browser displays the page from the top. Your Web visitors must scroll to any information rendered below the current screen. An HTML technique, however, links to a specific point anywhere on your page regardless of the display window's contents. This technique uses named anchors.

Using named anchors is a two-step process. First, you place a named anchor somewhere on your Web page. This placement is coded in HTML as an anchor tag using the name attribute, with nothing in between the opening and closing tags. In HTML, named anchors look like the following:

```
<a name= top ></a>
```

The second step includes a link to that named anchor from somewhere else on your Web page. If used, a named anchor is referenced in the final possible portion of an Internet address, designated by the hash mark (#), as follows:

```
<a href= http://www.idest.com/dreamweaver/index.htm#bible>
```

You can include any number of named anchors on the current page or another page. Named anchors are commonly used with a table of contents or index.

To insert a named anchor in Dreamweaver, follow these steps:

1. Place the cursor where you want the named anchor to appear.

2. Choose Insert ⇨ Named Anchor. You can also select the Insert Named Anchor button from the Invisibles panel of the Object Palette.

3. The Named Anchor dialog box opens (Figure 9-2). Type the anchor name into the text box.

Caution

Named anchors are case-sensitive and must be unique.

Insert Named Anchor button   Named Anchor symbol   Named Anchor Property Inspector

Figure 9-2: The Named Anchor tag lets you link to specific areas of a Web page.

When you press Enter (Return), Dreamweaver places a Named Anchor symbol in the current cursor location and opens the Named Anchor Property Inspector.

4. To change an anchor's name, click the Named Anchor symbol within the page and alter the text in the Property Inspector.

As with other invisible symbols, the Named Anchor symbol can be cut and pasted or moved using the drag-and-drop method.

Moving within the same document

One of the major advantages of using named anchors is the almost instantaneous response the viewer receives when they click them. The browser only needs to scroll to the particular place in the document, because the entire page is loaded. For long text documents, this capability is an invaluable time-saver.

Once you have placed a named anchor in your document — or all of them at once — you can link to these anchors. Follow these steps to create a link to a named anchor in the same document:

1. Select the text or image that you want to designate as a link.

2. In the Link text box of the Property Inspector, type a hash mark, #, followed by the exact anchor name. For example:

`#top`

Remember, anchor names are case-sensitive and must be unique in each document.

Tip You should place the named anchor one line above the heading or image to which you want to link the viewer. Browsers tend to be quite literal. If you place the named anchor on the same line, the browser renders it up against the top of the window. Placing your named anchor up one line gives your topic a bit of breathing room in the display.

In long documents with a table of contents or index linking to a number of named anchors, it's common practice — and a good idea — to place a link back to the top of the page after every screen or every topic. This technique allows your users to return to the menu quickly and pick another topic without having to scroll all the way back manually.

Using named anchors in a different page

If your table of contents is on a separate page from the topics of your site, you can use named anchors to send the viewer anywhere on a new page. The technique is exactly the same as already explained for placing named anchors, but there is one minor difference when it comes to linking. Instead of just placing a hash mark and name to denote the named anchor, you must first include the URL of the linked page.

Let's say you want to call the disclaimer section of a legal page from your table of contents. You could insert something like the following in the Link text box of the Property Inspector:

```
legal.htm#disclaimer
```

This link, when activated, first loads the referenced Web page (legal.htm) and then goes directly to the named anchor place (#disclaimer). Figure 9-3 shows how you would enter this in the Property Inspector. Keep in mind, you can use any form of addressing prior to the hash mark and named anchor.

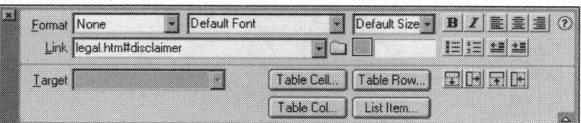

Figure 9-3: You can also link to any part of a separate Web page using named anchors.

Tip

One of the more obscure uses for named anchors comes into play when you are trying to use Dreamweaver's JavaScript Behavior feature. Because JavaScript needs to work with a particular type of tag to perform mouseOver and other events, one trick marks some text or image with a link to #nowhere. You can use any name for the nonexistent named anchor. In fact, you don't even have to use a name — you can just use a hash mark by itself.

Targeting Your Links

Thus far, all of this chapter's links have had a similar effect: they open another Web page or section in your browser's window. What if you want to force the browser to open another window and load that new URL in the new window? HTML lets you specify the target for your links.

Targets are most often used in conjunction with frames — that is, you can make a link in one frame open a file in another. (Chapter 14 covers the subject of frames in depth.) Here, though, let's take a look at one of the HTML predefined targets useful in the situation where you want to load another URL into a new window:

To specify a new browser window as the target for a link in Dreamweaver, follow these steps:

1. Select the text or image you want to designate as your new link.

2. In the Property Inspector, enter the URL into the Link text box.

3. If necessary, click the expander arrow to expand the Property Inspector so that the Target list box is visible.

4. Open the Target list box.

5. Choose the _blank option (see Figure 9-4).

   Now, when your link is activated, the browser spawns a new window and loads the referenced link into it. The user has both windows available.

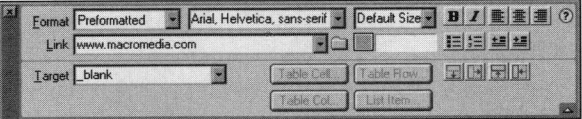

Figure 9-4: You can force a user's browser to open a separate window to display a specific link with the Target command.

The blank target is most often used when the originating Web page is acting as a jump station and has numerous links available. By keeping the original Web page open, the user can check out one site without losing the origin point.

You can even use the _blank target technique on named anchors in the same document, thereby emulating frames to some degree.

Summary

Whether they are links for Web site navigation or jumps to other related sites, hypertext links are an essential part of any Web page. Dreamweaver gives you full control over your inserted anchors.

✦ Through a unique URL, you can access virtually any Web page, graphic, or other item available on the Internet.

✦ The HyperText Transfer Protocol (HTTP) is the most common method of Web connection, but Web pages can link to most other formats, including FTP, e-mail, and newsgroups.

✦ Any of the three basic address formats — absolute, document relative, or site root relative — can be inserted in the Link text box of Dreamweaver's Property Inspector to create a link.

✦ Named anchors give you the power to jump to specific parts of any Web page, whether the page is the current one or located on another server.

✦ With the _blank target attribute, you can force a link to open in a new browser window, leaving your original available to the user.

In the next chapter, you'll see how to use the various types of lists in Dreamweaver.

✦   ✦   ✦

Creating Lists

In This Chapter

Bulleting your points

Using a numbered list

Building a glossary

Inserting menu and directory lists

Lists serve several different functions in all publications, including Web pages. A list can itemize a topic's points or catalog the properties of an object. A numbered list is helpful for giving step-by-step instructions. From a page designer's point-of-view, a list can break up the page and simultaneously draw the viewer's eye to key details.

Lists are an important alternative to the basic textual tools of paragraphs and headings. In this chapter, you study Dreamweaver's tools for designing and working with each of the three basic types of lists available under HTML:

- ✦ Unordered lists
- ✦ Ordered lists
- ✦ Definition lists

The various list types can be combined, as well, to create outlines. Dreamweaver supplies a straightforward method for building these *nested lists*.

Creating Bulleted (Unordered) Lists

What word-processing programs and layout artists refer to as bulleted lists are known in HTML as *unordered lists*. An unordered list is used when the sequence of the listed items is unimportant, as in a recipe's list of ingredients. Each unordered list item is set off by a leading character, and the remainder of the line is indented. By default, the leading character is the bullet; in HTML, you also can specify two other symbols by conventional means, and a custom bullet through Cascading Style Sheets.

You can either create the unordered list from scratch or convert existing text into the bulleted format.

To begin an unordered list from scratch, position the cursor where you want to start the list. Then click the Unordered List button supplied conveniently on the Text Property Inspector (see Figure 10-1), or use the Text ➪ Format ➪ Unordered List command.

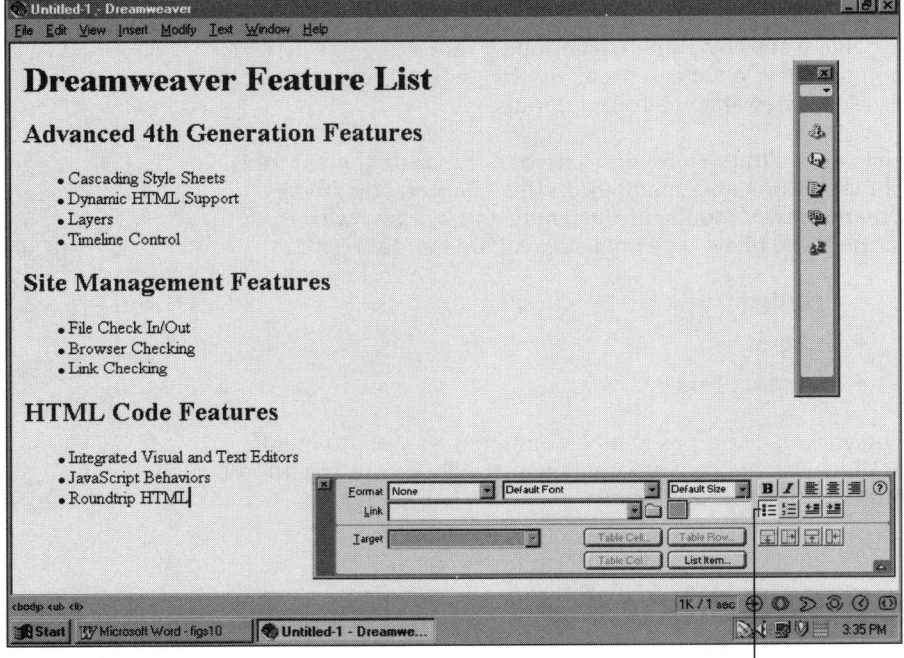

Unordered List button

Figure 10-1: An itemized list that doesn't need to be in any specific order is perfect to format as an unordered list.

If you are changing existing text into a list, select the paragraphs first and then execute the Unordered List button or menu command.

Dreamweaver creates one list item for every paragraph. As you can see from Figure 10-1, list items are generally rendered closer together than regular paragraphs. Unlike block elements such as paragraphs or headings, HTML doesn't insert additional lines above and space below each line of a list.

Caution

In terms of lists in Dreamweaver, the word *paragraph* is used literally to mean any text designated with a paragraph tag. Certainly you can apply a heading format to an HTML list, but you probably won't like the results: the heading format reinserts those additional lines below and above each list item — the ones generally not used by the list format. If you want your list items to appear larger in size, you should change the font size through the Property Inspector or with Text ➪ Size Increase.

Editing unordered lists

Once a series of paragraphs is formatted as an unordered list, you can easily add additional bulleted items. The basic editing techniques are the same for all types of lists:

✦ To continue adding items at the end of a list, simply press Enter (Return) to create each new paragraph. Another bullet is inserted.

✦ To insert an item in an unordered list, place your cursor at the end of the item above the desired position for the added item, and press Enter (Return).

✦ List items can be copied or cut and pasted in a different place on the list. Place your cursor in front of the list item below where you want the repositioned item to appear, and choose Edit ➪ Paste.

✦ To end a bulleted list, you can press Enter (Return) twice, or deselect the Unordered List button on the Text Property Inspector.

List tags

You may occasionally need to tweak your list code by hand. Two HTML tags are used in creating an unordered list. The first is the outer tag, which defines the type of list; the second is the item delimiter. Unordered lists are designated with the `<ul>...</ul>` tag pair, and the delimiter is the `<li>...</li>` pair. The unordered list code in the HTML Inspector looks like the following:

```
<ul>
   <li>Cascading Style Sheet Support</li>
   <li>Roundtrip HTML</li>
   <li>JavaScript Behaviors</li>
   <li>Repeatable Library Elements</li>
</ul>
```

If a list item is too long to fit in a single line, the browser indents the line when it wraps. By inserting a line break code, you can emulate this behavior even when you're working with lines that aren't long enough to need wrapping. To insert a line break, choose the Insert Line Break button from the Invisibles panel of the Objects Palette, or select Insert ➪ Line Break. Figure 10-2 shows examples of both approaches: the long paragraph that wraps naturally and the inserted line breaks to force the wrapping.

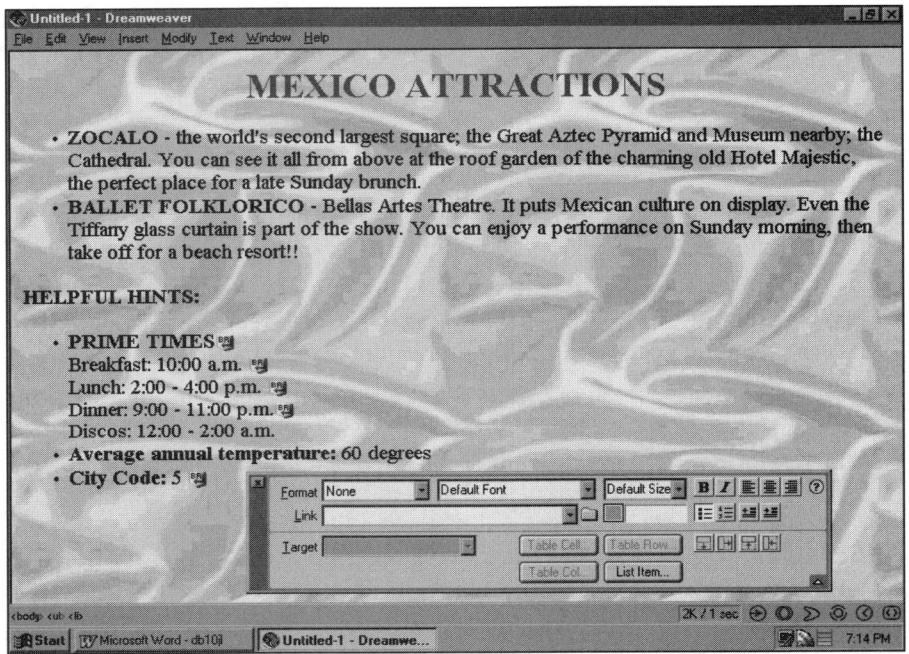

Figure 10-2: A list is indented if the text wraps around the screen or if you insert a line break.

Using other bullet symbols

Although HTML doesn't include a wide range of different symbols to use in an unordered list, you have a few options. Most browsers recognize three different bullet styles: bullet (the default), circle, and square. You can apply the style to the entire unordered list or to one list item at a time.

To change the bullet style of the overall unordered list, follow these steps:

1. Position your cursor where you want your new list to begin, or anywhere in an existing list.

2. If necessary, click the expander arrow on the Text Property Inspector to display the additional options. Click the List Item button.

3. In the List Properties dialog box that appears (Figure 10-3), open the Style options list.

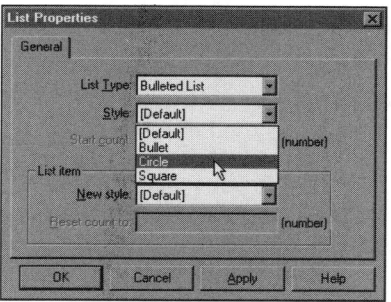

Figure 10-3: You can change the style of the entire list or just one list item through the List Properties dialog box.

4. Select one of the four options:

- **[Default]:** No style is listed and the browser applies its default, usually rendered as a bullet.
- **Bullet**: A solid circle.
- **Circle:** An open circle.
- **Square:** An open square.

5. Click OK.

Caution

If you find the List Item button inactive in your Text Property Inspector, make sure that you have — at most — one list item selected. Selecting more than one list item deactivates the List Item button.

When you try to change the style of just one list item, Dreamweaver alters all the successive list items as well. By default, list items don't specify a bullet style. Therefore, when a new style is inserted, all the following items adopt that style.

When you need to change the bullet style of just one item in a list, follow these steps:

1. Select the list item you wish to change.

2. Make sure the Text Property Inspector is expanded, and select the List Item button.

3. From the List Properties dialog box, in the List Item section, open the New Style drop-down list.

4. Select one of the four bullet options (described in the preceding steps).

You can alter the type of bullet used in two other ways. The time-tested solution substitutes a graphic for the bullet. Just as with graphical horizontal rules, the Web offers a substantial clip-art collection of bullets. You have to insert a graphic for each bullet, however. The quickest method is the drag-and-drop copy technique: Hold down the Ctrl (Command) key and then click and drag the bullet graphic — this sequence places a copy of the bullet wherever you release the mouse.

The newer technique for installing bullet styles uses style sheets. Style sheets can switch a list or list item's bullet style just as using the List Properties dialog box, but with a style sheet you can perform one additional task. You can assign the bullet style type to a specific file — in other words, you can customize your bullet image. The drawback to using this technique is that the list aspect of style sheets is currently only supported by Internet Explorer 4.0. Netscape browsers display the regular bullet symbol.

Cascading Style Sheets are covered in depth in Chapter 22. Here is a brief version of the steps for using a style sheet to assign a new bullet symbol:

1. Select the Style Palette button from the Launcher or choose Window ➪ Styles.
2. In the Style Inspector, select the Style Sheet button.
3. In the Edit Style Sheet dialog box, select the New button.
4. In the New Style dialog box, choose the Redefine HTML Tag radio button.
5. From the option list, choose the li tag and click OK.
6. In the Style Definition dialog box that appears, choose List in the Category list. See Figure 10-4.

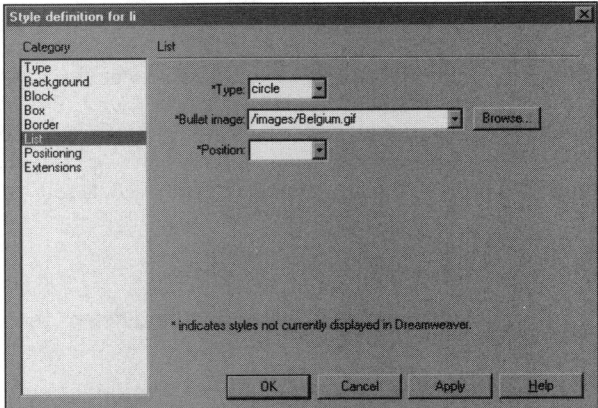

Figure 10-4: You can use Cascading Style Sheets to specify a bullet image for your Web page.

7. Find your graphics file by clicking the Browse button next to the Button Image text box (Figure 10-4).

8. Click OK, and then click Done in the Edit Style Sheet dialog box.

Note

Your newly defined bullet image doesn't preview in Dreamweaver, but you can view it in Internet Explorer 4.0.

Mastering Numbered Lists

Unlike a bulleted list, in which sequence is not vital, order is important in the numbered list. This relationship translates in HTML as "the opposite of an unordered list is an ordered list." The major advantage of an ordered list is the automatic generation of list item numbers and automatic renumbering when you're editing. If you've ever had to renumber a legal document because paragraph 14.b. became paragraph 2.a., then you recognize the timesaving benefits of this feature.

Ordered lists offer a slightly wider variety of built-in styles than unordered lists, but you cannot customize the leading character further. For instance, you cannot surround a character with parentheses or offset it with a dash. Once again, the browser is the final arbiter of how your list is viewed.

Many of the same techniques used with unordered lists work with ordered lists. To start a new numbered list in Dreamweaver, place your cursor where you want the new list to begin. Then, in the Text Property Inspector, select the Ordered List button or choose Text ➪ Format ➪ Ordered List.

As with unordered lists, you can also convert existing paragraphs into a numbered list. First select your text, and then select either the Ordered List button or the Text ➪ Format ➪ Ordered List command.

As shown in Figure 10-5, the default numbering system is Arabic numerals: 1, 2, 3, and so forth. In the following section, you learn how to alter this default.

Editing ordered lists

The HTML code for an ordered list is `<ol>`. Both the `<ol>` and the `<ul>` use the list item tag, `<li>`, to mark individual entries, and Dreamweaver handles the formatting identically:

```
<ol>
   <li>Stir in two sets of venetian blinds.</li>
   <li>Add one slowly rotating ceiling fan.</li>
   <li>Combine one flashing neon sign with one dangling light
bulb.</li>
   <li>Toss in 150 cubic yards of fog.</li>
   <li></li>
</ol>
```

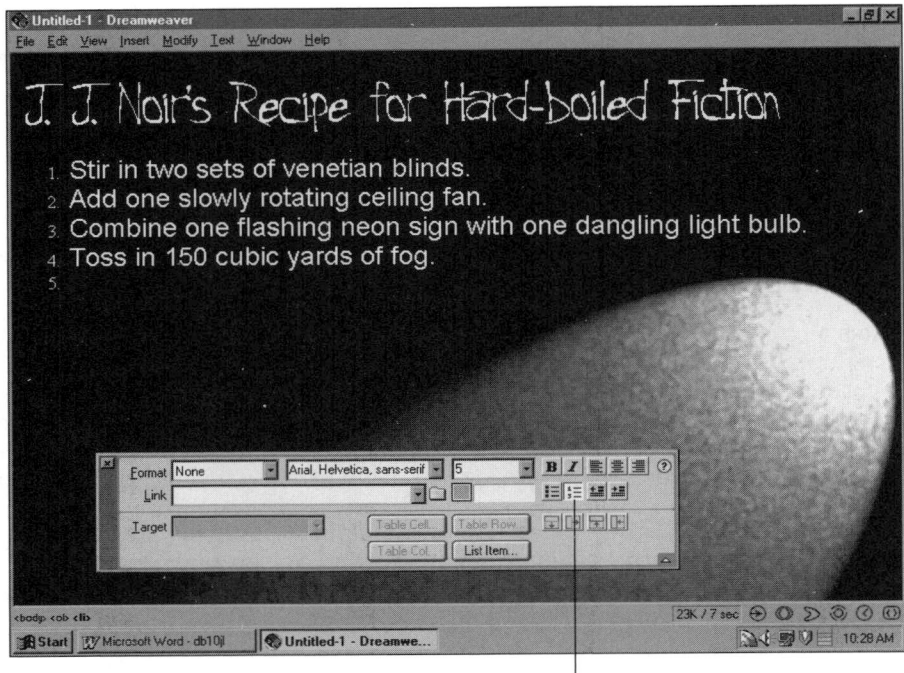

Ordered List button

Figure 10-5: Ordered lists are used on this page to create a numbered sequence.

The empty list item pair, $<$li$><$/li$>$, is displayed on the page as the next number in sequence.

Modifications to an ordered list are handled in the same manner as for an unordered list. The results are far more dramatic, however.

✦ To continue adding to the sequence of numbers, position your cursor at the end of the last item and press Enter (Return). The next number in sequence is generated, and any styles in use (such as font size or name) are carried over.

✦ To insert a new item in the list, put your cursor at the end of the item above where the new item will be positioned, and press Enter (Return). Dreamweaver inserts a new number in sequence and automatically renumbers the following numbers.

✦ To rearrange a numbered list, highlight the entire list item you want to move. Using the drag-and-drop method, release the mouse when your cursor is at the front of the item below the new location for the moved item.

✦ To end an item in a numbered list, press Enter (Return) twice or deselect the Ordered List button.

Using other numbering styles

In all, five different numbering styles can be applied to your numbered lists.

✦ *Arabic numerals (the default):* 1, 2, 3, and so forth.

✦ *Roman Small:* i, ii, iii, and so forth.

✦ *Roman Large:* I, II, III, and so forth.

✦ *Alphabet Small:* a, b, c, and so forth.

✦ *Alphabet Large:* A, B, C, and so forth.

You can restyle your entire list all at once, or you can just change a single list item. To change the style of the entire ordered list, follow these steps:

1. Position your cursor where you want the new list to begin or place the cursor anywhere in an existing list.

2. If necessary, click the expander arrow on the Text Property Inspector to display the additional options. Select the List Item button.

   The List Properties dialog box opens, with Numbered List showing as the List Type.

3. Open the drop-down list of Style options and choose any of the five preceding numbering types.

4. Click OK.

As with unordered lists, when you modify the style of one ordered list item, all the subsequent items adopt that style. To alter the style of a single and all subsequent items, follow these steps:

1. Select the item you wish to change.

2. In the expanded portion of the Text Property Inspector, select the List Item button.

3. In the List Properties dialog box from the List Item section, open the New Style list of options.

4. Select one of the five numbering options.

Cross-Reference

Although you can't automatically generate an outline with a different numbering system for each level, you can simulate this kind of outline with nested lists. See the following "Using Nested Lists" section in this chapter.

Making Definition Lists

A definition list is another list in HTML that doesn't use leading characters, such as bullets or numbers, in the list items. Definition lists are commonly used in glossaries or other types of documents where you have a list of terms followed by their description or explanation.

Browsers generally render a definition list with the definition term flush left and the definition data indented as shown in Figure 10-6. As you can see, no additional styling is added. You can, however, format either the item or the definition with the Text ⇨ Style options.

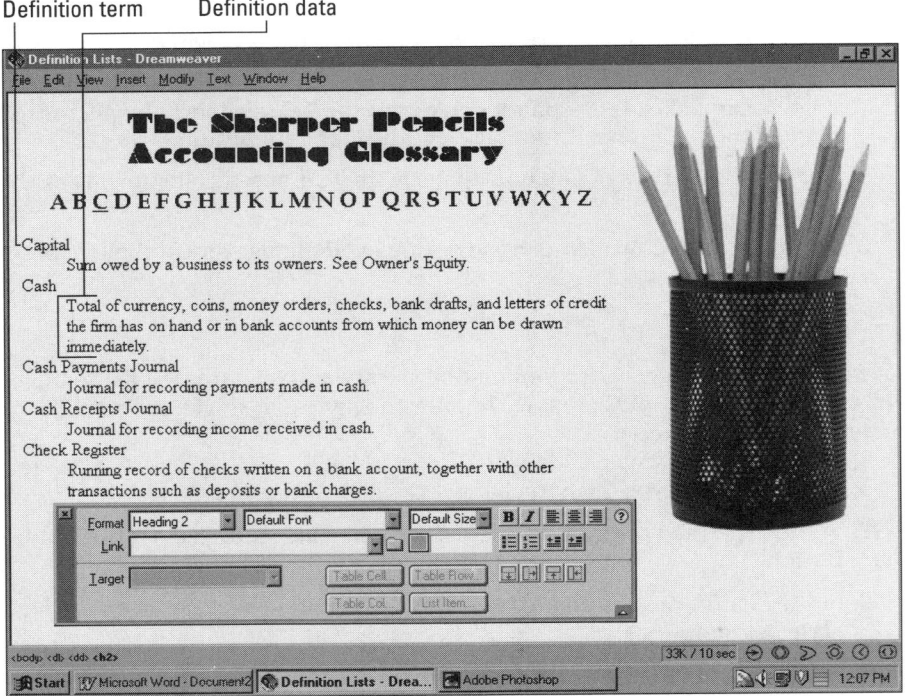

Figure 10-6: Definition lists are ideal for glossaries or other situations where you have a list of terms followed by their definition.

To begin your definition list in Dreamweaver, follow these steps:

1. Choose Text ➪ Format ➪ Definition List.

2. Type in the definition term and press Enter (Return) when you are finished. Dreamweaver indents the line.

3. Type in the definition data and press Enter (Return) when you are finished.

4. Repeat steps 2 and 3 until you have finished your definition list.

5. Press Enter (Return) twice to stop entering definition list items.

Tip If you have an extended definition, you may want to format it in more than one paragraph. Because definition lists are formatted with the terms and their definition data in alternating sequence, you have to use the line break tag, <br>, to create blank space under the definition if you want to separate it into paragraphs. Select the Insert Line Break button from the Object Palette to enter one or two <br> tags to separate paragraphs with one or two additional lines.

When you insert a definition list, Dreamweaver denotes it in code using the <dl>...</dl> tag pair. Definition terms are marked with a <dt> tag, and definition data uses the <dd> tag. A complete definition list looks like the following in HTML:

```
<dl>
  <dt>Capital</dt>
  <dd>Sum owed by a business to its owners. See Owner s
Equity.</dd>
  <dt>Cash</dt>
  <dd>Total of currency, coins, money orders, checks, bank
drafts, and letters
    of credit the firm has on hand or in bank accounts from
which money can be
    drawn immediately.</dd>
  <dt>Cash Payments Journal</dt>
  <dd>Journal for recording payments made in cash.</dd>
</dl>
```

When originally proposed by the World Wide Web Consortium, the <dt> column was intended to take up only one-third of the browser window, but the latest, most common browsers don't follow this design specification.

Tip You can vary the structure of a definition list from the standard definition term followed by the definition data format, but you have to code this variation by hand. For instance, if you want to have a series of consecutive terms with no definition in between, you need to insert the <dt>...</dt> pairs directly in the HTML Inspector.

Using Nested Lists

You can combine—*nest*—lists in almost any fashion. For instance, you can mix an ordered and an unordered list to create a numbered list with bulleted points. You can have one numbered list inside of another numbered list. You can also start with one numbering style such as Roman Large, switch to another style such as Alphabet Small, and return to Roman Large to continue the sequence (like an outline).

Dreamweaver offers an easy route for making nested lists. The Indent button in the Text Property Inspector—when used within a list—automatically creates a nested list. As an example, the ordered list in Figure 10-7 has a couple of bulleted points (or unordered list items) inserted within it. Notice how the new items are indented one level.

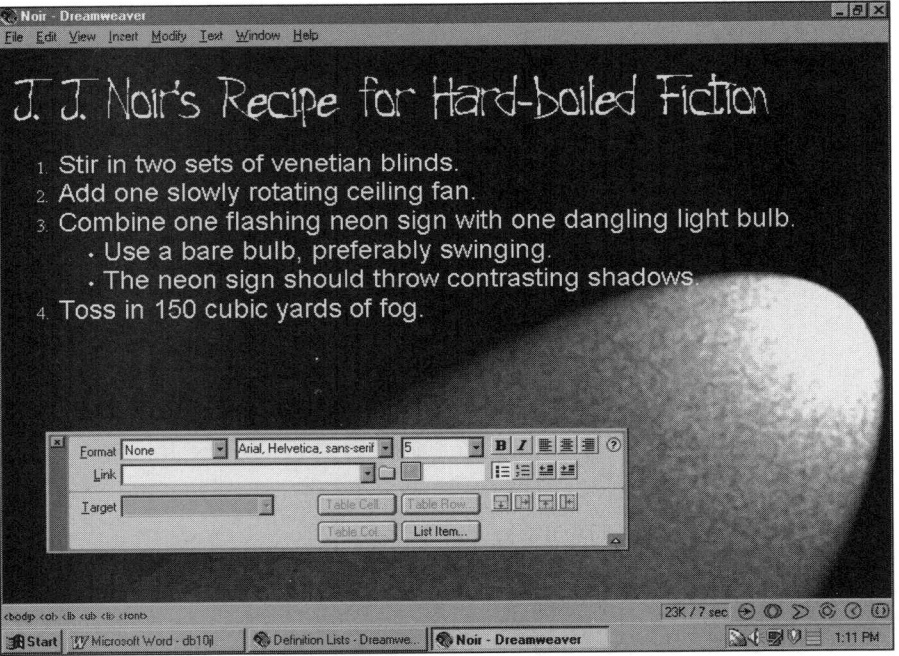

Figure 10-7: Dreamweaver automatically generates the code necessary to build nested lists when you use the Indent button on the Property Inspector.

Follow these steps to create a nested list in Dreamweaver:

1. Select the text in the Document Window that you want to reformat with a different style.

2. In the Text Property Inspector, choose the Indent button. You can also select the Text ➪ Indent command. Dreamweaver indents the selected text and creates a separate list in the HTML code with the original list's properties.

3. Go to the List Properties dialog box and select another list type or style, as described in preceding sections.

Caution

You can unnest your list and reverse the effects of the Indent button by selecting the Outdent button in the Text Property Inspector or choosing Text ➪ Outdent. Be careful, however, when selecting your text for this operation. When you use the mouse to perform a click-and-drag selection, Dreamweaver tends to grab the closing list item tag above your intended selection. A better way to highlight the text in this case uses the Tag Selector in the status bar. Place the cursor in the indented list you want to outdent, and choose the innermost `<ol>` or `<ul>` tag from the Tag Selector.

To examine the origins of the term *nested list*, take a look at the code created for this list type by Dreamweaver:

```
<ol>
   <li>Stir in two sets of venetian blinds.</li>
   <li>Add one slowly rotating ceiling fan.</li>
   <li>Combine one flashing neon sign with one dangling light
bulb.</li>
      <ul>
         <li>Use a bare bulb, preferably swinging.</li>
         <li>The neon sign should throw contrasting shadows.</li>
      </ul>
   <li>Toss in 150 cubic yards of fog.</li>
</ol>
```

Notice how the unordered tag pair, `<ul>...</ul>`, is completely contained between the ordered list items.

Caution

If you don't indent your list items before you change the list format, Dreamweaver breaks the current list into three separate lists: one for the original list above the selected text, another for the selected text itself, and a third list for the items following the selected text. If you don't want this arrangement, choose the Indent button in the Text Property Inspector, and Dreamweaver nests the list as described previously.

Accessing Special List Types

Dreamweaver gives you access to a couple of special-use list types: menu lists and directory lists. When the tags for these lists — `<menu>` and `<dir>`, respectively — were included in the HTML 2.0 specification, they were intended to offer several ways to present lists of short items. Unfortunately, browsers tend to render both tags in the same manner: as an unordered list. You can use Cascading Style Sheets to restyle these built-in tags for use in 4.0 and higher browsers.

Menu lists

A menu list generally comprises single items, with each item on its own individual line.

Tip   Because menu lists are rendered as unordered lists with leading bullets, you'll probably want to display the menu list in a more compact manner. Add the attribute `compact` as follows:

```
<menu compact>
```

To apply a menu list style, follow these steps:

1. In an existing list, select one item that you want to convert to a menu list.
2. In the expanded Text Property Inspector, select the List Item button.
3. In the List Properties dialog box, open the List Type drop-down list and choose Menu List, as shown in Figure 10-8.

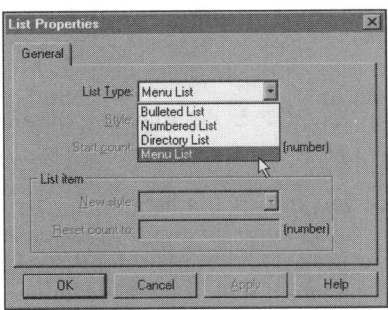

Figure 10-8: Making a menu list

4. Click OK.

Tip

To apply CSS techniques to either the `<menu>` or the `<dir>` tags in Dreamweaver, you must either hand-code all of the entry, or use a little trick to hand-code just a small portion. Here's the trick: because Dreamweaver doesn't list the menu or directory list tags in its list of HTML tags to redefine, you select an unused entry such as `<samp>` or `<var>` to redefine. You can still apply all the necessary style sheet changes, including list positioning. When you've finished, open the HTML Inspector, go to the Style definition section, and change your placeholder value ("samp") to "menu" or "dir".

Directory lists

The directory list was originally intended to provide Web designers with an easy way to create multiple-column lists of short items. Unfortunately, the most current browsers present the directory list's items in one long list rather than in columns.

The directory list format is applied in the same way as the menu list and, here as well, most browsers render the format as an unordered list with bullets.

To apply a directory list style, follow these steps:

1. In the current list, select one item you want to convert to a directory list.

2. In the expanded Text Property Inspector, select the List Item button.

3. In the List Properties dialog box, open the List Type list and choose Directory List, as shown in Figure 10-8.

4. Click OK.

Tip

Nested directory lists exhibit a cool feature in most browsers — they automatically change the list style for each level. In many browsers, the outermost level is displayed with a bullet, the second level with a circle, and the third level with a square. Automatic outlining from an unexpected source! One drawback to note: Dreamweaver doesn't preview the changing styles — it only shows the bullets.

Summary

Lists are extremely useful to the Web site designer from the perspectives of both content and layout. Dreamweaver offers point-and-click control over the full range of list capabilities.

✦ The three primary list types in HTML are unordered, ordered, and definition lists.

✦ Unordered lists are used when you want to itemize your text in no particular order. Dreamweaver can apply any of the three built-in styles to unordered lists or enable you to customize your own list style through style sheets.

✦ An ordered list is a numbered list. Items are automatically numbered when added, and the entire list is renumbered when items are rearranged or deleted. Dreamweaver gives you access to five different styles of numbering — everything from regular Arabic 1-2-3 to the Roman numerals I-II-III.

✦ Definition lists are designed to display glossaries and other documents in which terms are followed by definitions. A definition list is generally rendered without leading characters such as bullets or numbers; instead, the list terms are displayed flush left, and the definitions are indented.

✦ Dreamweaver gives you the power to nest your lists at the touch of a button — the Indent button on the Text Property Inspector. Nested lists enable you to show different outline levels, and to mix ordered and unordered lists.

✦ Menu and directory lists are also supported by Dreamweaver. Both of these special lists render in a similar fashion, but they can be adapted through style sheets for extensive use.

In the next chapter, you'll see how to create and use tables in Dreamweaver.

✦   ✦   ✦

Incorporating Advanced HTML

Setting Up Tables

Tables bring structure to a Web page. Whether used to align numbers in a spreadsheet or to arrange columns of text on a page, an HTML table brings a bit of order to otherwise free-flowing content. Initially, tables were implemented to present raw data in a more readable format. More recently, Web designers have taken up tables as the most capable tool to control page layout.

Dreamweaver's implementation of tables reflects this current trend in Web page design. Drag-and-drop table sizing, easy organization of rows and columns, and instant table reformatting all help get the job done in the shortest time possible. Although the absolute positioning capabilities offered by Dynamic HTML give Web designers a more exact layout control, the browsers that support tables are far more prevalent than those that support DHTML. In other words, HTML tables are going to be around for a long time.

HTML Table Fundamentals

A table is basically a grid that expands as you add text or images. Tables consist of three main components: rows, columns, and cells. *Rows* go across a table from left to right, and *columns* go up and down. A *cell* is the intersection of a row and a column; it's where you enter your information. Cells expand to fit whatever they hold. If you have enabled the table *border*, your browser shows the outline of the table and all its cells.

In HTML, all the structure and all the data of a table are contained between the table tag pair, `<table>` and `</table>`. The `<table>` tag can take numerous attributes to affect a table's width and height (which can be given in absolute measurement or as a percentage of the screen), as well as the border, alignment on the page, and background color. You can also control the size of the spacing between cells and the amount of padding within cells.

HTML uses a strict hierarchy when describing a table. You can see this very clearly in Listing 11-1 which shows the HTML generated from a default table in Dreamweaver.

Listing 11-1: Code for an HTML Table

```
<table border= 1  width= 75% >
  <tr>
    <td> </td>
    <td> </td>
    <td> </td>
  </tr>
  <tr>
    <td> </td>
    <td> </td>
    <td> </td>
  </tr>
  <tr>
    <td> </td>
    <td> </td>
    <td> </td>
  </tr>
</table>
```

Note

The   seen in the table code is HTML for a nonbreaking space. Dreamweaver inserts the code in each empty table cell because some browsers collapse the cell without it. Enter any text or image in the cell and Dreamweaver automatically removes the   code.

Rows

After the opening <table> tag comes the first row tag, <tr>. Within the current row, you can specify attributes for horizontal alignment or vertical alignment. In addition, recent browsers recognize row color as an added option.

Cells

Cells are marked in HTML with the <td>...</td> tag pair. There is no specific code for a column; rather, columns are seen as the number of cells within a row. For example, in Listing 1-1, notice there are three sets of <td> tags between each <tr> pair. This means the table has three columns. A cell can span more than one row or column—in these cases you'll see a rowspan=value or colspan=value attribute in the <td> tag.

Cells can also be given horizontal or vertical alignment attributes; these attributes override any like attributes specified by the table row. When you give a cell a particular width, all the cells in that column are affected. Width can be specified in either an absolute pixel measurement or as a percentage of the overall table.

Tip

After the initial <table> tag, you can place an optional caption for the table. In Dreamweaver, you have to enter the <caption> tag by hand or through your text editor. A third option is to use the Enhanced Table Object, included on this book's CD-ROM in the Dreamweaver/Configuration/Objects/Common folder.

Column/row headings

A special type of cell called a *table header* used for column and row headings. Information in these cells is marked with a <th> tag and is generally rendered in boldface, centered within the cell.

Inserting Tables in Dreamweaver

You can control almost all of a table's HTML features through Dreamweaver's point-and-click interface. To insert a Dreamweaver table in the current cursor position, use one of the following three methods:

✦ Select the Insert Table button in the Object Palette.

✦ Choose Insert ➪ Table from the menus.

✦ Use the keyboard shortcut: Ctrl-Alt-T or Command-Option-T.

The Insert Table dialog box, shown in Figure 11-1, contains default values when it is first displayed. The initial Dreamweaver table has 3 rows and 3 columns. Just replace the default values in the Rows and the Columns text boxes to change the number of rows and columns needed for your table. If you aren't sure of the number of rows/columns you'll need, put in your best guess — you can add or delete rows or columns as necessary.

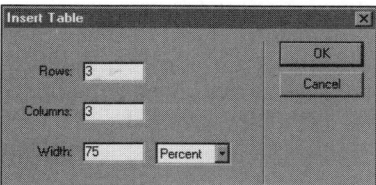

Figure 11-1: The Insert Table dialog box starts out with a default three columns and three rows; you can adjust as needed.

The default table is sized to take up 75 percent of the browser window. You can alter this percentage by changing the value in the Width text box. The table will maintain this proportion as you add text or images, except in two conditions:

✦ When an image is larger than the specified percentage.

✦ When the nowrap attribute is used for the cell or table row and there is too much text to fit.

In either case, the percentage set for the table is ignored and the cell and table expand to accommodate the text or image.

For further information on the nowrap attribute see the section on cell wrap, later in this chapter.

There's an Enhanced Table Object available on the accompanying CD-ROM that includes added general table attributes such as caption. It also supports font selection for every cell. You'll find the Enhanced Table Object in the Dreamweaver/Configuration/Objects/Common folder as the files etable.htm and etable.gif.

If you prefer to enter the table width as an absolute pixel value as opposed to the relative percentage, type the number of pixels in the Width text box and select pixels in the drop-down list of width options.

Figure 11-2 shows three tables: At the top is the default table with the width set to 75 percent. The middle table, set to 100 percent, will take up the full width of the browser window. The third table is fixed at 400 pixels — half of an 800×600 window.

You don't have to declare a width for your table at all. If you delete the value in the Width text box of the Insert Table dialog box, your table will start out as small as possible and will only expand to accommodate inserted text or images.

Setting table preferences

There are two preferences that directly affect tables. Both can be set by choosing Edit ⇨ Preferences and looking in the General category.

The first pertinent option is the Show Dialog when Inserting Objects check box. If this option is turned off, Dreamweaver will always insert a default table (3 rows by 3 columns at 75 percent width of the screen), without displaying a dialog box and asking for your input. Should you wish to change these values, you can adjust them from the Table Property Inspector once the table has been inserted.

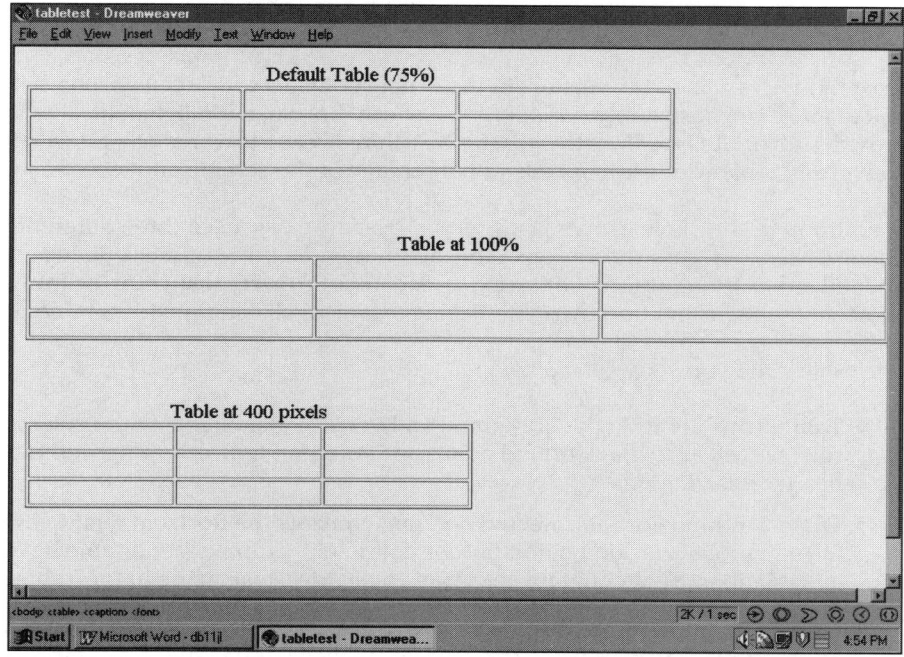

Figure 11-2: The width of a table can be relative to the browser window, or set to an absolute width in pixels.

Cross-Reference

The Insert Table dialog box is a Dreamweaver Object and can be modified to create new default settings. For more information on how to build and alter Dreamweaver Objects, see Chapter 16 "Creating and Using Objects."

The second notable preference is the one labeled Faster Table Update (Semi-WYSIWYG). Because tables expand and contract dynamically depending on their contents, Dreamweaver gives you the option to turn off the continual updating. (Depending on the speed of your system, the updating can slow down your table input.) If the Faster Update option is enabled, the table is updated whenever you click outside of it or when you press the keyboard shortcut, Ctrl-Space (Command-Space).

You'll want to decide whether to leave the Faster Update option on or turn it off, depending on your system and the complexity of your tables. Nested tables tend to update more slowly, and you may need to take advantage of the Faster Update option if tables aren't getting redrawn quickly enough. I recommend turning off Faster Update until it seems that you need it.

Modifying Tables

Most modifications to tables start in the Property Inspector. Dreamweaver helps you manage the basic table parameters — width, border, and alignment — as well as provides attributes for the other useful but more arcane features of a table, such as converting table width from pixels to percentage of the screen, and vice versa.

In addition to the Table Property Inspector, Dreamweaver uses three different dialog boxes to access the various table attributes. All three of these dialogs are opened either from buttons on the expanded Text Property Inspector, or from the shortcut menu brought up by right-clicking (Control-clicking) inside a table.

The table dialog boxes are as follows:

✦ **Table Row.** Controls the horizontal and vertical alignment for the selected row, as well as its background color, border color, text wrapping, and table header designations.

✦ **Table Column.** For the selected column, controls the horizontal and vertical alignment, background color, border color, text wrapping, and table header designations. Table Column selections override those made in the Table Row dialog box. The width of the column can also be specified here.

✦ **Table Cell:** Controls the horizontal and vertical alignment for the selected cell, as well as background color, border color, text wrapping, and table header designation. Table Cell selections override those made in *both* the Table Column and the Table Row dialog boxes.

In this section, you see how to edit a table's contents, modify its overall properties, and alter the attributes of a table row, column, and cell.

Editing a table's contents

Before you see how to change a table's attributes, let's look at basic editing techniques. Editing text in Dreamweaver tables is slightly different from editing text outside of tables. For example, you can only modify one cell at a time, as opposed to changing numerous paragraphs simultaneously.

When you begin to enter text into a table cell, the table borders expand to accommodate your new data. The other cells appear to shrink, but they, too, will grow once you start typing in text or inserting an image. Unless a cell's width is specified, the cell currently being edited expands or contracts, and the other cells are forced to adjust their width. Figure 11-3 shows the same table (with one row and three columns) in three different states. In the top table, only the first cell contains text; notice how the other cells have contracted. In the middle table, text has been entered into the second cell, as well, and you can see how the first cell is now smaller. Finally, in the bottom table, all three cells contain text, and the other two cells have adjusted their width to compensate for the expanding third cell.

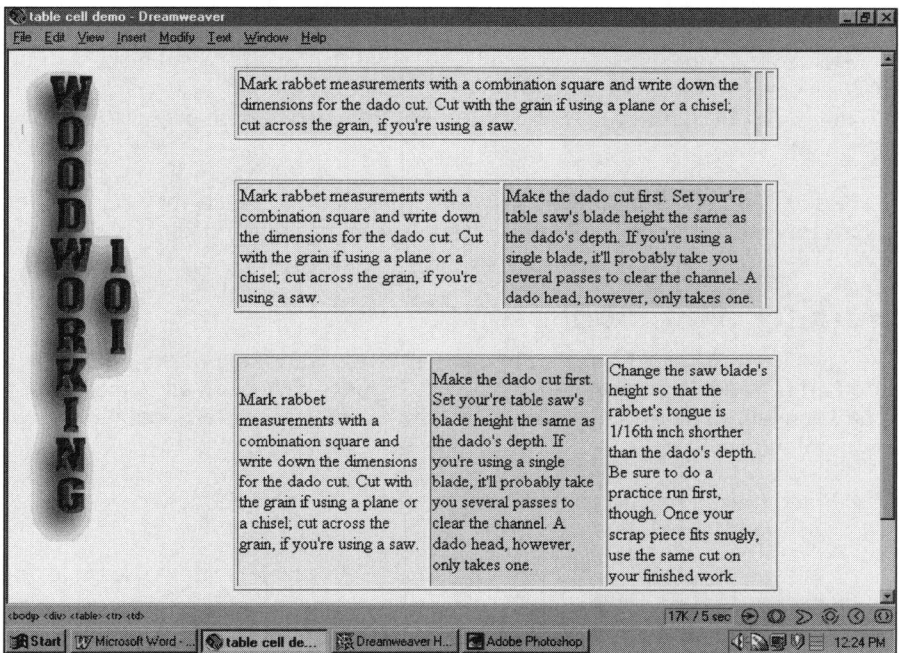

Figure 11-3: As text is entered into a cell, the cell grows; other cells get smaller, even if they already contain text.

If you look closely at the bottom table Figure 11-3, you can also see how the text doesn't line up vertically. That's because the default vertical alignment in Dreamweaver, as in most browsers, provides for entries to be positioned in the middle of the cell. (You'll see later in this section how to adjust the vertical alignment.)

Text in a table can be cut, copied, and pasted just like any other text. The drag-and-drop feature is especially useful when editing text in tables. Once you've selected any text — up to an entire cell — you can drag it to a new location. You can also copy text in this manner; just hold down the Ctrl (Option) key as you drag.

Tip

The fastest way to select all the text in the current cell is often by selecting the `<td>` tag from the Tag Selector in the Status Bar.

Moving through a table

When you've finished entering your text in the first cell, you can move to the next cell in the row by pressing the Tab key. When you reach the end of a row, pressing Tab takes your cursor to the first cell of the next row. To go backward, cell to cell, press Shift-Tab.

The Home and End keys take you to the beginning and end, respectively, of the cursor's current line. To move to the top of the current cell, press Ctrl-Home (Command-Home). And to get the bottom of the current cell, press Ctrl-End (Command-End).

Tip Pressing Tab has a special function when you're in the last cell of a row — it adds a new row, with the same column configuration as the current one.

Working with table properties

The `<table>` tag has a large number of attributes, and most of them can be modified through Dreamweaver's Property Inspector. As with all objects, the table must be selected before it can be altered. Because of the interdependencies of rows, columns and cells, you have to select the table in one of the following ways:

✦ Place the cursor anywhere in the current table and choose the `<table>` tag in the Tag Selector.

✦ Open the shortcut menu by right-clicking (Control-clicking) the table and choosing Select Table.

✦ Click just outside of the table, and then drag the mouse over the table until it is completely highlighted. If you accidentally select any additional tags, such as a `<p>` tag, the Property Inspector will not change to show the Table options.

Once you've selected the table, if the Property Inspector is open it will present the table properties as shown in Figure 11-4. Otherwise, you can open the Table Property Inspector by choosing Window ➪ Properties Inspector.

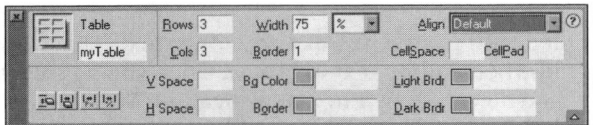

Figure 11-4: The expanded Table Property Inspector gives you control over all the tablewide attributes.

Setting Alignment

Aligning a table in Dreamweaver goes beyond the expected left, right and center options — you can also make a table into a free-floating object around which text can wrap to the left or right.

There are two different HTML methods to aligning a table, and each gives you a different effect. Using the text alignment method (Text ➪ Alignment) results in the conventional positioning (left, right, and center); and using the Table Property Inspector method lets you have text wrapped around your realigned table. Figure 11-5 compares some of the different results you get from aligning your table with the two methods.

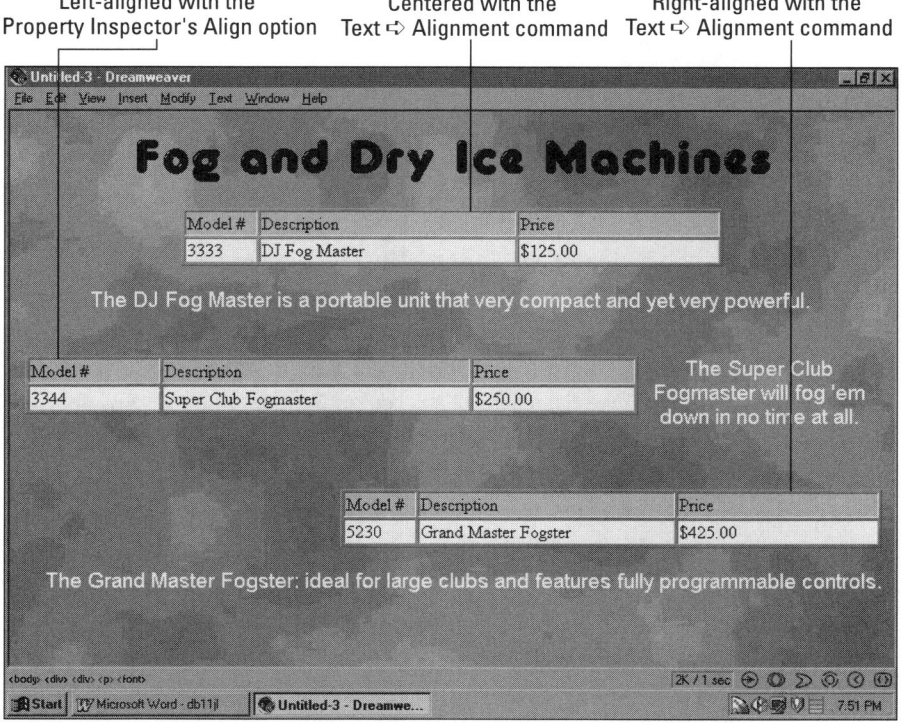

Figure 11-5: Tables can be centered, as well as aligned left or right — with or without text wrapping.

To align your table *without* text wrapping, follow these steps:

1. Select your table using one of the methods described earlier.

2. In the Property Inspector, make sure the Align option is set to Default.

3. Select the Text ➪ Alignment command, and then choose one of the three options: Left, Center or Right.

   Dreamweaver surrounds your table code with a division tag pair, `<div>...</div>`, with an `align` attribute set to your chosen value.

To align your table with text wrapping, making your table into a floating object, follow these steps:

1. Select the table.

2. In the Table Property Inspector, open the Align drop-down list and choose one of the four options:

Alignment Option	Result
Default	No alignment is written. Table aligns to the browser's default, usually left, with no text wrapping.
Left	Aligns the table to the left side of the browser window and wraps text around the right side.
Right	Aligns the table to the right side of the browser window and wraps text around the left side.
Center	The table aligns to the center of the browser window. Text does not wrap around either side. Note: This alignment option only works with 4.0 browsers and higher and it does not preview in Dreamweaver.

Dreamweaver codes these alignment attributes in the `<table>` tag. As with floating images, Dreamweaver places an anchor point for floating elements on the Web page. However, unlike most other Invisible symbols, you cannot drag-and-drop or cut-and-paste the anchor point for a floating table.

Caution   Bear in mind that choosing Center as the Align option in the Property Inspector is somewhat problematical in terms of browser compatibility. Until more browsers recognize this option, using the Text ➪ Alignment command for centering tables produces the widest browser compatibility.

Resizing a table

The primary sizing control on the Table Property Inspector is the Width text box. You can enter a new width value for the entire table in either a screen percentage or pixels. Just enter your value in the Width text box, and then select % or pixels in the drop-down list of options.

Dreamweaver also provides a very quick and intuitive way to resize the overall table width, column widths, or row height. Pass your pointer over any of the table's borders, and the pointer becomes a two-headed arrow; this is the *resizing pointer*. When you see the resizing pointer, you can click and drag any border to a new position.

As noted earlier, tables are initially sized according to their content. Once you move a table border in Dreamweaver, however, the new sizes are written directly into the HTML code and the column width or row height is fixed — unless the content cannot fit. If, for example, an inserted image is 115 pixels wide and the cell has a width of only 90 pixels, the cell expands to fit the image. The same is true if you try to fit an extremely long, unbroken text string, such as a complex URL, in a cell that's too narrow to hold the string.

With the exception of cell width set through the Table Column Properties dialog box, the only way to tell the measurement of a table or cell is to look at the HTML. When a table is resized, the width attribute in the <table> tag is altered. Changes to a cell or column's width are shown in the <td> tags, as are changes to a row's height, using the width and height attribute, respectively.

Here's the HTML for an empty table, resized:

```
<table border= 1  width= 70% >
  <tr>
    <td width= 21% > </td>
    <td width= 34% > </td>
    <td width= 45% > </td>
  </tr>
  <tr>
    <td width= 21%  height= 42 > </td>
    <td width= 34%  height= 42 > </td>
    <td width= 45%  height= 42 > </td>
  </tr>
  <tr>
    <td width= 21%  height= 42 > </td>
    <td width= 34%  height= 42 > </td>
    <td width= 45%  height= 42 > </td>
  </tr>
</table>
```

Notice how all the widths for the cells and the entire table are expressed as percentages. If the table width were initially set at a pixel value, the cell widths would have been, too. The row height values, on the other hand, are shown as an absolute measurement in pixels.

You can switch from percentages to pixels in all the table measurements, and even clear all the values at once — with the click of a button. There are four measurement controls in the lower-left portion of the expanded Table Property Inspector, as shown in Figure 11-6.

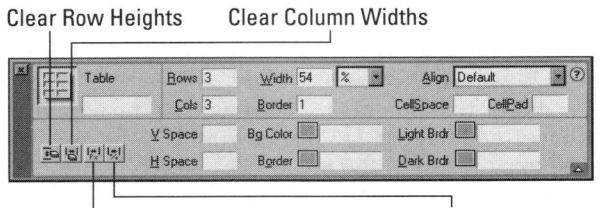

Figure 11-6: You can make tablewide changes with the four control buttons on the Table Property Inspector.

From left to right, the measurement controls are as described in the following table.

Measurement Control Buttons	Description
Clear Row Heights	Erases all the height attributes in the current table.
Clear Column Widths	Deletes all the width attributes found in the `<td>` tags.
Convert Table Widths to Pixels	Translates the current widths of all cells and for the full table from percentages to pixels.
Convert Table Widths to Percent	Translates the current widths of all cells and for the full table from pixels to percentages.

If you clear both row heights and column widths, the table goes back to its "grow as needed" format and, if empty, shrinks to its smallest possible size.

Caution   When converting width percentages to pixels, and vice versa, keep in mind that the percentages are relative to the size of the *browser* window — and in the development phase that browser window is Dreamweaver. You'll want to expand Dreamweaver's document window to the same size as what you expect to be seen in the browser.

Inserting and deleting rows and columns

The default Dreamweaver table configuration of three columns and three rows can be changed at any time. You can add rows or columns almost anywhere in a table, except above the top row or to the left of the first column.

There are three methods for adding a row:

✦ Position the cursor in the last cell of the last row, and press Tab to add a new row below the present one.

✦ Increase the number of rows indicated in the Rows text box of the Table Property Inspector. All new rows added in this manner appear below the last table row.

✦ Right-click (Control-click) to open the shortcut menu, and select Insert Row. Rows added in this way are inserted below the current row.

There are only two ways to add a new column to your table:

✦ Increase the number of columns indicated in the Cols text box of the Table Property Inspector. Columns added in this way appear to the right of the last column.

✦ Right-click (Control-click) to open the shortcut menu, and select Insert Column from the shortcut menu. The column is inserted to the right of the current column.

When you want to delete a column or row, you can use either the shortcut menu or the Table Property Inspector. On the shortcut menu, you can remove the current column or row by choosing Delete Column or Delete Row, respectfully. Using the Table Property Inspector, you can delete multiple columns and rows by reducing the numbers in the Cols or Rows text boxes. Columns are deleted from the right side of the table, and rows are removed from the bottom.

Caution   Watch out—exercise extreme caution when deleting columns or rows. Dreamweaver does not ask for confirmation and will remove these columns and/or rows whether or not there is data in them.

Setting table borders and backgrounds

Borders are the solid outlines of the table itself. A border's width is measured in pixels; the default width is 1 pixel. This width can be altered in the Border field of the Table Property Inspector.

You can make the border invisible by specifying a border of 0 width. You can still resize your table by clicking and dragging the borders, even when there are no borders visible.

When the border is visible, you can also see each cell outlined. The width of the outline around the cells stays constant, regardless of the width of the border. However, you can control the amount of space between each cell with the CellSpace value in the Table Property Inspector, covered later in this chapter.

To change the width of a border in Dreamweaver, select your table and enter a new value in the Border text box. With a wider border, you can see the default shading: the top and left side are a lighter shade, and the bottom and right sides are darker. This gives the table border a pseudo-3D appearance. Figure 11-7 shows single-cell tables with borders of various widths.

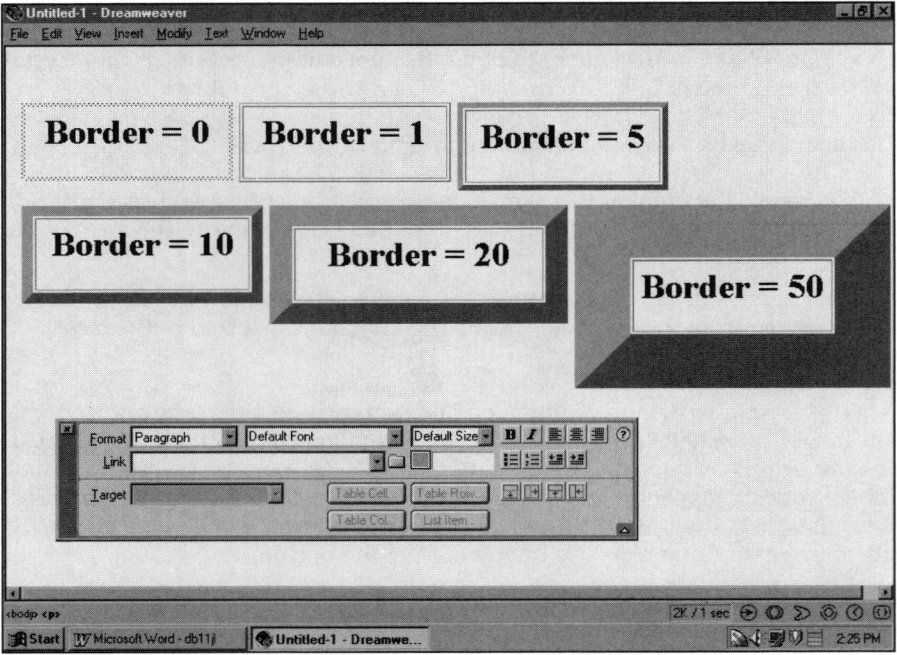

Figure 11-7: Changing the width of the border can give your table a 3D look.

In Dreamweaver, you can assign colors to the border, and to both the light and dark sides of the border. Each of these colors is chosen through the Table Property Inspector, as follows:

✦ To choose a color for the border, select the Border color swatch, or enter a color name in the adjacent text box.

✦ To choose a color for the light (top and left) border, select the Light Brdr color swatch or enter a color name in the adjacent text box.

✦ To choose a color for the dark (bottom and right) border, select the Dark Brdr color swatch or enter a color name in the adjacent text box.

If you assign a border color, it is overridden by any Light Brdr and/or Dark Brdr choices.

Tip

You can change the "light source" of the shadow for your table. To make the light appear to come from the bottom-right instead of the upper-left, choose a dark shade for the Light Brdr color and a light shade for the Dark Brdr color.

In addition to colored borders, a table can also have a colored background. (By default, the table is initially transparent.) Choose the background color in the Table Property Inspector, by selecting a color in the Bg Color color swatch or entering a color name in the adjacent text box. As you'll see later in the chapter, you can also assign background colors to rows, columns, and individual cells — if used, these specific colors all override the background color of the overall entire table.

Working with cellspacing and cellpadding

HTML gives you two methods to add white space in tables. *Cellspacing* controls the width between each cell, and *cellpadding* controls the margins within each cell. These values can be set independently through the Table Property Inspector.

Tip

Although not indicated in the Property Inspector, the default value is 2 pixels for both cellspacing and cellpadding. Some Web page designs call for a close arrangement of cells and are better served by changing either (or both) the CellSpace or CellPad values to one or zero.

To change the amount of white space *between each cell* in a table, enter a new value in the CellSpace text box of the Table Property Inspector. If you want to adjust the amount of white space *between the borders of the cell and the actual cell data,* alter the value in the CellPad text box of the Table Property Inspector. Figure 11-8 shows an example of a table with wide (20 pixels) cellspacing and cellpadding values.

Changing rowspan and colspan

You have seen how cells in HTML tables can extend across (*span*) multiple columns or rows. By default, a cell spans one column or one row. Increasing a cell's span lets you group any number of topics under one heading. To increase and decrease the cell's row or column span, you use the four buttons found at the lower-left of the Table Property Inspector, as described in Table 11-1.

Cellspacing⎯⎯⎯ Cellpadding⎯⎯⎯

Figure 11-8: You can add additional white space between each cell (cellspacing) or within each cell (cellpadding).

Table 11-1
Buttons for Controlling Row/Column Span

Button	Command	Description
	Increase Row Span	Joins the current cell with the cell below it.
	Decrease Row Span	Separates two or more cells previously spanned, from the bottom cell.
	Increase Column Span	Joins the current cell with the cell immediately to its right.
	Decrease Column Span	Separates two or more cells previously spanned, from the right edge.

Existing text or images are put in the same cell if the cells containing them are joined to span rows or columns. Figure 11-9 shows a table containing both row and column spanning.

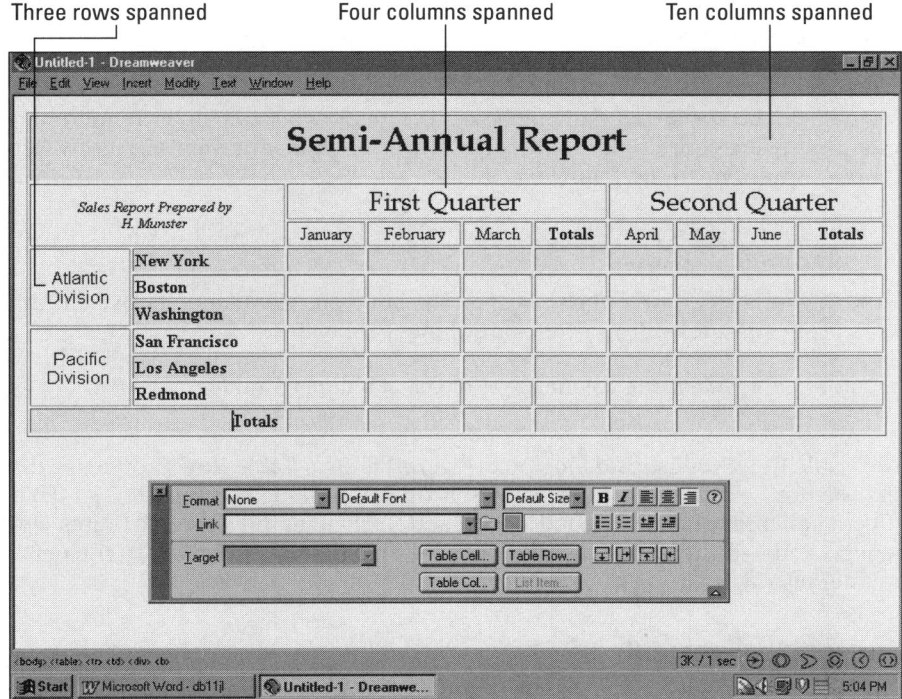

Three rows spanned   Four columns spanned   Ten columns spanned

Figure 11-9: This spreadsheet-like report was built using Dreamweaver's row- and column-spanning features.

Caution

When you need to build a complex table such as this one, it's best to try and map out your table before you begin constructing it. Keep in mind that Dreamweaver can't split a cell into two columns or rows; it can only combine existing ones. If you don't plan carefully, you'll find yourself having to move all of your data, one cell at a time.

One trick: Right-click (hold-click) the table and choose Insert Column or Increase Row from the shortcut menu. Now you can use the span buttons to create the table look you want without cutting and pasting data.

Setting cell, column, and row properties

In addition to the overall table controls, Dreamweaver helps you set numerous properties for individual cells one at a time, by the column or by the row. When there are overlapping or conflicting attributes, such as different background colors for a cell in the same row and column, the more specific target wins out. The hierarchy, from most general to most specific is as follows: tables, rows, columns, and finally cells.

You can call up the specific dialog boxes in one of two ways. In both methods, you must first place your cursor in the cell, row or column you want to modify. Then choose either one of the following:

- ✦ In the Table Property Inspector, click the Table Cell, Table Row, or Table Col (for column) button.
- ✦ Right-click (Control-click) to open the shortcut menu and choose either Cell Properties, Row Properties, or Column Properties.

Tip   You can only select one column, row, or cell at a time to modify.

The Table Cell Properties dialog box (Figure 11-10A), Table Row Properties dialog box (Figure 11-10B), and Table Column Properties dialog box (Figure 11-11C) each affect similar attributes. The following sections explain how the attributes work in general and — if there are any differences — specifically in regards to the cell, column or row.

Horizontal alignment

You can set the Horizontal Alignment attribute, `align`, to specify the default alignment, or Left, Right, or Center alignment, for the element in the cell, column, or row. This attribute can be overridden by setting the alignment for the individual line or image. Generally, Left is the default horizontal alignment for cells.

Vertical alignment

The HTML attribute, `valign`, determines whether the cell contents are vertically aligned at the cell's top, middle, bottom, or along the baseline. Typically, browsers align cells vertically in the middle by default. Select the Vertical Alignment option arrow in the Cell, Column, or Row Properties dialog box to specify a different alignment.

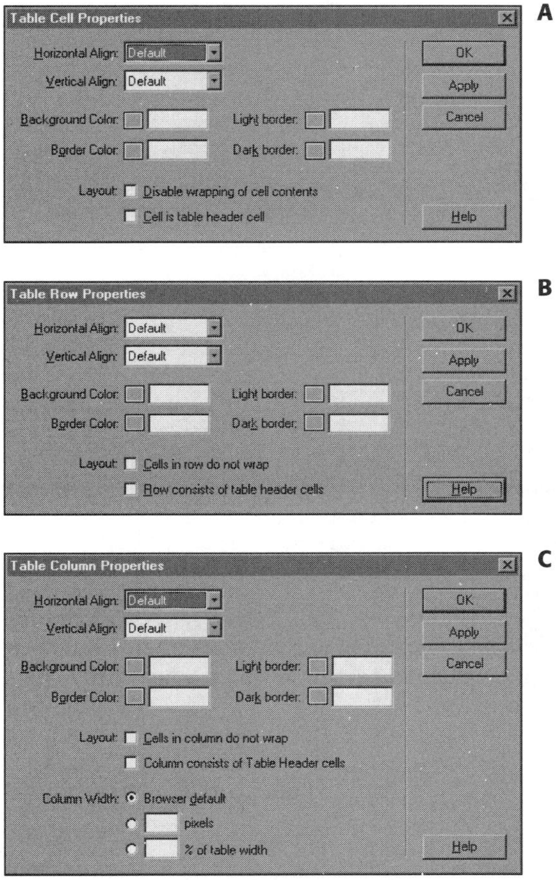

Figure 11-10: The dialog boxes for controlling attributes of cells (A), rows (B), and columns (C).

Top, Middle, and Bottom vertical alignments work pretty much as you would expect. A Baseline vertical alignment displays text near the top of the cell and positions the text — regardless of font size — so the baselines of all the text in the affected row, column, or cell are the same. You can see how images and text of various sizes are displayed under the various vertical alignment options in Figure 11-11.

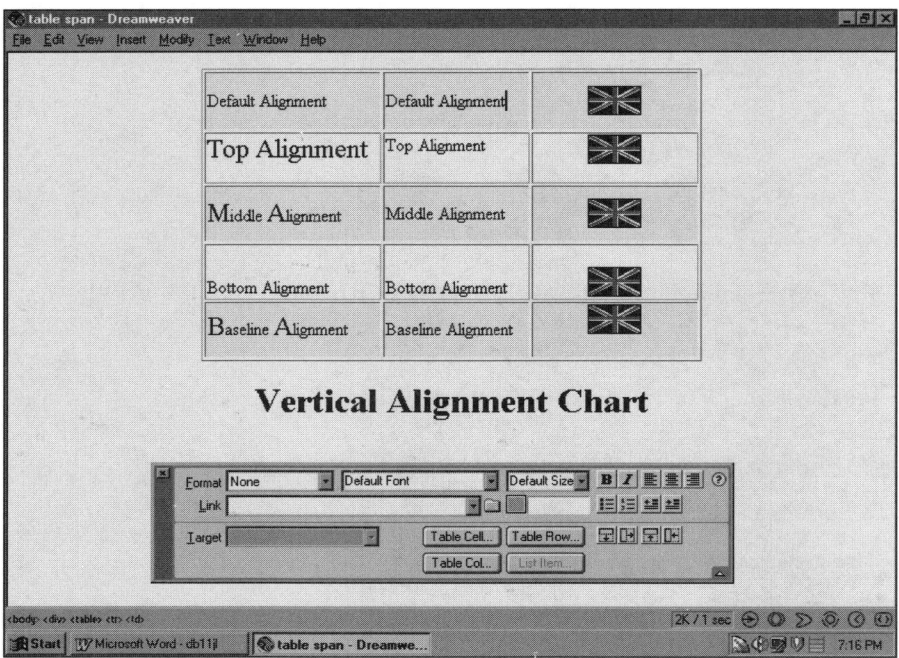

Figure 11-11: You can vertically align text and images in several arrangements in a table cell, row, or column.

Color elements

Just as you can specify color backgrounds and borders for the overall table, you can do the same for columns, rows or individual cells. Corresponding color swatches and text boxes are available in all dialog boxes for the following categories:

✦ **Background Color:** Specifies the color for the selected cell, row or column. Selecting the color swatch opens the standard 216 browser-safe color picker.

✦ **Border Color:** Controls the color of the single-pixel border surrounding each cell.

✦ **Light Border:** Sets the color for the bottom and right borders of each cell.

✦ **Dark Border:** Sets the color for the top and left borders of each cell.

Note

Notice that the light and dark shading concept for cell borders is reversed from the light and dark shading for table borders. However, the cell border attributes are just like the table attributes in that, if specified, the light and dark cell borders override any border color that might be chosen.

Cell wrap

Normal behavior for any cell is to automatically wrap text or a series of images within the cell's borders. You can turn off this automatic feature by selecting the appropriate disabling option in the Layout section of the Table Cell, Table Row, and Table Column Properties dialog boxes. For cells, the option is Disable Wrapping of Cell Contents; for rows, the option is Cells in Row Do Not Wrap; for columns, the option is Cells in Column Do Not Wrap.

Note

I've had occasion to use this option when I absolutely needed three images to appear side-by-side in one cell. In analyzing the results, I found that on some lower-resolution browsers the last image wrapped to the next line.

Table header cells

Quite often in tables, a column or row functions as the heading for that section of the table, labeling all the information in that particular section. Dreamweaver has an option for designating these cells: Mark As Table Header Cell. Table header cells are usually rendered in boldface and centered in each cell. Figure 11-12 shows an example of a table where both the first row and column are marked as table header cells.

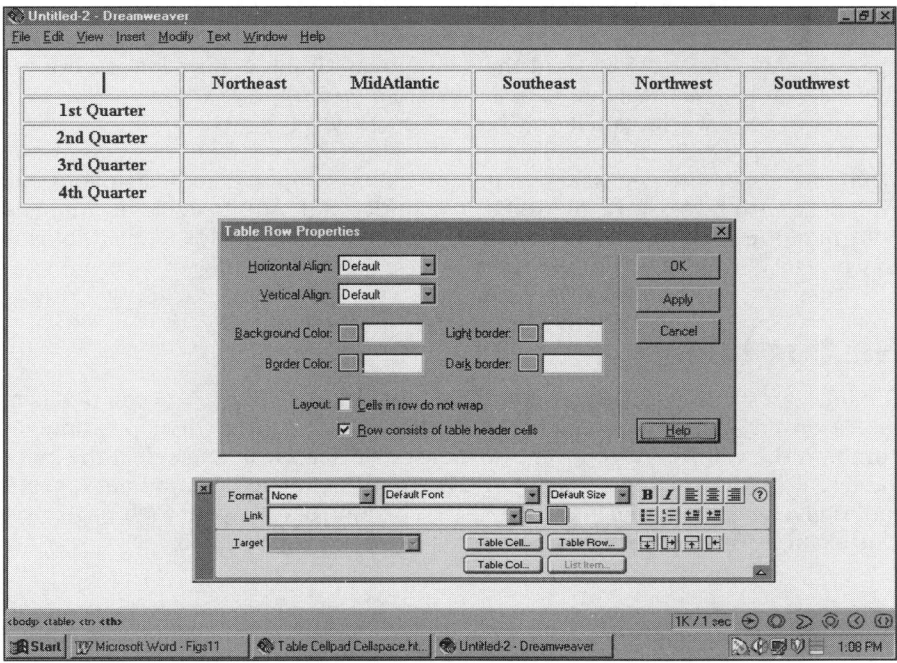

Figure 11-12: Table header cells are a good way to note a category's label, either for a row, a column, or both.

Tip

Sometimes your header columns and header rows intersect. In this case, if you first mark the row as table header cells, when you go to mark the column you'll probably find that the Mark As Table Header Cell option is already checked, even though the change isn't visible. To effect the change, first deselect the Table Header Cell option and then reselect it — in essence, turn it off and then turn it back on. Then select Apply or OK.

Column width

The gridlike structure of a table makes it impossible to resize only one cell in a multicolumn table. Therefore, the only way you can enter exact values for a cell's width is through the Column Width section available only in the Table Column Properties dialog box. In this section of the dialog, you can enter values in pixels or as a percentage of the table. The default allows cells to automatically resize with no restrictions outside of the overall dimensions of the table.

Structuring Your Web Page with Tables

At the beginning of this chapter I mentioned that experienced Web designers regard tables as one of their primary layout tools. This is because, outside of Dynamic HTML's layers, tables are the only way you can even get close to positioning your page elements the way you want them to appear. Granted, it's a lot of work to do this with tables, but designers are a persistent group — and when you have a vision to impart to the world, you'll do what's necessary.

What often becomes necessary, to get the look you want, is to design your entire Web page with tables — or, at least, the majority of it. And to achieve complete control of the page, you'll frequently put *nested tables* — tables within tables — to work.

Nesting tables

Dreamweaver has no practical restrictions on nesting tables. You can put as many tables within other tables as you can handle. All you have to do is position your cursor in the cell where you want the new table to appear, and select the Insert Table button in the Object Palette. Although it's not absolutely faultless, nesting tables give you an increasingly fine degree of control over your Web page layout. One example of a full-page table layout is shown in Figure 11-13.

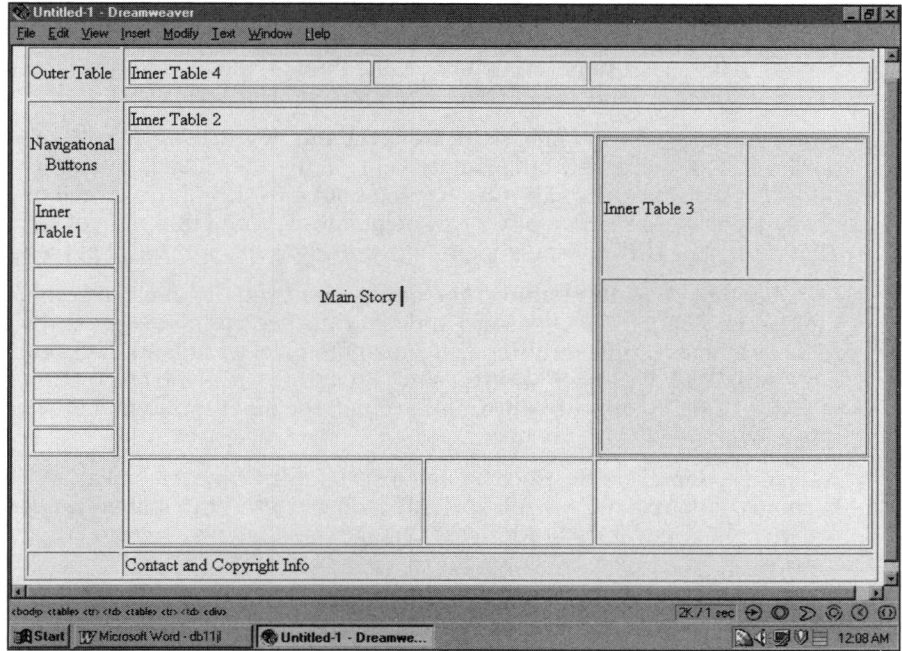

Figure 11-13: Nested tables can give the Web designer tighter command of the Web page elements.

Following are some pointers to consider when working with nested tables:

✦ **Sketch your work before you begin.** Even just a simple diagram can save you hours of experimentation and do-overs.

✦ **Work from the outside in.** Create your largest table first and then create the smaller tables within it.

✦ **Don't be afraid to move a table.** No matter how much you plan, you almost never get it right the first time. As long as you select your entire table, all the elements in it will remain intact. Unfortunately, you can't drag and drop a table. So after you've selected the table, choose Edit ➪ Cut, reposition the cursor, and then choose Edit ➪ Paste — or use those fabulous keyboard shortcuts.

✦ **Let the Tag Selector be your guide.** Because the Tag Selector displays tags in the nesting order (outside-to-inside is shown left-to-right), you can quickly select the table on which you need to work. Then you can switch to either the HTML Inspector or BBEdit, and the table will be highlighted in your code.

✦ **You can't split a cell, so nest a table.** If you've already begun embedding objects in your table and you find you need to split a cell in two or more parts, it's far easier to nest a two-cell table than to add an additional column to the entire table and readjust your column and row spans.

✦ **When resizing row heights, work from the top down.** Dragging a row's border to a new size sets an absolute value in the `<td>` tag. If you adjust the bottom row first — let's say you set it to about one fifth of the screen or 80 pixels high — and then modify a row height above, the table will get larger. That's because Dreamweaver maintains the 80 pixels, not the 20 percent.

✦ **Use absolute measurements on the outside and relative measurements on the inside.** Though it's not a hard-and-fast rule, I've found it is generally better to lock the outer table into a specific absolute pixel width and then set the inner table to 100 percent widths. Why? First, this saves the calculation time of trying to figure out the width, and second, the inner tables blend better this way.

✦ **Adjust the default table.** Because the Insert Table Object is, like all Dreamweaver objects, written in HTML, you can alter it to suit your needs. Are most of your tables borderless? Change the object code from `BORDER= 1` to `BORDER= 0` .

Want to make all your tables start at 100 percent instead of 75? Change the code

```
document.theform.width.value= 75
```

to:

```
document.theform.width.value= 100
```

For more information on how to modify an existing Object, see Chapter 16, "Creating and Using Objects.".

✦ **Remember the default cellspacing.** Trying to figure out why you can't close that gap? Could be because, even though the CellSpace text box is blank, Dreamweaver still inserts 2 pixels for cellspacing. Enter a zero as the CellSpace value to clear out the excess air.

Note

An interesting side note: Dreamweaver 1.2 adds the capability to convert a page that uses a fourth-generation browser feature — layers — to be HTML 3.2-compatible. Guess how Dreamweaver does it? Nested tables, of course. You can find out more about this conversion feature in Chapter 25, "Maximizing Browser Targeting."

Summary

Tables are an extremely powerful Web page design tool. Dreamweaver lets you modify both the appearance and the structure of your HTML tables through a combination of Property Inspectors, dialog boxes, and click-and-drag mouse movements. Mastering tables is an essential task for any modern Web designer, and worth the somewhat challenging learning curve. The key elements to keep in mind are as follows:

✦ An HTML table consists of a series of rows and columns, presented in a gridlike arrangement. Tables can be sized absolutely, in pixels, or relative to the width of the browser's window, in a percentage.

✦ Dreamweaver inserts a table whose dimensions can be altered through the Object Palette or the Insert ⇨ Table menu. Once in the page, the table needs to be selected before any of its properties can be modified through the Table Property Inspector.

✦ You can assign certain properties — such as background color, border color, and alignment — for a table's columns, rows, or cells through their respective dialog boxes. A cell's properties override those set for its column or row.

✦ Putting a table within another table — also known as nesting tables — is a powerful (and legal) design option in HTML. Nested tables offer a positioning alternative to Dynamic HTML's layers while retaining backward-browser compatibility.

In the next chapter, you see how to create and use client-side image maps.

✦ ✦ ✦

Making Client-Side Image Maps

By their very nature, HTML images are rectangular. Though you can make portions of a rectangular graphic transparent, giving the impression of an irregularly shaped picture, the image itself — and thus its clickable region — is still a rectangle. For more complex images in which shapes overlap and you want several separate areas of a picture to be hyperlinked, not just the overall graphic, you need an image map.

Dreamweaver includes an easy-to-use tool, the Image Map Editor, for delineating *client-side image maps* and inserting the proper code in your Web page. This chapter introduces you to that tool and also covers more advanced techniques for creating server-side and rollover image maps.

Client-Side Image Maps

As an almost literal example of an image map, imagine a map of the United States being used on a Web page. Suppose you want to be able to click each state and link to a different page in your site. How would you proceed? With the exception of Colorado and Wyoming, all the states have highly irregular shapes, so you can't use the typical side-by-side arrangement of rectangular images. You need to be able to specify a region on the graphic, to which you could then assign a link. This is exactly what an image map represents.

There are two different kinds of image maps: client-side and server-side. With a *server-side* image map, all the map data is kept in a file on the server. When the user clicks a particular spot on the image, often referred to as a *hotspot*, the server compares the coordinates of the clicked spot with its image-map data. If the coordinates match, the server loads the corresponding link. The key advantage to a server-side image map is that it will work with any image-capable browser. The disadvantages are that it consumes more of the server's processing resources and tends to be slower than the client-side version.

With *client-side* image maps, on the other hand, all the data that is downloaded to the browser is kept in the Web page. The comparison process is the same, but it requires a browser that is image-map savvy. Originally, only server-side image maps were possible. It wasn't until Netscape Navigator 2.0 was released that the client-side version was even an option. Microsoft began supporting client-side image maps in Internet Explorer 3.0.

In HTML, there are two parts to a client-side image map. In the `<img>` tag, Dreamweaver includes a `usemap=mapname` attribute. The `mapname` value refers to the second part of the image-map's HTML, the `<map>` tag. One of the first steps in creating an image map is to give it a unique name. Dreamweaver stores all of your mapping data under this map name. Here's an example of the code for an image map with three hot spots:

```
<img src= images/imagemap.jpg  width= 640  height= 480
usemap= #navbar ></p>
<map name= navbar >
  <area shape= poly
coords= 166,131,165,131,160,143,164,179,127,180,143,200,156,203
,118,229,119,236,158,229,177,217,199,238,212,247,220,242,196,20
3,232,190,241,189,241,182,223,177,185,182,175,134,166,132
href= /starpro.html  alt= High Risk Funds >
  <area shape= circle  coords= 312,202,56  href= /nestegg.html
alt= Mutual Funds >
  <area shape= rect  coords= 389,138,497,244
href= /prodfunds.html  alt= Money Markets >
</map>
```

Dreamweaver directly supports client-side image maps. Once you've inserted an image into your Web page, it can be an image map. Select any image and open the expanded version of the Property Inspector. In the lower-right corner you'll see the Map button, as shown in Figure 12-1. This button opens the Image Map Editor.

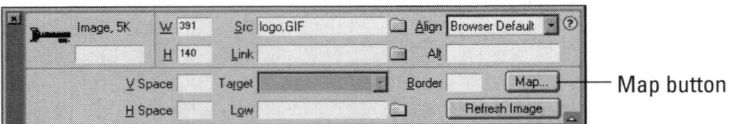

Figure 12-1: From the Image Property Inspector, select the Map button to open Dreamweaver's Image Map Editor.

Creating Image Hotspots

Image maps are created with tools similar to those you find in any drawing program. (They're described in detail in the section, "Using the drawing tools" later in this chapter.) After you've selected your graphic, you can click a tool to describe a rectangle, oval, or polygon shape.

You can make an image map from any graphic format supported by Dreamweaver: GIF, JPEG or PNG.

Tip

The window for the Image Map Editor can only display an area approximately 475 wide by 200 high. If your image is larger, horizontal and vertical scroll bars appear as needed.

Follow these steps to create hotspots on an image in Dreamweaver:

1. Select your image and open the Image Property Inspector.

2. Click the Map button to display the Image Map Editor with your selected graphic, as shown in Figure 12-2.

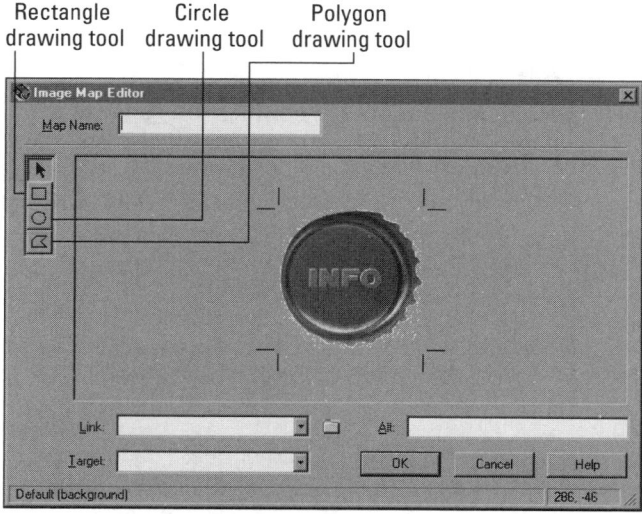

Figure 12-2: The Image Map Editor lets you draw the hotspots directly on your graphic.

3. Enter a unique name for your image map in the Map Name text box.

4. From the toolbar on the left of the Image Map Editor, choose the appropriate drawing tool to outline your hotspot: Rectangle, Circle, or Polygon (see Figure 12-2). Outline one hotspot.

5. Enter the URL for this image map in the Link text box, or click the Folder icon and browse for the file. Then press Tab to go to the next text box (Target).

6. If desired, enter a "go-to" or other target in the Target text box. Press Tab to go to the next text box (Alt).

Cross-Reference

A target can refer to a specific section of a frameset or to a new browser window. For more information on using targets in frames, see Chapter 14, "Using Frames and Framesets." To learn more about targeting a new browser window, see "Targeting Your Links" in Chapter 9, "Establishing Web Links."

7. In the Alt text box, you can enter text you want to appear as a tool tip that appears when the user's mouse moves over the area.

8. Repeat Steps 4 through 7 to add additional hotspots to the graphic.

9. Click OK when you're finished.

Tip

If the map area you're trying to define is larger than the Image Map Editor window, the solution is to create two or more overlapping areas. Set them all to the same Link and the user will never see the "seam."

Setting the default URL

In addition to joining specific hotspots to a hyperlink, you can also map any undefined areas of the image to a URL. Prior to defining any hotspots with the drawing tools, you notice the phrase "Default (background)" in the status bar of the Image Map Editor (you can see it in Figure 12-2). If you want to set up a default link for the undefined areas, enter the link's Internet address in the Link text box, along with the corresponding Target and Alt information, if any, in their respective text boxes.

When you establish a default, Dreamweaver sets the `shape` attribute of the `<area>` tag to `default` in your map data and lists whatever information you've specified.

Caution

Unfortunately, the `<area shape= default  href= url >` code doesn't work in the latest version of Internet Explorer 4.0, so setting the default in the Image Map Editor has no effect in that browser. One workaround to this drawback is to completely cover the graphic with an area, using the Rectangle drawing tool, and then assign the desired default URL.

Using the drawing tools

You'll find the drawing tools in the Image Map Editor to be straightforward and easy to use. Each one produces a series of coordinates that are incorporated into the HTML code. All three tools, when selected, display the crosshair cursor's coordinates in the lower-right corner of the Image Map Editor. These coordinates are also displayed for the arrow pointer.

In the following steps, you'll use the Image Map Editor's Rectangle drawing tool to outline a hotspot:

1. Select the Rectangle tool from the toolbar.
2. Click one corner of the area you want to map, and drag toward the opposite corner to draw a rectangle.
3. Release the mouse button. Dreamweaver inverts the defined area.
4. Fill in the Link, Target and Alt text boxes.

Follow these steps to use the Circle drawing tool in the Image Map Editor:

1. Select the Circle tool from the toolbar.
2. Click in the center of the area you want to define and drag out the circle until it reaches the correct size.
3. Release the mouse button. Dreamweaver inverts the defined area.
4. As before, complete the Link, Target and Alt text boxes.

To define an irregularly shaped hotspot, use the Polygon drawing tool. Follow these steps:

1. Select the Polygon tool from the toolbar.
2. Click the first point for your hotspot object.
3. Release the mouse button, and move the mouse to the next point.
4. Continue outlining the object by clicking and moving the mouse.
5. When the hotspot is completely outlined, double-click the mouse to close the area.
6. Fill in the Link, Target and Alt text boxes.

You can use the drawing tools in any combination. In Figure 12-3, all three drawing tools have been used to create three different hotspots. The star-shaped image is currently selected, as indicated by the inverted colors of that portion. The other two defined areas (the circular and rectangular objects) are shown with thin outlines around them.

Figure 12-3: The Image Map Editor's drawing tools let you define both regular and irregularly shaped areas.

Modifying an Image Map

Dreamweaver gives you limited options for modifying the image maps you create. First, you can move any previously defined area by selecting it and then clicking and dragging to a new location. For precise pixel-by-pixel movement, select the area and use the arrow keys to move it in any direction.

Dreamweaver also allows you to delete any existing area. Simply select the area and press the Delete or Backspace key.

Converting Client-Side Maps to Server-Side Maps

Although most Web browsers support client-side image maps, some sites still rely on server-side image maps. You can take the client-side image map generated by Dreamweaver and convert it to a server-side image map — you can even include pointers for both maps in the same Web page, to accommodate older browsers as well as the newer ones. Such a conversion does require, however, that you use a text editor to modify and save the file. You'll also need to add one more attribute, ismap, to the `<img>` tag; this attribute tells the server that the image referenced in the `src` attribute is a map.

Adapting the Server Script

First, let's examine the differences between a client-side and a server-side image map from the same graphic. The HTML for a client-side image map looks like this:

```
<map name= navbar >
  <area shape= rect  coords= 1,1,30,33  href= home.html
alt= Home Page >
  <area shape= circle  coords= 65,64,62  href= contacts.html
alt= Information >
  <area shape= default  href= index.html >
</map>
```

The same definitions for a server-side image map are laid out like this:

```
rect home.html 1,1 30,33
circle contacts.html 65,64 62
default index.html
```

As you can see, the server-side image map file is much more sparse. Notice first that all of the `alt= string` code is thrown out because tool tips can only be shown through client-side image maps.

A server expects the information in this form:

```
shape URL coordinates
```

So, you'll need to remove the `<area>` tag and its delimiters, as well as the phrases `shape=`, `coords=` and `href=`. Then you reverse the order of the URL and the coordinates.

The last step in this phase of adapting the server-side script is to format the coordinates correctly. The format depends on the shape that is being defined.

✦ For rectangles, group the x, y points into comma-separated pairs with a single space in between each pair.

✦ For circles, separate the center point coordinates from the diameter with a space.

✦ For polygons, group the x, y points into comma-separated pairs with a single space in between each pair — just like rectangles.

Your new map file should be stored on your server, probably in a subfolder of the cgi-bin directory.

Caution   Not all servers expect server-side image maps in the same format. The format offered here conforms to the NCSA HPPD standard. If you're unsure of the required format, or of where to put your maps on your server, check with your server administrator before creating a server-side image map.

Including the Map Link

The second phase of converting a client-side map to a server-side one involves making the connection between the Web page and the map file. A client-side image map link directly calls the URL associated with it. In contrast, all references from a server-side link call the map file—which, in turn, calls the specified URL.

The connection to a server-side map is handled in the normal fashion of adding a link to a graphic. You can, of course, do this directly in Dreamweaver. Simply select your graphic, and in the Image Property Inspector insert the map file URL in the Link text box. Be sure to set the image's Border property to zero to avoid the link outline.

The final addition to your script is the ismap attribute. Place the ismap attribute in the <img> tag of the graphic being used for the image map, like this:

```
<img href= images/biglogo.gif  width= 200  height= 350  ismap>
```

As noted earlier, it is entirely possible to use client-side and server-side image maps together. The easiest way to do it is to keep the image map data as written by Dreamweaver and add the ismap attribute. The HTML example seen in the first section, "Client-Side Image Maps," would then read as follows:

```
<a href= http://www.idest.com/cgi-bin/maps/imap.txt >
<img src= images/imagemap.jpg  width= 640  height= 480
usemap= #navbar  ismap><a/>
```

Dreamweaver Technique: Building an Image Map Rollover

One of the most popular Web page techniques today is known as a rollover. A *rollover* occurs when a user's mouse moves over a button or graphic in the page, and the button or graphic lights up or changes in some way. You'll see how to create these graphics rollovers in Chapter 20, "Inserting Shockwave Elements."

Here in this section, let's try out one method for applying the same technique to an image map. Portions of this technique were adopted from work by Peter Belesis's DHTML Tutorials at Mecklermedia's WebReference (`www.webreference.com`).

Caution The following method uses advanced techniques involving JavaScript behaviors and layers. If you're unfamiliar with these concepts, you might want to examine Chapters 20 ("Inserting Shockwave Elements") and 23 ("Working with Layers") before proceeding.

Before we get underway, keep in mind that this technique — because it uses layers — works only with 4.0 browsers and higher. Furthermore, though most of these steps can be accomplished in Dreamweaver's visual editor, you will need to tweak the code in your text editor to complete the project.

Step One: Create two images

As with behavior-based button rollovers, you'll use two images to represent the "off" and "on" states of the graphic. However, because we are using image maps here rather than separate graphics, you'll only need a total of two images (versus two for every button). In our example, there are three buttons "carved" from one graphic; but there very easily could have been eight or a dozen separate buttons, which would have required 16 or 24 separate images. All we need is our two image maps.

After building your first image, bring it into your favorite image processing program and make the alterations necessary to create the second image. Figure 12-4 shows examples of the two images you need, inserted into Dreamweaver. As you can see, all that was necessary to make the "on" image was to add a glow effect to each of the three hotspots.

Tip One of the methods used in this technique involves clipping a region of an image. Presently, layers only support rectangular clipping. Keep this in mind as you build your primary image, and avoid placing hotspots too close together.

Step Two: Set up the layers

This technique takes advantage of three different layer properties: absolute positioning, visibility, and clipping. The idea is to display just a portion of a hidden layer during a mouseOver event. So first, we need two layers — one for each of our images.

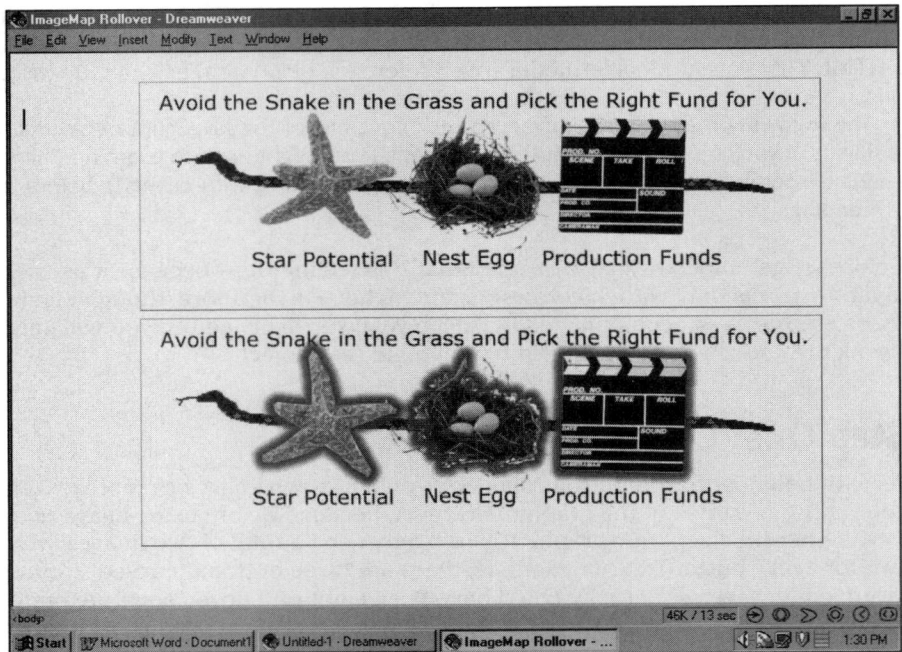

Figure 12-4: You'll need two separate images, representing "on" and "off," for a rollover image map.

Follow these steps to establish the initial layers:

1. Choose Insert ⇨ Layer or select the Insert Layer button in the Object Palette to create the onLayer. If you use the menu option instead of drawing out the layer, it will be created as a standard size and you won't have to spend as much time adjusting the layer sizes later.

2. Make sure the cursor is in the layer, and choose Insert ⇨ Image or select the Insert Image button in the Object Palette. Load your "on" graphic. If the layer is smaller than the image, the layer will automatically expand.

3. Repeat Step 1 to create the offLayer. Be sure to give it a unique name.

4. Repeat Step 2 and insert the "off" graphic.

5. If necessary, open the Layers Inspector by choosing Window ⇨ Layers or pressing F11, and make sure of the following:

   • Both layers must have unique names. In this example, we use offLayer and onLayer.

- The offLayer must be visible.
- The onLayer must be hidden.
- The onLayer must be on top of the offLayer, so that when you make a portion of the onLayer visible, it will obscure the offLayer.

Figure 12-5 shows how the screen looks with both layers in place and the visibility properties set correctly.

Figure 12-5: Two image maps are placed on top of each other in layers, and the top layer is hidden.

Step Three: Attach the Behavior

Currently, Dreamweaver doesn't support attaching a behavior to an image map. The workaround detailed here involves first attaching the behavior to the full images in each layer, and then cutting and pasting the code built by Dreamweaver. Dreamweaver includes a JavaScript Behavior called Show/Hide Layers that does exactly what we need.

Follow these steps to assign the Show/Hide Layers behavior to the layers:

1. Be sure the offLayer (the layer holding the basic, unchanged image) is visible, and the onLayer is hidden. You can select the visibility options in the Layer Inspector, to open and close the "eyes" of the respective layers.

2. Open the Behavior Inspector by clicking the Behavior button in the Launcher or selecting Window ➪ Behaviors.

3. Select the image in the offLayer.

4. If necessary, choose 4.0 Browsers from the Browser option list.

5. Still in the Behavior Inspector, click the + (Add) Event button in the Events pane and choose onMouseOver from the pop-up.

   Dreamweaver reminds you with a dialog box that this event can only be applied to an anchor tag, <a>, and proceeds to wrap one around the image targeted to "#".

6. From the Actions pane, select the + (Add) Action button and choose Show-Hide Layers from the pop-up list.

7. When the Show-Hide Layers dialog box opens, Dreamweaver searches for all the layers in your document. After they are displayed, select the onLayer and click the Show button (see Figure 12-6). Click OK when you've finished.

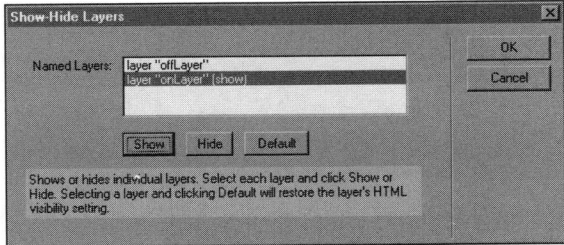

Figure 12-6: After you've selected a behavior event, choose the Show-Hide Layer action to make a hidden layer visible.

8. So far, we've assigned one behavior to make the onLayer visible when the pointer is over the image. Now we have to assign another behavior to hide the onLayer when the pointer moves away from the image.

   In the Events pane of the Behavior Inspector, click the Insert Event button again and this time choose (onMouseOut).

9. From the Actions pane, click the Insert Action button and again select Show-Hide Layers from the option list.

10. Now select the onLayer again and click the Hide button. Click OK when you're done.

So what we now have is two Behaviors assigned to one image. At this point the Dreamweaver code for the <body> of our Web page reads like this:

```
<body bgcolor= #FFFFFF >

<div id= offLayer  style= position:absolute; width:200px;
height:115px; z-index:1; visibility:visible >
  <a href= #  onmouseover =
 MM_showHideLayers( document.layers[\ onLayer\ ] ,
 document.all[\ onLayer\ ] , show )
onmouseout =  MM_showHideLayers( document.layers[\ onLayer\ ] ,
 document.all[\ onLayer\ ] , hide ) >
<img src= images/imagemap.jpg  width= 607  height= 191
border= 0 ></a>
</div>

<div id= onLayer  style= position:absolute; width:200px;
height:115px; z-index:2; overflow:visible; visibility: hidden >
  <img src= images/imagemap2.jpg  width= 607  height= 191 >
</div>

</body>
```

The MM_showHideLayers() JavaScript function called by both onMouseOver and onMouseOut is automatically written to the <head> section. Part of this technique involves adding and modifying that code a bit, which we'll cover in Step Five.

Step Four: Make the image maps

You may have noticed that I keep referring to "creating image maps" in the plural. In addition to the map that is used to provide the image-map coordinates, we'll use Dreamweaver's Image Map Editor to draw the coordinates necessary to perform the *clipping* function. When a layer is clipped to a specific rectangle, only that rectangular portion of the layer is visible; the remainder is hidden.

The first part of Step Four is to make the actual image map that will eventually be used to activate the onMouseOver and onMouseOut events. Follow these steps to complete this task:

1. Select the image in one of the layers. You can use either image (the "on" or the "off") to draw the image map. I preferred the onLayer, with the slightly fuzzier edges.

2. In the extended Image Property Inspector, click the Map button.

3. In the Image Map Editor, give your map a unique name.

4. Draw out the image maps using the drawing tools and give each area a URL in the Link box. Complete the Target and Alt text boxes, if desired. Click the OK button when you're done.

Normally, when building an image map, this is where you would stop. But we're going to stay with the Image Map Editor and use it a second time to find our clipping coordinates for us. Remember, only rectangular clipping is supported currently in Dynamic HTML and CSS; therefore, only the Rectangle tool is used when creating the clipping coordinates.

You can only have one image map per image, but in this technique you have planned ahead and created two identical images to work with. Now you can do the following steps to build your clipping map:

1. Temporarily reverse the visibility settings of the two layers, so that the layer containing the graphic used to build the image map is hidden.

2. Select the image in the now visible layer. In our example, this is the offLayer.

3. Click the Map button in the extended Image Property Inspector.

4. Give your new image map a temporary name.

5. Select the Rectangle drawing tool, and draw a rectangular area around each of the previously build image map areas. Note: It's important that these areas not overlap, but be drawn side-by-side as shown in Figure 12-7. Give each area a unique temporary link.

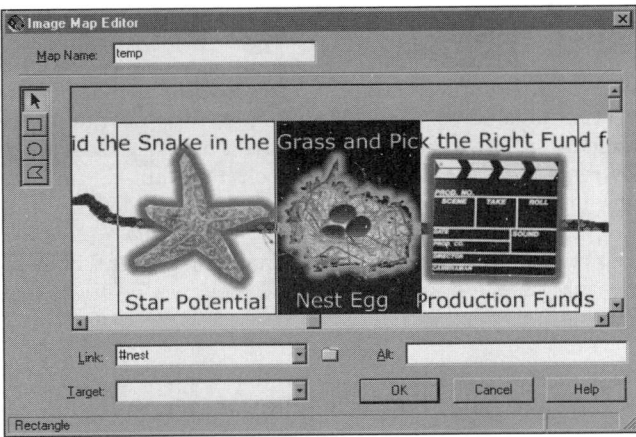

Figure 12-7: Place your rectangular clip regions side by side, without overlapping.

6. Click OK when you've finished.

When Dreamweaver builds code for an image map, it places the first item you define as the last item in the code list, and the last item defined as the first item in the code list. The rectangular coordinates are placed in this order: left, top, right, and bottom, as can be seen in this code fragment:

```
<map name= temp >
  <area shape= rect  coords= 365,0,506,176  href= #slate >
  <area shape= rect  coords= 236,0,365,176  href= #nest >
  <area shape= rect  coords= 93,0,234,176  href= #star >
</map>
```

Notice that, in defining the coordinates, I kept the top (0) and the bottom (176) constant for all three areas. Although this is not essential, it will result in code that is a tad simpler and, if possible, is recommended.

Step Five: Complete the Code

Let's review what we have done so far:

✦ Before we began working in Dreamweaver, we built two different images — one to depict the regular ("off") state, and another for the "on" state.

✦ We used Dreamweaver to create two identically sized and positioned layers. We then inserted our two images into the hidden layers, with the "on" graphic placed on top.

✦ Next, we used Dreamweaver to assign JavaScript behaviors that reveal the hidden layer when the user's pointer passes over the image.

✦ The last thing we did was to use Dreamweaver's Image Map Editor to build two image maps: one to provide clickable regions on the graphic, and one used to provide rectangular coordinates to be used for clipping.

All that is left to do now is to tweak the code. Granted, it's going to be a pretty big tweak, but Dreamweaver has really done all the hard work of inserting the layers and writing the cross-browser code for the behaviors. Now, it's time to move to your favorite text editor and customize the HTML.

Cut and Paste the Function Calls

First, you need to move the JavaScript function calls, onMouseOver and onMouseOut, away from the image and into each of the image map areas.

1. Cut the entire function call line from inside the `<a>` tag.

2. Delete the closing `</a>` tag that follows the `<img>` tag.

3. Move the cursor inside the first `<area>` tag at the end and paste the function calls into the tag. In our example, the code for the circle has been changed from this:

```
<area shape= circle  coords= 300,98,56  href= nest.htm >
```

to this:

```
<area shape= circle  coords= 300,98,56  href= nest.htm
onmouseout= MM_showHideLayers( document.layers[\ onLayer\
] , document.all[\ onLayer\ ] , hide )
onmouseover= MM_showHideLayers( document.layers[\ onLayer\
] , document.all[\ onLayer\ ] , show ) >
```

4. Repeat this cut-and-paste action for every `<area>` defined in your image map.

Point to the Right Map

You won't be able to test the above changes until you make one more minor change. Remember how, in Step Four of this Technique, you created a temporary image map to grab the clipping coordinates? Part of that process puts a `usemap=mapname` attribute in the `<img>` tag of one of the graphics. Now you need to find that reference and change the `usemap` value so that both images are pointing to the real image map. In the example I built, my two map names are "touch" and "t2" — the latter name is the one assigned to the temporary image map used to get the clipping coordinates. So I needed to change the img tag from this

```
<img src= imagemap.jpg  width= 607  height= 191  border= 0
usemap= #t2 >
```

to this:

```
<img src= imagemap.jpg  width= 607  height= 191  border= 0
usemap= #touch >
```

The section altered in both code lines is in boldface, to make it easy for you to see the change.

Once you've made this change, the image when tested in a 4.0 browser should only change when the pointer goes over the mapped areas. But it's still not quite right: You'll notice that all of the image changes instead of just one area. It's time to put that clipping function to work.

Build the Clipping Array

The next step involves taking the coordinates gathered from our pseudo-image map and plugging them into a JavaScript array. Because the top and bottom coordinates were kept constant, we only need to bring in the left and the right values. We also need an identifying number to mark each image map area.

In our example, only three image map buttons were included, so you see only three setParams statements. However, you can have as many buttons as you like.

The following code is included in the <script> section, above the Macromedia functions:

```
arClips = new Array();
function setParams(the_clip,from,to) {
    arClips[the_clip] = new Array();
    arClips[the_clip][0] = from;
    arClips[the_clip][1] = to;
}
setParams(1,93,234);
setParams(2,236,365);
setParams(3,365,506);
clTop = 0;
clBot = 176;
```

The two variables, clTop and clBot, hold the values for the clip top and the clip bottom range, respectively. Again, because these are constant, we can go ahead and set them.

Integrating the Code

Our last task is to tie all the disparate parts together. First we need to pass the identifying number from each image map area to the function. We do this by adding the number to the end of each function call in each <shape> tag. Previously, the code read as follows:

```
<area shape= rect  coords= 376,36,486,141  href= slate.htm
onmouseout= MM_showHideLayers( document.layers[\ onLayer\ ] , d
ocument.all[\ onLayer\ ] , hide )
onmouseover= MM_showHideLayers( document.layers[\ onLayer\ ] ,
document.all[\ onLayer\ ] , show ) >
```

Now, it reads like this (the additions are in bold for easy reference):

```
<area shape= rect  coords= 376,36,486,141  href= slate.htm
onmouseout= MM_showHideLayersIM( document.layers[\ onLayer\ ] ,
 document.all[\ onLayer\ ] , hide ,3)
onmouseover= MM_showHideLayersIM( document.layers[\ onLayer\ ]
, document.all[\ onLayer\ ] , show ,3) >
```

Be sure to use a unique number to identify each defined shape. In this example, the function name has also been slightly modified with the added IM for image map at the end. This is done to prevent Dreamweaver from overwriting the function should the same behavior be applied elsewhere on the page. Naturally, the name of the actual function needs to be modified as well.

The next step is to modify the Dreamweaver-generated function to read our new value and to act on our array. Listing 12-1 shows the basic Dreamweaver code for showing and hiding layers:

Listing 12-1: Macromedia's standard Show/Hide Layers Function

```
function MM_showHideLayers() { //v1.0
  var i, visStr, args;
  args = MM_showHideLayers.arguments;
  for (i=0; i<(args.length-2); i+=3) { //with arg triples
(objNS,objIE,visStr)
    visStr    = args[i+2];
    if (navigator.appName ==  Netscape ) {
      if (document.layers != null) eval(args[i]+ .visibility =
 +visStr+   );
    } else { //IE
      if (visStr ==  show ) visStr =  visible ; //convert vals
      if (visStr ==  hide ) visStr =  hidden ;
      if (document.all != null)
eval(args[i+1]+ .style.visibility =   +visStr+   );
  } }
}
```

Modifying the code involves the following:

✦ Modify the function name to prevent Macromedia from overwriting our customized code as mentioned at the beginning of this section.

✦ Add needed variables: clRight (Right Clip value), clLeft (Left Clip value) and the_clip (the identifying number of the defined area).

✦ Increase the number of arguments to examine, which is passed by the function call to account for the added value.

✦ Pull the identifying number of the clip from the arguments.

✦ Assign the value to the Left Clip variable, clLeft.

✦ Assign the value to the Right Clip variable, clRight.

✦ In the Netscape section, set the clipping range for the Left and the Right.

✦ In the Internet Explorer section, set the entire clipping range.

You can see the changes, marked in bold, in Listing 12-2. Once you've implemented these changes, test your object. You should see the type of reaction demonstrated in Figure 12-8.

Figure 12-8: The completed image map rollover technique in action.

Caution

Make sure that when you go to preview your work in a browser that the layer visibility is set correctly for each layer.

Listing 12-2: **Modified Image Map Rollover Function**

```
function MM_showHideLayersIM() { //v1.0 Modified by jlowery
  var i, visStr, args;
  var clRight, clLeft, the_clip;
  args = MM_showHideLayers.arguments;
  for (i=0; i<(args.length-2); i+=4) { //with 4 args
(objNS,objIE,visStr,the_clip)
    visStr   = args[i+2];
```

(continued)

Listing 12-2 *(continued)*

```
      the_clip = args[i+3];
      clLeft = arClips[the_clip][0];
      clRight = arClips[the_clip][1];
      if (navigator.appName ==  Netscape ) {
         document.onLayer.clip.left=clLeft
         document.onLayer.clip.right=clRight;
         if (document.layers != null) eval(args[i]+ .visibility =
   +visStr+   )
      } else { //IE
         if (visStr ==  show ) visStr =  visible ; //convert vals
         if (visStr ==  hide ) visStr =  hidden ;
         document.all.onLayer.style.clip = rect(  + clTop +      +
   clRight +      + clBot +      + clLeft +  ) ;
         if (document.all != null)
   eval(args[i+1]+ .style.visibility =   +visStr+   );
      } }
   }
```

Summary

Image maps provide a very necessary capability in Web page design. Without them, you wouldn't be able to link irregularly shaped graphics, or to group links all in one image. Dreamweaver's built-in Image Map Editor gives you all the tools you need to create simple, effective client-side image maps.

✦ Image maps let you define separate areas of one graphic and link them to different URLs. There are two kinds of image maps: client-side and server-side. Dreamweaver creates client-side image maps through its Image Map Editor.

✦ The Image Map Editor offers three basic drawing tools for creating rectangular, circular and irregularly shaped image maps.

✦ If your Web site uses server-side image maps, you can make them by modifying and converting Dreamweaver-generated client-side image maps.

✦ It's possible to create the effect of a graphic rollover, common on Web pages, using client-side image maps. This chapter's Dreamweaver Technique shows you how.

In the next chapter you learn about forms in Dreamweaver.

✦   ✦   ✦

Interactive Forms

A form, in the everyday world as well as on the Web, is a
type of structured communication. When you apply for
a driver's license, you're not told to just write down all your
personal info; you're asked to fill out a form that asks for
specific parts of that information, one at a time, in a specific
manner. Web-based forms are just as precise, if not more so.

Dreamweaver has a robust and superior implementation of
HTML forms — from the dedicated Forms panel in the Object
Palette to various form-specific Property Inspectors. In
addition to their importance as a tool for communication
between the browsing public and the Web site administrators,
forms are integral to building some of Dreamweaver's own
objects.

In this chapter you see how forms are structured and then
created within Dreamweaver. Each form object is explored in
detail — text fields, radio buttons, check boxes, menus and list
boxes, command buttons, hidden fields, and password fields.
Finally, you'll see one example of how forms work with the CGI
technique included with Dreamweaver.

How HTML Forms Work

Forms have a very special function in HTML: they support
interaction. Virtually all HTML elements apart from forms are
concerned with design and presentation — delivering the
content to the user, if you will. Forms, on the other hand, give
the user the ability to pass information back to Web site
creators and administrators. Without forms, the Web would be
a one-way street.

There are many, many uses for forms on the Web, including surveys, electronic commerce, guest books, polls, and even real-time custom graphic creation. For such feedback to be possible, forms require an additional component to what's seen on screen so that each form can complete its function. Every form needs some type of connection to a Web server, and usually this connection takes the form of a *common gateway interface* (CGI) script, although JavaScript and Java can also be used. This means that, in addition to designing your forms on screen, you or someone who works with you must implement a program that collects and manages the information from the form.

Forms, like HTML tables, can be thought of as self-contained units within a Web page. All the elements of a form are contained within the form tag pair, <form> and </form>. Unlike tables, you cannot nest forms, although there's nothing to stop you from having multiple forms on a page.

Form attributes

The <form> tag has three attributes, only two of which are commonly used:

✦ The method attribute tells the server how the contents of the form should be presented to the CGI program. The two possible method values are get and post. Get passes the information attached to a URL and is rarely used these days, because it places limitations on the amount of data that can be passed to the gateway program. Post causes the server to present the information as standard input and imposes no limits on the amount of passed data.

✦ The second <form> attribute is action. The action attribute determines what should be done with the form content. Most commonly, action is set to a URL for running a specific CGI program or for sending e-mail.

✦ The third, infrequently used attribute for <form> is enctype, which specifies the MIME media type.

Typical HTML for a <form> tag looks something like this:

```
<form method= post  action= http://www.idest.com/
cgi-bin/mailcall.pl >
```

Tip   The .pl extension in the example form tag just above stands for *Perl*—a scripting language often used to create CGI programs. Perl can be edited in any regular text editor.

Within each form are a series of input devices — text boxes, radio buttons, check boxes, and so on. Each type handles a particular sort of input; in fact, the main tag for these elements is the <input> tag. With one exception, the <textarea> tag, all form input types are called by specifying the `type` attribute. The text box tag, for example, is written as follows:

```
<input type=text value= lastname >
```

All form input tags have `value` attributes. The information input by the user is assigned to the given value. Thus, if I were to fill out a form with a text box asking for my last name, like the one produced by the foregoing tag, part of the message sent would include this string:

```
lastname=Lowery
```

Web servers send all the information from a form in one long text string to whatever program or address is specified in the `action` attribute. It's up to the program or the recipient of the form message to parse the string. For instance, if I were to fill out a small form with my name, e-mail address and a quick comment like "Good work!" the server would send a text string similar to this one:

```
name=Joseph+Lowery&address=jlowery@idest.com&comment=Good+work%21
```

As you can see, the various fields are separated by ampersands, and the individual words within the responses are separated by plus signs. Characters outside of the lower end of the ASCII set are represented by their hexadecimal value. Decoding this text string is called *parsing* the response.

Tip　　If you're not using the mailto method for getting your Web feedback, don't despair. Most CGI programs, including the one included with Dreamweaver, parse the text string as part of their basic functionality before sending it on its way.

Inserting a Form in Dreamweaver

A form is inserted just like any other object in Dreamweaver. Place the cursor where your want your form to start, and then either select the Insert Form button from the Forms panel of the Object Palette or choose Insert ➪ Form from the menus. Dreamweaver inserts a red dashed outline stretching across the Document Window to indicate the form.

If you have the Property Inspector open, the Form Property Inspector appears when you insert a form. As you can see from Figure 13-1, there are only three values that you can specify regarding forms: the form name, the Action and the Method.

Specifying a form name allows the form to be directly referenced from a JavaScript or by other language. Because of the interactive nature of forms, this feature is often used by Web programmers to gather information from the user.

Form outline   Insert Form button

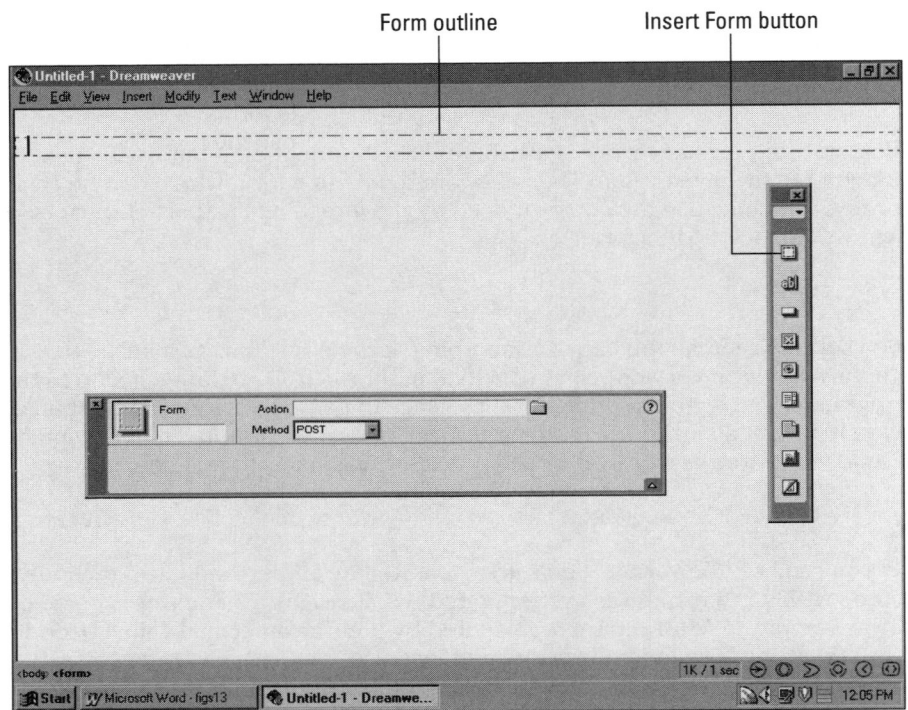

Figure 13-1: Inserting a form creates a dashed red outline of the form and displays the Form Property Inspector, if available.

In the Action text box, you can directly enter a URL or mailto address, or you can select the folder icon and browse for a file.

The Method defaults to Post, the most commonly used option. You can also choose Get; or Default, which leaves the Method up to the browser. In most cases, you should leave the Method set to Post.

Note   Forms cannot be placed inline with any other element such as text or graphics.

There are a few concerns to keep in mind when it comes to mixing forms and other Web page elements:

✦ Forms expand as objects are inserted into them; you can't resize a form by dragging its boundaries.

✦ The outline of a form is invisible; there is no border to turn on or off.

✦ Forms and tables can be used together only if the form either completely encloses or is completely enclosed inside the table. In other words, you can't have a form spanning part of a table.

✦ Forms can be inserted within layers, and multiple forms can be in multiple layers. However, the layer must completely enclose the form. As with forms spanning tables, you can't have a form spanning two or more layers. (A workaround for this limitation is discussed in the "Forms and Layers" section of Chapter 23, "Working with Layers.")

Tip You can turn off the red dashed form outline in Dreamweaver's preview, if you'd like. Choose Edit ➪ Preferences and, in the Invisible Elements panel, deselect the Form Delimiter option.

Using Text Boxes

Anytime you use a form to gather text information typed in by a user, you use a form object called a *text field*. Text fields can hold any number of alphanumeric characters. The Web designer can decide whether the text field is displayed in one line or several. When the HTML is written, a multiple-line text field uses a

```
<textarea>
```

tag, and a single-line text field is coded with

```
<input type=text>
```

Text fields

To insert a single-line text field in Dreamweaver, you can use any of the following methods:

✦ From the Forms panel of the Object Palette, select the Insert Text Field button to place a text field at your current cursor position.

✦ Choose Insert ➪ Form Object ➪ Text Field from the menus, which inserts a text field at the current cursor position.

✦ Drag the Insert Text Field button from the Object Palette to any existing location in the Document Window, and release the mouse button to position the text field.

When you insert a text field, the Property Inspector, when displayed, shows you the attributes that can be changed; see Figure 13-2. The size of a text field is measured in the number of characters it can display at one time. You can change the length of a text field by inserting a value in the Char Width text box. By default, Dreamweaver inserts a text field approximately 20 characters wide. The *approximately* is important here because the *final* size of the text field is ultimately controlled by the browser used to view the page. Unless you limit the number of possible characters by entering a value in the Max Chars text box, the user can enter as many characters as desired and the text box will scroll to display them.

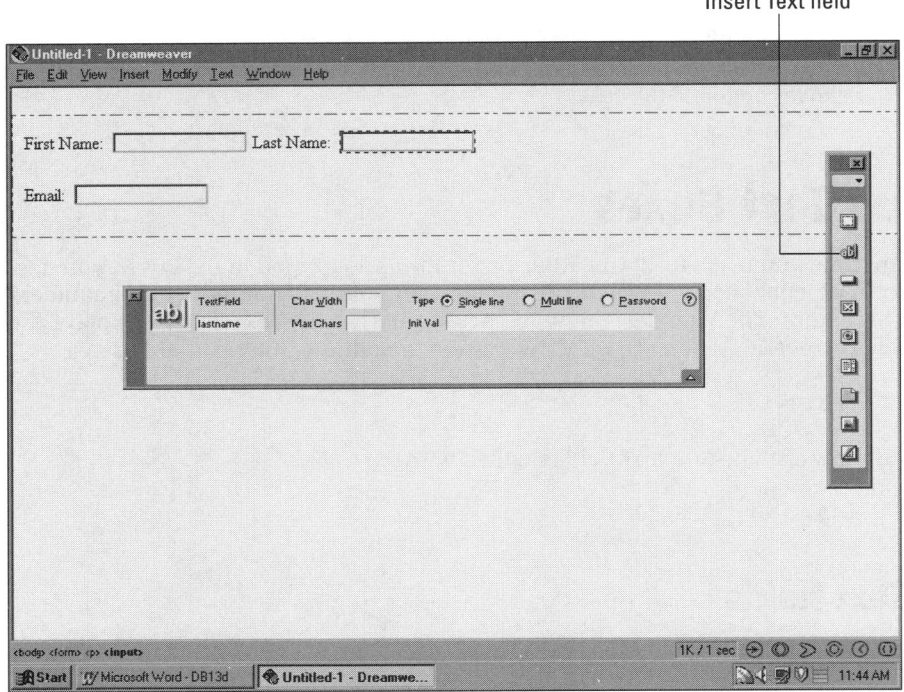

Figure 13-2: The text field of a form is used for allowing the user to type in any required information.

Note that the value in Char Width determines the visible width of the field, while the value in Max Chars actually determines the number of characters that can be entered.

The Init Value text box on the Text Field Property Inspector is used to insert a default text string. The user can overwrite this value, if desired.

Neat Forms

Text field width is measured in a monospaced character width. Because regular fonts are not monospaced, however, lining up text fields and other form objects can be problematic at best. There are two general workarounds: preformatted text and tables.

Switching the labels on the form to preformatted text allows you to insert any amount of white space to properly space out ("kern") your text and other input fields. Previously, Web designers were stuck with the default preformatted text format — the rather plain-looking Courier monospaced font. Now, however, newer browsers (3.0 and later) can read the `face=fontname` attribute. So you can combine a regular font with the preformatted text option and get the best of both worlds.

Going the preformatted text route requires you to insert a lot of spaces. So when you are working on a larger, complex form, using tables is probably a better way to go. Besides the speed of layout, the other advantage that tables offer is the ability to right-align text labels next to your text fields. Figure 13-3 gives examples of form layout using both preformatted text and tables.

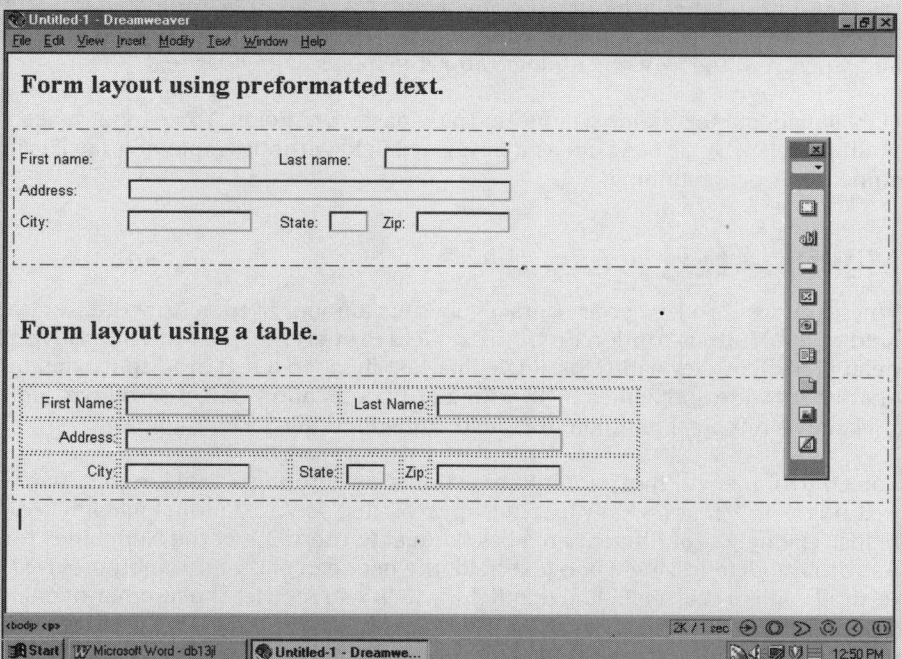

Figure 13-3: The top form uses preformatted text to get the different-sized form fields to line up properly. The bottom form uses a table.

(continued)

(continued)

Combining different size text fields on a single row — for example, when you're asking for a city, state, and ZIP code combination — can make the task of lining up your form even more difficult. Most often you'll spend a fair amount of time in a trial-and-error effort to make the text fields match. Be sure to check your results in the various browsers as you build your form.

Password fields

Normally, all text entered into a text field displays as you expect — programmers refer to this process as *echoing*. You can turn off the echoing by selecting the Password option in the Text Field Property Inspector. When a text field is designated as a password field, all text entered by the user will show up as asterisks in Window systems or as dots on Macintoshes.

Use the password field when you want to protect the user's input from prying eyes (as your PIN number is hidden when you enter it at an ATM, for instance). The information entered in a password field is not encrypted or scrambled in any way, and when sent to the Web administrator it displays as regular text.

Only single-line text fields can be set to be password fields. You cannot make a multiline `<textarea>` tag act as a password field without employing JavaScript or some other programming.

Multiline text areas

When you want to give your users a generous amount of room to write, set the text field to the Multiline option on the Text Field Property Inspector. This converts the default 20-character width for single-line text fields to a text area approximately 18 characters wide and 3 lines high, with a horizontal and vertical scroll bar. Figure 13-4 shows a typical multiline text field embedded in a form.

You control the width of a multiline text area by entering a value in the Char Width text box of the Text Field Property Inspector, just as you do for single-line text fields. The height of the text area is set equal to the value in the Num Lines text box. As with the default single line text field, the user can enter any amount of text desired. Unlike the single-line text field, which can restrict the number of characters that can be input through the Max Chars text box, you cannot restrict the number of characters the user enters into a multiline text area.

Tip   By default, text entered into a multiline text field does not wrap when it hits the right edge of the text area; rather, it keeps scrolling until the user presses Enter (Return). If desired, you can force the text to wrap by inserting the `wrap` attribute in the `<textarea>` tag, like this:

```
<textarea name= text6  cols= 50  rows= 8  wrap= virtual >
```

A `virtual` value wraps text on the screen but not when the response is submitted. To wrap text in both places, use `wrap= physical` . The `wrap` attribute must be entered by hand.

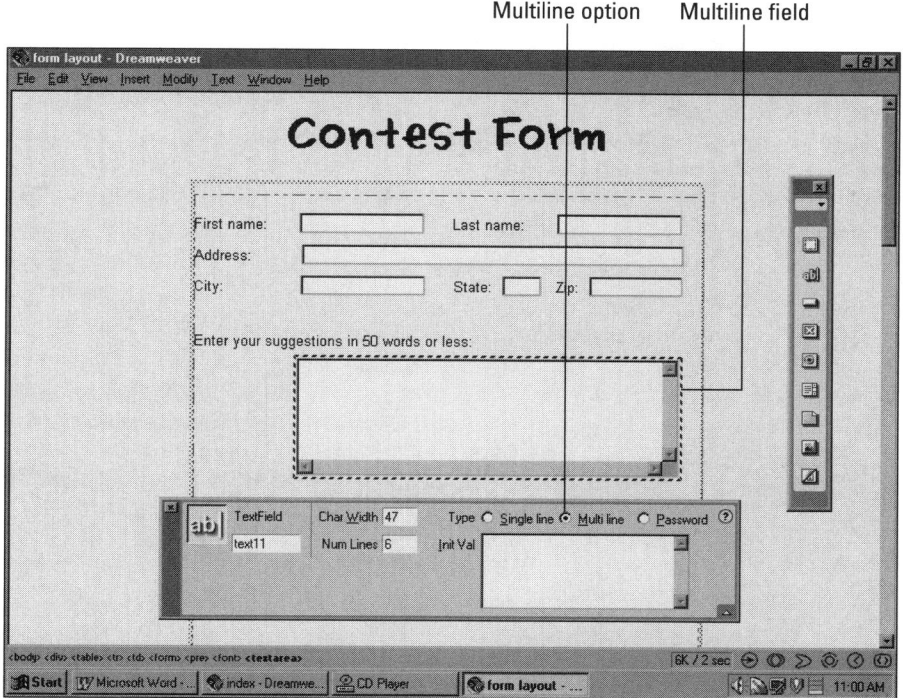

Figure 13-4: The Multiline option of the Text Field Property Inspector opens up a text box for more user information.

One other option is you can preload the text area with any default text you like. Enter this text in the Init Val text box of the Text Field Property Inspector. When Dreamweaver writes the HTML code, this text is not entered as a value, as for the single-line text field, but rather goes in between the `<textarea>...</textarea>` tag pair.

Providing Check Boxes and Radio Buttons

When you want your Web page reader to choose between a specific set of options in your form, one choice is to use either check boxes or radio buttons. Check boxes let you offer a series of options from which the user can pick as many as desired. Radio buttons, on the other hand, give your user a number of selections from which only one is chosen.

Tip   You can achieve the same functionality as check boxes and radio buttons with a different look by using the drop-down list and menu boxes. These options for presenting choices to the user are described shortly.

Check boxes

Check boxes are often used in a "Select All That Apply" type of section, when you want to allow the user to choose as many of the listed options as desired. You insert a check box in much the same way as you do a text box: Select or drag the Insert Check Box from the Object Palette, or choose Insert ⇨ Form Objects ⇨ Check Box.

Like other form objects, check boxes can be given a unique name in the text box provided in the Check Box Property Inspector (Figure 13-5). If you don't provide one, Dreamweaver inserts a generic one, such as checkbox4.

Insert Check Box

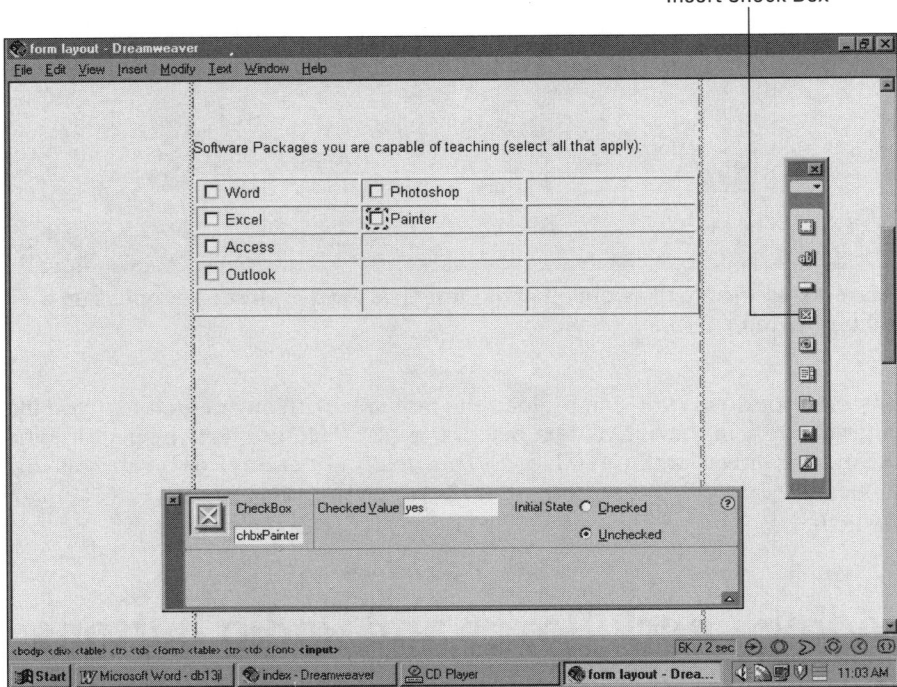

Figure 13-5: Check boxes are one way of offering the Web page visitor any number of options to choose.

In the CheckedValue text box, fill in the information you want passed to a program when the user selects the check box.

By default, a check box starts out unchecked, but you can change that by changing the Initial State option to Checked.

Radio buttons

Radio buttons on a form provide a distinct set of options, from which the user can only choose one. If users change their minds after choosing one radio button, selecting another one automatically deselects the first choice. You insert radio buttons in the same manner as check boxes. Choose or drag Insert Radio Button from the Forms panel of the Object Palette, or choose Insert ➪ Form Objects ➪ Radio Button.

Unlike check boxes and text fields, each radio button in the set does not have a unique name — instead, each *group* of radio buttons does. Giving the entire set of radio buttons the same name allows browsers to assign one value to the radio button set. That value is determined by the contents of the Checked Value text box. In the form example in Figure 13-6, there are two different sets of radio buttons. One is named `rbComputers` and the other, `rbOpSys`.

To designate the default selection for each radio button group, you select the particular radio button and make the Initial State option Checked instead of Unchecked. In the form shown in Figure 13-6, the default selection for the rbOpSys group is Macintosh.

Tip

Because you must give radio buttons in the same set the same name, you can speed up your work a bit by creating one button, copying it, and then pasting the others. Don't forget to change the Checked Value for each button, though.

Creating Form Lists and Menus

Another way to offer your user choices, in a more compact form than radio buttons and check boxes, is with form lists and menus. Both objects can create single-line entries in your form that expand or scroll to reveal all the available options. You can also determine how deep you want the scrolling list to be; that is, how many options you want displayed at a time.

Insert Radio Button

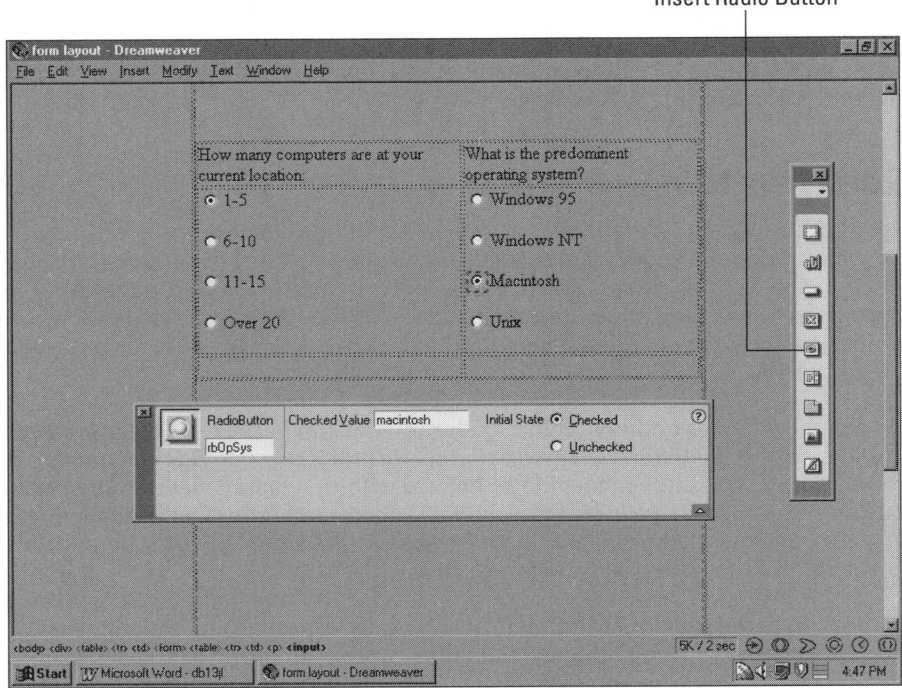

Figure 13-6: Radio buttons allow a user to make just one selection from a group of options.

Drop-down menus

A drop-down menu is very familiar to everyday users of computers: the menu is initially displayed as a single-line text box with an option arrow button at the right end; when the button is clicked, the other options are revealed in a list or menu. (Whether the list "pops up" or "drops down" depends on its position in the browser window at the time it is selected. Normally the list drops down, unless it is close to the bottom of the screen.) The user selects one of the listed choices and, when the mouse is released, the list closes up and the selected value remains displayed in the text box.

Insert a drop-down menu in Dreamweaver as you would any other form object, with one of these actions:

✦ From the Forms panel of the Object Palette, select the Insert List/Menu button to place a drop-down menu at the current cursor position.

✦ Choose Insert ➪ Form Object ➪ List/Menu from the menu to insert a drop-down menu at the current cursor position.

✦ Drag the Insert List/Menu button from the Property Inspector to any location in the Document Window, and release the mouse button to position the drop-down menu.

With the list/menu object inserted, make sure the Menu option (versus the List option) is selected in the Property Inspector as shown in Figure 13-7. You can also name the drop-down menu by typing a name in the Name text box; if you don't, Dreamweaver supplies a generic "select" name.

Insert List/Menu

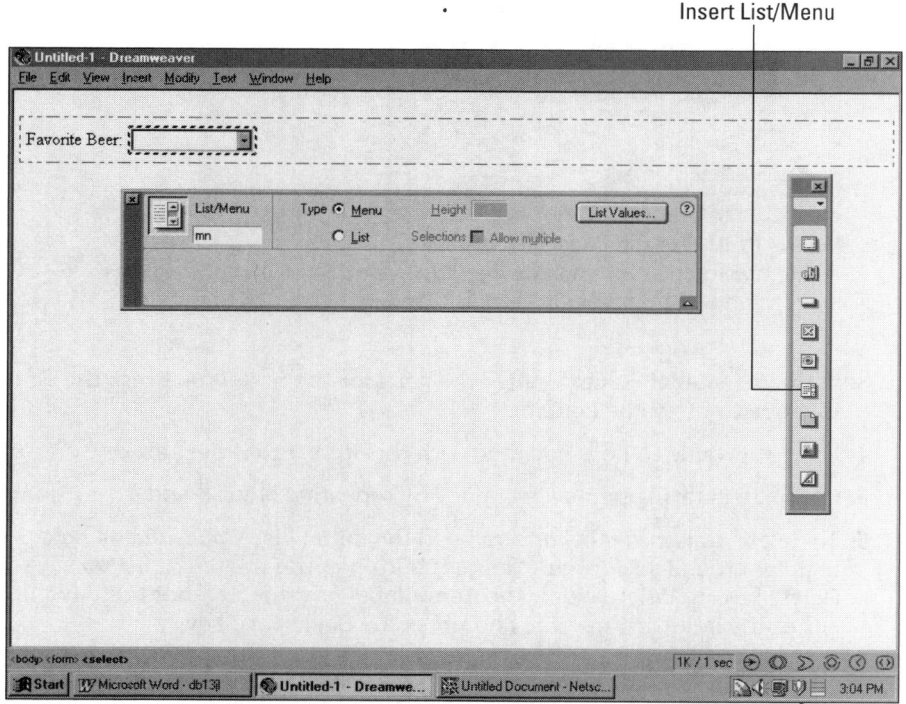

Figure 13-7: Drop-down menus are created by inserting a List/Menu object and then selecting the Menu option in the List/Menu Property Inspector.

Menu values

The HTML code for a drop-down menu uses the `<select>`...`</select>` tag pair surrounding a number of `<option>`...`</option>` tag pairs. Dreamweaver gives you a very straightforward user interface for entering labels and values for the options on your menu. The menu item's *label* is what is displayed on the drop-down list; its *value* is what is sent to the server-side processor when this particular option is selected.

To enter the labels and values for a drop-down menu — or for a scrolling list — follow these steps:

1. Select the menu for which you want to enter values.

2. From the List/Menu Property Inspector, select the List Values button. The Initial List Value dialog box appears (Figure 13-8).

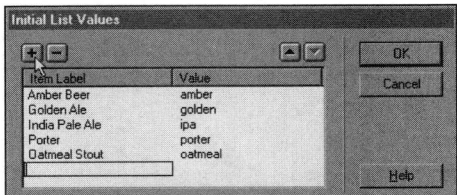

Figure 13-8: Use the Initial List Value dialog box to enter and modify the items in a drop-down menu or scrolling list.

3. In the Item Label column, enter the label for the first item. Press the Tab key to move to the Value column.

4. Enter the value to be associated with this item. Press the Tab key.

5. Continue entering items and values by repeating Steps 3 and 4.

6. To delete an item's label *and* value in the Initial List Values dialog box, highlight it and select the – (minus) button at the top of the list, or press the Delete key. To delete either the item's label *or* value, but not both, highlight either the label or the value and press the Backspace key.

7. To continue adding items, select the + (Add) button (as shown in Figure 13-8).

8. To rearrange the order of items in the list, select an item and then press the up or down keys to reposition it.

9. Click OK when you've finished.

If you haven't entered a value for every item, the server-side application receives the label instead. Generally, however, it is a good idea to specify a value for all items.

Tip

In the browser (you don't see it in the Document Window), an unopened drop-down list usually displays the first item of the menu. You can, however, choose another item for this display by using the `selected` attribute in the `<option>` tag, like this:

```
<option value= ipa  selected>India Pale Ale</option>
```

The `selected` attribute must be entered in the HTML code by hand.

Scrolling lists

A scrolling list differs from a drop-down menu in three respects. First, and most obviously, the scrolling list field has up- and down-arrow buttons rather than an option arrow button, and the user can scroll the list, showing one item at a time, instead of the entire list. Second, you can control the height of the scrolling list, enabling it to display more than one item — or all available items — simultaneously. Third, you can allow the user to select more than one item at a time, as with check boxes.

A scrolling list is inserted in the same manner as a drop-down menu — through the Object Palette or the Insert ➪ Form Object menu. Once the object is inserted, select the List option in the List/Menu Property Inspector.

You enter items for your scrolling list just as you do with a drop-down menu, by starting with the List Values button and filling in the Initial List Values dialog box.

As it does for drop-down menus, Dreamweaver automatically shows the first list item in the scrolling list's single-line text box. However, all the list items are displayed in the Document Window, as shown in Figure 13-9.

By default, the check box for Allow multiple selections is enabled in the List/Menu Property Inspector, and the Height box (which controls the number of items visible at one time) is empty. When multiple selections are enabled, the user can then make multiple selections by using two keyboard modifiers, the Shift and Control key:

✦ To select several adjacent items in the list, the user must click the first item in the list, press the Shift key, and select the last item in the list.

✦ To select several nonadjacent items, the user must hold down the Control key while selecting the items.

Other than the highlighted text, no other acknowledgment (such as a check mark) appears in the list.

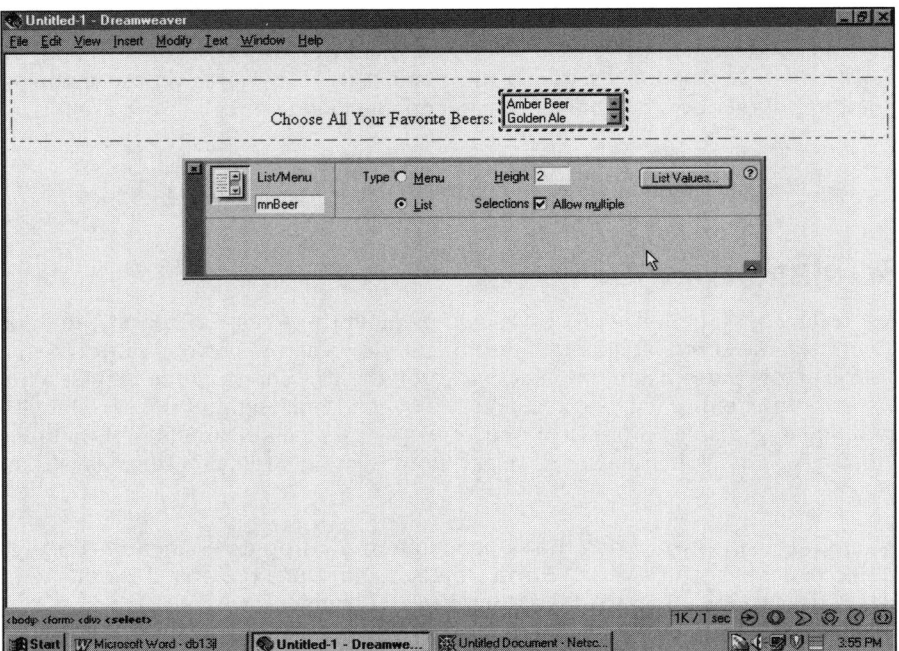

Figure 13-9: Scrolling lists allow multiple selections.

Tips for scrolling lists

There are several factors to keep in mind as you are working with scrolling lists:

✦ If you disable the Allow Multiple Selections box and do not set a Height value greater than 1, the list appears as a drop-down menu.

✦ If you do not set a Height value at all, the number of items that appear on screen is left up to the browser. Internet Explorer, by default, shows four items at a time, and Navigator displays *all* the items in your list. To exercise control over your scrolling list, it is best to insert a Height value.

✦ The widths of both the scrolling list and the drop-down menu are determined by the number of characters in the longest label. To widen the list/menu object, you must directly enter additional spaces in the HTML code; Dreamweaver does not recognize additional spaces entered through the Initial List Values dialog box. For example, to expand the Favorite Beer list/menu object in our example, you'd need use the HTML Inspector or another editor to change this code:

```
<option value= oatmeal >Oatmeal Stout </option>
```

to this:

```
<option value= oatmeal      >Oatmeal Stout </option>
```

Activating Your Form with Buttons

Command buttons are essential to HTML forms. You can place all the form objects you want on a page, but until your user presses that Submit button, there's no interaction between the client and the server. HTML provides three basic types of buttons: Submit, Reset, and command buttons.

Submit, Reset, and command buttons

A Submit button sends the form to the specified Action (generally a URL of a server-side program, or a mailto address) using the noted Method (generally post). A Reset button clears all the fields in the form. Submit and Reset are both reserved HTML terms used to invoke specific actions.

A command button permits the execution of functions defined by the Web designer, as programmed in JavaScript or other languages.

To insert a button in Dreamweaver, follow these steps:

1. Position the cursor where you want the button to appear. Then either select the Insert Button icon from the Form pane of the Object Palette, or choose Insert ➪ Form Objects ➪ Button from the menus. Or you can simply drag the Insert Button button from the Objects Palette and drop it into place on an existing form.

2. Choose the button type. As shown in Figure 13-10, the Button Property Inspector indicates that the Submit Form button type is selected. (This is the default.) To make a Reset button, select the Reset Form option. To make a command button, select the None option.

3. To change the name of any button as you want it to appear on the Web page, enter the new name in the Label text box.

Tip

When working with command buttons, it's not enough to just insert the button and give it a name. You have to link the button to a specific function. A common technique is to use JavaScript's onClick event to call a function detailed in the <script> section of the document, like this:

```
<input type= BUTTON  name= submit2  value= yes
onClick= doFunction( ) >
```

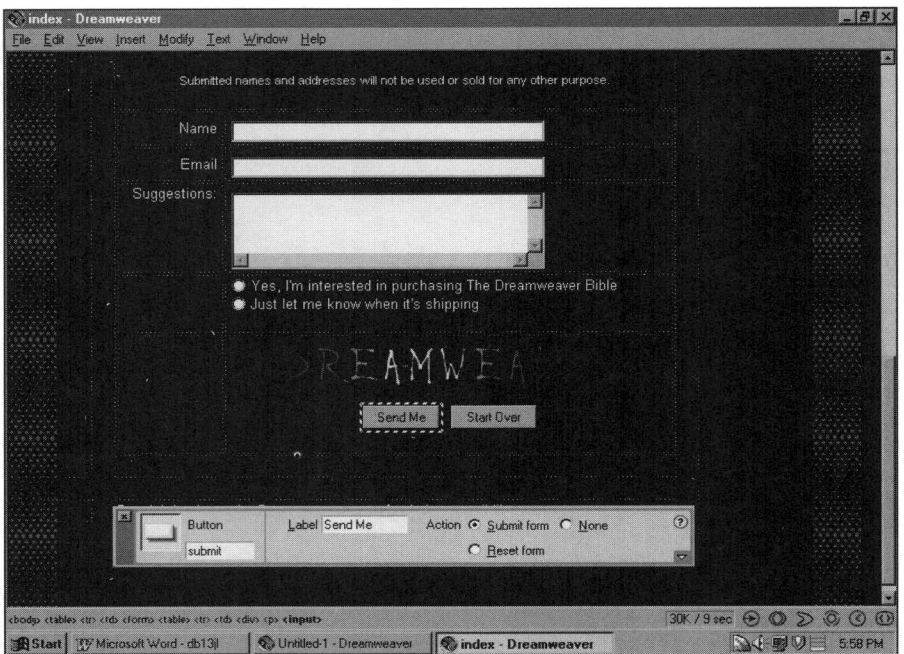

Figure 13-10: You can choose a function and a label for a button through the Button Property Inspector.

Graphical buttons

HTML doesn't limit you to the browser-style default buttons. You can also use an image as a Submit, Reset or command button. Dreamweaver 1.2 adds the capability to include an Image field. You add an image field as you do other form elements: Place the cursor in the desired position, and choose Insert ⇨ Form Object ⇨ Image Field or select the Image Field button from the Forms panel of the Object Palette. You can use multiple image fields in a form to give the user a graphical choice, as shown in Figure 13-11.

When the user clicks the picture that you've designated as an image field for a Submit button, the form is submitted. Any other functionality, such as resetting the fields, must be coded in JavaScript or another language and triggered by attaching an onClick event to the button. This can be handled through the Dreamweaver Behaviors, covered in Chapter 17, "Creating and Using Behaviors," or by hand-coding the script and inserting the onClick code.

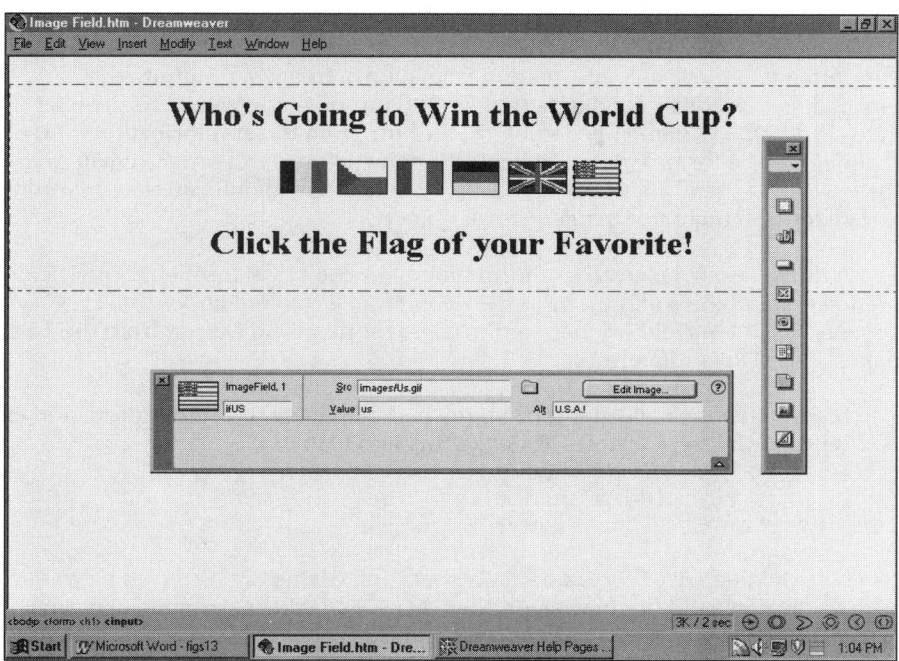

Figure 13-11: Each flag in this page is not just an image; it's an image field that also acts as a Submit button.

Note

In fact, when the user clicks a graphical button, not only will it submit your form, but it will also pass along the x, y coordinates of the image. The x coordinate is submitted using the name of the field and a `.x` attached; likewise, the y coordinate is submitted with the name of the field and a `.y` attached. Although this latter feature isn't often used, it's always good to know all the capabilities of your HTML tools.

Using the Hidden Field and the File Field

There are a couple of other special-purpose form fields that you should be aware of. The *hidden field* and *file field* are supported through all major browsers. The hidden field is extremely useful for passing variables to your gateway programs, and the file field allows the user to attach a file to the form being submitted.

The hidden input type

Very often when passing information from a form to a CGI program, the programmer needs to send data that should not be made visible to the user. The data could be a variable needed by the CGI program to set information on the recipient of the form, or it could be a URL to which the CGI program will redirect the user after the form is submitted. To send this sort of information unseen by the form user, you must use a *hidden* form object.

The hidden field is inserted in a form much like the other form elements. To insert a hidden field, place your cursor in the desired position and choose Insert ➪ Form Objects ➪ Hidden Field or choose the Insert Hidden Field button from the Forms panel of the Object Palette.

The hidden object is another input type, just like the text, radio button, and check box types. A hidden variable looks like this in HTML:

```
<input type= hidden  name= recipient
value= jlowery@idest.com >
```

As you would expect, there is no representation of this tag when it's viewed though a browser. However, Dreamweaver does display a Hidden Form Element Invisible symbol in the Document Window. You can turn off the display of this symbol by deselecting the Hidden Form Element option from the Invisible Elements panel of Preferences.

The file input type

Much more rarely used than the *hidden* input type is the *file* input type, which allows any stored computer file to be attached to the form and sent with the other data. Used primarily to allow for the easy sharing of data, the file input type has been largely supplanted by modern e-mail methods, which also allow for files to be attached to any message.

The file field is inserted in a form much like the other form elements. To insert a file field, place your cursor in the desired position, and choose Insert ➪ Form Objects ➪ File Field or choose the Insert File Field button from the Forms panel of the Object Palette. Dreamweaver automatically inserts a text box for the filename to be input, with a Browse button on the right. In a browser, the user's selection of the Browse button displays a standard Open File dialog box, from which a file can be selected to go with the form.

Applying Dreamweaver's Form/CGI Technique

Dreamweaver includes a simple form and CGI demonstration with both HTML and Perl code. To view the files from a browser, open the file testform.htm in the Dreamweaver/Techniques/form_cgi folder.

The basic file illustrates a form layout and contains code to send the processed data to a CGI program called mailform.pl. As with all Dreamweaver Techniques, you'll be able to examine the actual code as well as follow the step-by-step instructions. At the top of the Dreamweaver Technique window, just select either See the Code or Do It in Dreamweaver, as shown in Figure 13-12. Be sure to select the available links that describe how to use Dreamweaver and the mailform CGI program. There are essential steps included in that file that must be followed for the form and CGI program to work.

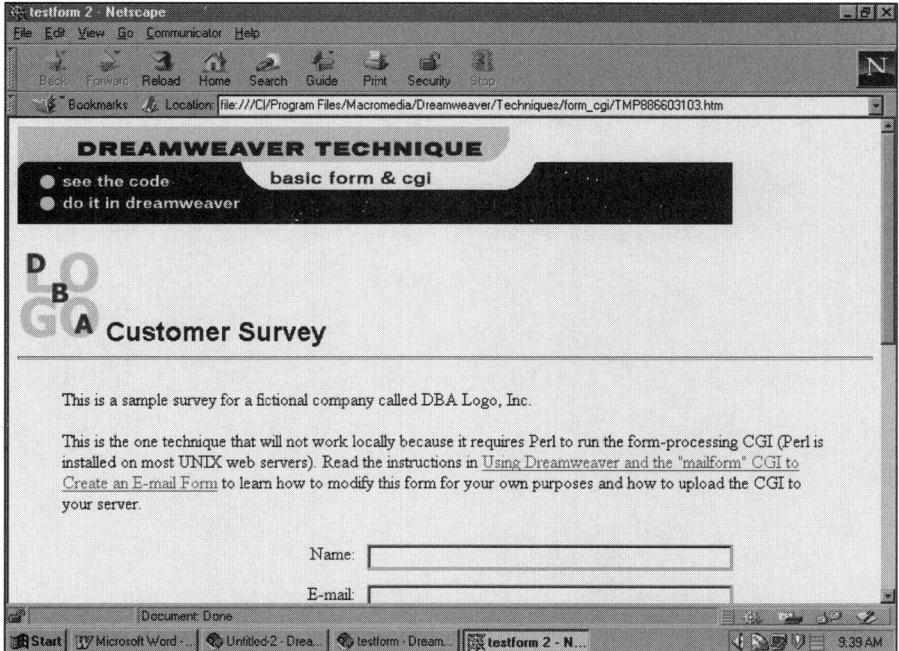

Figure 13-12: This Dreamweaver Technique teaches you how to use a form and CGI program together.

Summary

HTML forms provide a basic line of communication from Web page visitor to Web page creator. With Dreamweaver you can enter and modify most varieties of form inputs, including text fields and check boxes.

✦ For the most part, a complete form requires two working parts: the form object inserted in your Web page, and a CGI program stored on your Web server.

✦ To avoid using a server-side script, you can use a mailto address rather than a URL pointing to a program in a form's `action` attribute. However, you will still have to parse the form reply to convert it to a usable format.

✦ The basic types of form input are text fields, text areas, radio buttons, check boxes, drop-down menus, and scrolling lists.

✦ Once a form is completed is must be sent to the server-side application. This is usually done through a Submit button on the form. Dreamweaver also supports Reset and user-definable command buttons.

In the next chapter, you'll learn how to use Dreamweaver to develop frames and framesets.

✦   ✦   ✦

Using Frames and Framesets

The first time I fully appreciated the power of frames I was visiting a site that displayed examples of what the Webmaster considered "bad" Web pages. The site was essentially a jump-station with a series of links — the author used a frameset with three frames: one that ran all the way across the top of the page, displaying a logo and other basic information; one narrow panel on the left with a scrolling set of links to the sites themselves, and the main viewing area, which took up two-thirds of the center screen. Selecting any of the links caused the site to appear in the main viewing frame.

I was astounded when I finally realized that each frame was truly an independent Web page, and that you didn't have to use only Web pages on your own site — you could link to any page on the Internet. That was when I also realized the amount of work involved in establishing a frame Web site: Every page displayed on that site used multiple HTML pages.

Dreamweaver takes the head-pounding complexity out of coding and managing frames with a point-and-click interface. You get easy access to the commands for modifying the properties of the overall frame structure as well as each individual frame. This chapter gives you an overview of frames, as well as all the specifics you'll need for inserting and modifying frames and framesets. Special attention is given to defining the unique look of frames through borders, scroll bars, and margins.

Frames constitute one of the Webmaster's major design tools. A frame is a Web page that is subdivided into both static and changing HTML pages. Not too long ago, the evolution of frames was right where Dynamic HTML is today, in terms of general acceptance. The use of frames and framesets has become even more widespread over the last year or so, and the technology is now supported through every major browser version. It's safe to say that every Web designer today needs a working knowledge of frames to stay competitive.

Frames and Framesets: The Basics

It's best to think of frames in two major parts: the frameset and the frames. The *frameset* is the HTML document that defines the framing structure — the number of individual frames that make up a page, their initial size, and the shared attributes among all the frames. A frameset by itself is never displayed. *Frames*, on the other hand, are complete HTML documents that can be viewed and edited separately or together in the organization described by the frameset.

A frameset takes the place of the `<body>` tags in an HTML document, where the content of a Web page is found. Here's what the HTML for a basic frameset looks like:

```
<frameset rows= 50%,50% >
  <frame src= top.html >
  <frame src= bottom.html >
</frameset>
```

Notice that the content of a `<frameset>` tag consists entirely of `<frame>` tags, each one referring to a different Web page. The only other element that can be used inside of a `<frameset>` tag is another `<frameset>` tag.

Columns and rows

Framesets, much like tables, are made of columns and rows. The columns and rows attributes (`cols` and `rows`) are lists of comma-separated values. The number of values indicates the number of either columns or rows, and the values themselves establish the size of the columns or rows. Thus, a `<frameset>` tag that looks like this:

```
<frameset cols= 67,355,68 >
```

denotes that there are three columns of widths 67, 355, and 68, respectively. And this frameset tag:

```
<frameset cols= 270,232  rows= 384,400 >
```

declares that there are two columns with the specified widths (270 and 232) and two rows with the specified heights (384 and 400).

Sizing frames

Column widths and row heights can be set as absolute measurements in pixels, or expressed as a percentage of the entire screen. HTML frames also support an attribute that assigns the size relative to the other columns or rows. In other words, the relative attribute (designated with an asterisk) assigns the balance of the remaining available screen space to a column or row. For example, the following frameset:

```
<frameset cols= 80,* >
```

sets up two frames, one 80 pixels wide and the other as large as the browser window allows. This assures that the first column will always be a constant size — making it perfect for a set of navigation buttons — while the second is as wide as possible.

The relative attribute can also be used proportionally. When preceded by an integer, as in n*, this attribute specifies that the frame is allocated *n* times the space it would have received otherwise. So frameset code like this:

```
<frameset rows= 4*,* >
```

will assure that one row is proportionately four times the size of the other.

Creating a Frameset and Frames

Dreamweaver offers two ways to divide your Web page into frames and make your frameset. The first method uses the menus. Choose Modify ➪ Frameset, and from the submenu, select the direction in which you would like to split the frame: left, right, up, or down. Left or right splits the frame in half vertically; up or down splits it horizontally in half.

To create a frameset visually using the mouse, follow these steps:

1. Turn on the frame borders in your Dreamweaver Document Window by selecting View ➪ Frame Borders.

   A three-pixel-wide inner border appears along the edges of your Document Window.

2. Position the cursor over any of the frame borders.

3. Press Alt (Option).

   If your pointer is over a frame border, the pointer changes into a two-headed arrow when over an edge and a four-headed arrow (or a drag-hand on the Mac) when over a corner.

4. Drag the frame border into the Document Window. Figure 14-1 shows a four-frame frameset being created.

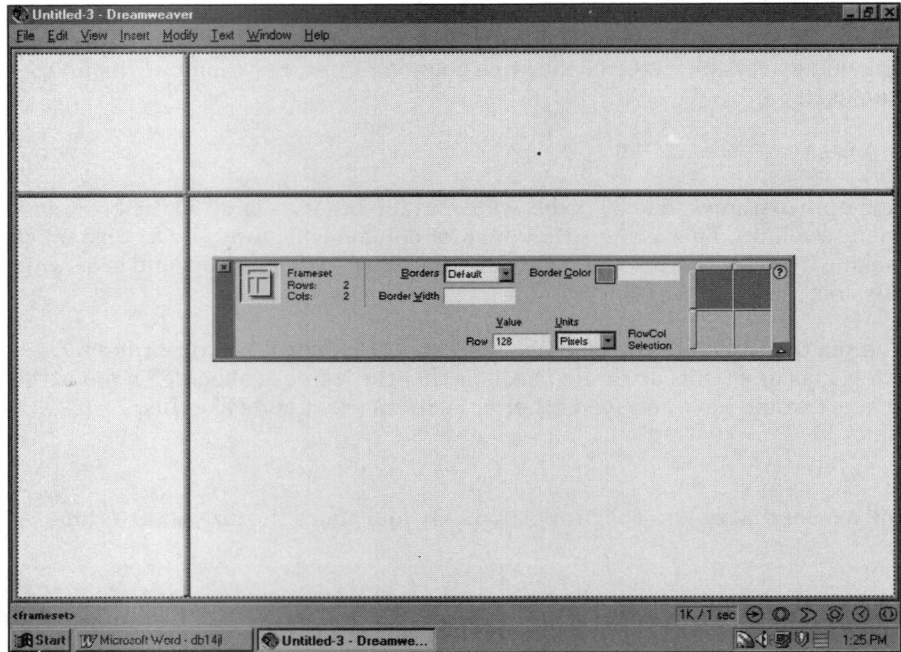

Figure 14-1: After you've enabled the frame borders, you can drag out your frameset structure with the mouse.

Dreamweaver assigns a temporary filename and an absolute pixel value initially to your HTML frameset code. Both can be modified later, if you wish.

Tip   With the menu method of frameset creation, you can only create a two-way frame split, initially. To further split the frame using the menu commands, you must first select each frame. However, by Alt-dragging (Option-dragging) the corner of the frame border, you can quickly create a four-frame frameset.

When the frameset is selected Dreamweaver displays a black dotted line along all the frame borders and within every frame. You can easily reposition any frameset border by clicking and dragging it. If you just want to move the border, make sure you don't press the Alt or Option key while dragging the border; this action creates additional frames.

Caution   If you create a four-frame frameset in two stages, by first splitting the Web page in one direction and then dragging a frame border to split it in another, you'll find a small aberration in the HTML code. Dreamweaver adds the relative indicator (*) to the second set of frames, as shown in this code:

```
<frameset rows= 265,237  cols= 323*,455 >
```

Although, in most cases, this coding will not create any problems for the user, it could lead to undesired results when the window is resized. To avoid this possible problem, when you know you are building a four frame frameset, drag the frame border from the corner to create the frameset all at once. If you must create the frameset in two steps, change the relative value to a pixel or percentage value.

Adding more frames

You're not at all limited to your initial frame choices. In addition to being able to move them visually, you can also set the size through the Frameset Property Inspector, as described in the next section. Furthermore, you can continue to split either the entire frame or each column or row as needed. When you divide a column or row into one or more frames, you are actually nesting one frameset inside another.

Tip   Once you've created the basic frame structure, you can select View ➪ Frame Borders again (it's a toggle) to turn the borders off and give a more accurate preview of your page.

Using the menus

To split an existing frame using the menus, position the cursor in the frame you want to alter, and choose Modify ➪ Frameset ➪ Split Frame Left, Right, Up or Down. Figure 14-2 shows a two-row frameset in which the bottom row was split into two columns and then repositioned. The Frameset Property Inspector indicates that the inner frameset (2 columns, 1 row) is selected.

You can clearly see the "nested" nature of the code in this HTML fragment describing the frameset in Figure 14-2.

```
<frameset rows= 163,333  cols= 784 >
  <frame src= file://Dev/UntitledFrame-34 >
  <frameset cols= 115,663  rows= * >
    <frame src= file://Dev/UntitledFrame-57 >
    <frame src= file://Dev/UntitledFrame-35 >
  </frameset>
</frameset>
```

Tip   You can also split an existing frame by Alt-dragging (Option-dragging) the current frame's border, but you have to choose an inner border that does not extend across the page.

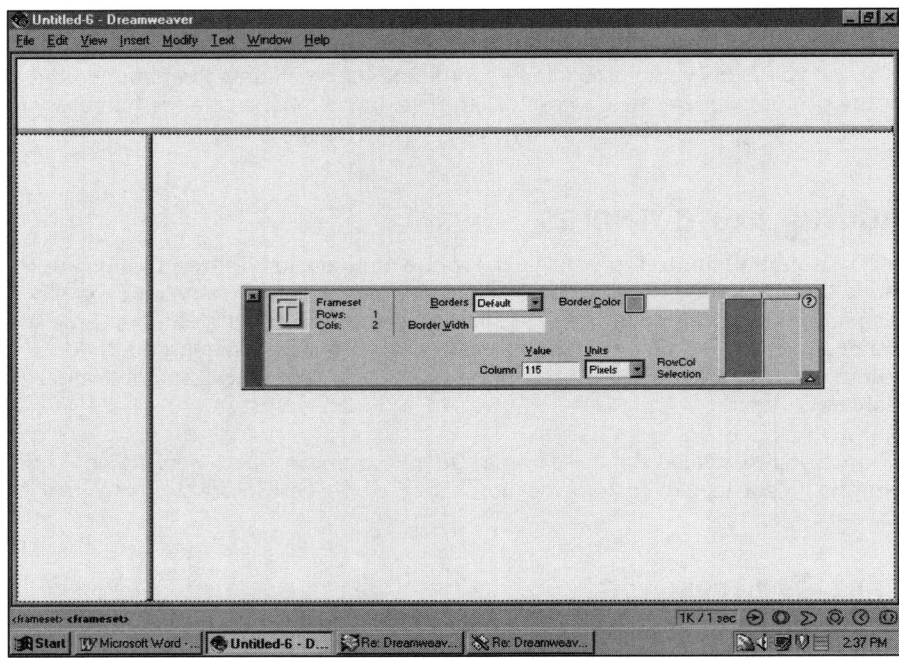

Figure 14-2: Use the Modify ➪ Frameset menu option to split an existing frame into additional columns or rows and create a nested frameset.

Using the mouse

When you need to create additional columns or rows that span the entire Web page, use the mouse method instead of the menus. Option-drag or Alt-drag any of the current frame's borders that go across the entire page, such as one of the outer borders. Figure 14-3 shows a new row added along the bottom of our previous frame structure.

Tip

You can also split a smaller frame by first selecting it and then Alt- or Option-dragging one of its borders. As you'll see in this chapter, you select a frame by Alt-clicking (Windows) or Option-Shift-clicking (Macintosh) inside the frame.

The new row

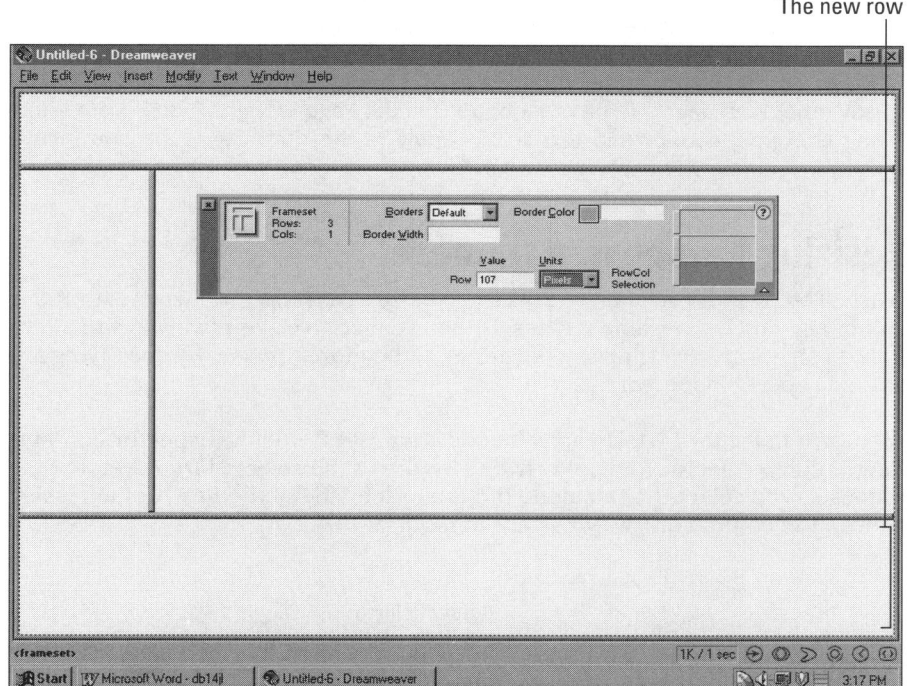

Figure 14-3: An additional frame row was added using the Alt-drag (Option-drag) method.

Working with the Frameset Property Inspector

The Frameset Property Inspector manages those elements, such as the borders, that are common to all the frames within a frameset; it also offers more precise sizing control over individual rows and columns than you can do visually. To access the Frameset Property Inspector, choose Window ⇨ Properties if the Property Inspector is not already open, and then select any of the frame borders.

Tip

When a browser visits a Web page that uses frames, it displays the title found in the frameset HTML document for the entire frame. You can set that title in Dreamweaver by selecting the frameset and then choosing Modify ➪ Page Properties. In the Page Properties dialog box, enter your choice of title in the Title text box, as you would for any other Web page. All the other options in the Page Properties dialog box — including background color and text color — apply to the `<noframes>` content, covered later in "Handling Frameless Browsers."

Resizing frames in a frameset

With HTML, when you want to specify the size of a frame, you work with the row or column in which the frame resides. Dreamweaver gives you two ways to alter a frame's size — by dragging the border or, to be more precise, by specifying a value in the Property Inspector.

As shown in Figure 14-4, Dreamweaver's Frameset Property Inspector contains a Row/Column selector to display the structure of the selected frameset. For each frameset, you select the tab along the top or left side of the Row/Column selector to choose the column or row you want to modify.

Row/Column
Selector tabs

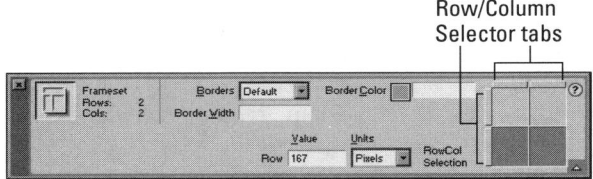

Figure 14-4: In the Frameset Property Inspector, you use the Row/Column Selector tabs to choose which frame you are going to resize.

Tip

The Row/Column Selector only shows one frameset at a time. So if your design uses nested framesets, you won't see an exact duplicate of your entire Web page in the Row/Column Selector.

Whether you need to modify just a row, a column, or both a row and a column depends on the location of the frame.

✦ If your frame spans the width of an entire page, like the top or bottom row in Figure 14-4, select the corresponding tab on the left side of the Row/Column selector.

✦ If your frame spans the height of an entire page, select the equivalent tab along the top of the Row/Column selector.

✦ If your frame does not span either height or width, like the middle two rows in Figure 14-4, you need to select both its column and its row, and modify the size of each in turn.

Once you have selected the row or column, follow these steps to specify its size:

1. To specify the size in pixels, enter a number in the Property Inspector's Value text box, and select Pixels as the Units option.

2. To specify the size as a percentage of the screen, enter a number from 1 to 100 in the Value text box, and select Percent as the Units option.

3. To specify a size relative to the other columns or rows, first select Relative as the Units option. Then:

   • To set the size to occupy the remainder of the screen, delete any number that may be entered in the Value text box; optionally, you can enter a 1.

   • To scale the frame relative to the other rows or columns, type the scale factor in the Value text box. For example, if you want the frame to be twice the size of another relative frame, put a 2 in the Value text box.

Tip

The Relative size operator is generally used to indicate you want the current frame to take up the balance of the frameset column or row. This makes it easy to specify a size without having to calculate pixel widths, and ensures that the frame will have the largest possible size.

Manipulating frameset borders

By default, Dreamweaver sets up your framesets so all the frames have gray borders that are 6 pixels wide. You can alter the border color, change the width, or eliminate the borders altogether. All of the border controls are handled through the Frameset Property Inspector.

Tip

There are also border controls for individual frames. Just as table cell settings can override options set for the entire table, the individual frame options override those determined for the entire frameset, as described in the section "Working with the Frame Property Inspector" later in this chapter. Use the frameset border controls when you want to make a global change to the borders, like turning them all off.

If you are working with nested framesets, it's important that you select the outermost frameset before you begin making any modifications to the borders. You can tell that you've selected the outermost frameset by looking at the Dreamweaver

Tag Selector; it will show only one `<frameset>` in bold. If you select an inner nested frameset, you'll see more than one `<frameset>` in the Tag Indicator.

Eliminating borders

When a frameset is first created, Dreamweaver leaves the borders display up to the browser's discretion. You can expressly turn the frameset borders on or off through the Property Inspector.

To eliminate borders completely, enter a zero in the Border Width text box. Even if there is no width value displayed, the default is a border 6 pixels wide. If you turn off the borders for your frameset, you can still work in Dreamweaver with the View ➪ Frame Borders enabled, which gives you quick access to modifying the frameset. The borders will not display, however, when your Web page is previewed in a browser.

Border appearance options

You can control the appearance of your borders to a limited degree. In the Borders drop-down list of options, choosing Yes causes browsers to draw the borders with a 3D appearance. Select No, and the frameset borders will be drawn as a single color. The Default option is generally interpreted by browsers as the three-dimensional look.

Border color options

To change the frameset border color, select the Border Color text box and then enter either a color name or hexadecimal color value. You can also select the color swatch and choose a new border color from the browser-safe color picker. Clicking the Palette icon on the color picker opens the extended color selector, just as for other color swatches in Dreamweaver.

Caution   If you have nested framesets on your Web page, make sure you've selected the correct frameset before you make any modifications through the Property Inspector. You can move from a nested frameset to its "parent" by using the keyboard shortcut Alt-Up Arrow (Command-Up Arrow). Likewise, you can move from a parent frameset to its "child" by pressing Alt-Down Arrow (Command-Down Arrow).

Saving a frameset and frames

As mentioned earlier, when you're working with frames, you're working with multiple HTML files. You must be careful to not only save all the individual frames that make up your Web page, but also to save the frameset itself.

Dreamweaver makes it easy to save framesets and included frames by providing several special commands. To save a frameset, choose File ➪ Save Frameset to open the standard Save File dialog box. You can also save a copy of the current frameset by choosing File ➪ Save Frameset As. You don't have to select the frameset border or position your cursor in any special place to activate these functions.

Saving each frame in the frameset can be a chore unless you choose File ➪ Save All. The first time this command is invoked, Dreamweaver cycles through each of the open frames and displays the Save File dialog box. Each subsequent time you choose File ➪ Save All, Dreamweaver automatically saves every file in the frameset that has been updated.

To copy an individual frame, you must use the regular File ➪ Save As command.

Closing a frameset

There's one small trick to closing a Dreamweaver frameset and keeping your Dreamweaver window open: You have to select the frameset border first, before you choose File ➪ Close. Otherwise, Dreamweaver just closes the current frame. Naturally, if there are any unsaved modifications to either the frameset or any of the frames, Dreamweaver asks if you'd like to save the file before closing.

Modifying a Frame

What makes the whole concept of a Web page frame work so well is the flexibility of each frame.

- ✦ You can design your page so that some frames are fixed in size while others are expandable.

- ✦ You can attach scroll bars to some frames and not others.

- ✦ Any frame can have its own background image, and yet all frames can appear as one seamless picture.

- ✦ Borders can be enabled — and colored — for one set of frames, but left off for another set.

Dreamweaver uses a Frame Property Inspector to specify most of a frame's attributes. Others are handled through devices already familiar to you, such as the Page Properties dialog box.

Joining Background Images in Frames

One popular technique is to insert background images into separate frames so they blend into a seamless single image. This takes careful planning and coordination between the author of the graphic and the designer of the Web page.

To accomplish this image consolidation operation, you must first "slice" the image in an image processing program, such as Adobe PhotoShop or Fireworks. Then save each part as a separate graphic, making sure that there is no border around these image sections — each cut-up piece will become the background image for a particular frame. Next, set the background image of each frame to the matching graphic. Be sure to turn off the borders for the frameset, and set the Border Width to zero.

Correct sizing of each piece is important, to ensure that no gaps appear in your joined background. A good technique is to use absolute pixel measurements for images that fill the frame and, where the background images tile, set the frame to Relative spacing. In Figure 14-5, the corner frame has the same measurement as the background image (107×126 pixels), and all the other frames are set to Relative.

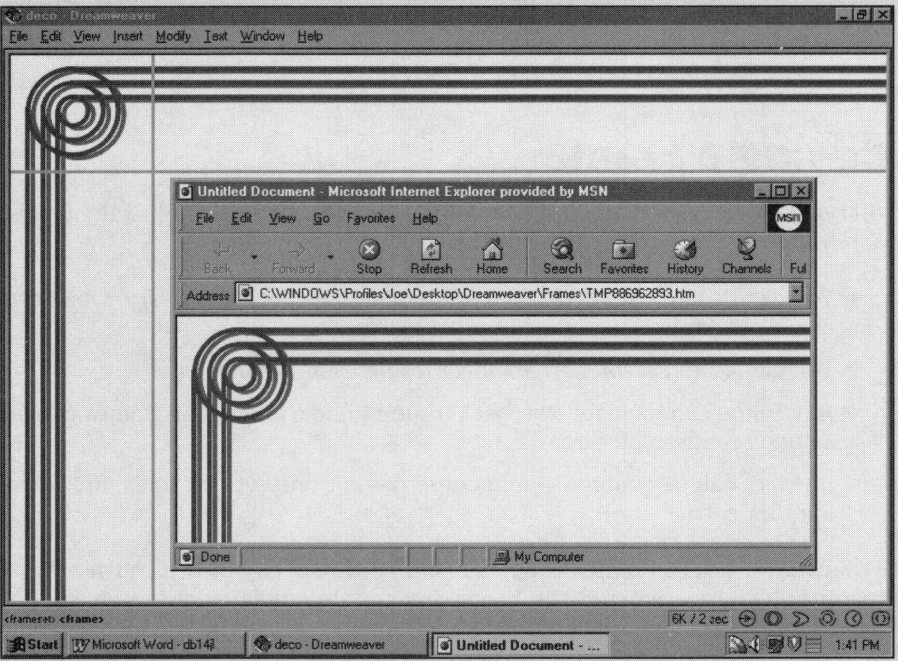

Figure 14-5: You can join frame backgrounds to create a seamless pattern. In the Dreamweaver window, View ⇨ Frame Borders is turned on, but no gap can be seen in the Internet Explorer preview.

Page properties

Each frame is its own HTML document and, as such, each frame can have independent page properties. To alter the page properties of a frame, position the cursor in the frame and then choose Modify ⇨ Page Properties. You can also use the keyboard shortcuts, Ctrl-J or Command-J. Or you can select Page Properties from the shortcut menu by right-clicking (Control-clicking) any open space on the frame's page.

From the Page Properties dialog box, you can assign a title, although it will not become visible to the user unless the frame is viewed as a separate page. If you plan on using the individual frames as separate pages in your <noframes> content (see "Handling Frameless Browsers" at the end of this chapter), it's good practice to title every page. You can also assign a background and the various link colors by selecting the appropriate color swatch or entering a color name into the correct text box.

Working with the Frame Property Inspector

To access the Frame Property Inspector, you must first select a frame. And selecting a frame is different from just positioning the cursor in the frame. There are two ways to properly select a frame: using the Frames Inspector or using the mouse.

The Frames Inspector shows an accurate representation of all the frames in your Web page. Open the Frames Inspector by choosing Window ⇨ Frames. As you can see in Figure 14-6, the Inspector displays names, if assigned, in the individual frames, and (no name) if not. Nested framesets are shown with a heavier border.

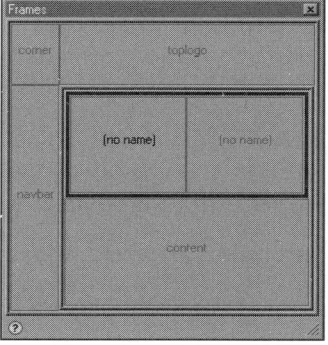

Figure 14-6: Use the Frames Inspector to visually select a frame to modify.

To select a frame, click directly on its represented image in the Frames Inspector. If the Frame Property Inspector is open, it will reflect the selected frame's options. For more complex Web pages, you can resize the Frames Inspector to get a better sense of the page layout. To close the Inspector, select the Close button or choose Window ➪ Frames again.

Tip   When you are working with multiple framesets, use the Tag Selector together with the Frame Inspector to identify the correct nested frameset. Selecting a frameset in the Tag Selector causes it to be identified in the Frame Inspector with a heavy black border.

To select a frame with the mouse, press Alt (Option-Shift) and click into the desired frame. Once the frame is selected, you can move from one frame to another by pressing Alt (Command) and then using the arrow keys.

Naming your frames

Naming each frame is essential to get the most power from a frame-structured Web page. The frame's name is used to make the content inserted from a hyperlink appear in that particular frame.

Cross-Reference   For more information about targeting a link, see "Targeting Frame Content" later in this chapter.

Frame names must follow specific guidelines, as explained in the following steps:

1. Select the frame that you want to name. You can either use the Frames Inspector or Alt-click (Option-Shift-click) inside the frame.

2. If necessary, open the Property Inspector by choosing Window ➪ Properties.

3. In the Frame Property Inspector, shown in Figure 14-7, add the frame's name in the text box next to the frame logo. Frame names have the following restrictions:

   • Use one word, with no spaces.

   • Do not use special characters such as quotation marks, question marks, and hyphens.

   • The underscore character *is* allowed.

   • Certain frame names are reserved: _blank, _parent, _self and _top.

Frame name

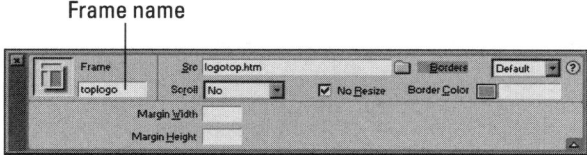

Figure 14-7: The Frame Property Inspector allows you
to name your frame and control all of a frame's attributes.

Opening a Web page into a frame

You don't have to build all Web pages in frames from scratch. You can load an
existing Web page into any frame. If you've selected a frame and the Frame Property
Inspector is open, just type the link directly into the Src text box or choose the
folder icon to browse for your file. Or, you can position your cursor in a frame
(without selecting the frame), and choose File ➪ Open in Frame.

Setting borders

You can generally set most border options adequately in the Frameset Property
Inspector; you can also override some of those options, such as color, for each
frame. There are, however, practical limitations to these possibilities.

To set borders from the Frame Property Inspector for a selected frame, you can
make the borders three-dimensional by choosing Yes in the Borders drop-down
option list, or use the monochrome setting by choosing No. Leaving the Borders
option at Default gives control to the frameset settings. You can also change a
frame's border color by choosing the Border Color swatch in a selected frame's
Property Inspector.

Now, about those limitations: They come into play when you try to implement one
of your border modifications. Because frames share common borders, it is difficult
to isolate an individual frame and have the change affect just the selected frame. As
an example, Figure 14-8 shows a frameset where the borders are set to No for all
frames, except the one on the lower-right. Notice how the top border of the lower-
right frame extends to the left, all the way over the adjacent frame. There are two
possible workarounds for this problem. First, you can design your frames so that
borders do not touch, as in a multirow frameset. Second, you can create a
background image for a frame that includes a border design.

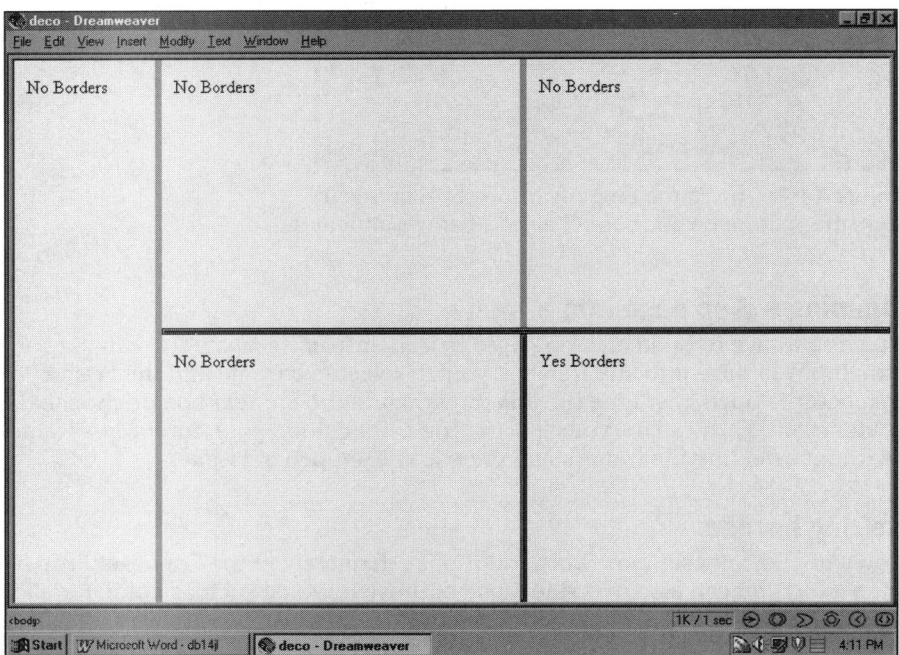

Figure 14-8: If you want to use isolated frame borders, you have to carefully plan your Web page frameset to avoid overlapping borders.

Adding scroll bars

I think one of the features that have given frames the wide use they enjoy of late is the ability to enable or disable scroll bars for each frame. Scroll bars are used when the browser window is too small to display all the information in the Web page frame. The browser window size is completely user-controlled, so the Web designer must apply the various scroll bar options on a frame-by-frame basis, depending on the look desired and the frame's content.

There are four options selectable from the Scroll drop-down list on the Frame Property Inspector:

✦ **Default:** Leaves the use of scroll bars up to the browser.

✦ **Yes:** Forces scroll bars to appear regardless of the amount of content.

✦ **No:** Disables scroll bars.

✦ **Auto:** Turns scroll bars on if the content of the frame extends horizontally or vertically beyond what the browser window can display. Figure 14-9 uses an automatic vertical scroll bar in the lower frame; you can see it on the far right.

Automatic scroll bar enabled

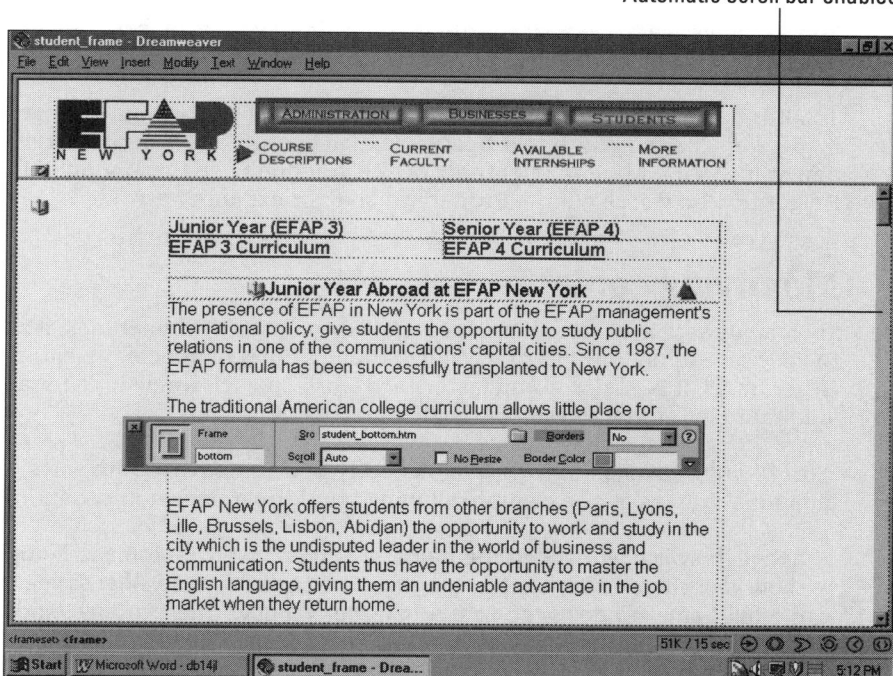

Figure 14-9: Here, the top frame of the Web page has the scroll bars turned off, and the bottom frame has scroll bars enabled.

Resizing

By default, all frames are resizable by the user; that is, a visitor to your Web site can widen, narrow, lengthen, or shorten a frame by dragging the border to a new position. You can disable this resizing capability, however, on a frame-by-frame basis. In the Frame Property Inspector, select the No Resize option to turn off the resizing feature.

Tip

Although it might be tempting to select No Resize for every frame, it's best to allow resizing except in frames that require a set size to maintain their functionality (for instance, a frame containing navigational controls).

Setting margins

Just as you can pad table cells with additional space to separate text and graphics, you can offset content in frames. Dreamweaver lets you control the left/right margins and the top/bottom margins independently. By default, there is normally about 6 pixels of space between the content and the left or right frame borders, and about 15 pixels of space between the content and the top or bottom frame borders. You can increase or decrease these margins, but even if you set the values to zero, there is still some room between the borders and the content.

To alter the left and right margins, change the value in the Frame Property Inspector's Margin Width text box; to change the top and bottom margins, enter a new value in the Margin Height text box. If you don't see the Margin Width and Height text boxes, select the Property Inspector expander arrow.

Modifying content

You can update a frame's content in any way you see fit. Sometimes, it's necessary to keep an eye on how altering a single frame's content affects the entire frame. Other times, it is easier — and faster — to work on each frame individually and later load them into the frameset to see the final result.

With Dreamweaver's multiwindow structure you can have it both ways. Work on the individual frames in one or more windows, and the frameset in yet another.

Although switching back to the frameset window won't automatically update it to show your changed frames, there is one shortcut you can use. After saving changes in the full frame windows, go to the frameset window. Then, in any window you've altered elsewhere, make another small change, such as inserting a space. Finally, choose File ➪ Revert. This command is normally used to revert to the previously saved version, but in this case you're using it to update your frames.

To preview changes made to a Web page using frames, you must first save the changed files. Currently, Dreamweaver creates a temporary file of the frameset but not any of the included frames.

Deleting frames

As you're building your Web page frame, inevitably you'll try a frame design that does not work. How do you delete a frame once you've created it? Click the frame border and drag it into the border of the enclosing or parent frame. When there is no parent frame, drag the frame border to the edge of the page. If the frame that is being deleted contains any unsaved content, Dreamweaver asks if you'd like to save the file before closing it.

Tip

Because the enclosing frameset and each individual frame are all discrete HTML pages, each keeps track of its own edits and other changes — and therefore each has its own Undo memory. If you are in a particular frame and try to Undo a frameset alteration, such as adding a new frame to the set, it won't work. To reverse an edit to the frameset, you have to select the frameset and then choose File ➪ Undo, or use one of the keyboard shortcuts (Ctrl-Z or Command-Z).

Targeting Frame Content

One of the major uses of frames is for navigation control. One frame acts as the navigation center, offering links to various Web pages in a site. When the user selects one of the links, the Web page appears in another frame on the page; and that frame, if necessary, can scroll independently of the navigation frame. This technique keeps the navigation links always visible and accessible.

When you assign a link to appear in a particular frame of your Web page, you are said to be assigning a *target* for the link. You can target specific frames in your Web page, and you can target structural parts of a frameset. In Dreamweaver, targets are assigned through the Text and Image Property Inspectors.

Targeting sections of your frameset

In the earlier section on naming frames, you learned that certain names are reserved. These are the four special names HTML reserves for the parts of a frameset that are used in targeting: _blank, _parent, _self and _top. With them, you can cause content from a link to overwrite the current frame or to appear in an entirely new browser window.

To target a link to a section of your frameset, follow these steps:

1. Select the text or image you want to use as your link.

2. Expand the Text (or Image) Property Inspector, and enter the URL and/or named anchor in Link text box. Alternatively, you can select the folder icon to browse for the file.

3. Press the Tab key twice to accept the entry and to move to the Target text box. (Or just select the Target text box.)

4. Select one of the following reserved target names from the drop-down list of Target options (Figure 14-10), or type an entry into the text box:

   • **_blank** opens the link into a new browser window and keeps the current window available.

- **_parent** opens the link into the parent frameset of the current frame, if any.

- **_self** opens the link into the current frame, replacing its contents (this is the default).

- **_top** opens the link into the outermost frameset of the current Web page, replacing all frames.

The generic nature of these reserved target names allows them to be used repeatedly on different Web pages, without your having to code a particular reference each time.

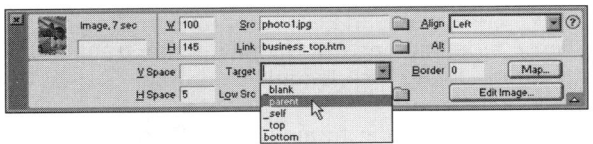

Figure 14-10: Choose your frame target from the Property Inspector's Target drop-down list.

Note   For an example of structural targeting, look at the code for the Dreamweaver Help system. The Index frame, for example, uses the implied _self target whenever a major help topic is selected, to open an HTML document that shows all the subtopics.

Caution   There is a phenomenon known as *recursive frames* that can be dangerous to your site setup. Let's say you have a frameset named index_frame.html. If you include in any frame on your current page a link to index_frame.html, and set the target as _self, when the user selects that link the entire frameset loads into the current frame — including another link to index_frame.html. Browsers can handle about three or four iterations of this recursion before they crash. To avoid the problem, set your frameset target to _top.

Targeting specific frames in your frameset

Earlier I stressed the importance of naming each frame in your frameset. Once you have entered a name in the Name text box of the Frame Property Inspector, Dreamweaver dynamically updates the Target list to include that name. This feature allows you to target specific frames in your frameset in the same manner that you target the reserved names noted above.

Although you can always type the frame name directly in the Name text box, the drop-down option list comes in handy for this task. Not only do you avoid having to keep track of the various frame names in your Web page, but you avoid typing errors as well. Targets *are* case-sensitive, and names must match exactly or the browser won't be able to find the target.

Updating two frames or more at once

Sooner or later, most Web designers using frames have the need to update more than frame with a single click. The problem is, you can't group two or more URLs together in an anchor tag. Here is an easy-to-implement solution, thanks to Dreamweaver's behaviors.

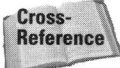 **Cross-Reference** If you're not familiar with Dreamweaver's JavaScript behaviors, you might want to look over Chapter 17, "Creating and Using Behaviors," before continuing.

To update more than one frame target from a single link, follow these steps:

1. Select your link in the frame.

2. Open the Behavior Inspector from the Launcher or by choosing Window ➪ Behaviors.

3. Make sure that 4.0 Browsers is selected in the Event pane of the Behavior Inspector.

4. Select the + (Add) Event button and choose onClick from the drop-down option list.

5. In the Actions pane, choose the + (Add) Actions button and choose Go To URL from the drop-down option list.

6. Dreamweaver displays the Go To URL dialog box (Figure 14-11) and scans your document for all named frames. Select a target frame from the list of windows or frames.

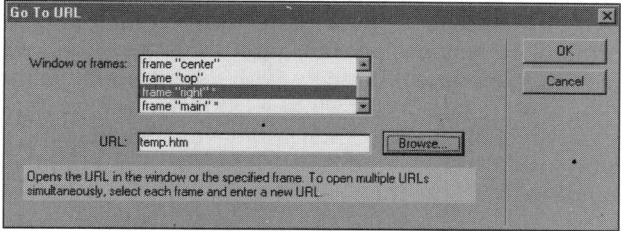

Figure 14-11: You can cause two or more frames to update from a single link by using Dreamweaver's Go To URL behavior.

7. Enter a URL, or choose the Browse button to select one.

Dreamweaver places an asterisk after the targeted frame, to indicate that a URL has been selected for it. You can see this in Figure 14-11.

8. Repeat Steps 6 and 7 for any additional frames you want to target.

9. Click OK when you're finished.

Now, whenever you click your one link, the browser opens the URLs in the targeted frames in the order specified.

Handling Frameless Browsers

Not all of today's browsers support frames. Netscape began supporting frames in Navigator version 2.0; Microsoft didn't start until IE version 3.0 — and a large number of earlier versions for both browsers are still in use. There are also other less prevalent browsers that don't support frames at all. HTML has a built-in mechanism for working with browsers that are not frame-enabled: the `<noframes>...</noframes>` tag pair.

When you begin to construct any frameset, Dreamweaver automatically inserts a `<noframes>` area just below the closing `</frameset>` tag. If a browser is not frames-capable, it ignores the frameset and frame information and renders what is found in the `<noframes>` section.

What should you put into the `<noframes>` section? To ensure the widest possible audience, Webmasters typically insert links to a nonframe version of the site. The links can be as obvious or as discreet as you care to make them. Many Webmasters also include links to current versions of Communicator or Internet Explorer, to encourage their non-frame-capable visitors to upgrade.

Dreamweaver includes a facility for easily adding and modifying the `<noframes>` content. Choose Modify ➪ Frameset ➪ Edit NoFrames Content to open the NoFrames Content window. As you can see in Figure 14-12, this window is identical to the regular Dreamweaver Document Window, with the exception of the "NoFrames Content" in the title bar. In this window you have access to all the same objects and palettes as you do normally. When you have finished editing your `<noframe>` content, Choose Modify ➪ Frameset ➪ Edit NoFrames Content again to deselect the option and return to the frameset.

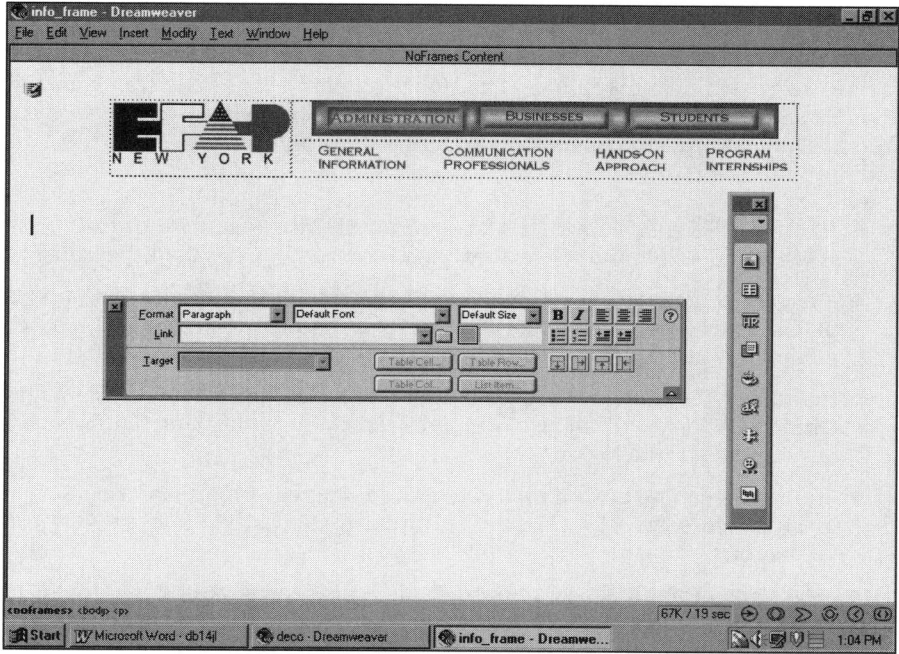

Figure 14-12: Through the Edit NoFrames Content command, Dreamweaver lets you specify what's seen by visitors whose browsers are not frames-capable.

Here are some pointers to keep in mind when working in the NoFrames Content window:

✦ The page properties of the `<noframes>` content are the same as the page properties of the frameset. You can select the frameset and then choose Modify ➪ Page Properties to open the Page Properties dialog box. While in the NoFrames Content window, you can also right-click (Control-click) in any open space to access the Page Properties command.

✦ Dreamweaver disables the File ➪ Open commands when the NoFrames Content window is on screen. To move existing content into the `<noframes>` section, use Dreamweaver's Copy and Paste features.

✦ The `<noframes>` section is located in the frameset page, which is the primary page examined by search engine "spiders." It's a good idea to enter `<meta>` tag information detailing the site, as described in Chapter 6, "How HTML Works," in the frameset page. While you're in the NoFrames Content window, you can open the HTML Inspector and add the `<meta>` tags.

Summary

Frames are a significant Webmaster design tool. With frames and framesets you can divide a single Web page into multiple, independent areas. Dreamweaver gives the Web designer quick and easy access to frame design through the program's drag-and-drop interface.

✦ A framed Web page consists of a separate HTML document for each frame and one additional file that describes the frame structure, called the frameset.

✦ A frameset comprises columns and rows, which can be sized absolutely in pixels, or as a percentage of the browser window, or relative to the other columns or rows.

✦ Dreamweaver allows you to reposition the frame borders by dragging them to a new location. You can also add new frames by Alt-clicking (Option-clicking) any existing frame border.

✦ Framesets can be nested to create more complex column and row arrangements. Selecting the frame border displays the Frameset Property Inspector.

✦ Select any individual frame through the Frame Inspector or by Alt-clicking (Option-Shift-clicking) within any frame. Once the frame is selected, the Frame Property Inspector can be displayed.

✦ You make your links appear in a specific frame by assigning targets to the links. Dreamweaver supports both structured and named targets. You can update two or more frames with one link by using a Dreamweaver JavaScript behavior.

✦ You should include information and/or links for browsers that are not frames-capable, through Dreamweaver's Edit NoFrames Content feature.

In the next chapter, you learn how to add video to your Web pages in Dreamweaver.

✦   ✦   ✦

Extending HTML Through Dreamweaver

P A R T

IV

◆ ◆ ◆ ◆

In This Part

Chapter 15
Accessing External
Programs

Chapter 16
Creating and Using
Objects

Chapter 17
Creating and Using
Behaviors

◆ ◆ ◆ ◆

Accessing External Programs

Until recently, you could create relatively static Web pages made of text and images with "basic" HTML, but you needed additional code for more action. Without using some of the advanced capabilities of Dynamic HTML — viewable only with a fourth-generation browser — animated GIFs have been your sole option for any sort of motion on a self-contained Web page. HTML need not stand alone, however; the language allows for several methods to extend its capabilities.

Using external programs along with HTML, you can:

✦ Collect data from the user

✦ Add multimedia elements such as audio, video, animation, and virtual reality

✦ Allow a Web browser to present almost any kind of information in its native format

✦ Dynamically create Web pages based on a user's request

Dreamweaver gives you various methods — some specific to the file type and others more generic — for accessing a full range of external programs invaluable to the Web author. In this chapter, you learn how to send information to and from the server through CGI programs, install feature-extending plug-ins and ActiveX controls, incorporate custom-built Java applets, and work with scripting languages such as JavaScript and VBScript.

Generally, the techniques for melding any of the external capabilities with your Web page are quite straightforward. Often, however, learning to use the outside program takes a fair amount of time — whether that progam is writing your CGI script or encoding your digital video. You may want to approach each specific technique on a project-by-project basis rather than try to master all of the disciplines at once. No matter how you choose to work, you can always count on Dreamweaver's own extensibility to incorporate every new technology.

Using CGI Programs

When someone clicks a link to a Web page, a message is sent to a particular Web server, which then sends the components of that Web page — the HTML file and any associated graphic files — back to the user. Usually most information is sent over the Web from the server to the client. But how do you send information in the opposite direction, from the client to the server?

The standard method is to use a Common Gateway Interface (CGI) program. CGI programs or scripts (the terms are used interchangeably) perform many different kinds of Internet functions, but they all entail collecting data from the user and passing it to the server. Whether the server stores the information in a database, manipulates and passes it on to another system, or generates a new Web page to be sent to the user depends on the design of the CGI program.

Creating and calling scripts

CGI programs can be written in any number of computer languages, including C/C++, Fortran, Perl, TCL, UNIX shell, Visual Basic, AppleScript, and others. The only requirement is that the program must be executable by the type of server processing the information. Perl (Program Extraction and Report Language) is one of the most popular languages used to write CGI programs. Perl is an *interpreted* language — that is, the source code is an ordinary text file compiled at run-time, unlike Java or C++ code, which is previously compiled. Because it is text-based, Perl is easy to modify and particularly strong in parsing and manipulating text — an important capability for interpreting data from forms and other Web-based tasks.

Perl is also difficult to debug, however — you don't get much in the way of error reporting from the Perl interpreter.

Every CGI script must be customized to some extent in order to communicate with a particular server. You can develop your custom CGI program in two ways: build it from scratch yourself or modify an existing script. Modifying an existing script is much easier and a customary practice on the Web. Someone else has probably already developed a CGI script for your situation, and it is probably available for download on the Internet.

Tip

Two great sources for CGI scripts are Matt's Script Archives (`www.worldwidemart`
`.com/scripts/`) and Selena Sol's Public Domain CGI Script Archive (`selena.`
`mcp.com/Scripts/`).

Once your CGI program is completed, three steps remain before it can be used:

✦ The CGI script must be uploaded to your Web server and stored in a special
   directory — often named cgi-bin.

✦ The file permissions need to be set depending on the program's function. File
   permissions determine whether a file can be read, written to, and/or executed
   and by whom. File permissions are explained in the following section.

✦ The CGI program must be referenced or called from the Web page.

Web designers most often use the HTML <form> structure to call a CGI script and
simultaneously pass the data from the user to the server. Dreamweaver enables you
to specify the necessary information through various form objects.

Setting file permissions in Dreamweaver

An important aspect of installing CGI programs is properly setting the file
permissions for the CGI file. Because of security concerns, most Web servers
restrict access on certain files to particular users. A file can either be read,
overwritten, or executed. With UNIX servers, you can set these three operations for
each of three different groups of people: the creator or owner of the file, the group
administering the Web server, and outside visitors. These settings are called the file
permissions.

Typically, a CGI file is set to the following parameters:

✦ It can be read, overwritten, or executed by its owner

✦ It can be read and executed by the administrative group, but not overwritten

✦ It can be read and executed by the outside visitors, but not overwritten

File permissions are set on a UNIX machine through the site chmod command
issued directly to the server. The permissions previously listed are accomplished
when the site chmod command is set to 755 and the filename is referenced; an
example follows:

```
site chmod 755 mailer.pl
```

To set the file permissions in Dreamweaver, follow these steps:

1. Open the Site Window: Choose File ➪ Open Site and then select the site you want to work with from the submenu.

2. Go on line and select the Connect button from the Site Window.

3. From the Site Window menus, choose Window ➪ Site Log.

4. In the Site Log window's FTP command line, use the `site chmod` command with the appropriate code number and filename reference (see the example in Figure 15-1) and press Enter (Return).

The code command

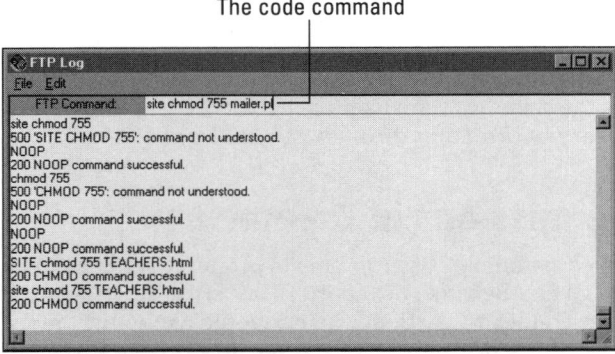

Figure 15-1: Before a CGI program can be used, the file permissions must be set through Dreamweaver's Site Log window.

Sending data to CGI programs

Two primary methods send data to the Web server for processing by a CGI script. The first technique attaches the information directly to a selected URL; another method uses a form to post the data when the user selects the Submit button. The URL method is useful when you need to send known data.

The form method is useful for sending variable or user-supplied information. Both techniques can be used within the Dreamweaver interface.

Passing data through a URL

Although the URL route is not as commonly employed as the forms method, certain information lends itself well to being passed to the server directly through a URL. Anytime you need to send a specific value to your CGI program, you can use the URL method.

Following is the general syntax of the statement that sends data to the URL. You use a question mark to separate the CGI program address from the data itself. The data takes the following form:

```
1st_field=value+2nd_field=value
```

In practice, information passed to a program via a link looks like the following:

```
<a href= http://www.testcenter.com/cgi-
bin/response.pl?choice=left+entry=nada_ad >
```

In Dreamweaver, enter the data as part of the Link information, as shown in Figure 15-2. Most often, you should enter the URL to a CGI program as an absolute address, with the full `http://domain/path` attached.

Figure 15-2: In the Link text box, enter the specific information to be passed directly to a CGI program.

Using forms to send information

Forms are the most common method to transmit data from the user to a CGI program on a server. With the push of a single Submit button, all of the information the user has filled in or selected on the form — text, menu options, radio button options, and so forth — is sent. The data arrives in the program's standard input. The CGI script manipulates the data before sending it on to a database or in an e-mail message.

Cross-Reference

To find out more about building forms in Dreamweaver and the various form fields, see Chapter 13, "Interactive Forms."

Most CGI scripts require that the form use the post method (as opposed to get) to send data to the server. When you first insert a form in Dreamweaver, you notice that the default method listed in the form's Property Inspector is POST, as shown in Figure 15-3.

Aside from choosing a method, the only other task to ready a form for submission is to assign an Action — which, oddly enough, is really the URL of the CGI program (see the Action box in Figure 15-3).

Figure 15-3: Use the POST method to send information via a form to most CGI programs.

Again, this URL is most often supplied in absolute address form, like the following:

```
http://www.idest.com/cgi-bin/mailer.pl
```

Posting form data with a Submit button

Once you have set up the form properly and installed the Web page and corresponding CGI program, data is sent to the server when the user selects the Submit button. You don't need to assign an onClick or another event to the button.

As noted in Chapter 13, "Submit" and "Reset" are the default names for these two buttons. You can easily modify the name of a button by entering new text in the Label text box, as shown in Figure 15-4.

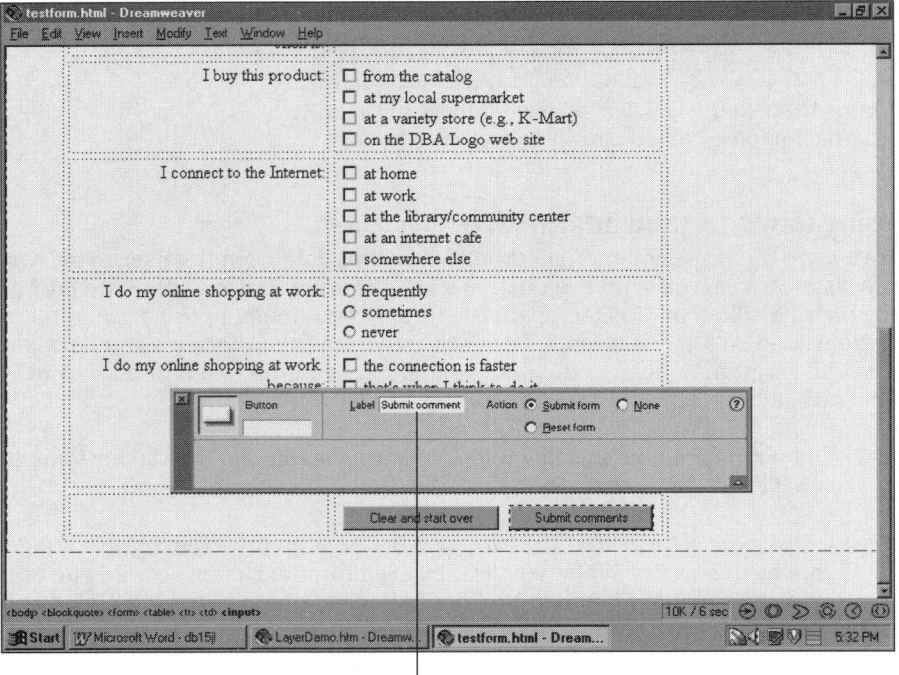

Button name

Figure 15-4: Change the text of the Submit and Reset buttons by entering a name in the Label field of the Property Inspector.

Since Dreamweaver 1.2, you can also use an image to create a graphical button to handle the submitting chores. To use an image for a submit button, follow these steps:

1. Choose Insert ➪ Form Object ➪ Image Field or select the Insert Image Field button from the Forms panel of the Object Palette.

2. In the Insert Image Field dialog, enter the path to your image or select the folder icon to locate the file. The image can be any GIF, JPEG, or PNG format graphic.

3. Optionally, you can give the image field a name, value, and alternative text using the appropriate text boxes in the Property Inspector (see Figure 15-5).

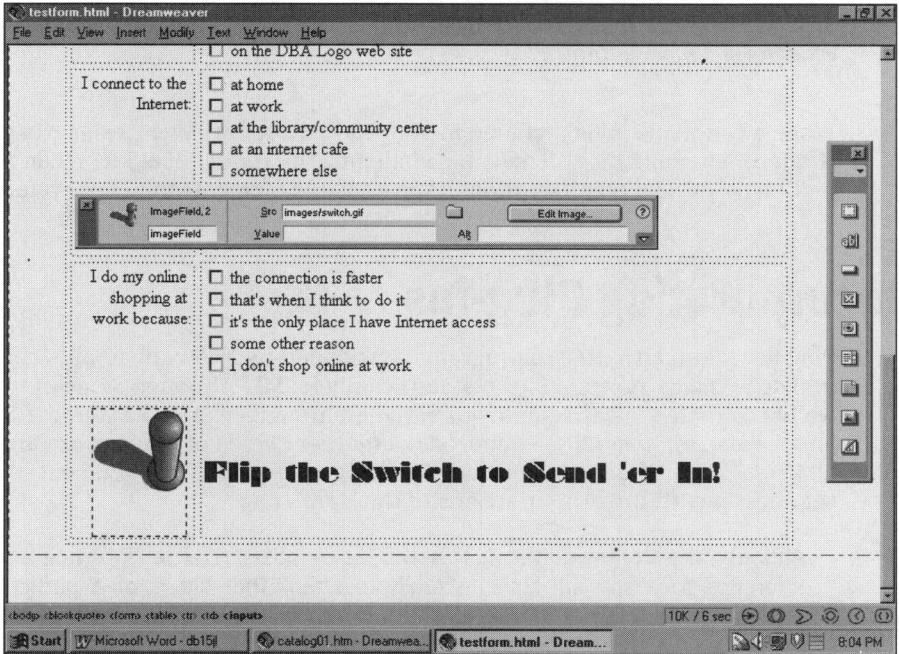

Figure 15-5: You can substitute any valid graphic for the Submit button by using the Image Field.

Using the Hidden Field

Many CGI scripts require that certain information not input by the user be submitted in order to process the form properly. A good example is a text string that tells the CGI program which fields of the form are required. This type of data is hidden from the user and passed to the program through the unseen form object, the appropriately-named Hidden Field.

Although generally placed at the top of the form, Hidden Fields can be included anywhere between the <form> tag pair. You can include a Hidden Field by choosing the Insert Hidden Field button in the Forms panel of the Object Palette or by selecting Insert ➪ Form Object ➪ Hidden Field. Enter the information you want to pass to the CGI program in the Value text box of the Property Inspector, as shown in Figure 15-6.

Figure 15-6: Pass variables that you want to be unseen by your Web page visitor by using the Hidden Field in your form.

When a Hidden Field is included in your form, Dreamweaver designates it with a Hidden Field icon. Like all invisible elements, the Hidden Field icon can also be hidden by deselecting its option in the Invisible Elements panel of Preferences.

Incorporating Plug-ins

Plug-ins are small software programs introduced by Netscape to allow its browser to display many types of files instead of only HTML. Although some of the most well-known plug-ins are employed in the multimedia world — Macromedia's Shockwave, for example — hundreds of different kinds of plug-ins are available for all kinds of files. Plug-ins are generally designed so that the document blends seamlessly with the other portions of the HTML page.

Note Although the Dreamweaver menus and dialog boxes refer to "inserting a plug-in," a reference to a specific file is actually inserted. That file is of a particular MIME (Multipurpose Internet Mail Extension), which tells the browser what kind of file is being called. Once the browser knows the file's MIME type, it can invoke the correct plug-in. Keep in mind that you're not really inserting a plug-in, but instead you're inserting a file that requires a plug-in.

Just like plug-ins, the code used to insert the plug-in was also originally developed by Netscape. Plug-ins are incorporated into HTML through the <embed> tag. Although plug-in features and their associated attributes vary widely, the minimum requirements for a plug-in are the source file and the dimensions (height and width) of the object. Typical HTML for a plug-in looks like the following:

```
<embed src= movies/oscars.avi  height=200 width=300>
```

Beyond the excitement and novelty that plug-ins can add to your page, one inescapable fact remains: if a user doesn't have the plug-in installed, the plug-in file can't be experienced. Users generally have to download and install the plug-in — and then restart their browsers — before they can perceive any new material. While this sequence is not a particularly difficult task, it nevertheless stops many people from easily viewing your creation in its entirety.

Tip   Plug-in Plaza (www.browserwatch.com/plugins) is an excellent resource for links to the entire spectrum of plug-ins. You can access plug-ins by category or by searching the entire list.

Dreamweaver has an open-ended approach to plug-ins. After you've inserted the Plug-in object, Dreamweaver displays a placeholder for it and enables you to enter the basic attributes through the Property Inspector (see Figure 15-7). Custom attributes are inserted through the Parameters dialog box. You can enter as many attributes as necessary.

Plug-in Property Inspector   Plug-in placeholder   Insert Plug-in

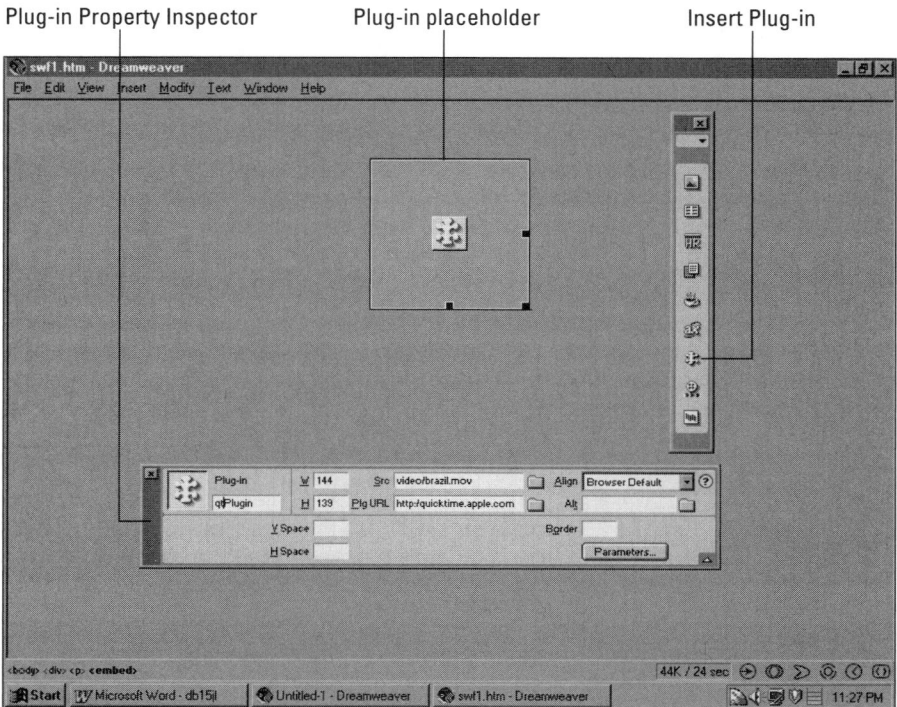

Figure 15-7: Use the Plug-in object from the Object Palette to begin the process of embedding your plug-in.

Embedding a plug-in

Dreamweaver provides a generic Plug-in object available through the menus or through the Object Palette. Like any other HTML object, a plug-in can be aligned with text or an image, or even included in a table. Some plug-ins work automatically with no user interaction; others come with their own control panel.

To embed a plug-in into your Web page, follow these steps:

1. Insert the Plug-in object by choosing Insert ➪ Plug-in or by selecting the Plug-in object from the Object Palette. You can also drag the Plug-in object from the Object Palette to any place in the Document Window with any existing text or object.

2. In the Insert Plug-In dialog box, enter the path and filename for your plug-in file in the Plug-in Source text box, or select the Browse button to locate your file in the Select File dialog box.

   A placeholder icon for the plug-in appears in the Document Window.

3. Size the plug-in placeholder by either of these methods:

   • Enter the appropriate values in the W (Width) and the H (Height) text boxes of the Property Inspector.

   • Click the resizing handles on the plug-in placeholder and dragout the placeholder to a new size.

4. In the Plg URL text box, enter the Internet address where visitors to your Web page can be directed if they do not have the necessary plug-in installed. For example, in the case of QuickTime movies, you would use `http://quicktime.apple.com`.

5. To name the plug-in, enter a unique name in the unlabeled text box on the left side of the Property Inspector. Such names are useful when the plug-in is addressed from a JavaScript function.

6. To change the alignment relative to other inline objects, click the Align arrow button and choose one of the options in the drop-down list.

7. To add additional white space around the plug-in, enter pixel values in the V Space text box for the top and bottom of the object, and in the H Space text box for the left and right sides.

8. To surround the plug-in with a border, enter a pixel value in the Border text box.

9. You may want to display some text or an image as an alternative to the plug-in when the user's browser does not have the plug-in available. Enter a file source for this alternative content in the Alt text box, or use the folder icon to locate a file.

10. To add additional attributes, select the Parameters button. These options are discussed in the following section, "Setting plug-in parameters."

Once you've entered the basic values for your plug-in, you have to preview it through the appropriate browser; Dreamweaver never displays anything more than the placeholder.

Setting plug-in parameters

Because individual attributes for plug-ins can take any form, Dreamweaver offers a completely generic method of entering parameters and associated values. Parameters generally fall into one of two categories: those that take a value and those that stand alone. You can enter both types through the Parameters dialog box.

To set additional parameters to a plug-in, follow these steps:

1. Insert the Plug-in object by choosing Insert ⇨ Plug-in or dragging the Plug-in object from the Object Palette to a place on your Web page.

2. From the extended Property Inspector, select the Parameters button.

The Parameters dialog box is displayed with its two columns: Parameters and Values.

3. Click in the Parameter column and type in the first parameter. Press Tab to move to the Value column, and enter the desired value. If the attribute is a stand-alone and doesn't take a value, simply press Tab again to return to the Parameter column.

4. Repeat step 3 until all parameters are entered. Press Shift-Tab to move backwards through the list.

5. To delete a parameter, highlight it and select the Minus button.

6. To move a parameter from one position in the list to another, highlight it and select the Up or Down arrow buttons in the Parameters dialog box as shown in Figure 15-8.

7. When you are finished inserting your parameters, select the OK button.

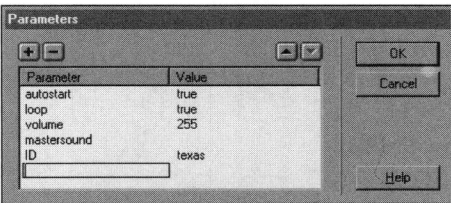

Figure 15-8: Enter specific attributes for each plug-in through the Parameters dialog box.

Many plug-ins require that the Web server recognize the affiliated MIME types. MIME types are a standard method of various file formats. If your plug-in works locally but not remotely, the server probably needs to be configured for the particular MIME type. Contact your server administrator for further details.

Detecting particular plug-ins

When a user visits your Web site using Netscape Navigator 3.0 or higher, you can find out what plug-ins are installed and act accordingly. You may, for example, want to redirect a user who can't accommodate Shockwave files to a separate, less media-intensive page. You can achieve this redirection by creating a mechanism within your page to recognize the Shockwave plug-in.

To detect the presence of a specific plug-in, you need to use a little JavaScript in the `<head>` section of your document. You also need to know either the official name of the plug-in or its MIME type. As an example, the following code checks for a Shockwave Director plug-in by name; if that name isn't found, the user is redirected to another page.

```
<script language= javascript >
if (!navigator.plugins[ director ]){
location= http://www.nadaville.com/simple.html
}
</script>
```

You can also have your document discover whether a particular MIME type is supported, regardless of which plug-in is used. This next example checks for anything that can play a .wav audio file and, if the means is found, plays some background music:

```
<script language= javascript >
if (navigator.mimetypes[ audio/wav ]){
document.write( <embed name= audioBG  src= moody.wav  loop=true
autostart=true hidden=true volume=100 height=2 width=2> );
}
</script>
```

Both of these `if` statements can be used to detect any plug-in and MIME type by simply substituting the appropriate plug-in name and the MIME type you attempt to detect.

To see which plug-ins are installed in your own system — and their proper names and MIME types — choose Help ➪ About Plug-ins from within Navigator or Communicator.

Working with ActiveX Components

Microsoft developed ActiveX components largely in response to Netscape's plug-ins, and although the two technologies are similar, some significant differences exist. Standing on the shoulders of Microsoft's Object Linking and Embedding (OLE) technology, ActiveX controls work only with Internet Explorer 3 and later. A plug-in that allows Navigator to run ActiveX components is available, but not widely used.

ActiveX controls, though difficult to develop, are fairly easy to implement in any Web page. Aside from the usual attributes such as a source file and the object dimensions, ActiveX uses two special parameters: a Class ID and the codebase property.

The Class ID is a unique code used to identify the specific ActiveX control. Every ActiveX control has a Class ID that must be used when calling the control. The Class ID is a lengthy combination of numbers and letters; here's the ActiveMovie ActiveX Class ID code:

```
CLSID:05589FA1-C356-11CE-BF01-00AA0055595A
```

To escape the considerable risk of typing errors when entering a Class ID code, you should cut and paste the code.

The codebase property is an Internet location where the ActiveX control can be automatically downloaded and installed if the browser does not find the control on the user's system. The primary difference between the ActiveX's codebase parameter and a plug-in's pluginspage attribute is that the ActiveX control can be transferred and installed without requiring the browser to close and restart. A typical codebase value follows — the Shockwave Director ActiveX control value:

```
http://active.macromedia.com/director/cabs/sw.cab#version=
6,0,0,0
```

Microsoft uses the <object>...</object> tag pair to include ActiveX controls in the HTML code. Unlike Netscape's <embed> tag, the <object> tag is recognized by the W3C as a valid specification for HTML 3.2 and later.

Note   Optimally, everyone would adhere to the same standard; however, because neither browser recognizes the other's tag, you can actually combine an <object> and an <embed> tag to cover both browsers. This procedure is explained in the following section.

Dreamweaver provides a separate object for adding ActiveX controls to your Web pages. In addition, Dreamweaver makes it easy to add those complex Class ID codes by maintaining a user-definable list — accessible right from the ActiveX Property Inspector.

Incorporating an ActiveX control

As with plug-ins, Dreamweaver includes an ActiveX object to simplify inserting ActiveX controls. The primary difference between an ActiveX object and a Plug-in object — aside from the two special ActiveX parameters previously noted — is the location for the ActiveX source file. For example, if you want to embed an ActiveX control to show a digital video in AVI format, you first insert the control object by selecting the Insert ActiveX button from the Object Palette. Then you see the ActiveX Property Inspector (rather than an Insert ActiveX file dialog box). The source file is actually one of the parameters of the <object> tag, FileName, and must be entered through the Parameters dialog box (Embed Src text box).

Follow these steps to insert an ActiveX control into your Web page:

1. Position the cursor where you want the ActiveX file to appear. Choose Insert ➪ ActiveX or select the Insert ActiveX button from the Object Palette.

   An ActiveX placeholder appears in the Document window, and the Property Inspector displays the ActiveX options (see Figure 15-9).

2. In the Class ID text box, enter the Microsoft ID for the ActiveX control.

   If you've previously entered this particular Class ID, select the arrow button and choose the ID from the drop-down list, as shown in Figure 15-9.

3. Change the Width and Height values in the W and H text boxes to match the desired control display.

4. If you know the codebase URL, enter it in the Base text box.

5. Enter other relative parameters for the object as needed (see Table 15-1).

6. Click the Parameters button to display the Parameters dialog box.

7. Click the + (Add) button and enter the first parameter: FileName. Press Tab to move to the Value column, and enter the path and filename for your file.

8. Press Tab, and continue entering the desired parameters in the left column and their values in the right column. Click OK when you're finished.

9. Preview your ActiveX control in action through Internet Explorer 3 or 4.

ActiveX placeholder   Insert ActiveX   ActiveX Property Inspector

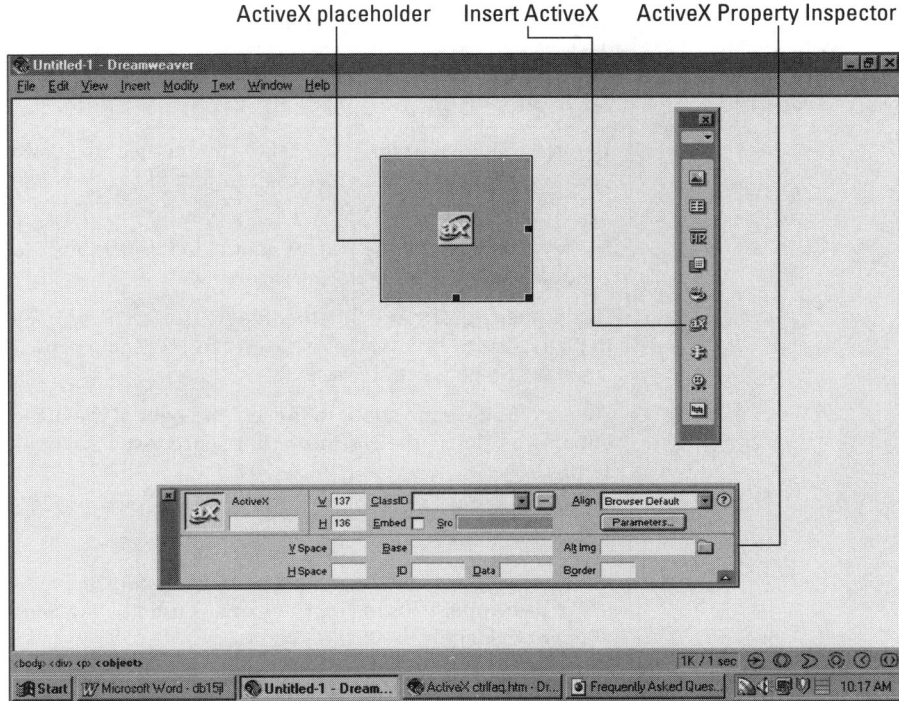

Figure 15-9: ActiveX controls are inserted with the help of Dreamweaver's ActiveX object and its Property Inspector.

Table 15-1
ActiveX Object Properties

ActiveX Object Property	Description
Align	To alter the alignment of the ActiveX control, choose an option from the Align drop-down list. In addition to the Browser Default, your options include Baseline, Top, Middle, Bottom, Texttop, Absolute Middle, Absolute Bottom, Left, and Right.
Alt Image	Enter a path to an alternative image for display to users who do not have the correct ActiveX control installed. You can also select the folder icon to open a Select Image Source dialog box. This image does not display in Dreamweaver.

(continued)

Table 15-1 (continued)

ActiveX Object Property	Description
Border	To place a border around your control, enter a number in the Border text box. The number determines the width of the border in pixels. The default is zero or no border.
Data	Specify a data file for the ActiveX control in this text box. Not all ActiveX controls use this attribute.
Embed	This property designates whether the matching code for the plug-in is to be included (as described in the section "Combining ActiveX controls and plug-in objects" in this chapter).
H Space	You can increase the space to the left and right of the object by entering a value in the H (Horizontal) Space text box. The default is zero.
ID	The ID field is used to define the optional ActiveX ID parameter, most often used to pass data between ActiveX controls.
Name	If desired, you can enter a unique name in the unlabeled field at the left of the Property Inspector. The name is used by JavaScript and VBScript to identify the ActiveX control.
Src	This sets the source for the plug-in, if the Embed check box is selected (as described in the following section "Combining ActiveX controls and plug-in objects").
V Space	To increase the amount of space between the top and bottom of the ActiveX object and the other elements on the page, enter a pixel value in the V (Vertical) Space text box. The default is zero.

Combining ActiveX controls and plug-in objects

Dreamweaver takes advantage of the fact that Netscape browsers do not recognize the `<object>` tag, and that Microsoft browsers do not recognize the `<embed>` tag placed inside the `<object>` tag. How could this be an advantage, you ask? Because of their mutual exclusivity, you can include both types of tags in the same Web page and still avoid conflicts.

The following example code shows you how the approach works in HTML. The `<embed>` section is bolded to view how one tag fits within another.

```
<object width= 137  height= 136  classid= clsid:CFCDAA03-8BE4-
11cf-B84B-0020AFBBCCFA >
    <param name= FileName  value= images/braz.wav >
    <embed width= 137  height= 136  filename= images/braz.wav
    src= images/braz.wav ></embed>
</object>
```

Notice the values common to both tags, including the dimensions and the source file. (The source file is the `src` attribute in `<embed>`, and the `FileName` parameter in the `<object>` tag.) Dreamweaver automatically inserts these values when you enable the Embed option on the ActiveX Property Inspector.

Tip

If you're going to use the Embed option with your ActiveX object, you should wait until you've entered the necessary `FileName` parameter (through the Edit Parameters button) before you select the Embed check box. When the `FileName` parameter is already specified, Dreamweaver automatically writes the same value in the Embed Scr text box. If you forget and turn on the Embed option before entering the `FileName` parameter, just turn off Embed, reselect it, and the proper value appears as the Embed source file.

Adding Java Applets

Java is a platform-independent programming language developed by Sun Microsystems. Although Java can also be used to write entire applications, its most frequent role is on the Web in the form of an applet. An *applet* is a self-contained program that can be run within a Web page.

Java is a compiled programming language similar to C++. Once a Java applet is compiled, it is saved as a class file. Web browsers call Java applets through, aptly enough, the `<applet>` tag. When you insert an applet, you refer to the primary class file much as you call a graphic file for an image tag.

Each Java applet has its own unique set of parameters — and Dreamweaver enables you to enter as many as necessary in the same manner as for plug-ins and ActiveX controls. In fact, the Applet object works almost identically to the Plug-in and ActiveX objects.

Note

Keep two caveats in mind if you're planning to include Java applets in your Web site. First, most (but not all) browsers support some version of Java—the newest release, Java 1.2, has the most features but the least support. Second, all the browsers that support Java enable the user to disable it, because of security issues. You make sure to use the Alt property to designate an alternative image or some text for display by browsers that do not support Java.

Specifying the Java parameters

A Java applet can be inserted in a Web page with a bare minimum of parameters: the code source and the dimensions of the object. Java applets instead derive much of their power from their configurability, and most of these little programs have numerous custom parameters. As with plug-ins and ActiveX controls, Dreamweaver lets you specify the basic attributes through the Property Inspector, and the custom ones via the Parameters dialog box.

To include a Java applet in your Web page, follow these steps:

1. Position the cursor where you want the applet to originate and choose Insert ➪ Applet. You can also select the Insert Applet button from the Object Palette.

   The Insert Applet dialog box opens.

2. From the Insert Applet dialog box, enter the path to your class file in the Java Class Source text box or select the Browse button to locate the file.

   An Applet object placeholder appears in the Document Window. In the Applet Property Inspector (Figure 15-10), the selected source file appears in the Code text box and the folder appears in the Base text box.

   Caution The path to your Java class files cannot be expressed absolutely, but must be given as an address relative to the Web page that is calling it.

3. Enter the height and width of the Applet object in the H and W text boxes, respectively. You can also resize the Applet object by clicking and dragging any of its three sizing handles.

4. You can enter any of the usual basic attributes, such as a name for the object, as well as values for Align, V Space, and/or H Space, Border, and Alt in the appropriate text boxes in the Property Inspector.

5. To enter any custom attributes, select the Parameters button to open the Parameters dialog box.

6. Select the + (Add) button and enter the first parameter. Press Tab to move to the Value column.

7. Enter the value for parameter, if any. Press Tab.

8. Continue entering desired parameters in the left column and their values in the right. Click OK when you're finished.

Applet placeholder   Insert Applet   Applet Property Inspector

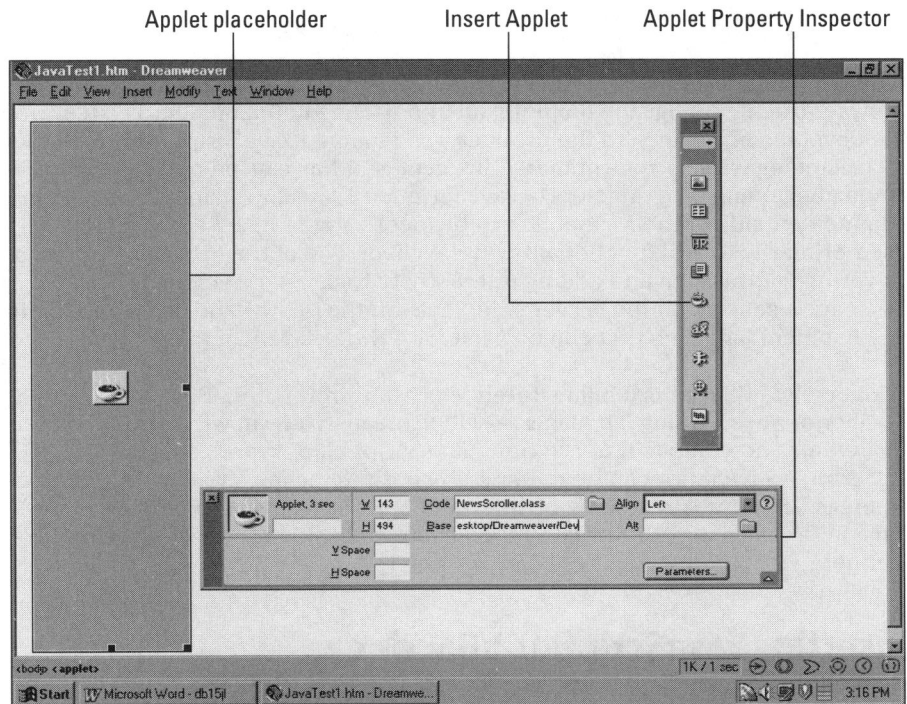

Figure 15-10: Use the Insert Applet button to insert a Java Applet object and display the Applet Property Inspector.

Tip

Because of the importance of displaying alternative content for users not running Java, Dreamweaver provides a method for displaying something for everyone. To display text, enter your message in the Alt text box of the Applet Property Inspector. To display an image, enter the URL to a graphics file in the Alt text box. Also, you can combine the two approaches with a little hand-coding. First, select a graphics file to insert in the Alt text box, and then open the HTML Inspector. In the `<img>` tag found between the `<applet>` tags, add an `alt= your_message` attribute by hand (where the text you want to display is the value for the `alt` attribute). Now your Java applet displays an image for browsers that are graphics-enabled but not Java-enabled, and text for text-only browsers such as Lynx.

Some Java class files have additional graphics files. In most cases, you need to store both the class files and the graphics files in the same folder.

Adding JavaScript and VBScript

When initially developed by Netscape, JavaScript was called LiveScript. This browser-oriented language did not gain importance until Sun Microsystems joined the development team and the product was renamed JavaScript. Although the rechristening was a stroke of marketing genius, it has caused endless confusion among beginning programmers — JavaScript and Java have almost nothing in common outside of their capability to be incorporated in a Web page. JavaScript is used primarily to add functionality on the client side of the browser (for tasks such as verifying form data and adding interactivity to interface elements), or to script Netscape's servers on the server side. Java, on the other hand, is an application development language that can be used for a wide variety of tasks.

Conversely, VBScript is a full-featured Microsoft production. Both VBScript and JavaScript are scripting languages — which means you can write the code in any text editor and compile it at run time. JavaScript enjoys more support than VBScript — JavaScript can be rendered by both Netscape and Microsoft browsers, whereas VBScript is read only by Internet Explorer — but both languages have their fans. In Dreamweaver, both types of code are inserted in the Web page in the same manner.

Inserting JavaScript or VBScript

If only mastering JavaScript or VBScript itself were as easy as inserting the code in Dreamweaver! Simply go to the Object Palette's Invisibles pane and select the Insert Script button, or choose Insert ⇨ Script from the menus, and enter your code in the small Insert Script window. After you click OK, a Script icon appears in place of your script.

Of course, any JavaScript or VBScript instruction is beyond the scope of this book, but any working Web designer must have an understanding of what these languages can do. Both languages refer to and, to varying degrees, manipulate the information on a Web page. Over time, you can expect significant growth in the capabilities of the JavaScript and VBScript disciplines.

Cross-Reference

Dreamweaver, through the application of its Behaviors, goes a long way toward making JavaScript useful for nonprogrammers. To learn more about Behaviors, see Chapter 17, "Creating and Using Behaviors."

Use the Script Property Inspector (Figure 15-11) to select an external file for your JavaScript or VBScript code. You can also set the language type by opening the Language drop-down list and choosing either JavaScript or VBScript.

Insert Script window   Script icon   Insert Script   Script Property Inspector

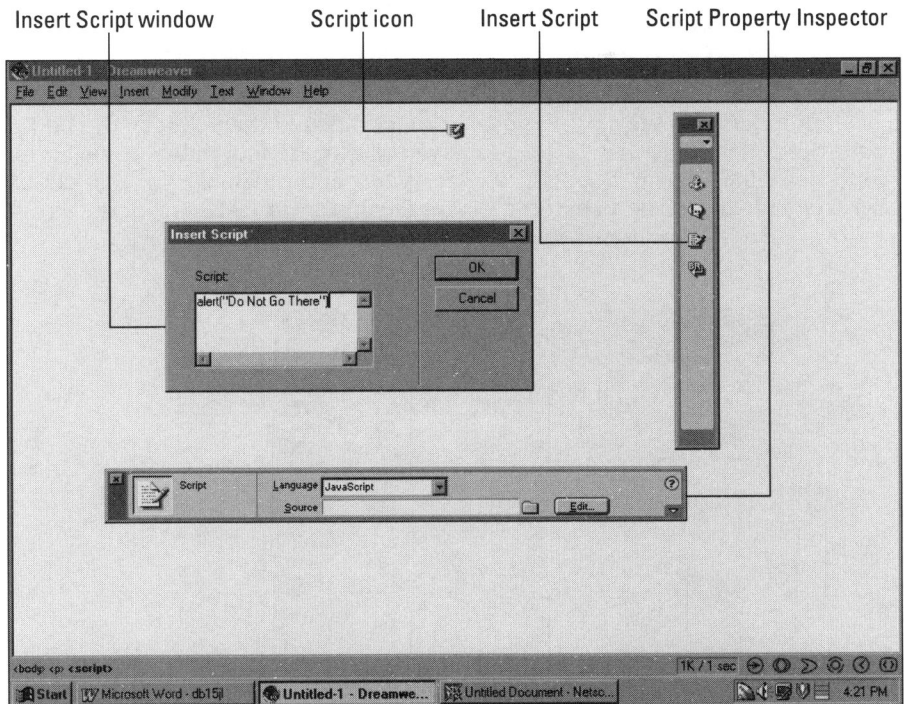

Figure 15-11: Insert either JavaScript or VBScript through the Object Palette's Script object available on the Invisibles panel.

When you choose JavaScript or VBScript as your Language type, Dreamweaver writes the code accordingly. Both languages use the `<script>` tag pair, and each is specified in the `language` attribute, as follows:

```
<script language= JavaScript >alert( Look Out! )</script>
```

Dreamweaver can only insert script code in the `<body>` section of your Web page. Many JavaScript and VBScript functions must be located in the `<head>` section. To complete this insertion, you must currently enter the code through the HTML Inspector or your external editor.

On the CD-ROM

Want to attach a quick JavaScript command to a mouse click or another event? Copy Andrew Wooldrich's Behavior to Execute Custom Code into your Dreamweaver\ Configuration\Behaviors\Actions\ folder, and restart Dreamweaver. With this behavior installed, you can attach any JavaScript sequence to any valid event.

Editing JavaScript or VBScript

As shown in Figure 15-12, Dreamweaver provides a large editing window for modifying your script code. To open this Script Properties window, select the placeholder icon for the script you want to modify and then choose the Edit button on the Script Property Inspector. You have the same functionality in the Script Properties window as in the Script Property Inspector; namely, you can choose your language or link to an external script file. In Figure 15-12, the Script Properties window (currently) only has a vertical scroll bar — not a scroll bar.

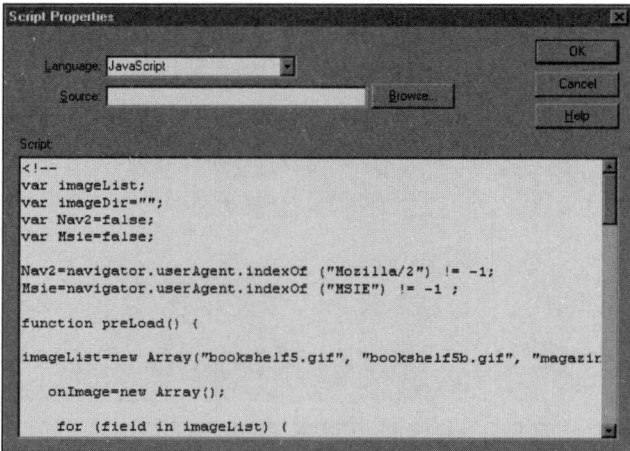

Figure 15-12: The generous Script Properties window provides plenty of room for modifying your JavaScript or VBScript.

Tip

Some older browsers "break" when loading a JavaScript Web page and display the code written between the `<script>...</script>` tag pair. Although Dreamweaver doesn't do it by default, you can use a trick to prevent this anomaly. In the HTML Inspector or your external editor, insert the opening comment tag (`<--`) right after the opening `<script>` tag. Then insert the closing comment tag (`-->`), preceded by two forward slashes, right before the closing `</script>`. An example follows:

```
<script language= Javascript >
<!--
[JavaScript code goes here]
//-->
</script>
```

The comment tags effectively tell the older browser to ignore the enclosed content. The two forward slashes in front of the closing comment tag are JavaScript's comment indicator and tell it to ignore the rest of the line.

Summary

To paraphrase a popular commercial, "Web pages aren't just for HTML anymore." The horizons of possibility expand tremendously when you start to explore any of the technologies discussed in this chapter: CGI, plug-ins, ActiveX, Java, and JavaScript or VBScript. Dreamweaver maintains an open-ended design for external programs.

✦ CGI scripts are primarily used to send information back and forth between the user and the Web server. The Web server can then, under direction of the CGI program, store the information in a database or forward it to another URL or e-mail address.

✦ Plug-ins allow Netscape browsers to display formats other than HTML. A plug-in can display multimedia content inline with other HTML objects like images and tables. Dreamweaver supports a Plug-in object that can allows the <embed> code to be customized through the Parameters dialog box.

✦ ActiveX controls are employed by Microsoft browsers in a manner similar to Netscape's plug-ins. Each ActiveX control has its own unique Class ID, as well as a codebase attribute that enables users to get the control without interrupting their workflow.

✦ Java applets can be inserted as Applet objects in a Dreamweaver Web page. Java source files, called classes, can be linked to the Applet object through the Property Inspector.

✦ Dreamweaver offers a simple method for including both JavaScript and VBScript code in the <body> section of your HTML page. Script functions that need to be inserted in the <head> section must be coded by hand.

In the next chapter, you see how you can use and create your own Dreamweaver objects.

✦   ✦   ✦

Creating and Using Objects

Sometimes the simplest ideas are the most powerful. The Dreamweaver development team had a simple idea: Why not code the insertable objects in HTML? After all, when you choose to insert anything into a Web page — from a horizontal rule to a Shockwave Director movie — you are just putting HTML in the page. If the objects are just HTML files, what are the possible benefits? For one, the objects can be easily modified. Also, HTML requires no special program to code, and coding the language itself is not extraordinarily difficult. In addition, the core users of Dreamweaver are experts in HTML. Now, the simple idea is turned into a powerful tool.

All the objects included with Dreamweaver can be modified and customized to fit any Web designer's working preferences. Furthermore, custom objects can easily be created. This capability not only enables you to include regular HTML tags that repeatedly occur in your designs, but it also opens the door to a vast level of expandability. Dreamweaver's capability to accommodate any number of custom objects means you can take advantage of new technologies immediately.

Building a site that needs the latest tags just released by the W3C? Go right ahead — make an object that inserts any or all of the tags. You may not be able to see the result in Dreamweaver, but if your browser can handle the tags, you can preview them there.

Find yourself including the same ActiveX control over and over again, with only one change in the parameters? Create a custom object that inserts that control, with all the constant attributes — and add a parameter form to enter the variable attributes.

This chapter shows the tremendous potential of Dreamweaver objects. After studying the use of the standard objects, you learn how you can customize your object working environment. Then, you find out how to create your own objects and take advantage of the new features in Dreamweaver 1.2.

Inserting Dreamweaver Objects

If you've been using Dreamweaver, you've been using objects. Even if your first exposure to Dreamweaver has been working through the first 15 chapters of this book, you've already used several types of objects. Aside from text, everything inserted in a Web page can be considered an object: images, comments, plug-ins, named anchors — they're all objects and are all extremely easy to use.

Dreamweaver offers several ways to include any object. For a few objects, you even have as many as four different techniques from which to choose. Here are your options:

✦ From the main menu, choose Insert and then any of the listed objects.

✦ From the Object Palette (Figure 16-1), click any button on the three standard panes — Common, Forms, and Invisibles — to insert an object in the current cursor position.

✦ Drag any button off the Object Palette and drop it next to any existing content on your Web page.

✦ Many objects have a keyboard shortcut, such as Ctrl-Alt-I (Command-Alt-I) for Image or Ctrl-Alt-F (Command-Alt-F) for a Flash movie. Keyboard shortcuts insert the chosen object at the current cursor location.

Figure 16-1: You'll find yourself returning to the Object Palette as an easy way to include HTML elements.

Tip   When you insert one of the objects from the Invisibles panel — such as the Line-Break, Comment, or Named Anchor — Dreamweaver by default inserts an icon to show the object's placement. If you find these placeholders distracting, you can turn them all off by choosing the toggle command, View ⇨ Invisible Elements. If you have an Invisible Element "turned off" in Preferences, you will never see the icon, regardless of the status of the View menu command.

Modifying the Object Palette

The Object Palette is one of the most customizable of all of Dreamweaver's features. In addition to the flexibility of having it "float" anywhere on the screen, you can also resize and reshape the Palette to your liking. Most important, you can rearrange its contents, add new panes, and, as noted earlier, include custom objects.

Moving and reshaping the Object Palette

If you work with your Document Window fully expanded, you'll often find yourself repositioning the Object Palette. Just click-and-drag the title bar on top of the palette to move it out of the way quickly. You can also press F4 to send the Object Palette (and any other open palette or inspector) behind the Document Window. Pressing F4 again brings them back to the front.

If you don't like the long, vertical shape that Dreamweaver uses by default for the Object Palette, you can change its appearance. Place your pointer over any border of the Palette until the usual pointing arrow changes into a two-headed arrow — now you can click and drag the Object Palette into a new shape. You can drag any corner to form a rectangular shape, as shown in Figure 16-2, or you can make the Palette extend horizontally instead of vertically.

Figure 16-2: Reshape the Object Palette to your liking.

When screen real estate is at a premium, you can reduce the overall size of the Object Palette — even down to just a one-button size. If you shrink it down small enough so that all the buttons don't show at once, one or two scroll arrows appear. Click an arrow to see the next button in the palette.

Reorganizing the objects and adding panes

The three panes of the Object Palette—Common, Forms, and Invisibles—correspond to the three folders found in the Dreamweaver Configuration\Objects directory. Each folder has two items for each object: an HTML file and a GIF file. The HTML file is the source code for the object, and the GIF file is the button image. If you want to move an item from one Object Palette pane to another, just transfer the two files related to that object from one folder to the other.

For example, let's say you're doing a lot of JavaScript work and you want to move the Insert Script object from the Invisibles pane to the Common pane. To accomplish this task, you need to move `script.htm` and `script.gif` from the Invisibles folder to the Common folder. You can click and drag the files, or cut and paste them. You must restart Dreamweaver to see the changes.

You're not limited to the three panes on the Object palette. The standard panes—Common, Forms, and Invisibles—correspond to identically named subfolders in the Objects directory. If you want to add another pane, simply add a new subfolder. For example, I've developed a number of custom Objects for inserting sound and digital video files, which I wanted to group on a new pane of the Object palette. In my file management program, I created a folder called Media within the Dreamweaver\Configuration\Objects\ folder and moved all my special Object files into the new folder. After restarting Dreamweaver, Media appears as my fourth pane in the Object palette.

Caution   Dreamweaver only recognizes one level of subfolders within the Objects folder as new Object Palette panes. You cannot, for instance, create a subfolder called Videos within the Media subfolder.

Tip   Dreamweaver alphabetizes the Object panes by folder name. If you want your new custom pane to appear first on the Object Palette, you must name its folder so that it appears further down alphabetically (that is, closer to *A*) than the Common folder. Use one of two tricks: you can start the custom folder name with a tilde (~), like ~Media for instance, or you can rename the Common folder so that its name appears later in the alphabet.

Customizing the Insert Menu

Just as you can reorganize the Object Palette to your working style, you can also restructure the Insert menu. To a degree, the Insert menu can control the appearance of the Object Palette. You can create keyboard shortcuts for objects, and make subfolders for existing and new objects. The capability to create custom objects is an invaluable design feature—as a significant bonus, Dreamweaver enables you to reference custom objects.

The key to the Insert menu is a file called InsertMenu.htm, stored in Dreamweaver's Configuration\Object folder. Because InsertMenu.htm is an HTML file, you can make your modifications directly in Dreamweaver. After you're done, just save the file and restart Dreamweaver to see your changes take effect.

Altering the InsertMenu file

The InsertMenu file uses basic HTML — bulleted lists and underlining — to build the familiar drop-down menu. The following lists the three items that make up each item in the list, in order:

1. The object name as it appears in the Insert menu. In Windows systems, one letter, unique to the list, is underlined; this letter is used together with the Alt key to call the object.

2. A single letter used in combination with the Ctrl-Alt (Command-Alt) keys to make up the keyboard shortcut.

3. The object HTML file.

The standard InsertMenu file, shown in Figure 16-3, begins as follows:

- Image, I, image.htm

- Table, T, table.htm

- Horizontal Rule,H, horizontal_rule.htm

- ----------

- Layer, , layer.htm

- ----------

- Applet, , applet.htm

- ActiveX, , activex.htm

- Plug-in, , plugin.htm

Caution

Before you alter the InsertMenu.htm file, save a spare copy of the file. Open the file in Dreamweaver, choose File ➪ Save As, and enter a different name in the File name text box — something like **InsertMenu-Original** (the .htm extension is automatically attached). Then, just to make sure that copy is left unchanged, close your renamed file and reopen InsertMenu.htm.

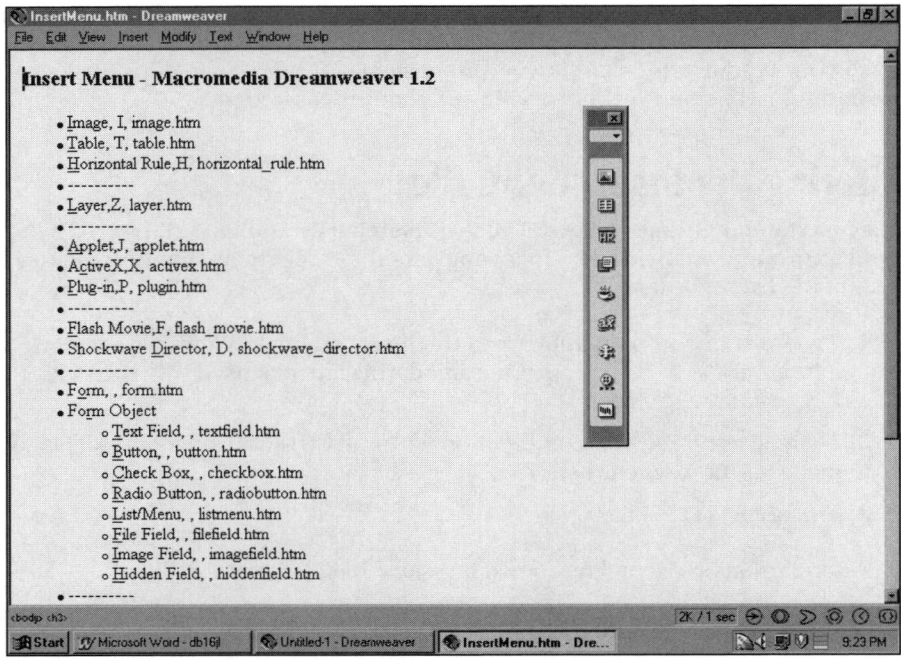

Figure 16-3: You can edit the InsertMenu.htm file right in Dreamweaver.

Once you have the InsertMenu.htm file open, take a look at the HTML. Notice that each object is one list item, <li>, in an unordered list, <ul> — even the separator lines made up of dashes are list items. To rearrange one or more items to a different location in the list, select the entire line for the object you want to move. Then choose Edit ➪ Cut or use the keyboard shortcut, Ctrl-X (Command-X). Move your cursor to the front of the line below where you want your cut line to appear, and choose Edit ➪ Paste or Ctrl-V (Command-V).

Tip   Dreamweaver even lets you specify the order of the buttons that appear in the Object Palette. The order is the same as in the Insert menu, which is determined by the InsertMenu.htm file. When you alter the order of the items in this file, the Object Palette buttons reflect the same sequence the next time you start Dreamweaver.

You can also group items in submenus, such as the submenu for Form Objects. To achieve this effect, highlight the item you want to appear in a submenu and, from the Property Inspector, choose the Indent button — you can also select Text ➪ Indent in the menus. Because all items are in an unordered list, the submenu items appear with a different bullet in the HTML file, but render normally in the list.

Adding items and keyboard shortcuts

Once you start making your own objects — and installing other prebuilt ones like those included on this book's CD-ROM — you'll eventually want to modify the InsertMenu.htm file to incorporate your creations. Again, this procedure is straightforward; just follow the format of the objects already in the file.

Tip

In addition to adding new objects with keyboard shortcuts, you can also add a keyboard shortcut to any existing object that doesn't have a shortcut. The single letter that denotes the shortcut can be uppercase or lowercase; Dreamweaver doesn't care. You can also use the single-digit numbers, 0–9.

To add a new object to the InsertMenu.htm file, follow these steps:

1. From within Dreamweaver, open the file Dreamweaver\Configuration\Objects\InsertMenu.htm.

2. Position the text cursor at the end of the line above where you want to insert the object.

3. Press Enter (Return) to make a new bulleted entry.

4. Enter the object name, the shortcut letter (if any), and object source file — separated by commas. Even if you don't use a shortcut letter, you still must include both commas.

   The format for this entry follows:

   `Objectname, X, objectfile`

   where *Objectname* is the name of the object, with the Alt- letter underlined; *X* is the Ctrl-Alt- (Command-Alt) shortcut letter; and *objectfile* is the .htm filename of the object.

5. When you've completed your editing of the InsertMenu.htm file, choose File ⇨ Save or press Ctrl-S (Command-S) to save the file.

6. Quit and restart Dreamweaver.

Adding Additional Objects

Before you begin building your own custom objects, you may want to look around and see if someone else has already created something similar. In addition to the standard objects that ship with Dreamweaver, several Web sites that have objects (and behaviors) are available for download. Of course, a wide variety of objects are available on the CD-ROM accompanying this book. Find these objects in the folder Dreamweaver\Configuration\Objects.

No matter where you get your objects, the procedure for installing them is the same. To incorporate new objects into your Dreamweaver system, follow these steps:

1. Uncompress the files if necessary. Object files come with an HTML file and a GIF file, and the two files are usually compressed for easy download or transfer.

2. If necessary, make a new folder for your objects. All objects must be stored in a subfolder of the Dreamweaver\Configuration\Objects folder. You can either store the object files in an standard subfolder (Common, Forms, or Invisibles, for instance) or in a new folder that you create.

3. Transfer the object files to the desired folder. Be careful: make sure you transfer both the HTML and the GIF file together.

4. Open InsertMenu.htm in Dreamweaver, and modify the file to include your new objects. Follow the steps described in the preceding section "Altering the InsertMenu file."

5. Restart Dreamweaver.

Online Sources for Objects and Behaviors

As of this writing, there are five main online sources for new objects and behaviors:

Macromedia

```
http://www.macromedia.com/support/dreamweaver/upndown/objects
```

The official Object and Behavior Exchange site accepts objects submitted from all over. After evaluations by the Dreamweaver engineers, objects are posted for downloading. Before you can access this area of the Macromedia site, you must accept the terms of a licensing agreement.

Dreamweaver Depot

```
http://people.netscape.com/andreww/dreamweaver/
```

Run by Andrew Woolridge, the Dreamweaver Depot specializes in Netscape-only objects and behaviors, although the site offers cross-browser and Internet Explorer-specific objects as well. The Depot also has a forum and a chat room for Dreamweaver aficionados.

Excellent Dreamweaver Supply Bin

```
http://home.att.net/%7EJCB.BEI/Dreamweaver/
```

This site is chaired by James Bartz and focuses primarily on objects and behaviors that take advantage of Internet Explorer's special features. The Supply Bin also has a good supply of cross-browser objects and behaviors.

Webmonkey Editor Extensions Collection

```
http://www.hotwired.com/webmonkey/javascript/code_library/ed_ext
```

Although this area on the Hot Wired site could potentially hold other Web authoring tools' extensions, Dreamweaver is currently the only one on the market with the capability. You'll find several professional-quality objects and behaviors, both cross-browser and browser-specific.

Dreamweaver, etc.

```
http://www.idest.com/dreamweaver/
```

Maintained by Joseph Lowery, author of this book, the Dreamweaver etc. site includes all the objects found on this book's CD-ROM, plus new ones posted after this book's publication.

Creating Custom Objects

Each custom object, like standard objects, is made from two files: an HTML file describing the object, and a GIF file depicting the button. The complexity of the HTML depends on the complexity of the object. You can build just about anything — from a simple object that replicates a repeatedly used item, to a high-end object that uses advanced JavaScript techniques for creating special function layers and windows. You can even make objects that create other objects.

To support the "higher end" of the custom object scale, Dreamweaver includes extensions to JavaScript and a Document Object Model (DOM), which is a subset of Netscape Navigator 3.0's DOM. You study these techniques further into the chapter. As the following section shows, however, many objects don't require any JavaScript and are easy to construct.

Making simple objects

To make a simple object that inserts any HTML-created item, put only the code necessary to create the object into a file, and then save the file in one of the object folders. The key phrase in the preceding sentence is *just the code necessary*. Unlike a regular Web page, for a simple custom object you don't include the framing <html>...<body>...</body>...</html> sections — all you need is the essential code necessary to make the object.

For example, let's say you are asked to enhance 100 Web pages and make each page capable of showing a different VDOLive movie. Each of the .avi files is different, so you can't use Dreamweaver's Library feature. The easiest way to handle this situation is to create a dummy version of what you need and then turn that dummy into an object.

Step 1: Create the item

First, create your item as you normally would in Dreamweaver. For this example, let's insert a plug-in and add all the standard attributes: name, height and width, pluginspage, border, v space, and h space — and even a few special parameters like autostart and stretch. The only attribute that the example omits is the attribute that changes: the file source. You also want the movie to be centered, wherever it's located, and you center the plug-in. When finished, the complete code for the page and plug-in, as generated by Dreamweaver, looks like the following:

```
<html>
<head>
<title>Untitled Document</title>
<meta http-equiv= Content-Type  content= text/html;
charset=iso-8859-1 >
</head>
<body bgcolor= #FFFFFF >
<div align= center >
  <embed src=  width= 135  height= 135  name= vdoMovie
pluginspage= http://www.vdo.net/download/  vspace= 5
hspace= 5  border= 5  stretch= true  autostart= false ></embed>
</div>
</body>
</html>
```

Step 2: Create the object

To create a simple object from the preceding, just cut everything in the code but the item (or items) you want repeated. In the HTML Inspector, select all the code from the opening <html> tag up to and including the <body> tag, and then delete. Then delete the closing tags, </body> and </html>. The only remaining code is the following:

```
<div align= center >
  <embed src=  width= 135  height= 135  name= vdoMovie
pluginspage= http://www.vdo.net/download/  vspace= 5
hspace= 5  border= 5  stretch= true  autostart= false ></embed>
</div>
```

Tip

After you eliminate all the code except for your object's code and return to the visual editor, the Document Window changes from a white background to a dark-gray background. This change occurs because Dreamweaver makes the bgcolor attribute of the <body> tag white by default — to create a simple object, you need to delete the entire <body> tag, including the color information.

Step 3: Save the object

Now your object is ready to be saved. For Dreamweaver to recognize this or any other snippet of code as an object, the file must be saved in the Configuration\ Objects folder. You can choose to save your object in any of the existing subfolders —Common, Forms, or Invisibles—or you can create a new folder within the Objects folder. For this example, create a new folder called Media for this and other similar objects.

Caution

You must save your new Object in a subfolder within the Objects folder. Dreamweaver doesn't recognize objects saved individually in the Objects folder.

After the file is saved, you must restart Dreamweaver to test your object. Then, by selecting its name in the Insert menu ⇨ or clicking its button from the Object Palette, you can insert your object as needed. The object creation task is not quite finished, however.

Step 4: Create a button for the object

As shown in Figure 16-4, Dreamweaver displays an "image not found" placeholder in the Object Palette, because you haven't yet made a button image for the vdoMovie object. In addition, unless you specifically include the new object in the InsertMenu.htm file, the object is listed in the bottom portion of the Insert menu. This arrangement is fine for debugging, but if you want to continue using your object, it's more efficient to create a button image for it and revise the InsertMenu.htm file to include it. The following section shows you how to complete this task.

Building an object button

Object buttons are GIF files, ideally sized at 16 pixels square. To make the object button, you can use any graphics-creation program that can save GIF files. If your button image file is not 16 pixels by 16 pixels, Dreamweaver resizes it to those dimensions. Although Dreamweaver uses a muted grayscale color scheme, you are not limited to the same palette. Your button can be as colorful as you want—as long as it can still fit in a 16-pixel square.

Tip

To create an object button, you can open and modify any of the existing GIF files for the standard buttons. Just be sure to use the Save As command of your paint program—and not the Save command—to save your modified version.

After you've created your button image, save the GIF file in the same folder as the HTML file for the new object. At this time, you may also want to modify the InsertMenu.htm file as described in the preceding "Altering the InsertMenu file" section.

The "image not found" placeholder

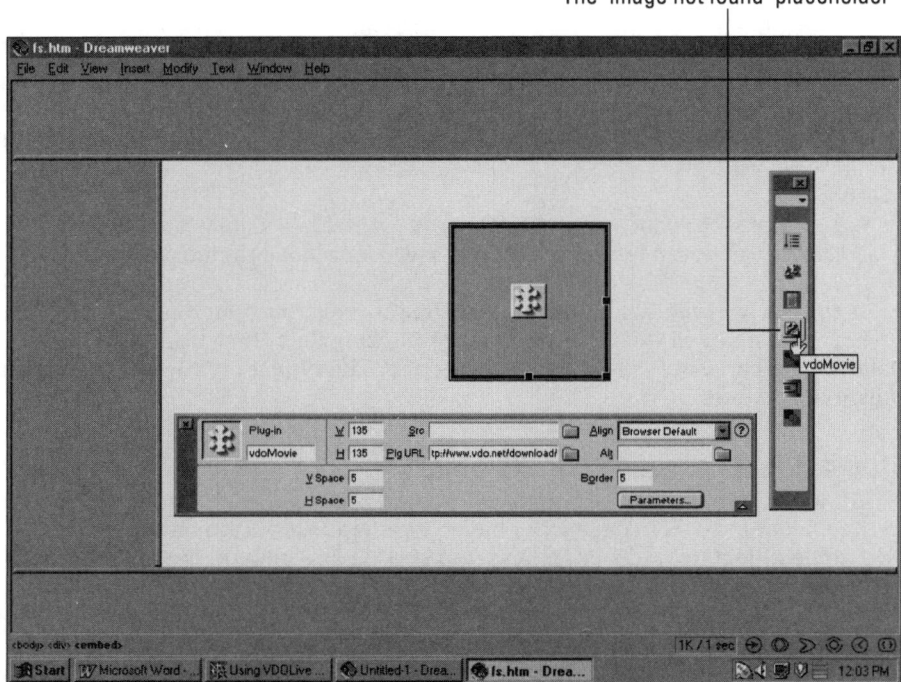

Figure 16-4: You can create custom objects like the vdoMovie object shown here.

Putting JavaScript to Work in Custom Objects

The remaining sections of this chapter deal with using JavaScript to create more complex objects.

Caution

If you're totally unfamiliar with JavaScript, you might want to review this section with a good supporting resource at hand. An excellent choice is *JavaScript Bible*, published by IDG Books Worldwide.

Using the objectTag() function

When Macromedia built a JavaScript interpreter into Dreamweaver, a number of extensions were included to facilitate object and behavior creation. One of these functions, objectTag(), is the key to building advanced objects. All of the standard Dreamweaver-built objects use the objectTag() function. This function has a single purpose: it writes the specified value into the <body> of an HTML document.

You can see a simple use of the objectTag() function by looking at the source code for Dreamweaver's Insert Line-break object. In the Objects\Invisibles folder, open line_break.htm and look at the code for this object in the HTML Inspector. Just like most JavaScript functions that can affect any portion of the page, the objectTag() function is written in the <head> section. Here's the function in its entirety:

```
function objectTag() {
  // Return the html tag that should be inserted
  return  <BR> ;
}
```

Tip

You can designate a ToolTip to appear when your mouse passes over your new object's button. Enter the desired name in the <title> section of the HTML object file.

Aside from the comment line, objectTag() only returns a value. In the preceding example, the value happens to be "<BR>". You can insert any HTML code as the return value. However, because JavaScript formats any value as a string, you need to apply JavaScript string-formatting syntax, as follows:

✦ To use the objectTag() function to return an HTML tag and a variable, use quotes around each string literal but not around the variable, and join the two with a plus sign. For example, the following objectTag() function code inserts <img src=images/whatzit.gif> in the current cursor position:

```
nada =  images/whatzit.gif
return  <img src=  + nada +  > ;
```

✦ To make an object that returns separate lines of code, put each tag on its own line with the symbol for a newline, \n, at the end of the string, surrounded by quotes; then add a plus sign at the end of the line. For example, this objectTag() function inserts a Flash movie of a particular size and shape:

```
function objectTag() {
  // Return the html tag that should be inserted
  return \n  +
 <object classid= clsid:D27CDB6E-AE6D-11cf-96B8-
444553540000  \n  +
 codebase= http://active.macromedia.com/flash2/cabs/swflas
h.cab#version=2,0,0,0  width= 145  height= 135 > \n  +
  <param name= movie  value= .swf > \n  +
  <param name= PLAY  value= false > \n  +
  <embed src= .swf  \n  +
 pluginspage= http://www.macromedia.com/shockwave/download
/  width= 145  height= 135  play= false ></embed> \n  +
 </object>
}
```

✦ Use single quotes to surround the return values that include double quotes. Make sure that for every opening quote of one kind, there is a matching closing quote of the same kind. For example:

```
return <img src= images/eiffel.jpg >
```

✦ Use the backslash character, \, to display special inline characters such as double and single quotes or newline.

```
return <strong>You\ re Right!</strong>
```

Tip

Unless you're mixing variables with the HTML you're using for your object, you should use the "object-only" method described in the prior section, "Making simple objects." Reserve the objectTag() function for your intermediate-to-advanced object-creation projects.

Attaching a parameter form

To be truly useful, many objects require additional attributes. Several of the standard objects in Dreamweaver use parameter forms to simplify entry of these attributes. A *parameter form* is the portion of the object code that creates a dialog box. Dreamweaver uses the HTML form commands for handling the parameter form duties.

To see how a parameter form is structured, look at the parameter forms used in the standard objects. Select the Insert Plug-in button in the Object Palette. The familiar Insert Plug-in dialog box that appears on the screen is a basic parameter form. Both the Image and Plug-in objects use this type of parameter form, with its essential capability of locating a source file.

Next, open the Plug-in object source file (Objects\Common\plugin.htm) in Dreamweaver to see how the parameter form is built. As shown in Figure 16-5, the <body> of the file consists of a single <form> element with two items inside, a text field and a Browse button.

The HTML source code for the Plug-in object contains only one element in the <body> section: the <form> with its two <input> fields, as follows.

```
<FORM NAME= theform >
  <TABLE>
    <TR>
      <TD nowrap>  Plugin Source:<BR>
        <INPUT TYPE= text  name= pluginfilename  size= 30 >
        <INPUT TYPE= button  value= Browse...  onclick=
        browseFile()  name= button >
      </TD>
    </TR>
  </TABLE>
</FORM>
```

Parameter form   Insert Plug-in dialog box

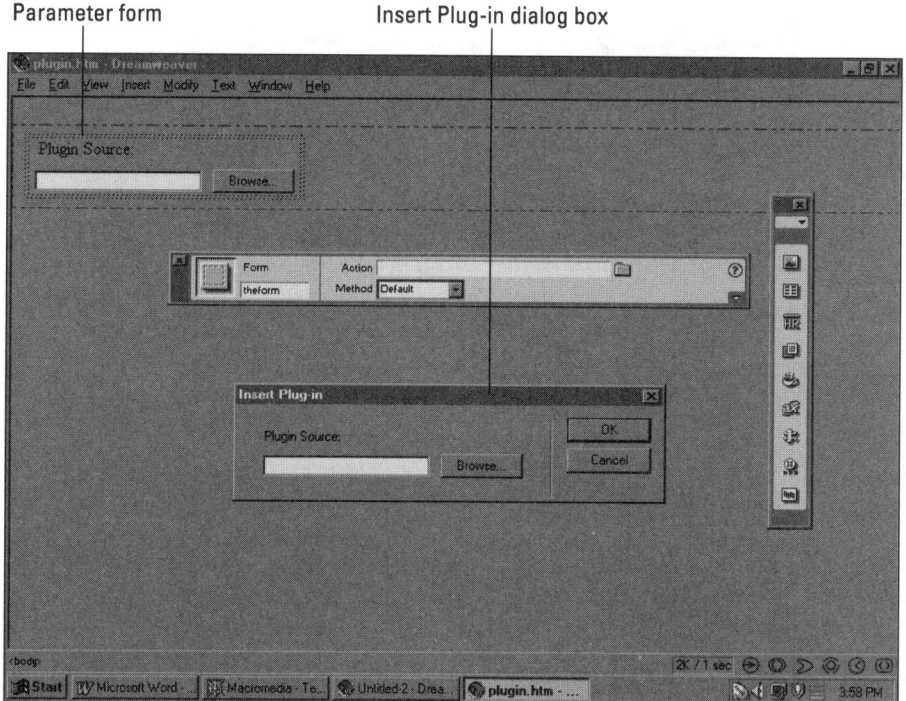

Figure 16-5: To see how the parameter form is used, compare the Plug-in source file to its completed object.

When selected, the Browse button calls the browseFile() function, which in turn calls one of the Dreamweaver JavaScript extensions, browseForFileURL(). These functions open a standard Select File dialog box and enable the user to locate a source file. The path and name of the source file are then displayed in the form's text box.

When the parameter form is displayed as an object, Dreamweaver automatically adds the OK and Cancel buttons. When you select the OK button, the objectTag() function combines the value in the text box (the filename) with the necessary HTML tags to write the plug-in code.

Sizing the Parameter Form Dialog Box

Although you cannot control all aspects of your parameter form — Dreamweaver automatically inserts the OK and Cancel buttons on the upper-right — you can designate the dimensions of the parameter's dialog box. Normally, Dreamweaver automatically sizes the dialog box, but for a complex object, you can speed up the display by using the windowDimensions() function. Moreover, if your object is intended for general distribution, you can set different window dimensions for the Macintosh and Windows platforms.

The windowDimensions() function takes one argument, platform, and returns a string in the form:

```
width_in_Pixels,height_in_Pixels
```

The size specified should not include the area for the OK and Cancel buttons. If dimensions offered are too small to display all the options in the parameter form, scroll bars automatically appear.

The following example of the windowDimensions() function creates a parameters dialog box 324 pixels by 233 pixels if viewed on a Macintosh, and 376 pixels by 252 pixels if viewed on a Windows system:

```
function windowDimensions(platform){
    if (platform.charAt(0) == m ){ // Macintosh
      return 324,233 ;
    }
    else { // Windows 95 or NT
      return 376,252 ;
    }
}
```

Macromedia recommends that you not use the windowDimensions() function unless performance for your object is a problem. Like all Dreamweaver extensions to the Application Programming Interface (API), the windowDimensions() function can be used to build both objects and actions.

Using the form controls

Dreamweaver uses the HTML <form> tag and all of its various input types to gather attribute information for objects. To use the form elements in a parameter form, their input data must be passed to the JavaScript functions. Because Dreamweaver uses a subset of the Navigator 3.0 Document Object Model (DOM) as shown in Table 16-1, you are restricted to using specific methods for the various input types to gather this information. Properties marked with an asterisk are read-only.

Table 16-1
Form Elements in the Dreamweaver Document Object Model

Object	Properties	Methods	Events
form	elements* (an array of button, checkbox, password, radio, reset, select, submit, text, and text area objects) child objects by name	None	None
button reset submit	form*	blur() focus()	onClick
checkbox radio	checked form*	blur() focus()	onClick
password text textarea	value form*	blur() focus() select()	onBlur onFocus
select	form* options[n].defaultSelected* options[n].index* options[n].selected* options[n].text* options[n].value* selectedIndex	blur() (Windows only) focus()	onBlur (Windows only) onChange

Note

JavaScript uses a hierarchical method of addressing the various elements on any given Web page. Moving from most general to most specific, each element is separated by a period. For example, the background color property of a page would be document.bgColor. The status of a checkbox named "sendPromo" on a form called "orderForm" would be document.orderForm.sendPromo.checked. The more complex your objects, the more important it is for you to master this syntax.

Text, textarea, and password fields

When information is entered in one of the text input type fields, the data is stored in the value property of the specific object. For example, look again at the code for the Plug-in object, and notice the text field where the selected file's name is displayed:

```
<INPUT TYPE= text  name= pluginfilename  size= 30 >
```

When the objectTag() function is run, the contents of that text box is assigned to a variable, and that variable is included in the output written to the Web page:

```
function objectTag() {
  // Return the html tag that should be inserted
  var retval = <EMBED SRC=   +
escape(document.forms[0].pluginfilename.value) +   ></EMBED> ;

  // clear the field for next insertion
  clearForm();
  return retval;
}
```

In the preceding case, the input filename is located in `document.forms[0].pluginfilename.value`. Because the form was also named ("theForm"), this same value could also be written as follows:

```
document.theForm.pluginfilename.value
```

Note

> The "escape" function is a JavaScript internal function that converts a text string so that it can be read by a Web server. Any special characters are encoded into their hexadecimal ASCII equivalents. A single space between words, for instance, is converted to %20.

The text input types recognize two events in the Dreamweaver Document Object Model: `onBlur` and `onFocus`. When a user selects a text field, either by tabbing or clicking into it, that text field is said to have *focus* — and the `onFocus` event is fired. When the user leaves that field, the field loses focus or *blurs* — and the `onBlur` event is triggered. Because the DOM does not recognize the `onChange` event handler with text fields, you can use a combination of the `onFocus` and `onBlur` to check for changes and act accordingly.

Submit, reset and command buttons

The button input types are used in parameter forms to trigger custom JavaScript functions. Instead of sending data to an external server, the data is sent to a specified internal function. The buttons respond only to `onClick` events and cannot pass any particular properties of their own, such as value or name.

Command buttons are used extensively in the Character Entities object shown in Figure 16-6. (The object is available on this book's CD-ROM.) Each character entity is a separate command button, written in the following form:

```
<input type= BUTTON  value= &#161;
onClick= getChar( &amp;#161; , &#161; ) >
```

Each character entity symbol in each line has a specific purpose. The value is the character displayed on the button; the first argument in the getChar() function is written to a hidden field and eventually sent to the Web page; and the second argument is used to display the selected character in a text box.

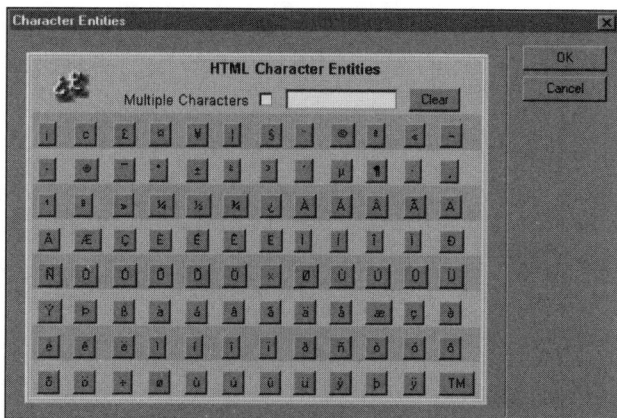

Figure 16-6: This custom Character Entities object (available on the CD-ROM) uses 97 separate command buttons.

```
function getChar(val,val2) {
  document.theForm.charValue.value=val
  document.theForm.txChar.value=val2
}
```

When this object is at work, the user makes a selection and clicks OK, and the objectTag() function reads the value from the hidden field and writes it into the Web page:

```
function objectTag() {
  return document.theForm.charValue.value;
}
```

Command buttons can be used to fire any custom JavaScripts and pass any necessary information to be eventually processed by the objectTag() function.

Check boxes

Check boxes allow an option to be selected or deselected, so the only information that a function needs from a check box is whether it has been selected. Dreamweaver's DOM lets you read the checked property of the check box object and act accordingly. The Character Entities object discussed in the preceding section, for instance, uses a check box to turn on and off the Multiple Characters option. If the check box (named `cbMultiple`) is selected, then `document. theForm.cbMultiple.checked` is true and one set of statements is executed; otherwise, the second set of statements is run. The code for check boxes follows:

```
function getChar(val,val2) {
if(document.theForm.cbMultiple.checked) {
  document.theForm.charValue.value=
  document.theForm.charValue.value+val
  document.theForm.txChar.value=
  document.theForm.txChar.value+val2
  } else {
  document.theForm.charValue.value=val
  document.theForm.txChar.value=val2
  }
}
```

Check boxes are excellent for setting up either/or situations. You can also use check boxes to set (turn on) particular attributes. You may, for instance, use a check box to let the user enable an automatic startup for an .avi movie, or to turn on/off the control panel.

Radio buttons

Radio buttons are a means for offering a group of choices, from which the user can only select one. The group is composed of `<input type=radio>` tags with the same `name` attribute; there can be as few as two in the group or as many as necessary.

The input type `radio`, like `checkbox`, makes use of the `checked` property to see which option was selected. The method used to figure which of the radio buttons was chosen depends on the number of buttons used on the form:

✦ With just two or three buttons, you may want to use a simple if-else construct to find which radio button was selected.

✦ If you are offering many options, you can use a loop structure to look at the `checked` property of each radio button.

With only a couple of radio buttons in a group, you can examine the one radio-type item in the array (starting with 0) and see if it was checked. In the following code, if one radio button is selected, the variable (`theChoice`) is set to one value—otherwise, it is set to the other value:

```
if (document.forms[0].comm[0].checked ==  1 )
    theChoice =  left ;
  else
    theChoice =  right ;
```

When you have many radio buttons, or you don't know how many radio buttons you will have, use a counter loop such as this next example from the Enhanced LineBreak object (available on the CD-ROM).

```
for (var i = 0; i < document.theForm.lbreak.length; i++) {
    if (document.theForm.lbreak[i].checked) {
        break
    }
}
```

In this example, `lbreak` is the name of the group of radio buttons on the parameter form, and the `length` property tells you how many radio buttons are in the group. When the loop finds the selected radio button in the array, the loop is broken and the program proceeds to the next group of statements.

Unfortunately, once you know which radio button is checked, there's no easy way to get its value. The Dreamweaver DOM doesn't support the value property for the radio input type. As a result, you have to assign the value to a variable based on which radio button was selected. You can complete this task in a simple series of if-else statements:

```
if (i == 0){
val =
    } else {
    if (i == 1) {
    val =  left
        } else {
        if (i == 2) {
        val =  right
            } else {
            val =  all
            }
        }
    }
```

Alternatively, you can put all the values in an array and assign them in a statement like the following:

```
return  <br clear=  + newValue[i].name +  >
```

List boxes and drop-down menus

List boxes and drop-down menus are perfect for offering a variety of choices in a compact format. Drop-down menus enable the user to choose an option from a scrolling list; list boxes offer multiple choices from a similar list. Both use the `<select>` tag to set up their available options. When you include a list box or drop-down menu from Dreamweaver, you enter the options by selecting the List Value button and entering the item labels and their associated values in the dialog. The code for the Direction list box — taken from Matthew David's Marquee object, which is shown in Figure 16-7 and is available on the CD-ROM — is written as follows:

```
<select name= direction >
     <option value= LEFT  selected>LEFT</option>
     <option value= RIGHT >RIGHT</option>
     <option value= UP >UP</option>
     <option value= DOWN >DOWN</option>
</select>
```

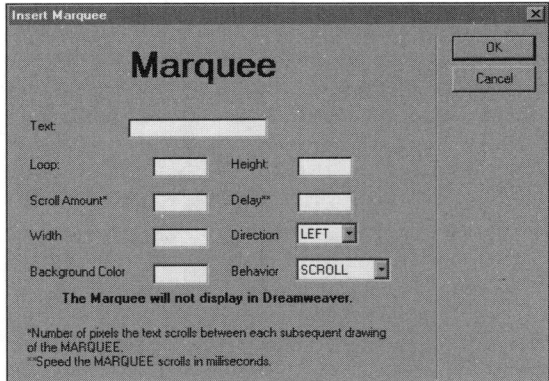

Figure 16-7: The Marquee custom object is designed to take advantage of an Internet Explorer special function: the capability to make a scrolling text display.

Each list box or drop-down menu must have a unique name — in the preceding code, that name is "direction" given in the `<select>` tag. To discover which option the user selected when working with a drop-down menu, you need to examine the `selected Index` property of the named `<select>` object. Each `<option>` in a `<select>` tag is placed in an array in the order listed in the displayed menu. Remember, arrays always start with a 0 in JavaScript.

The following code looks at each member of the array; if that option is the one in which the `selectedIndex` property is true, then the proper value is assigned to a variable.

```
if(document.forms[0].direction.selectedIndex == 0) {
  direct_choice =  LEFT
   } else {
   if(document.forms[0].direction.selectedIndex == 1) {
  direct_choice =  RIGHT
  } else {
      if(document.forms[0].direction.selectedIndex == 2) {
      direct_choice =  UP
  } else {
      if(document.forms[0].direction.selectedIndex == 3) {
      direct_choice =  DOWN
  }
 }
}
}
```

The process is slightly different when you allow multiple options in a list box. In this situation, you should set up a loop to examine the `options[n].selected` property. All the options in a `<select>` tag set have additional properties that can be read by Dreamweaver's DOM, as follows:

Select Options	Description
`options[n].defaultSelected`	Returns True for the option (or options, when multiple selections are enabled) for every `<option>` tag with a `selected` attribute.
`options[n].index`	Returns the option's position in the array.
`options[n].selected`	Returns True if the option is chosen by the user.
`options[n].text`	Returns the text of the item as it appears in the list.
`options[n].value`	Returns the value of the item assigned in the `<option>` statement.

The following method cycles through all of the `<options>` to find which one(s) were selected:

```
for (var i = 0; i < document.theForm.optList.length; i++) {
  if (document.theForm.optList.options[i].selected) {
      result += n\   + document.theForm.optList.options[i].
      value
```

```
        }
    }
    return result
}
```

Adding images to your objects

Custom objects don't have to be just text, of course. You can include images in your object, just as you would in a regular Web page — with one catch: Dreamweaver has to be able to find your image files. If you are not distributing your custom object, you can use images from any folder on your system. On the other hand, if your objects are going out to other users, you have to either include the image files with the object or use existing graphics stored in known locations.

What existing graphics are on every Dreamweaver system in specific locations? The GIF files for each object, of course. The example uses the GIF file from the Character Entities object (shown in Figure 16-6) in the object itself. Because the two files always have to be in the same folder, you can include the image file on the same level. The size of the GIF files is fairly small (16 pixels by 16 pixels), so you can simply double the size of the image and let Dreamweaver rescale it.

Of course, you can create your own custom graphics for your objects and include those files with the associated HTML and GIF button files. You can even spice up your Dreamweaver standard objects, as in Figure 16-8.

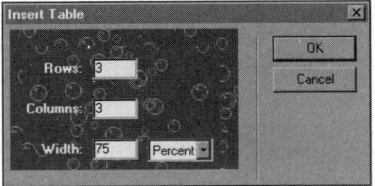

Figure 16-8: You can include graphics in custom objects — in this Insert Table dialog box, the standard Dreamweaver object is altered.

Tip   You can count on two other useful graphical objects: the "plus" and "minus" buttons used in the Dreamweaver dialog boxes for behaviors and parameters. The GIF files for these buttons are found in the Configuration\Behaviors\Actions folder.

Using layers in objects

The capability to use layers in Dreamweaver objects and behaviors is new to Dreamweaver 1.2. With the expansive possibilities of layers, you can build a Wizard-type object that leads the users through a series of complex steps, with instructions on every screen. You could also use layers to describe the effect of the user's choices.

Layers and forms (the essence of a Dreamweaver object) can coexist, but only if you dot all your i's and cross all your t's. Keep the following pointers to keep in mind:

✦ Make sure your forms do not span any layers. The form must be completely within the layer — and not vice versa.

✦ Because of a code discrepancy, you can't use the regular Show-Hide Layer Behavior when designing objects. Instead, use the custom Show-Hide Layer for objects included on the CD-ROM in the Dreamweaver\Configuration\ Behaviors\Actions folder.

✦ Be careful using forms on separate layers. When you switch among layers, making one visible and hiding the others, the data on the forms is cleared. You need to add JavaScript code to read and restore the data on each change.

✦ To pull a value from a form object in a layer: name the form, the layer, and the object, and then use the following syntax:

```
document.layers[ layerName ].document.formName.objectName.
property
```

This syntax is the object reference used by Navigator and the Dreamweaver object engine.

✦ Use hidden form fields to consolidate input from various layers and then reference those hidden fields for your final object output. See "Using the Hidden Field" in Chapter 15.

Summary

In one sense, objects are analogous to the macros in a word-processing program that allow repetitive work to be greatly simplified. Objects can be so much more than just duplication tools, however — they can extend the reach of Dreamweaver's power and instantly incorporate new standards and technology. The standard Dreamweaver objects can be used effortlessly. Just like all objects, they are simply HTML files, and thus provide excellent examples for creating custom objects.

✦ Objects can be inserted from either the Object Palette or the Insert menu.

✦ Both the Object Palette and the Insert menu can be easily modified by adjusting the InsertMenu.htm file.

✦ Simple objects can be created by inserting the HTML code necessary to make the object into a file, and then saving the file in one of the Objects subfolders.

✦ More complex objects can take advantage of Dreamweaver's built-in JavaScript interpreter, its Document Object Model, special JavaScript functions, and enhanced Application Programming Interface (API). Dreamweaver 1.2 even allows layers to be used in the construction of custom objects.

In the next chapter, you see how to use and create Dreamweaver Behaviors.

✦   ✦   ✦

Creating and Using Behaviors

Behaviors are truly the power tools of Dreamweaver. With Dreamweaver behaviors, any Web designer can make layers appear and disappear, execute 3-button rollovers, or control a Shockwave movie — all without even knowing even a snippet of JavaScript. In the hands of an accomplished JavaScript programmer, Dreamweaver behaviors can be customized or created from scratch to automate the most difficult Web effect.

Creating behaviors is one of the more challenging Dreamweaver features to master. Implementing these gems, however, is a piece of cake. This chapter is split evenly between these two concepts. The first portion examines the concepts and the reality of using behaviors — detailing the use of all the behaviors included with Dreamweaver — and from other notable third-party sources. The chapter's second half offers step-by-step instructions for creating your own behaviors. You also find insights into Macromedia's Behavior Development Kit (BDK), and an overview of the library of useful functions already available to speed your coding.

Once you get the hang of using Dreamweaver behaviors, your Web pages will never be the same.

Understanding Behaviors, Events, and Actions

A *behavior*, in Macromedia parlance, is the combination of an event and one or more actions. In the electronic age, one pushes a button (the event) and something (the action) occurs — like changing the channel on the TV. In Dreamweaver, events can be anything as interactive as a user's click on a link, or something as automatic as the loading of a Web page.

Let's examine the five essential steps for adding a behavior to your Web page to help you understand conceptually how behaviors are structured:

Step 1. Pick a tag. All behaviors are connected to a specific HTML element. You can attach a behavior to everything from the <body> to the <textarea> of a form.

Step 2. Choose your target browser. Different browsers — and the various browser versions — support different events. Dreamweaver lets you choose either a specific browser, such as Internet Explorer 4, or a browser range, such as 3.0 and 4.0 browsers.

Step 3. Select an event. The list of possible events depends on the browser you chose and the tag selected. Generally, the older the browser, the fewer events are available to you. Events can be based on the user's action (such as moving a mouse over an image) or on something that happens in the Web page (such as resizing).

Step 4. Select an action. Dreamweaver makes active only those actions available to your specific page. You can't, for instance, choose the Show-Hide Layer action until you insert one or more layers. Behaviors guide you to the workable options.

Step 5. Enter the parameters. Behaviors get their power from their flexibility. Each action comes with a specific parameter form (which represents the dialog box that the user sees) designed to customize the JavaScript code output. Depending on the action, you can choose source files, set attributes, and enable features. The parameter form can even dynamically update to reflect your current Web page.

Dreamweaver 1.2 comes with 18 cross-browser-compatible actions, and third-party developers have made many additional actions available, with even more are in the works. Behaviors can greatly extend the range of possibilities for the modern Web designer — without learning to program JavaScript. All you need to know about attaching behaviors is presented in the following section.

Attaching a Behavior

When you see the code generated by Dreamweaver, you understand why setting up a behavior is also referred to as attaching a behavior. As previously noted, Dreamweaver needs a specific HTML tag to assign the behavior (Step 1). The link tag <a> is often used because, in JavaScript, links can respond to several different events, including onClick. Here's an example:

```
<a href= # onClick= MM_popupMsg( Thanks for coming! ) >Exit
Here</a>
```

You're not restricted to one event per tag or even one action per event. Multiple events can be attached to a tag to handle various user actions. For example, you may have an image that does all of the following things:

✦ Highlights when the user's pointer moves over the image.

✦ Reveals a hidden layer in another area of the page when the user clicks the mouse button down on the image.

✦ Makes a sound when the user releases the mouse button over the image.

✦ Starts a Flash movie when the user's pointer moves away from the image.

Likewise, a single event can trigger several actions. Updating multiple frames though a single link used to be difficult — but no more. Dreamweaver makes it easy by enabling you to attach several Go to URL actions to the same event, onMouseClick. In addition, you are not restricted to attaching multiple instances of the same action to a single event. For example, in a site that uses a lot of multimedia, you could tie all of the following actions to a single onClick event:

✦ Begin playing an audio file (with the Control Sound action).

✦ Move a layer across the screen (with the Play Timeline action).

✦ Display a second graphic in place of the first (with the Swap Image action).

✦ Show the copyright information for the audio piece in the status bar (with the Display Status Message action).

You can even determine the order in which the actions are executed.

With Dreamweaver behaviors, hours of complex JavaScript coding is reduced to a handful of mouse clicks and a minimum of data entry. All behavior assigning and modification is handled through the Behavior Inspector.

Using the Behavior Inspector

The Behavior Inspector is a two-paned window (Figure 17-1) that neatly sums up the behaviors concept in general. A list of assigned events is located on the left side of the window. The selected tag is displayed at the top of the events pane, with a drop-down list of browsers. The options follow:

✦ 3.0 and 4.0 Browsers

✦ 4.0 Browsers

✦ IE 3.0

✦ IE 4.0

+ Netscape 3.0

+ Netscape 4.0

When you select one of these choices, a pop-up menu shows you which events are available for the browser. Select any event in the menu to see the associated actions in the right half of the window (the Actions pane). Double-click the action to open the associated Parameter window, where you can modify the action's attributes.

Selected tag   Browser drop-down list

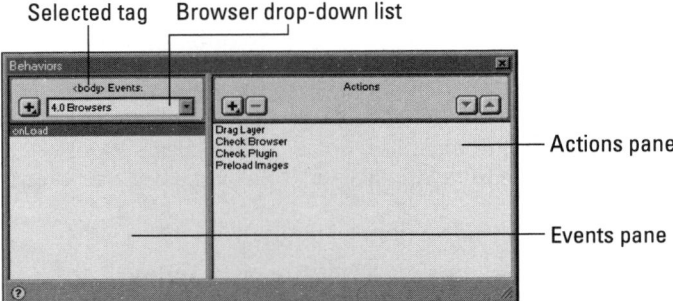

Actions pane

Events pane

Figure 17-1: You can handle everything about a behavior through the Behavior Inspector.

As usual in Dreamweaver, you have your choice of methods for opening the Behavior Inspector:

+ Choose Window ➪ Behaviors.

+ Select the Show Behaviors button from either Launcher.

+ Use the keyboard shortcut, F8 (an on/off toggle).

Tip

The Behavior Inspector can be closed by toggling it off with F8, or hidden with the other floating windows by pressing F4.

After you have attached a behavior to a tag and closed the associated action's parameter form, Dreamweaver writes the necessary HTML and JavaScript code into your document. Because it involves functions which can be called from anywhere in the document, the JavaScript code is placed in the `<head>` section of the page, and the code that links the selected tag to the functions is written in the `<body>` section. A few actions, including Control Sound, place additional JavaScript code at the top of the `<body>`, but most of the code — there can be a lot of code to handle all the cross-browser contingencies — is placed in the `<head>` HTML section.

Adding a behavior

Now let's look more closely at the procedure for adding (or attaching) a behavior. As noted earlier, you can only assign certain events to particular tags, and those options are further defined by the type of selected browser.

Note Even in the latest browsers, key events such as onMouseDown, onMouseOver, and onMouseOut only work with anchor tags. To circumvent this limitation, Dreamweaver can enclose an element, like <img>, with an anchor tag that links to nowhere — src= # . Events that use the anchor tag in this fashion are seen in parentheses in the pop-up menu of events.

To add a behavior to your Web page, follow these steps:

1. Select an object in the Document Window.

   Tip If you want to assign a behavior to the entire page, select the <body> tag from the Tag Selector.

2. Open the Behavior Inspector by choosing Window ⇨ Behaviors or selecting the Show Behaviors button from either Launcher. You can see the selected tag at the top of the Events pane.

3. If necessary, select a different browser target from the drop-down list in the Events pane.

4. Select the + (Add) Event button to reveal the available options for the selected browser, as shown in Figure 17-2. Choose one from the pop-up menu.

5. In the Actions pane, select the + (Add) Action button to see the list of possible actions. Choose one from the pop-up menu to open the Action dialog box.

6. Enter the necessary parameters in the Action dialog box.

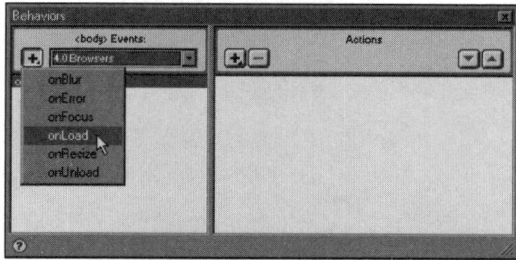

Figure 17-2: The Add Events pop-up dynamically changes according to the tag and browser selected.

The standard events

Dreamweaver ships with a set list of events recognized by particular browsers. The Dreamweaver\Configuration\Behavior\Events folder contains HTML files corresponding to the six browsers offered in the Events pane's drop-down list. You can open these files in Dreamweaver, but Macromedia asks that you not edit them. Each file contains the list of tags that have supported *event handlers* (the JavaScript term for events) in that browser.

The older the browser, the fewer event handlers are included — unfortunately, this also means that if you want to reach the broadest Internet audience, your event options are limited. In the broadest category, 3.0 and 4.0 Browsers, only 13 different tags can receive any sort of event handler.

If you do open and examine an event file in Dreamweaver, notice a group of yellow tags and a few form objects, as shown in Figure 17-3. The yellow tags identify what Dreamweaver sees as invalid HTML. Those form objects — the buttons, checkbox, radio button, and text — render normally but aren't active.

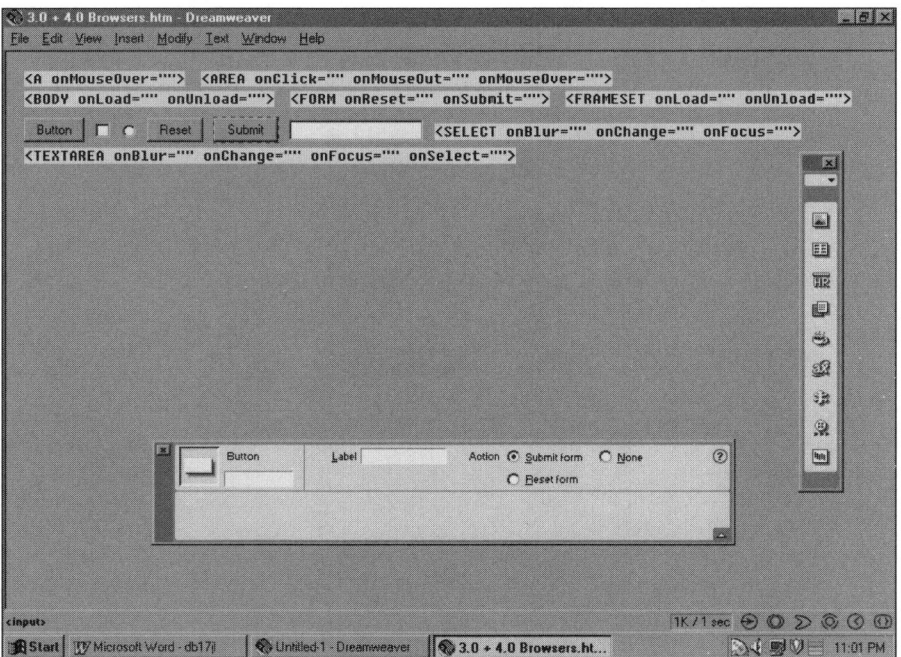

Figure 17-3: The Event files define the tags that support particular event handlers in a selected browser.

In this case, viewing the HTML is far more instructive than the Document Window, as you can see by looking at Listing 17-1. This example gives the event handler definitions for the 3.0 and 4.0 Browsers category.

Listing 17-1: **The Events file for 3.0 and 4.0 Browsers**

```
<A onMouseOver=  >
<AREA onClick=    onMouseOut=    onMouseOver=  >
<BODY onLoad=    onUnload=  >
<FORM onReset=    onSubmit=  >
<FRAMESET onLoad=    onUnload=  >
<INPUT TYPE= Button   onClick=  >
<INPUT TYPE= Checkbox   onClick=  >
<INPUT TYPE= Radio   onClick=  >
<INPUT TYPE= Reset   onClick=  >
<INPUT TYPE= Submit   onClick=  >
<INPUT TYPE= Text   onBlur=    onChange=    onFocus=
onSelect=  >
<SELECT onBlur=    onChange=    onFocus=  >
<TEXTAREA onBlur=    onChange=    onFocus=    onSelect=  >
```

By contrast, the events file for Internet Explorer 4.0 shows support for every tag under the HTML sun — 79 in all — with almost every tag able to handle any type of event.

Tip

Although any HTML tag could potentially be used to attach a behavior, the most commonly used by far are the `<body>` tag (for entire-page events such as `onLoad`), the `<img>` tag when used as a button, and the link tag, `<a>`.

The standard actions

As of this writing, 18 standard actions ship with Dreamweaver 1.2. Three new actions were added in the 1.2 release: Check Browser, Drag Layer, and Preload Images. A preload option has also been added to `Swap Image`. Each action operates independently and differently from the others, although many share common functions. Each action is associated with a different dialog box or parameter form to allow easy attribute entry.

Following is a discussion of the standard actions: what the action does, what requirements must be met for it to be activated, what options are available, and most importantly of all, how to use it. Each action is written to work with all 4.0 browsers; however, some actions do not work as designed in the older browsers. The charts included with every action show the action's compatibility in older browsers. (The information in these charts was adapted from the Dreamweaver Help pages and used with permission.)

Change Property

The Change Property action enables you to alter dynamically a property of one of the following tags:

<layer>   <div>   <form>

<span>   <img>   <select>

You can also alter the following <input> types:

radio   checkbox   text

textarea   password

Exactly which properties can be altered depends on the tag as well as on the browser being targeted. For example, the <div> tag and Internet Explorer 4.0 combination enables you to change virtually every style sheet option on the fly. The Change Property dialog box (Figure 17-4) offers a list of the selected tags in the current page.

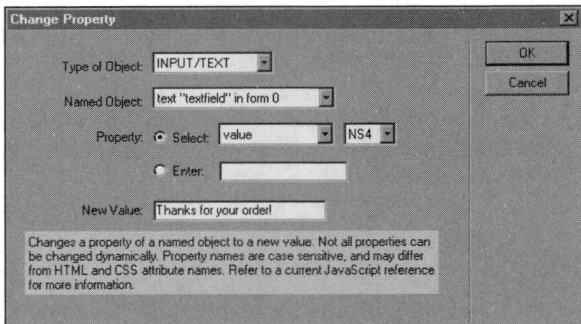

Figure 17-4: The Change Property action enables you to alter attributes of certain tags dynamically.

To use the Change Property action, follow these steps:

1. Select an event to trigger the action, and then choose Change Property from the Add Action pop-up.

2. In the parameter form, choose an object type from the Type of Object drop-down list.

3. In the dynamic Named Object drop-down list, choose the object you wish to affect.

4. Click the Select radio button. Select the target browser in the small list box on the far right, and then choose the Property to change. If you don't find the property in the drop-down list box, you can type it yourself into the Enter text box.

   Note: Many properties in the various browsers are read-only and cannot be dynamically altered.

5. In the New Value text box, type the property's new value to be inserted when the event is fired.

Note

About the browser compatibility charts: some language in the following and subsequent charts detailing the action's behavior in older browsers needs a little explanation. The phrase "fails without error" means that the action won't work in the older browser, but neither does it generate an error message for the user to see. Where the table indicates "error," it means the user receives a JavaScript alert message.

Here's the browser compatibility chart for the Change Property behavior:

Change Property	*Netscape 2.x*	*Netscape 3.x*	*Internet Explorer 3.0*	*Internet Explorer 3.01*
Macintosh	OK; fails without error for objects in layers	OK; fails without error for objects in layers	Fails without error	OK
Windows	OK; fails without errorfor objects in layers	OK; fails without error for objects in layers	OK	OK

Check Browser

Increasingly, Web sites are splitting into multilevel versions of themselves to handle the variety of browsers in operation gracefully. The Check Browser action acts as a type of browser "router" capable of sending browsers to appropriate URLs, or just letting them stay on the current page. Generally, the Check Browser action is assigned to the `<body>` tag and uses the onLoad event.

The Check Browser parameter form (Figure 17-5) is quite flexible and enables you to specify decimal version numbers for the two main browsers. For instance, you may want to let all users of Navigator 4.04 or later stay on the current page and send everyone else to an alternative URL. The URLs can be either relative, like `alt/index.html`, or absolute, like `http://www.idest.com/alt/index.html`.

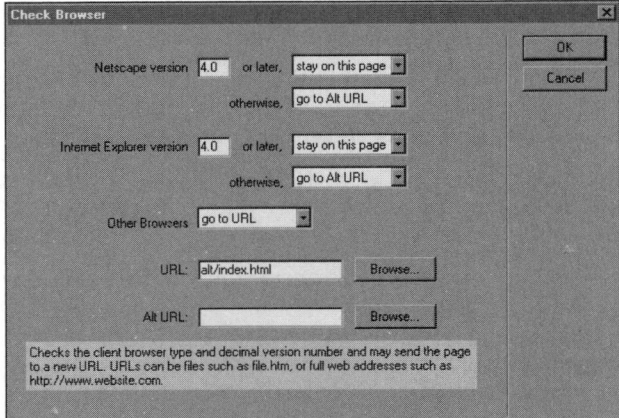

Figure 17-5: The Check Browser action is a great tool for segregating old and new browsers.

To use the Check Browser action, follow these steps:

1. Select an event to trigger the action, and then choose Check Browser from the Add Action pop-up.

2. Specify the Netscape Navigator and Internet Explorer versions, and whether you want the browser to stay on the current page, go to another URL, or proceed to a third alternative URL.

   Note: With both major browsers, you can specify the URL that the lower version numbers should visit.

3. Set the same options for all other browsers, such as Opera and Linux.

4. Enter the URL and alternate URL options in their respective text boxes, or select the Browse buttons to locate the files.

The Check Browser action works well with another Dreamweaver 1.2 feature: Convert to 3.0 Compatible. Learn all about this new capability in Chapter 27, "Publishing via FTP."

Here's the browser compatibility chart for the Check Browser behavior:

Change Browser	Netscape 2.x	Netscape 3.x	Internet Explorer 3.0	Internet Explorer 3.01
Macintosh	OK; fails without error for objects in layers	OK; fails without error for objects in layers	Fails without error	OK
Windows	OK; fails without error for objects in layers	OK; fails without error for objects in layers	OK	OK

Check Plugin

If certain pages on your Web site require the use of one or more plug-ins, you can use the Check Plugin action to see if a visitor has the necessary plug-in installed. Once this has been examined, Check Plugin can route users who have the appropriate plug-in to one URL, and users without it to another URL. You can only look for one plug-in at a time, but you can use multiple instances of the Check Plugin action, if needed.

By default, the parameter form for Check Plugin (Figure 17-6) offers five plug-ins: Shockwave Flash 2.0, Shockwave Director, LiveAudio, Netscape Media Player, and QuickTime. You can check for any other plug-in by entering its name in the Enter text box; use the name that appears when choosing Help ➪ About Plugins in the Navigator menus.

Tip

If you use a particular plug-in regularly, you may want to also modify the Check Plugin.htm file. Add your new plug-in name to the PLUGIN_NAMES variable found in the Global section.

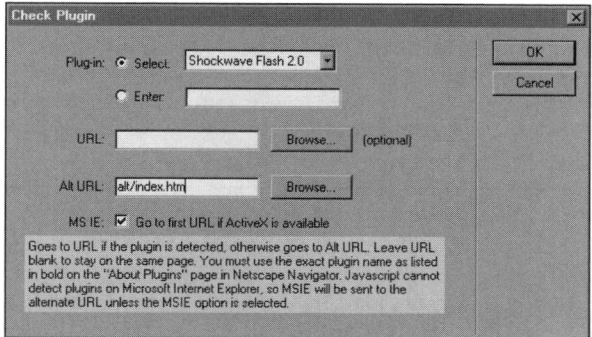

Figure 17-6: Running a media-intensive site? Use the Check Plugin action to divert visitors without plug-ins to alternative pages.

Although Check Plugin cannot check for specific ActiveX controls, this action can route the Internet Explorer user to the same page as users who have plug-ins. The best way to handle both browsers is to use both ActiveX controls and plug-ins, through the ⟨object⟩ and ⟨embed⟩ methods explained in Chapter 15, "Accessing External Programs."

On the CD-ROM

Another method for determining whether a plug-in or other player is available is to use the Check MIME action included in the CD-ROM. This action works in the same way as the Check Plugin action, except you enter the MIME type. For example: application\x-shockwave-flash — which, incidentally, is necessary for checking to see if the user has the Flash 3 plug-in installed.

To use the Check Plugin action, follow these steps:

1. Select an event to trigger the action, and then choose Check Plugin from the Add Action pop-up.

2. Select a plug-in from the drop-down list. You can also type another plug-in name in the Enter text box.

3. If you want to send users who are confirmed to have the plug-in to a different page, enter that URL (absolute or relative) in the URL text box (or use the Browse button to locate the file). If you want them to stay on the current page, leave the text box empty.

4. In the Alt URL text box, enter the URL for users who do not have the required plug-in.

5. If you do not want Internet Explorer users to go to the same location chosen for users with the plug-in, deselect the MS IE check box. In this case, users are sent to the Alt URL address.

Here's the browser compatibility chart for the Check Plugin behavior:

Change Plugin	Netscape 2.x	Netscape 3.x	Internet Explorer 3.0	Internet Explorer 3.01
Macintosh	OK	OK	Fails without error	OK
Windows	OK	OK	OK	OK

End tableControl Shockwave

The Control Shockwave action enables you to command your Director and Flash Shockwave movies through external controls. With Control Shockwave, you can build your own interface for your Shockwave material. This action can be used in conjunction with the autostart=true attribute (entered through the Property

Inspector's Parameter dialog box for the Shockwave or Flash file), to allow a replaying of the movie.

You must have a Shockwave Director or Flash movie inserted in your Web page in order for the Control Shockwave action to be available. The parameter form for this action (Figure 17-7) lists all the Shockwave Director or Flash movies by name that are found in either an `<embed>` or `<object>` tag. You can set the action to control the movie in one of four ways: Start, Stop, Rewind, or Go to Frame. You can only choose one option each time you attach an action to an event. If you choose the last option, you need to specify the frame number in the text box. Note that specifying a Go to Frame number does not start the movie there; you will need to attach a second Control Shockwave action to the same event to play the file.

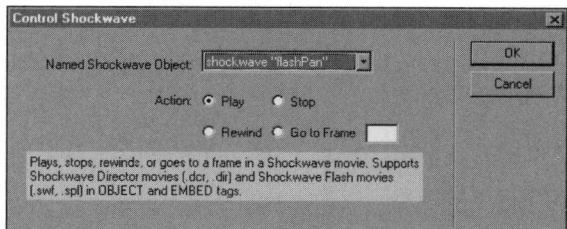

Figure 17-7: Build your own interface, and then control a Shockwave Director and Flash movie externally with the Control Shockwave action.

Tip   Be sure to name your Shockwave Director or Flash movie. Otherwise, the Control Shockwave action lists both `unnamed <embed>` and `unnamed <object>` for each file, and you cannot write to both tags as you can with a named movie.

To use the Control Shockwave action, follow these steps:

1. Select an event to trigger the action, and then choose Control Shockwave from the Add Action pop-up.

2. Select a movie from the Named Shockwave Object drop-down list.

3. Select a control by choosing its radio button:
    - Play: To begin playing the movie at the current frame location.
    - Stop: To stop playing the movie.
    - Rewind: To return the movie to its first frame.
    - Go to Frame: To display a specific frame in the movie. Note: for this option, you must enter a frame number in the text box.

Here's the browser compatibility chart for the Control Shockwave behavior:

Control Shockwave	Netscape 2.x	Netscape 3.x	Internet Explorer 3.0	Internet Explorer 3.01
Macintosh	Fails without error	OK	Fails without error	Fails without error
Windows	Fails without error	OK	Fails without error	Fails without error

Control Sound

The Control Sound action is used to add external controls to an audio file that normally uses the Netscape LiveAudio plug-in. Supported audio file types include .wav, .mid, .au, and .aiff files — generally to add background music with a hidden sound file. The Control Sound action inserts an `<embed>` tag with the following attributes set:

✦ loop=false

✦ autostart=false

✦ mastersound

✦ hidden=true

✦ width=0

✦ height=0

Instead of automatically detecting which sound files have been inserted in the current Web page, Control Sound needs the sound file to be inserted though the action's parameter form (Figure 17-8). Once the file has been inserted through the Control Sound action, the file appears in the Stop Sound drop-down list when you next invoke this action.

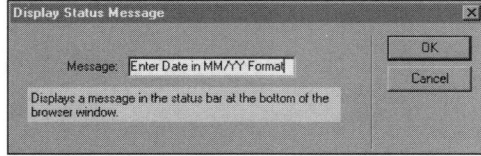

Figure 17-8: Give your Web page background music and control it with the Control Sound action.

To use the Control Sound action, follow these steps:

1. Select an event to trigger the action, and then choose Control Sound from the Add Action pop-up.

2. To play a sound, select the Play Sound radio button, and enter the path to the audio file in the Play Sound text box (or select the Browse button to locate the file).

3. To stop a sound, select the Stop Sound radio button and select the audio file to control from the Stop Sound drop-down list.

    Note: only audio files that have been previously inserted through the Play Sound option are listed.

Here's the browser compatibility chart for the Control Sound behavior:

Control Sound	Netscape 2.x	Netscape 3.x	Internet Explorer 3.0	Internet Explorer 3.01
Macintosh	Error	OK	Fails without error	Fails without error
Windows	Fails without error	OK	Fails without error	Fails without error

Display Status Message

Use the Display Status Message action to show your choice of text in a browser's status bar, based on a user's action such as moving the pointer over an image. The message stays displayed in the status bar until another message replaces it. System messages, such as URLs, tend to be temporary and only visible when the user's mouse is over a link.

The only limit to the length of the message is the size of the browser's status bar; you should test your message in various browsers to make sure that it is completely visible.

Tip

> To display a message only when a user's pointer is over an image, use one Display Status Message action, attached to an onMouseOver event, with your associated text. Use another Display Status Message action, attached to an onMouseOut event, that has a null string (a couple of spaces) as the text.

All text is entered in the Display Status Message parameter form (see Figure 17-9) in the Message text box.

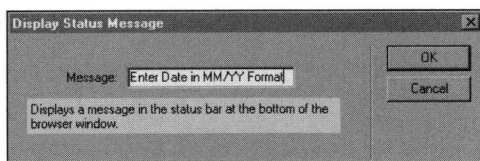

Figure 17-9: Use the Display Status Message action to guide your users with instructions in the browser window's status bar.

To use the Display Status Message action, follow these steps:

1. Select an event to trigger the action, and then choose Display Status Message from the Add Action pop-up.

2. Enter your text in the Message text box.

Here's the browser compatibility chart for the Display Status Message behavior:

Display Status Message	*Netscape 2.x*	*Netscape 3.x*	*Internet Explorer 3.0*	*Internet Explorer 3.01*
Macintosh	Fails without error	OK	Fails without error	OK
Windows	Fails without error	OK	OK	OK

Drag Layer

New to Dreamweaver in Version 1.2, the Drag Layer action provides some spectacular effects with little effort. Drag Layer enables users to move layers — and all that they contain — around the screen with the drag-and-drop technique. With the Drag Layer action, you can easily set up the following capabilities for the user:

✦ Allow layers to be dragged anywhere on the screen.

✦ Restrict the dragging to a particular direction or combination of directions — a horizontal sliding layer can be restricted to left and right movement, for instance.

✦ Limit the drag handle to a portion of the layer such as the upper bar, or allow the whole layer to be used.

✦ Provide an alternative clipping method by allowing only a portion of the layer to be dragged.

✦ Allow changing of the layers' stacking order while dragging or on mouse release.

✦ Set a snap-to target area on your Web page for layers that the user releases within a defined radius.

✦ Program a JavaScript command to be executed when the snap-to target is hit, or every time the layer is released.

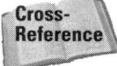

Cross-Reference
Layers are one of the more powerful features of Dreamweaver. To get the most out of the layer-oriented behaviors, familiarize yourself with layers by examining Chapter 23, "Working with Layers."

Layers must be inserted in your Web page before the Drag Layer action becomes available for selection from the Add Action pop-up. Because Drag Layer initializes the system to make the dragging possible, it should be attached to the `<body>` tag. This action's parameter form (see Figure 17-10) includes a Get Current Position button that puts the left and top coordinates into the appropriate boxes for the Get Target parameters. If you plan on using targeting, place your layer at the target location before attaching the behavior.

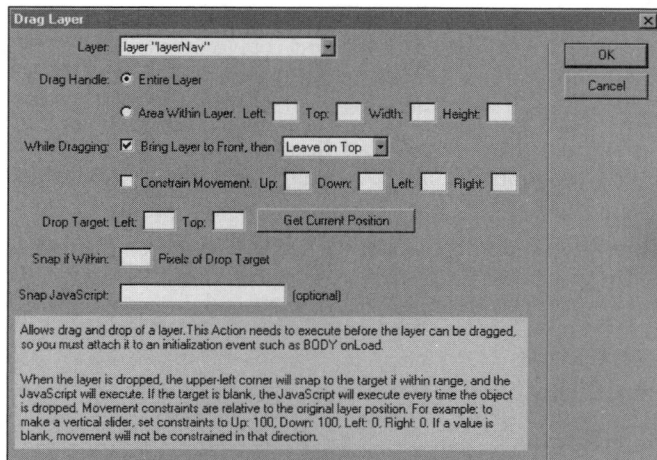

Figure 17-10: With the Drag Layer action, you can set up your layers to be repositioned by the user.

To use the Drag Layer action, follow these steps:

1. Select an event (usually onLoad) to trigger the action, and then choose Drag Layer from the Add Action pop-up.

2. In the Layer drop-down list of the parameter form, select the layer you want to make draggable.

3. If you want to limit the area to be used as a drag handle, select the radio button for Drag Handle: Area Within Layer. In the appropriate text boxes, enter the Left and Top coordinates of the drag handle, as well as the Width and Height dimensions.

Note: If you want to allow the whole layer to act as a drag handle, make sure the Drag Handle: Entire Layer radio button is selected.

4. Positioning of the dragged layer is controlled with the While Dragging options.

- To keep the layer in its current depth and not bring it to the front when it is dragged, deselect the check box for While Dragging: Bring Layer to the Front.

- To change the stacking order of the layer when it is released, select either Leave on Top or Restore z-order from the drop-down list.

- To limit the movement of the layer, select the Constrain Movement check box. Then enter the direction(s) to which you want to limit the movement by selecting the appropriate checkbox(es): Up, Down, Left, and/or Right.

5. To establish a location for a target for the dragged layer, enter coordinates in the Drop Target: Left and Top text boxes. Select the Get Current Position button to fill these text boxes with the layer's present location.

6. To set a snap-to area around the target coordinates where the layer falls, if released, in the target location, enter a pixel value in the Snap if Within text box.

7. To execute a JavaScript command when the layer is dropped on the target, enter the code in the Snap JavaScript text box. If you want the JavaScript to execute every time the layer is dropped, leave the Drop Target: Left and Top text boxes empty.

Here's the browser compatibility chart for the Drag Layer behavior:

Drag Layer	*Netscape 2.x*	*Netscape 3.x*	*Internet Explorer 3.0*	*Internet Explorer 3.01*
Macintosh	Fails without error	Fails without error	Fails without error	Fails without error
Windows	Fails without error	Fails without error	Fails without error	Fails without error

Go to URL

Dreamweaver brings the same power of links — with a lot more flexibility — to any event with the Go to URL action. One of the trickier tasks in using frames on a Web page is updating two or more frames simultaneously with a single button click. The Go to URL action handily streamlines this process for the Web designer. Go to URL can also be used as a preload router that sends the user to another Web page once the onLoad event has finished.

The parameter form for Go to URL (Figure 17-11) displays any existing anchors or frames in the current page or frameset. To load multiple URLs at the same time, open the drop-down list and select the first frame that you want to alter; then enter the desired page or location in the URL text box. Select the second frame from the list and enter the next URL (or Browse to find it). If you select a frame to which you have previously assigned a URL, that address appears in the URL text box.

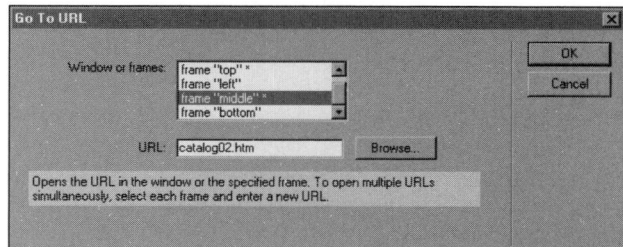

Figure 17-11: Update two or more frames at the same time with the Go to URL action.

Here's the browser compatibility chart for the Go to URL behavior:

Go to URL	Netscape 2.x	Netscape 3.x	Internet Explorer 3.0	Internet Explorer 3.01
Macintosh	Works in a frame. In main window, fails without error if applied to a link.	OK	Fails without error.	OK
Windows	OK	OK	OK	OK

Open Browser Window

Want to display your latest design in a borderless, nonresizeable browser window that's exactly the size of your image? With the Open Browser Window action, you can open a new browser window and specify its exact size and attributes. You can even set it up to receive JavaScript events.

You can also open a new browser window with a regular link by specifying a `target= _blank`, but you can't control any of the window's attributes with that method. You do get this control with the parameter form of the Open Browser Window Action (Figure 17-12); here you can set Width and Height, Navigation Toolbar, Location Toolbar, Status Bar, Menu Bar, Scrollbars, and Resize Handles.

If you don't select any of the attributes, the browser uses its default options. Keep in mind, however, that if you check even one of the Attributes check boxes, then none of the other Attributes is used unless you specifically check it. In this case, your new browser window contains only the Attributes you've checked, plus basic window elements like a title bar and a close button.

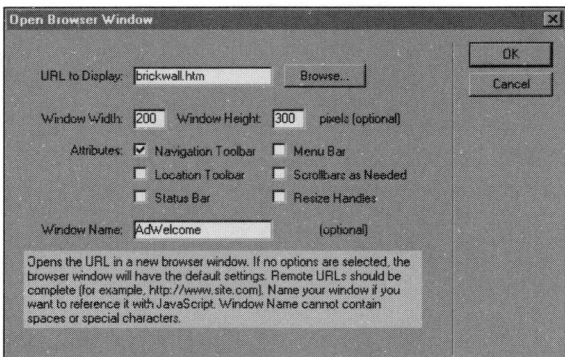

Figure 17-12: Use the Open Browser Window action to program in a pop-up advertisement or remote control.

To use the Drag Layer action, follow these steps:

  1. Select an event to trigger the action, and then choose `Open Browser Window` from the Add Action pop-up.

  2. In the URL to Display text box, enter the address of the Web page you want to display in the new window. (You can also select the Browse button to locate the file.)

  3. To specify the window's size and shape, enter the Width and Height values in the appropriate text boxes.

 **Caution**

You must enter both a Width and Height measurement, or the new browser window opens to its default size.

4. Check the appropriate Attributes check boxes to enable the parameters you want.

   Note: If you select any attribute, you must select every other one that you want included. Otherwise, the new window uses its default attributes.

5. If you plan on using JavaScript to address or control the window, type a unique name in the Window Name text box. This name cannot contain spaces or special characters. Dreamweaver alerts you if the name you've entered is unacceptable.

Here's the browser compatibility chart for the Open Browser Window behavior:

Open Browser Window	*Netscape 2.x*	*Netscape 3.x*	*Internet Explorer 3.0*	*Internet Explorer 3.01*
Macintosh	OK	OK	Fails without error	OK
Windows	OK	OK	OK	OK

Popup Message

You can send a quick message to your users with the Popup Message Action. When triggered, this action opens a JavaScript Application Alert with your message. You enter your message in the Message text box on the action's parameter form (Figure 17-13).

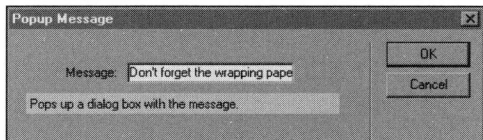

Figure 17-13: Send a message to your users with the Popup Message action.

To use the Popup Message action, follow these steps:

1. Select an event to trigger the action, and then choose Pop-up Message from the Add Action pop-up.

2. Enter your text in the Message text box.

Here's the browser compatibility chart for the Popup Message behavior:

Popup Message	Netscape 2.x	Netscape 3.x	Internet Explorer 3.0	Internet Explorer 3.01
Macintosh	Fails without error	OK	Fails without error	OK
Windows	OK	OK	OK	OK

Preload Images

Designs commonly require a particular image or images to be displayed immediately when called by an action or a timeline. Because of the nature of HTML, all graphics are separate files that normally are downloaded when needed. To get the snappy response required for certain designs (such as a rollover)

graphics need to be *preloaded* or *cached* so that they will be available. The Preload Images action performs this important service. You designate the images you want to cache for later use through the Preload Images parameter form (Figure 17-14).

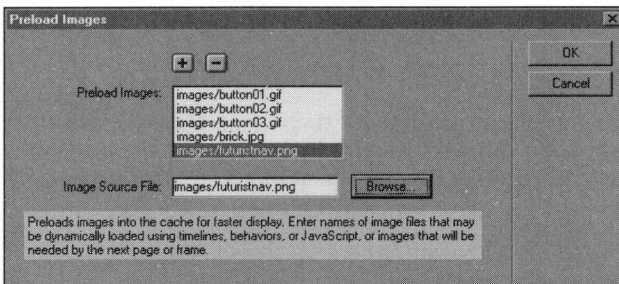

Figure 17-14: Media-rich Web sites respond much faster when the images have been cached with the Preload Images action.

To use the Preload Images action, follow these steps:

1. Select an event to trigger the action, and then choose Preload Images from the Add Action pop-up.

2. In the action's parameter form, enter the path to the image file in the Image Source File text box, or select the Browse button to locate the file.

3. To add another file, click the + (Add) button and repeat step 2.

Caution After you've specified your first file to be preloaded, be sure to press the + (Add) button for each successive file you want to add to the list. Otherwise, the highlighted file is replaced by the next entry.

4. To remove a file from the Preload Images list, select it and click the – (Delete) button.

Here's the browser compatibility chart for the Preload Images behavior:

Preload Images	Netscape 2.x	Netscape 3.x	Internet Explorer 3.0	Internet Explorer 3.01
Macintosh	Fails without error	OK	Fails without error	OK
Windows	Fails without error	OK	Fails without error	Fails without error

Show-Hide Layer

One of the key features of Dynamic HTML layers is the ability to appear and disappear on command. The Show-Hide Layer action gives you easy control over the visibility attribute for all layers in the current Web page. In addition to explicitly showing or hiding layers, this action can also restore layers to the default visibility setting.

Typically, the Show-Hide Layer Action reveals one layer while concealing another; however, you are not restricted to hiding or showing just one layer at a time. The action's parameter form (Figure 17-15) shows you a list of all the layers in the current Web page, from which you can choose as many as you want to show or hide.

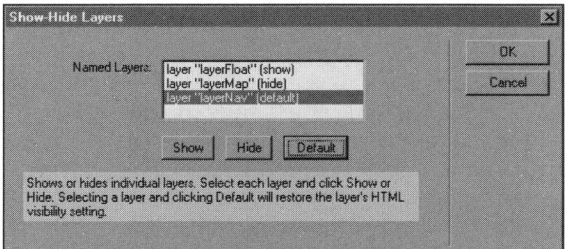

Figure 17-15: The Show-Hide Layer action can make any number of hidden layers visible, hide any number of visible layers, or both.

To use the Show-Hide Layer action, follow these steps:

1. Select an event to trigger the action, and then choose `Show-Hide Layer` from the Add Action pop-up.

   The parameter form shows a list of the available layers in the open Web page.

2. To reveal a hidden layer, select the layer from the Named Layers list and click the Show button.

3. To hide a visible layer, select its name from the list and click the Hide button.

4. To restore a layer's default visibility value, select the layer in the list and click the Default button.

Here's the browser compatibility chart for the Show-Hide Layer behavior:

Show-Hide Layer	Netscape 2.x	Netscape 3.x	Internet Explorer 3.0	Internet Explorer 3.01
Macintosh	Fails without error	Fails without error	Fails without error	Fails without error
Windows	Fails without error	Fails without error	Fails without error	Fails without error

Swap Image and Swap Image Restore

Button rollovers are one of the most commonly used techniques in Web design today. In a typical button rollover, a user's pointer moves over one image and the graphic appears to change in some way, seeming to glow or change color. Actually, the onMouseOver event triggers the almost instantaneous swapping of one image for another. Dreamweaver automates this difficult coding task with the Swap Image action and its companion, the Swap Image Restore action.

When the parameters form for the Swap Image Action opens, it automatically loads all the images it finds in the current Web page (see Figure 17-16). You select the image you want to change — which could be the same image to which you are attaching the behavior — and enter the address for the file you want to replace the rolled-over image. You can swap more than one image with each Swap Image Action. For example, if you want an entire submenu to change when a user rolls over a particular choice, you can use a single Swap Image Action to switch all of the submenu button images.

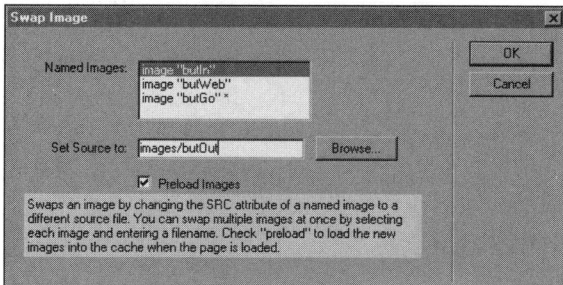

Figure 17-16: The Swap Image action is used primarily for handling button rollovers.

Note that the Swap Image Action only changes one image to another; it does not change the image back to the original. For that task, you need to attach the Swap Image Restore Action to another event. The Swap Image Restore Action can be used only after a Swap Image Action. No parameter form exists for the Swap Image Restore action—just a dialog box confirming your selection.

Tip If the swapped-in image has different dimensions than the image it replaces, the swapped-in image is resized to the height and width of the first image.

To use the Swap Image action, follow these steps:

1. Select an event to trigger the action, and then choose `Swap Image Action` from the Add Action pop-up.

2. In the parameter form, choose an available image from the Named Images list of graphics on the current page.

3. In the Set Source To text box, enter the path to the image that you want to swap in. (You can also select the Browse button to locate the file.)

4. To preload all images involved in the Swap Image Action when the page loads, make sure the Preload Images option is checked. Click OK.

5. Next you need to set up the action to bring back the original image after the rollover. Select an event (such as onMouseOut) and choose the Swap Image Restore action from the Add Action pop-up. Click OK from the dialog box.

Here's the browser compatibility chart for Swap Image and Swap Image Restore behaviors:

Swap Image & Swap Image Restore	Netscape 2.x	Netscape 3.x	Internet Explorer 3.0	Internet Explorer 3.01
Macintosh	Fails without error	OK	Fails without error	OK
Windows	Fails without error	OK	Fais without error	Fails without error

Timelines: Play Timeline, Stop Timeline, and Go to Timeline Frame

Any Dynamic HTML animation in Dreamweaver happens with timelines, but a timeline can't do anything without the actions written to control it. The three actions in the timeline set — Play Timeline, Stop Timeline and Go to Timeline Frame — are all you need to set your Web page in motion.

Before the Timeline actions become available, there must be at least one timeline on the current page. All three of these related actions are located in the Timeline pop-up. Generally, when you are establishing controls for playing a timeline, you first attach the Go to Timeline Frame action to an event and then attach the Play Timeline Action to the same event. By setting a specific frame before you allow the timeline to start, you ensure that the timeline always begins at the same point.

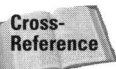

Cross-Reference   For more detailed information on using timelines, see Chapter 24, "Working with Timelines."

The Play Timeline and Stop Timeline actions have only one element on their parameter forms: a drop-down list box offering all timelines in the current page.

The Go to Timeline Frame action's parameter form (Figure 17-17), aside from enabling you to pick a timeline and enter a specific go-to frame, also gives you the option to loop the timeline a set number of times.

Tip   If you want the timeline to loop an infinite number of times, leave the Loop text box empty, and turn on the Loop option in the Timeline Inspector.

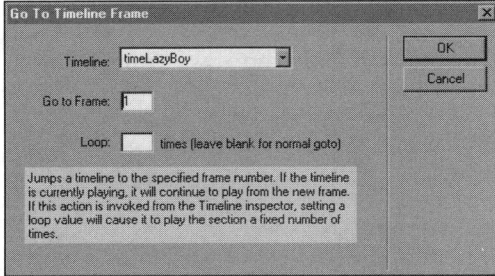

Figure 17-17: Control your timelines through the three Timeline actions. The Go to Timeline Frame parameter form lets you choose a go-to frame and designate the number of loops for the timeline.

To use the Go to Frame action, follow these steps:

1. Select an event to trigger the action, and then choose Timeline ⇨ Go to Frame from the Add Action pop-up.

2. In the parameter form's Timeline list, choose the timeline for which you want to set the start frame.

3. Enter the frame number in the Go to Frame text box.

4. If you want the timeline to loop a set number of times, enter a value in the Loop text box.

To use the Play Timeline action, follow these steps:

1. Select an event to trigger the action, and then choose Timeline ⇨ Play Timeline from the Add Action pop-up.

2. In the parameter form's Timeline list, choose the timeline that you want to play .

To use the Stop Timeline action, follow these steps:

1. Select an event to trigger the action, and then choose Timeline ⇨ Stop Timeline from the Add Action pop-up.

2. In the parameter form's Timeline list, choose the timeline that you want to stop.

Here's the browser compatibility chart for the Timeline behavior:

Timeline	*Netscape 2.x*	*Netscape 3.x*	*Internet Explorer 3.0*	*Internet Explorer 3.01*
Macintosh	Error	Image source animation and invoking behaviors works, but layer animation fails without error.	Fails without error	Fails without error
Windows	Error	Image source animation and invoking behaviors works, but layer animation fails without error.	Fails without error	Fails without error

Validate Form

When you set up a form for user input, each field is established with a purpose: the name field, the e-mail address field, the zip code field — each has its own requirements for input. Usually, unless the CGI program is specifically written to check the user's input, forms take input of any type. Even if the CGI program can handle it, this server-side method ties up server time, and is relatively slow. The Validate Form action checks any text field's input and return the form to the user if any of the entries are unacceptable. You can also use this action to designate any text field as a required field. For the Validate Form action to return the form to the user if unacceptable input is encountered, the action must be linked to the form's Submit button.

When opened, the Validate Form action's parameter form (Figure 17-18) reads all the text fields in all the forms in the current Web page. Each text field is displayed in the Named Fields list. An unnamed form within that list is represented as "form *n*," where *n* represents the number of the form on the page. JavaScript begins counting forms at zero; if there is only one form on the page, it is listed as "form 0."

The Validate Form parameters let you designate any text field as required, and you can evaluate its contents. You can require the input of a text field to be a number, an e-mail address (for instance, jdoe@anywhere.com), or a number within a range. The number range you specify can include positive whole numbers, negative numbers, or decimals.

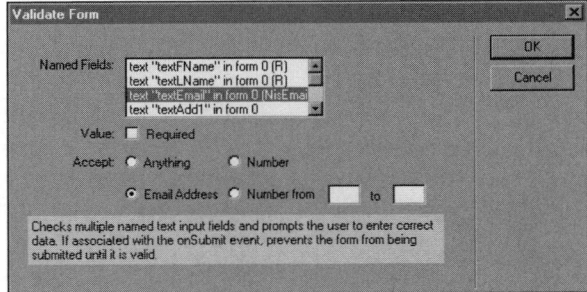

Figure 17-18: The Validate Form action can check your form's entries without CGI programming.

To use the Validate Form action, follow these steps:

1. Select the Submit button in your form.

2. Select an event to trigger the action, and then choose Validate Form from the Add Action pop-up.

3. Select a text field from the Named Fields list.

4. To make the field required, select the Value: Required check box.

5. To set the kind of input expected, choose from one of the following Accept options:

   • Anything: accepts any input.

   • Number: allows any sort of numeric input. You cannot mix text and numbers, however, as in a telephone number like (212) 555-1212.

   • Email Address: looks for an e-mail address with the @ sign.

   • Number Range: lets you enter two numbers, one in each text box, to define the number range.

Here's the browser compatibility chart for the Timeline behavior:

Validate Form	Netscape 2.x	Netscape 3.x	Internet Explorer 3.0	Internet Explorer 3.01
Macintosh	Fails without error	OK	Fails without error	OK
Windows	Fails without error	OK	Fails without error	Fails without error

Managing and modifying your behaviors

The standard behaviors that come with Dreamweaver are indeed impressive — but they're really just the beginning. Because existing behaviors can be modified and new ones created from scratch, you can continue to add behaviors as you need them.

The process of adding a behavior is simplicity itself. Just copy the HTML file to the Configuration\Behaviors\Actions folder and restart Dreamweaver.

Tip

If you find that your Add Action pop-up list is starting to get a little awkward with lots of files in a row, you can create subfolders to organize the actions better. When you create a folder within the Actions folder, that subfolder appears on the Add Action pop-up as a submenu, as you saw when you worked with the Timelines actions in a preceding section. Figure 17-19 shows a sample arrangement. This example has a subfolder called New to centralize the nonstandard but useful actions. You can even create sub-subfolders to maintain several levels of nested menus.

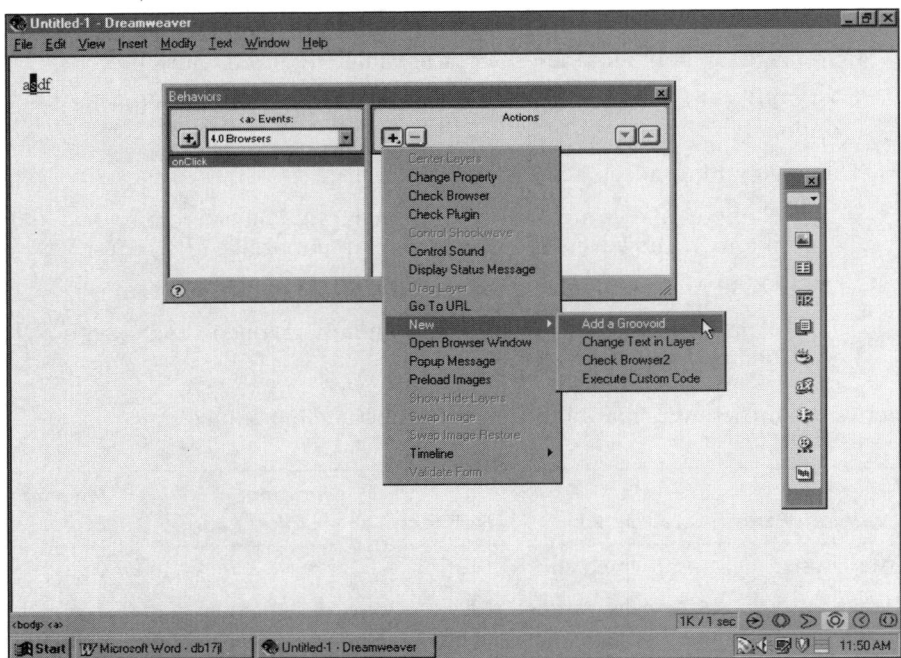

Figure 17-19: To create a new submenu in the Action pop-up, just create a folder in the Actions directory.

Altering the parameters of a behavior

You can alter any of the attributes for your inserted behaviors at any time. To modify a behavior you have already attached, follow these steps:

1. Open the Behavior Inspector (go to Window ➪ Behaviors, or click the Show Behaviors button in either Launcher, or press F8).

2. Select the tag to which your behavior is attached.

3. Select the event, if there is more than one, in the Events pane of the Behavior Inspector.

4. In the Action page, double-click the action that you want to alter. The parameter form opens.

5. Make any modifications to the existing settings for the action, and click OK when you are finished.

Sequencing your behaviors

When you have more than one action attached to a particular event, the order of the actions is often important. For example, you should generally implement the Go to Frame Action ahead of the Play Timeline Action. To specify the sequence in which Dreamweaver triggers the actions, reposition as necessary in the Actions page by highlighting one and using the up- and down-arrow buttons to reposition it in the list.

Deleting behaviors

To remove a behavior from your list of actions attached to a particular event, simply highlight the behavior and select the – (Delete) button. If the removed behavior is the last action added, the event is also removed from the list; this process occurs after you select any other tag or click anywhere in the Document Window.

Note

As noted in Chapter 16, "Creating and Using Objects," several Web sites — maintained by Dreamweaver as well as third parties — feature new Dreamweaver objects and behaviors available for download or purchase. In addition to those sites listed in Chapter 16, one commercial developer (Alapi) has readied new behaviors for the Dreamweaver market. The Alapi behaviors are of professional quality and they introduce some exciting new actions. As of this writing, the Alapi Behaviors cost $50 for a CD-ROM with ten new actions. You can examine the Alapi Behaviors at the company's Web site (www.alapi.com).

Creating a Behavior from Scratch

Dreamweaver behaviors are an open standard, and anyone with the requisite JavaScript and HTML skills can write one. To talk about "writing" a behavior, though, is a bit of a misnomer. You never actually touch the event portion of the behavior — you only work on the Action file. To help the creation process, Macromedia has a complete Behavior Development Kit (BDK) that documents the custom functions, JavaScript extensions, and Document Object Model (DOM) that Dreamweaver recognizes. The remainder of this chapter takes a step-by-step approach to building a behavior and then explores the BDK, including new features in Version 1.2 not officially documented as of this writing.

Writing a behavior is not so complex when you take it one step at a time. In all, there are six basic stages to creating a behavior from scratch:

1. **Define your behavior.** A behavior is an automatic method of incorporating a particular JavaScript function. The best way to begin building your behavior is to write that function. The function that you write is actually incorporated into the Dreamweaver Action.

2. **Create the action file**. One of the key functions in Dreamweaver behaviors is, aptly enough, the behaviorFunction(). The behaviorFunction() inserts your function into the <head> section of the Web page. Recent advances in Dreamweaver 1.2 make this task into a trivial effort.

3. **Build the user interface.** As you look through the standard Dreamweaver Behaviors, you see a dialog box that acts as the user interface in all but a few instances. The user interface that you create is based on HTML forms and is generally referred to as a parameter form.

4. **Apply the behavior.** Both an event and an action are required to make up a behavior. Next, write the applyBehavior() function, which ties your function to a specific tag and event. The applyBehavior() function also passes the necessary arguments to the function in the <head> section.

5. **Inspect the behavior.** Building a Web page is often a trial-and-error process. You try one approach and if it doesn't work, you try another. To modify your settings for a particular behavior, just double-click the action name to reopen the parameter form and change your settings. The inspectBehavior() function handles the restoration of your previous values to the parameters form.

6. **Test your behavior.** The final step, as in any software development, is testing. You need to try out your new behavior in a variety of Web browsers and debug it, if necessary. (It's always necessary.)

To demonstrate the process of creating a behavior, the next few sections take you through a real-world example: the construction of an Add a Groovoid action. A Groovoid is one of 50 sound effects incorporated into the Beatnik plug-in. Groovoids can be used for one-shot user interface feedback or for seamlessly repeating background music.

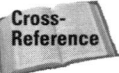 For more on Beatnik and Groovoids, see the "Making Music with Beatnik" section of Chapter 19, "Using Audio on Your Web Page."

Defining the behavior

Behaviors are born of either need, desire, or a combination of both. After repeating a single operation a thousand times, you probably find yourself thinking, "There's got to be a better way." The better way usually automates the process in any possible way. In the case of inserting JavaScript functions into Web pages, the better way is to create a behavior.

Starting from this vantage point already accomplishes the first phase of behavior creation: defining the behavior. For example, suppose you've been using the Groovoid feature of the Beatnik plug-in to attach particular user-interface sounds to particular events, mostly onMouseOver and onClick. Rather than continue to enter the function by hand repeatedly, and having to look up the exact titles of the Groovoid samples, it would be easier to incorporate them into an action.

Here's a complete listing of my Groovoid-adding function as I routinely use it:

```
<html>
<head>
  <title>Groovoid Sample</title>
  <meta http-equiv= Content-Type  content= text/html;
charset=iso-8859-1 >
<script SRC= images/music-object.js ></script>
<script language=JavaScript>
function doGroovoid(looping,groovoidName) {
      myMusicObject.playGroovoid(looping,groovoidName);
}
myMusicObject = new musicObject ( myMusicObject )
myMusicObject.stubEmbed( images/stub.rmf )
</script>
</head>
<body bgcolor= #FFFFFF >
<a href= #  onClick= doGroovoid(false, Fanfare-Arrival ) ><img
src= images/button01.gif  width= 63  height= 37
name= playButton  border= 0 ></a>
</body>
</html>
```

Notice the lines in boldface. These are the key parts in the file: the function in the <script> section (the action) and the run-time function call attached to the button image (the event). After testing in several browsers, I know my function is sound (no pun intended, but welcome) and can be made into a behavior.

When you define your behavior in this manner it tells you the arguments you need to generalize. In my Groovoid example, there are two: `looping` and `groovoidName`. Ideally, your action should be flexible enough to allow for any argument to be user defined. So now I know that in my user interface, I'll have at most two attributes to take in through my parameter form and pass to my function.

Once you've created and tested your function in Dreamweaver, save it. I've found it helpful to go back to the original file as I build my action and verify that I have everything in working order.

Creating the Action file

In the next phase of behavior creation, you build the skeleton of the Action file and begin filling in the necessary JavaScript functions. Each action file must have, at a minimum, these four functions:

✦ `canAcceptBehavior()`: Determines if the behavior should be available. If it is not to be available, the entry in the Add Action pop-up is not selectable.

✦ behaviorFunction(): Inserts the general function in the <head> section of the Web page.

✦ applyBehavior(): Attaches the run-time function to the selected tag and inserts the chosen event.

✦ inspectBehavior(): Allows the user to reopen the parameter form and make modifications to the original settings.

The easiest way to start an Action file is to adapt one that is already built. You can open and modify any of the existing Dreamweaver standard actions, as long as you remember to use the File ➪ Save As feature and give your file a new name.

Here are the steps to follow in this phase, with descriptions of what I'll do in creating the Add a Groovoid action:

1. Open a simple Action file to serve as a template. I choose the Display Status Message action.

2. Choose File ➪ Save As to save your file under a new name.

3. Open the HTML Inspector or your favorite text editor to work on the code for your new action.

4. Replace every instance of the old primary function name and arguments with the name of your function — normally this occurs in two functions: behaviorFunction() and applyBehavior(). In my case, the original function was MM_displayStatusMsg(msgStr) and the new one was doGroovoid(looping, groovoidName).

   Whenever you first open the Behavior Inspector, Dreamweaver checks to see if there are multiple function names. If you don't replace the run-time functions, Dreamweaver recognizes the earlier file, but not the later one.

5. Replace the original function with your new function copied from your function test file. It's easiest to just copy and paste from one document to the other.

Note

You'll notice that nothing was done with the canAcceptBehavior() function. This function determines whether or not the action is available based on the elements in the current page. For instance, the Swap Image and Swap Image Restore actions are not available unless the Web page contains one or more images. In many cases, including our Groovoid example, you won't have to modify this function at all. Should you have to, look at the standard files that use this criteria, including Drag Layer, Control Shockwave, and Swap Image.

Enhancements to behaviorFunction() in Dreamweaver 1.2

Prior to Dreamweaver 1.2, the steps to alter the `behaviorFunction()` were quite elaborate. Because the function returned a definition of the run-time function formatted as a single string, the entire run-time function had to be in quotes. JavaScript syntax enables you to send newline characters with a `\n`, and plus signs to connect the individual lines. With Dreamweaver 1.0, the `behaviorFunction()` for my Add a Groovoid Action read as follows:

```
function behaviorFunction() {
return   +
 function doGroovoid(looping,groovoidName) {\n+
 myMusicObject.playGroovoid(looping,groovoidName);
}
```

An advance in the Behavior Application Programming Interface (API) for Dreamweaver 1.2 allows the `behaviorFunction()` to return function names instead of definitions. Now, my more efficient behaviorFunction()reads

```
function behaviorFunction(){
   return  doGroovoid ;
}
```

Not much change is evident in this example, but many other functions consist of dozens of lines of code, and converting them to a string is tedious at best. Moreover, `behaviorFunction()` is no longer limited to returning just one function but can now return multiple functions. For more on this capability, see the section later in this chapter, "Behavior Changes in Dreamweaver 1.2."

Building the user interface

The user interface of a behavior is a parameter form, constructed with HTML form elements. The key indicator of what you'll need to include in your action's parameter form is the number and type of arguments required by your completed function.

In the Groovoid example, the function requires two arguments, `looping` and `groovoidName`. The interface needs to enable the user to choose the looping parameter (whether or not to loop the sample and, if so, for how many times) and the Groovoid name. One of the time-consuming elements of attaching a Groovoid to an event is entering the exact name—there are 50 Groovoids and using the exact name is essential. To be useful, the action should make it easy to find and select a Groovoid name, automatically placing it in the function.

All user interface constructions are contained in the `<body>` section of your action file. You can use Dreamweaver's visual editor to create and modify your form quickly. Many Web designers use tables to line up the various form elements; if you use this approach, be sure to place the table inside the form and not the other way around. Although you could insert a form in the cell of a table, you are limited to just entering form elements in that cell — and you return to no structure at all.

Follow these steps to create your user interface:

1. Open your Action file in Dreamweaver.

2. Choose Insert ⇨ Form or select the Insert Form button from the Forms panel of the Object palette. Name the form for easy JavaScript identification.

3. For better alignment, place a table in your form by choosing Insert ⇨ Table or selecting the Insert Table button from the Common panel of the Object palette.

4. Enter your form elements as needed. Be sure to name each one individually (with the exception of a radio button grouping) for JavaScript purposes.

Note As with Dreamweaver objects, you don't see the OK and Cancel buttons that appear when the parameter form is actually used. Dreamweaver automatically applies these buttons to the upper-right part of your interface.

The interface for the Add a Groovoid action uses a series of list boxes and radio buttons, as shown in Figure 17-20, to select the Groovoid name. Another couple of radio buttons and a check box handle the looping parameters. Because the example has two different sets of radio buttons, each set has its own unique name.

The last part of setting up the user interface writes a function that activates the interface and sets the cursor in the right text box, if applicable. To complete this task, use the initializeUI() function, generally located in the Local Functions sections of the JavaScript code. Because the object is not using any text boxes, the initializeUI() function is simple:

```
function initializeUI(){
   document.theForm.menuUI.focus();
}
```

This function puts the highlight on the first list box in the form. If you have a text box in which you want to place the cursor, add a line similar to the following:

```
document.theForm.textName.select();
```

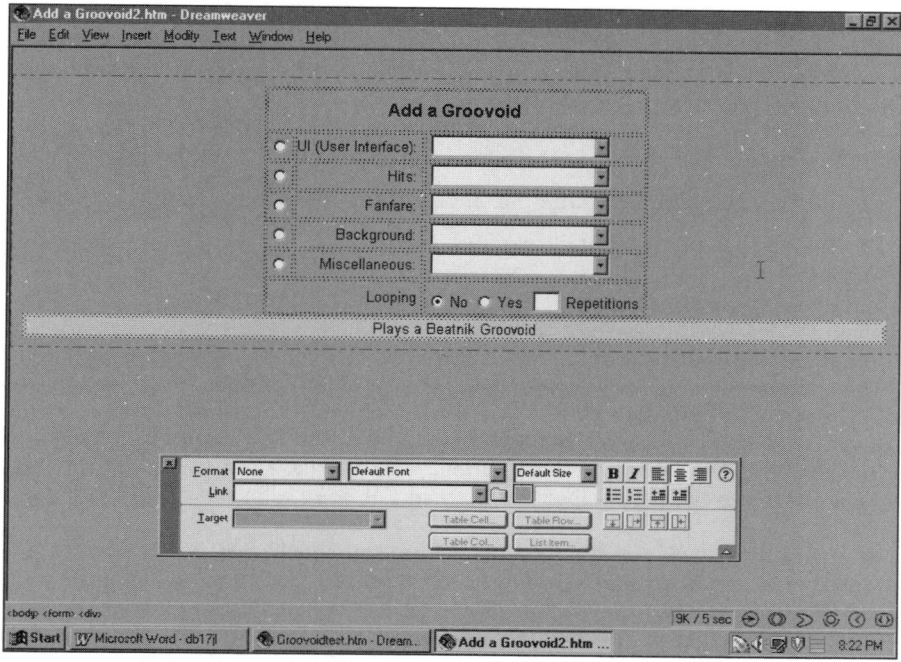

Figure 17-20: The parameter form uses a form to gather the user input and transmit it to the proper functions.

Finally, you need to activate the initializeUI() to `<body>` with an onLoad event. You can proceed in one of two ways. First, you can locate the `<body>` tag and amend it so that it reads as follows:

```
<body onLoad= initializeUI() >
```

The second method uses a handy custom action called Execute Custom Code, designed by Andrew Woolridge and included on this book's CD-ROM. To use this method, first select the `<body>` from the Tag Selector and then choose the onLoad event from the Add Events pop-up in the Behavior Inspector. In the Add Actions pop-up, choose Execute Custom Code and enter initializeUI() in the text area. Select OK when you are done. In essence, the onLoad event calls the Execute Custom Code function, which in turn calls the initializeUI() function.

Applying the behavior

Now you can write the code that links your function to a specific tag and event. You can think of this process in three steps:

1. Check to make sure that the user entered information in the right places.

2. Put the user's input on the parameter form into a more usable format.

3. Return the run-time function call.

All of these steps are contained in the applyBehavior() function.

You gather information from an action's parameter form in the same way that you gather data from a custom object. Using the same techniques discussed in Chapter 17, "Creating and Using Objects," you receive the input information and usually convert it to local variables that are easier to handle. The number of variables is equal to the number of arguments expected; in the case of the Add a Groovoid action, there are two variables: `looping` and `groovoidName`.

Tip   If any of the input from the parameter form potentially may be sent out to a Web server — say, a URL or a file — you need to encode the text string so that it can be read by UNIX servers. Use the built-in JavaScript function `escape` to convert space and special characters in the URL to UNIX-friendly strings. The companion function, unescape(), reverses the process and is used in the inspectBehavior() function.

Follow these steps to build your applyBehavior() function:

1. Make the necessary variables.

   ```
   var looping
   var nameGroovoid
   ```

2. Get the information from the form. This process depends on the type of input field used. For the radio buttons, you can use a simple if-else test:

   ```
   if (document.theForm.radioLoop[0].checked ==  1 )
       looping =  false ;
   else
       looping =  true ;
   ```

3. Return the function run-time call, incorporating the variables. The applyBehavior() function must return a complete string. Enclose the argument variables with single quotes. If you use any internal quotes, they should be preceded by or escaped with a backslash.

4. Run an error check to see if values are entered where necessary; if not, inform the user.

```
if (nameGroovoid) {
return  doGroovoid(\   + looping +  \ ,\   + groovoidName
+  \ ) ;
} else {
return  Please pick a Groovoid.
```

Only one more step remains before you're ready to begin testing your action.

Inspecting the behavior

Now you can add the inspectBehavior() function to your file. Basically, this function restores the information already entered through the parameter form and enables the user to change the parameters. This function can be considered the reverse of the applyBehavior() function: rather than reading the form and writing the information to the Web page, inspectBehavior() reads the information and writes the information back to the form.

Interpreting the string of information from a form is referred to as *parsing the string*. The Add a Groovoid function passes a message string similar to the following:

```
doGroovoid( false , Fanfare-Arrival )
```

Dreamweaver uses several built-in functions to aid the parsing process, but the key function is getTokens(). The getTokens() function accepts a string to parse and the separators for which to look. It returns an array of strings. You can call getTokens(), passing the function call string as the first argument. The second argument should contain parentheses, a quote, and a comma as separators, as follows:

```
var argArray = getTokens(msgStr, () , );
```

Once the string arguments are in an array, they can be extracted and placed back in the parameter form. Follow these steps to write the inspectBehavior() function:

1. Declare a variable and set it equal to the getTokens() function.

2. Assign the array elements to the same variables you used in the applyBehavior() function.

```
If (argArray.length == 3) {
    var looping = argArray[1];
    var groovoidName = argArray[2];
```

3. Now put the variables back in the form.

```
document.theForm.radioLoop = looping
document.theForm.radioCat = groovoidName
```

4. The complete inspectBehavior() function looks like the following:

```
function inspectBehavior(msgStr) {
    var argArray = getTokens(msgStr, () , );
    If (argArray.length == 3) {
    var looping = argArray[1];
        var groovoidName = argArray[2];
document.theForm.radioLoop = looping
document.theForm.radioCat = groovoidName
    }
}
```

Tip

This example is a fairly simple inspectBehavior() function. Keep in mind that the more input you allow from your user, the more complicated it is to restore the information through this function. As with many aspects of building behaviors, one of the best methods of constructing your inspectBehavior() function is by examining the code of working examples provided in the Macromedia-built behaviors, as well as those examples contributed by other developers.

Testing the behavior

Testing and debugging is the final, necessary phase of building an action. To test your behavior, follow these steps:

1. Restart Dreamweaver.

2. Insert an image or a link in a blank Web page.

3. Select the element to use as your trigger.

4. Open the Behavior Inspector.

5. Select onClick from the Add Event pop-up.

6. Select the + (Add) Action button and choose your behavior.

7. Fill out the parameters form as required. Your action's name appears in the Action pane.

8. Double-click the action to verify that your prior choices have been restored.

9. Test the behavior in various Web browsers.

Caution

When you first select an event to add, Dreamweaver examines all of the actions in the Actions folder. If a problem is found, such as two files having the same function name, you are alerted to the conflict and the list only displays the older file. You have to correct the problem with the other action and restart Dreamweaver before the file appears in the list again.

If your action is intended for distribution and not your own personal use, you should expand your testing considerably, especially on the user interface side. As the action programmer, you know what values are expected and know — often subconsciously — how to avoid the pitfalls into which a new user may easily stumble. Be especially mindful of accepting input through a text box. Unless you're just passing a message to be displayed on screen or in the browser status bar, you often have to validate the incoming text string. Just because you tell the user to enter a number in a particular range, these instructions don't guarantee correct results.

Debugging the behavior

Finding a bug is every programmer's least favorite moment — but getting rid of that bug can be the best. Basic JavaScript debugging techniques, including using the alert() function to keep track of variables, are without a doubt your first course of action. With its built-in JavaScript interpreter, Dreamweaver can give you error messages in the same manner as a browser.

If the errors are severe enough to stop Dreamweaver from recognizing your Action file as such, the file is not listed in the Action pop-up until the problem is resolved. Generally this situation means that you must restart Dreamweaver after each modification until the problem is resolved. Once you are debugging and modifying the minor errors, the following technique enables you to make changes without restarting Dreamweaver:

1. First, open your Action file and make the necessary changes. Save the file.

2. Assign your action to an event, and enter the needed parameters. Click OK to close the parameter form.

3. Remove the action from the Action pane by selecting the Delete button.

4. Reassign your action, and Dreamweaver reloads the new version.

Tip

Remember that JavaScript is extremely case-sensitive. If you get a message that a function cannot be found, make sure the names match exactly.

The Behavior Development Kit

To help developers create behaviors, Macromedia has released the Behavior Development Kit (BDK). The BDK is the background documentation of the various functions available for building behaviors. As such, it provides a useful framework for discussing the underpinnings of Dreamweaver Behaviors and how the extensions and built-in functions can be used.

The BDK contains three main sections, thus reflecting the three intertwined aspects of behavior development: the Document Object Model, the Dreamweaver JavaScript Extensions, and the Behavior API. The more you understand about each of the various components and their included functions, the more flexibility you have in building your behaviors.

 **Caution** The material in this section is intended for programmers familiar with JavaScript and, as such, it's fairly advanced.

Document Object Model

JavaScript is an interpreted programming language that addresses elements in the browser and on the Web page in a hierarchical fashion. To access the properties of any object on the page, JavaScript employs a Document Object Model (DOM). The DOM breaks down the page into successively smaller parts, until each element and its specific properties are identified.

When referencing a specific tag, the DOM syntax goes from the most general to the most specific. For example, let's say you want to find out what a user entered into a specific text box, a property called *value*. You need to start from the document itself and work your way down, as follows:

```
var theText = document.theForm.textboxName.value
```

The DOM dictates what properties are accessible and in what form. The Document Object Model built into Dreamweaver's JavaScript interpreter is a subset of that available for Netscape Navigator 3.0. Not all properties and methods are supported. You can't, for instance, directly reference the value of a button on a form. Instead, you have to assign that value to a hidden or other text field, and access that value.

The portion of the DOM relating directly to forms and form elements is discussed in Chapter 16, "Creating and Using Objects." The same rules of use and the same restrictions for implementing forms in objects apply likewise to implementing forms in behaviors. Additionally, the Dreamweaver DOM addresses other major objects as outlined in Table 17-1.

Table 17-1
Additional Elements in the Dreamweaver
Document Object Model

Object	Properties	Methods	Events
window	document (read-only) navigator (read-only)	alert() rescape() unescape()	None
document	forms (an array of form objects) (read-only); child objects by name	None	onLoad
array boolean date function rmath number object string	Same as Netscape 3	Same as Netscape 3	None

Tip   Certain objects, such as forms or radio buttons in a group, can be referred to either by name or by their array number. For example, if you have more than one form on a Web page, the first form is seen as document.forms[0]. Using arrays rather than specific names allows for a more generalized code, which can be reused in other behaviors.

Dreamweaver JavaScript extensions

To make the behavior programmer's life a little easier, Dreamweaver has several built-in extensions to the regular set of JavaScript functions. These functions, described in the following sections, can be used in the main behavior JavaScript section or in Objects.

Function	Role
getTokens()	Useful for parsing a string.
browseForURL()	Enables a user to locate a file through a dialog box.
getObjectTags()	Returns an array of specified tags in a document.
getObjectRefs()	Returns an array of specified tags in a browser-specific format.

The getTokens() function

The `getTokens()` function is often used in the `inspectBehavior()` function because it does such a good job of parsing a string. A *token* is a group of text characters that do not contain any of the specified separators. Generally, the *separators* in a function are the parentheses that surround the arguments and the commas that separate them.

The `getTokens()` function takes two arguments — the string to be parsed and the separators — and puts the results in an array. For example, note the following string:

```
doGroovoid( false , Fanfare-Arrival )
```

To extract the two arguments from this statement, use the `getTokens()` function as follows:

```
getTokens( doGroovoid( false , Fanfare-Arrival ) , (), )
```

If you set this function equal to an array called argArray, you get the following results:

```
argArray[0] = doGroovoid
argArray[1] = false
argArray[2] = Fanfare-Arrival
```

Usually the first element of the array, the function name, is ignored.

The browseForURL() function

The `browseForURL()` function enables the user to locate a file via the Select File dialog box rather than entering the entire path by hand. The function does not take any arguments; it returns the path and filename in the form of a relative URL.

The `browseForURL()` function is generally contained within another function that is called by an onClick event attached to a Browse button. For instance, the code for a Browse button may read as follows:

```
<input value= Browse... type= button  onClick= browseFile()
name= button >
```

The `browseFile()` function then calls the built-in browseForFileURL() function, which opens the Select File dialog box and, if the dialog is returned with a filename, assigns that filename to a particular value or variable. In the following example, the returned filename is assigned to a textbox value, which makes the name appear in the text box.

```
function browseFile(){
  fileName = browseForFileURL();
  if (fileName !=  ) {
    document.theForm.sndFile.value = fileName;
  }
}
```

The `browseForFileURL()` function does not return absolute URLs.

The getObjectTags() function

The `canApplyBehavior()` function often uses the `getObjectTags()` function to see if particular HTML objects exist on the current page. If `getObjectTags()` doesn't find them, the behavior cannot be applied and the item is inactive on the Add Action pop-up. Because the `getObjectTags()` function places the found tags in an array, the function can also be used to extract the unique names of those tags. This procedure is used in both the Control Shockwave and Show-Hide Layers actions.

The `getObjectTags()` function takes two arguments: either document or parent, and a list of tags for which to search. If the first argument is document, then the current page is assumed to be searched; the parent argument is used when the Web page is a member of a frameset. Each tag in the second argument is surrounded by quotes and separated by commas. For example, note the following statement:

```
getObjectTags( document , embed )
```

The preceding looks for all the `<embed>` tags in the current document and returns the entire tag in an array. The array can then be examined to see if it has the desired property—say a Flash movie file extension.

Two special cases are in use with the `getObjectTags()` function. First, if `layer` is specified, the function returns all `<layer>` and `<ilayer>` tags and all absolutely positioned `<div>`, `<span>`, and `<img>` tags. Second, if `input` is in the tag list, all `<input>` types are returned. To get a specific input type (like a radio button), you specify input/*type*, where *type* is button, text, radio, checkbox, password, textarea, select, hidden, reset, or submit.

The getObjectRefs() function

Netscape and Internet Explorer format some tags differently, especially those dealing with layers. To look for the appropriate tags coded for a particular browser, you need to use the `getObjectRefs()` function. The `getObjectRefs()` function examines the current Web page using the DOM of either Netscape 4.0 or Internet Explorer 4.0 as its guide.

The getObjectRefs() function takes three arguments:

✦ NS 4.0 or IE 4.0: Sets the browser conditions for which to look.

✦ Document or parent: The parent argument is used if the page to be examined is in a frameset.

✦ The tag list: Tags are enclosed in quotes and separated by commas. If no list is given, all the tags are put into the array.

The getObjectRefs() function is used in the Change Property action to look for the various layer tag formats.

Caution The getObjectRefs() function does not return references for unnamed objects. If an object does not contain either a name or an id attribute, Dreamweaver returns unnamed <tag>. As always, you should name any object potentially referenced by JavaScript.

Behavior API

You've seen most of the Behavior API functions applied in the preceding section, "Creating the Action file." The API is used to create a behavior. The primary functions are as follows:

Function	Role
canAcceptBehavior()	Determines whether an action is available.
WindowDimensions()	Sets the width and height of the parameter form.
applyBehavior()	Attaches the behavior function to the selected tag.
InspectBehavior()	Restores user selected values to the parameter form for reediting.
BehaviorFunction()	Writes a function into the <head> of the HTML file.
behaviorObjects()	Writes a function into the <body> of the HTML file.
getBehaviorTag()	Returns the HTML source for the selected tag for the action currently being edited.
getBehaviorEvent()	Returns the JavaScript name for the selected event currently being edited.

For discussions of the use of the canAcceptBehavior(), applyBehavior(), inspectBehavior(), and behaviorFunction() functions, see the preceding "Creating a Behavior" sections. Following are discussions of the other Behavior API functions.

The windowDimensions() function

To speed display, the `windowDimensions()` function sets specific dimensions for the parameters form that the user sees as the dialog box. If this function is not defined, the window dimensions are computed automatically. This function takes one argument, `platform`, which is used to specify whether the user system is Macintosh or Windows. The function returns a string with the width and height in pixels. For example:

```
function windowDimensions(platform){
if (platform.charAt(0) ==  m ){ // Macintosh
     return  324,233 ;
     }
     else { // Windows 95 or NT
     return  376,252 ;
}
}
```

You can see this function in most of the standard behaviors.

The behaviorObjects() function

Just as `behaviorFunction()` returns information that is included in the `<head>` section, the `behaviorObjects()` function returns information that is included in the `<body>` section of the current Web page. The `behaviorObjects()` function can only be placed at the very top of the section, just after the `<body>` tag. You can see this function in the Control Sound Action where an `<embed>` tag is written into the `<body>` section, as follows:

```
<!-- #BeginBehavior MM_controlSound1 -->
<embed name= MM_controlSound1  src= /images/Braz.mid
loop=false autostart=false mastersound hidden=true width=0
height=0></embed>
<!-- #EndBehavior MM_controlSound1 -->
```

The comments that surround the implanted `<embed>` tag are used as identifiers so that Dreamweaver can remove the tag later if necessary. The function takes one argument, uniquename, which in the preceding example is expressed as `MM_controlSound1`. The uniquename is generated by Dreamweaver and is in the form of function-number. If you place another Control Sound Action in the same document, the unique name increments to `MM_controlSound2`.

The getBehaviorTag() and getEventTag() functions

New in Dreamweaver 1.2, the `getBehaviorTag()` and `getEventTag()` functions are proprietary. They return the tag and event to which the current behavior is being attached. Currently, the `canApplyBehavior()` function is used to disable certain behaviors, but you cannot tell the user why they are inactive. With these two new functions, the programmer can give some feedback as to the problem and advise the user of steps to be taken.

A second possible use for these functions takes advantage of a new feature in Dreamweaver 1.2: layers in behaviors. Because you can now use layers in both Objects and behaviors, you can use `getBehaviorTag()` and `getEventTag()` to determine which layer the user sees in the parameter form. This approach allows a more complex and multifaceted user interface to be built.

Neither `getBehaviorTag()` nor `getEventTag()` takes an argument.

Dreamweaver Restrictions on Behaviors

Dreamweaver behaviors can handle a great number of situations and have exceptional flexibility in extending a user's capabilities and automating programming tasks. Behaviors have some restrictions, however. Save yourself a lot of wasted effort by reviewing these restrictions before you begin programming your next behavior.

Currently, Dreamweaver behaviors cannot do any of the following:

✦ Change HTML tags in the document

✦ Control where a function is inserted

✦ Read or write files

✦ Manage other behaviors

✦ Insert VBScript

Another restriction stems from the method in which Dreamweaver writes the `behaviorFunction()`. This function always encloses whatever it writes in the `<script language= javascript >...</script>` tag pair. As a result, you cannot programmatically insert `<meta>` tags or separate `<script src= file . js >...</script>` tags to call independent JavaScript files. Currently, these elements must be inserted by hand.

Behavior Changes in Dreamweaver 1.2

The Macromedia software engineers made some enhancements to the underlying behavior engine for Dreamweaver 1.2. These changes work together to make behaviors more flexible and more responsive to real-world needs — with just a little razzamatazz tossed in. In all, there are seven significant changes:

✦ URLs in a behavior can be corrected should the file be moved to a different folder.

✦ Layers can be used in the Behavior dialog box.

✦ A behavior can return multiple functions.

✦ External JavaScripts can be referenced.

✦ Name functionality has been extended.

✦ A behavior can return a behavior function rather than a definition.

✦ Two additional JavaScript functions have been added: `getBehaviorTag()` and `getBehaviorEvent()`.

Restoring a behavior's URLs after a file is moved

If you've ever had to relocate a Web site from one directory to another, you know the laborious job of making sure all your references are intact. Dreamweaver 1.2 takes some of the tedium out of this chore. When you use Save As from Dreamweaver, all of the file paths within HTML attributes, such as the image source files and links, are automatically updated. Dreamweaver now extends the same functionality to URLs contained within behaviors.

For example, say you have constructed a Web page that uses the Check Browser action to route users to various URLs, depending on the browser they are using. Should you elect to save your Web page in a different folder, for whatever reason, Dreamweaver automatically updates the referenced URLs.

For this property to work correctly, a new function must be included in the behavior. The function, `identifyBehaviorArguments()`, passes the argument structure to Dreamweaver so it can update the URLs, if necessary. The function also identifies the layer objects in the behavior that Dreamweaver must correct if the Convert Layers to Tables command is used.

The `identifyBehaviorArguments()` function accepts a string that contains the behavior function call, with arguments. The function then extracts the arguments into an array and identifies which arguments in the array are URLs, which ones are layer objects, and which ones are neither. The four identifying values that are returned are as follows:

✦ URL—when the argument is a file or file path.

✦ `NS4.0ref`—when the argument identifies a layer in Netscape syntax, such as `document.layers[\ Layer1\ ]`.

✦ `IE4.0ref`—when the argument identifies a layer in Internet Explorer syntax, `document.all[\ Layer1\ ]`.

✦ Other—when the argument is none of the above.

You can see an example of the `identifyBehaviorArguments()` function in the Check Plugin action:

```
function identifyBehaviorArguments(fnCallStr) {
  var argArray;

  argArray = extractArgs(fnCallStr);
  if (argArray.length == 5) {
    return  other,URL,URL,other ;
  }
}
```

As with the `inspectBehavior()` function, the array for the function-call string is one element longer than the number of arguments — the initial array element is the function name itself.

Behaviors can use layers

Your custom behaviors (and objects) are now capable of displaying layers in their dialog boxes. As in regular HTML pages, layers in behaviors greatly extend the potential for displaying a user interface. You can stack layers and dynamically change their visibility and position in your behavior parameter form. This approach opens up the possibility for creating dialog boxes with step-by-step "wizards" to guide the user through a complex behavior or a series of explanatory panels that appear depending on the choices made.

Cross-Reference

The processes of incorporating layers in objects and in behaviors have many parallels. See the section, "Using Layers in Objects" in Chapter 16 for some insights into the process.

Watch out: Because of a code discrepancy in this new functionality, you can't use the regular Show-Hide Layer Behavior when designing objects. Instead, use the custom Show-Hide Layer for Objects included on the CD-ROM in the Dreamweaver\Configuration\Behaviors\Actions folder.

Inserting multiple functions for a single behavior

When a new behavior is added to a Web page, Dreamweaver uses `behaviorFunction()` to insert the function definition. With Dreamweaver 1.0, you could only return a single function that is uniquely named (among all the installed behaviors). Dreamweaver 1.2 now permits multiple function definitions to be returned by `behaviorFunction()`. Moreover, all but the last function definition can be shared by other behaviors.

The `applyBehavior()` function still inserts a single function call into the selected tag's event handler, as follows:

```
<body onLoad= resizePatch() >
```

The function referenced can, in turn, call additional functions.

Caution

When a behavior is deleted from a page, Dreamweaver erases all the code associated with it. Because functions can now be shared among behaviors, Dreamweaver can leave code associated with one behavior when the program finds the function name in another behavior. This technique may leave some unused JavaScript code in your file.

Support for the <script> src attribute

In addition to sharing behavior functions, Dreamweaver 1.2 can now share entire JavaScript files. In JavaScript, when you want to include the code in an external file in your Web page, use the following syntax:

```
<script src= buttonjump.js ></script>
```

No additional code is specified between the `<script>...</script>` tag pairs because the code referenced in the `src` attribute is read into the Web page. The file referenced contains only JavaScript code, as indicated by the .js filename extension. Because the file is external, it can be referenced by several behaviors — much like an #include file in C programming. This support extends to objects as well as behaviors.

Function name extensions

Custom Dreamweaver functions used in creating behaviors and objects are now grouped under the new `dreamweaver` object in the DOM. Thus, when referring to the `getObjectsTag()` function, developers should use the following syntax:

```
dreamweaver.getObjectsTag()
```

To ensure backwards compatibility, all currently defined functions can be called without referencing the `dreamweaver` object. This new naming syntax is better JavaScript and clears the way for current functions to continue working, even if Macromedia creates a new Dreamweaver function with the same name.

Returning function names instead of function definitions

As covered earlier in the sidebar "Enhancements to `behaviorFunction()` in Dreamweaver 1.2," you can now return just the function name instead of restating the entire definition. The function has to be defined elsewhere in the `<script>` section — or in the newly available `<script src= file.js >` attribute — but that's the only restriction.

New JavaScript functions

The new functions `getBehaviorTag()` and `getBehaviorEvent()` are discussed in a preceding section. These tags return the tag and event to which the current behavior is attached. They can be used to make the current behavior unavailable if a certain tag or event is chosen or to select a particular layer for an interface.

Summary

Dreamweaver behaviors can greatly extend the Web designer's palette of possibilities — even a Web designer who is an accomplished JavaScript programmer. Behaviors simplify and automate the process of incorporating common, and not so common, JavaScript functions. The versatility of the behavior format enables anyone proficient in JavaScript to create custom actions that can be attached to any event. When considering behaviors, keep the following points in mind:

✦ Behaviors are a combination of events and actions.

✦ Behaviors are written as in HTML and are completely customizable from within Dreamweaver.

✦ Different browsers support different events. Dreamweaver enables you to select a specific browser or a browser range, such as all 4.0 browsers, on which to base your event choice.

✦ Dreamweaver includes 18 standard actions. Some actions are not available unless a particular object is on the current page.

✦ You can use Dreamweaver's built-in JavaScript extensions and API functions to build your own actions.

In the next chapter, you examine how to extend HTML capabilities by accessing external programs.

✦   ✦   ✦

Adding Multimedia Elements

Adding Video to Your Web Page

In a world accustomed to being entertained by moving
images 50 feet high, it's hard to see why people are thrilled
to see a grainy, jerky, quarter-screen-sized video on a Web
page. And in truth, it's the *promise* of video on the Web, not
the current state of it, that has folks excited. Many of the
industry's major players, including Microsoft and Apple, are
spending big bucks to bring that promise a little closer to
reality.

No one standard for video on the Web has yet to emerge,
although QuickTime is the most popular format on the Web
and is cross-platform. Dreamweaver therefore handles the
various flavors through open-ended HTML commands. Video
can be downloaded to the user and then automatically played
with a helper application, such as Microsoft's MediaPlayer or
QuickTime's MoviePlayer.

Streaming video, which enables the movie to begin playing as
it is being downloaded, is a relatively recent innovation but
one that appears to be gaining ground rapidly. This chapter
looks at all the different methods for incorporating video —
whether you're downloading an MPEG file or streaming a
RealVideo movie — into your Web pages through
Dreamweaver.

Video on the Web

It may be hard for folks not involved in the technology of
computers and the Internet to understand why the high-tech
Web doesn't always include something as "low-tech" as video.
After all, television has been around for over 50 years, right?
The difficulties arise from the fundamental difference between
the two media: television and radio signals are analog, and
computers work with digital signals. Sure, you can convert an
analog signal to a digital one — but that's just the beginning of
the solution.

Any digital equivalent of an analog file is enormous by comparison: A two-hour movie fits on a single video cassette, but uncompressed digital video uses roughly 27 megabytes per second; a two-hour show equals almost 2,000,000MB of storage. And large file sizes translate into enormous bandwidth problems when you are transmitting video over the Web.

To resolve this issue of mega-sized files, industry professionals and manufacturers have developed various strategies or *architectures* for the creation, storage, and playback of digital media. Each architecture has a different file format, and thus each requires the user to have a playback system—whether a plug-in, ActiveX control, or Java applet—capable of handling that particular format.

The leading digital video architectures are described briefly in the following section.

MPEG

Developed by the Motion Picture Experts Group, MPEG is to moving pictures as JPEG is to still images. Several different versions of MPEG have been developed by the standards group. Of these, MPEG-1 is the most widely supported, although MPEG-2 probably has enough market penetration to be useful. Filename extensions are either .mpg or .mpeg.

QuickTime

Originally developed by Apple as a multiplatform multimedia solution, QuickTime has proved so successful that version 3.0 is the basis for the latest MPEG standard. Aside from the regular QuickTime, Apple has also released QuickTime VR, which provides panoramic views. Filename extensions are either .qt or .mov.

RealVideo

RealNetworks (originally Progressive Networks) released the first streaming media system—RealAudio—in 1995. The current version, RealVideo, supports streaming playback for both audio and video, as well as Flash, Macromedia's vector animation format. Filename extensions include .ra and .ram.

Video for Windows

Years ago, in the light of QuickTime's success on the Macintosh, Microsoft released its own video format, Video for Windows. All Windows systems are equipped with players for any .avi file. These .avi files are not cross-platform, however. So although the format is standard for all Windows systems, its inability to "play well with others" has made Video for Windows less popular on the Web. Full-size, full-motion video is not yet available for the Web.

In an effort to keep file sizes as small as possible, Web videos are often presented relatively small. It's not uncommon to display a video in one-quarter of the screen or less. Furthermore, in terms of smoothness of the action you'll notice a major difference between conventional and Web-based video. Film is shown at 24 frames per second, while video uses roughly 30 frames per second. The best Web video rarely gets above 15 frames per second — almost guaranteeing a choppiness of motion depending on the footage. The faster the action, the more noticeable the frame rate is.

Given all the restrictions that video on the Web suffers, why use it at all? Simply because there is nothing else like it, and when you need video you have to use video. Take heart, though. Advances are occurring at a very rapid rate, both in the development of new video architectures and codecs, as well as in new, higher-speed Internet delivery systems such as cable modems. What you learn in this chapter enables you to include video in your Dreamweaver-built Web pages today, and gives you a good foundation for accommodating future enhancements.

Inserting Simple Video Capabilities

Once you've digitized your video, the easiest way to make it available on your Web page is to treat it as an ordinary link. Then, when the link is selected, the video downloads to the user's machine. What happens next depends on what helper applications are on the user's system. Most modern systems come equipped with multimedia players that can handle the common video file formats: MPEG, QuickTime, and Video for Windows.

To include a digitized video file on your Web page in Dreamweaver, follow these steps:

1. Select the text or image that you want to serve as the link to the video file.

2. In the Property Inspector, enter the name of the video file in the Link text box, or select the folder icon to browse for the file.

3. Because video files can be quite large, it's also good practice to note the file size next to the link name or enter it in the Alt text box as shown in Figure 18-1.

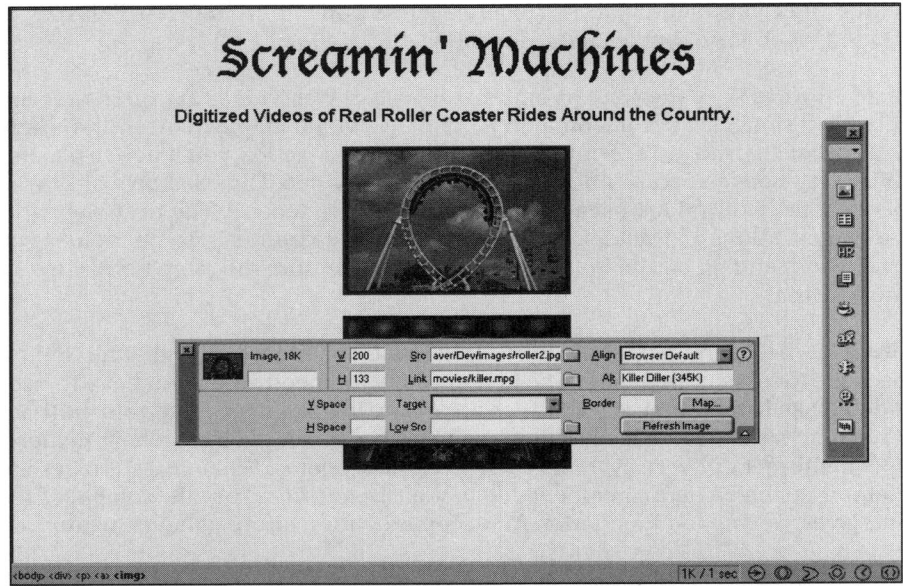

Figure 18-1: You can insert any video file for user download by including it as a link to a selected graphic or text.

Tip

Don't expect to automatically see an image from the linked video file in Dreamweaver's Document Window or in your browser preview. Many Web designers grab a still image from the video, convert it to GIF or JPEG format, and use that as the linked graphic.

Using Inline Video

Microsoft's Internet Explorer has a very useful proprietary attribute capable of producing *inline video*. Inline video is digital video that can be played back within the Web page itself, "in line with" other elements such as text and graphics. You can't depend on it for full Internet access; nevertheless, the dynamic source attribute, `dynsrc`, enables a Web designer working with an Internet Explorer intranet to easily include and control any Video for Windows (.avi) file. The attribute is inserted in the `<img>` tag, like this:

```
<img src= images/logo.gif  dynsrc= images/logo.avi >
```

A browser not supporting the `dynsrc` attribute displays the normally referenced image source, and an Internet Explorer browser automatically displays the image after it is transferred. Like the linked video files noted in the preceding section, a dynamic source video has to be completely downloaded before it can begin playing. Unless you're using a custom object in Dreamweaver, you have to code all the dynamic source attributes by hand. The dynamic source attribute enables some degree of control in displaying your .avi file.

Additional attributes of the `<img>` tag are described in Table 18-1. You can also use any of the regular `<img>` tag attributes, including `height`, `width`, `border`, `hspace`, and `vspace`.

Table 18-1
Attributes for Internet Explorer Inline Video

<img> Attribute	Purpose
start	By default, the video begins playing once the file download from the Web server is completed. Using the `start` attribute, you can specify when you want the video to play, either on `fileopen` or `mouseover`. You can also include both values to make your video play when it is first downloaded and then repeat whenever the user's mouse is passed over the image.
controls	To add the standard control panel to your video, insert the attribute `controls` by itself in any dynamic source object.
dynsrc	This attribute sets the .avi file to be displayed.
loop	Set the number of times you want your video clip to repeat by giving a value to the `loop` attribute. To make your video repeat continuously, use either `loop=-1` or `loop=infinite`.
loopdelay	Use this attribute to insert a delay between each repeat of a video clip. Insert `loopdelay=n` where *n* is the time in milliseconds; for example, `loopdelay=5000` would create a five-second delay between loops.

On the
CD-ROM

Dreamweaver's interface doesn't by default support the `<dynsrc>` dynamic source attribute, so normally you'd have to enter these attributes and values by hand. You can, however, use the Dynamic Source Object found on the CD-ROM to easily insert your .avi video clip. Just transfer dynsrc.htm and dynsrc.gif from the Dreamweaver/Configuration/Objects/Media folder.

Installing QuickTime and QuickTime VR Movies

QuickTime has become a leading format for cross-platform multimedia content. Developed by Apple, the QuickTime architecture encompasses still pictures, digitized video, audio, drawing, and even panoramic virtual reality environments. Because QuickTime output can be played on multiple platforms, it has substantial support in the industry. If I had to guess which architecture would become the standard, I'd bet on QuickTime.

QuickTime attributes

To view a QuickTime movie in your Web page, your users need to have a QuickTime plug-in installed. The HTML command for incorporating a QuickTime movie (or any other media that requires a plug-in) is the <embed> tag. Because so many different types of plug-ins exist, Dreamweaver uses a generic Plug-in Inspector that enables an unlimited number of parameters to be specified.

Only three parameters are really required for a QuickTime movie: the source of the file, the movie's width, and the movie's height. If you don't know the dimensions of your QuickTime movie, open the file with the MoviePlayer program that comes with QuickTime and choose Movie ➪ Get Info.

Note   When specifying the height of the movie, add 24 pixels to leave room for the controller panel, unless you've specifically turned off the controller.

To insert a QuickTime movie in your Web page, follow these steps:

1. First, insert the Plug-in object. Choose Insert ➪ Plug-in.

2. Either select the Plug-in object from the Common pane of the Object palette, or drag the Plug-in object to a location on your Web page.

3. In the Insert Plug-in dialog box, enter the QuickTime file's path and name in the Plug-in Source text box, or select the folder to browse for the file. Click OK when you're done.

4. In the Plug-in Inspector (see Figure 18-2), enter the width and height values in the W and H text boxes, respectively. Alternatively, you can drag any of the sizing handles on the Plug-in placeholder in the Document Window to a new size. Remember to add 24 pixels to the height if you are using the controller panel.

Figure 18-2: When inserting a QuickTime movie, specify
the properties and values in the Plug-in Inspector.

5. In the Plg URL text box, enter the Internet address to which you want visitors
   to your Web page directed if they do not have the necessary plug-in installed.
   (*Note:* In the case of QuickTime movies, use `http://quicktime.apple.com`.)

6. Select the Parameters button to open the Parameters dialog box. Enter the
   QuickTime parameters in the left column and the desired values in the right
   column. Press Tab to move from one column to another. Table 18-2 describes
   the available parameters for a QuickTime movie.

7. Dreamweaver's Plug-in Inspector also enables you to enter several other
   attributes generally used with other objects, such as images. These other
   attributes include `Align` (alignment), `Alt` (alternative text), `V Space` (vertical
   space), `H Space` (horizontal space), and `Border`. You can also enter a name in
   the Plug-in text box if you plan on referring to your QuickTime file in a
   JavaScript or other program.

On the CD-ROM

While you can certainly use the Plug-in Inspector to fill out your QuickTime parameters, you can also make your life a little easier by using the QuickTime Object found
on the CD-ROM. Just copy the two files from Dreamweaver/Configuration/Objects/
Media (qtime.htm and qtime.gif) to your folder and restart Dreamweaver. You'll find
all the parameters necessary for including a QuickTime or QuickTime VR movie.

Table 18-2 QuickTime Movie Parameters	
QuickTime Parameter	**Description**
autoplay	Enables the QuickTime movie to start playing as soon as the movie data has sufficiently downloaded. You can set autoplay to either true or false (the default).
bgcolor	Sets the background color for the QuickTime movie (QuickTime 3 only).
cache	Informs the user's browser to cache the movie, as with other documents. The values for cache are true (the default) or false. *Note:* This parameter is currently supported only by Netscape 3.0 browsers.

(continued)

Table 18-2 (continued)

QuickTime Parameter	Description
controller	Displays the controller panel attached to the QuickTime movie. You can set controller to either true (the default) or false. If the controller is enabled, add 24 pixels to the height of the movie.
hidden	If hidden is included as a parameter, the QuickTime movie is not displayed, but the audio soundtrack is played. This parameter does not take any values.
href	Establishes a link to a URL when the movie is selected by the viewer. You can supply either an absolute or a relative Internet address.
loop	Causes the movie to loop continuously. In addition to true and false (the default) values, the loop parameter also can take a palindrome value, which causes the QuickTime movie to play alternately forward and backward.
playeveryframe	When enabled, this parameter forces the movie to play every frame, even if it must do so at a slower rate than is optimum. Possible values are true and false (the default). Do not enable playeveryframe if the QuickTime movie includes an audio or MIDI track, because it will disable the sound.
scale	Resizes the QuickTime movie. By setting scale to tofit, you can scale the movie to the dimensions of the embedded box as specified by the height and width values. Setting scale to aspect resizes the movie to the height and width dimensions, but maintains the aspect ratio of the original movie. You can also set scale to a number; if, for example, you want to resize the movie to two-and-a-half times the original size, you would set the scale value to 2.5. The default is scale=1.
target	Enables the link specified in the href parameter to be targeted to a specific frame or named anchor. You can use any of the standard target values, including _self, _parent, _top or _blank.
volume	Controls the volume of the QuickTime audio track. Possible values are 0 (no sound) to 256 (loudest). The default is volume=256.

QuickTime VR

QuickTime has one feature that no other video architecture can match: QuickTime VR (QTVR). QuickTime VR enables the user to "look around" in the view being offered — this range is often a 180° panoramic view and sometimes has complete 360° capability. QTVR is also used for "object movies," in which the camera rotates around an object at its center point in three dimensions. In addition, QuickTime VR enables the designer to designate certain areas as *hotspots* that, when selected by the user, activate a link to another page or another movie. Though purists will argue that QTVR is not *really* virtual reality, the technology has made tremendous progress toward acceptance on the Web.

QuickTime VR's attributes are entered in the same manner as the regular QuickTime movie attributes — through the Parameters button in the Plug-in Parameters dialog box (see Figure 18-3).

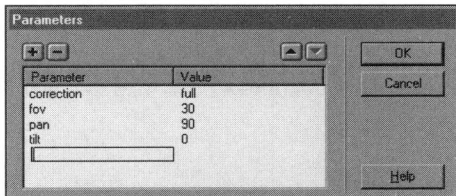

Figure 18-3: Use the Plug-in Parameters dialog box to enter attributes for any plug-in. This example is for a QuickTime VR movie.

QTVR's special capabilities require special attributes, as listed in Table 18-3:

<table>
<tr><td colspan="2" align="center">Table 18-3
Parameters for QuickTime VR Movies</td></tr>
<tr><td>*QuickTime VR
Parameter*</td><td>*Description*</td></tr>
<tr><td>correction</td><td>Applies the correction filter. Settings are none, partial, or full (the default).</td></tr>
<tr><td>fov</td><td>Specifies the initial field-of-view angle. The range of values goes from 0 (maximum zoom) to 90 (narrowest zoom). The default is fov=0.</td></tr>
</table>

(continued)

Table 18-3 *(continued)*	
QuickTime VR Parameter	**Description**
hotspot	Defines the URL for any designated hotspot. The syntax is hotspot n=URL, where n is the identification number given the hotspot during QTVR authoring, and URL is any valid Internet address. *Note:* Because of this attribute's syntax, you can't use the Parameters dialog box to enter a hotspot; you must either enter its value by hand or through a custom object.
node	Determines the initial node for a QTVR multinode movie. Nodes are specified during QTVR authoring and given numeric IDs. Set node to a new integer to override the default initial node.
pan	Sets the initial pan angle, in degrees, of a QuickTime VR movie. The range of values for a typical movie is from 0.0° to 360.0°. The default is pan=0.
tilt	Sets the initial tilt angle, in degrees, of a QuickTime VR movie. The range of values for a typical movie is from −42.5 to 42.5 degrees. The default is tilt=0.

As with a regular QuickTime movie, the only *required* parameters for a QTVR movie are the source file, movie width, and movie height. Remember to add an additional 24 pixels to the height measurement for the controller.

 **Caution**   Some parameters that are meaningful to regular QuickTime movies are not appropriate for QuickTime VR movies. These include autoplay, controller, hidden, href, loop, playeveryframe, target, and volume.

Working with Streaming Video

If you've ever downloaded a few minutes of digital video over a slow modem connection, you know the reason why streaming video was invented. In an age where immediacy rules, waiting until the complete video file is transferred and then loaded into the video player can seem to last an eternity. *Streaming*, on the other hand, enables the multimedia content to begin playing as soon as the first complete packet of information is received, and then to continue playing as more digital information arrives. Video is just one form of media to get the streaming treatment: You can also stream audio and animation.

As with other digital video, no clear standard exists for streaming video. Most solutions require special software on the server side, as well as client-side plug-ins. Many companies are competing in the market. Dreamweaver uses the Plug-in object and Plug-in Inspector to insert and configure the parameters for the various streaming video formats: RealVideo, NetShow, VXtreme, and VDOLive to name a few.

Tip   All of the video solutions require that the digital content be compressed or *encoded* with a system-specific encoder. Visit specific companies' Web sites to get more information — and, in some cases, the necessary software — for this process.

Regardless of which streaming video protocol you use, the procedure for incorporating the file on your Web page is basically the same, although the details (such as filename extensions) differ. In order to demonstrate the general technique and still offer some specific information you can use, the next section gives a detailed account of how to include streaming RealVideo clips with Dreamweaver. Check with the streaming video developer you plan to use to get the precise installation details.

A RealVideo example

The earliest streaming system (and one of today's most prevalent) was developed by Progressive Networks (www.real.com). This company recently changed its name to RealNetworks in honor of its leading products, RealAudio and RealVideo. RealNetworks offers a free multimedia player, RealPlayer, for anyone wishing to see or hear the content of these systems. An enhanced player product is also available at low cost.

When incorporating RealVideo into your Web pages, you have a variety of playback options. You can set the video so that a free-floating RealPlayer is invoked, or you can specify that the video appear inline on your Web page. You can also customize the controls that appear on your Web page so that only the ones you want — at the size you want — are included.

Creating RealVideo metafiles

RealVideo uses its own specialized server software to transmit encoded video files called RealServer. Rather than call this server and the digital video file directly, RealVideo uses a system of *metafiles* to link to the RealVideo server and file. A metafile is an ordinary text file containing the appropriate URL pointing to the RealServer and video file.

The metafiles are distinguished from the media files by their filename extensions, as follows:

.rm   RealVideo files

.ra   RealAudio files

.ram   Metafile that launches the independent RealPlayer

.rpm   Metafile that launches the RealPlayer plug-in.

 **Caution**   For your RealVideo file to play properly, the Web server administrator must configure your Web server to understand that the extensions .ra and .ram refer to the MIME type x-pn-realaudio, and that the extension .rpm refers to the MIME type x-pn-realaudio-plugin.

To create the metafile, open your favorite text editor and insert one or more lines pointing to your server and the video files. Instead of using the http:// locator seen with most URLs, RealVideo files address the server with a pnm:// (Progressive Networks Metafile) indicator. The contents of the file should take this form:

```
pnm://hostname/path/file
```

where *hostname* is the domain name of the server where the RealVideo files are stored, *path* is the path to the file, and *file* is the name of the RealVideo file. For example, to display a training video, the metafile contents might look like this:

```
pnm://www.trainers.com/videos/training01.rm
```

You can include multiple video clips by putting each one on its own line, separated by a single return. RealVideo plays each clip in succession and the user can skip from one clip to another.

Inserting RealVideo in your Web page

Once you've created both the encoded RealVideo file and the metafiles, you're ready to insert them into your Web page. You have two basic techniques for including RealVideo: as a link, and using the <embed> tag.

Using a Link

Generally, if you want to invoke the free-floating RealPlayer, you use a link; the href attribute is set to an address for a metafile, like this:

```
<a href= videos/howto01.ram >Demonstration</a>
```

When the link is selected, it calls the metafile that, in turn, calls the video file on the RealServer. As the file begins to download to the user's system, the RealPlayer program is invoked and starts to display the video as soon as possible through the independent video window, as shown in Figure 18-4. The link can be inserted in Dreamweaver through either the Text or Image Property Inspector.

Figure 18-4: You can set up your RealVideo clip so that it plays inline, or in a separate player as illustrated here.

Using <embed>

If, on the other hand, you'd like to make the video appear inline with the Web page's text or graphics, you use Dreamweaver's Plug-in object to insert an <embed> tag. Position the pointer where you want the RealVideo to be displayed, and either choose Insert ⇨ Plug-in or select Insert Plug-in from the Object Palette. After the Insert Plug-in dialog box appears, enter the path and filename for the video's metafile in the Plug-in Source text box.

When the Plug-in object representing the RealVideo clip is selected, the Property Inspector lets you enter values for the <embed> tag. As with the QuickTime object, the only attributes required for a RealVideo clip are the file source and the width and height of the movie. And, also like QuickTime, you can choose from a healthy number of attributes to control your RealVideo movie. Attributes are entered by selecting the Parameters button on the Plug-in Inspector, and entering attributes and their values in the Parameters dialog box (shown earlier in Figure 18-3).

RealVideo attributes are listed in Table 18-4.

Table 18-4	
Parameters for RealVideo Movies	
RealVideo Parameter	*Description*
autostart	Enables the RealVideo clip to start playing as soon as content is available. You can set autostart to either true (the default) or false.
console	Determines the console name for each control in a Web page having multiple controls. To force controls on a page to refer to the same file, use the same console=name attribute. The console name _master links to all controls on a page, whereas _unique connects to no other instances.
controls	Enables the placement of individual control panel elements in the Web page. You can use multiple controls in one attribute or multiple <embed> tags to build a custom RealVideo interface. The separate controls are as follows: all controlpanel imagewindow infovolumepanel infopanel playbutton positionslider positionfield statuspanel statusbar stopbutton statusfield volumeslider
nolabels	Suppresses the Title, Author, and Copyright labels in the Status panel. If you set nolabels to true, the actual data is still visible. The default is nolabels=false.

HTTP Streaming

To gain the maximum throughput of your RealVideo files, it's best to use the RealServer software. Occasionally, however, you'll encounter Web site clients who must economize and can't afford the specialized server. Not widely known is the fact that you can use a regular World Wide Web server to stream RealVideo and other RealMedia files.

Two prerequisites exist for HTTP streaming: 1. Your system administrator must first correctly configure the MIME types, and 2. You must provide multiple files to match the right user-selectable modem speeds. The proper MIME types are as follows:

✦ audio/x-pn-RealAudio (for .ra, .rm or .ram files)

✦ audio/x-pn-RealAudio-plugin (for .rpm files)

✦ video/x-pn-RealVideo (for .ra, .rm or .ram files)

✦ video/x-pn-RealVideo-plugin (for .rpm files)

RealServer automatically selects the right file for the user's modem connection. If you are using HTTP streaming capabilities, you should offer multiple files to accommodate the various modem connection rates, such as 28.8K and 56K.

Other than a reduction in download speed, the other disadvantage to using HTTP streaming over RealServer streaming is the reduced number of simultaneous users who can be served. RealServer can handle hundreds of connections at the same time; HTTP streaming is far more limited.

Summary

Digital video on the Web is in its infancy. Bandwidth is still too tight to enable full-screen, full-motion movies, no matter what the format. However, you can include downloadable as well as streaming video content through Dreamweaver's Plug-in object and Plug-In Inspector.

✦ Converting analog video to digital video requires special compressing or encoding systems. Even with the highest degree of compression, digital video has enormous storage and download requirements.

✦ You can include a digital video movie to be downloaded in your Web page by using the anchor tag, <a>, and setting the href attribute to the file's location on your Web server.

✦ Use Dreamweaver's Plug-in object when you want your video to be presented inline on your Web page. The Plug-in Inspector then lets you alter the video's parameters for any video architecture.

✦ QuickTime is an excellent example of cross-platform digital video that offers a full range of options — including QuickTime VR for displaying panoramic movies.

✦ To have your visitors view your digital video clips as soon as possible, use a streaming video technology such as RealVideo. RealVideo files can be displayed either in a separate player or embedded in the Web page.

In the next chapter you'll see how Dreamweaver helps you incorporate background music, sound effects, and streaming audio into your Web pages.

✦   ✦   ✦

Using Audio on Your Web Page

Web sites tend to be divided into two categories: those totally without sound and those that use a lot of it — there's not much middle ground. Music and entertainment sites rely heavily on both downloadable and streaming audio.

You'll likely find that the major stumbling block for putting audio on the Web is not the HTML implementation, but achieving the conversion from analog to digital sound. Once you have the necessary equipment and the expertise for this task, however, the ability (via Dreamweaver) to add an audio layer to a site will greatly enhance your Web designer palette of skills.

In this chapter you'll learn how to use audio in the Web pages you design with Dreamweaver. You'll be able to include simple audio that must be fully downloaded before it can play, as well as streaming audio that starts playing as soon as the opening bars have been transferred. In addition to the better-known music formats such as .wav, MIDI, and RealAudio, this chapter also examines a relative newcomer to the audio scene: Rich Music Format, including its plug-in component, Beatnik, and its advanced JavaScript capabilities.

Digital Audio Fundamentals

Audio on the Internet has been around longer than video, but there's still no one standard. Outside of a single proprietary Internet Explorer tag, no direct HTML command exists to include sound in your Web page. Dreamweaver, therefore, uses a generic plug-in approach to handle the various audio options.

Like digital video, digital audio requires all analog signals — voice, music, and sounds — to be converted. And, again like digital video, the resulting files can be quite hefty. Many different formats for digital audio files are in use today across the various computer platforms. These formats can be identified by their unique filename extensions, described in Table 19-1.

Table 19-1 Digital Audio File Formats	
Audio Filename Extension	**Format Description**
.au	Used by NeXT and Sun UNIX systems, the .au format is important because many of the earliest Internet audio files were available for UNIX only.
.aiff	The Audio Interchange File Format was developed by Apple and is also used by Silicon Graphics machines.
.midi or .mid	The MIDI format consists of instructions on re-creating a sound score rather than specific notes.
.mp3	The MPEG3 format features high-quality digital audio files with excellent compression. Used very heavily for downloading long audio samples.
.ra or .ram	RealAudio, developed by Progressive Networks, was the first streaming audio format.
.rmf	The Rich Music Format was developed by musician Thomas Dolby and his company, Headspace, and is used by the Beatnik plug-in.
.swa	Shockwave Audio, developed by Macromedia and based on MPEG3; this format can be streamed or downloaded.
.wav	Codeveloped by Microsoft and IBM, the waveform audio file format is heavily used in Windows systems.

Which audio format should you choose? That depends on a combination of factors, including your target audience, the available bandwidth, and the purpose of the audio's content. Live broadcasts over the Internet, for example, must be created in RealAudio (or one of the other streaming technologies). Short sound effects can be handled by most of the formats, so you'll need to weigh the more prevalent accessibility of .wav files against the higher fidelity of a plug-in such as Beatnik. It's not uncommon for a sound file to be offered in multiple formats.

Linking Audio Files

If you're working with .wav, MIDI, or other common audio files, you can easily incorporate them into your Web design. The simplest way to add these sound files to a Web page is to include them as a link. From Dreamweaver's Text or Image Property Inspector, you enter the path to your audio file in the Link text box or select the folder icon to browse for the file. When the user selects that link, the sound file downloads, and whatever program has been designated to handle that type of file opens in a separate window and begins playing the music. See Figure 19-1.

Figure 19-1: The audio file included in this page can be downloaded and played by the user. The file has been entered as a link through the Dreamweaver Property Inspector.

Tip

Dreamweaver 1.2 lets you search for files of a specific type with a simple trick. Limit the selection that appears in the Select File dialog box by typing the asterisk (*) wildcard character, followed by the filename extension of the desired type of files. For example, if you were looking for MIDI files, you would enter ***.mid**. Only MIDI files will be displayed for your selection.

Both the Netscape and Microsoft browsers come with their own players — or
connections to multimedia players — for handling the various audio formats,
including .wav, MIDI, .au, and .aiff. Each player is a little different, but they all offer
simple, familiar controls such as Pause, Stop, and Volume buttons (you can see the
Netscape player in Figure 19-1). Each audio link in your Web page opens a separate
player.

Caution If you're having trouble playing a .wav file through Netscape Navigator on your
Macintosh, the problem may be your plug-in types. If the QuickTime plug-in is set to
handle the audio/wav MIME type, the audio file won't play back properly. To see if
this is the case, choose Help ➪ About Plug-ins in Navigator/Communicator, and con-
sult the online Navigator Help system for information on how to modify your plug-in
set-up.

When you use the link technique for incorporating sound, you have no control over
the position or appearance of the floating player window. However, you can control
these factors and more by *embedding* your audio. Let's see how that works.

Embedding Sounds and Music

To truly integrate the audio files into your Web page — and to avoid a free-floating
sound control panel — the files must be embedded. Embedding the sound files also
gives you a much higher degree of control over every element of audio
presentation, including:

✦ The clip's play volume

✦ Which part, if any, of the controls are visible

✦ The starting and ending points of the music clip

As with any other embedded object, you can present the visual display inline with
other text elements — aligned to the top, middle, or bottom of the text, or blocked
left or right to allow text to flow around it. Dreamweaver controls all of these
various parameters through two different objects: the Plug-in object and the
ActiveX object. Each type of object calls a specific type of player. For example,
the default Plug-in object calls the LiveAudio Plug-in in a Netscape browser, and
the ActiveMovie control in Internet Explorer. Calling ActiveMovie as an ActiveX
object explicitly enables you to modify a great number of parameters for Internet
Explorer — which are completely ignored by Navigator. You'll learn all of your
embedding options, including techniques for cross-browser audio, in the next few
sections.

Basic audio embedding

As with the basic video file, Dreamweaver uses the generic Plug-in object to embed audio in your Web page. The object requires only three parameters: the source of the audio file, and the width and height of the object. To embed an audio file in your Web page, follow these steps in Dreamweaver:

1. Position the cursor where you want the control panel for the audio file to appear.

2. Insert the Plug-in object by choosing Insert ⇨ Plug-in or by selecting the Plug-in object from the Object Palette.

3. In the Property Inspector, enter the path and filename for your audio file in the Plug-in Source text box. Or select Browse to choose your file from the Select File dialog box.

4. Use either of the following techniques to size the plug-in placeholder:

   • Enter the appropriate values in the W (Width) and the H (Height) text boxes of the Property Inspector; or

   • Click the resizing handles on the plug-in placeholder and drag it out to a new size.

For a default audio plug-in, use a width of 144 pixels and a height of 60 pixels. These dimensions are slightly larger than necessary for Internet Explorer's audio controls, but they fit Navigator's controls perfectly, and the control panel will not appear to be "clipped" when viewed through any browser.

When the Plug-in object is inserted, Dreamweaver displays the generic plug-in icon instead of any control panel (as with other placeholders). The type of control panel displayed depends on the browser used, as shown in Figure 19-2. Here you can see the differences between Dreamweaver in the top window, Netscape Navigator in the lower-left, and Internet Explorer in the lower-right.

Incorporating Enhanced Plug-ins

Because there's really no one standard yet for Internet audio, you can exercise a much finer degree of control of the audio in your pages by calling specific plug-ins. The trade-off, unfortunately, is that by designating a plug-in, you reduce the size of your potential audience. Some plug-ins are specific to a browser, or to a browser version. Moreover, plug-ins that aren't distributed with the major browsers face an uphill battle in terms of market penetration. If you use a plug-in, you can always expect some folks to be resistant to downloading the necessary software. Before you incorporate any plug-in, you must weigh these issues against your overall design plan.

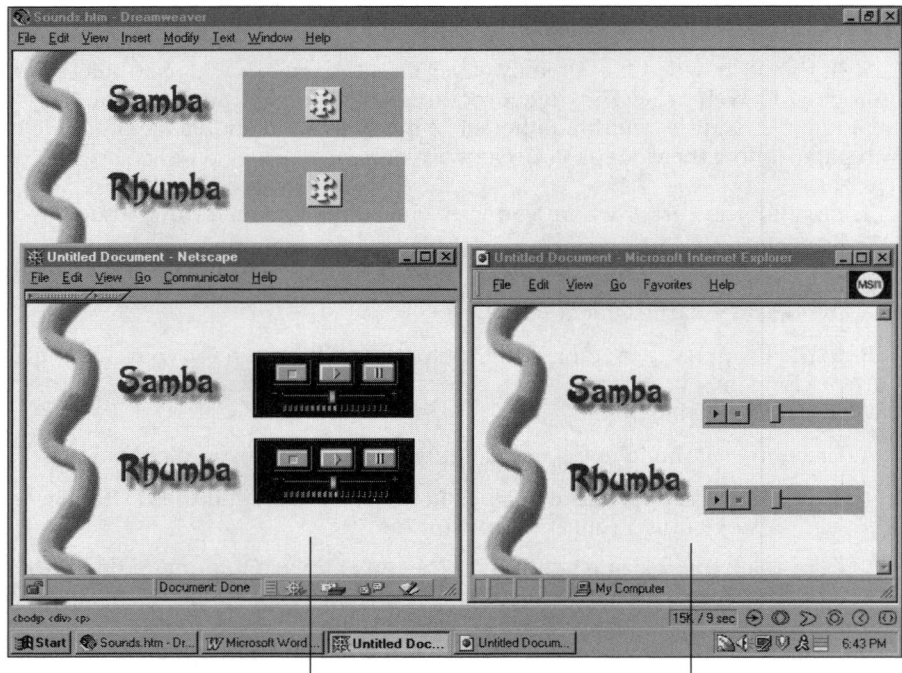

Netscape Navigator's player   Internet Explorer's player

Figure 19-2: With a basic embedding technique, the type of player is set by the browser.

Tip

> A great number of audio plug-ins are available and offer a broad variety of functionality and features. A good place to see a list of those available is the Plug-in Plaza (www.browserwatch.com/plug-in.html). In addition to offering complete descriptions, this site also has links direct to the download areas.

To represent the wide range of audio plug-ins, this chapter examines two of the major players in the field: Netscape's LiveAudio and Headspace's Beatnik. LiveAudio has the advantage of being included with Netscape Navigator/Communicator (since Navigator 3.0), and Beatnik provides excellent fidelity and next-generation features.

Using Netscape's LiveAudio plug-in

LiveAudio is Netscape's default audio player and is used when you do basic embedding of an audio file, as well as when you attach a sound file to a URL. Both of these methods of incorporating audio, however, barely scratch the surface of what

LiveAudio is capable of doing. LiveAudio uses up to 13 different parameters to shape its appearance and functionality in the Web page, and also accepts a full range of JavaScript commands.

To take advantage of LiveAudio's full capabilities, you must enter the audio file's parameters and values (we'll discuss these shortly) through Dreamweaver's Property Inspector. Follow these steps to specify the parameters for your Plug-in object:

1. Insert the Plug-in object — either by choosing Insert ⇨ Plug-in or by dragging the Plug-in object from the Object Palette to a place on your Web page.

2. From the extended Property Inspector, select Parameters.

   The Parameter dialog box is displayed with its two columns: Parameter and Value (see Figure 19-3).

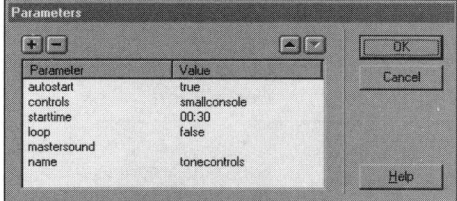

Figure 19-3: Enter all the LiveAudio attributes and their values through the Parameters dialog box.

3. Click in the Parameter column and type in the first parameter. Press Tab to move to the Value column and enter the desired value. Press Tab again to move to the next parameter.

   • Press Shift-Tab if you need to move backwards through the list.

   • To delete a parameter, highlight it and select the – (minus) button at the top of the parameters list.

   • To move a parameter from one position in the list to another, highlight it and select the Up or Down arrow buttons at the top of the parameters list.

Tip

For most plug-ins, including LiveAudio, the order of the parameters is irrelevant.

4. Repeat Step 3 until all parameters are entered.

5. Click OK when you're done.

LiveAudio parameters

The parameters for LiveAudio affect either the look of the player or the qualities of the sound. The main parameter for altering the player's appearance is `controls`. Depending on the value used, you can display the default control panel, a smaller version or individual controls.

You can embed individual controls anywhere on your Web page. To link the various controls, you use the `mastersound` keyword in each `<embed>` statement and set the `name` parameter to one unique value for all files. Finally, set the source in one `<embed>` tag to the actual sound file, and the other sources in the other files to a dummy file called a *stub* file.

Table 19-2 contains all the parameters available for LiveAudio, *except* those set by Dreamweaver's Property Inspector (source, height, width, and alignment).

<table>
<tr><td colspan="3" align="center">Table 19-2
LiveAudio Parameters</td></tr>
<tr><td>*Parameter*</td><td>*Acceptable Values*</td><td>*Description*</td></tr>
<tr><td>autostart</td><td>true or false</td><td>If autostart is set to true, the audio file begins playing as soon as the download is completed. The default is false.</td></tr>
<tr><td>controls</td><td>console, smallconsole, playbutton, pausebutton, stopbutton, or volumelever</td><td>Sets the sound control to appear. The default is console.</td></tr>
<tr><td>endtime</td><td>minutes:seconds; for example, 00:00</td><td>Determines the point in the sound clip at which the audio stops playing.</td></tr>
<tr><td>hidden</td><td>true</td><td>Expressly hides all the audio controls; sound plays in the background.</td></tr>
<tr><td>loop</td><td>true, false, or an integer</td><td>Setting loop to true forces the sound file to repeat continuously until the Stop button is selected or the user goes to another page. To set the number of times the sound repeats, set loop equal to an integer. The default is false.</td></tr>
</table>

Parameter	Acceptable Values	Description
mastersound	None	Enables several `<embed>` tags to be grouped and controlled as one. Used in conjunction with the `<name>` attribute.
name	A unique name	Links various `<embed>` tags in a file to control them as one. Used in conjunction with the `<mastersound>` attribute.
starttime	minutes:seconds; for example, 00:00	Determines the point in the sound clip at which the audio begins playing.
volume	1 to 100	Sets the loudness of the audio clip on a scale from 1 to 100 percent.

Caution   Although LiveAudio enjoys the distribution of being bundled with Netscape Navigator, keep in mind that most plugs-ins by themselves don't work in Internet Explorer.

Making music with Beatnik

Beatnik is a recent but very powerful entry into the audio plug-in field. Developed by Headspace, Inc., an audio technology company headed by musician Thomas Dolby, Beatnik plays Rich Music Format (RMF) files. RMF playback compares favorably with high-end PC wavetable sound cards, even though the processing is entirely software-based. Beatnik can also play all other major audio-file formats, including .wav, .aiff, MIDI, and MOD.

In addition to offering excellent sound, the other advantage that Beatnik offers is interactivity. Beatnik supports a comprehensive JavaScript command set. With Beatnik, you can play sounds or music in response to mouse clicks, mouse movements and other user events. In addition, the audio can be altered in its tempo, volume, pitch, or mix.

Beatnik includes one additional special feature worth noting. Included with each Beatnik plug-in are 50 user-interface sounds, known as *Groovoids*. Groovoids are short sounds — a cash register ring, teletypes, fanfares, chimes, and musical snippets — built into the Beatnik memory. Because they are incorporated in the plug-in, there's no additional download time. Thus a Web designer can use the Groovoids to provide aural feedback for user selections, or as a type of hold music while a Web page is loading.

Dreamweaver comes with the Beatnik plug-in as well as a Beatnik object. The only downside to Beatnik is that it is subject to the quirks inherent to advanced plug-ins.

First, the Beatnik plug-in only works with Netscape Navigator browsers, 3.0 and higher, because Beatnik relies on JavaScript. Second, your users must have the plug-in installed before they can experience the RMF and Groovoid sounds.

As of this writing, the Headspace company (www.headspace.com) has announced that an ActiveX Beatnik control is in development and should be available shortly.

Installing the Beatnik object

Before you can use the Beatnik object in Dreamweaver, you have to install it. Follow these steps:

1. Close Dreamweaver if it is running.

2. Copy the two Beatnik files, beatnik.htm and beatnik.gif, from the original Dreamweaver CD-ROM to an object folder.

The object folders are located in this path on your system: Dreamweaver\Configuration\objects\. Dreamweaver ships with three object folders, which correspond to the three panels on the Object Palette — Common, Forms, and Invisibles. You can either copy the Beatnik files into one of the existing folders or create a new one. I recommend creating a new folder called Media for all your multimedia objects.

3. After you've finished copying the Beatnik files, restart Dreamweaver.

4. Be sure to install the Beatnik plug-in, if you haven't already done so.

5. Double-click the Beatnik icon on the your original Dreamweaver CD-ROM to begin the install process.

If you don't have a fairly recent version of Dreamweaver, use the Beatnik plug-in (now officially called the Beatnik Player) located on this book's CD-ROM in the External Programs folder.

Embedding a Beatnik object in your page

Once the Beatnik object is installed in Dreamweaver, you'll find that incorporating RMF and other files to use the plug-in is a very straightforward process. As with other plug-ins, simply position the cursor where you want the Beatnik object to appear, and select it from the Object Palette. (You can also choose Insert ⇨ Beatnik from the menus.) When the Insert Beatnik dialog box opens, enter a file source in the RMF File Source text box. This can be the name of any RMF file or other audio format file. As usual, you can also select Browse to choose your file from a Select File dialog box. Click OK when you're finished.

Once you've learned how to include a Beatnik object, you can really indulge yourself. You can embed — and play! — up to eight Beatnik objects on a page (although some systems may have problems playing more than four at a time).

After you've picked your file, the Property Inspector displays your filename in the src text box, along with other information about the Beatnik object, including the following attributes:

✦ **Width and Height.** The preset dimensions conform to the size of the default Beatnik controls. As with LiveAudio objects, you can vary the size and number of Beatnik controls through the parameters.

✦ **Plg URL.** When a user doesn't have the appropriate plug-in, this attribute provides a link to get one. The Beatnik plug-in URL address is http://www.headspace.com/beatnik/?plug-in.

Caution

At a minimum, always keep the Width and Height attributes set to a value of at least 2, even when using the hidden parameter. Enter the Width and Height pixels size in the W and H text boxes on the Property Inspector, respectively.

Beatnik parameters

When you click Parameters in the Beatnik object's Property Inspector, you get access to the parameters described in Table 19-3.

<table>
<tr><td colspan="2" align="center">Table 19-3
Beatnik Object Parameters</td></tr>
<tr><td>**Beatnik
Parameter**</td><td>**Description**</td></tr>
<tr><td>autostart</td><td>This attribute is set to true, which allows the audio to begin playing as soon as the file has completely downloaded. Use false if you want to control the playing of the audio independently.</td></tr>
<tr><td>Display</td><td>Determines which graphic is used to represent the Beatnik object. Options are song, which shows copyright information, or system (the default), which enables the user to toggle between the song information, output meters, or oscilloscope.</td></tr>
<tr><td>Hidden</td><td>Hides the controls; no value is specified.</td></tr>
<tr><td>Type</td><td>Sets the MIME type. If the audio file is in RMF format, this attribute is set to audio/rmf.</td></tr>
<tr><td>mode</td><td>Sets which of three graphics is to be displayed initially as the Beatnik plug-in — scope, meters, or copyright. When display=song, then only the copyright value is available.</td></tr>
<tr><td>loop</td><td>If set to true, this attribute causes the file to repeat continuously. If set to false (the default) the file plays once only. The value for loop can also be an integer to determine the number of times the file repeats.</td></tr>
<tr><td>volume</td><td>Preset to the loudest value (100); this attribute can be any number from 1 to 100.</td></tr>
</table>

Playing a Groovoid

As mentioned earlier, Groovoids are short musical riffs and sound effects intended to add an interactive sound dimension to your Web page. The Beatnik plug-in includes 50 such samples in five categories: User Interface, Hits, Fanfare, Background, and Miscellaneous. How you incorporate a Groovoid in your Web page depends on how you plan to use it:

✦ To use a Groovoid as a repeating background theme, an attribute is added to the parameters of your Beatnik object.

✦ To activate your Groovoid sound according to a user's actions, you have to call a JavaScript function.

A Groovoid background

To include a Groovoid as a repeating theme playing in the background, follow these steps:

1. Insert a Beatnik object by choosing Insert ⇨ Beatnik or selecting the Beatnik object from the Object Palette.

2. Select a dummy RMF format file as your source.

You'll find a dummy RMF format file on the CD-ROM. It's called `stub.rmf` in the Dreamweaver Bible Code section; you can copy it to your system.

3. In the Property Inspector, select Parameters.

4. Change the value for `autostart` to `true`.

5. If you want the audio clip to repeat continuously, change the value for `loop` to `true`.

6. Select the + button to add a new attribute.

7. Type **groovoid** in the Parameter column, and tab to the Value column.

8. As the value for the Groovoid, enter one of the Groovoid names. Example names are Background-StillWaiting, Background-Clock, and Background-Funky. *Note:* Groovoid names are case-sensitive! Press Tab when you're done.

9. In the Parameters column, enter the `hidden` attribute. Press Tab, leaving the value column blank for this attribute.

10. Click OK to process the parameter values and close the Parameters dialog box.

To experience the complete list of Groovoids, try out the Interactive Groovoid Web page available on the CD-ROM in the Web Resource folder.

Interactive Groovoids

Getting your Groovoid to play interactively requires a modicum of JavaScripting, but it pays off in big dividends. Not only do the interactive Groovoids add a cool sonic dimension to your Web page, but understanding the process of getting them to play opens the door to far more elaborate musical Web explorations.

To play a Groovoid interactively, you have to include a JavaScript library called *musicObject* on your Web site. The musicObject library contains the `playGroovoid` command — as well as over 40 other commands to make and shape Web audio. The technique described here also needs a dummy RMF file — a stub file — as used in the preceding section.

Note In the following procedure, you'll use Dreamweaver behaviors. You may want to review Chapter 17, "Creating and Using Behaviors."

The concept of "including a JavaScript library" may sound daunting to you, but all that is involved is simply copying a file to your Web site and referencing that file in the code — in the same way that you copy an image and refer to that file in code. The musicObject library is contained in the file musicObject.js, and your Web server must be set up to recognize the .js extension as an application/x-javascript MIME type. Contact your Web site administrator for further assistance.

On the CD-ROM To simplify the task of adding interactive Groovoids to your Web page, you'll find an Add a Groovoid action in the Dreamweaver Behaviors folder of the CD-ROM, as well as a copy of the musicObject.js file. Install the action by copying it to the Dreamweaver\Configuration\Behaviors\Actions folder; then restart Dreamweaver.

After you've installed the Add a Groovoid action, follow these steps to incorporate an interactive Groovoid:

1. Select the image or link you want to act as a trigger for your Groovoid.

2. Open the Behavior Inspector by selecting Show Behaviors from the Launcher, by choosing Windows ⇨ Behaviors, or by pressing F8.

3. In the Behavior Inspector, click the Add Events (+) button to choose an event, such as `onMouseOver` or `onClick`.

4. In the Actions pane, click the Add Action (+) button and choose Add a Groovoid from the drop-down list.

5. In the Add a Groovoid dialog box, shown in Figure 19-4, enter the path to the musicObject.js file in the musicObject Source text box, or click Browse to locate the file.

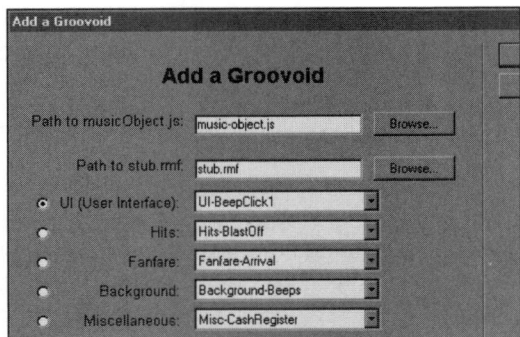

Figure 19-4: Set up your Web page to groove interactively, through the Add a Groovoid behavior.

6. In the Stub Source text box, enter the path to a dummy music file, or select Browse to find the file.

7. Select your Groovoid from any of the category drop-down lists: User Interface, Hits, Fanfare, Background, or Miscellaneous.

8. Select OK when you're finished.

You can preview your Groovoid in any Navigator browser, 3.0 or higher.

Tip

For detailed information on using the musicObject library with Beatnik, visit the Headspace Web site (www.headspace.com) and get the latest Beatnik documentation pack.

Using ActiveMovie to Play Audio

ActiveMovie — although it sounds visually oriented — is Internet Explorer's multimedia player. As such, you can use it to play the standard audio files, including .wav, .midi, .aiff or .au. In fact, when you add an audio file as a link, or embed it without any other specifications, Internet Explorer automatically calls ActiveMovie to play the file. Calling ActiveMovie directly as an ActiveX control, however, gives you far more flexibility over your player's appearance and functionality.

Caution

If you're unfamiliar with ActiveX controls, you might want to look over the "Incorporating an ActiveX control" section of Chapter 15 before proceeding.

Calling the ActiveMovie ActiveX control

To incorporate the ActiveMovie ActiveX control, follow these steps:

1. Position the cursor where you would like the ActiveMovie control panel to appear. Choose Insert ⇨ ActiveX or select Insert ActiveX from the Object Palette.

   The Property Inspector displays the ActiveX options (Figure 19-5).

Figure 19-5: Once you've inserted an ActiveX object, you can select the appropriate Class ID from the drop-down list.

2. In the ClassID text box, enter the ID for the ActiveMovie control: **CLSID:05589FA1-C356-11CE-BF01-00AA0055595A**.

   If you've entered this *long* ActiveMovie Class ID previously, you can click the arrow button and choose the ID from the drop-down list, as shown in Figure 19-5.

3. Change the Width and Height values in the W and H text boxes to match the desired control display.

   The ActiveMovie display resizes to match your dimensions as closely as possible.

   If you want to show both the controls and the timer display, you can use a value of 100 for both width and height dimensions. If you want to just show the control panel, without the timer display, make the height a minimum of 20 pixels.

4. Click Parameters in the Property Inspector.

5. Select the Add (+) button and enter the first parameter: FileName. Press Tab to move to the Value column.

6. Enter the path and filename for your audio file. Press Tab.

7. Continue entering the desired parameters and their values for your audio file.

8. Click OK when you're finished.

Like LiveAudio, the ActiveX ActiveMovie control has many parameters to choose from — 34, to be exact. Explaining all of these parameters is beyond the scope of this book, but Table 19-4 lists the key ones that parallel the LiveAudio attributes.

For more detailed information on using the ActiveMovie ActiveX control, visit Microsoft's Web site DirectX section, at `http://www.microsoft.com/directx/`.

Table 19-4 ActiveMovie Parameters		
ActiveMovie Parameter	**Possible Values**	**Description**
AutoStart	true or false	Determines if the sound begins playing when the download is complete. The default is true.
FileName	Any valid URL	Specifies the sound file to be played.
PlayCount	Any integer	Sets the number of times the file should repeat. If the value is 0, the sound loops continuously. The default is 1.
SelectionStart	Number of seconds	Determines the beginning point for the audio clip, relative to the start of the file.
SelectionEnd	Number of seconds	Determines the ending point for the audio clip, relative to the start of the file.
ShowControls	true or false	Hides the control panel if set to true. The default is false.
ShowDisplay	true or false	Hides the display panel if set to true. The default is false.
Volume	Any integer, from −10000 to 0	Sets the loudness of the audio playback. The default is the highest volume, 0.

On the CD-ROM

To hasten the process of inserting an ActiveX media control, you'll find an ActiveMovie object on the CD-ROM. Just copy the ActiveMovie files from the Dreamweaver\Configuration\Objects\Media folder to your system, and restart Dreamweaver.

Using Embed with ActiveX

All ActiveX controls are included in HTML's `<object>`...`</object>` tag pair. Dreamweaver codes this for you when you insert any ActiveX control. Of course, Netscape doesn't recognize the `<object>` tag, just as Internet Explorer doesn't recognize Netscape's plug-ins. However, you can use a simple technique in Dreamweaver to ensure cross-browser compatibility for ActiveX objects.

After you've entered the `FileName` parameter/value for the ActiveX ActiveMovie control, select the Embed checkbox in the Property Inspector. The same name that you specified as the `FileName` now appears in the Embed text box. Dreamweaver takes advantage of the fact that Netscape doesn't recognize the `<object>` tag by inserting the `<embed>` tag inside the `<object>...</object>` tag pair. The resulting HTML looks like this:

```
<object width= 200  height= 18  classid= CLSID:05589FA1-C356-
11CE-BF01-00AA0055595A  border= 2 >
      <param name= FileName  value= images/Braz.mid >
      <param name= ShowDisplay  value= False >
      <embed width= 200  height= 18  border= 2
filename= images/Braz.mid  showdisplay= False
src= images/Braz.mid ></embed>
      </object>
```

Note that Dreamweaver picks up the attributes and parameters from the ActiveX control to use in the `<embed>` tag. Often you'll have to adjust these, especially when specifying a narrow ActiveX control and a taller Netscape object.

Playing Background Music

Background music, played while the user is viewing online material, is one of the Web's hidden treasures. When used tastefully, background music can enhance the overall impact of the page. Two methods are necessary to cover the major browsers in use: the `<bgsound>` tag for Internet Explorer, and a hidden `<embed>` tag for Netscape. You can use both without fear of conflict.

For Internet Explorer: <bgsound>

Microsoft uses a proprietary HTML command to implement background sound, `<bgsound>`. The `<bgsound>` tag must be coded by hand or through a custom object in Dreamweaver. The background sound command takes the following attributes:

<bgsound> Attribute	Description
src	Sets the URL of the background sound to be played.
loop	Determines the number of times that a file repeats. You can set the value to any integer. To cause the audio clip to repeat continually, make loop=infinite or loop=-1.

The complete HTML for a continuously looping background sound looks like this:

```
<bgsound src= sounds/bgtrack1  loop=infinite>
```

As noted earlier, the `<bgsound>` tag is ignored by all browsers except Internet Explorer.

For other browsers: Hidden <embed>

To make sure your background sound is heard by Netscape and other browsers besides Internet Explorer, use a hidden `<embed>` tag. You embed a background sound as described in the earlier section, "Basic audio embedding." All you need do, once the sound is embedded, is to add the necessary parameters, and you have instant background music.

Follow these steps to embed background music in a Web page to be viewed in browsers other than Internet Explorer:

1. Position the cursor near the top of your Web page. Choose Insert ⇨ Plug-in or select the Plug-in object from the Object Palette.

2. Enter the path to your audio file in the Plug-in Source text box, or select Browse to locate the file.

3. In the Property Inspector, enter a **2** in both the H (Height) and W (Width) text boxes.

4. Click Parameters.

5. In the Parameters dialog box, select the Add (+) button and enter `hidden` in the Parameter column. Press Tab and enter `true` in the Value column.

6. Enter `autostart` as the next parameter and give it the value `true`.

7. To make the audio clip repeat, enter `loop` as the next parameter, and in the Value column enter the number of times you want the sound to repeat. To make the audio repeat endlessly (or until the user goes to another Web page), enter `true` as the value.

8. Click OK when you're finished.

Dreamweaver automatically adds the necessary parameters, such as `hidden` and `autostart`, to hide and automatically play the file.

Caution   To preserve backward-compatibility with earlier Netscape versions, it's important to enter a small value in the Height and Width text boxes for the background music object, even though the control is hidden.

Installing Streaming Audio

Although audio files are not as time-consuming as video, downloading them can take a long time. Audio-on-demand — or *streaming audio* — has emerged as an alternative to such lengthy downloads. The recognized leader in the streaming audio field is RealAudio, a format developed by RealNetworks (www.real.com).

Streaming audio files work much the same as streaming video files, as covered in Chapter 18, "Adding Video to Your Web Page." Both these streaming formats use metafiles to call the actual media files. For details on creating metafiles, see the "Creating RealVideo metafiles" section in Chapter 18.

As with RealVideo, you can either have the RealAudio player appear to be free-floating or embedded in the Web page. To insert a RealAudio streaming audio file with a free-floating player, follow these steps:

1. Select the link or image that you want to use to begin the RealAudio file.

2. In the Property Inspector, enter the path to the RealAudio metafile in the Link text box or select Browse to locate the file.

Make sure that the metafile has the .ram extension.

To embed a RealAudio streaming audio file in your Web page, follow these steps:

1. Position the pointer where you want the RealAudio player to be displayed. Either choose Insert ➪ Plug-in or select Insert Plug-in from the Object Palette.

2. From the Property Inspector, enter the path and filename for the video's metafile in the Plug-in Source text box.

3. Enter the width and height values in the W and H text boxes, respectively.

4. To specify additional attributes, click Parameters and enter the parameters with their values.

5. Click OK when you're done.

Only the source of the player and the dimensions are required, but it will come as no surprise to you that a great number of attributes are available for a RealAudio file. See Table 19-5.

	Table 19-5 RealAudio Parameters	
RealAudio Attributes	**Possible Values**	**Description**
autostart	true or false	Enables the RealVideo clip to start playing as soon as content is available. The default is autostart=true.
console	_master or _unique	Determines the console name for each control in a Web page that uses multiple controls. To force controls on a page to refer to the same file, use the same console=name attribute. The console name _master links to all controls on a page; _unique connects to no other instances.
controls	all, controlpanel, infovolumepanel, infopanel, statuspanel, statusbar, playbutton, stopbutton, volumeslider, positionslider, positionfield, or statusfield	Enables the placement of individual control panel elements in the Web page. You can use multiple controls in one attribute, or multiple <embed> tags to build a custom RealAudio interface.
nolabels	true or false	Suppresses the Title, Author, and Copyright labels in the Status panel. If you set nolabels to true, the actual data is still visible. The default is nolabels=false.

Summary

Adding sound to a Web page indeed brings it into the realm of multimedia. Dreamweaver gives you numerous methods to handle the various different audio formats, both static and streaming. With custom Dreamweaver objects and actions, enhancing your Web site with audio is, quite literally, a snap.

✦ Audio must be digitized before it can be sent over the Web. The leading audio file formats are .wav, .au, .aiff, .rmf, and .midi (for sound that must be downloaded before it can be played).

✦ You can either link to a sound or embed it in your Web page. With standard audio, the linking technique calls an independent, free-floating player, and the embedding technique incorporates the player into the design of the page.

✦ Plug-ins offer far greater control over the appearance and functionality of the sound than relying on common players; to use a plug-in, however, your user must download it.

✦ The Beatnik plug-in provides excellent fidelity and JavaScript interaction.

✦ You can include a background sound for both major browsers by using two separate but compatible techniques.

✦ Streaming audio gives almost instant access to large audio files; RealAudio is the recognized standard in the field.

In the next chapter you'll learn how to incorporate Shockwave Director and Flash multimedia elements in your Dreamweaver Web pages.

✦   ✦   ✦

Inserting Shockwave Movies

To the mind of many Web designers, Shockwave has represented the state-of-the-art in Internet multimedia since Macromedia first released the compression scheme in 1995. With Shockwave, multimedia files created in Macromedia's flagship authoring package, Director, could be compiled to run in a browser window. This gave Web designers the ability to build just about anything — from interactive Web interfaces with buttons that look indented and clicked when pushed, to arcade-style games, multimedia Web front-ends, and complete Web sites built entirely in Director — bringing a CD-ROM "look and feel" to the Web.

Macromedia's strategy was to enable the output of *all* of its products to the Web. Soon Web sites sported "Shocked" real-time scalable maps and diagrams from Freehand (a vector graphics package), and tutorials from Authorware (an instructional design package). In short order, a vector-based animation package called Future Splash was acquired as a source of Shocked animations for Web pages, and repackaged as Macromedia Flash. Today the company offers options for streamed animation, audio, and multimedia, as well.

As you might expect, Macromedia carefully paved the way for Shockwave Director and Flash files to be incorporated into Dreamweaver. Both of these formats have special objects that provide control over virtually all of their parameters through the Property Inspector — and each format is cross-browser-compatible by default. To take full advantage of Shockwave's multimedia capabilities, you need to understand the differences between Director and Flash as well as the various parameters available to each format. In addition to covering this material, this chapter also shows you how to use independent controls — both inline and with frames — for your Shockwave Director and Shockwave Flash movies.

Shockwave Director and Shockwave Flash: What's the Difference?

Because both Director and Flash movies can be "shocked" and saved as Shockwave files, how do you choose which program to use? Each has its own special functions, and each excels at producing particular types of effects. Director is more full-featured, with a complete programming language (Lingo). And, with the help of a Macromedia Xtra, Director movies can include Flash animations. Director also has a much steeper learning curve than does Flash. Flash is terrific for short, low-bandwidth animations with or without a synchronized audio track; however, the interactive capabilities in Flash are limited.

Director is really a multimedia production program used for combining various elements: backgrounds, foreground elements called *sprites*, and various media such as digital audio and video. With Director's Lingo programming language, you can build extraordinarily elaborate demos and games — you can even use an extension called *NetLingo* with Internet-specific commands. When you need to include a high degree of interactivity, build your movie with Shockwave Director.

One of the primary differences between Director and Flash is the supported graphic formats. Director is better for *bitmap graphics*, in which each pixel is mapped to a specific color; both GIF and JPEG formats use bitmap graphics. Flash, on the other hand, uses primarily *vector graphics*, which are drawing elements described mathematically. Because vector graphics use a description of a drawing — a blue circle with a radius of 2.5 centimeters, for instance — rather than a bitmap, the resulting files are much smaller. An animation included with Flash might be only 40K — however, a comparable QuickTime movie (for which the vector graphics are converted to bitmap graphics) would be over ten times larger at 430K.

Aside from file size, the other feature that distinguishes vector from bitmap graphics is the smoothness of the line. When viewed with sufficient magnification, bitmap graphics always display tell-tale "stair-steps" or "jaggies," especially around curves. Vector graphics, on the other hand, are almost smooth. In fact, Shockwave Flash takes special advantage of this characteristic and enables users to zoom into any movie — an important effect that saves a lot of bandwidth when used correctly.

Director can, with the assistance of a plug-in called the Flash Xtra, show vector graphics, but Flash needs to convert bitmaps to vectors before it can display them. Luckily, the new version, Flash 2, has enhanced bitmap capabilities so that the conversions are quite workable.

Flash animations can be used as special effects, cartoons, and navigation bars within (or without) frames. Although Flash isn't the best choice for games and other complex interactive elements, you can use Flash to animate your navigation system — complete with sound effects for button-pushing feedback.

The AfterShock Utility

To play Director's and Flash's Shockwave files, a plug-in or an ActiveX control is required. If a user doesn't have the necessary plug-in or control, one will have to be downloaded and installed before the user can view your Shockwave page. Macromedia does, however, offer a plug-in-less alternative: the AfterShock utility.

AfterShock enables Flash movies to be converted to Java applets, which can be played through any browser that supports Java without a plug-in. It's even possible to build your Shockwave Flash Web pages so that they gracefully "degrade," depending on the user's system. If the user has the Flash plug-in, play the regular Flash movie; if the user doesn't have the plug-in but is Java-enabled, show the Java version; if neither the plug-in nor Java is available, show the Flash movie in an animated GIF format. For more information about using this utility, visit the AfterShock support center on Macromedia's Web site at the following URL:

`http://www.macromedia.com/support/flash/how/subjects/aftershock/`

Including Shockwave Movies in Dreamweaver Projects

Dreamweaver makes it easy to bring Shockwave Director and Shockwave Flash files into your Web pages. The Object Palette provides an object for both types of movie, located in the Common panel. As with other elements requiring plug-ins or ActiveX controls, Dreamweaver does not display the movie or a frame of the movie in the Document Window, but shows a plug-in placeholder icon instead (see Figure 20-1).

Before you can successfully include a Shockwave file, you need to know one small bit of information — the dimensions of your movie. Almost all the other parameters are selectable right from the Property Inspector. Here's how to check the width and height of your movie:

✦ In Director, load your file and then choose Modify ➪ Movie ➪ Properties to open the Movie Properties dialog box.

✦ In Flash, open the file in question and choose Modify ➪ Movie to view the Movie Properties dialog box.

Tip   It is essential to have the movie's height and width before you can include it successfully in Dreamweaver-built Web pages. During the development phase of a Dreamweaver project, I often include the movie dimensions in a filename, as an instant reminder to take care of this detail. For example, if I'm working with two different Flash movies, I can give them names like navbar125x241.swf and navbar400x50.swf. (The .swf extension is automatically appended by Flash when you save a movie as a Shockwave file.) By consistently putting width before height in the filename, this trick saves me the time it would take to reopen Flash, load the movie, and go Modify ➪ Movie to check the measurements in the Movie Properties dialog box.

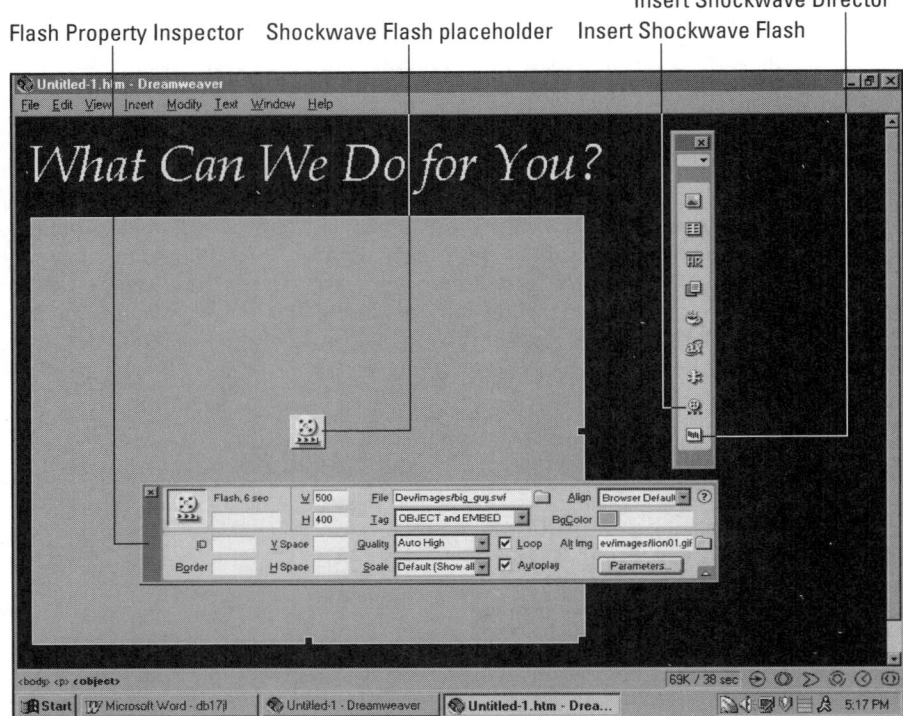

Flash Property Inspector   Shockwave Flash placeholder   Insert Shockwave Flash
Insert Shockwave Director

Figure 20-1: Lay out your Flash or Director Shockwave movie and preview it in any compatible browser.

To include either a Shockwave Director or Shockwave Flash file in your Web page, follow these steps:

1. Position the cursor in the Document Window at the point where you'd like the movie to appear.

2. Insert the movie by any of these methods:

    • Choose Insert ➪ Shockwave Director or Insert ➪ Shockwave Flash from the menus.

    • In the Common panel of the Object Palette, select either the Insert Shockwave Director or Insert Shockwave Flash button.

    • Drag the movie object from the Object Palette to any location in the Document Window.

3. In the Insert Shockwave Director or Insert Flash Movie dialog box enter the path and the filename in the Movie Source text box or select the Browse button to locate the file. Click OK.

   Dreamweaver inserts a small plug-in placeholder in the current cursor position, and the Property Inspector displays the appropriate information for Shockwave Director or Shockwave Flash.

As noted earlier, you must specify the dimensions of your file in the Property Inspector before you can preview the movie in a browser. Although they produce basically the same kind of file, Shockwave Director and Shockwave Flash have some different features in the Dreamweaver Property Inspector. These differences are covered separately in the following sections.

Specifying Shockwave Director properties

Once you've inserted your Shockwave Director file, you're ready to begin entering the specific parameters in the Property Inspector. The Property Inspector takes care of all but one Shockwave Director attribute, the `palette` parameter. Some of the information, including the ActiveX Class ID, is automatically set in the Property Inspector when you insert the movie.

To set or modify the parameters for a Shockwave Director file, follow these steps:

1. Select the Shockwave Director placeholder icon.

2. In the Shockwave Director Property Inspector, enter the width and the height values in the W and H text boxes, respectively, as shown in Figure 20-2. Or you can click and drag any of the three resizing handles on the placeholder icon. *Note:* Pressing the Shift key while dragging the corner resizing handle maintains the current aspect ratio, a square.

3. To designate how the Shockwave Director HTML code is written, select one of these three options from the Tag drop-down list:

Tag Option	Result
OBJECT and EMBED	This is the default choice and ensures that code is written for both Internet Explorer and Netscape Navigator/Communicator. Use this option unless your page is on an intranet where only one browser is used.
OBJECT only	Select this option to enable your movie to be viewed by Internet Explorer-compatible browsers.
EMBED only	Select this option to enable your movie to be viewed by Navigator/Communicator-compatible browsers.

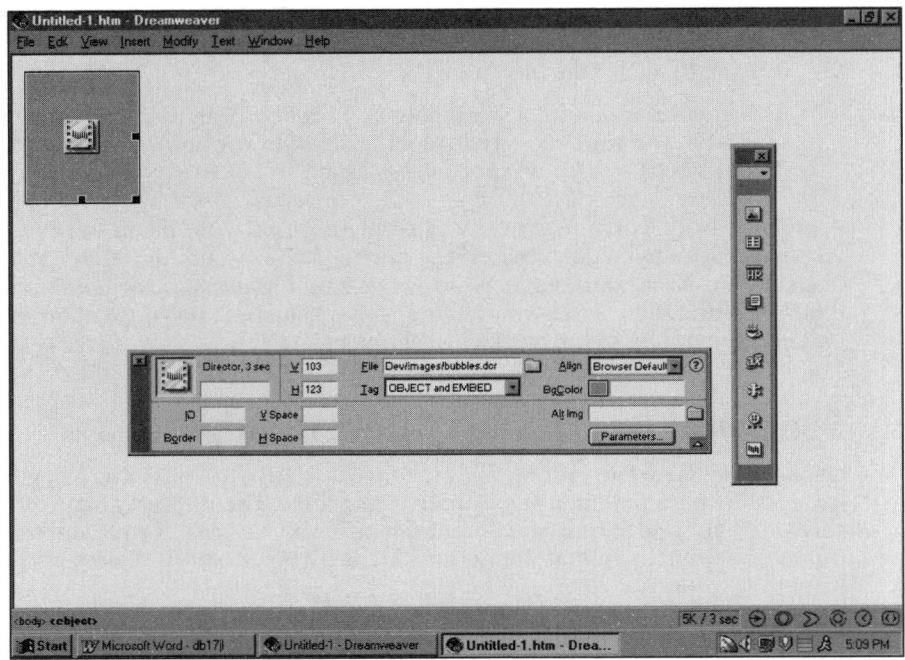

Figure 20-2: Modify parameters for a Shockwave Director property through the Property Inspector.

4. Set and modify other object attributes as needed; see Table 20-1 for a list.

Table 20-1
Property Inspector Options for Shockwave Director Objects

Shockwave Director Property	Description
Align	Choose an option to alter the alignment of the movie. In addition to the Browser Default, your options include Baseline, Top, Middle, Bottom, Texttop, Absolute Middle, Absolute Bottom, Left, and Right.
Alt Image	The Alt Image file is displayed to users who do not have the appropriate plug-in installed. This image does not display in Dreamweaver. Enter the path to the alternate image, or select the folder icon to open a Select Image Source dialog box.

Shockwave Director Property	Description
BgColor	The background color only is visible if the width and height of the plug-in are larger than the movie. To alter the background color of your plug-in, choose the color swatch and select a new color from the pop-up menu; or enter a valid color name in the BgColor text box.
Border	To place a border around your movie, enter a number in the Border text box. The number determines the width of the border in pixels. The default is zero or no border.
H Space	You can increase the space to the left and right of the movie by entering a value in the H (Horizontal) Space text box. The default is zero.
ID	The ID field is used to define the optional ActiveX ID parameter, most often used to pass data between ActiveX controls.
(Name)	If desired, you can enter a unique name in this unlabeled field on the far left of the Property Inspector. The name is used by JavaScript and other languages to identify the movie.
V Space	To increase the amount of space between other elements on the page, and the top and bottom of the movie plug-in, enter a pixel value in the V (Vertical) Space text box. Again, the default is zero.

Additional parameters for Shockwave Director

As with other plug-ins, you can pass other attributes to the Shockwave Director movie via the Parameters dialog box — available by clicking the Parameters button on the Property Inspector. Press the Add (+) button to begin inserting additional parameters. Enter the attributes in the left column and their respective values in the right. To remove an attribute, highlight it and select the Delete (–) button.

Automatic settings for Shockwave files

When you insert a Shockwave Director or Shockwave Flash file, Dreamweaver writes a number of parameters that are constant and necessary. In the <object> portion of the code, Dreamweaver includes the ActiveX Class ID number as well as the codebase number; the former calls the specific ActiveX control, and the latter enables users who don't have the control installed to receive it automatically. Likewise, in the <embed> section, Dreamweaver fills in the pluginspage attribute, designating the location where Navigator users can find the necessary plug-in. Be sure you don't accidentally remove any of this information — however, if you should, all you have to do is delete and reinsert the object.

The palette parameter

Only one other general attribute is usually assigned to a Shockwave Director file, the `palette` parameter. This parameter takes a value of either `foreground` or `background`.

✦ If `palette` is set to `background`, the movie's color scheme does not override that of the system; this is the default.

✦ When `palette` is set to `foreground`, then the colors of the selected movie are applied to the user's system — which includes the desktop, scroll bars, and so forth.

Note that `palette` is not supported by Internet Explorer.

Caution Web designers should take care when specifying the `palette=foreground` parameter. This effect is likely to prove startling to the user; moreover, if your color scheme is sufficiently different, the change may render the user's system unusable. If you do use the `palette` parameter, be sure to include a Director command to restore the original system color scheme in the final frame of the movie.

Designating Shockwave Flash attributes

Shockwave Flash movies require the same basic parameters as their Director counterparts — and Flash movies have a few additional optional ones, as well. As it does for Shockwave Director files, Dreamweaver sets almost all the attributes for Shockwave Flash movies through the Property Inspector. The major difference you'll notice is that several more parameters are available than for Shockwave Director.

To set or modify the attributes for a Shockwave Flash file, follow these steps:

1. After your Shockwave Flash movie has been inserted in the Document Window, make sure it's selected. Then insert the width and height dimensions in the W and H text boxes of the Property Inspector.

2. Set the other attributes in the Property Inspector, as needed for your Flash movie. (Refer to the previous descriptions of these attributes in the "Specifying Shockwave Director parameters" section.) In addition, you can also set the parameters described in Table 20-2.

Table 20-2
Property Inspector Options for Shockwave Flash Objects

Shockwave Flash Parameter	Possible Values	Description
Autoplay	Checked (default) or unchecked	Enables the Shockwave Flash movie to begin playing as soon as it has completely downloaded or, if streaming, as soon as enough has loaded.
Loop	Checked (default) or unchecked	If Loop is checked, the movie plays continuously; if unchecked, the movie plays once.
Quality:		Controls anti-aliasing during playback.
	High	Anti-aliasing is turned on.
	Low	No anti-aliasing is used; this setting is best for animations that must be played quickly.
	AutoHigh (default)	The animation begins in high quality (with anti-aliasing) and switches to normal if the host computer is too slow.
	AutoLow	Starts the animation in normal quality (no anti-aliasing) and then switches to high quality if the host machine is fast enough.
Scale:		Scale determines how the movie fits into the dimensions as specified in the width and height text boxes.
	ShowAll (default)	Displays the entire movie in the given dimensions while maintaining the file's original aspect ratio. Some of the background may be visible with this setting.
	ExactFit	Scales the movie precisely into the dimensions without regard for the aspect ratio. It is possible that the image could be distorted with this setting.
	NoBorder	Fits the movie into the given dimensions so that no borders are showing, and maintains the original aspect ratio. Some of the movie may be cut off with this setting.

Setting the scale in Shockwave Flash movies

Be careful with your setting for the Scale parameter. It is important that you supply the exact dimensions of your Shockwave Flash movie. Take a look at Figure 20-3 and notice the comments below each of the four examples. The example in the lower-right corner of this figure is the only one with the exact measurements and the only one that is displayed properly.

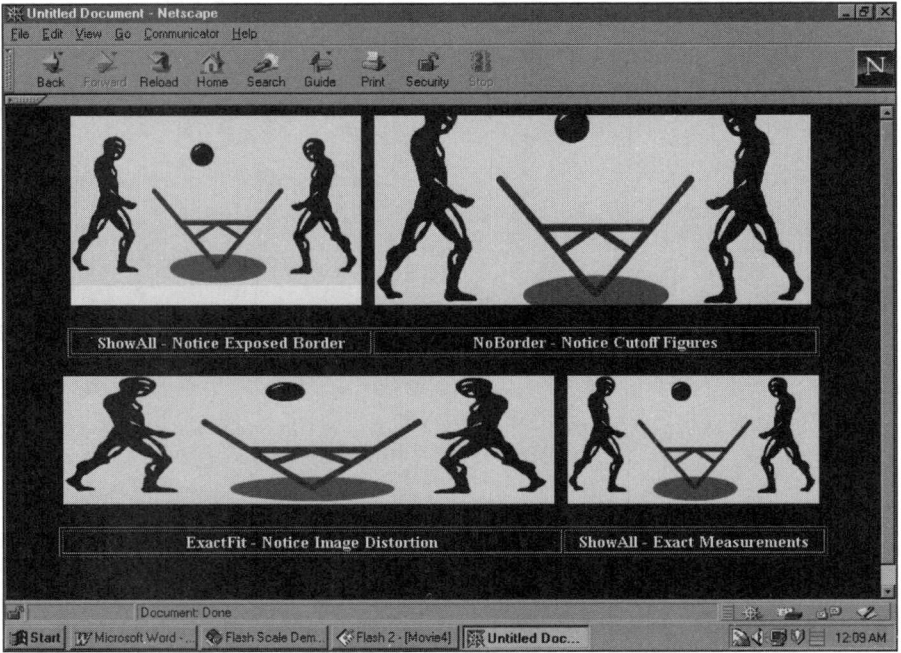

Figure 20-3: Your setting for the Scale attribute determines how your movie is resized within the plug-in width and height measurements.

Tip

Dreamweaver 1.2 makes it easy to rescale a Shockwave Flash movie. First, from the Property Inspector, enter the precise width and height of your file in the W and H text boxes. Then, while holding the Shift key, click and drag the corner resizing handle of the Shockwave Flash placeholder icon to the new size for the movie. By Shift-dragging, you retain the aspect ratio set in the Property Inspector. This lets you quickly enlarge or reduce your movie without distortion.

Additional parameters for Shockwave Director

Shockwave Flash has one additional attribute that can be entered through the Parameters dialog box (click the Parameters button on the Property Inspector). The `salign` attribute determines how the movie aligns itself to the surrounding frame when the Scale attribute is set to ShowAll. In addition, `salign` determines which portion of the image gets cut off when the Scale attribute is set to NoBorder. The alignment can be set to L (left), R (right), T (top), or B (bottom). You can also use these values in combination. For example, if you set `salign=RB`, the movie aligns with the right-bottom edge or the lower-right corner of the frame.

Configuring MIME Types

As with any plug-in, your Web server has to have the correct MIME types set before Shockwave files can be properly served to your users. If your Web page plays Shockwave Director and Flash movies locally, but not remotely, chances are the correct MIME types need to be added. Configuring MIME types is generally handled by the system administrator.

The system administrator needs to know the following information in order to correctly configure the MIME types:

Application	MIME Type	File Extension
Shockwave Director	application/x-director	*.dcr, *.dir, *.dxr
Shockwave Flash	application/x-shockwave-flash	*.swf

Shockwave is a very popular plug-in, and it's likely that the Web server is already configured to recognize the appropriate file types. Use of Flash, especially in its new version, is not as widespread, however.

Tip

Movies made by an earlier version of Flash, called FutureSplash, can also be played by the Flash plug-in — but only if the correct MIME type is added: application/futuresplash with the file extension, *.spl.

Providing User Interaction with Shockwave Movies

What happens once you've installed your Director or Flash Shockwave files? Many movies are set to play automatically or upon some action from the user, such as a mouse click on a particular hotspot within the movie. The Show Me movies used in the Dreamweaver Help Pages are good examples of the kind of interactivity that can be programmed within a Director Shockwave movie. But what if you want the user to be able to start or stop a movie in one part of the page, using controls in another part? How can controls in one frame affect a movie in a different frame?

Dreamweaver includes a Control Shockwave behavior that makes inline controls — controls on the same Web page as the movie — very easy to set up. However, establishing frame-to-frame control is slightly more complex in Dreamweaver 1.2 and requires a minor modification to the program-generated code. You'll find all you need to know in this section, for using both techniques.

Cross-Reference

Both of the following step-by-step techniques rely on Dreamweaver behaviors. If you're unfamiliar with using behaviors, you will want to review Chapter 17, "Creating and Using Behaviors" before proceeding.

Dreamweaver Technique: Creating Inline Shockwave Controls

Certainly it's perfectly acceptable to make your Director or Flash movies with built-in controls for interactivity, but sometimes you'll want to separate the controls from the movie. Dreamweaver includes a JavaScript behavior called Control Shockwave. With this behavior, you can set up external controls to start, stop, and rewind Shockwave Director and Shockwave Flash movies.

Creating Inline Shockwave Controls

1. Insert your Shockwave file by choosing either the Insert Shockwave Director or Insert Shockwave Flash button from the Object Palette.

2. From the Insert Shockwave dialog box, enter the path to your file in the Movie Source text box, or select the folder icon to locate your file using the Select File dialog box.

3. In the Property Inspector, enter the width and height of your movie in the W and H text boxes, respectively.

4. Enter a unique name for your movie in the text box provided.

5. If you are inserting a Shockwave Flash movie, deselect the Autoplay and Loop options.

6. To insert the first control, position the cursor where you'd like the control to appear on the page.

7. Select Insert Image from the Object Palette.

8. In the Link box of the Property Inspector, enter a dummy link or just a hash symbol, #, to create an empty target.

9. Open the Behavior Inspector by selecting the Behavior button from the Launcher or by pressing F8.

10. If necessary, change the selected browser to 4.0 Browsers; you can do this by opening the drop-down list in the Events pane.

11. Select the + (Add) Event button, and choose onClick from the drop-down list of events. The onClick event is displayed in the Events pane.

12. In the Action pane, select the + (Add) Action button and choose Control Shockwave from the drop-down list.

13. In the Control Shockwave dialog box (see Figure 20-4), select the movie you want to affect from the Named Shockwave Object drop-down list.

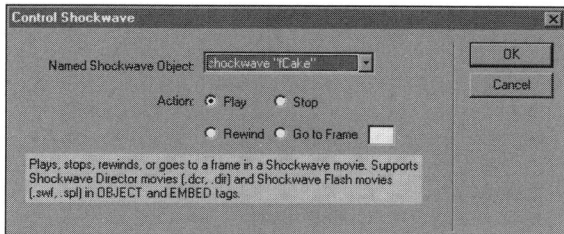

Figure 20-4: In the Control Shockwave dialog box, you assign a control action to an image button or link.

14. Now select the desired action for your control. Choose from the four options: Play, Stop, Rewind, and Go to Frame. If you choose the Go to Frame option, enter a frame number in the text box.

15. Click OK to close the Control Shockwave dialog box.

16. Repeat steps 6–15 for each movie control you'd like to add. Figure 20-5 shows a sample Web page with three different controls in various places on the page.

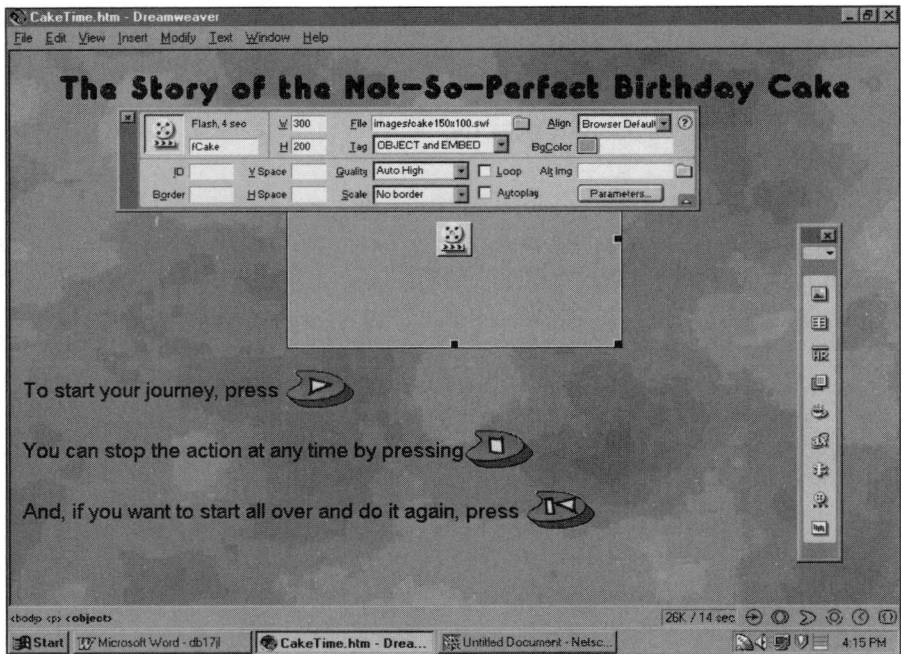

Figure 20-5: This Web page contains three controls — Play, Stop, and Rewind — inserted via the inline Control Shockwave technique.

Dreamweaver Technique: Playing Shockwave Movies in Frames

Framesets and frames are great for Web sites in which you want your navigation and other controls kept in one place, in one frame, and the freedom to vary the content in another frame. It's entirely possible to set up your movie's playback buttons in one frame and the Shockwave movie in another. The method and the tools used are very similar to those used in the preceding technique for adding same-page controls to a Shockwave movie. For this technique using frames, some HTML hand-coding is necessary, but it is relatively minor — only one additional line per control!

As you saw in the previous section, Dreamweaver's Control Shockwave behavior lists all the Shockwave movies, both Flash and Director, on the Web page and lets you choose the one you want to affect (see Figure 20-4). Unfortunately, the behavior as currently constructed only looks on one page and not through an entire frameset. However, with a little sleight-of-hand and a bit of JavaScript, we can get the effect we want.

Tip

Before you begin applying this technique, you should have constructed (and saved) your frameset and individual frames. Be sure to name each frame uniquely, because you'll have to provide the names in order to address the correct frames.

Placing Shockwave Controls in Frames

1. In one frame, insert the images or links that are going to act as the Shockwave controls. (For this demonstration, the control frame is named `frControl`.)

2. In another frame, insert the Shockwave file (either Shockwave Director or Shockwave Flash) by choosing the appropriate object from the Object Palette. (For this demonstration, the movie frame is named `frMovie`.) In Figure 20-6, `frControl` is on the left of the page, and `frMovie` is on the right.

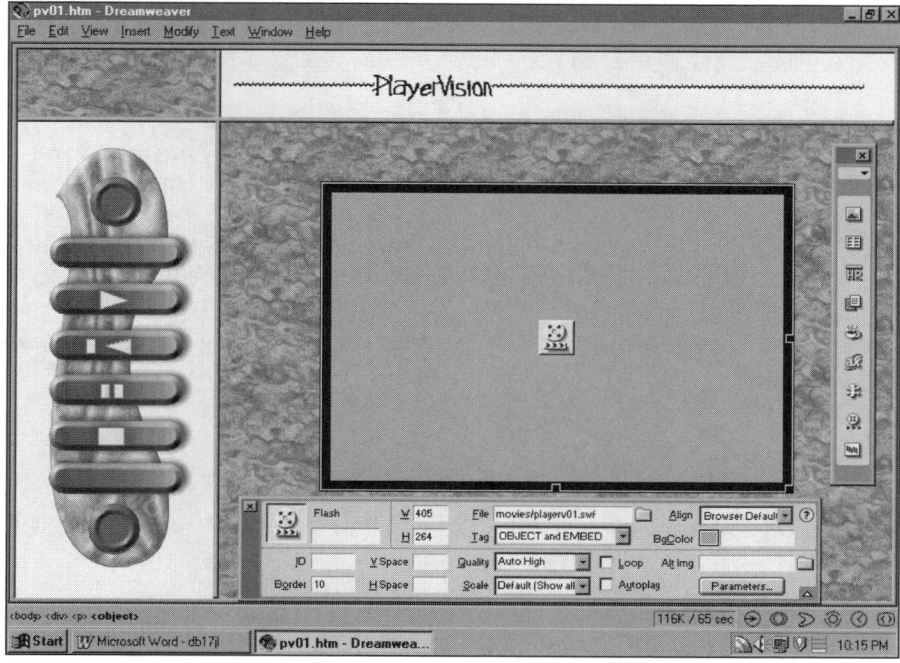

Figure 20-6: With some minor code modification, you can control your Shockwave movies from a different frame.

(continued)

3. Be sure to modify the Shockwave Property Inspector with the necessary parameters: name, width, height, and source; and, if you're inserting a Shockwave Flash file, deselect the Autoplay and Loop check boxes.

4. Copy the Shockwave placeholder by selecting it and choosing Edit ➪ Copy.

5. Position the cursor in the frControl frame, and paste the placeholder in a temporary position by choosing Edit ➪ Paste. At this point, the placement for the placeholder is not critical, as long as it is in the same frame as the images or links your are going to use as controls. The placeholder will be deleted shortly.

Instead of using the Copy and Paste commands, you can hold down Ctrl (Command), and click and drag the placeholder to its new temporary position.

6. Now select the first image or link you want to use as a control. As described in the preceding technique, attach the Control Shockwave behavior to the selected object. As you learned in the preceding exercise, this entails the following actions:

- With the image or link selected, open the Behavior Inspector.

- Add the onClick event.

- Add the Control Shockwave action.

- In the Control Shockwave dialog box, specify the movie and select the required action (Play, Rewind, Stop, or Go to Frame).

7. The major work is finished now. All we still need to do is add a little HTML. Open the HTML Inspector or use your favorite external editor to edit the file.

8. Locate the image or link controls in the code. Each JavaScript routine is called from within an <a> tag and will read something like the following, where fMovie is the name of our Shockwave Flash movie:

```
<a href= #  onClick= MM_controlShockwave( document.fMovie ,
 document.fMovie , Play ) >
```

9. Wherever you see the JavaScript reference to document, change it to

```
parent.frameName.document
```

where frameName is the unique name you gave to the frame in which your movie appears. In our example, frameName is frMovie; So, after the replacement is made the tag reads as follows:

```
<a href= #  onClick= MM_controlShockwave( parent.frMovie.
document.fMovie , document.fMovie , Play ) >
```

By making this substitution, you've pointed the JavaScript function first to the "parent" of the current document — and the parent of a frame is the entire frameset. Now that we're looking at the entire frameset, the next word (which is the unique frame name) points the JavaScript function directly to the desired frame within the frameset.

10. After you've made the alterations to all of your controls, close the HTML Inspector or external editor.

11. Finally, delete the temporary Shockwave movie that was inserted into the frame containing the controls.

Test the frameset by pressing F12 (primary browser) or Shift-F12 (secondary browser). If you haven't changed the Property Inspector's default Tag attribute (the default is OBJECT and EMBED), the Shockwave movie should work in both Netscape Navigator and Internet Explorer.

Summary

Shockwave makes a strong case for being the king of all multimedia. Together, the interactive power of Shockwave Director and the speedy glitz of Shockwave Flash can enliven a Web page's content like nothing else. Dreamweaver is extremely well-suited for integrating and displaying Shockwave movies.

✦ Shockwave is a compression/playback system developed by Macromedia. Both Director and Flash enable creations called movies to be exported into the Shockwave format. Shockwave movies are played on the Web with the help of a plug-in or ActiveX control.

✦ Dreamweaver has built-in objects for both Director and Flash versions of Shockwave files. All the important parameters are accessible directly through the Property Inspector.

✦ You only need three parameters to incorporate a Shockwave movie: the file's location, its height, and its width. You can get the exact measurements of a Shockwave movie in either Director or Flash.

✦ Dreamweaver comes with a JavaScript behavior for controlling Shockwave movies. This Control Shockwave behavior can be used as-is for adding external controls to the same Web page or — with a minor modification — for adding the controls to another frame in the same frameset.

In the next chapter you'll begin to learn about Dynamic HTML.

✦　　✦　　✦

Dynamic HTML and Dreamweaver

What's Dynamic HTML?

◆ ◆ ◆ ◆

In This Chapter

Dynamic HTML
fundamentals

Using the DHTML
features of Navigator

Applying DHTML
techniques in Internet
Explorer

◆ ◆ ◆ ◆

Dynamic HTML sounds like an ad slogan for the latest technology, doesn't it? In this case, the word *dynamic* refers to the capability to change, evolve, grow, shift, and otherwise metamorphose into a different state. With Dynamic HTML (or DHTML), almost everything on the heretofore static Web page can change. Moreover, these dynamic transitions are not generated from the server side of the Internet, but inherent in the programming language itself.

Depending on the implementation, Dynamic HTML allows an amazing range of effects to take place:

- ✦ Objects fly in from all corners of the screen and assemble into a coherent, integrated portion of the page.
- ✦ Text and logos suddenly materialize and instantly disappear from the screen.
- ✦ Web pages aren't two-dimensional — now objects can be in front of or behind other objects.
- ✦ Outlines expand to reveal details, and collapse to provide an overview; content changes with the interactive click of a button.
- ✦ The design on the Web appears as it was designed off the Web; designers can make their Web layouts appear just the way they want, without complicated tables or single-pixel spacers.
- ✦ Tables are automatically generated according to the data returned from a query, and then updated globally with input from the user.

These capabilities barely scratch the surface of the Dynamic HTML possibilities. With Dreamweaver's advanced interface, challenging and code-intensive projects become intuitively achievable. Dreamweaver is among the first Web authoring tools to take full advantage of Dynamic HTML capabilities.

With its history of open standards and competing commercial visions, however, the Web doesn't yet have a smooth road with Dynamic HTML. In theory, both Netscape and Microsoft have fully embraced DHTML, but the reality is that both companies have adopted divergent models of the standard. Dreamweaver rises above the fray and makes cross-browser Dynamic HTML really work — with little or no assistance from the Web designer.

This chapter has a dual purpose. First and foremost, it introduces you to the concepts of DHTML and provides an overview of the current state of implementation in the two primary browsers. Second, it examines the browser-specific Dynamic HTML features and shows how to employ them in Dreamweaver.

Tip

For a taste of the possibilities with Dynamic HTML, visit Macromedia's Dynamic HTML Zone at `www.dhtmlzone.com` and select the Tutorials option. Once you're in the tutorial screen, click the Launch Superfly button. This demo not only shows the excitement Dynamic HTML can generate, but also acts as an excellent tutorial. (While you're in the Dynamic HTML Zone, be sure to also check out the Spotlight sites for further demonstrations.)

Fundamentals of Dynamic HTML

What makes Dynamic HTML so, well... dynamic? No single factor can take all the credit. Rather, DHTML is really a combination of new technologies that are coming to be regarded as the next generation of Web development. In this section, you examine the roles of the components that make up DHTML:

✦ Cascading Style Sheets: CSS gives the Web designer control over the characteristics of any text group, whether designated by a standard or custom HTML tag.

✦ Absolute positioning: This feature allows pixel-precise placement of any Web object.

✦ Dynamic content: The Web page can have content added or deleted on the fly.

✦ Downloadable fonts: Web designers can embed specific fonts to control a Web page's typography.

✦ Data binding: Server-side data is linked to a table or form on a Web page, which can dynamically update without redrawing the entire page.

Not all of this functionality is cross-browser, but all these features are possible in one configuration or another. As a whole, Dynamic HTML brings a more responsive, media-rich Web environment to the Web designer's palette that more closely resembles multimedia CD-ROM productions, while still maintaining the unique hyperconnectivity of the Internet. Best of all, Dynamic HTML is far more internalized than earlier HTML implementations, relying less on helper applications and plug-ins to achieve its state-of-the-art effects.

Cascading Style Sheets

As sanctioned by the HTML-governing body, the World Wide Web Consortium (W3C), the Cascading Style Sheet (CSS) specification is at the core of DHTML. CSS was the first step toward making traditional HTML more flexible and malleable. In a nutshell, CSS enables a Web designer to specify the attributes of an HTML tag — whether in a single page or through an entire site — with one command.

Take the `<h1>` tag, for instance. Does management want all headlines across the company's Web site during July to be Helvetica 24-point and blue-green? CSS can handle this request in one line:

```
h1 {  font: 24pt Helvetica; color: green}
```

If you're a print-oriented layout artist who has been trying to adjust to HTML, you'll appreciate not only the flexibility and control of Cascading Style Sheets, but also their implementation. CSS uses the well-established language of print designers. Fonts, for example, can be sized in points or picas instead of with relative sizes 1–6.

The Cascading Style Sheets technology not only affects the standard attributes of HTML tags, but also extends the number and variety of properties that can be modified. For instance, CSS now enables Web designers to specify the line height of any given tag, whether to make a paragraph of text double-spaced, or to tighten the leading (line-spacing) for subheads. CSS offers entire categories of new elements, such as boxes, that can be added to the designer's palette and the Web page. Moreover, CSS power is not limited to existing standard tags — you can create custom styles and assign them special characteristics. For instance, a large organization may define a "legal" style to be used in disclaimers and other fine print.

The important aspect of CSS from the standpoint of DHTML is that CSS begins to control the elements on the page in a systematic fashion. In the fullest implementation of CSS, scripting languages such as JavaScript can address any declared style and modify its properties interactively.

 **Cross-Reference** Dreamweaver uses an intuitive interface for working with CSS. To learn more about this topic, see Chapter 22, "Building Style Sheet Web Pages."

Absolute positioning

From a print designer's viewpoint, perhaps the single most aggravating circumstance of working on the Web has been the inability to easily place type or graphics anywhere on the page. Designers have had to go to elaborate lengths, using complex nested tables and one-pixel images as spacers, in attempts to achieve a faithful online representation of their designs.

An extension of Cascading Style Sheets now provides a more elegant solution: absolute positioning. Known as CSS-P, the standard for positioning has been adopted fully by Microsoft and to a lesser extent by Netscape. CSS-P forms the basis for layers.

Layers are invisible containers that can hold any type and amount of Web elements — most importantly, they can be positioned anywhere on a Web page to exact pixel coordinates.

The power of layers goes farther than absolute positioning, however. Layers and their contents can be made invisible or visible with a change of one property. Because CSS employs a concept known as *inheritance,* in which related styles take on the characteristics of the parent style, many layers can be manipulated at once. As the term implies, layers bring an illusion of depth to the Web page. By design, each layer exists in its own three-dimensional plane. You can stack one layer on top of another or you can change their stacking order interactively.

Just as regular CSS elements can be updated dynamically, so can the position of layers — which makes the look of animation possible. Just as one second in a movie is actually 24 static images shown rapidly, layers can be quickly repositioned, appearing to move from point A to point B. This animation quality is one of the most striking features of Dynamic HTML. For the first time, movement on the Web is not generated from an source external to the Web page itself, whether it is server-push, an animated GIF, or a plug-in. This capability accelerates the display of pages online and allows Web pages to be viewed offline in a more easy and complete manner.

Cross-Reference To learn more absolute positioning and layers, refer to Chapter 23, "Working with Layers."

Dynamic content

So far, Dynamic HTML can change the look of a Web page's elements with CSS, and control the placement of a Web page's objects with layers — but what about the content? Only Microsoft has currently taken the challenge of creating dynamic content. Because Internet Explorer 4.0 has complete control over the Document

Object Model (DOM), any element or tag can be updated on the fly. This capability includes the content or value of tags.

Dynamic content is extremely useful when working with outline-based documents. With dynamic content links, you can show only the headings of a document which, when selected by the user, expands to present the substance—no matter how many paragraphs exist. Select the same heading again, and the expanded outline collapses. Expanding and collapsing outlines can be implemented in both primary 4.0 browsers. Only Microsoft, however, uses true dynamic content; Netscape uses a technique involving layers.

When you build an expanding outline in a Web page, you initially include all the content. Then you designate the heading and the content, and apply the appropriate styles, as illustrated in Figure 21-1.

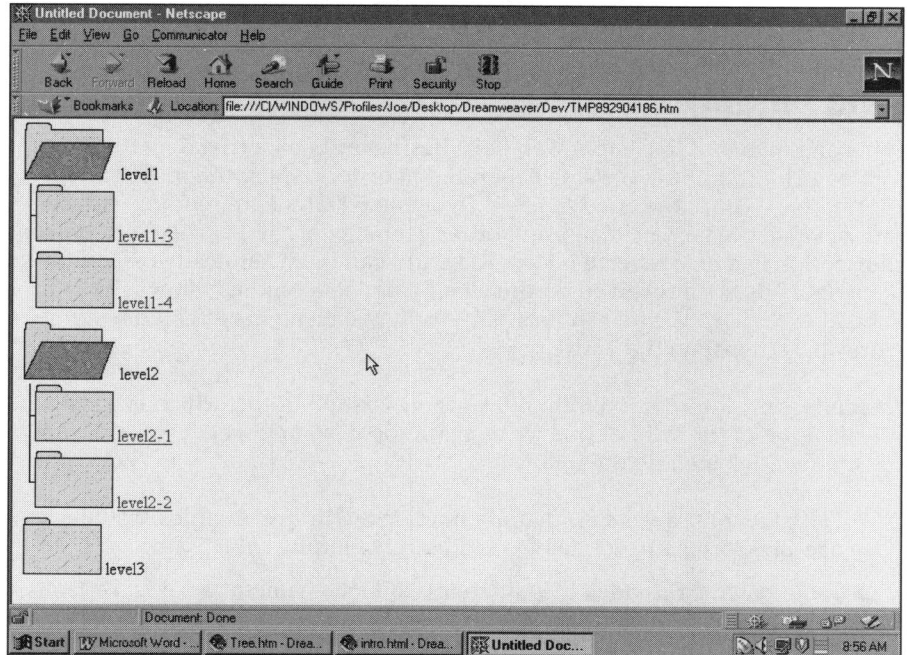

Figure 21-1: Dynamic content lets you create expanding and collapsing outlines.

Downloadable fonts

Increased font control tops the wish list for most Web designers — and this capability does not mean font size or color. For too long, Web pages have been limited to the most generic of typefaces (primarily Times and Helvetica), because HTML could only access the fonts on the user's system. Dynamic HTML promises to change this deficiency with downloadable fonts. As the term implies, *downloadable fonts* enable the Web designer to embed a specific font within a DHTML page, and the font is temporarily transferred to the Web site visitor's system.

Unfortunately, at the present time, the key word in the preceding paragraph is "promises." Both Microsoft and Netscape have implemented their own mutually incompatible versions of downloadable fonts. The demand for this capability is so strong, however, that it is only a matter of time before downloadable fonts become a cross-browser reality and a working standard. In the meantime, you can apply Open Font in Internet Explorer 4.0 and Dynamic Font technology in Communicator 4.0 simultaneously.

Data binding

Tying an online database to a Web page has never been a trivial matter. Any Web page had to be server-side generated in order to post the most current information — until the emergence of Dynamic HTML's data binding feature. With *data binding*, the tables, forms, and other elements of the page used to present the information can also receive information and can be dynamically restructured. Once data has been received on the client side, data binding allows the information to be filtered, sorted, and represented — only the elements affected need be redrawn, rather than the entire page.

Presently, only Internet Explorer 4.0 supports data binding, which is a proposed specification of the W3C at this writing. Microsoft's support is extensive, however; key innovations include the following:

✦ Full object model access to data binding attributes: Enables Web designers to use JavaScript to add, delete, and modify bindings at runtime.

✦ Table paging: Provides the capability to limit the number of records displayed in a repeated table and move the starting record forward and backward in the data set.

✦ Table and form generation: Offers automatic building of table rows from data records and data-bound form fields.

For more on data binding, see the section "Delivering Data Binding" later in this chapter.

Accessing DHTML in Netscape Communicator

The Navigator 4 component of Communicator contains three features that comprise Netscape's Dynamic HTML effort: style sheets, positionable content, and dowloadable fonts. The Netscape version of DHTML only partially conforms to the standard outlined by the W3C. For instance, Netscape supports two different types of style sheets: the W3C-standard Cascading Style Sheets, and the company's own JavaScript Style Sheets (JSS).

The following sections discuss the Netscape way of implementing Dynamic HTML and show you how to implement those methods in Dreamweaver.

Creating style sheets

Let's take a closer look at Netscape's support of the standard Cascading Style Sheet as well as its own proprietary JSS method. In brief, CSS uses the `<style>` tag to apply new attributes to an existing HTML tag or a custom tag known as a *class*. The CSS style tag format looks like the following:

```
<STYLE TYPE= text/css >
<!--
P {font-size:18pt; margin-left:20pt;}
H1 {color:blue;}
-->
</STYLE>
```

JavaScript Style Sheets also use the `<style>` tag but take advantage of the DOM to format the JSS specifications. The DOM is a hierarchical system that identifies each page element by its type of object (or by its assigned name). Once you have properly identified an element, you can then change its properties. The preceding CSS style sheet example looks like the following in JSS:

```
<STYLE TYPE =  text/javascript >
tags.P.fontSize =  18pt ;
tags.P.marginLeft =  20pt ;
tags.H1.color =  blue ;
</STYLE>
```

Caution

Do not use the HTML comment tags with JavaScript Style Sheets.

Dreamweaver outputs CSS formatted code and previews the changes as well. Although you cannot preview JSS formatted code within Dreamweaver, JSS renders properly when previewed in a compatible browser.

To be frank, JSS has not received serious support in the Web developer community, and since the standard CSS format works in both browsers, JSS has little chance of becoming popular. If, however, you develop pages that use JSS, you can continue to code them in Dreamweaver — just not as conveniently.

Making positionable content

With positionable content, Netscape again supports two possibilities. Although Navigator 4.0 essentially supports the CSS-P style layers created using the `<div>` and `<span>` tags with the style attributes, it also puts forth its own proprietary `<layer>` and `<ilayer>` tags. Aside from these syntax differences, some differences also exist between what Navigator 4.0 supports in the properties for CSS-P style positioning and the proprietary `<layer>` tags. That said, all of the tags form the basis for layers, which can be placed anywhere on the page.

Relative positioning represents perhaps the biggest difference between the two implementations. When you usually place a layer in your Web page, the `left` and `top` attributes define the layer's absolute position on the screen. When the `position` attribute is set to `relative`, however, the `left` and `top` values relate to whatever contains the layer, whether it is a table or another layer. Relative positioning using the CSS convention of `position:relative` simply doesn't work in the current release of Navigator 4.05. Instead, you should use the `<layer>` and `<ilayer>` tags. The `<layer>` is used for absolute positioning and the `<ilayer>` is used for relative positioning — or what Netscape calls inflow-positioning. Dreamweaver supports all four of the layer tag variations.

Several other properties for positionable content are supported differently in Netscape than in the CSS standard. In most cases, when Netscape doesn't support the CSS standard, it offers its own variation for the `<layer>` and `<ilayer>` tags and for the CSS style use. Table 21-1 describes these equivalents.

Tip   You can include both the CSS standard and the Netscape variation of an attribute in a `<style>` tag for cross-browser compatibility without dire consequences. In Dreamweaver, however, you need to add the Netscape syntax by hand, preferably after the CSS standard syntax.

Table 21-1
Differences Between CSS and Netscape Layer Properties

CSS Term	Layer Property	Netscape Equivalent
include-source:url (filename.htm)	SRC= filename.htm	source-include:url (filename.htm)

CSS Term	Layer Property	Netscape Equivalent
background-color:colorname	BGCOLOR= colorname	layer-background-color:colorname
background-image:url (filename)	BACKGROUND= filename	layer-background-image:filename

Using downloadable fonts

Fonts in HTML have only recently started to get a little respect. A <font> tag wasn't supported until HTML 3.2 — and the support is strictly limited. Attributes for the <font> tag enable you to specify a number of font face options from which the user's system can choose, like the following:

```
<font face= Arial, Helvetica, sans-serif >
```

Until Dynamic HTML, however, a designer could not use a typeface that the user did not have on their system and still expect to have the layout viewed correctly. Netscape's method for implementing downloadable fonts requires that the fonts be contained in a font definition file on the same Web server as the Web page. When the page is served to the user, the font definition file is downloaded with the HTML file, in the same way as a GIF or JPEG file. The font definition file is loaded asynchronously so that the HTML page doesn't have to wait while the fonts are loading.

Note

> To protect the copyrights of font designers, the downloaded font remains on the user's system only while the page is in the browser's cache; the fonts cannot be copied for personal use.

Font definition files are generated with a special authoring tool, such as Typograph from HexMac (www.hexmac.com) or the Font Composer Plug-in for Communicator. The process involves opening your Web page in the authoring tool, selecting text, and applying the font to it. You then burn (process) the file, which saves the document, creates a font definition file containing the fonts used by the file, and also links the font definition file into the document. Font definition files can only be used by one domain at a time, and the domain is specified at the time you burn the file.

Once the font definition file is created, you link the font either through a style tag, like the following:

```
<STYLE TYPE= text/css ><!--
@fontdef url(http://home.netscape.com/fonts/sample.pfr);
--></STYLE>
```

You can also use a `<link>` tag, as follows:

```
<LINK HXBURNED REL= fontdef  SRC= fontdef1.pfr >
```

The final step in getting the user's system to recognize Netscape downloadable fonts adds a new MIME type to the Web server, `application/font-tdpfr`, with a filename extension of .pfr.

To support the new capabilities of downloadable fonts, Netscape includes two new attributes: `point-size` and `weight`. The `point-size` attribute enables you to set exact sizes for your font (unlike the regular `size` attribute for the `<font>` tag, which works relatively). The weight attribute enables you to alter the boldness of the font. The weight value is from 100 to 900, inclusive (in steps of 100), where 100 indicates the least bold value, and 900 indicates the boldest value. Specifying the `<b>` tag causes Netscape to render the boldest font possible.

The amount of work involved to achieve downloadable fonts is a factor in Web designers' reluctance to use the technique. As you can see in Figure 21-2, however, the results can be spectacular.

Tip

You can certainly use Netscape's downloadable fonts in Dreamweaver, but keep in mind that you do have to add all the special code by hand. Also, Dreamweaver does not preview the font changes.

Working with DHTML and Internet Explorer

With Internet Explorer 4.0, Microsoft adopted Dynamic HTML with a vengeance. Supporting all the W3C official recommendations as well as numerous proposals, Internet Explorer 4.0 advances DHTML to the extreme. Included in Microsoft's rendition are the following features:

✦ Dynamic Styles: Includes a full implementation of the CSS, Level 1 specification for controlling style sheets.

✦ Dynamic Content: Allows the Web page to be redrawn after it has been downloaded.

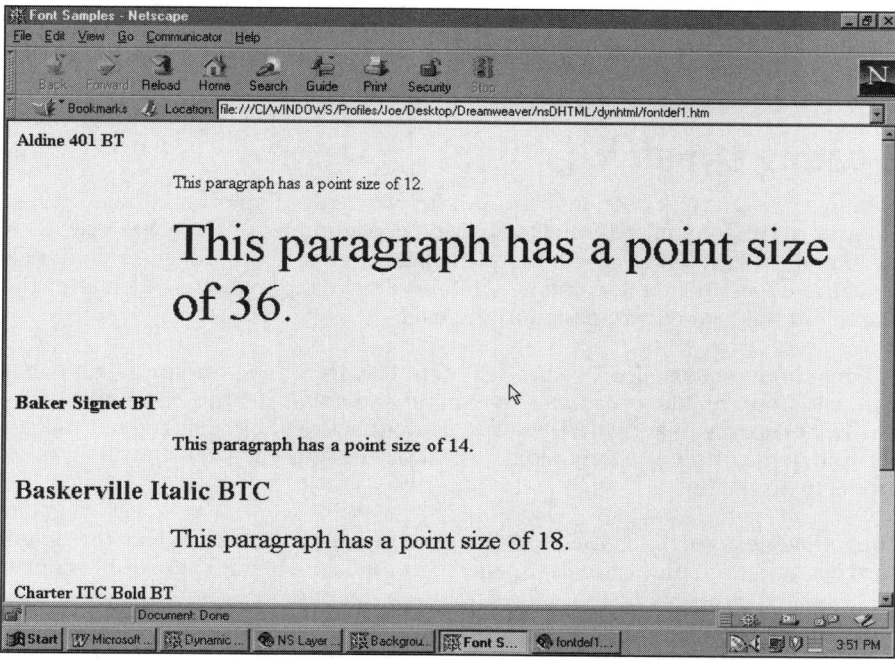

Figure 21-2: You can access a wide range of fonts and font sizes with Netscape's downloadable font technology.

✦ Positioning and Animation: Provides a full implementation of the CSS-P specification for layers and movement.

✦ Filters and Transitions: Permits designers to use special effects applied to images, text, or entire Web pages.

✦ Open Fonts: Lets the Web page specify a font that is automatically downloaded, used for that page, and then discarded.

✦ Data Binding: Links Web elements such as tables to an external source — either a server database or a comma-delimited file for automatic updating.

✦ Dynamic HTML Object Model: Gives complete access to all of the page elements and their properties through an extensive list of events.

Dreamweaver directly supports all the Internet Explorer 4.0 Dynamic HTML features that are cross-browser-compatible, including style sheets, layers, and a large portion of the Object Model. Other elements, such as filters and transitions, can be applied through Dreamweaver's Style Sheet Inspector, but cannot be previewed in the Document Window.

This book does not cover all the details of the Internet Explorer 4.0's DHTML implementation, but the remainder of this section covers those features not duplicated in any other browser.

Creating Dynamic Content

Dynamic Content has been made possible by Internet Explorer 4.0's complete support of the Dynamic HTML Object Model, a superset of Netscape's own Document Object Model. Essentially, the DHTML Object Model gives you full access to all the elements in a document — and here's the innovation — even after the document has been downloaded to the user.

The most obvious use for Dynamic Content is with outline-oriented Web pages. Dynamic Content allows outlines to expand and collapse at the click of a mouse. The key property to activate Dynamic Content is the display property, because you can name or identify any block of text or element and then alter its display property on the fly.

The following code hides the <ul> list elements until the user clicks the heading above it, and then hides the list again when the same heading is double-clicked:

```
<a href=# onClick= javascript:document.all.MyList.style.display
=
onDblClick= javascript:document.all.MyList.style.display= none
  border=0>
<h1>Notes on Installation</h1>
</a>
<ul ID=MyList STYLE= display:none  >
  <li>Item #1...</li>
  <li>Item #2...</li>
  <li>Item #3...</li>
</ul>
<p>More information to follow...</p>
```

When viewed in Dreamweaver's Document Window, you see all the elements, and you must preview it in Internet Explorer 4.0 to see the Dynamic Content in action. Currently, you have to code this sort of structure in Dreamweaver by hand or through a custom object.

Using filters and transitions

Looking for a little sparkle in your Web page? Internet Explorer 4.0's filters and transitions are quite spectacular. A filter is a special effect, such as a drop shadow, that can be applied to an element (usually text or an image) through CSS. Transitions are used when one image is exchanged with another, or one Web page with another.

The number of available filters and the range of their parameters is mind-boggling. The list shown in Table 21-2 gives an overview of the filters, but doesn't hint at the amount of variety available from changing their attributes.

Table 21-2 CSS/Internet Explorer 4.0 Filters	
Filter	**Description**
Alpha	Sets a uniform transparency level.
Blend	Sets a transition blending between two objects.
Blur	Creates the impression of moving at high speed.
Chroma	Makes a specific color transparent.
DropShadow	Creates a solid silhouette of the object.
FlipH	Creates a horizontal mirror image.
FlipV	Creates a vertical mirror image.
Glow	Adds radiance around the outside edges of the object.
Gray	Drops color information from the image.
Invert	Reverses the hue, saturation, and brightness values.
Light	Projects a light source onto an object.
Mask	Creates a transparent mask from an object.
Shadow	Creates an offset solid silhouette.
Reveal	Sets a transition's revealing of a hidden object
Wave	Creates a sine wave distortion along the horizontal axis.
Xray	Shows just the edges of the object.

Filters can be coded in the `<style>` tag or as a `style` attribute and is generally applied to a class object. The syntax follows:

```
filter:filtername(parameter_1, parameter_2, ...)
```

As you can see from Figure 21-3, the effects are quite amazing — especially when you keep in mind that they all can be performed interactively.

Figure 21-3: Internet Explorer 4.0's filters and transitions offer a full spectrum of graphic effects.

Delivering Data Binding

Much of the business of the Web depends on database-driven Web sites — virtual storefronts, online catalogs, and special information servers all require a strong connection between client-side requests and server-side answers. Microsoft's Dynamic HTML Data Binding links individual elements in your document, such as tables and forms, to data from another source, such as a database on a server or a comma-delimited text file. When the Web page with the data-bound tag is loaded, the data is automatically retrieved from the source, formatted, and displayed within the tag.

You can use Internet Explorer 4.0's Data Binding feature to generate tables in your Web page automatically and dynamically by binding a <table> tag to a data source. When the Web page is viewed, a new row is created in the table for each record retrieved from the source, and the cells of each row are filled with text and data from the fields of the record. Because this generation is dynamic, the user can view the document even while new rows in the table are being created. Moreover, once all the table data is present, you can sort or filter it without requiring the server to send additional data. The table is simply regenerated, using the previously retrieved data to fill the new rows and cells of the table.

You can also bind one or more tags in the Web page to specific fields of a record. When the page is browsed, the tags are filled with text and data from the fields in the current record. This technique can be used to generate form letters on the Web from a remote database. You can also bind the form tags to record fields, which gives the user the opportunity to view the information and, if necessary, change it. Then the record can be submitted to the server and reentered into the database.

Data Binding requires that a data source object be included in the Web page. A *data source object* is an ActiveX control (or a Java applet) capable of communicating with the data source. Internet Explorer 4.0 offers two data source objects with Internet Explorer 4.0: one for comma-delimited data in text files, and the other for SQL data in SQL Servers and other ODBC sources.

Summary

Dynamic HTML is a quantum leap forward in Web development. Style sheets, layers, dynamic content, downloadable fonts and more features make 4.0 generation browsers faster, more client-side oriented, and more designer-friendly.

✦ Dynamic HTML features work only with Internet Explorer 4.0 and Navigator 4.0 browsers and above.

✦ Much of the DHTML feature set is based on the Cascading Style Sheet specification recommended by the World Wide Web Consortium.

✦ The Dynamic HTML components of Netscape Navigator 4.0 are a blend of W3C standards and proprietary tags.

✦ Microsoft's Internet Explorer 4.0 offers the widest support of Dynamic HTML innovations through its Dynamic HTML Object Model, along with complete support of the CSS, Level 1 standard.

In the next chapter, you study more specifics on how to use Cascading Style Sheets.

✦　　✦　　✦

Building Style Sheet Web Pages

All publications, whether on paper or the Web, need a balance of style and content to be effective. Style without content is all flash with no real information. Content with no style is flat and uninteresting, thus losing the substance. Traditionally, HTML has tied style to content wherever possible, preferring logical tags like `<strong>` for bold to physical tags like `<b>`. But while this emphasis on the logical worked for many single documents, its imprecision made it unrealistic, if not impossible, to achieve style consistency across a broad range of Web pages.

The Cascading Style Sheets specification has changed this situation—and much more. As support for Cascading Style Sheet (CSS) grows, more Web designers are able to alter font faces, type size and spacing, and many other page elements with a single command—and have the effect ripple not only throughout the page, but also throughout a Web site. Moreover, an enhancement of CSS called CSS-P (for positioning) is the foundation for what has commonly become known as layers.

Dreamweaver is one of the first Web authoring tools to make the application of Cascading Style Sheets user-friendly. Through Dreamweaver's intuitive interface, the Web designer can access over 70 different CSS settings affecting everything from type specs to multimedia-like transitions. Dreamweaver lets you work the way you want: create your style sheet all at once and then link it when you're ready, or make up your styles one by one as you build your Web page.

In this chapter, you find out how CSS works and why you need it. A Dreamweaver Technique for removing underlines from links walks you through a typical style sheet session. With that experience under your belt, you're ready for the sections with detailed information on the current CSS commands and how to apply them to your Web page and site. Also, the section on defining styles helps you understand what's what in the Style Definition dialog box.

The Cascading Style Sheets system is a rapidly evolving specification, and this chapter also includes some insights into the CSS future.

Understanding Cascading Style Sheets

The Cascading Style Sheet system significantly increases the design capabilities for a Web site. If you are a designer used to working with desktop publishing tools, you will recognize many familiar features included in CSS, including the following:

✦ Commands for specifying and applying font characteristics

✦ Traditional layout measurement systems and terminology

✦ Pinpoint precision for page layout

Cascading Style Sheets are able to apply many features with a simple syntax that is easy to understand. If you're familiar with the concept of using styles in a word processing program, you'll have no trouble grasping style sheets.

Here's how the process works: CSS instructions are given in rules; a style sheet is a collection of these rules. A *rule* is a statement made up of an HTML or custom tag called a selector and its defined properties, referred to as a declaration. For example, a CSS rule that makes the contents of all <h1> tags (the selector) red in color (the declaration) looks like the following:

```
h1 {color:red}
```

In the following sections, you see the various characteristics of CSS — grouping, inheritance, and cascading — working together to give style sheets their flexibility and power.

Grouping properties

A Web designer often needs to change several style properties at once. CSS allows declarations to be grouped by separating them with semicolons. For example:

```
h1 {color:red; font-family:Arial,Helvetica; font-size:18pt}
```

The Dreamweaver interface provides a wide range of options for styles. Should you ever need to look at the code, you'll find that Dreamweaver groups your selections exactly as shown in the preceding example. Although Dreamweaver keeps each selector in its own rule, when you are hand-coding your style sheets you can group selectors as well as declarations. Grouped selectors are separated by commas rather than semicolons. For example:

```
h1, h2, p, em {color:green; text-align:left}
```

Inheritance of properties

CSS rules can also be applied to more than one tag through inheritance. Most, but not all, CSS declarations can be inherited by the HTML tags enclosed within the CSS selector. Suppose you set all `<p>` tags to the color red. Any tags included within a `<p>...</p>` tag pair then inherits that property and is also colored red.

Inheritance is also at work within HTML tags that involve a parent-child relationship, as with a list. Whether numbered (or ordered, `<ol>`) or bulleted (or unordered `<ul>`), a list comprises any number of list items, designated by a `<li>` tag. Each list item is considered a child of the parent tag, `<ol>` or `<ul>`. If you set the following CSS rules:

```
ol {color:red}
ul {color:blue}
```

With the preceding example, all ordered list items appear in red, while all unordered list items appear in blue. One major benefit to this parent-child relationship is that you can change the font for an entire page with one CSS rule. The following statement accomplishes this change:

```
body {font-family: Arial}
```

The change is possible in the previous example because the `<body>` tag is considered the parent of every HTML element on a page.

Cascading characteristics

The term *cascading* describes the capability of a local style to override a general style. Think of a stream flowing down a mountain; each ledge encountered by the stream has the potential to change its direction. The last ledge determines the final direction of the stream. In the same manner, one CSS rule applying generally to a block of text can be overridden by another rule applied to a more specific part of the same text.

For example, let's say you've defined, using style sheets, all normal paragraphs — <p> tags — to be in a particular font in a standard color, but you mark one section of the text using a little-used tag such as <samp>. If you make a CSS rule that alters both the font and the color of the <samp> tag, that section takes on the characteristics of that rule.

The cascading aspect of style sheets also works on a larger scale. One of the key features of CSS is the capability to define external style sheets that can be linked to individual Web pages, acting on their overall look-and-feel. Indeed, you can use the cascading behavior to fine-tune the overall Web site style based on a particular page or range of pages. Your company may, for instance, define an external style sheet for the entire company intranet, and each division could then build upon that overall model for its individual Web pages. For example, let's say that the company style sheet dictates that all <h2> headings are in Arial and black. One department could output their Web pages with <h2> tags in Arial, but colored red rather than black, while another department could make them blue.

Defining new classes for extended design control

Redefining existing HTML tags is a step in the right direction toward consistent design, but the real power of CSS comes into play when you define custom tags. In CSS-speak, a custom tag is called a *class*, and the selector name always begins with a period. Here's a simple example: To style all copyright notices at the bottom of all pages of a Web site to be displayed in Helvetica, 8-point type, and all caps, you could define a tag like this:

```
.cnote {font-family:Helvetica; font-size:8pt; font-
transform:uppercase}
```

If you define this style in an external style sheet and apply it to all 999 pages of your Web site, you only have to alter just one line of code (instead of all 999 pages) when the edict comes down from management to make all the copyright notices a touch larger. Once a new class has been defined, you can apply it to any range of text, from one word to an entire page.

How styles are applied

CSS applies style formatting to your page in one of three ways:

- ✦ Via an internal style sheet
- ✦ Via an external, linked style sheet
- ✦ Via embedded style rules

Internal style sheets

An internal style sheet is a list of all of the CSS styles for a page.

Dreamweaver inserts all of the style sheets at the top of a Web page within a
`<style>...</style>` tag pair. Placing style sheets within the header tags has
become a convention that many designers use, although you can also apply a style
sheet anywhere on a page.

The `<style>` tag for a Cascading Style Sheet identifies the type attribute as
`text/css`. A sample internal style sheet looks like the following:

```
<style type= text/css >
<!--
p {  font-family: Arial, Helvetica, sans-serif; color: #000000}
.cnote {  font: 8pt Arial, Helvetica, sans-serif; text-
transform: uppercase}
h1 {  font: bold 18pt Arial, Helvetica, sans-serif; color:
#FF0000}
-->
</style>
```

The HTML comments `<!--` and `-->` prevent older browsers that can't read style
sheets from displaying the CSS rules.

External style sheets

An external style sheet is a file that contains the CSS rules and links one or more
Web pages. One benefit of linking to an external style sheet is that you can
customize and change the appearance of a Web site quickly and easily from one file.

Two different methods exist for working with an external style sheet: the link and
the import method. Dreamweaver lets you choose your preferred method.

For the link option, a line of code is added outside of the `<style>` tags, as follows:

```
<link rel= stylesheet  href= mainstyle.css >
```

The import method writes code within the style tags, as follows:

```
<style type= text/css >
@import  newstyles.css ;
</style>
```

Between the link and the import methods, the link method is generally better
supported among browsers.

Embedded rules

The final method of applying a style inserts it within HTML tags using the `style` attribute. This method is the most "local" of all the techniques; that is, it is closest to the tag it is affecting and therefore has the ultimate control — because of the cascading nature of style sheets as previously discussed.

When you create a layer within Dreamweaver, you notice that the positioning attribute is a Cascading Style Sheet embedded within a `<div>` tag like the following:

```
<div id= Layer1  style= position:absolute; visibility:inherit;
left:314px; top:62px; width:194px; height:128px; z-index:1 >
</div>
```

For all its apparent complexity, the Cascading Style Sheets system becomes straightforward in Dreamweaver. Often, you won't have to write a single line of code — even if you don't have to write code, you should understand the CSS fundamentals of grouping, inheritance, and cascading.

Creating and Applying a Style Sheet in Dreamweaver

Dreamweaver uses three primary tools to implement Cascading Style Sheets: the Styles Palette, the Edit Style Sheet dialog box, and the Style Definition dialog box. Specifically, the Styles Palette is used to apply styles created in the Edit Style Sheet dialog box and specified with the Style Definition dialog box. With these three interfaces, you can:

✦ Apply styles to selected text or to a particular tag surrounding that text.

✦ View and edit many of the attributes included in the official release of CSS Level 1.

✦ Modify any styles you have created.

✦ Link or import all of your styles from an external style sheet.

Caution

The fourth-generation browsers support many of the attributes from the first draft of the Cascading Style Sheets standard. Neither Netscape Navigator 4.0 nor Microsoft Internet Explorer 4.0 fully supports CSS Level 1, however. Of the earlier browsers, only Internet Explorer 3.0 supports a limited set of the CSS Level 1 features: font attributes, indents, and color. Netscape Navigator 3.0 does not support any of the features of CSS Level 1.

Dreamweaver Technique: eliminating underlines from links

Because Dreamweaver's interface for CSS has so many controls, initially creating and applying a style can be a little confusing. Before delving into the details of the various palettes, dialog boxes, and floating windows, let's quickly step through a typical style sheet session. Then you'll have an overall feeling for how all the pieces fit together.

Note

Don't panic if you encounter unfamiliar elements of Dreamweaver's interface in this introductory Technique. You see them at work again and again as you work through the chapter.

One of the modifications most commonly included in style sheets is disabling the underline for the anchor tag, <a>, which is normally associated with any hyperlinked text. To accomplish this task, follow these steps:

1. Open the Styles Palette by choosing Windows ⇨ Styles or selecting the Show Styles button from either Launcher.

2. In the Styles Palette, select the Style Sheet button. This sequence opens the Edit Styles dialog box.

3. In the Edit Styles dialog box, select the New button. This sequence opens the New Style dialog box.

4. In the New Style dialog box, select Redefine HTML Tag and choose the anchor tag, a, from the drop-down list. Click OK, and the Style Definition window opens.

Tip

You can also select the Use CSS Selector option and choose a:link from the drop-down list. You cannot preview this altered style in Dreamweaver, however.

5. In the Style Definition window, make sure that the correct pane is displayed by selecting Type from the list of categories.

6. In the Decoration section of the Type pane, select the none option. You can also make any other modifications to the anchor tag style, like color or font size. Click OK when you're done.

   The Style Definition window closes, and the style changes instantly take effect on your page. If you have any previously defined links, the underline disappears from them.

7. In the Edit Style dialog box, select the Done button.

Now, any links that you insert on your page still function as links — the user's pointer still changes into a pointing hand, and the links are active — but no underline appears.

> **Tip**
>
> This technique works for any text used as a link. To eliminate the border around an image that is designated as a link, set the image's Border to zero in the Property Inspector.

Using the Styles Palette to apply styles

The Styles Palette, shown in Figure 22-1, is a flexible and easy-to-use interface with straightforward command buttons listing all available style items. Like all of Dreamweaver's primary palettes, you can open the Styles Palette in several ways:

✦ Choose Windows ➪ Styles.

✦ Select the Show Styles button from either Launcher.

✦ Press F7.

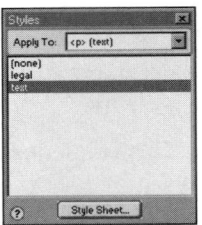

Figure 22-1: The Dreamweaver Styles Palette helps you apply consistent styles to a Web page.

The Styles Palette has three simple but important elements. The Apply To drop-down list shows the current tags available to the present cursor location. The tags in this list correspond to those found in the Tag Selector at any given time. One other item in the Apply To list is Selection, which attaches any defined style to any selected portion of your HTML page. The Apply To list enables you to focus quickly on whatever portion of the Web page to which you're applying a new style.

The main part of the Styles Palette is the list of defined custom styles or classes. Every custom tag you create is listed alphabetically in this window. Once you've chosen the portion of your HTML document that you're stylizing, you can choose one of the custom styles listed here by simply selecting it.

At the bottom of the Styles Palette is the Style Sheet button. Clicking this button opens the multifaceted Edit Style Sheet dialog box, in which you create a new style, link a style sheet, edit or remove an existing style, or duplicate a style that you can then alter. Before you can begin applying styles to a Web page or site, the styles must be defined, and the Edit Style Sheet dialog box is the pain-free method of accomplishing this task. You can, of course, open the HTML Inspector and add the style by hand, but you can avoid this process with the Edit Style Sheet dialog box. You'll get a good close look at this tool in the upcoming section "Editing and managing style sheets."

To apply an existing style, follow these steps:

1. Choose Windows ⇨ Styles or select the Show Styles button from either Launcher to open the Styles Palette.
2. To apply the style to a section of the page enclosed by an HTML tag, select the tag from the Apply To drop-down list or from the Tag Selector.

   To apply the style to a section that's not enclosed by a single HTML tag, use your mouse to select that section in the Document Window. The section is highlighted, and a Selection option then appears in the Apply To list.
3. To apply the style you want to the chosen section of the page, simply select it in the Styles Palette.

As you might expect, Dreamweaver offers a second way of applying a style to your pages. The following quick method, using the menus, does not employ the Styles Palette:

1. Highlight the text to which you're applying the style, either through the Tag Selector or by using the mouse.
2. Select Text ⇨ Custom Styles ⇨ Your Style.

Editing and managing style sheets with the Edit Style Sheet dialog box

The Edit Style Sheet dialog box, shown in Figure 22-2, displays all of your current styles — including HTML and custom styles — and provides various controls to link a style sheet and edit, create, duplicate, or remove a style.

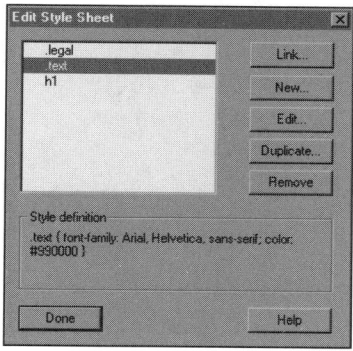

Figure 22-2: The Edit Style Sheet dialog box lists and defines any given style, in addition to presenting several command buttons for creating and managing styles.

Tip

To start editing one of your styles immediately, double-click the style in the list window of the Edit Style Sheet dialog. This sequence takes you to the Style Definition dialog box, in which you redefine your selected style.

Use the five command buttons along the right side of the Edit Style dialog box to create new external sheets or manage your existing style sheets.

Link	Lets you create an external style sheet or link to an existing external style sheet.
New	Begins the creation of a new style by first opening the New Style dialog box, described in the following section.
Edit	Modifies any existing style.
Duplicate	Makes a copy of the selected style as a basis for creating a new style.
Remove	Deletes an existing style.

Defining new styles with the New Style dialog box

Selecting the New button in the Edit Styles dialog box brings up a new dialog box called New Style (Figure 22-3). In this dialog box, you specify the type of style you're defining along with its name. The following sections explain the three style types:

✦ Make Custom Style (class)

✦ Redefined HTML Tag

✦ Use CSS Selector

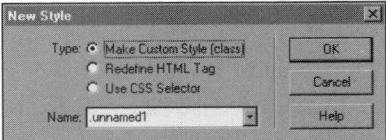

Figure 22-3: The first step in defining a new style is to select a style type and enter a name for the style.

Make Custom Style (class)

Making a custom style is the most flexible way to define a style on a page. The first step in creating a custom style is to give it a name; this name is used in the `class` attribute. The name for your class must start with a period and must be alphanumeric without punctuation or special characters. If you do not begin the name of your custom style with a period, Dreamweaver inserts one for you.

Typical names you can use follow:

```
.master
.pagetitle
.bodytext
```

Caution

Although you can use names such as `body`, `title`, or any other HTML tag, this approach is not a good idea. Dreamweaver warns you of the conflict if you try this method.

Redefine HTML Tags

The second radio button in the New Style dialog is Redefine HTML Tags. This type of style is an excellent tool for quick, global changes made to existing Web pages. Essentially, the Redefine HTML Tags style enables you to modify the features of your existing HTML tags. When you select this option, the drop-down list displays over 40 HTML tags in alphabetical order. Select a tag from the drop-down list and click OK.

Use CSS Selector

When you use the third style type, Use CSS Selector, you define what are known as pseudo-classes. A *pseudo-class* is a cross between a custom style and a redefined HTML tag. The pseudo-classes in CSS are associated with the `<a>` tag used to create hypertext links.

When you choose Use CSS Selector, the drop-down list box contains four customization options:

`a:active`	Customizes the style of a link when selected by the user.
`a:hover`	Customizes the style of a link while the user's mouse is over it. Note: This pseudo-class is a CSS Level 2 specification and is currently only supported by Internet Explorer 4.0.
`a:link`	Customizes the style of a link that has not been visited recently.
`a:visited`	Customizes the style of a link to a page that has been recently visited.

Note

Dreamweaver does not preview pseudo-class styles, although they can be previewed through a supported browser.

Styles and Their Attributes

After you've selected a type and name for a new style or chosen to edit an existing style, the Style Definition dialog box opens. A Category list from which you select a style category (just as you select a category of preferences in Dreamweaver's Preferences dialog) is located on the left side of this dialog.

Dreamweaver offers you eight categories of CSS Level 1 styles to help you define your style sheet:

Type	Box	Positioning
Background	Border	Extensions
Block	List	

You can apply styles from one or all categories. The following sections describe each style category and its available settings.

Note   Dreamweaver 1.2 doesn't yet preview all the possible CSS attributes. Those attributes that can't be seen in the Document Window are marked with an asterisk in the Style Definition dialog boxes.

Type options

The Type category (Figure 22-4) specifies the appearance and layout of the typeface for the page in the browser window. The Type category is one of the most widely used and supported categories — it can be rendered in Internet Explorer 3.0 and above and Navigator 4.0 and above. Table 22-1 explains the settings available in this category.

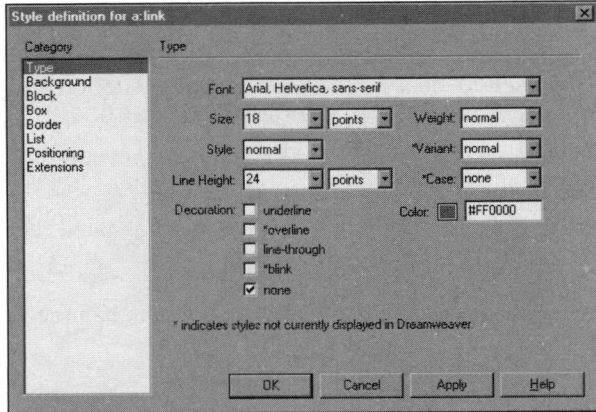

Figure 22-4: Type settings for your style.

Table 22-1
CSS Type Attributes

Type Setting	Description
Font	Specifies the font or a collection of fonts, known as a font family. You can edit the font list by selecting Edit Font List from the drop-down list. (This sequence takes you to Font Editing Land, as described in Chapter 7.)
Size	Selects a size for the selected font. If you enter a value, you can then select the measurement system in the adjacent text box (default is points). The relative sizes, such as small, medium, and large, are set relative to the parent element.
Style	Specifies normal, oblique, or italic attribute for the font. An oblique font may have been generated in the browser by electronically slanting a normal font.
Line Height	Sets the line height of the line (known as leading in traditional layout). Typically, line height is a point or two more than the font size, although you can set the line height the same or smaller than the font size for an overlapping effect.
Decoration	Changes the decoration for text. Options include underline, overline, line-through, blink, and none. The blink decoration is only displayed in Netscape browsers.
Weight	Sets the boldness of the text. You can use the relative settings (light, bold, bolder, and boldest) or apply a numeric value. Normal is around 400; Bold is 700.
Variant	Switches between normal and small caps. Small-caps is a font style that displays text as uppercase, but the capital letters are a slightly larger size. The Variant option is not currently fully supported by either primary browser.
Case	Forces a browser to render the text as uppercase, lowercase, or capitalized.
Color	Sets a color for the selected font. Enter a color name or select the color swatch to choose a browser-safe color from the pop-up menu.

Background options

Since Netscape Navigator 2, Web designers have been able to use background images and color. Thanks to CSS Background attributes, designers can now use background images and color with increased control. Whereas traditional HTML background images are restricted to a single image for the entire browser window,

CSS backgrounds can be specified for a single paragraph or any other CSS selector. (To set a background for the entire page, apply the style to the <body> tag.) Moreover, instead of an image automatically tiling to fill the browser window, CSS backgrounds can be made to tile horizontally, vertically, or not at all (see Figure 22-5). You can even position the image relative to the selected element.

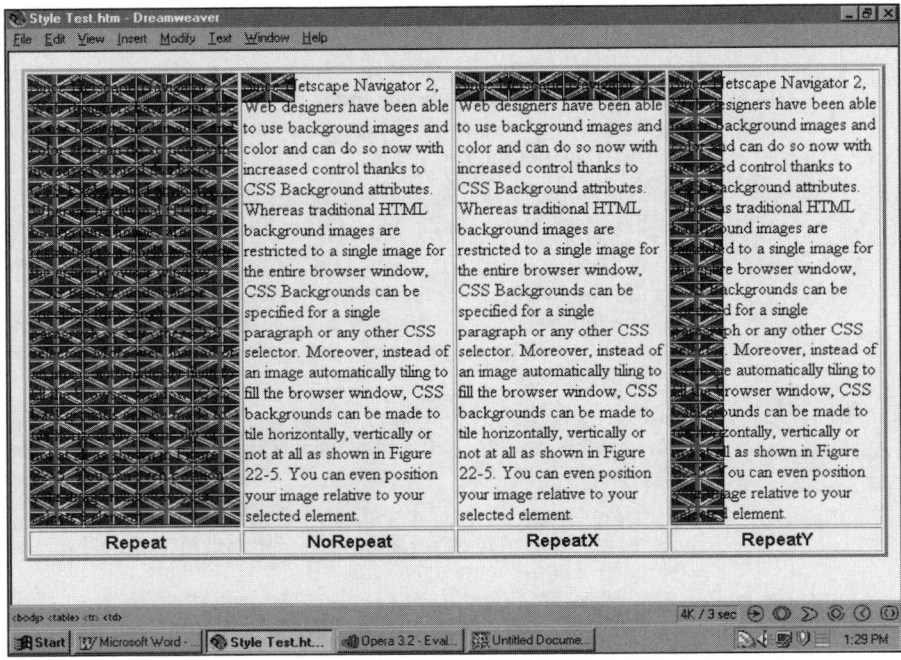

Figure 22-5: You can achieve a number of different tiling effects by using the Repeat attribute of the CSS Background category.

Neither of the primary browsers fully supports the CSS Background attributes shown in Figure 22-6 and listed in Table 22-2. The Repeat attribute enjoys full support, but Positioning and Scroll are only rendered in Internet Explorer 4.0.

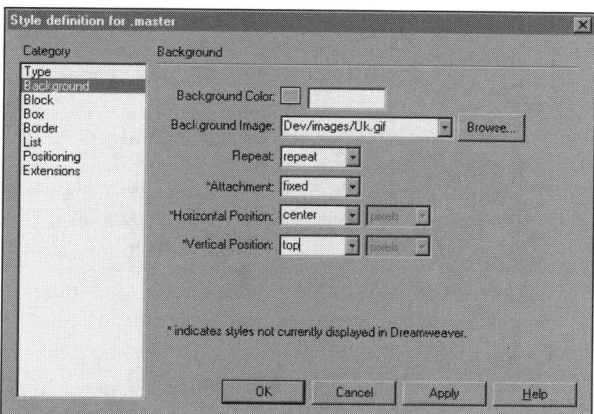

Figure 22-6: The CSS Background options allow a much wider range of control over background images and color.

Table 22-2
CSS Background Attributes

Background Setting	Description
Background Color	Sets the background color for a particular style. Note that this setting enables you to set background colors for individual paragraphs or other elements.
Background Image	Specifies a background image.
Repeat	Tiling options for a graphic is tiled.
	no repeat: displays the image in the upper-left corner of the applied style.
	repeat: tiles the background image horizontally and vertically across the applied style.
	repeat-x: tiles the background image horizontally across the applied style.
	repeat-y: tiles the background image vertically down the applied style.

(continued)

Table 22-2 *(continued)*	
Background Setting	**Description**
Attachment	Determines whether the background image remains fixed in its original position or scrolls with the page. This setting is useful for positioned elements. Often, if you use the overflow attribute, you want the background image to scroll in order to maintain layout control.
Horizontal Positioning	Controls the positioning of the background image in relation to the style sheet elements (text or graphics) along the horizontal axis.
Vertical Positioning	Controls the positioning of the background image in relation to the style sheet elements (text or graphics) along the vertical axis.

Block options

One of the most common formatting effects in traditional publishing long absent from Web publishing is justified text — text that appears as a solid block. Justified text is now possible with the Text Align attribute, one of the six options available in the CSS Block category, as shown in Figure 22-7. Indented paragraphs are also a new possibility. Table 22-3 lists the CSS Block options.

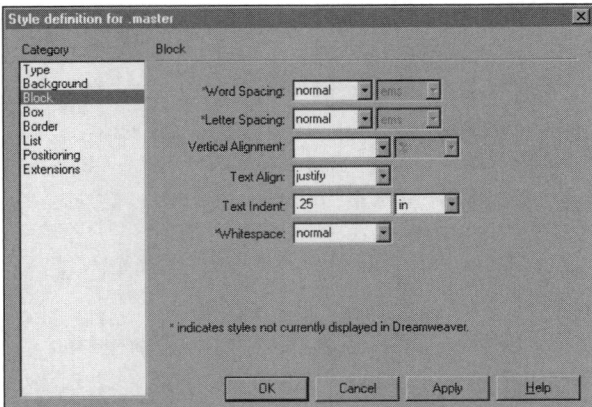

Figure 22-7: The Block category gives the Web designer enhanced text control.

Table 22-3
CSS Block Attributes

Block Setting	Description
Word Spacing	Defines the spacing between words. You can increase or decrease the spacing with positive and negative values.
Letter Spacing	Defines the spacing between the letters of a word. You can increase or decrease the spacing with positive and negative values.
Vertical Alignment	Sets the vertical alignment of the style. Choose from baseline, sub, super, top, text-top, middle, bottom, text-bottom, or add your own value.
Text Align	Sets text alignment (left, right, center, and justified).
Text Indent	Indents the first line of text on a style by the amount specified.
Whitespace	Controls display of spaces and tabs. The normal option causes all whitespace to collapse. The pre option behaves similarly to the `<pre>` tag; all whitespace is preserved. The nowrap option allows text to wrap if a ` ` tag is detected.

Box options

The Box attribute defines the placement and settings for elements (primarily images) on a page. Many of the controls (shown in Figure 22-8) emulate spacing behavior similar to that found in `<table>` attributes. If you are already comfortable using HTML tables with cell padding, border colors, and width/height controls, you will quickly learn how to use these Box features, which are described in Table 22-4.

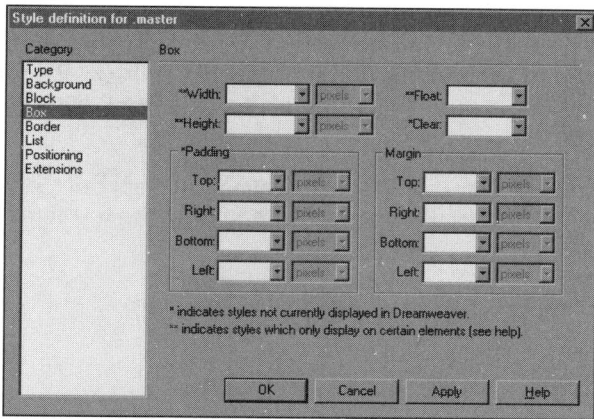

Figure 22-8: The CSS Box attributes define the placement of HTML elements on the Web page.

Dreamweaver imposes some specific restrictions on which Box attributes can and cannot be previewed in the Document Window. For example, the Float and Clear attributes can only be previewed when applied to an image. The Margin attributes can be previewed when applied to block level elements, such as any of the <h1> through <h6> tags or the <p> tag. Padding is not displayed within Dreamweaver.

Table 22-4 CSS Box Attributes	
Box Setting	**Description**
Width	Sets the width of the element.
Height	Defines the height of the element.
Float	Places the element at the left or right page margin. Any text that encounters the element wraps around it.
Clear	Sets the side on which layers are not allowed to be displayed next to the element. If a layer is encountered, the element with the Clear attribute places itself beneath the layer.
Margin	Defines the amount of space between the border of the element and other elements in the page.
Padding	Sets the amount of space between the element and the border or margin, if no border is specified. You can control the padding for the left, right, top, and bottom independently.

Border options

With Cascading Style Sheets, you can specify many parameters for borders surrounding text, images, and other elements like Java Applets. In addition to specifying separate colors for any of the four box sides, you can also choose the width of each side's border, as shown in the CSS Border panel (Figure 22-9). You can use eight different types of border lines, including solid, dashed, inset, and ridge. Table 22-5 lists the Border options.

Tip

The CSS Border attributes are especially useful for highlighting paragraphs of text with a surrounding box. Use the Box panel's Padding attribute to inset the text from the border.

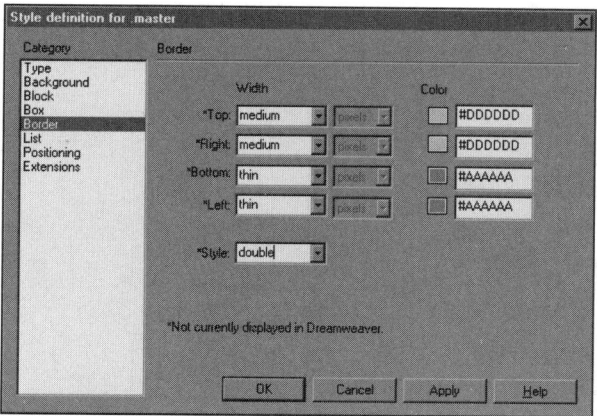

Figure 22-9: Borders are useful when you need to highlight a section of text or a graphic.

Table 22-5
CSS Border Attributes

Border Setting	Description
Top	Sets the color and settings for a border along the top of an element.
Right	Sets the color and settings for a border along the right-hand side of an element.
Bottom	Sets the color and settings for a border along the bottom of an element.
Left	Sets the color and settings for a border along the left-hand side of an element.
Style	Sets the style of the border. You can use any of the following as a border: Dotted, Dashed, Solid, Double, Groove, Ridge, Inset, and Outset.

List options

CSS gives you greater control over bullet points. With Cascading Style Sheets, you can now display a specific bullet point based on a graphic image, or you can choose from the standard built-in bullets including disc, circle, and square. The CSS List pane also lets you specify the type of ordered list to use, including decimal, roman numerals, or A-B-C order.

Figure 22-10 shows and Table 22-6 describes the settings for lists.

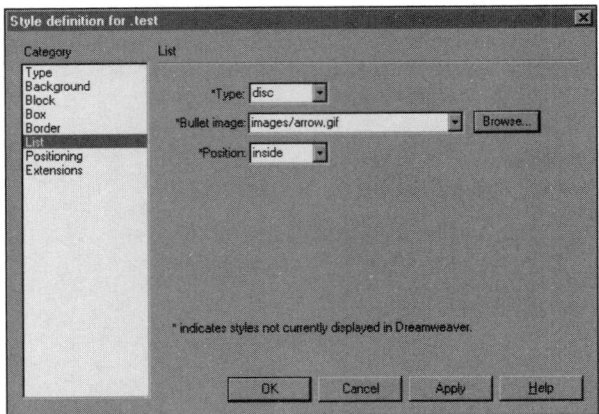

Figure 22-10: Specify a graphic to use as a bullet through the CSS List pane.

Table 22-6	
List Category for Styles	
List Setting	**Description**
Type	Selects the built-in bullet type. The options includes: disc, circle, square, decimal, lowercase roman, uppercase roman, lowercase alpha, and uppercase alpha.
Bullet Image	Sets an image to be used as custom bullet. Enter the path to the image in the text box.
Position	Determines if the list item wraps to an indent (the default) or to the margin.

Positioning options

For many designers, positioning has increased creativity in page layout design. With positioning, you have exact control over where an element will be placed on a page. Figure 22-11 shows the various attributes that provide you with this pinpoint control of your elements on a page. The options are described in Table 22-7.

Dreamweaver layers are built upon the foundation of CSS positioning. For a complete explanation of layers and their attributes, see Chapter 23, "Working with Layers."

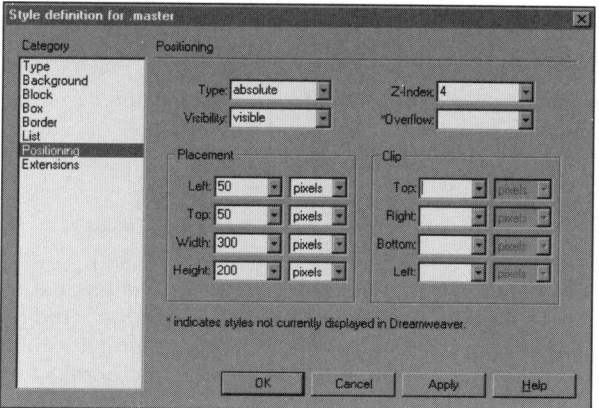

Figure 22-11: Control over the placement of elements on a page frees the Web designer from the restrictions imposed with HTML tables and other old style formats.

Table 22-7
CSS Positioning Attributes

Positioning Setting	Description
Type	Determines whether an element can be positioned absolutely or relatively on a page. The third option, static, does not allow positioning.
Visibility	Determines whether the element is visible, hidden, or inherits the property from its parent.
Z-index	Sets the apparent depth of a positioned element. Higher values are closer to the top.
Overflow	Specifies how the element is displayed when it's larger than the dimensions of the element. Options include: Clip, where the element is partially hidden; none, where the element is displayed and the dimensions are disregarded; and Scroll, which inserts scroll bars to display the overflowing portion of the element.

(continued)

Table 22-7 *(continued)*	
Positioning Setting	**Description**
Placement	Sets the styled element's placement with the left and top attributes, and the dimensions with the width and height attributes.
Clip	Sets the visible portion of the element through the left, top, width, and height attributes.

Extensions options

The specifications for Cascading Style Sheets are rapidly evolving, and Dreamweaver has grouped some cutting-edge features in the Extensions category. As of this writing, Extensions attributes (see Table 22-8) are only supported by Internet Explorer 4.0, although support is planned for Netscape Navigator 5.0. The Extensions settings in Figure 22-12 affect three different areas: page breaks for printing, the user's cursor, and special effects called filters.

One of the problems with the Web's never-ending evolution of page design is evident when you begin to print the page. The pagebreak attribute alleviates this problem by allowing the designer to designate a style that forces a page break when printing; the break can occur either before or after the element is attached to the style. While no browser currently supports this feature, it's a good candidate for support by future browsers.

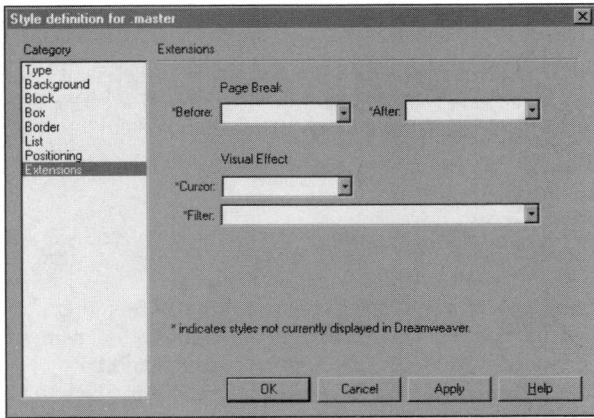

Figure 22-12: The CSS Extensions panel.

Table 22-8 CSS Extensions Attributes	
Extensions Setting	**Description**
Pagebreak	Inserts a point on a page where a printer sees a page break. Not supported by any current browser.
Cursor	Defines the type of cursor that appears when the user moves the cursor over an element. Currently supported only by Internet Explorer 4.0.
Filter	Filters enable you to customize the look and transition of an element without having to use graphic or animation files. Currently supported only by Internet Explorer 4.0.

The Filter attribute offers 16 different special effects that can be applied to an element. Many of these effects, such as wave and xray, are quite stunning. Several effects involve transitions, as well; Table 22-9 details all of these effects.

Table 22-9 CSS Filters		
Filter	**Syntax**	**Description**
Alpha	alpha(Opacity=*opacity*, FinishOpacity=*finishopacity*, Style=*style*, StartX=*startX*, StartY=*startY*, FinishX=*finishX*, FinishY=*finishY*) *Opacity* is a value from 0 to 100, where 0 is transparent and 100 is fully opaque. *style* can be 0 (uniform), 1 (linear), 2 (radial), or 3 (rectangular).	Sets the opacity of a specified gradient region. This can have the effect of creating a burst of light in an image.
BlendTrans*	blendtrans(duration=*duration*) *Duration* is a time value for the length of the transition, in the format of *seconds.milliseconds*.	Causes an image to fade in or out over a specified time.

(continued)

	Table 22-9 *(continued)*	
Filter	*Syntax*	*Description*
Blur	blur(Add=*add*, Direction=*direction*, Strength=*strength*) *Add* is any integer other than 0. *Direction* is any value from 0 to 315 in increments of 45. *Strength* is any positive integer representing the number of pixels affected.	Emulates motion blur for images.
Chroma	chroma(Color= *color*) *Color* must be given in hexadecimal form, for example, #rrggbb.	Makes a specific color in an image transparent.
DropShadow	dropshadow(Color=*color*, OffX=*offX*, OffY=*offY*, Positive=*positive*) *Color* is a hexadecimal triplet. *OffX* and *OffY* are pixel offsets for the shadow. *Positive* is a Boolean switch; use 1 to create shadow for nontransparent pixels, and 0 to create shadow for transparent pixels.	Creates a drop shadow of the applied element, either image or text, in the specified color.
FlipH	FlipH	Flips an image or text horizontally.
FlipV	FlipV	Flips an image or text vertically.
Glow	Glow(Color=*color*, Strength=*strength*) *Color* is a hexadecimal triplet. *Strength* is a value from 0 to 100.	Adds radiance to an image in the specified color.
Gray	Gray	Converts an image in grayscale.
Invert	Invert	Reverses the hue, saturation, and luminance of an image.
Light*	Light	Creates the illusion that an object is illuminated by one or more light sources.

Filter	Syntax	Description
Mask	Mask(Color=*color*)	Sets all the transparent pixels to the specified color and converts the nontransparent pixels to the background color.
	Color is a hexadecimal triplet.	
RevealTrans*	RevealTrans(duration=*duration*, transition=*style*)	Reveals an image using a specified type of transition over a set period of time.
	Duration is a time value that the transition takes, in the format of *seconds.milliseconds.*	
	Style is one of 23 different transitions.	
Shadow	Shadow(Color=*color*, Direction=*direction*)	Creates a gradient shadow in the specified color and direction for images or text.
	Color is a hexadecimal triplet.	
	Direction is any value from 0 to 315 in increments of 45.	
Wave	Wave(Add=*add*, Freq=*freq*, LightStrength=*strength*, Phase=*phase*, Strength=*strength)*	Adds sine wave distortion to the selected image or text.
	Add is a Boolean value, where 1 adds the original object to the filtered object and 0 does not.	
	Freq is an integer specifying the number of waves.	
	LightStrength is a percentage value.	
	Phase specifies the angular offset of the wave, in percentage (for example, 0% or 100% = 360 degrees, 25% = 90 degrees)	
	Strength is an integer value specifying the intensity of the wave effect.	
Xray	Xray	Converts an image to inverse grayscale for an x-rayed appearance.

*These three transitions require extensive documentation beyond the scope of this book.

Linking to an External Style Sheet

The external style sheet is an essential tool in the Web designer's CSS toolbox. Certainly, with Cascading Style Sheets, you can change all of a particular tag's attributes in a single page fairly quickly. But changing all the pages on a large Web site can still take an enormous amount of time. With an external style sheet linked to most, if not all, of a Web site's pages, the workload is cut down substantially.

To link to a separate style sheet, follow these steps:

1. Open the Styles Palette.

2. Select the Style Sheet button.

3. In the Edit Style dialog box, select the Link command button.

4. The Add Remote Style Sheet dialog box pops up, where you can access all your style sheets, by browsing and linking (Figure 22-13).

5. Either type in the file/URL path or select the Browse button to locate a style sheet; the Cascading Style Sheet file has the .css filename extension on your hard drive. If you have not already created a style sheet, you can do so by locating the place you want to have the style sheet and then creating a name for it. Useful names for style sheets can be master.css, contents.css, or body.css.

6. Choose either the Link or Import radio button.

   To add a CSS style to a page, you have to either link or import the file. Both of these features work for linking a style sheet; however, the link method is supported in more browsers.

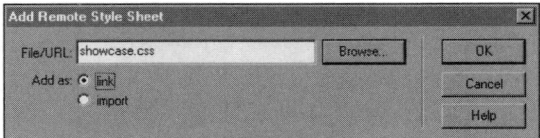

Figure 22-13: You can link an external style sheet to one Web page or your entire site through the Add Remote Style Sheet dialog box.

When you go back to the Edit Style Sheet dialog box, you see a link file referenced in the listing above all of the styles. You can double-click the linked file to open a new Edit Style Sheet dialog box for your linked style sheet file. The defined styles within the linked style sheet then appears in the Styles Palette.

The Future for Cascading Style Sheets

While still in their infancy, Cascading Styles Sheets are growing up fast. Standard HTML has many restrictions in terms of styles and media, and only some of those restrictions are resolved with CSS Level 1. Recently, the World Wide Web Consortium released a publication outlining Cascading Style Sheets Level 2. The new specification addresses many issues, including support for Extensible Markup Language (XML), media types, and increased graphical control.

Extensible Markup Language is a relative newcomer to the Web. Both Microsoft Internet Explorer and Netscape Navigator plan support for XML in future browsers. Essentially, XML is a markup language that does not concern itself with the layout of a page. Rather, it focuses on what the page contains — the so-called metadata, which is handled by the development of custom tags allowed by XML. Once you have developed these tags, however, you need to define them with a style sheet. For instance, consider the following XML:

```
<MESSAGE>
<TITLELINE>The Truth and Beauty of XML</TITLELINE>
<WRITER>J. Lowery</WRITER>
<TEXTAREA>XML is a very flexible and diverse language, however
it requires CSS to enable the layout of the text within the
tags on the browser window.</TEXTAREA> </MESSAGE>
```

A Web browser cannot interpret the display for these XML tags. You need to insert a CSS style sheet as follows:

```
MESSAGE, TEXTAREA, WRITER, TITLELINE { font: Arial }
```

With the style sheet inserted, the browser knows to display the XML as the font Arial.

The future for CSS includes a multitude of media-driven devices that will interpret style sheets. Printers, projectors, and television and aural devices will have the capability of understanding styles. In particular, aural devices will enable a hearing-impaired audience to listen to your Web pages.

In other areas of expansion, extended support for page layout elements will be added to CSS Level 2. Features such as the angle of an element will continue to increase the CSS bounty.

Summary

In this chapter, you have discovered how you can easily and effectively add and modify Cascading Style Sheets. You can now:

✦ Update and change styles easily with the Styles Palette.

✦ Easily apply generated styles to an element on a page.

✦ Apply a consistent look and feel with linked style sheets.

✦ Position fonts and elements, such as images, with pinpoint accuracy.

✦ Exercise control over the layout, size, and display of fonts on a page.

In the next chapter, you will see how to position elements on a page in Dreamweaver using layers.

✦   ✦   ✦

Working with Layers

For many years, page designers have taken the capability of placing text and graphics anywhere on a printed page for granted — even allowing graphics, type, and other elements to "bleed off" a page. This flexibility in design has eluded Web designers until recently. Lack of absolute control over layout has been a high price to pay for the universality of HTML, which makes any Web page viewable by any system, regardless of the computer or the screen resolution.

Lately, however, the integration of positioned layers within the Cascading Style Sheets specification has brought true absolute positioning to the Web. Page designers with a yen for more control can move to the precision offered with Cascading Style Sheets-Positioning (CSS-P).

Dreamweaver's implementation of layers turns the promise of CSS-P into an intuitive, designer-friendly, layout-compatible reality. As its name implies, layers offer more than pixel-perfect positioning. You can stack one layer on another, hide some layers while showing others, move a layer across the screen — and even move several layers around the screen simultaneously. Layers add a tremendous depth to the Web designer's palette.

This chapter explores every aspect of how layers work in HTML — except for animation, which is saved for Chapter 24, "Working with Timelines." With the fundamentals under your belt, you learn how to create, modify, populate, and activate layers on your Web page.

Layers 101

When the World Wide Web first made its debut in 1989, few people were concerned about the aesthetic layout of a page. In fact, because the Web was a descendant of SGML — a multiplatform, text document, and information markup specification — layout was trivialized. Content and the newfound capability to use hypertext to jump from one page to another were emphasized. After the first graphical Web browser software (Mosaic) was released, it quickly became clear that a page's graphics and layout could enhance a Web site's accessibility as well as marketability. Content was still king, but design was moving up quickly.

The first attempt at Web page layout was the server-side imagemap. This item was a typically large graphic (usually too hefty to be downloaded comfortably) with hotspots. A click on a hotspot sent a message to the server, which returned a link to the browser. The download time for these files was horrendous, and the performance varied from ordinary to awful, based on the server's load.

The widespread adoption of tables, released with HTML 2.0 and enhanced with HTML 3.2, radically changed layout control. Designers gained the ability to align objects and text — but a lot of graphical eye candy was still left to graphic files strategically located within the tables. The harder designers worked at precisely laying out their Web pages, the more they had to resort to workarounds such as nested tables and one-pixel-wide GIFs used as spacers. To relieve the woes of Web designers everywhere, the W3C included a feature within the new Cascading Styles Sheet specifications that allows for absolute positioning of an element upon a page. Absolute positioning allows an element, such as an image or block of text, to be placed anywhere on the Web page. Both Microsoft Internet Explorer 4.0 and Netscape Navigator 4.0 support layers under the Cascading Style Sheet-Positioning specification.

The addition of the third dimension, depth, truly turned the positioning specs into layers. Now objects can be positioned side-by-side, and they have a *z-index* property as well. The z-index gets its name from the geometric practice of describing three-dimensional space with *x*, *y*, and *z* coordinates; z-index is also called the stacking order because objects can be stacked upon one another.

Positioning Measurement

Positioning of layers is determined by aligning elements on an x-axis and a y-axis. In CSS, the x-axis (defined as "Left" in CSS syntax) begins at the left-hand side of the page, and the y-axis (defined as "Top" in CSS syntax) is measured from the top of the page down. As with many of the other CSS features, you have your choice of measuring systems for Left and Top positioning. All measurements are given in Dreamweaver as a number followed by the abbreviation of the measurement system (without any intervening spaces). The measurement system choices follow:

Unit	Abbreviation	Measurement
Pixels	px	Relative to the screen
Points	pt	1 pt = 1/72 in
Inches	in	1 in = 2.54 cm
Centimeters	cm	1 cm = 0.3937 in
Millimeters	mm	1 mm = 0.03937 in
Picas	pc	1 pc = 12 pt
EMS	em	The height of the element's font
Percentage	%	Relative to the screen

If you don't define a unit of measurement for layer positioning, Dreamweaver defaults to pixels. If you decide to edit out the unit of measurement, the Web browser defaults to pixels.

HTML structure of layers

A single layer in HTML looks like the following:

```
<div id= Layer1  style= position:absolute; visibility:inherit;
width:200px; height:115px; z-index:1 ></div>
```

Positioned layers are most commonly placed within the `<div>` tag. Another popular location is the `<span>` tag. These tags were chosen because they are seldom used in the HTML 3.2 specification (Dreamweaver supports both tags). Both Microsoft and Netscape encourage users to employ either of these tags, because the two primary browsers are designed to credit full CSS-P features to either the `<div>` or `<span>` tag. You should generally use the `<div>` tag when cross-browser compatibility is important.

Note

Netscape has developed two additional proprietary tags for using layers: `<layer>` and `<ilayer>`. The primary difference between the two tags has to do with positioning: the `<layer>` tag is used for absolute positioning, and the `<ilayer>` tag for relative positioning. Unfortunately, layers created by the `<div>` tag and the `<layer>` tag have different feature sets. Because Netscape recognizes both tags to some degree, you cannot combine them in the same way that you can use both the `<object>` and `<embed>` tags.

Creating Layers with Dreamweaver

Dreamweaver enables you to create layers creatively and precisely. You drag out a layer, placing and sizing it by eye, or choose to do it by the numbers — it's up to you. Moreover, you can combine the methods, quickly eyeballing and roughing out a layer layout and then aligning the edges precisely. For Web design that approaches conventional page layout, Dreamweaver even includes rulers and a grid to which you can snap your layers.

Creating layers in Dreamweaver can be handled in one of three ways:

✦ You can drag out a layer, after selecting the Marquee Layer button from the Object palette.

✦ You can put a layer in a predetermined location by choosing Insert ➪ Layer.

✦ You can create a layer with mathematical precision through the Style Sheet Inspector.

The first two methods are quite intuitive and explained in the following section. The Style Sheet Inspector method is examined later in this chapter.

Tip   Why is it called a Marquee Layer? Marquee refers to the outline of moving dashes that appears as you click and drag out the layer shape. A bit of trivia: Marquee outlines were also known as "crawling ants."

Inserting a layer object

When you want to draw out your layer quickly, use the object approach. If you come from a traditional page-designer background and are accustomed to using a program like Quark Express or PageMaker, you're already familiar with drawing out frames or text boxes with the click-and-drag technique. Dreamweaver uses the same method for placing and sizing new layer objects.

To draw out a layer as an object, follow these steps:

1. From the Common pane of the Object palette, select the Marquee Layer button. Your pointer becomes a crosshair. (If you decide not to draw out a layer, you can press Esc at this point to abort the process.)

2. Click anywhere in your document to position the layer, and drag out a rectangle. Release the mouse button when you have an approximate size and shape with which you're satisfied (see Figure 23-1).

Layer icon

Marquee Layer button

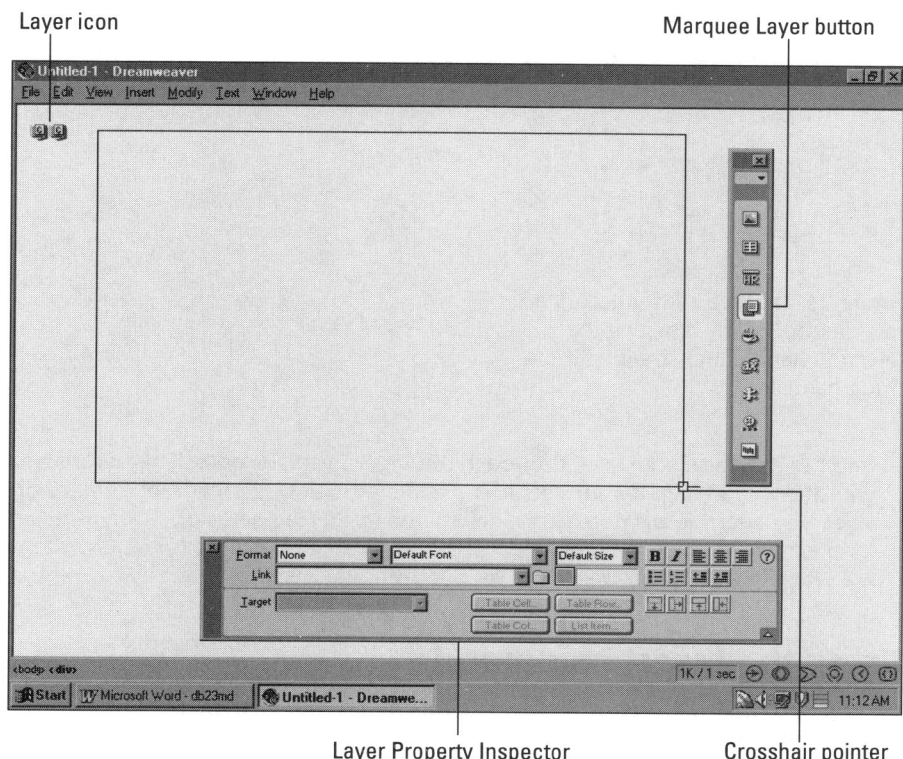

Layer Property Inspector

Crosshair pointer

Figure 23-1: After selecting the Layer object in the Object Palette (Common), the pointer becomes a crosshair when you are working on the page. Click and drag to create the layer.

After you've dragged out your layer, notice several changes to the screen. First, the layer now has a small box on the outside of the upper-left corner. This box, shown in Figure 23-2, is the selection handle, which is used to move an existing layer around the Web page. When you click on the selection handle, eight sizing handles appear around the perimeter of the layer.

Another subtle but important addition to the screen is the Layer icon. Like the other Invisibles icons, the Layer icon can be cut, copied, pasted, and repositioned. When you move the Layer icon, however, its corresponding layer does not move — you are actually only moving the code for the layer to a different place in the HTML source. Generally, the layer code's position in the HTML is immaterial — however, you may want to locate your layer source within another structure such as a form. Dragging and dropping the Layer icon inside the form outline is a quick way to achieve this task.

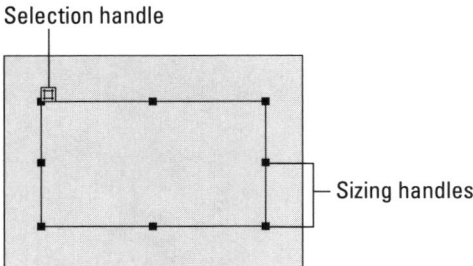

Selection handle

Sizing handles

Figure 23-2: Once a layer is created, you can move it by dragging the selection handle and size it with the sizing handles.

Tip

Another way to select a layer is through the Tag Selector. By default, layers are created with the `<div>` tag. If your cursor is positioned below the code placement of the layer, you see one or more `<div>` elements in the Tag Selector. Select one, and a layer is highlighted in the Document Window. This feature comes in handy when you are working with layers where the visibility attribute is set to `hidden`.

Using the Insert command

The second method to create a layer is through the menus. Instead of selecting an object from the Object palette, choose Insert ⇨ Layer. Unlike the click-and-drag method, inserting a layer through the menu automatically creates a layer in the upper-left corner; the default size is 200 pixels wide and 115 pixels high.

Although the layer is by default positioned 28 pixels from the top and 15 pixels from the left, it does not have any coordinates listed in the Property Inspector. The position coordinates are added when you drag the layer into a new position. If you repeatedly add new layers through the menus, without moving them to new positions, each layer is offset to the right by approximately 17 pixels.

Setting characteristics of a default layer

You can designate the default size — as well as other features — of the layer that is inserted with Insert ⇨ Layer. Choose Edit ⇨ Preferences or use the keyboard shortcut Ctrl-U (Command-U) to open the Preferences dialog box. Select the Layers category. The Layers Preferences panel (see Figure 23-3) helps you to set the following layer attributes listed in Table 23-1.

Table 23-1
Layer Preferences

Layer Preferences	Description
Tag	Sets the HTML code to use when creating layers. The options are `<div>` (the default), `<span>`, `<layer>`, and `<ilayer>`.
Visibility	Determines the initial state of visibility for a layer. The options are `default`, `inherit`, `visible`, and `hidden`.
Width	Sets the width of the layer in the measurement system of your choice. The default is 200 pixels.
Height	Sets the height of the layer in the measurement system of your choice. The default is 115 pixels.
Background Color	Sets a color for the layer background. Select the color swatch and choose an option from the pop-up menu.
Background Image	Sets an image for the layer background. In the text box, enter the path to the graphics file, or click the Browse button to locate the file.
Nesting Option	If you want to nest layers when one layer is placed in the other automatically, check the Always Nest When Created Within an Existing Layer check box.

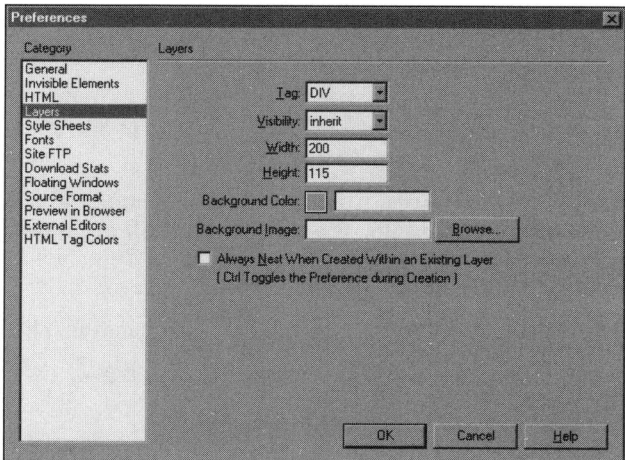

Figure 23-3: If you're building layers to a certain specification, use the Layers Preferences panel to designate your options.

Embedding a layer with style sheets

In addition to laying out your layer by eye, or inserting a default layer with Insert ⇨ Layer, you can also specify your layers precisely through style sheets. Although this method is not as intuitive as either of the preceding methods, creating layers through style sheets has notable advantages:

✦ You can enter precise dimensions and other positioning attributes.

✦ The placement and shape of a layer can be combined with other style factors such as font family, font size, color, and line spacing.

✦ Layer styles can be saved in an external style sheet, which allows similar elements on every Web page in a site to be controlled from one source.

If you haven't yet read Chapter 22, "Building Style Sheet Web Pages," you may want to look it over before continuing here.

To create a layer with style sheets, follow these steps:

1. Choose Window ⇨ Styles or select the Show Styles button from the Launcher. This selection opens the Styles Palette.

2. From the Styles Palette, select the Style Sheet button. This selection opens the Edit Style Sheet dialog box.

3. From the Edit Style Sheet dialog box, select the New button.

4. From the New Style dialog box, keep the Type option set to Make Custom Style (class). Enter a name for your new style and click OK.

5. Next up is the Style Definition dialog box. Select the Positioning category.

6. From the Positioning panel (see Figure 23-4), enter the desired attributes: Type, Visibility, Z-Index, Overflow, Placement (Left, Top, Width, and Height), and the Clip settings (Top, Right, Bottom, Left).

   The Type attribute allows three choices: Absolute, Relative, and Static. While you are familiar with the first two options, the third choice, Static, is probably new to you. Use Static when you don't want to add a layer or specify a position, but you still want to specify a rectangular background.

7. If appropriate, select other categories and enter any additional style sheet attributes desired. Click OK when you're done.

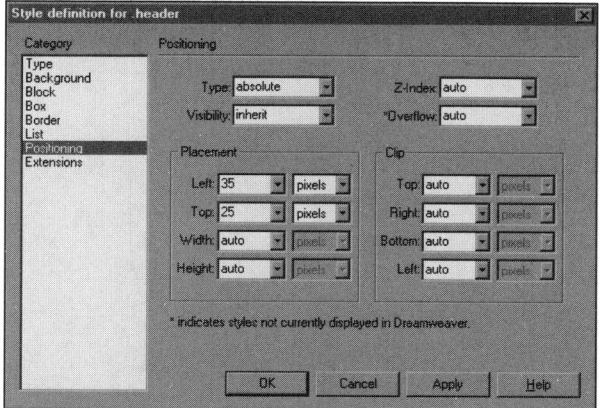

Figure 23-4: Use the Positioning panel of the Style Definition dialog box to set layer attributes in an internal or external style sheet.

Keep in mind that layers are part of the overall Cascading Style Sheet specification and can benefit from all of the features of style sheets. You may decide that a specific area of text — a header, for instance — must always be rendered in a bold, red, 18-point Arial font with a green background, and that it should always be placed 35 pixels from the left margin and 25 pixels from the top of the page. You can place the style sheet within a .CSS file, have your Web pages link to this file, and receive a result similar to Figure 23-5. Within one component — the Cascading Style Sheetfile — you can contain all of your positioning features for a page's headers, titles and other text, graphics, or objects. This capability gives you the benefit of controlling the position and look of every title linked to one style sheet.

Choosing relative instead of absolute positioning

In most cases, absolute positioning uses the top-left corner of the Web page or the position where the <body> tag begins as the point of origin from which the Web browser determines the position of the text, image, or object. You can also specify measurements relative to objects. Dreamweaver offers two methods to accomplish relative positioning.

Using the relative attribute

In the first method, you select Relative as the Type attribute in the Style Sheet Positioning category. Relative positioning does not force a fixed position; instead, the positioning is guided by the HTML tags around it. For example, you may place a list of some items within a table and set the positioning relative to the table. You can see the effect of this sequence in Figure 23-6. In this illustration's Positioning Panel, the Type attribute is set to Relative and the Placement/Left value is set to .5 inch for a style applied to the listed items.

Figure 23-5: You can apply the layer style to any element on any Web page linked to the style sheet.

Note

Dreamweaver 1.2 doesn't preview relative positioning, so you should check your placement by previewing the page in a browser, as in Figure 23-6.

Relative attributes can be useful, particularly if the designer wants to place the positioned objects within free-flowing HTML. Free-flowing HTML repositions itself if the browser window is larger or smaller than the designer is aware. When you're using this technique, remember to place your relative layers within absolutely positioned layers. Otherwise, when the end user resizes the browser, the relative layers position themselves relatively to the browser and not to the absolutely positioned layers. This situation can produce messy results — use relative positioning with caution when mixed with absolute layers.

Using nested layers

The second technique for positioning layers relatively uses nested layers. Once you nest one layer inside another, the inner layer uses the upper-left corner of the outer layer as its orientation point. For more details about nesting layers, refer to the following "Nesting with the Layer Inspector" section.

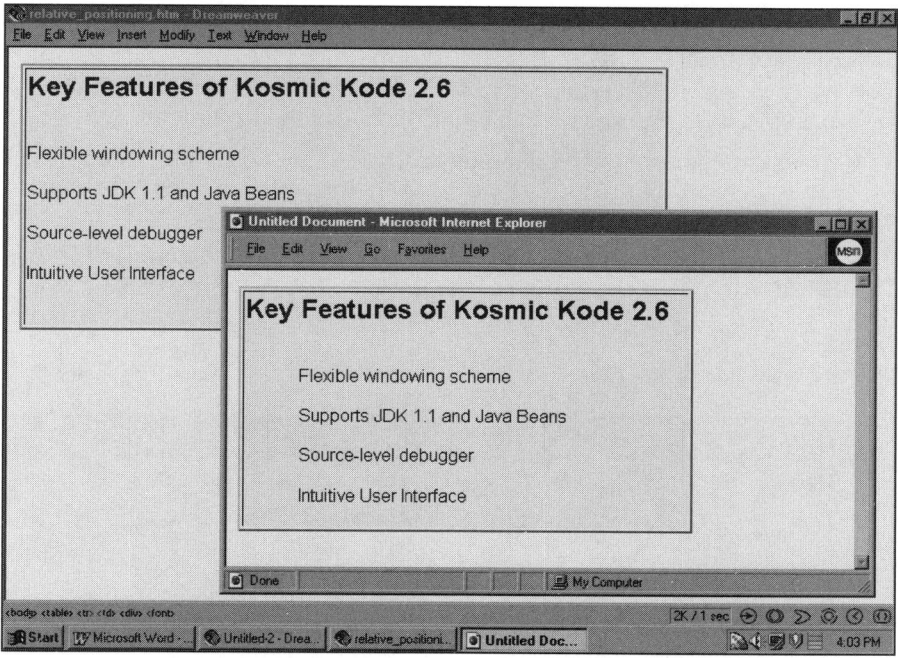

Figure 23-6: Relative positioning through styles can give your document a clean look, although the effect is not previewed in Dreamweaver.

Modifying a Layer

Dreamweaver helps you deftly alter layers once you have created them. Because of the complexity of managing layers, Dreamweaver offers an additional tool to the usual Property Inspector: the Layers Inspector. This tool enables you to select any of the layers on the current page quickly, change layer relationships to one another, modify their visibility, and adjust their stacking order. You can also alter the visibility and stacking order of a selected layer in the Property Inspector, along with many other attributes. Before any modifications can be accomplished, however, you have to select the layer.

Selecting a layer

You can choose from several methods to select a layer for alteration (see Figure 23-7). Your choice will most likely depend on the complexity of your page layout.

✦ When you have only a few layers that are not overlapping, just click the selection handle of the layer with which you want to work.

✦ When you have layers placed in specific places in the HTML code (for example, a layer embedded in a form), choose the Layer icon.

✦ When you have many overlapping layers that are being addressed by one or more JavaScript functions, use the Layers Inspector to choose the desired layer by name.

✦ When you're working with invisible layers, click the <div> tag in the Tag Selector to reveal the outline of the layer.

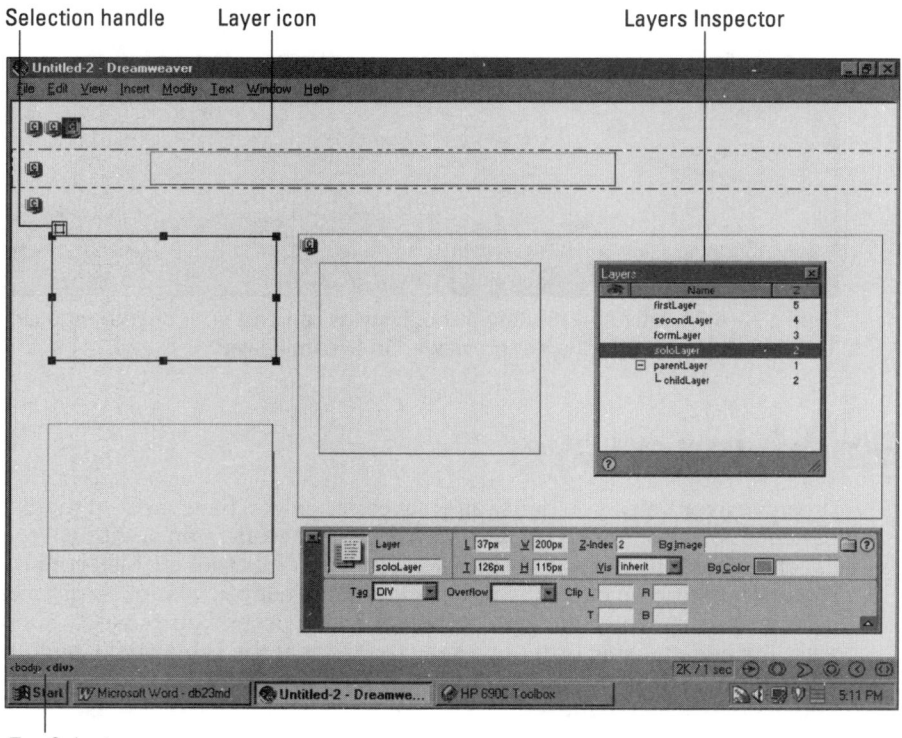

Figure 23-7: You have four different methods for selecting a layer to modify.

Resizing a layer

To resize a layer, position the pointer over one of the eight sizing handles surrounding a selected layer. When over the handles, the pointer changes shape to a two- or four-headed arrow. Now click and drag the layer to a new size and shape.

You can also use the arrow keys to resize your layer with more precision. The following keyboard shortcuts change the width and height dimension while the layer remains anchored by the upper-left corner.

✦ When the layer is selected, press Ctrl-arrow (Option-arrow) to expand or contract the layer by one pixel.

✦ Press Shift-Ctrl-arrow (Shift-Option-arrow) to increase or decrease the selected layer by the current grid increment. The default grid increment is 5 pixels.

Tip   You can quickly preview the position of a layer on a Web page without leaving Dreamweaver. Deselecting the View ➪ Layer Borders option leaves the layer outline displayed when the layer is selected.

Moving a layer

The easiest way to reposition a layer is to drag the selection handle. If you don't see the handle on a layer, click anywhere in the layer. You can drag the layer anywhere on screen — or off the bottom or right side of the screen. To move the layer off the left side or top of the screen, enter a negative value in the left and top (L and T) text boxes of the Layer Property Inspector.

Tip   To hide the layer completely, match the negative value with the width or height of the layer. For example, if your layer is 220 pixels wide and you want to position it off screen to the left (so that the layer can slide on at the click of a mouse), set the Left position at –220 pixels.

As with resizing layers, you can also use the arrow keys to move the layer more precisely:

✦ Press any arrow key to move the selected layer one pixel in any direction.

✦ Use Shift-arrow to move the selected layer by the current grid increment.

Using the Layer Property Inspector

You can modify almost all the CSS-P attributes for your layer right from the Layer Property Inspector (Figure 23-8). Certain attributes, such as width, height, and background image and color are self-explanatory or recognizable from other objects. Other layers-only attributes such as visibility and inheritance require further explanation. Table 23-2 describes all the Layer properties, and the following sections discuss the features that are unique to layers.

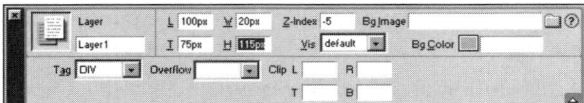

Figure 23-8: The Layer Property Inspector makes it easy to move, resize, hide, and manipulate all of the visual elements of a layer.

Table 23-2
Layer Property Inspector Options

Layer Attribute	Possible Values	Description
BgColor	Any hexadecimal or valid color name	Background color for the layer.
BgImage	Any valid graphic file	Background image for the layer.
Clip (Top, Bottom, **Left, Right**)	Any positive integer	Measurements for the displayable region of the layer. If the values are not specified, the entire layer is visible.
H (Height)	Any integer measurement in pixels, centimeters, millimeters, inches, points, percentage, ems, or picas	Vertical measurement of the layer.
L (Left)	Any integer measurement in pixels, centimeters, millimeters, inches, points, percentage, ems, or picas	Distance measured from the origin point on the left.
Name	Any unique name without spaces or special characters	Labels the layer so that it can be addressed by style sheets or JavaScript functions.
Overflow	visible, scroll, hidden, or auto	Determines how text or images larger than the layer should be handled.

Layer Attribute	Possible Values	Description
T (Top)	Any integer measurement in pixels, centimeters, millimeters, inches, points, percentage, ems, or picas	The distance measured from the origin point on the top.
Tag	span, div, layer, or ilayer	Type of HTML tag to use for the layer.
Vis (Visibility)	default, inherit, visible or hidden	Determines whether a layer is displayed. If visibility is set to inherit, then the layer takes on the characteristic of the parent layer.
W (Width)	Any integer measurement in pixels, centimeters, millimeters, inches, points, percentage, ems, or picas	The horizontal measurement of the layer.
Z-Index	Any integer	Stacking order of the layer in relation to other layers on the Web page. Higher numbers are closer to the top.

Name

Names are important when working with layers. To refer to them properly for both CSS and JavaScript purposes, each layer must have a unique name: unique among the layers and unique among every other object on the Web page. Dreamweaver automatically names each layer as it is created in sequence: Layer1, Layer2, and so forth. You can enter a name that is easier for you to remember by replacing the provided name in the text box on the far left of the Property Inspector.

Caution

Netscape Note: Netscape Navigator 4.0 is strict with its use of the ID attribute. You must ensure that you call the layer with an alphanumeric name that does not use spacing or special characters such as the underscore or percentage sign. Moreover, make sure your layer name begins with a letter and not a number—in other words, layer9 works but 9layer can cause problems.

Tag attribute

The Tag drop-down list contains the HTML tags that can be associated with the layer. By default, the positioned layer has <div> as the tag, but you can also choose <span>, <layer>, or <ilayer>. As previously noted, the <div> and <span> tags are endorsed by the World Wide Web Consortium Group as part of their CSS standards. The <layer> and <ilayer> tags are Netscape Navigator proprietary tags, although Netscape also supports the CSS tags.

Indeed, if you are working on a Navigator-based intranet, you may want to change the default layer tag. Choose Edit ➪ Preferences and then, from the Layers category, select either `<layer>` or `<ilayer>` from the Tag drop-down list.

Visibility

Visibility (`Vis` in the Property Inspector) defines whether or not you can see a layer on a Web page. Four values are available:

Default	Allows the browser to set the visibility attribute. Most browsers use the `inherit` value as their default.
Inherit	Sets the visibility to the same value as that of the parent layer, which allows a series of layers to be hidden or made visible by changing only one layer.
Visible	Causes the layer and all of its contents to be displayed.
Hidden	Makes the current layer and all of its contents invisible.

Remember the following when you're specifying visibility:

✦ Whether or not you can see a layer, you must remember that the layer still occupies space on the page and demands some of the page loading time. Hiding a layer does not affect the layout of the page, and invisible graphics take just as long to download as visible graphics.

✦ When you are defining the visibility of a positioned object or layer, you should not use `default` as the visibility value. The designer does not necessarily know whether the site's end-user has set the default visibility to `visible` or `hidden`. Designing an effective Web page can be difficult without this knowledge.

Overflow

Normally, a layer expands to fit the text or graphics inserted into it. You can restrict the size of a layer by changing the height and width values in the Property Inspector, however. What happens when you define a layer to be too small for an image, or when an amount of text depends on the setting of the layer's `overflow` attribute? CSS layers (the `<div>` and `<span>` tags) support four different `overflow` settings:

Visible	Default. All of the overflowing text or image is displayed, and the height and width settings established for the layer are ignored.
Hidden	The portion of the text or graphic that overflows the dimensions is not visible.

Scroll	Horizontal and vertical scroll bars are added to the layer regardless of the content size or amount, and regardless of the layer measurements.
Auto	When the content of the layer exceeds the width and/or height values, horizontal and vertical scroll bars appear.

Currently, support for the `overflow` attribute is spotty at best. Dreamweaver doesn't display the result in the Document Window, and this result must be previewed in a browser to be seen. Navigator offers limited support: only the attribute's hidden value works correctly and, even then, just for text. Only Internet Explorer 4.0 renders the `overflow` attribute correctly, as shown in Figure 23-9.

Caution

Netscape Note: The Overflow property is not recognized by the Netscape proprietary layer tags, `<layer>` and `<ilayer>`.

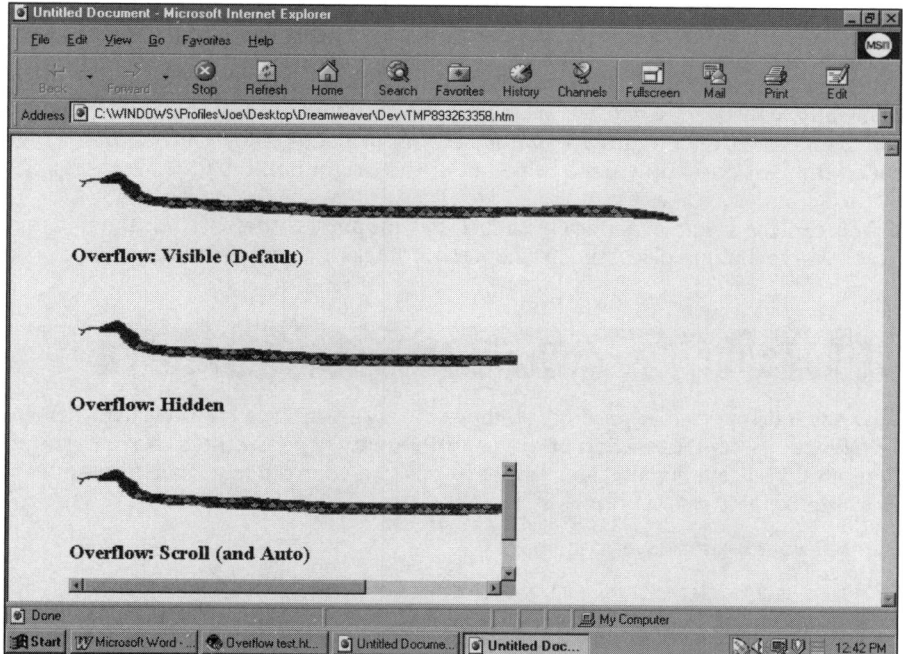

Figure 23-9: When your content is larger than the dimensions of your layer, you can regulate the results with the `overflow` attribute.

Clipping

If you're familiar with the process of cropping an image, you'll quickly grasp the concept of clipping layers. Just as desktop publishing software hides but doesn't delete the portion of the picture outside of the crop marks, layers can mask the area outside the clipping region defined by the Left, Top, Right, and Bottom values in the Clip section of the Layer Property Inspector.

All clipping values are measured from the upper-left corner of the layer. You can use any CSS standard measurement system: pixels (the default), inches, centimeters, millimeters, ems, or picas.

The current implementation of CSS only supports rectangular clipping. When you look at the code for a layer that has been clipped, you see the values you inserted in the Layer Property Inspector in parentheses following the clip attribute, with the rect (for rectangular) keyword, as follows:

```
<div id= Layer1  style= position:absolute; left:54px; top:24px;
width:400px; height:115px; z-index:1; visibility:inherit; clip:
rect(10 100 100 10) >
```

Generally, you specify values for all four criteria: Left, Top, Right, and Bottom. You can also leave the Left and Top values empty or use the keyword auto — which cause the Left and Top values to be set at the origin point: 0,0.

Tip   You can clip layers dynamically. In fact, this property is the basis for the image map rollover technique discussed in Chapter 12, "Making Client-Side Image Maps."

A Visual Clipping Technique

Dreamweaver doesn't allow you to draw the clipping region visually — the values have to be explicitly input in the Clip section of the Layer Property Inspector. That said, a trick using a second temporary layer can make it easier to position your clipping. Follow these steps to get accurate clipping values:

1. Insert your original layer and image.

2. Nest a second, temporary layer inside the first, original layer (select Marquee Layer button in the Object Palette and draw out the second layer inside the first).

   If you have your Layer Preferences set so that layers do not automatically nest when created inside another layer, press the Ctrl key while you draw your layer to override the preference.

3. Position the second layer over the area you want to clip. Use the layer's sizing handles to alter the size and shape, if necessary.

4. Note the position and dimensions of the second layer (the Left, Top, Width, and Height values).

5. Delete the second layer.

6. In the Property Inspector for the original layer, enter the Clip values as follows:

L—Enter the Left value for the second layer.

T—Enter the Top value for the second layer.

R—Add the second layer's Left value to its Width value.

B—Add the second layer's Top value to its Height value.

Dreamweaver displays the clipped layer after you enter the final value. Figure 23-10 shows the original layer and the temporary layer on the left, and the final clipped version of the original layer on the right.

Figure 23-10: You can use a temporary second layer—and the relative positioning capabilities of Dreamweaver's layers—to figure out your clipping values quickly.

Z-Index

One of a layer's most powerful features is its capability to appear above or below other layers. You can change this order, known as the *z-index*, dynamically. Whenever a new layer is added, Dreamweaver automatically increments the z-index — layers with higher z-index values are positioned above layers with lower z-index values. The z-index can be adjusted manually in either the Layer Property Inspector or the Layer Palette. The z-index must be an integer, either negative or positive.

Tip Although some Web designers use high values for the z-index, such as 3000, the z-index is completely relative. The only reason for increasing a z-index to an extremely high number is to ensure that that particular layer remains on top.

The z-index is valid for the CSS layer tags as well as the Netscape proprietary layer tags. Netscape also has two additional attributes that can affect the apparent depth of either the `<layer>`- or `<ilayer>`-based content: above and below. With above and below, you can specify which existing layer is to appear directly on top of or beneath the current layer. You can only set one of the depth attributes, the z-index, to above or below.

Caution Certain types of objects — including Java Applets, plug-ins and ActiveX controls — ignore the z-index setting when included in a layer, and always appear as the uppermost layer.

When you designate the layer's tag attribute to be either `<layer>` or `<ilayer>`, the Property Inspector displays an additional field: the A/B attribute for setting the above or below value as shown in Figure 23-11. Choose either attribute from the A/B drop-down list and then select the layer from the adjacent list. The layer you choose must be set up in the code before the current layer. You can achieve this condition in the Document Window by moving the icon for the current layer to a position after the other layers. Although you must use either `<layer>` or `<ilayer>` to specify the above or below attribute, the layer specified can be either a CSS or Netscape type.

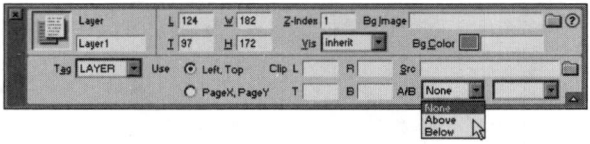

Figure 23-11: Choosing the Netscape-specific tags LAYER or ILAYER from the Property Inspector causes several new options to appear, including the A/B switch for the Above/Below depth position.

Caution Working with the `above` and `below` attributes can be confusing. Notice that they determine which layer is to appear on top of or underneath the current layer, and not which layer the present layer will be above or below.

Background image or color

Inserting a background image or color with the Layer's Property Inspector works in a similar manner as changing the background image or color for a table (as explained in Chapter 11). To insert an image, enter the path to the file in the Bg Image text box, or select the folder icon to locate the image file on your system or network. If the layer is larger than the image, the image will be tiled, just as it would in the background of a Web page or table.

To give a layer a background color, enter the color name (either in its hexadecimal or nominal form) in the Bg Color text box. You can also select the color swatch to pick your color from the color picker.

Note Netscape Note: When your layer is based on the `<div>` tag, Netscape Navigator doesn't handle background color correctly. Dreamweaver writes the regular CSS syntax for a background color as follows:

```
background-color:color
```

Netscape Navigator only colors the background behind the actual text in the layer, however, as shown in the left in Figure 23-12. To force Navigator to color all of the layer, you must add its specific syntax:

```
layer-background-color:color
```

For cross-browser compatibility, you can safely have both versions in the HTML code for your layer, as follows:

```
<div id= Layer2  style= position:absolute; left:408px;
top:56px; width:357px; height:190px; z-index:1; background-
color:#FFCCFF; layer-background-color:#FFCCFF;
visibility:inherit >
```

Caution Unlike much of HTML, the order in which you place the standard CSS attribute and Netscape's proprietary version does matter. Always place the CSS attribute before the Netscape form.

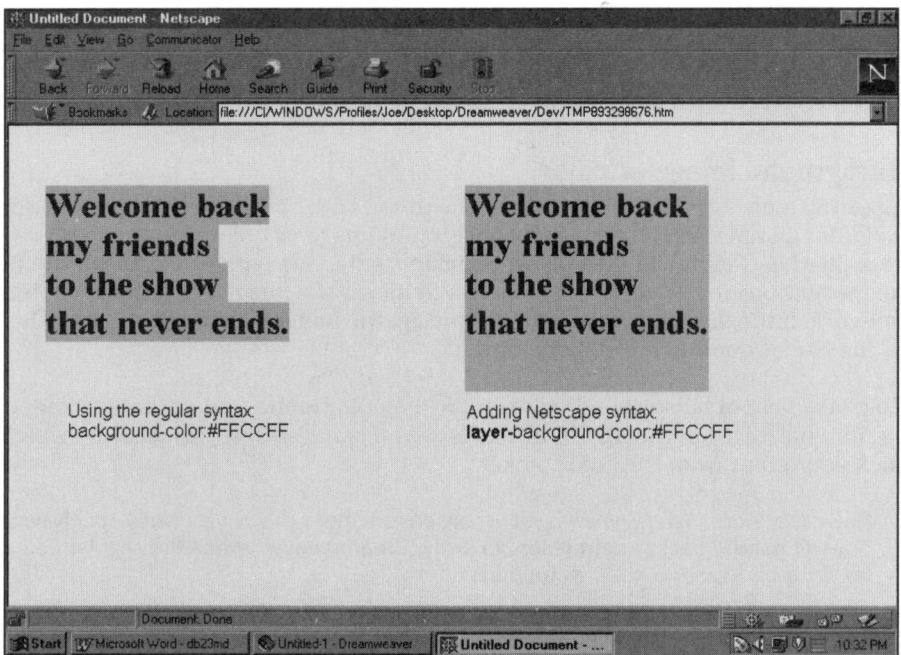

Figure 23-12: Navigator doesn't correctly recognize the normal background color attribute when rendering <div> tags. You can compensate by adding a special Netscape-only syntax (shown on the right).

Additional Netscape properties

In addition to the above and below values for the z-index attribute, two other Netscape variations are worth noting — both of which appear as options in the Property Inspector when either <layer> or <ilayer> is selected as the layer tag.

First, you can set your measurements to be based either on the Left and Top of a page, or on the Page X and Page Y. When either <layer> or <ilayer> is selected, these options become available as radio buttons in the Property Inspector. With Netscape layers, Left and Top place the layer relative to the top-left corner of its parent (whether that's the page or another layer). Page X and Page Y, on the other hand, position the layer based on the top-left corner of the page, regardless of whether the layer is nested.

The other additional Netscape layer attribute is the source property. You can specify another HTML document to appear within a <layer> or <ilayer> — much like placing other Web pages in frames. To specify a source for a Netscape layer, enter the path to the file in the Src text box, or select the folder icon to locate the file.

The Layer Inspector

Dreamweaver offers another tool to help manage the layers in your Web page: the Layer Inspector. Although this tool doesn't display as many properties about each element as the Property Inspector, the Layer Inspector gives you a good overview of all the layers on your page. It also provides a quick method of selecting a layer — even when it's off screen — as well as enabling you to change the z-index and the nesting order.

The Layer Inspector, shown in Figure 23-13, can be opened either through the Window menu (Window ⇨ Layer) or by pressing the keyboard shortcut, F11.

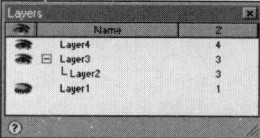

Figure 23-13: Use the Layer Inspector to select quickly or alter the visibility or relationships of all the layers on your page.

Modifying properties with the Layer Inspector

The Layer Inspector lists the visibility, name, and z-index settings for each layer. All of these properties can be modified directly through the Layer Inspector.

The visibility of a particular layer is noted by the eye symbol in column one of the Inspector. Selecting the eye symbol cycles you through three different visibility states:

✦ Eye Closed: the layer is hidden.

✦ Eye Open: the layer is visible.

✦ No Eye: the visibility attribute is set to the default (which, for both Navigator 4.0 and Internet Explorer 4.0, means inherit).

You can also change a layer's name (in the second column of the Layer Inspector). Just double-click the current layer name in the Inspector; the name will be highlighted. Type in the new name and press Enter (Return) to complete the change.

The z-index (stacking order) in the third column can be altered in the same manner. Double-click on the z-index value; then type in the new value and press Enter (Return). You can enter any positive or negative integer. If you're working with the Netscape proprietary layer tags, you can also alter the above or below values previously set for the z-index through the Property Inspector. Use A for Above and B for Below.

Nesting with the Layer Inspector

Another task managed by the Layer Inspector is nesting or unnesting layers. This process is also referred to as creating parent-child layers. To nest one layer inside another through the Layer Inspector, follow these steps:

1. Choose Window ⇨ Layers or press F11 to open the Layer Inspector.

2. Click on the name of the layer to be nested (the child) and drag it on top of the other layer (the parent).

3. When you see a rectangle form around the parent layer's name, release the mouse.

   The child layer is indented underneath the parent layer, and the parent layer has a minus sign (a down-pointing triangle on the Mac) attached to the front of its name.

4. To hide the child layer(s) from view, select the minus sign (down-pointing triangle) in front of the parent layer's name. Once the child layer is hidden, the minus sign turns into a plus sign (a right-pointing triangle on the Mac).

5. To reveal the child layer(s), select the plus sign (right-pointing triangle on the Mac).

6. To undo a nested layer, select the child layer and drag it to a new position in the Layer Inspector. Make sure that no rectangle (indicating a nesting relationship) is showing when you release the mouse button.

You can use the nesting features of the Layer Inspector to hide many layers quickly. If the visibility for all the child layers is set to default — with no eye displayed — then by hiding the parent layer you cause all the child layers to inherit that visibility setting and also disappear from view.

You can also delete a layer from the Layer Inspector. Just highlight the layer to be removed and press Delete. Dreamweaver does not enable you to delete nested layers as a group, however — you have to remove each one individually.

Aligning layers with the ruler and grid

With the capability to position layers anywhere on a page comes additional responsibility and potential problems. In anything that involves animation, correct alignment of moving parts is crucial. As you begin to set up your layers, their exact placement and alignment becomes critical. Dreamweaver includes two tools to simplify layered Web page design: the ruler and the grid.

Rulers and grids are familiar concepts in the arena of traditional desktop publishing. Dreamweaver's ruler shows the x- and y-axis in pixels, inches, or centimeters along the outer edge of the Document Window. The grid crisscrosses the page with lines to support a visual guideline when you're placing objects. You can even enable a snap-to-grid feature to ensure easy, absolute alignment.

Using the ruler

Until now, "eyeballing it" was the only option available for Web page layout. The absolute positioning capability of layers has changed this deficiency, however. Now online designers have a more precise and familiar system of alignment: the ruler. Dreamweaver's ruler can be displayed in several different measurement units and with your choice of origin point.

To enable the ruler in Dreamweaver, choose View ⇨ Ruler ⇨ Show or use the keyboard shortcut Ctrl-Alt-Shift-R (Command-Option-Shift-R). Horizontal and vertical rulers appear on along the top and the left sides of the Document Window, as shown in Figure 23-14. As you move the pointer, a light-gray line indicates the position on both rulers.

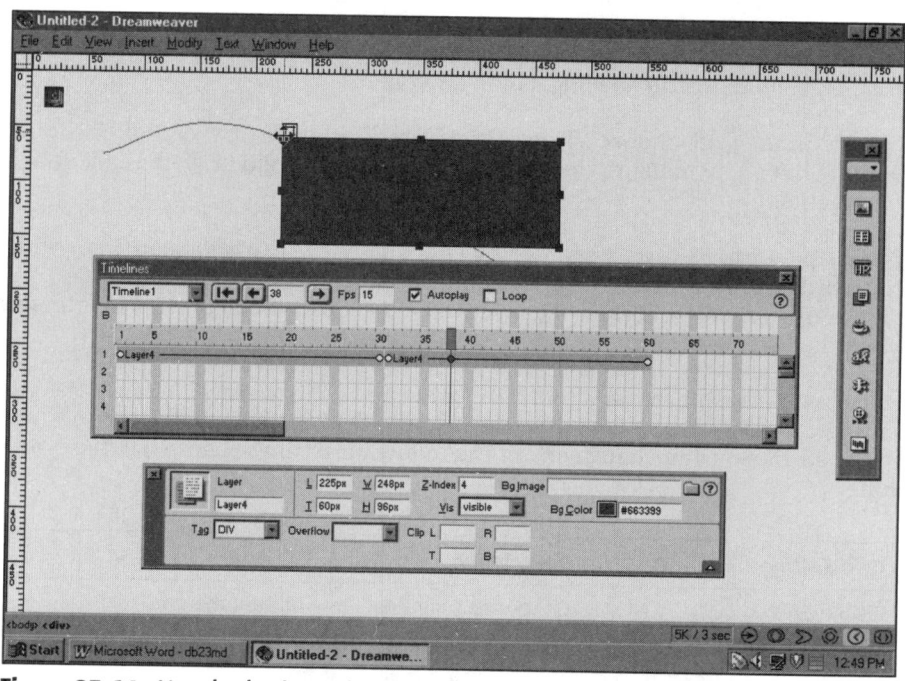

Figure 23-14: Use the horizontal and vertical rulers to assist your layer placement and overall Web page layout.

By default, the ruler uses pixels as its measurement system—you can change the default by selecting View ➪ Rulers and choosing either inches or centimeters.

Dreamweaver also lets you move the ruler origin to a new position. Normally, the upper-left of the page acts as the origin point for the ruler. On some occasions, it's helpful to start the measurement at a different location—at the bottom-right edge of an advertisement, for example. To move the origin point, select the intersection of the horizontal and the vertical rulers and drag the crosshair to a new location. When you release the mouse button, both rulers are adjusted to show negative values above and to the right of the new origin point. To return the origin point to its default setting, choose View ➪ Rulers ➪ Reset Origin.

Tip   You can access a ruler shortcut menu by right-clicking (Ctrl-clicking) the ruler itself. The shortcut menu lets you change the system of measurement, reset the origin point, or hide the rulers.

Lining up with the grid

Rulers are generally good for positioning single objects, but a grid is extremely helpful when aligning one object to another. With Dreamweaver's grid facility, you can align elements visually or snap to the grid. You can set many of the grid's other features, including grid spacing, color, and type.

To turn on the grid, choose View ➪ Grid ➪ Show or press Ctrl-Alt-Shift-G (Command-Option-Shift-G). By default, the grid is displayed with solid gray lines set at 5-pixel increments.

The snap-to-grid feature is enabled by choosing View ➪ Grid ➪ Snap To or with the keyboard shortcut Ctrl-Alt-G (Command-Option-G). When activated, Snap To Grid causes the upper-left corner of a layer to be placed at the nearest grid intersection when the layer is moved.

Like most of Dreamweaver's tools, the grid can be customized. To alter the grid settings, choose View ➪ Grid ➪ Settings. In the Grid Settings dialog box, shown in Figure 23-15, you can change any of the following settings. Click OK when you're done.

Grid Setting	Description
Visible Grid	Check box toggle to show or hide the grid.
Spacing	Adjust the distance between grid points by entering a numeric value in the text box.
Spacing Unit of Measure	Select Pixels, Inches, or Centimeters from the Spacing drop-down box.

Grid Setting	Description
Color	Change the default color (gray) by entering a color name in the text box or by selecting the color swatch to use the color picker.
Display	Choose either solid lines or dots for the gridlines.
Snapping	Check box toggle to enable or disable the Snap To Grid feature.
Snap Every	Adjust the distance between snap-to points (the points to which Dreamweaver snaps selected objects). Enter a number in the text box, and select the distance measurement unit from the drop-down list.

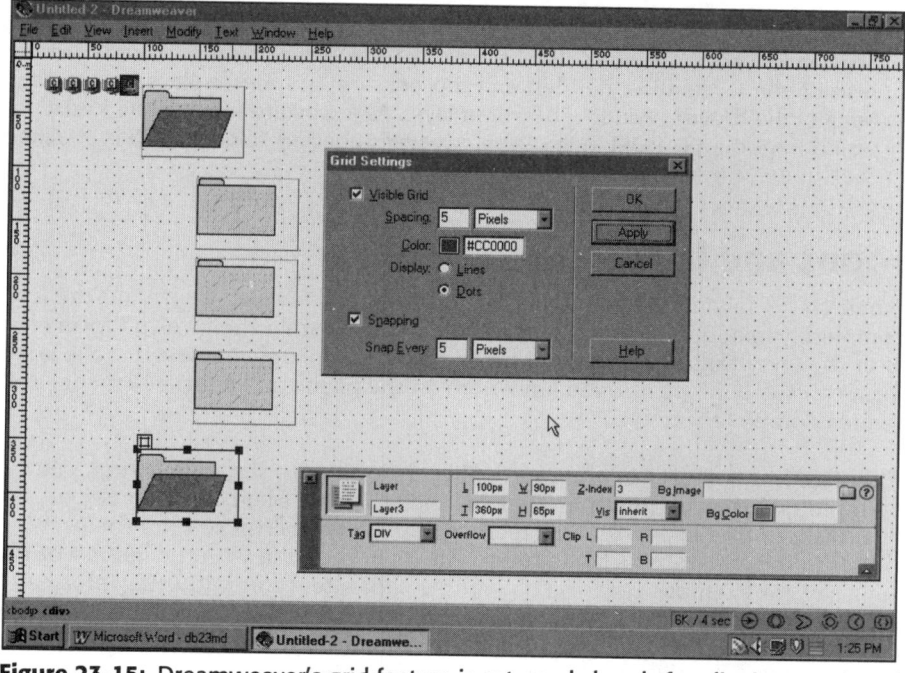

Figure 23-15: Dreamweaver's grid feature is extremely handy for aligning a series of objects.

Adding Elements to a Layer

Once you have created and initially positioned your layers, you can begin to fill them with content. Inserting objects in a layer is just like inserting objects in a Web page. The same insertion methods are available to you:

✦ Position the cursor inside a layer, choose Insert in the menu bar, and select an object to insert.

✦ With the cursor inside a layer, select any object from the Object Palette. Note: you cannot select the Marquee Layer object.

✦ Drag an object from the Object Palette and drop it inside the layer.

Netscape Note: A known problem exists with Netscape Navigator 4.0 and nested layers — and layers in general — using the `<div>` tag. Whenever the browser window is resized, the layers lose their left and top position and are displayed along the left edge of the browser window or parent layer. As a workaround, use the Resize Patch action from the CD-ROM in the Dreamweaver Behaviors folder, which is attached to the `<body>` tag and uses the onLoad event.

Forms and layers

When you're mixing forms and layers, follow only one rule: always put the form completely inside the layer. If you place the layer within the form, all form elements after the layer tags are ignored. With the form completely enclosed in the layer, the form can safely be positioned anywhere on the page and all form elements still remain completely active.

Although this rule means you can't split one form onto separate layers, you can set up multiple forms on multiple layers — and still have them all communicate to one final CGI or other program. This technique uses JavaScript to send the user-input values in the separate forms to hidden fields in the form with the Submit button. Let's say, for example, that you have three separate forms gathering information in three separate layers on a Web page. Call them formA, formB, and formC on layer1, layer2, and layer3, respectively. When the Submit button in formC on layer3 is selected, a JavaScript function is first called by means of an onClick event in the button's `<input>` tag. The function, in part, looks like the following:

```
function gatherData() {
        document.formC.hidden1.value = document.formA.text1.value
        document.formC.hidden2.value = document.formB.text2.value
}
```

Notice how every value from the various forms gets sent to a hidden field in formC, the form with the Submit button. Now, when the form is submitted, all the hidden information gathered from the various forms is submitted along with formC's own information.

Netscape Note: The code for this separate-forms approach, as written in the preceding listing, works in Internet Explorer. Navigator, however, uses a different syntax to address forms in layers. To work properly in Navigator, the code must look like the following:

```
document.layers[ layer3 ].document.formC.hidden1.value
=document.layers[ layer1 ].document.formA.text1.value
```

To make the code cross-browser-compatible, you can use an initialization function that allows for the differences, or you can build it into the onClick function.

For more information on building cross-browser-compatible code, see Chapter 25, "Maximizing Browser Targeting."

Activating Layers with Behaviors

While absolute positioning is a major reason to use layers, there are other motives to use this capability. All the properties of a layer — the coordinates, the size and shape, the depth, the visibility, and the clipping — can be altered dynamically and interactively, as well. Normally, resetting a layer's properties dynamically entails some fairly daunting JavaScript programming. Now, with one of Dreamweaver's hallmarks — those illustrious behaviors — activating layers is possible for nonprogrammers as well.

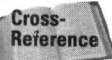

In case you missed it, Chapter 17 describes Dreamweaver's rich behaviors feature.

Behaviors consist of two parts, the event and the action. In Dreamweaver 1.2, two standard actions are designed specifically for working with layers:

✦ Drag Layer — so the user can move the layer and get a response to that movement.

✦ Show-Hide Layers — so the user can turn the layer on and off.

You can find detailed information on these actions in their respective sections in Chapter 17. In the following sections, you find an overview and outline of how to use these behaviors to activate your layers.

Drag Layer

For the Web designer, positioning a layer is easy: click the selection handle and drag the layer to a new location. For the readers of your pages, moving a layer is next to impossible — unless you incorporate the Drag Layer Action into the page's design.

With the Drag Layer Action, you can set up interactive pages in which the user can rearrange elements of the design to achieve an effect or make a selection. Drag Layer includes an option that enables you to execute a JavaScript command if the user drops the layer on a specific target. In the example shown in Figure 23-16, each pair of shoes is in its own layer. When the user drops a pair in the bag, a one-line JavaScript command opens the desired catalog page and order form.

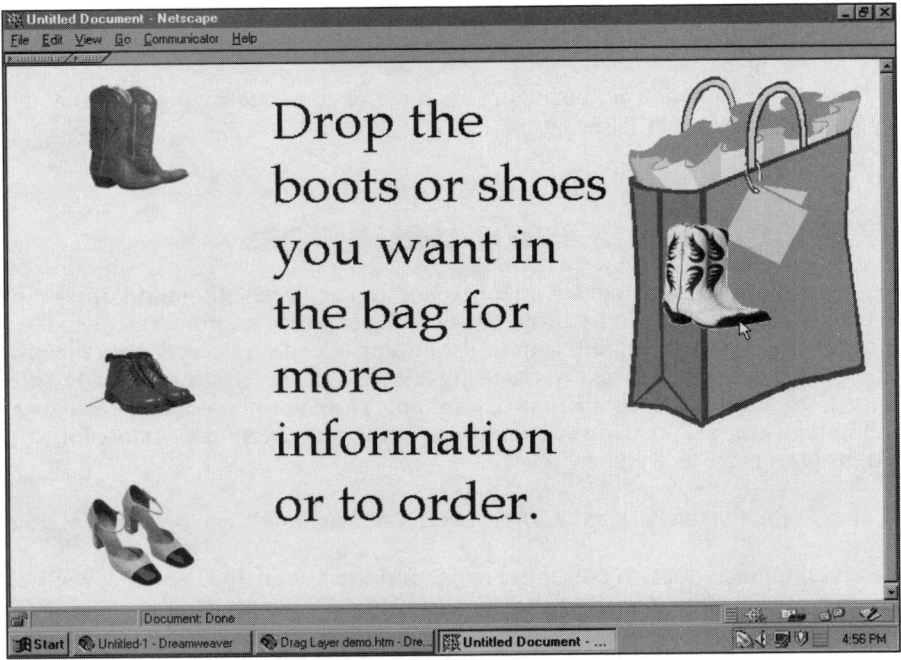

Figure 23-16: On this interactive page, visitors can drop merchandise into the shopping bag; this feature is made possible with the Drag Layer Action.

After you've created all your layers, you're ready to attach the behavior. Because Drag Layer initializes the script to make the interaction possible, you should always associate this behavior with the <body> tag and the onLoad Event.

Follow these steps to use the Drag Layer action, and to designate the settings for the drag operation:

1. Choose the `<body>` tag from the Tag Selector in the status bar.

2. Choose Window ➪ Behaviors or select the Show Behaviors button from either Launcher. The Behavior Inspector opens.

3. In the Behavior Inspector, make sure that 4.0 Browsers is displayed in the browser list.

4. Click the + (Add) Event button and select an event (usually onLoad) from the pop-up.

5. Click the + (Add) Action button and choose Drag Layer from the Add Action from the pop-up.

6. In the Drag Layer dialog box, select the layer you want to make available for dragging.

7. Designate the drag handle:

    • If you want to limit the area to be used as a drag handle, select the radio button for Drag Handle: Area within Layer. Enter the Left and Top coordinates as well as the Width and Height dimensions in the appropriate text boxes.

    • To allow the whole layer to act as a drag handle, select the radio button for Drag Handle: Entire Layer.

8. If you want to keep the layer in its current depth and not bring it to the front, deselect the check box for While Dragging: Bring Layer to the Front. To change the stacking order of the layer when it is released after dragging, select either Leave on Top or Restore Z-order from the drop-down list.

9. To limit the movement of the dragged layer, select the Constrain Movement check box. Then mark the appropriate check boxes to specify the direction(s) to which you want to limit the movement: Up, Down, Left, and/or Right.

10. To establish a location for a target, enter coordinates in the Drop Target: Left and Top text boxes. You can fill these text boxes with the selected layer's present location by clicking the Get Current Position button.

11. You can also set a snap-to area around the target's coordinates. When released in the target's location, the dragged layer snaps to this area. Enter a pixel value in the Snap if Within text box.

12. To execute a JavaScript command when the layer is dropped on the target, enter the code in the Snap JavaScript text box. If you want the script to execute every time the layer is dropped, leave the Drop Target: Left and Top text boxes empty.

Targeted JavaScript Commands

The following simple yet useful JavaScript commands can be entered in the Snap JavaScript text box of the Drag Layer dialog box.

✦ To display a brief message to the user after the layer is dropped, use the alert() function:

```
alert( You hit the target )
```

✦ To send the user to another Web page when the layer is dropped in the right location, use the JavaScript location object:

```
location = http://www.yourdomain.com/yourpage.html
```

The location object can also be used with relative URLs.

Show-Hide Layers

The ability to implement interactive control of a layer's visibility offers tremendous potential to the Web designer. The Show-Hide Layers Action makes this implementation straight-forward and simple to set up. With the Show-Hide Layers Action, you can simultaneously show one or more layers while hiding as many other layers as necessary. Create your layers and name them a unique name before invoking the Show-Hide Layers Action.

To use Show-Hide Layers, follow these steps:

1. Select an image, link, or other HTML tag to which you'll attach the behavior.

2. Choose Window ➪ Behaviors or select the Show Behaviors button from either Launcher to open the Behavior Inspector.

3. From the Add Events pop-up, select an event to trigger the action.

4. Choose Show-Hide Layers from the Add Action pop-up. The parameters form (Figure 23-17) shows a list of the available layers in the open Web page.

5. To cause a hidden layer to be revealed when this event is fired, select the layer from the list and choose the Show button.

6. To hide a visible layer when this event is fired, select its name from the list and select the Hide button.

7. To restore a layer's default visibility value when this event is fired, select the layer and choose the Default button.

8. Click OK when you are done.

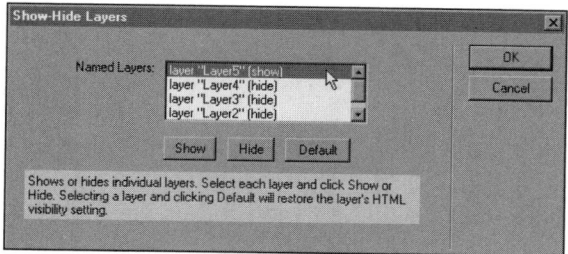

Figure 23-17: With the Show-Hide Layers behavior attached, you can easily "program" the visibility of all the layers in your Web page.

Dreamweaver Technique: Creating a Loading Layer

As Web creations become more complex, most designers want their layers to zip on and off screen or appear and disappear as quickly as possible for the viewer of the page. A layer can act only when it has finished loading its content — the text and images. Rather than have the user see each layer loading in, some designers use a loading layer to mask the process until everything is downloaded and ready to go.

A loading layer is fairly easy to create. The trick is to make the layer large enough to cover the entire screen so that no user interaction can interfere with the procedure. This arrangement can be handled in several ways; you can use a large table with a set background color, for example. This method sidesteps the difficulties with Navigator 4.0's layer-background rendering and allows placement of other simple objects (like a "Loading... Please Wait" message). Use the following steps to create a loading layer using a table.

1. Create all of your layers with the content in place, and the visibility property set as normal.

2. Create the loading layer. (Choose Insert ⇨ Layer or select the Marquee Layer button from the Object Palette.)

3. Insert a table in the layer, and through the Property Inspector set the following properties:

   • Change the Width to 800 pixels.

   • Select a background color from the Bg Color swatch.

   • If desired, enter 0 in the Border attribute to remove the border.

4. Enter and position whatever content you want displayed while the other layers are loading.

5. Click and drag the bottom border of the table until it fills the screen. If you are working at a resolution lower than 800×600, open the HTML Inspector and change the row height attribute to <td height=600> or more.

6. Select the loading layer through the Layer Inspector (F11).

7. In the Layer Property Inspector, set following properties:

- Set the left and top (L and T) attributes to 0, so that the layer starts at the upper-left of the browser window.

- Choose Visible from the Vis drop-down list.

- In the Z-Index text box, enter the highest value for any layer on the current page.

8. Select the `<body>` tag from the Tag Selector.

9. Choose Window ⇨ Behaviors or select Show Behaviors from either Launcher to open the Behavior Inspector.

10. Select the + (Add) Event button and choose onLoad from the pop-up.

11. Select the + (Add) Action button and choose Show-Hide Layers from the pop-up.

12. In the Show-Hide Layers dialog box, select the loading layer and then click the Hide button. Click OK when you are done.

Now, when you test your Web page, you should see only your loading layer until everything else is loaded, and then the loading layer disappears.

Summary

Layers are effective placement tools for developing the layout of a page. Anyone used to designing with desktop publishing tools can quickly learn to work layers effectively.

✦ Layers are only visible on fourth-generation and later browsers.

✦ Layers can be used to place HTML content anywhere on a Web page.

✦ You can stack layers on top of one another. This depth control is referred to as the stacking order or the z-index.

✦ Layers can be constructed so that the end-user can display or hide them interactively, or alter their position, size, and depth dynamically.

✦ Dreamweaver gives you rulers and grids to help with layer placement and alignment.

✦ Layers can easily be activated by using Dreamweaver's built-in JavaScript behaviors.

In the next chapter, you'll learn how to develop timelines, which enable layers and their contents to move around the Web page.

✦　　✦　　✦

Working with Timelines

Motion implies time. A static object, like an ordinary HTML Web page, can exist either in a single moment or over a period of time. Conversely, moving objects (such as a Dynamic HTML layer flying across the screen) need a few seconds to complete their path. All of Dreamweaver's DHTML animation effects use the Timeline feature to manage this conjunction of movement and time.

Timelines can do much more than move a layer across a Web page, however. A timeline can coordinate an entire presentation: starting the background music, scrolling the opening rolling credits, and cueing the voice-over narration on top of a slideshow. These actions are all possible with Dreamweaver because, in addition to controlling a layer's position, timelines can also trigger any of Dreamweaver's JavaScript behaviors on a specific frame.

This chapter explores the full and varied world of timelines. After an introductory section brings you up to speed on the underlying concepts of timelines, you learn how to insert and modify timelines to achieve cutting-edge effects. A Dreamweaver Technique shows you, step-by-step, how to create a multiscreen slideshow complete with fly-in and fly-out graphics. From complex multilayer animations to slideshow presentations, you can do it all with Dreamweaver timelines.

Note   Because timelines are so intricately intertwined with layers and behaviors, you need to have a good grasp of these concepts. Before examining the topic of timelines, make sure to read Chapter 19, "Creating and Using Behaviors," and Chapter 23, "Working with Layers."

Into the Fourth Dimension with Timelines

Until recently, Web designers have had little control over the fourth dimension and their Web pages. Only animated GIFs, Java, or animation programs such as Macromedia's Flash could create the illusion of motion events. Unfortunately, all of these technologies have some limitations.

The general problem with animated GIF images is related to file size. An animated GIF starts out as an image for every frame. Therefore, if you incorporate a three-second, 15-frames-per-second animation, you are asking the user to download the compressed equivalent of 45 separate images. Even though an animated GIF is an index color file with a limited 256 colors and uses the format's built-in compression, the GIF file is still a relatively large graphic file. Moreover, for all their apparent animated qualities, GIFs allow no true interaction other than as a link to another URL. Animations created with Dynamic HTML and Dreamweaver's Timelines, on the other hand, do not significantly increase the overall size of the Web page and are completely interactive.

DHTML is not the only low-bandwidth approach to animations with interactive content for the Web. You can create animations, complete with user-driven interactions, with Java—as long as you're a Java programmer. Certainly Java development tools are making the language easier to use, but you still must deal with the rather long load time of any Java applet and the increasing variety of Java versions. As another option, Macromedia Director movies can be compressed or "shocked" to provide animation and interactivity to your pages. Like Java, the Director approach requires a bit of a learning curve. Shockwave movies can also have long load times and require the user to have a plug-in to be viewed.

Macromedia's Flash is another alternative to GIF images, though Flash has its own set of caveats to keep in mind. On the plus side, Flash files are small and can be streamed through RealNetwork's Real Player 5. This arrangement is tempting, and if you just want animation on a page, Flash is probably a superior choice to any of the approaches previously described. On the minus side, Flash is limited to its own proprietary features and functions, and every user must have the Flash plug-in or ActiveX control installed. Moreover, a Flash image cannot execute behavior commands, and you cannot layer Flash animation on top of other layers on a page. Once you or another designer has created a Flash animation, the animation must be edited with the same animation package.

Timeline capabilities

Dreamweaver timelines are part of the HTML code. For the movement of one layer straight across a Web page, Dreamweaver generates about 70 lines of code devoted to initializing and playing the timeline. But just what is a timeline? A timeline is composed of a series of frames. A frame is a snapshot of what the Web page — more specifically, the objects on the timeline — look like at a particular moment. You probably know that a movie is made up of a series of still pictures; when viewed quickly, the pictures create the illusion of movement. Each individual picture is a frame; movies show 24 frames per second, and video uses about 30 frames per second. Web animation, on the other hand, generally displays about 15 frames per second (fps). Not surprisingly, Dreamweaver's timeline is similar to the one used in Macromedia's timeline-based, multimedia authoring tool and animation package, Director 6.0.

If you have to draw each frame of a 30-second animation, even at 15 fps, you won't have time for other work. Dreamweaver uses the concept of keyframes to make a simple layer movement workable. Each keyframe contains a change in the timeline object's properties, such as position. For example, let's say you want your layer to start at the upper-left (represented by the coordinates 0,0) and travel to the lower-right (at 750,550). To accomplish this task, you need only specify the layer's position for the two keyframes — the start and the finish — and Dreamweaver generates all the frames in between.

Timelines have three primary roles:

✦ A timeline can alter a layer's position, dimensions, visibility, and depth.

✦ Timelines can change the source for any image on a Web page and cause another graphic of the same height and width to appear in the same location.

✦ Any of Dreamweaver's JavaScript behaviors can be triggered on any frame of a timeline.

A few ground rules

Keep the following basic guidelines in mind when you're using timelines in the Web pages you create with Dreamweaver:

✦ Timelines require a 4.0 or later browser.

✦ For a timeline to be able to animate an object, such as text, the object must be within a layer. If you try to create a timeline with an element that is not in a layer, Dreamweaver warns you and prevents you from adding the object to the timeline.

✦ Events don't have to start on the beginning of a timeline. If you want to have an action begin five seconds after a page has loaded, you can set the behavior on frame 60 of the timeline, with a frame rate of 15 frames per second.

✦ You can include multiple animations on one timeline. The only restriction: you can't have two animations affecting the same layer at the same time. Dreamweaver prevents you from making this error.

✦ You can have multiple timelines that animate different layers simultaneously or the same layer at different times. Although you can set two or more timelines to animate the same layer at the same time, the results are difficult to predict and generally unintended.

Creating Animations with Timelines

Dreamweaver provides an excellent tool for managing timelines — the Timeline Inspector. Open this tool by choosing Window ➪ Timelines, selecting the Show Timelines button from either Launcher, or using the keyboard shortcut, F9.

The Timeline Inspector uses VCR-style controls combined with a *playback head,* which is a visual representation that shows which frame is the current one. As shown in Figure 24-1, the Timeline Inspector gives you full control over any of the timeline functions. The Timeline Inspector has four major areas:

Timeline Controls	Includes the Timeline pop-up menu for selecting the current timeline; the Rewind, Back, and Play buttons, the Fps (framerate) text box; and the Autoplay and Loop check boxes.
Behavior Channel	Shows the placement of any behaviors attached to specific frames of the timeline.
Frames	Displays the frame numbers for all timelines, and the playback head showing the current frame number.
Animation Channels	Represents the animations for any included layers and images.

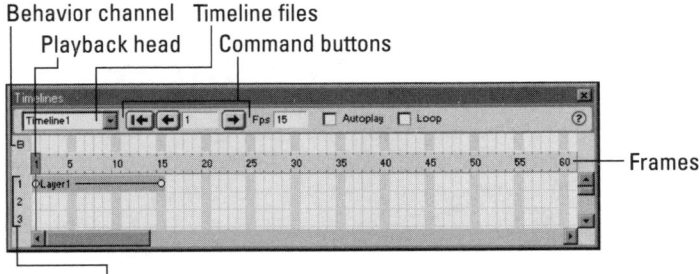

Figure 24-1: The Dreamweaver Timeline Inspector lets you quickly and easily master animation control.

Adding Layers to the Timeline Inspector

As with many of Dreamweaver's functions, you can add a layer or an image to the Timeline Inspector in more than one way. You can either insert a layer into a timeline through the menus (Modify ➪ Add Object to Timeline), or you can drag and drop an object into a timeline. The default timeline is set at a frame rate of 15 fps. When you add an object to a timeline, Dreamweaver inserts an animation bar of 15 frames in length, labeled with the object's name. The animation bar shows the duration (the number of frames) for the timeline's effect on the object. An animation bar is initially created with two initial keyframes, the start and the end.

To add a layer or image to the Timeline Inspector through the menus, follow these steps:

1. Choose Window ➪ Timelines, or select the Show Timelines button from either Launcher to open the Timeline Inspector.

2. In the Document Window, select the layer or image you want to add to the timeline.

3. Choose Modify ➪ Add Object to Timeline. An animation bar appears in the first frame of the timeline, as shown in Figure 24-2.

4. To add another object, repeat steps 2 and 3. Each additional animation bar is inserted beneath the preceding bar.

Tip

The first time you add an image or layer to the Timeline Inspector, Dreamweaver displays an alert message that details the limitations of timelines. If you don't want to see this alert, turn it off by checking the Don't Show Me This Message Again check box.

As previously noted, you can add as many objects to a timeline as you desire. If necessary, increase the size of the Timeline Inspector by dragging any border of its window.

Dragging an object onto the timeline

You have a little more flexibility when you add an object by dragging it into the timeline. Instead of the animation bar always beginning at frame 1, you can drop the object in to begin on any frame. This approach is useful, especially if you are putting more than one object into the same animation channel.

Animation bar

Figure 24-2: The default animation bar is set at 15 frames, but can easily be modified.

To place an object in a timeline with the drag-and-drop method, follow these steps:

1. Open the Timeline Inspector by choosing Window ➪ Timelines or selecting the Show Timelines button from either Launcher.

2. In the Document Window, select the object you want to add to the timeline and drag it to the Timeline Inspector. As soon as the object is over the Timeline Inspector, a 15-frame animation bar appears.

3. Holding the mouse button down, position the animation bar so that the animation begins in the desired frame. Release the mouse button to drop the object into the timeline.

   Note: your placement does not have to be exact; you can modify it later.

Placing a layer or image on a timeline is just the beginning. To begin using your timeline in depth, you have to make changes to the object for the keyframes and customize the timeline.

Modifying a Timeline

When you add an object—either an image or a layer—to a timeline, you'll notice that the animation bar has an open circle at its beginning and end. An open circle marks a keyframe. As previously explained, the designer specifies a change in the state of the timeline object in a keyframe. For example, when you first insert a layer, the two generated keyframes have identical properties—the layer's position, size, visibility, and depth are unchanged. For any animation to occur, you have to change one of the layer's properties for one of the keyframes.

For example, let's move a layer quickly across the screen. Follow these steps:

1. Create a layer. If you like, add an image or a background color so that the layer will be more noticeable.

2. Open the Timeline Inspector (go Window ⇨ Timelines, select the Show Timelines button from either Launcher, or press F9).

3. Drag the layer into the Timeline Inspector and release the mouse button.

4. Select the ending keyframe of the layer's animation bar. The playback head moves to the new frame.

5. In the Document Window, grab the layer's selection handle and drag the layer to a new location. A thin line connects the starting position of the layer to the ending position, as shown in Figure 24-3. This line is the animation path.

6. To play your animation, first click the Rewind button in the Timeline Inspector; then click and hold down the Play button.

If you want to change the beginning position for your layer's movement, select the starting keyframe and then move the layer in the Document Window. To alter the final position for your layer's movement, select the ending keyframe and then move the layer.

Tip

For more precise control of your layer's position in a timeline, select a keyframe and then, in the layer's Property Inspector, change the Left and/or Top values. You can also select the layer and use the arrow keys to move it.

Altering the animation bars

A Web designer can easily stretch or alter the range of frames occupied by a layer or image in an animation bar. You can make an animation longer, smoother, or have it start at an entirely different time. You can also move the layer to a different animation channel so it runs before or after another animation.

Animation path

Figure 24-3: When you move a layer on a timeline, Dreamweaver displays an animation path.

Use the mouse to drag an animation bar around the timeline. Click on any part of the bar except on the keyframe indicators, and move it as needed. To change the length of an animation, select the final keyframe and drag it forward or backward to a new frame.

You can remove an animation bar in two ways: select it and press Delete, or choose Modify ➪ Timeline ➪ Remove Object.

Using the timeline controls

As you probably noticed if you worked through the example in the preceding section, you don't have to use a browser to preview a timeline. The Timeline controls shown in Figure 24-4 enable you to fine-tune your animations before you view them through a browser.

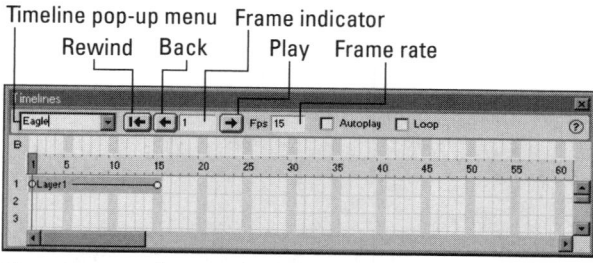

Figure 24-4: The Timeline controls let you move back and forth in your timeline, easily and precisely.

At the top-left corner is the Timeline pop-up menu, which is used to indicate the current timeline. By default, every new timeline is given the name Timeline*n*, where *n* indicates how many timelines have been created. You can rename the timeline by selecting it and typing in the new name. As you accumulate and use more timelines, you should give them recognizable names.

Tip

If you change the timeline name, you must enter a one-word name using alphanumeric characters that always begins with a letter. Netscape Navigator 4.0 cannot read spaces or special characters in JavaScript.

The next three buttons in the control bar enable you to move through the frames of a timeline. From left to right:

✦ **Rewind:** Moves the playback head to the first frame of the current timeline.

✦ **Back:** Moves the playback head to the previous frame. You can hold down the Back button to play the timeline in reverse.

✦ **Play:** Moves the timeline forward one frame at a time; hold down the Play button to play the timeline normally. When the last frame is reached, the playback head moves to the first frame of the current timeline and continues playing it.

The field between the Back and Play buttons is the frame indicator text box. To jump to any specific frame, enter the frame number in this box.

The next item in the control bar is the Fps (frames per second) text box. To change the frame rate, enter a new value in the Fps text box and press Tab or Enter (Return). The frame rate you set is an ideal number that a user's browser attempts to reach. The default rate of 15 frames per second is a good balance for both Macintosh and Windows systems.

Tip

Because browsers play every frame regardless of the frame rate setting, increasing the frame rate does not necessarily make your animations smoother. A better method for creating smooth animation is to drag the end keyframe farther out and therefore increase the number of frames used by your animation.

The next two check boxes, Autoplay and Loop, affect how the animation is played.

Autoplay

If you mark the Autoplay check box, the current timeline begins playing as soon as the Web page is fully downloaded. Dreamweaver alerts you to this arrangement by telling you that the Play Timeline action is attached to an onLoad event. The Autoplay is achieved by inserting code into the <BODY> tag that looks similar to the following:

```
<body bgcolor="#FFFFFF" onload="MM_timelinePlay('timeline1')">
```

Note

If you don't use the Autoplay feature, you must attach the Play Timeline Action to another event and tag, such as an onMouseClick event and a button graphic. Otherwise, the timeline does not play.

Looping

Mark the Loop check box if you want an animation to repeat once it has reached the final frame. When Loop is enabled, the default is for the layer to replay itself an infinite numbers of times — you can change this setting, however.

When you first enable the Loop check box, Dreamweaver alerts you that it is placing a Go to Frame Action after the last frame of your current timeline. To set the number of repetitions for a timeline, follow these steps:

1. In the Timeline Inspector, check the Loop check box.

2. Dreamweaver displays an alert informing you that the Go to Timeline Frame action is being added one frame past your current final frame. To disable these alerts, select the Don't Show Me This Message Again option.

3. In the Behavior channel (above the Frame numbers and playback head), double-click the behavior you just added.

   The Behavior Inspector opens, with an onFrame event in the Events pane and a Go To Timeline Frame Action showing in the Actions pane.

4. Double-click the Go to Timeline Frame Action. The Go to Timeline Frame dialog box opens (see Figure 24-5).

5. Enter a positive number in the Loop text box to set the number of times you want your timeline to repeat. To keep the animation repeating continuously, leave the Loop text box blank.

6. Click OK when you are finished.

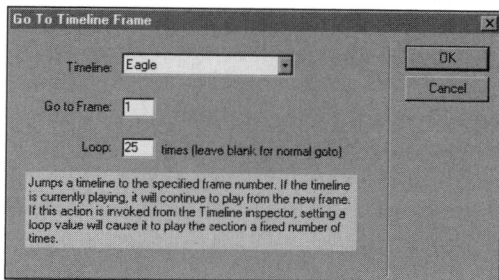

Figure 24-5: Selecting the Loop option on the Timeline Inspector adds a Go to Timeline Frame Action, which you can customize.

Tip   Your animations don't have to loop back to the beginning each time. By entering a different frame number in the Go to Frame text box of the Go to Timeline Frame dialog, you can repeat just a segment of the animation.

Adding keyframes

Animating a timeline can go far beyond moving your layer from point A to point B. Layers (and the content within them) can dip, swirl, zigzag, and generally move in any fashion — all made possible by keyframes in which you have entered some change for the object. Dreamweaver calculates all the differences between each keyframe, whether the change is in a layer's position or size. Each timeline starts with two keyframes, the beginning and the end; you have to add other keyframes before you can insert the desired changes.

You can add a keyframe to your established timeline in three different ways. The first two methods use the Dreamweaver menus, while the third method is clicking and dragging.

Adding keyframes with the Add Keyframe command

To add a keyframe with the menus, follow these steps:

1. In the Timeline Inspector, select the animation bar for the object with which you are working.

2. Select the frame where you want to add a keyframe.

3. Add your keyframe by either of the following methods:

  • Choosing Modify ⇨ Timeline ⇨ Add Keyframe.

  • Right-clicking (Control-clicking) the frame in the animation bar and, from the shortcut menu, choose Add Keyframe.

A new keyframe is added on the selected frame, signified by the open circle in the animation bar.

While your new keyframe is selected, you can alter the layer's position, size, visibility, or depth. For example, if your animation involves moving a layer across the screen, you can drag the layer to a new position while the new keyframe is selected. The animation path is redrawn to incorporate this new positioning, as illustrated in Figure 24-6.

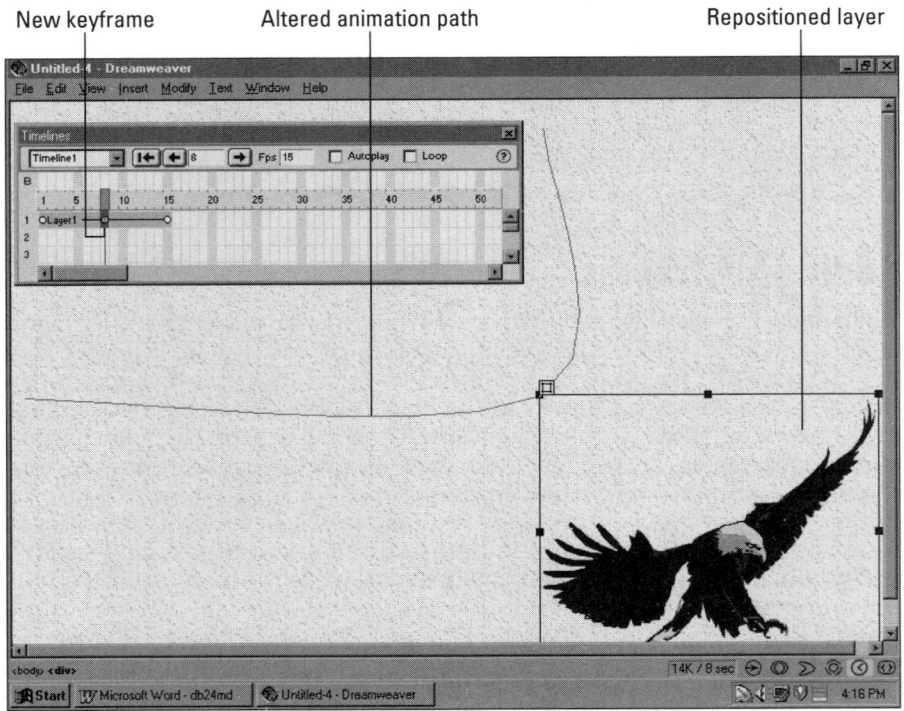

Figure 24-6: Repositioning a layer while a keyframe is selected can redirect your animation path.

Adding a keyframe by moving an object

The second method for adding a keyframe is a little more intuitive; however, it only works when you are moving a layer in the Document Window. To add a keyframe using the Document Window method, follow these steps:

1. In the Timeline Inspector, select the frame where you want to add the new keyframe.

2. Select the layer and move it to a new location. A new keyframe with the new position is automatically added to the animation bar.

Tip   What if you want to move the keyframe? Simply click and drag the keyframe to a new frame, sliding it along the animation bar in the Timeline Inspector.

Tip   If, after plotting out an elaborate animation with a layer, you discover that you need to shift the entire animation — say, 6 pixels to the right — you don't have to redo all your work. Just select the animation bar in the Timeline Inspector and then, in the Document Window, move the layer in question. Dreamweaver shifts the entire animation to your new location.

Removing timeline elements

The easiest way to remove an object, keyframe, or behavior from the Timeline Inspector selects the element and presses Delete. You cannot use this technique to delete individual frames or entire timelines, however. For these situations, you must use the menus:

✦ To remove the whole timeline, choose Modify ➪ Timeline ➪ Remove Timeline.

✦ To remove an individual frame, choose Modify ➪ Timeline ➪ Remove Frame.

The Timeline Inspector's shortcut menu also contains all the removal commands. Right-click (Control-click) the Timeline Inspector anywhere below the control bar, and in the shortcut menu (Figure 24-7) choose the removal command you need: Remove Keyframe, Remove Behavior, Remove Object, Remove Frame, or Remove Timeline.

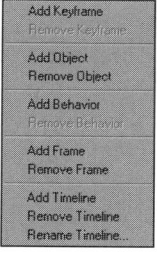

Figure 24-7: The Timeline Inspector's shortcut menu is extremely handy for doing quick edits.

Changing the speed of the animation

You can alter your Dynamic HTML animation speed with two different methods that can be used separately or together.

✦ Drag the final keyframe in the animation bar out, to cover additional frames, or back, to cover fewer frames. Any keyframes within the animation bar are kept proportional to their original settings. This method works well when altering the speed of an individual animation bar.

✦ Change the frames per second value in the Fps text box of the Timeline Inspector. Increasing the number of frames per second accelerates the animation, and vice versa. Adjusting the Fps value affects every layer contained within the timeline; you cannot use this method for individual layers.

Caution

Browsers play every frame of a Dynamic HTML animation, regardless of the systems resources. Some systems, therefore, play the same animation faster or slower than others. Don't depend on every system to have the same timing.

Triggering Behaviors in Timelines

Adding a behavior to a timeline is similar to adding behaviors to any object on a Web page. Because timelines are written in JavaScript, they behave exactly the same as any object enhanced with JavaScript.

You'll use the behaviors channel section of the Timeline Inspector to work with behaviors in timelines.

You can attach a behavior to a timeline in three ways:

✦ Highlight the frame in which you wish to have the behavior, and then right-click (Control-click). Select Add Behavior from the shortcut menu.

✦ Highlight the frame in which you want to activate the behavior, and choose Modify ⇨ Add Behavior to Timeline.

✦ Open the Behavior Inspector, and click the frame you wish to modify in the Behavior channel.

After a behavior is attached to a frame and you open the Behavior Inspector, you see that the event inserted in the Events pane is related to a frame number, for example onFrame20. Each frame can trigger multiple actions.

Cross-Reference

For more specifics about Dreamweaver behaviors, see Chapter 17, "Using and Creating Behaviors."

The timeline behaviors

Behaviors are essential to timelines. Without these elements, you cannot play or stop your timeline-based animations from running. Even when you select the Autoplay or Loop options in the Timelines Inspector, you are enabling a behavior. The three behaviors always deployed for timelines are Play Timeline, Stop Timeline, and Go to Timeline Frame.

If you are not using the Autoplay feature for your timeline, you must explicitly attach a Play Timeline Behavior to an interactive or another event on your Web page. For example, a timeline is typically set to start playing once a specific picture has loaded, if the user enters a value in a form's text box, or — more frequently — when the user selects a Play button. You could use the Stop Timeline Behavior to pause an animation temporarily.

To use the Play Timeline or Stop Timeline Behavior, follow these steps:

1. In the Document window, select a tag, link, or image that you want to trigger the event.

2. Choose Window ➪ Behavior or select the Show Behavior button from either Launcher to open the Behavior Inspector.

3. In the Behavior Inspector, select the + (Add) Event button, and choose an event from the pop-up to trigger the behavior.

4. Click the + (Add) Action button, and from the pop-up choose either of the following methods:

   • Timeline ➪ Play Timeline to start a timeline.

   • Timeline ➪ Stop Timeline to end a timeline.

5. In the Play Timeline or Stop Timeline dialog box (see Figure 24-8), choose the timeline that you want to play (or stop) from the Timeline drop-down list.

6. Click OK when you are finished.

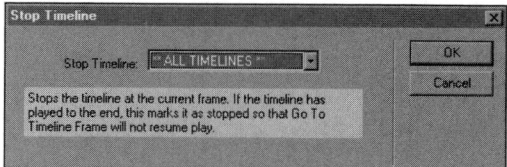

Figure 24-8: The Stop Timeline Behavior can be used to stop all timelines from playing or a specific timeline.

When you select the option to loop your timeline, Dreamweaver automatically inserts a Go to Frame behavior — with the first frame set as the target. You can display any frame on your timeline by inserting the Go to Frame behavior manually. To use the Go to Frame behavior, follow these steps:

1. In the Document Window, select a tag, link, or image that you want to trigger the event.

2. Choose Window ⇨ Behavior or select the Show Behavior button from either Launcher to open the Behavior Inspector.

3. In the Behavior Inspector, select the + (Add) Event button and choose an event from the pop-up to trigger the behavior.

4. Select the + (Add) Action button and choose Timeline ⇨ Go to Frame from the Add Behavior drop-down list.

5. In the Go to Timeline Frame dialog box, choose the timeline you want to affect.

6. Enter the frame number in the Go to Frame text box.

7. If you'd like the timeline to loop a set number of times, enter a value in the Loop text box.

8. Click OK when you are finished.

Tip

Depending on the type of effect desired, you may want to use two of the Timeline Behaviors together. To ensure that your timeline always starts from the same point, first attach a Go to Timeline Frame behavior to the event, and then attach the Play Timeline behavior to the same event.

Dreamweaver Technique: Creating a Multiscreen Slideshow

Moving layers around the screen is pretty cool, but you've probably already figured out that you can do a lot more with timelines. One of the possibilities is a graphics slideshow displaying a rotating series of pictures. The Dreamweaver Web site has an excellent tutorial that shows you how to do a single-screen slideshow. To demonstrate the range of potential available to timelines, the following sample project shows you how to construct a slideshow with more than one screen, complete with moving layers and triggered behaviors.

This technique has four steps:

1. Prepare the graphic elements. The process is easier if you have most (if not all) of your images for the slideshow — as well as the control interface — ready to go.

2. Create the slideshow timeline. In this project, one timeline is devoted to rotating images on four different "screens."

3. Create the moving layers timeline. The slideshow begins and ends with a bit of flair, as the screens fly in and fly out.

4. Add the behaviors. The slideshow includes controls for playing, pausing, restarting, and ending the slideshow, which then takes the user to another Web page.

This technique is intended to act as a basis for your own creations, not as an end in itself. You can add many variations and refinements; for example, you can preload images, make rollover buttons, and add music to the background. Following is a fundamental structure focused on the use of timelines, which you can expand with additional objects as needed.

Note   The end result of this Dreamweaver Technique can only be viewed by 4.0 browsers or better.

Step 1: Prepare the graphic elements

You'll find only one restriction to using a timeline for a slideshow presentation, but the qualification is significant — all the graphics in one "screen" must have the same dimensions. The timeline doesn't actually change the image tag; it only changes the file source for the tag. Thus, the height and width of the last image inserted overrides all the values for the foregoing graphics.

Luckily, all major image-processing software can resize and extend the canvas of a picture with little effort. When creating a slideshow, you may find it useful to do all of the resizing work at one time. Load in your images with the largest width and largest height — they may or may not be the same picture — and use these measurements as your common denominators for all graphics.

Go ahead and create your interface buttons earlier rather than later. Experience shows that the more design elements you prepare ahead of time, the less adjusting you have to do later. Also, activating a timeline with a behavior is a straightforward process, and a finished interface enables you to incorporate the buttons quickly.

Finally, you should create and place the layers you'll be using. The sample Web page in this Technique is built of four screens, all of the same dimensions. The four different layers are uniquely named, but they all have the same size.

Tip   If you are making multiple versions of the same layer, consider changing the default layer size to fit your design. Choose Edit ⇨ Preferences and open up the default Layers preferences. Once you've customized the height and width values, all the layers incorporated in the Web page with the Insert ⇨ Layer command automatically size correctly. You only have to position these layers.

To recap, use the following steps to prepare your graphics:

1. Create all the images to be used as slides. All the slides must be the same height and width.

2. Prepare and place your interface buttons.

3. Create the number of layers that you'll need for the different screens in the slideshow.

4. Position your layers so that each can hold a different slide. The preceding example has four layers, centered on the screen in two rows.

5. Insert your opening slides into each of the layers.

   Note: Your opening slide doesn't have to be a graphic image. You could also use a solid-colored GIF or a slide with text.

Try to work backward from a final design whenever layer positioning is involved. At this stage, all of the elements are in their ending placement, ready for the slideshow to begin (see Figure 24-9). Next, you can begin to activate the slideshow.

Figure 24-9: Before activating any layers or setting up the slideshow, design the layout.

Step 2: Create the slideshow timeline

For all the attention that timelines and layers receive, you may be surprised that one of the best features of Dreamweaver timelines has nothing to do with layers. You can use timelines to change images anywhere on your Web page—whether or not they are in layers. As explained in Step 1, the timeline doesn't actually replace one <img> tag with another, but rather alters an image by swapping the src attribute value. The src changes just as changes in a layer's position, shape, or depth must happen at a keyframe.

In planning your slideshow, you need to decide how often a new slide appears, because you need to set keyframes at each of these points. If you are changing your slides every few seconds, you can change the frame rate to 1 fps. This setting helps you easily keep track of how many seconds occur between each slide change (and because no animation is involved with this timeline, a rapid frame rate is irrelevant). Note, however, that on the other timeline—involving moving layers— the frame rate should be maintained at around 15 fps. Each timeline can have its own frame rate.

The only other choices involve the Autostart and Loop options. As with frame rate, you can set each timeline to its own options without interfering with another timeline. This example has the slideshow loop but not start automatically. Use the Play button to enable the user to start the show. But first, let's add the images to the slides.

To put images into a slideshow on a timeline, follow these steps:

1. Choose Window ⇨ Timelines or select the Show Timelines button from either Launcher to open the Timeline Inspector.

2. If desired, rename Timeline1 by selecting the name and typing your own unique name.

3. Select one image from those on screen in the positioned layers, and drag the graphic to the Timeline Inspector.

    Be sure to grab the image—not the layer.

4. Release the animation bar at the beginning of the timeline.

5. Repeat steps 3 and 4 for each image until all images are represented on the timeline.

6. Change the frame rate by entering a new value in the Fps text box. This example changes the frame rate to 1.

7. Select the Loop or Autostart option, if desired.

8. On one of the animation bars representing images, select the frame for a keyframe.

9. Choose Modify ➪ Timeline ➪ Add Keyframe, or right-click (Ctrl-click) the frame on the timeline and choose Add Keyframe from the shortcut menu. Alternatively, you can choose the keyframe and press the keyboard shortcut, Shift-F9.

10. In the Image Property Inspector, select the Src folder to locate the graphic file for the next slide image.

11. Repeat steps 9 and 10 until every animation bar has keyframes for every slide change, and each keyframe has a new or different image assigned.

This example changes slides every five seconds, as you can see in Figure 24-10 by looking at the keyframe placement. Although the slideshow has all four images changing simultaneously, you can also stagger the timing of the image changes. Simply drag one or more of the animation bars a few frames forward or backward after the keyframes have been set.

Figure 24-10: Each keyframe on each animation bar signals a change of the slide image.

Tip

To preview your slide changes, you don't have to go outside of Dreamweaver. Just click and hold down the Play button on the Timeline Inspector.

Step 3: Create the moving layers timeline

At this stage, the slideshow is functional, but a little dull. To add a bit of showmanship, you can "fly in" the layers from different areas of the Web page to their final destination. This task is easy — to complete the effect, the layers "fly out" when the user is ready to leave.

You can achieve these fly-in/fly-out effects in several ways. You can put the opening fly-in on one timeline and the ending fly-out on another. A more concise method combines the fly-in and fly-out for each layer on one timeline — separating them with a Stop Timeline Behavior. After the fly-in portion happens when the page has loaded (because the example selects the Autostart option for this timeline), the fly-out section does not begin to play until signaled to continue with the Play Timeline Behavior.

To create the moving layers' opening and closing for the slideshow, follow these steps:

1. Choose Modify ⇨ Timeline ⇨ Add Timeline or right-click (Ctrl-click) the Timeline Inspector and choose Add Timeline from the shortcut menu.

2. Rename your new timeline if desired.

3. Select the Autostart check box so that this timeline begins playing automatically when the Web page is loaded.

4. Select any one of the layers surrounding your images and drag it onto the Timeline Inspector.

This time, make sure you move the layers — not the images.

5. To set the amount of time for the fly-in section to span, drag the final keyframe of the animation bar to a new frame. The example sets the end at 30 frames, which at 15 fps lasts two seconds.

6. From the Document Window, select the same layer again and drag it to the Timeline Inspector. Place it directly behind the first animation bar. This animation bar becomes the fly-out portion.

7. Drag the final keyframe to extend the time, if desired.

8. At this point, all four keyframes — two for each animation bar — have exactly the same information. Now change the positions for two keyframes to allow the layer to move. Select the first keyframe in the opening animation bar.

9. Reposition the layer so that it is off screen. Although you can complete this task manually to the right or bottom of the screen by dragging the layer to a new location, you can also use the Layer Property Inspector to input new values directly for the Left and Top attributes.

Use negative numbers to move a layer off screen on the left or top of the browser window.

10. From the Timeline Inspector, select the last keyframe of the closing animation bar.

11. Reposition the layer off screen. If you want the layer to return in the same manner as it arrived, enter the same values for the Left and Top attributes as in the first keyframe of the opening animation bar.

12. Repeat steps 4 through 11 for every layer.

Now, when you preview this timeline, the layers fly in and immediately fly out again. Figure 24-11 shows the layers in the example in midanimation. In the final phase of the technique, you add behaviors to put the action under user control.

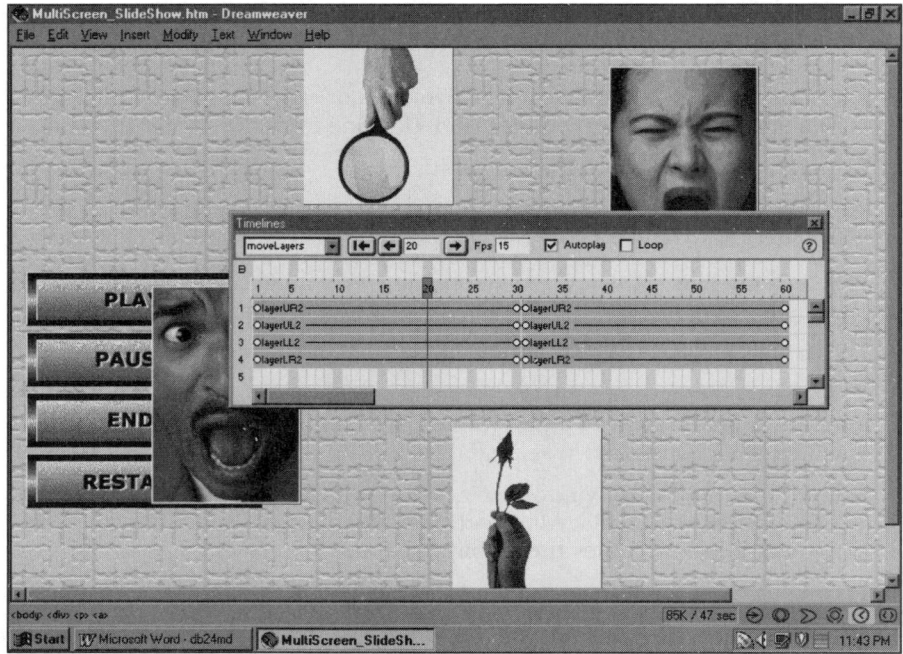

Figure 24-11: You can use two animation bars side-by-side to achieve a back and forth effect.

Step 4: Add the behaviors

Although it may be fun to watch an unexpected effect take place, giving the user control over aspects of a presentation is much more involving — for the designer as well as the user. The example is ready to incorporate the user-interaction aspect by attaching Dreamweaver behaviors to the user interface and to the behavior channel of the Timeline Inspector.

Two timeline behaviors have already been attached to the example — when the Loop option is selected in step 2 for the slideshow timeline, Dreamweaver automatically includes a Go to Timeline Frame Behavior after the final frame that sends the timeline back to the first frame. In the moving layers timeline, enabling the Autostart option causes Dreamweaver to attach a Play Timeline Behavior to the onLoad event of the Web page's `<body>` tag. To complete the project, five behaviors need to be added.

First, you need a behavior to stop the moving layers from proceeding after the fly-in portion of the animation:

1. From the Timeline Inspector, double-click the final frame of the first animation bar in the Behavior channel. The Behavior Inspector opens with an onFrame event displayed.

2. In the Behavior Inspector, add the Timeline ⇨ Stop Timeline action.

3. From the Stop Timeline dialog box, select the timeline that contains the moving layers.

Second, you need a behavior to let the user begin playing the slideshow:

1. In the Document Window, select the Play button.

2. In the Behavior Inspector, add the onClick or (onClick) event.

3. Add the Timeline ⇨ Play Timeline action.

4. In the Play Timeline dialog box, choose the layer representing the slideshow.

The next behavior enables the user to stop the slideshow temporarily:

1. In the Document Window, select the Pause button.

2. In the Behavior Inspector, add the onClick or (onClick) event.

3. Add the Timeline ⇨ Stop Timeline action.

4. Choose the layer representing the slideshow in the Stop Timeline dialog box.

To enable the user to begin the slideshow from the beginning, follow these steps:

1. In the Document Window, select the Restart button.

2. In the Behavior Inspector, add the onClick or (onClick) event.

3. Add the Timeline ⇨ Go to Timeline Frame action.

4. In the Go to Timeline Frame dialog box, enter a 1 in the Frame text box and click OK.

5. In the Behavior Inspector, add the Timeline ⇨ Start Timeline action.

6. In the Start Timeline dialog box, choose the layer representing the slideshow.

To end the presentation and move the user on to the next Web page, follow these steps:

1. In the Document Window, select the End button.

2. In the Behavior Inspector, add the onClick or (onClick) event.

3. Add the Timeline ⇨ Start Timeline action.

4. Choose the layer representing the moving layers in the Start Timeline dialog box, and click OK. The timeline begins playing where it last stopped — just before the layers are about to fly out.

5. Add the Go to URL action.

6. In the Go to URL dialog box, enter the path to the new page in the URL text box (or select the Browse button to locate the file). Click OK when you are finished.

The project is complete and ready to test. Feel free to experiment and try out different timings to achieve different effects.

You can test the final working version by just using your browser to view the Multiscreen Slideshow Demo in the Dreamweaver Bible Code section of the CD-ROM.

Summary

Timelines are effective tools for developing pages in which events need to be triggered at specific points in time.

✦ Timelines can affect particular attributes of layers and images, or they can start any Dreamweaver behavior.

✦ Use the Timeline Inspector to set an animation to play automatically, to have it loop indefinitely, and to change the frames-per-second display rate of the timeline.

✦ You must use one of the timeline behaviors to activate your timeline if you don't use the Autoplay feature.

In the next chapter, you'll learn how to handle browser targeting, as well as cross-browser and backwards-browser compatibility.

✦   ✦   ✦

Web Site Management Under Dreamweaver

Maximizing Browser Targeting

Each new release of a browser is a double-edged sword. On one hand, an exciting new array of features is made possible. On the other, Web designers have to cope with yet another browser-compatibility issue. In today's market, you'll find in use all of the following:

◆ A host of 3.0 browsers, widely varying in their capabilities

◆ A growing number of fourth-generation (and, soon, fifth-generation) browsers

◆ A small group of 2.0 browsers in the machines of determined users who have never (and may never) upgrade

◆ A diverse assortment of browsers outside the mainstream, including Opera, WebTV, and Linux

The browser compatibility issue is one of a Web designer's primary concerns (not to mention the source of major headaches); there are many strategies evolving to deal with this matter. Dreamweaver is in the forefront of cross-browser Web page design, both in terms of the type of code it routinely outputs and in its specialty functions. This chapter examines the browser-targeting techniques available in Dreamweaver. From multibrowser code to conversion innovations to browser validation capabilities, Dreamweaver helps you get your Web pages out to the widest audience with the most features.

Converting Pages in Dreamweaver

DHTML's gifts of layers and Cascading Style Sheets are extremely tempting to use because of their enhanced typographic-control and absolute-positioning capabilities. Many Web designers, however, have resisted using these features because only fourth generation browsers can view them. Though Dreamweaver can't change the capabilities of 3.0 browsers, it can make it easy for you to create alternative content for them.

Dreamweaver 1.2 makes it possible to convert Web pages designed with layers and CSS into pages that can be rendered by 3.0 browsers. Moreover, if you're looking to upgrade your site from nested tables to layers, you don't have to do it by hand. Dreamweaver also includes a command to convert tables to layers, preserving their location but allowing greater design flexibility and dynamic control. A Webmaster's life just got a tad easier.

Making 3.0-compatible pages

It's a slight misstatement that Dreamweaver converts 4.0 feature-laden pages into pages that can be read by 3.0 browsers. Actually, Dreamweaver creates a *new* 3.0-compatible page based on the 4.0 page—and does it in almost no time at all. Once you've converted your page, you can use Dreamweaver 1.2's Check Browser behavior to route users to the appropriate pages, based on their browser version.

Preparing your page for conversion

When Dreamweaver makes a new 3.0-compatible page, layers are converted to nested tables and Cascading Style Sheet references are converted to inline character styles. You have the option to convert either or both features. To accomplish this conversion of your 4.0 Web page, the document must meet the following conditions:

✦ **All content must be in layers.** Because Dreamweaver converts layers to tables, it must start with everything absolutely positioned.

✦ **Layers must not overlap.** During the conversion process, Dreamweaver warns you when it finds overlapping layers and even tells you which ones they are.

✦ **Nesting layers are not allowed.** When one layer is inside another, the inner layer is placed relative to the outer layer. Dreamweaver cannot convert relative-positioned layers.

✦ **The `<ilayer>` tag cannot be used.** Because the `<ilayer>` tag is based on relative positioning, Dreamweaver cannot convert it. Use `<layer>`, `<div>` or `<span>` instead.

Some Web pages you'd like to convert — or *devolve* — from 4.0 to 3.0 applicability have content both in and out of layers. And, as noted, Dreamweaver needs to have all the Web page elements in a layer before proceeding with conversion. Fortunately, this is not that difficult to set up. Depending on where on your page the layers are, you may be able to move all of the regular content at once; or you may have to move it in smaller sections. Regardless, the process for moving content from the regular position on a page into a layer is the same. Follow these steps:

1. Select all the content in your page that you want to transfer to a layer.

2. Use Edit ⇨ Cut or Ctrl-X (Command-X) to move the selected content to the Clipboard.

3. Choose Insert ⇨ Layer to open a new layer near the top of the page. You can also draw out your layer by selecting the Marquee Layer button from the Object Palette.

4. Paste the selected content into the layer, with Edit ⇨ Paste or Ctrl-V (Command-V).

   Be careful: Make sure that the cursor is *inside* the layer you are using.

5. Adjust your layer's position, if necessary, by clicking a selection handle and dragging it to a new location.

6. Repeat steps 1–5 until all of your content is moved into layers.

Running the conversion

Once your page is prepped, generating a 3.0-compatible Web page from a 4.0 version is straightforward. You only have a couple of options — whether to convert layers, CSS styles, or both — and once you make your choice and click OK, the rest of the process is almost instantaneous.

To a create 3.0-compatible version of a Web page with 4.0 features, follow these steps:

1. Choose File ⇨ Convert ⇨ 3.0 Browser Compatible; or use the keyboard shortcut, Ctrl-F6 (Command-F6).

   The Convert into 3.0 Browser Compatible File dialog box opens, as shown in Figure 25-1.

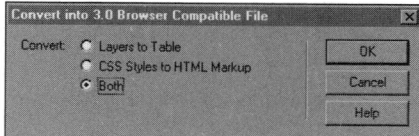

Figure 25-1: Begin to build your cross-browser compatible site with the Dreamweaver 1.2 new Convert Layers to Tables command.

2. From the Convert into 3.0 dialog box, select your options. If you are:

   - Converting layers to tables only, choose the Layers to Tables radio button.

   - Converting Cascading Style Sheet styles to HTML tags only, choose the CSS Styles to HTML Markup radio button.

   - Making all conversions, select the Both radio button.

3. Click OK, and Dreamweaver starts the conversion. A dialog box informs you if a problem is encountered, such as a nested layer or overlapping layers. If the Web page has overlapping layers, another dialog box (shown in Figure 25-2) tells you which layers are overlapping. Dreamweaver cannot proceed until all conflicts are resolved.

   If there are no problems, Dreamweaver creates the page in a new window.

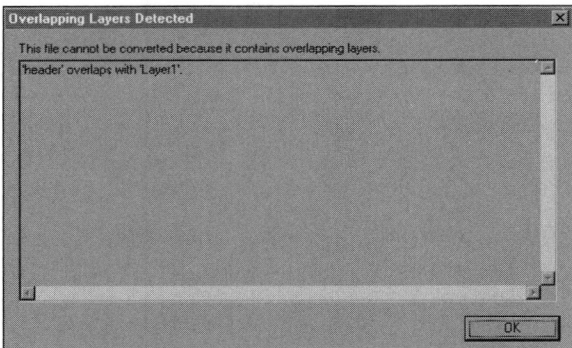

Figure 25-2: On a page with multiple layers, Dreamweaver spots the "illegal" overlapping ones when you try to convert the page to tables.

Note   The CSS-to-HTML conversion disregards any CSS feature, such as line spacing, that is not implemented in regular HTML. In addition, the exact point size that can be specified in CSS is roughly translated to the relative size equivalents in HTML. Any font over 36 points is set to the largest HTML size, which is 7.

Evolving 3.0 pages to 4.0 standards

Web sites are constantly upgraded and modified. Eventually you'll need to enhance a more traditional site with new features, such as layers. Some of the older 3.0-oriented sites used elaborately nested tables on their pages to create a semblance of absolute positioning; normally, upgrading these Web pages would take hours and hours of tedious cutting and pasting. Now, however, Dreamweaver can bring these older pages up to speed with the ConvertTables to Layers command.

Introduced in Dreamweaver 1.2, the Convert Tables to Layers command can also be used to make a version of a page created by another Web authoring program that uses nested tables for positioning (Net Objects Fusion, for example). Once tables have been transformed into layers, the layout of the entire page is much easier to modify. It's even possible to make the switch from 3.0 to 4.0 capabilities, modify your page and then, with the Convert to 3.0 Browser Compatible command, re-create your 3.0-compliant page.

The name of the Convert Tables to Layers command is another one that's a little misleading. Once you issue this command, every HTML element in the new page — not just the tables — is placed in a layer. Moreover, every cell with content in every table is converted into it's own layer, In other words, if you are working with a 3x3 table where one cell is left empty, Dreamweaver creates eight different layers for just the table. The only criteria for converting a page is that it contains at least one table.

Tip

If you want to convert a 3.0-compatible page to a page with layers but the page has no tables, you can add a dummy table with no data in it and choose File ⇨ Convert ⇨ Tables to Layers. Dreamweaver makes the conversion without the table, because the table was empty.

To convert a 3.0-browser-compatible Web page with tables to a 4.0-browser-compatible Web page with layers, choose File ⇨ Convert ⇨ Tables to Layers. Or use the keyboard shortcut, Ctrl-Shift-F6 (Command-Shift-F6). If there are no tables in the page, Dreamweaver alerts you to this fact and aborts the process. If, on the other hand, one or more tables are found in the page, Dreamweaver creates a new page with your content in layers.

Ensuring Browser Compatibility

As more browsers and browser versions become available, a Web designer has two basic approaches to take to stay on the road to compatibility: internal and external.

◆ The *internal* method uses scripts on the same Web page that deliver the proper code depending on the browser detected. Many of Dreamweaver's own behavior functions manage the browser issue internally.

◆ The *external* approach examines each visitor's browser right off the bat and reroutes the user to the most appropriate Web page.

Both the internal and the external methods have their pluses and minuses, and both are better suited to particular situations. For example, it is impractical to use the external method of creating multiple versions of the same Web pages when you are working with a large site. Suddenly, you've gone from managing 300 pages of information to 900 or 1,200. Of course, you don't have to duplicate every page — but because of the open nature of the Web, where any page can be bookmarked and entered directly, you have to plan carefully and provide routing routines at the key locations. Conversely, sometimes you have no choice but to use multiple versions, especially if a page employs many browser-specific features.

Don't get the idea that the internal and external strategies are mutually exclusive. Several sites today are routing 3.0 browsers to one page, and using internal coding methods to differentiate between the various 4.0 browser versions on another page. This section examines techniques for implementing browser compatibility from both the internal and external perspective.

Internal coding for cross-browser compatibility

Imagine the shouts of joy when the Web development community learned that the 4.0 versions of Navigator and Internet Explorer both supported Cascading Style Sheet layers! Now imagine the grumbling when it became apparent that each browser uses a different JavaScript syntax for calling them. You get the picture: it all boils down to differences in each browser's Document Object Model.

Tip

Dreamweaver's BDK includes a very large table that documents all of these differences. It's called "Object References in 4.0 Browsers," and it's available in the BDK version on the CD-ROM.

Calling layers

For example, when referring to a layer, Navigator uses this syntax:

```
document.layers[ layerName ]
```

while Internet Explorer uses this:

```
document.all[ layerName ]
```

The trick to internal code-switching is to assign the variations — the "layers" from Navigator and the "all" from Internet Explorer — to the same variable, depending on which browser is being used. Here's a sample function that does just that:

```
function init(){
if (navigator.appName ==  Netscape ) {
var layerRef= document.layers ;
}else {
```

```
var layerRef= document.all ;
  }
}
```

In this function, if the visitor is using a Netscape browser, the variable `layerRef` is assigned the value `document.layers`; otherwise, `layerRef` is set to `document.all`.

Calling properties

However, if we're looking to assign or read a layer property, one variable is only half the battle. There is another difference: in the way properties are called. With Navigator, it's done like this:

```
document.layers[ layerName ].top
```

while with Internet Explorer, it's:

```
document.all[ layerName ].style.top
```

Internet Explorer inserts another hierarchical division, called `style`, whereas Navigator doesn't use anything at all. The solution is another variable, styleRef, which for Internet Explorer would be set like this:

```
var styleRef= style
```

And the Navigator `styleRef` is actually set to a *null string* or nothing. You can combine the two variables into one initialization function, which is best called from an onLoad event in the `<body>` tag:

```
function init(){
if (navigator.appName ==  Netscape ) {
var layerRef= document.layers ;
var styleRef =   ;
}else {
var layerRef= document.all ;
var styleRef= style ;
  }
}
```

Once these differences are accommodated, the variables are ready to be used in a script. To do this, you can use JavaScript's built-in eval() function to combine the variables and the object references. Here's an example that sets a new variable, varLeft, to whatever is the `left` value of a particular layer:

```
varLeft = eval(layerRef +  [ myLayer ]  + styleRef +  .left );
```

Luckily, the variations between the Navigator and the Internet Explorer DOM are consistent enough that a JavaScript function can assign the proper values with a minimum of effort.

Calling objects within layers

There's one other area where the two DOMs diverge. When you are attempting to address almost any entity inside a layer, Navigator uses an additional hierarchical layer to reference the object. Thus, a named image in a named layer in Navigator is referenced like this:

```
document.layers[ layerName ].document.imageName
```

whereas the same object in Internet Explorer is called like this:

```
document.imageName
```

This is why the Show-Hide Layers Behavior passes two arguments with the affected layers' name: one in the Navigator format and the other in the Internet Explorer syntax.

Designing Web pages for backwards compatibility

The previous section describes a technique for dealing with the differences between 4.0 browsers, but how do you handle the much larger gap between third- and fourth- generation browsers? When this gap becomes a canyon, with DHTML-intensive pages on one side and noncompatible browsers on the other, the ultimate answer is to use redirection to send a particular browser to an appropriate page. However, there are plenty of cases where browsers can coexist — with a little planning and a little help from Dreamweaver.

When designing backwards-compatible Web pages, browsers generally offer one major advantage: ignorance. If a browser doesn't recognize a tag or attribute, it just ignores it and renders the rest of the page. Because many of the newer features are built on new tags, or on tags such as <div> that previously were little used, your Web pages can gracefully devolve from 4.0 to 3.0 behavior, without causing errors or grossly misrendering the page.

Take layers, for instance. One advantage offered by this DHTML feature is the capability to make something interactively appear and disappear. Although that's not possible in 3.0 browsers (without extensive image-swapping), it is possible to display the same material and even allow some degree of navigation. The key is proper placement of the layer code, and not the layer itself.

Browsers basically read and render the code for a Web page from top to bottom. You can, for example, make several layers appear one after another in a 3.0 browser, even if they appear to be stacked on top of one another in a 4.0 browser. All you have to do is make sure the code — not the position of the layers — appears in the document sequentially. You can see this effect in Figure 25-3, where there are three layers all with the same `left` and `top` coordinates. However, the layer symbols inserted by Dreamweaver to represent the actual code appear one after the other with a little white space in between. The navigational links in the upper-left have two roles: they are linked to the named anchor next to the layer's code and, through the Behavior Inspector, are set to show and hide the appropriate layers when selected (using the onClick event).

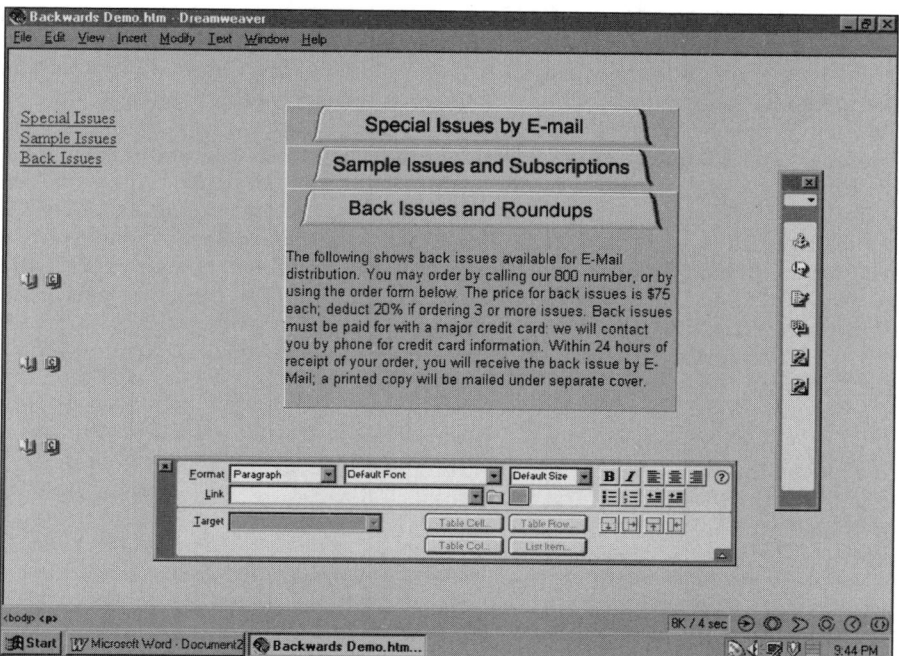

Figure 25-3: Careful placement of the code for layers can be an effective tool for backwards compatibility.

Because the code for three layers is spaced one after the other, browsers that do not understand the `style` attribute in the `<div>` tags — which create the layers — simply render the information contained within all three tags, one after another.

The Dreamweaver Technique in the upcoming section is based on methods used by George Olsen, Design Director of 2-Lane Media (www.21m.com), and an article by Trevor Lohrbeer in the Dynamic HTML Zone (www.dhtmlzone.com).

Tip   It's even possible to animate your layers for the benefit of Dynamic HTML-enabled browsers and at the same time allow 3.0 browsers to just show the static images. The key is to make sure that your animations begin and end in the same locations.

Dreamweaver Technique: Browser Checking

Because of the major differences between third- and fourth- generation browsers, it is increasingly popular practice to create a Web page geared to each browser and then use a *gateway* script to direct users to the proper page. A gateway script uses JavaScript to determine a visitor's browser version and route the page accordingly. Dreamweaver includes the Check Browser behavior (see Chapter 17, "Creating and Using Behaviors"), which makes this process relatively effortless.

For maximum efficiency, the best strategy is to use three pages: one page for 4.0 browsers, one page for 3.0 browsers, and a blank page that serves as your home page. Then, the Check Browser action can be assigned to the onLoad event of the blank page and can execute immediately. The other alternative is to use only two pages, one for each browser, and then run the Check Browser routine after the page is loaded and send the users of one browser version off to the other page. The disadvantage to this approach is that a good portion of your visitors have to sit through the loading process of one page, only to be whisked off to another and start again.

The following Technique takes you through the conversion of a layers-based page to a 3.0-compatible page; the creation of a new gateway page; and the incorporation of a Check Browser action that automatically directs users to a new page depending on their browser type.

Building a Web Page Gateway

1. In Dreamweaver, construct the fourth-generation browser version of your Web page — the one that uses layers and Cascading Style Sheets — first.

   Remember: Be sure no layers overlap and that the Web page otherwise meets the criteria noted in the preceding section, "Preparing your page for conversion."

2. Choose File ➪ Convert ➪ 3.0 Browser Compatible. Save the new version of the page, created by Dreamweaver, with a name similar to the original (4.0) page, but with a different prefix or suffix. For example, you might call the page intended for 4.0 browsers **index40.html** and the 3.0 version **index30.html**.

3. Choose File ⇨ New to create a new page. This page will serve as the gateway for the other two pages.

4. By default, Dreamweaver makes new pages with a white background. To make the gateway page as unobtrusive as possible, it's best to remove any background color options. To do this, choose Modify ⇨ Page Properties. In the Page Properties dialog box, select the #FFFFFF value in the Background Color text box and press Delete. Click OK, and the Web page is seen without any background color selected.

5. In your blank gateway page, choose Window ⇨ Behaviors to open the Behavior Inspector.

6. From the Tag Selector in the status bar of the Document Window, select the `<body>` tag.

7. In the Behavior Inspector, select the + (Add) Event button and choose the onLoad event from the pop-up.

8. In the Actions pane, select the + (Add) Action button and choose the Check Browser action from the pop-up.

9. In the Check Browser parameter form:

- Enter the URL for your 4.0 browser page in the URL text box or select the Browse button to locate the file.

- Enter the URL for your 3.0 browser page in the Alt URL text box or select the Browse button to locate the file.

    Click OK when you are done. If you haven't changed any of the other Check Browser default settings, both 4.0 browsers will go to the address in the URL text box, and all other browser versions will be directed to the address in the Alt URL text box. See Figure 25-4.

10. Save your gateway page. If this page is to serve as the gateway for the home page(s) for your domain, save it as **index.html**.

11. The gateway can now be preliminarily tested. However, because any Web page can be an entry point to a site, we also have to use the Check Browser action on each of the version-specific pages. Reopen the 4.0 browser page.

12. If necessary, open the Behavior Inspector by choosing Window ⇨ Behaviors or selecting the Show Behaviors button from the Launcher.

13. Repeat steps 6–8 to get to the Check Browser parameter form.

(continued)

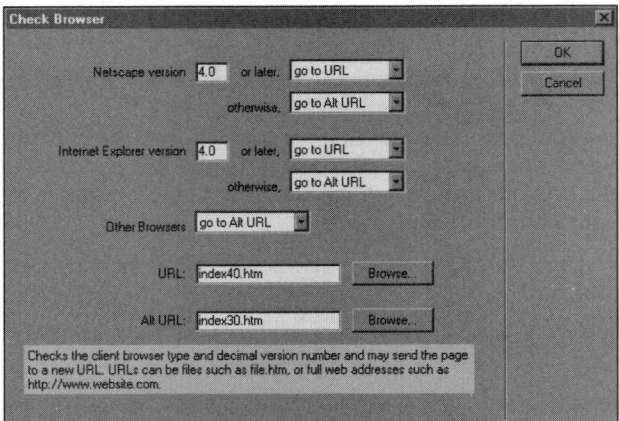

Figure 25-4: The Check Browser Behavior can build a gateway script for you with no coding.

14. This time, enter the URL for your 3.0 browser page in the Alt URL text box (or select the Browse button to locate the file).

15. In the sections for both Netscape and Internet Explorer 4.0 (or later), choose the Stay on This Page option from the drop-down list.

16. Select OK when you are finished and save the file.

17. Open the 3.0 browser page. Repeat steps 13–16, except when you get to the Check Browser parameter form, enter the URL for the 4.0 browser page in the Alt URL text box.

Now visitors can come in through the front door of your home page, or through any side door, and be served the correct page. Generally, not all the pages in your site will use the high-end features available to the 4.0 browsers, so you only have to create gateways for those pages that do. If you plan your site with this strategy in mind — avoid putting a moving layer on every page as a logo, for instance — you can manage your site more effectively.

Testing Your Page with a Targeted Browser

Testing is an absolute must when building a Web site. It's critical that you view your pages on as many browsers and systems as possible. Variations in color, gamma, page offset, and capabilities must be observed before they can be adjusted.

There is also a more basic, preliminary type of testing that can be done right from within Dreamweaver: code testing. Browsers usually ignore tags and attributes they do not understand. However, sometimes these tags can produce unexpected and undesirable results, such as exposing code to the viewer.

Dreamweaver's *browser targeting* feature, File ➪ Check Target Browsers, enables you to check a Web page — or an entire Web site — against any number of browser profiles. Dreamweaver 1.2 comes with profiles for the following browsers:

Internet Explorer 2.0	Navigator 2.0
Internet Explorer 3.0	Navigator 3.0
Internet Explorer 4.0	Navigator 4.0

You can choose to check your page or site against a single browser profile, all of them, or anything in between. Though not a substitute for real-world testing, browser targeting gives you an overview of potential errors and problematical code to look out for.

Testing browser compatibility for a Web page

To check a single Web page against specific browser targets, follow these steps.

Caution

With browser targeting, Dreamweaver checks the saved version of a Web page. So if you've made any modifications to your current page, save it *before* beginning the following process.

1. Choose File ➪ Check Target Browsers.

   The Check Target Browser(s) dialog box opens as shown in Figure 25-5.

2. Select the browser profiles against which you want the current page to be checked. The usual selection techniques work in this list: To choose various browsers, press Ctrl (Command) while selecting. To specify a contiguous range of browsers, select the first one, press Shift, and then select the last one.

3. After you've chosen the target browsers, click the Do Check button. Dreamweaver opens your primary browser, if necessary, and outputs the report to the browser window (see Figure 25-6).

4. Note: Dreamweaver only stores the browser profile report file temporarily and deletes the file after its use. To keep a record of the report, use your browser's File ➪ Print or File ➪ Save command.

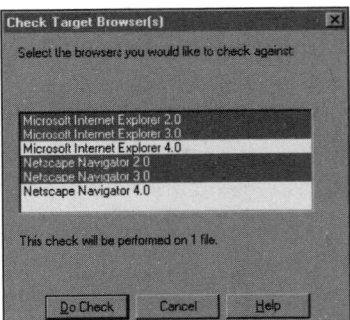

Figure 25-5: Select the browsers on which you'd like to check the code of your current page.

The Dreamweaver Target Browser Check offers both a summary and a detail section. The summary, shown in Figure 25-6, lists the browser being tested and any errors or warnings. Totals for each category are listed beneath the columns.

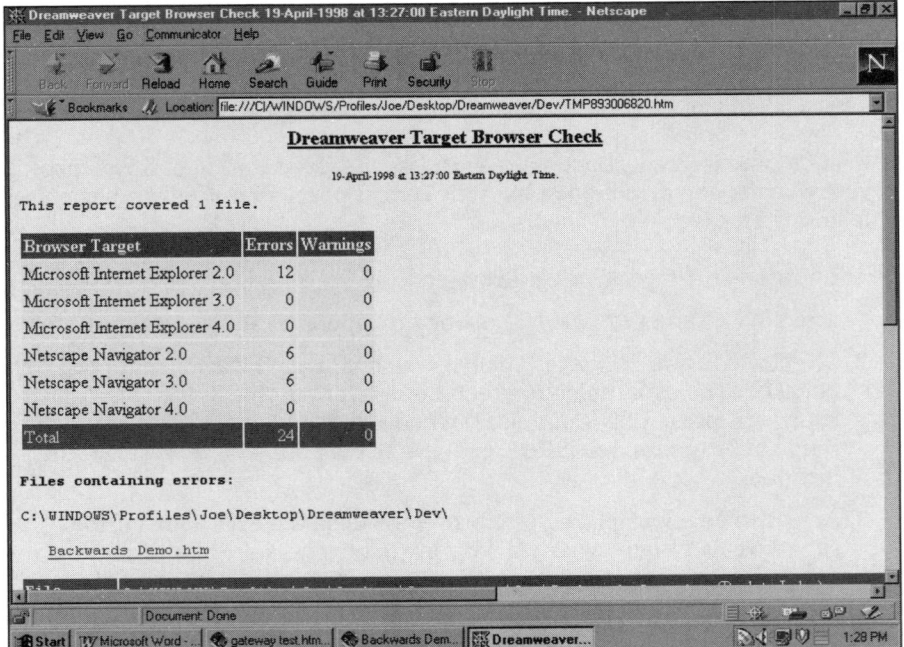

Figure 25-6: The Dreamweaver Target Browser Check displays a summary of all the errors it finds in your selected page. It's a good idea to print out the report or save it in a file.

The detail section of the browser check report, shown in Figure 25-7, lists the following:

✦ Each offending tag or attribute

✦ The browsers that do not support the tag or attribute

✦ An example HTML line

✦ Additional line numbers where the error occurred

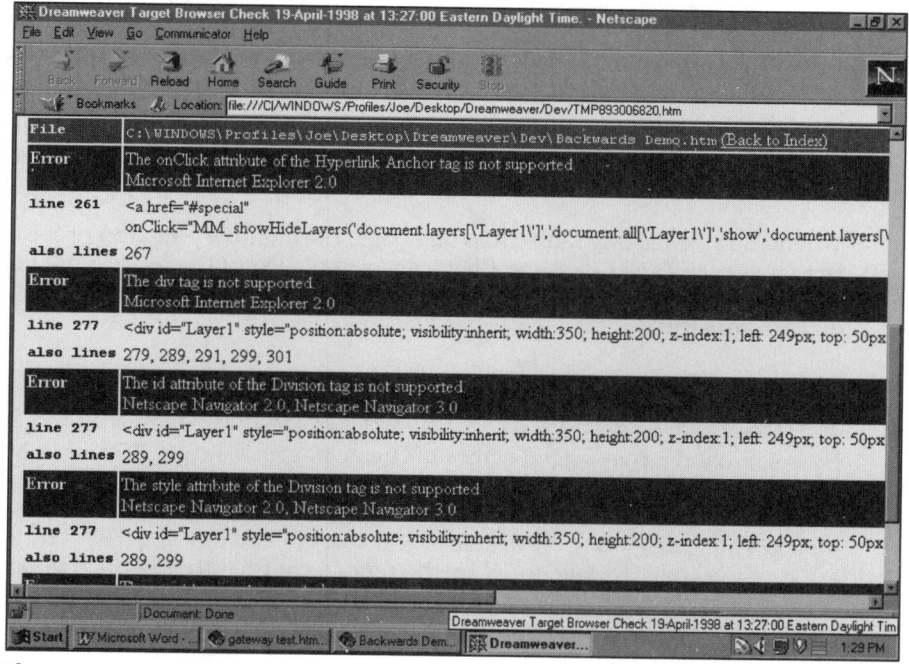

Figure 25-7: Detailed information can be found on the lower half of the Dreamweaver Target Browser Check report.

Testing browser compatibility for an entire site

With Dreamweaver, you can check the browser compatibility for an entire Web site as easily as you can check a single page. Dreamweaver checks all the HTML files in a given folder, whether they are actually used in the site or not.

To check an entire site against specific browser targets, follow these steps:

1. Choose File ⇨ Site or select the Show Site FTP button from the Launcher. The Site FTP window opens.   .

2. In the Site FTP window, select a folder from the Local Directory pane, or choose one of the listed sites from the Remote Site drop-down list.

3. Choose File ⇨ Check Target Browsers. The Check Target Browser(s) dialog box opens, shown earlier in Figure 25-5. Below the list of Browser Profiles, there's a statement of how many pages are to be checked.

4. Select the Browser Profiles against which you want the current site checked.

5. When you're ready, select the Do Check button. Dreamweaver opens your primary browser, if necessary, and outputs the report to the browser window.

6. Note: Dreamweaver only stores the Browser Profile report file temporarily and deletes the file after its use. To keep a record of the report, use your browser's File ⇨ Print or File ⇨ Save command.

When you're checking more than one page, the summary section of the Dreamweaver Target Browser Check gives you a list of the files containing errors as well as an error count. The summary section displays the errors for each file grouped together.

Using the results of the browser check

How you handle the flagged errors in Dreamweaver's Target Browser Check report is entirely dependent on the design goals you have established for your site. If your mission is to be totally accessible to every browser on the market, then you need to look at your page/site with the earliest browsers and pay special attention to those areas of possible trouble noted by the report. On the other hand, if your standards are a little more relaxed, then you can probably ignore the 2.0 browser warnings and concentrate on those appearing in the 3.0 and 4.0 categories.

Customizing a Browser Profile

For Dreamweaver's browser targeting feature to be effective, you must have access to profiles for all the browsers you need to check. You can create custom browser profiles to cover any new browser versions or browsers as they become available. The Browser Profile file is a text file and can be created or altered in any text editor.

In this section, we look at the required structure and format for a Browser Profile file, and the steps for building one based on an existing file.

Understanding the Browser Profile structure

In order for Dreamweaver to properly process an HTML file using any browser profile, the profile must follow a precise format. Here's a sample taken from the Internet Explorer 3.0 browser profile:

```
<!ELEMENT H1 name= Heading 1  >
<!ATTLIST H1
        Align ( left | center | right )
        Class
        ID
        Style
>
```

As you can see, the HTML tag is listed in a very specific syntax. Here's how the syntax is formed:

```
<!ELEMENT htmlTag Name= tagName  >
<!ATTLIST htmlTag
unsupportedAttribute1  !Error  !msg= The unsupportedAttribute1 of
the htmlTag is not supported. Try using thisAttribute for a
similar effect.
supportedAttribute1
supportedAttribute2    ( validValue1 | validValue2 | validValue3
)
unsupportedAttribute2  !Error  !htmlmsg= <b>Don t ever use this
unsupportedAttribute2 of the  htmlTag !!</b>
>
```

The variables in the syntax are as follows:

✦ htmlTag: The tag as it appears in an HTML document.

✦ tagName: Optional; how the tag is known. For example, the <applet> tag is called the "Java Applet." If it's noted in the file, the tagName is used in the error message; otherwise, htmlTag is used.

✦ unsupportedAttribute: Indicates invalid attributes so that a custom error message can be offered. Otherwise, all attributes not specifically listed are assumed to be unsupported.

✦ supportedAttribute: A valid attribute; all valid attributes must be listed. Only attributes listed without an !Error designation are supported.

✦ validValue: A value supported by the attribute.

Several other, not-so-obvious rules must be followed for Dreamweaver to correctly read the profile:

✦ The name of the profile must appear in the first line of the file, followed by a single carriage return. This is the profile name that appears in the Check Target Browser(s) dialog box and in the report.

✦ The key phrase `PROFILE_TYPE=BROWSER_PROFILE` must appear in the second line.

✦ On the `!ELEMENT` line, a single space must be used before the closing angle (>) bracket, after the opening parentheses, before the closing parentheses, and before and after each pipe (|) character in the list of values.

✦ There must be an exclamation point, without an intervening space, before the words `ELEMENT`, `ATTLIST`, `Error`, `msg` and `htmlmsg`. For example:

```
!ELEMENT, !ATTLIST, !Error, !msg, and !htmlmsg.
```

✦ You can only use plain text in `!msg` messages, but a `!htmlmsg` message can use any valid HTML, including links.

✦ Don't use HTML comment tags, `<!-- -->`, because they interfere with the regular Dreamweaver processing of the file.

Creating a Browser Profile

As you can see, Dreamweaver browser profiles do have a very specific structure. Consequently, it's far easier to modify an existing profile than to write one from scratch. The basic procedure takes three steps:

✦ Choose an existing profile for a browser similar to the one for which you are creating a new profile. Open the profile in a text editor.

✦ Add any tags and attributes that are supported in the target browser but not in the existing profile.

✦ Remove any tags or attributes not supported by your target browser. Or, you can add an `!Error` message after any attribute to flag it for Dreamweaver's Target Browser Check operation.

For example, take a look at the code fragment illustrated in Listing 25-1; it contains a portion of the browser profile I created for WebTV. Note the custom error messages after the `<applet>` tag and the `rel` attribute of the `<a>` tag.

Caution

When saving a new browser profile in Windows, there's a small trick to getting the version number to appear correctly at the end of the browser name, as in "Navigator 3.0." Choose File ➪ Save As from your text editor. Then in the filename box enter your browser name with the filename extension (.txt), all enclosed in quotes. For example, to save the Web TV 1.0 file, I entered **"WebTV_1.0.txt"** in the Filename text box.

Listing 25-1: **Excerpt from Browser Profile file for WebTV**

```
WebTV 1.0
PROFILE_TYPE=BROWSER_PROFILE
-- Copyright 1997 Macromedia, Inc. All rights reserved.

<!ELEMENT A Name= Hyperlink Anchor  >
<!ATTLIST A
        Class                   !Error
        HREF
        ID
        Name
        OnClick
          OnMouseOut
        OnMouseOver
          Rel                       !Warning !msg  The rel
attribute has been modified by WebTV.
        Style                   !Error
          Selected              !Error
        Target                  !Error
>

<!ELEMENT Address >
<!ATTLIST Address
        Class                   !Error
        ID                      !Error
        Style                   !Error
>

<!ELEMENT APPLET Name= Java Applet  > !Error !msg  WebTV does
not support Java Applets.
<!ATTLIST APPLET
        Align ( top | middle | bottom | left | right |
absmiddle | absbottom | baseline | texttop )
        Alt
        Archive         !Error
        Code
        Codebase
        Height
        HSpace
        Name
        VSpace
        Width
        Class
        ID
        Style
```

(continued)

Listing 25-1 *(continued)*

```
>

<!ELEMENT AREA Name= Client-side image map area  >
<!ATTLIST AREA
        Alt                     !Error
        Class                   !Error
        Coords
        HREF
        ID
          Name
        NoHREF
          NoTab
          OnMouseOut
        OnMouseOver
        Shape
        Style                   !Error
        Target
>

<!ELEMENT AUDIOSCOPE Name= Audioscope  >
<!ATTLIST AUDIOSCOPE
        Align
        Border
        Gain
        Height
        LeftColor
        LeftOffset
        MaxLevel
        RightColor
          RightOffset
        Width
>

<!ELEMENT B Name= Bold  >
<!ATTLIST B
        Class                   !Error
        ID                      !Error
        Style                   !Error
>

<!ELEMENT Base >
<!ATTLIST Base
        HREF
        Target
>

<!ELEMENT BaseFont >
```

```
<!ATTLIST BaseFont
        Size
>

<!ELEMENT BGSOUND Name= Background sound  >
<!ATTLIST BGSOUND
        Loop
        Src
>

<!ELEMENT Big >
<!ATTLIST Big
        Class
        ID
        Style
>

<!ELEMENT Blackface >

<!ELEMENT Blink !Error >

<!ELEMENT Blockquote >

<!ELEMENT Body >
<!ATTLIST Body
        ALink                        !Error
        Background
        BGColor
        BGProperties
          Credits
        LeftMargin
        Link
          Logo
        OnBlur                               !Error
        OnFocus                              !Error
        OnLoad
        OnUnload
        Style                                !Error
        Text
        VLink
>

<!ELEMENT BQ Name= Block Quote  >

<!ELEMENT BR Name= Line break  >
<!ATTLIST BR
        Clear ( left | right | all )
>
```

Summary

Unless you're building a Web site for a strictly controlled intranet, in which case you know everyone is using the BrandX 4.03 browser, it's critical that you address the browser compatibility issues that your Web site is certain to face. Whether it's cross-browser or backwards compatibility you're trying to achieve, Dreamweaver has features and techniques in place to help you get your Web pages viewed by the maximum number of users.

✦ Dreamweaver takes a Web page built with 4.0 features, including layers and CSS, and creates another Web page that is 3.0-compatible.

✦ Dreamweaver can take a Web page created with tables and create another Web page that uses layers instead.

✦ You can use JavaScript within a Web page to handle cross-browser-compatibility problems with 4.0 browsers.

✦ Careful placement of your HTML objects can help with backwards compatibility.

✦ Dreamweaver lets you check your Web page or Web site against a browser profile to look for tags and attributes that will not work in a particular browser version.

✦ Browser profiles can be customized or copied and modified for a new browser or browser version.

In the next chapter, you see how to use Dreamweaver's Library feature to reuse repeating elements.

✦   ✦   ✦

Using the Repeating Elements Library

One of the challenges of designing a Web site is ensuring that buttons, copyright notices, and other cross-site features always remain consistent. Fortunately, Dreamweaver offers a useful feature called *Library items* which helps you insert repeating elements, such as a navigation bar or a company logo, into every Web page you create. With one command, you can update and maintain Library items efficiently and productively.

In this chapter you examine the nature and the importance of repeating elements, and find out how to effectively use the Dreamweaver Library feature for all of your sites.

Dreamweaver Libraries

Library items within Dreamweaver are another means for you as a designer to maintain consistency throughout your site. Suppose you have an navigation bar on every page that contains links to all of your site's other pages. It's highly likely that you'll eventually (and probably more than once) need to make changes to the navigation bar. In a traditional Web development environment, you must modify every single page. There are lots of opportunities for making mistakes, missing pages, and adding code to the wrong place. Moreover, the whole process is tedious — ask anyone who has had to modify the copyright notice at the bottom of every Web page for a site with over 200 pages.

Another traditional method of updating repeating elements is using server-side includes. A *server-side include* causes the server to place a component, say a copyright notice, in a specified area of a Web page when it's sent to the user. This arrangement, however, increases the strain on your already overworked Web server. Not to mention you have to know how to install server-side scripts. To add to the designer's frustrations, you can't lay out a Web page in a WYSIWYG format and simultaneously see the server-side scripts. So you either take the time to calculate that a server-side script will take up a specific space on the Web page, or you cross your fingers and guess.

There is a better way in Dreamweaver, using the important innovation called the Library. The Library is designed to make repetitive updating quick, easy, and as error free as possible. The Library's key features include the following:

✦ Any item — whether text or graphic — that goes in the body of your Web page can be designated as a Library item.

✦ Once created, Library items can be placed instantly in any Web page in your site, without your having to retype, reinsert, or reformat text and graphics.

✦ Library items can be altered at any time. After the editing is complete, Dreamweaver gives you the option to update the Web site immediately or postpone the update until later.

✦ If you are making a number of alterations to your Library items, you can wait until you're finished with all the updates and then make the changes across the board in one operation.

✦ You can update one page at a time, or you can update the entire site all at once.

✦ A Library item can be converted back to a regular non-Library element of a Web page at any time.

✦ Library items can be copied from one site to another.

Using the Library Palette

Dreamweaver's Library control center is, of course, the Library Palette. There you find the tools for creating, modifying, updating and managing your Library items. Shown in Figure 26-1, the Library Palette is as flexible and easy-to-use as all of Dreamweaver's primary palettes, with straightforward command buttons, an alphabetical listing of all available Library items, and a handy preview pane.

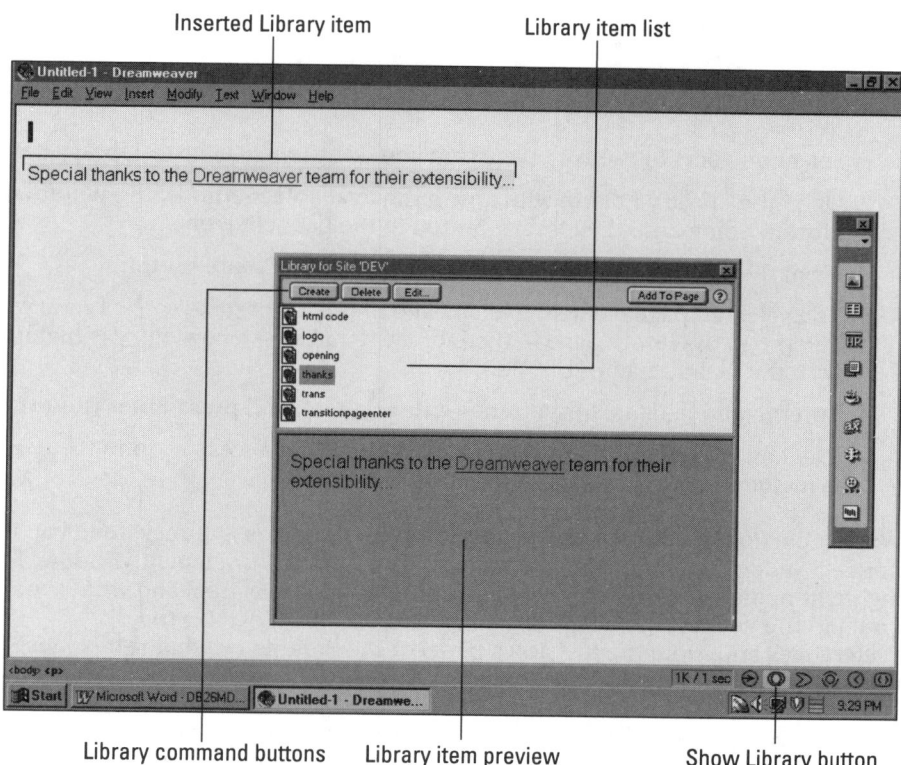

Figure 26-1: With the Dreamweaver Library Palette, you can easily add and modify consistent objects to an entire Web site.

As usual, you can open the Library Palette in several ways:

✦ Choose Windows ➪ Library.

✦ Select the Library button from the Launcher.

✦ Press F7.

Caution

To use Library items, you must first create a site root folder for Dreamweaver, as explained in Chapter 5, "Setting Up Your First Site." A separate Library folder is created to hold the individual Library items and is used by Dreamweaver during the updating process.

Ideally, you could save the most time by creating all your Library items before you begin constructing your Web pages, but most Web designers don't work that way. Feel free to include, modify, and update your Library items as much as you need to as your Web site evolves — that's part of the power and the flexibility you gain because of Dreamweaver's Library.

Adding a Library item

Before you can insert or update a Library item, that item must be designated as such within the Web page. To add an item to your site's Library, follow these steps:

1. Select any part of the Web page that you want to make into a Library item.

2. Open the Library Palette with any of the available methods: the Windows ⇨ Library command, the Library button in the Launcher, or F7.

3. From the Library Palette (Figure 26-1), select the Create button.

    The selected page element is displayed in the lower pane of the Library Palette. In the upper pane — the Library item list — a new entry is highlighted with the default name "Untitled."

4. Enter a unique name for your new Library item, and press Enter (Return).

    The Library item list is resorted alphabetically, if necessary, and the new item is included.

When a portion of your Web page has been designated as a library item, you'll notice a yellow highlight over the entire item within the Document Window. The highlight helps you to quickly recognize what is a Library item and what is not. If you find the yellow highlight distracting, you can disable it. Go to Edit ⇨ Preferences and, from the Invisibles panel of the Preferences dialog box, deselect the Library Item Highlight check box.

Caution   At this writing, Dreamweaver can include Library items only in the <body> section of an HTML document. You cannot, for instance, create a series of <meta> tags for your pages that must go in the <head> section.

Drag-and-Drop Creation of Library Items

A second option for creating Library items is the drag-and-drop method. Simply select an object or several objects on a page and drag them to the Library item list of the Library Palette; release the mouse button to drop them in.

You can drag any object into the Library Palette: text, tables, images, Java applets, plug-ins, and/or ActiveX controls. Essentially anything in the Document Window that can be HTML code can be dragged to the Library. And, as you might suspect, the reverse is true: library items can be placed in your Web page by dragging them from the Library Palette list and dropping them anywhere in the Document Window.

Moving Library items to a new site

Although Library items are specific to each site, they can be used in more than one site. When you make your first Library item, Dreamweaver creates a folder called Library in the local root folder for the current site. To use a particular Library item in another site, simply open the Library folder from your system's desktop and copy the item to the new site's Library folder.

Inserting a Library item in your Web page

When you create a Web site, there are always certain standard features you need to incorporate, including a standard set of link buttons along the top, a consistent banner on various pages, and a copyright notice along the bottom. To add these items to a page with the Library Palette can be as easy as dragging and dropping them.

You must first create a Web site and then designate Library items (as explained in the preceding section). Once these items exist, you will be able to add the items to any page created within your site.

To add Library items to a document, use the following steps:

1. Position the cursor where you want the Library item to appear.
2. From the Library Palette, select the item you wish to use.
3. Select the Add to Page button. The Library item appears on the Web page, highlighted in yellow.

Tip   As noted earlier, you can also use the drag-and-drop method to place Library items in the Document Window.

When you add a Library item to a page, you notice a number of immediate changes. As mentioned, the added Library item will be highlighted in light yellow. If you click anywhere on the item, the whole of the Library item will be selected.

It's important to understand that Dreamweaver treats the entire Library item entry as an external object being linked to the current page. You cannot modify Library items directly on a page. For information on editing Library entries, see "Editing a Library Item" later in this chapter.

While the Library item is highlighted, you will also notice that the Property Inspector changes. Instead of displaying the properties for the HTML object that is selected, the item is identified as a Library item as shown in Figure 26-2.

Figure 26-2: The Library item Property Inspector identifies the source file for any selected Library entry.

The HTML for a Library item

You can also see evidence of Library items in the HTML for the current page. Open the HTML Inspector, and you see that several lines of code have been added. The following code example indicates one Library item (in boldface):

```
<!-- #BeginLibraryItem /Library/title.lbi -->
<font color= #FF6633 face= Verdana, Arial, Helvetica, sans-
serif size= +4 >
<b>Copyright &copy; 1998</b></font>
<!-- #EndLibraryItem -->
```

In this case the Library item happens to be a phrase: "Copyright © 1998." (The character entity © is used to represent the c-in-circle copyright mark in HTML.) In addition to the code that specifies the font face, color and size, notice the text before and after the HTML code. These are commands within the comments that tell Dreamweaver it is looking at a Library item. One line marks the beginning of the Library item:

```
<!--#BeginLibraryItem /Library/title.lbi -->
```

and another marks the end:

```
<!--#EndLibraryItem -->
```

Two items are of interest here. First, notice how the Library demarcation surrounds not just the text ("Copyright © 1998"), but all of its formatting attributes. Library items can do far more than just cut-and-paste raw text. The second thing to note is that the Library markers are placed discreetly within HTML comments. Web browsers ignore the Library markers and render the code in between them.

The value in the opening Library code, /Library/title.lbi , is the source file for the Library entry. This file would be located in the Library folder, inside of the current site root folder. Library source (.lbi) files can be opened with a text editor or Dreamweaver; they consist of plain HTML code without the <html> and <body> tags.

The .lbi file for our title example would contain the following:

```
<font color= #FF6633 face= Verdana, Arial, Helvetica, sans-
serif size= +4 >
<b>Copyright &copy; 1998</b></font>
```

The power of repeating elements is that they are simply HTML. There is no need to learn proprietary languages to customize Library items. Anything, except for information found in the header of a Web page, can be included in a library file.

The importance of the `<!-- #BeginLibraryItem>` and `<!-- #EndLibraryItem>` tags become extremely evident when you start to update Library items to a site. You examine how Dreamweaver can be used to automatically update your entire Web site in the later section, "Updating your Web site with Libraries."

Deleting an item from the Library

Removing an entry from your site's Library is a two-step process. First, you must delete the item from the Library Palette. Then, if you want to keep the item on your page, you must make it editable again. Without completing the second step, Dreamweaver maintains the Library highlight and, more important, prevents you from modifying the element.

To delete an item from the Library, follow these steps:

1. Open the Web page containing the Library item you want to delete.

2. Open the Library Palette by choosing Window ⇨ Library or selecting the Library button from the Launcher.

3. Select the Library item in the Library Palette's list, and click the Delete button or press Delete.

4. Dreamweaver asks if you are sure you want to delete the item. Select Yes, and the entry is removed from the Library item list. (Or select No to cancel.)

5. In the Document Window, select the element you are removing from the Library.

6. In the Property Inspector, click the Make Editable button.

7. As shown in Figure 26-3, Dreamweaver warns you that if you proceed, the item cannot be automatically updated (as a Library element). Select OK to proceed. The yellow Library highlight vanishes and the element can now be modified individually.

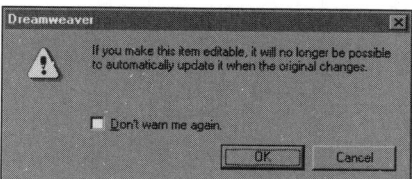

Figure 26-3: When removing an entry from the Library, Dreamweaver alerts you that, if you proceed, you won't be able to update the item automatically using the Library function.

Tip

Should you unintentionally delete a Library item in the Library Palette, you can restore it if you still have the entry included in a Web page. Select the element within the page and, in the Property Inspector, choose the Recreate [sic] button. Dreamweaver restores the item to the Library item list, with the original Library name.

Renaming a Library item

It's easy to rename a Library item, but you should exercise caution when doing so. Renaming a Library item only renames that item in the Library folder — it does not rename the item in any Web page where the item has already been inserted. Should you attempt to modify and update the renamed item, occurrences of the same item under the old name in existing pages will not be updated.

To give an existing Library entry a new name, open the Library Palette and click once on the name of the item. The name is highlighted and a small box appears around it. Enter the new name and press Enter (Return).

The best strategy to follow when renaming a Library item is to rename it *before* you insert the entry into any Web pages. If you should rename the item after it has been included in one or more Web pages, there are two approaches to the renaming task:

✦ If the renamed item is included in only a few Web pages: Open every Web page containing the Library item that you've renamed. Delete the original entry from the Web page, and insert the renamed item.

✦ If the renamed item has been included on a number of pages in your Web site: Use your external editor's extended search-and-replace feature to change the item's name within the HTML code.

Let's look at an example of the second option. Suppose you've included a Library entry, originally called LibraryItem01, on six or seven Web pages within a site. Later you decide to change the name to something more descriptive, like CopyrightLine. After you've renamed the item in the Library, so all future uses of the entry will be correct, you need to correct the previously inserted entries. Because you have numerous entries to fix, you decide to use the extended search-and-replace method to change the name within the HTML. In your external editor, you would search for

```
<!-- #BeginLibraryItem  /Library/LibraryItem01.lbi  -->
```

and replace it with

```
<!-- #BeginLibraryItem  /Library/CopyrightLine.lbi  -->
```

Note

Both HTML editors included with Dreamweaver, HomeSite and BBEdit, have powerful extended search-and-replace features that allow you to quickly change all the entries in all the pages of a Web site.

Editing a Library Item

Rarely will you create a Library item that is perfect from the beginning and never needs to be changed. Whether it is due to site redesign or the addition of new sections to a site, you'll find yourself going back to Library items and modifying them, sometimes over and over again. You can use the full power of the Dreamweaver's design capabilities to alter your Library items, within the restraints of Library items in general. In other words, you can modify an image, reformat a body of text, add new material to a boilerplate paragraph, and have the resulting changes reflected across your Web site. However, you can not add anything to a Library item that is not contained in the HTML <body> tags.

Dreamweaver uses a special editing window for modifying Library items that is identifiable by its gray background. You access this editing window through the Library Palette. Follow these steps to modify an existing Library item:

1. In the Library Palette, select the item you wish to modify from the list of available entries.

2. Click the Edit button. The Library editing window opens with the selected entry, as shown in Figure 26-4.

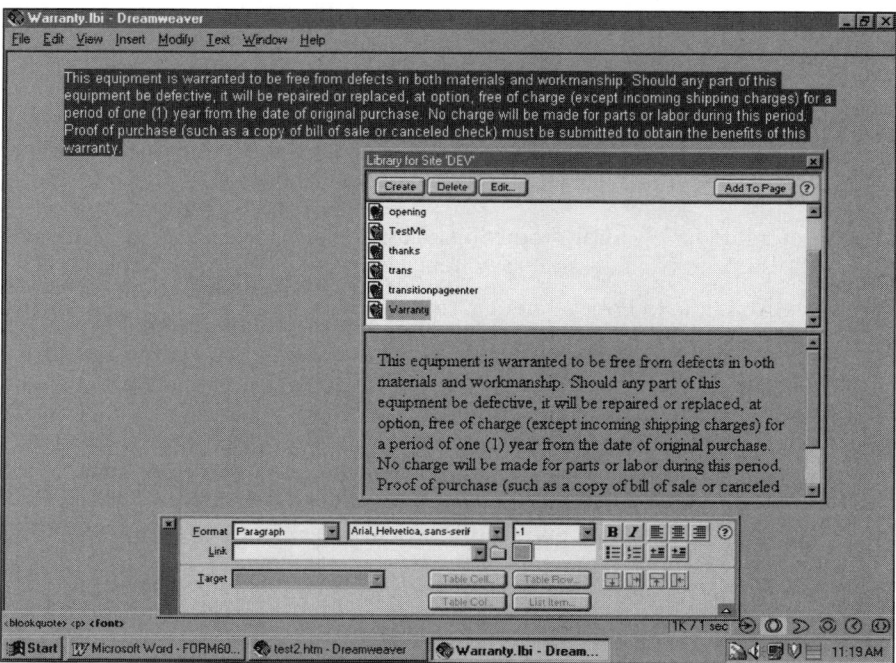

Figure 26-4: Use the Library editing window to modify existing Library items.

3. Make any necessary modifications to the Library entry.

4. When you are finished with your changes, choose File ➪ Save or press Ctrl-S (Command-S).

5. Dreamweaver notes that your Library item has been modified and asks if you would like to update the Web pages containing the item. Select Yes to update all the Library items, including the one just modified; or choose No to postpone the update. (See the upcoming section, "Updating Your Web Site's Library Items.")

6. Close the editing window by selecting the Close button or choosing File ➪ Close.

Once you've completed the editing operation and closed the editing window, you can open any Web page containing the modified Library item to view the changes.

Caution

There are some features that you will not be able to use when editing Library items. These include Timelines, Behaviors, Layers and Styles. Each of these modifications requires a JavaScript function to be placed in the `<head>` tags of a page — a task that the Dreamweaver Library function cannot currently handle. As a workaround, you can use a Dreamweaver template to add entire pages with JavaScript functions included, as described in Chapter 28, "Using Dreamweaver Templates."

Updating Your Web Sites with Libraries

The effectiveness of the Dreamweaver Library feature becomes more significant when it comes time to update an entire multipage site. Dreamweaver offers two opportunities for you to update your site:

✦ Immediately after modifying a Library item, as explained in the preceding steps for editing a Library item.

✦ At a time of your choosing, through the Modify ➪ Library command.

An immediate update to every page on your site can be accomplished when you edit a Library item. After you save the alterations, Dreamweaver asks if you'd like to apply the update to Web pages in your site. If you click Yes, Dreamweaver not only applies the current modification to all pages in the site, but it applies any other alterations, as well, that you have made previously in this Library.

The second way to modify a Library item is by using the Modify ➪ Library command, and when you use this method you can choose to update the current page or the entire site.

To update just the current page, choose Modify ⇨ Library ⇨ Update the Current Page. Dreamweaver makes a quick check to see what Library items you are managing on the current page and then compares them to the site's Library items. If there are any differences, Dreamweaver modifies the page accordingly.

To update an entire Web site, follow these steps:

1. Choose Modify ⇨ Library ⇨ Update the Entire Site. The Update Site dialog box opens (Figure 26-5).

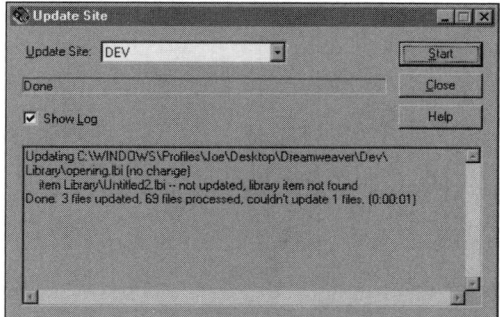

Figure 26-5: The Update Site dialog allows you to apply any changes to your Library items across an entire site, and informs you of the progress.

2. Select the Web site you want to update from the drop-down list.

3. If you want to see the results from the update process, leave the Show Log check box selected. (Turning off the Log reduces the size of the Site Update dialog box.)

4. Choose the Start button. Dreamweaver processes the entire site for Library updates. Any Library items contained will be modified to reflect the changes.

Note   Although Dreamweaver does modify Library items on currently open pages during an Update Site operation, you will have to save the pages to accept the changes.

The Update Site log displays any errors encountered in the update operation. In the example shown in Figure 26-5, this notation:

```
item Library\Untitled2.lbi -- not updated, library item not
found
```

indicates that one Web page contains a reference to a Library item that has been removed. Though this is not a critical error, you might want to use an external HTML editor (HomeSite or BBEdit, for instance) to search your Web site for the code and remove it.

Dreamweaver Technique: Creating Server-Side includes with the Library

At the beginning of this chapter I mentioned the conventional method for inserting the same HTML element in each Web page, using server-side includes. Server-side includes are instructions embedded in a Web page that, when processed by the Web server, cause the server to insert a specific bit of HTML code before presenting it to the client browser. Dreamweaver Libraries replace much of the functionality of server-side includes, yet some Web designers will find that they need to keep using the earlier technology — whether by choice or because it has been mandated by the client or management. This section describes a technique by which you combine Dreamweaver's Library items with conventional server-side includes in such a way that simplifies the creation and maintenance of the #include mechanism.

When inserted into the HTML code, a server-side include looks like this:

```
<!--#include file= legal.html  -->
```

Because an #include uses the HTML comment structure, adding it to a Dreamweaver site Library is a simple matter. However, you need to know a trick or two before you can make any modifications to the item. Here's how it works.

Here's how to convert a server-side include to a Dreamweaver Library item:

1. Before proceeding, make sure that your Dreamweaver Preferences option to show a Comment icon is enabled. Choose Edit ➪ Preferences and select the Invisible Elements category in the Preferences dialog box. The Comment check box should be selected.

2. If it's not already on your Web page, enter your server-side include. You can do this through the HTML Inspector or with your external text editor. Another option is to go to the Object Palette's Invisibles panel and select Comment, and then enter the #include information in the dialog box.

3. Open the Library Palette by choosing Window ➪ Palette or selecting the Library button from the Launcher.

4. In the Document Window, select the Comment icon for your server-side include.

5. In the Library Palette, click the Create button, or drag-and-drop the Comment icon into the Library Palette's list pane.

6. Name your new Library entry.

You can now insert the server-side include as you would any other Library item. If, however, you ever need to modify the entry, there is one difference to the usual method.

Here's how to modify a Library item for a server-side include:

1. Select the item in the Library Palette list and choose the Edit button. When the Library editing window opens, it will appear to be empty.

2. Open the HTML Inspector by choosing Window ➪ HTML or selecting HTML button from the Launcher. The server-side include code is revealed in the HTML Inspector as shown in Figure 26-6.

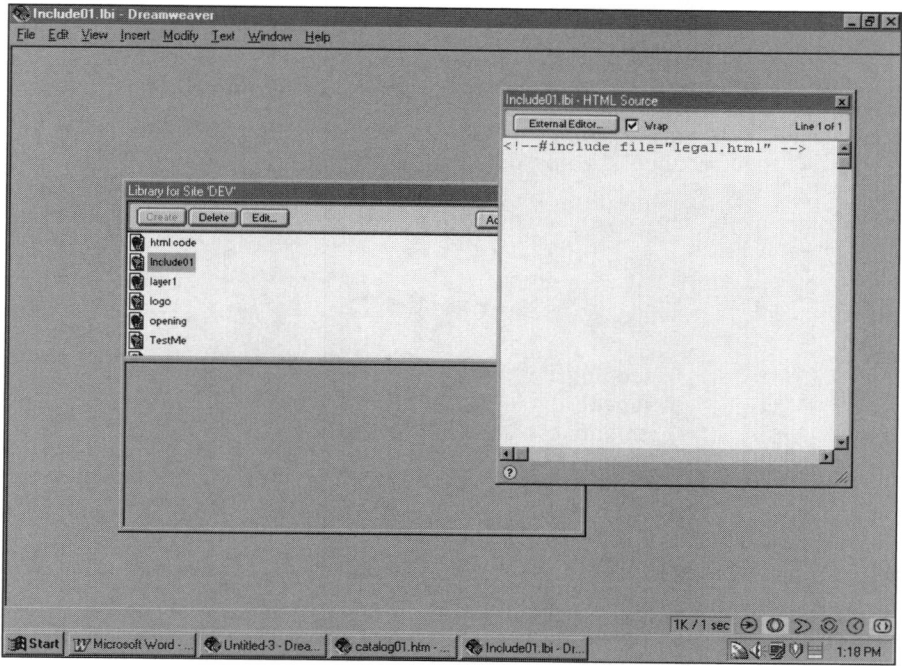

Figure 26-6: You must open the HTML Inspector to modify a server-side include that has been converted to a Library item.

3. Make the necessary modifications to your server-side include.

4. When finished, choose File ➪ Save or Ctrl-S (Command-S). Dreamweaver notes that your Library item has been modified and asks if you would like to update the Web pages containing the item.

5. Select Yes to update all the Library items, including the server-side include just modified, or No to postpone the update.

6. Close the editing window by selecting the Close button or choosing File ➪ Close.

Summary

In this chapter you have discovered how you can easily and effectively create Library items that can be repeated throughout an entire site to help maintain consistency.

✦ Library items can consist of any text, object or HTML code that is contained in the <body> of a Web page.

✦ The quickest method to create a Library item is to drag the code from the Dreamweaver Document Window into the Library Palette's list area.

✦ Editing Library items is also very easy with the Library Palette. Just click the Edit button, and you can swiftly make all of your changes.

✦ The Modify ➪ Library ➪ Update the Entire Site command allows for easy maintenance of your Web site.

In the next chapter you see how to publish your site to the Internet in Dreamweaver.

✦   ✦   ✦

Publishing via Site FTP

Site management is an essential part of a Webmaster's job description. Far from static designs, the Web site is not like a magazine advertisement that you're done with as soon as you send the file to the printer. Publishing your Web site pages on the Internet is really just the first step in an ongoing, often day-to-day, management task.

Dreamweaver includes an integrated but separate process called Site FTP to handle all your Web management needs. With Site FTP, you can:

- ✦ Transfer files to your remote site from your local development site and back again.
- ✦ Issue system commands to enable CGI programs on the server.
- ✦ Monitor your Web site for broken links and orphaned files.
- ✦ Check a file in or out during team Web development.

This chapter covers these site management functions and more. However, before you begin exploring the Site FTP features, it's helpful to know a little more about site management in Dreamweaver.

Site Management with Dreamweaver

At the simplest level, *site management* means transferring your files from the local drive to a publishing server. This is standard File Transfer Protocol (FTP), and many designers are accustomed to working with tools such as WS_FTP and Fetch. These utilities, however, only help you to move files back and forth — there are other issues that must be addressed in a medium-to-large Web site. For instance:

✦ What happens when a large group is working on a single Web site? What prevents the graphics designer from altering the same file the JavaScript programmer is modifying?

✦ How can you tell which version of your logo is the final one among the 15 working versions in your local site root folder?

✦ Do you have to update all your files every time some change is made to a few? Or can you only update those that have changed? How can you tell which ones have changed?

To help the Dreamweaver developer cope with these issues and avoid the type of frustration they can produce, a useful site-management tool is included within Dreamweaver: Site FTP. Its key features include the following:

✦ A quick, visual view of the elements of your site, on your local *and* remote directories.

✦ Fast drag-and-drop functionality for transferring files with dependent file support.

✦ Site management check-in and check-out tools for groups working on files within the same Web site.

✦ A Link Checker that helps you identify broken or unused objects being posted to your site.

Site FTP runs as a connected but independent process, so that you can close your Document Window when you're finished designing and then publish your files to the Web through the Site FTP window.

Setting Up a New Site

The first step in developing an effective site — one that links to other Web pages, uses images, and library files, and offers other site-root-relative links — is, of course, to first establish a site. Dreamweaver has made this very easy to do.

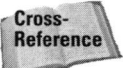

For complete, detailed information on establishing your initial site, see Chapter 5, "Setting Up Your First Site."

You'll need to create a folder on your development system that contains all the HTML, as well as graphics, media, and other files needed by the site. To create a new site, choose File ➪ Open Site ➪ Edit Sites. The Site Window opens with the Site Information dialog box shown in Figure 27-1. Here you'll find the information and settings for the current site you are developing. Once you've entered this information, you'll seldom need to modify it.

Host site directory information
Local directory information

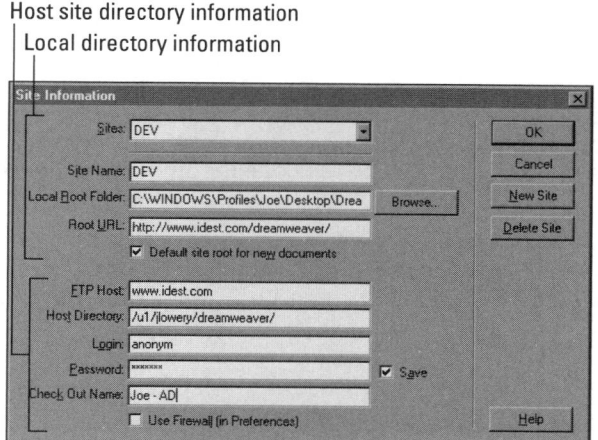

Figure 27-1: The Site Information dialog box, containing settings for the current site you are developing.

The New Site button presents a blank form for a new site, and the Delete Site button deletes the information contained for the current site — but not the files you have created.

The data in the Site Information dialog box is divided into two sections: Local Site information and Host Site information.

Local directory information

The local directory is in a folder on your development system, either on your own hard drive or on a network server.

Site Name

This is the name that appears in the File ➪ Open Sites drop-down list. The site name is a reference only you need to know and can be as fancy as you want. There are no hard and fast rules for creating a site name, except you should keep the name simple so you can easily reference it later. In a large Web design firm, you may need to develop more structured methods for naming various clients' Web sites.

Local Root Folder

The Local Root Folder is the location on your hard drive, or a network folder, where you will be placing your HTML pages, images, plug-in files, and library items. Remember, the root folder is essential to an effective Dreamweaver site. As you add links to other Web pages and images, Dreamweaver needs to maintain the relative links between files. The benefit of this becomes very apparent when you upload your files to a Web server. By maintaining a root-relative relationship, you ensure that all of the files and associated images will transfer seamlessly together onto any Web site. You won't have to go back and replace the code for any broken images.

Root URL

The information entered in the Root URL field is used when you access the Link Checker (new in Dreamweaver 1.2). In this field you'll enter the remote URL that corresponds to the local root folder, as if it were a regular Web address.

For example, say you are developing a Web site for *My Frozen Custard Inc.* For the Root URL field you would enter the URL for the Web site, like this:

```
http://www.myfrozencustard.com/
```

Let's say you're working on a subsite of a larger site. You can include the path as well, like this:

```
http://www.myfrozencustard.com/contest/
```

With this information, the Link Checker can compare absolute addresses embedded in your Web page to see whether those addresses refer to internal or external files.

Host site directory information

The host directory section contains all of the information required for you to post your files to a remote server. The setup allows for any type of host directory. Typically, though, you will be uploading your files to either a UNIX or NT Web server.

Tip   If you don't know the name of your FTP host server or any other of the required host site information (directory, login ID, password, and firewall preferences), contact your ISP or system administrator.

FTP Host

The FTP Host is the name of the server on which you will be placing your files. The names for the host will be something like these:

```
www.yourdomain.com
FTP.yourdomain.com
```

Do not include the protocol information, such as `http://`, in the FTP Host name.

Host Directory

The host directory is the one in which publicly accessible documents are stored on the server. Your remote site root folder will be a subfolder of the host directory. Check with your Web server administrator for the proper directory path.

Login and password

A login ID and password are required to transfer your files from your local root folder to the host. Your login ID is a unique name that tells the host who you are. Your password should be known only by you and the host. Every time you upload or download a file from the host server, you will be asked for your password. If you don't want to have to retype your password each time you log on, just select the Save check box next to your password and Dreamweaver will remember it.

Caution   For security reasons, it is highly recommended that you do not allow anyone to know your password.

Check Out Name

The name you enter in the Check Out Name field is used to allow others in your group to know when you have downloaded a file from the host server. Because the Check Out Name is one of several columns of information in the local and remote panes of the Site Window, it's a good idea to keep the name relatively short. (Your initials are an ideal choice for Check Out Name, if that is appropriate.)

Firewall preferences

Firewalls are useful security features used by many companies to prevent unwanted access to internal documents. There are many different types of firewalls, and all have a multitude of security settings. For instance, some firewalls allow people within a company to move documents back and forth through the firewall without any problems. Other companies will not allow Java or ActiveX controls to be moved through the firewall.

If you have a firewall that requires additional security to upload and download files, you will want to enable the Use Firewall check box in the Site Management Window.

Selecting this check box requires that you go to the Dreamweaver Preferences and fill out additional information on *proxy servers*. A proxy server allows you to navigate files through a firewall.

To make the appropriate proxy server changes, go to Edit ➪ Preferences and choose the Site FTP category. This page of settings contains selections for Firewall Information. Enter the firewall host name and port number, which will have been provided to you from your ISP or system administrator. By default, most firewalls use port 21.

Cross-Reference

For detailed information on the Site FTP preferences, see Chapter 3, "Setting Your Preferences."

Using the Site Window

Dreamweaver's Site FTP utility runs in the Site Window. You can open the Site Window by any of the following methods:

✦ Choose File ➪ Open Site ➪ Your Site.

✦ Select the Show Site FTP button from either Launcher.

✦ Choose Window ➪ Sites.

✦ Press the keyboard shortcut, F5.

The Site Window is your vehicle for moving files back and forth between your local and remote folders. Figure 27-2 illustrates the various parts of the Site Window.

Remote Site and Local Root Directory Windows

The Site Window is arranged in two main windows to represent the remote site on the left and the local root directory on the right. These two windows allow you to view all of the files that are contained within the two directories.

You can toggle the two windows on and off when you only need to see either the Remote Site Window or Local Root Directory Window. Use the View menu to do this, choosing from the commands Show Local, Show Remote, or Show Both.

The View command also enables you to refresh the two windows. This can be useful when other people are working on the same site at the same time — refreshing your screen allows you to see if any additional files have been added or removed during your FTP session. You also need to refresh the site windows if you have modified a file during the FTP session. The two refresh commands, Refresh Local and Refresh Remote, are on the View menu.

Connect to/Disconnect from server

Retrieve files from host Transfer files to host Check-Out option Preview your page

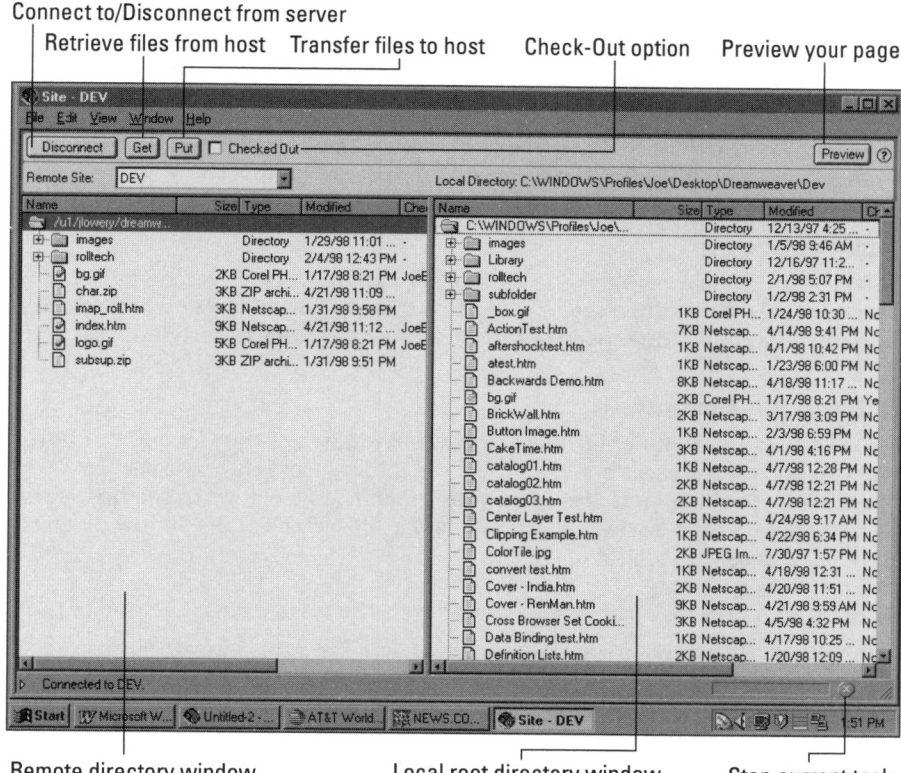

Remote directory window Local root directory window Stop current task

Figure 27-2: The Site Window is used for transferring files to and from your remote Web server.

Another helpful view lets you see which files have been most added or modified since the last FTP transfer. Choose either Select Newer Local or Select Newer Remote in the View menu, and Dreamweaver compares the files within the two folders to see which ones have been saved since the last FTP session. The newer files are highlighted and can be easily transferred by selecting the Get or Put button (described in a later section).

Connect/Disconnect button

The Connect/Disconnect button lets you begin or end a live session with a remote Host server. By clicking the Connect button, you start a new FTP session. You must currently be connected to the Internet when you select Connect. You won't see any information in the Remote Site pane until you connect to it.

After Dreamweaver has made the connection to your Remote site — as identified in the Site Information dialog box — the Connect button becomes the Disconnect button. To end your FTP session with the Host server, click the Disconnect button.

Tip　You can monitor all of your site management transactions by looking at the FTP Log. Select Window ➪ Site FTP Log from within the Site Window. A new window pops up and shows you all your transactions as you perform them.

Preview button

The Preview button displays the Web page you are working on in your Dreamweaver default browser. This is the same as pressing F12 when you are working on an individual page in the Dreamweaver Document Window.

Get and Put buttons

Two of the most useful controls on the Site Window are the Get and Put buttons. The Get button retrieves selected files and folders from the host server. The Put button transfers selected files from your local root directory to the host server. Dreamweaver offers several ways to transfer files in the Site Window during an active FTP session.

To transfer file(s) from the Local Directory to the host server, use one of the following methods:

- ✦ Select files from the Local Root Directory pane and drag it over to the Remote Directory pane.
- ✦ Use the keyboard shortcut: Select the files and press Ctrl-Shift-U (Command-Shift-U).
- ✦ Highlight the files and choose File ➪ Put.
- ✦ Select the file in the Local Root Directory pane and click the Put button.

If the file you are transferring has any dependent files, such as inserted images or Java applets, the Dependent Files dialog box (Figure 27-3) asks if you want to include dependent files. If you select Yes, all such files are transferred. Select No to move only the file you selected.

Caution　The Dependent Files dialog box includes a check box asking if you want to be reminded of this feature again. It is strongly recommended that you do not select this option. If you do you can never move a single HTML file that has embedded images or the like without moving the dependent files as well.

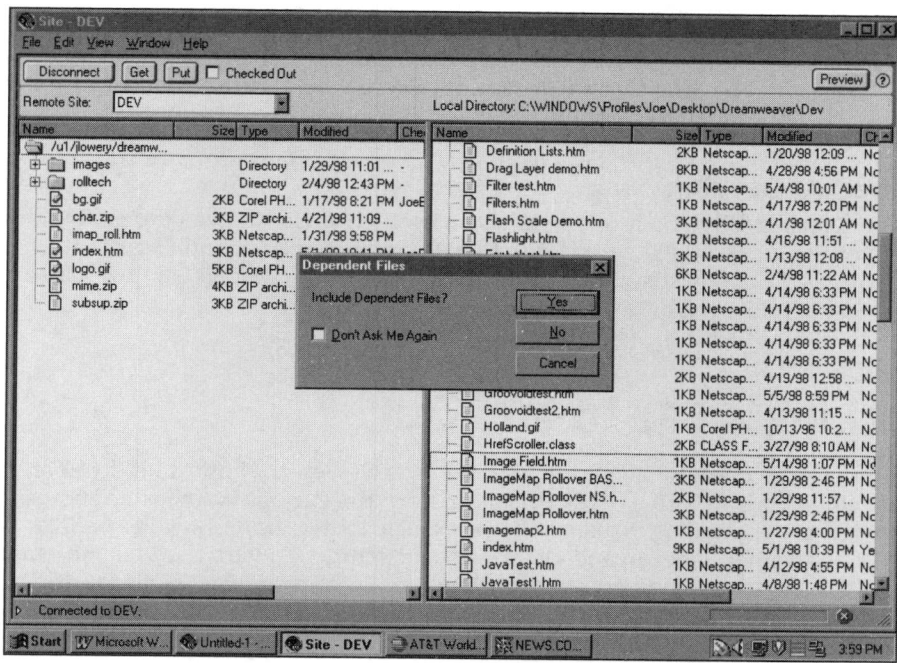

Figure 27-3: You only need select the HTML files and say Yes to the Dependent File dialog box to transfer all the needed files.

To transfer file(s) from the host server to the local folder, use one of these techniques:

✦ Select a file from the Remote Site pane and drag it over to Local Directory pane.

✦ Use the keyboard shortcut: Select the files and press Ctrl-Shift-D (Command-Shift-D).

✦ Highlight the files and select File ➪ Get.

✦ Select the files in the remote directory and click the Get button.

Caution

If you select either File ➪ Get or the Get button without having selected any files in the Remote Site pane, all of the files from your host server will be moved.

Stop Current Task button

Use the Stop Current Task button to halt the current transfer of files in an active FTP session. The Stop Current Task button is the red X button located in the lower-right corner of the Site Window.

Checked Out check Box

The Check In/Check Out option allows a user to officially check out an item from either the local or host server. The Checked Out check box indicates that a file is currently in use by someone with access to the server. Details on how to use this feature are covered in the next section.

Checking a File In and Out

Your control over the files used for your Web site is very important if you are developing a site with a team. On larger sites, the various Webmaster chores — design, programming, management — are distributed among several people. Without proper check-in and check-out procedures, it's very easy for the same HTML page to get updated by more than person, and you can wind up with incompatible versions.

Dreamweaver's Check-In/Check-Out facility solves this file-control problem by permitting only one person at a time to modify a Web page or graphic. Once a file has been checked out — accessed by someone — the file must be checked in again before another person using Site FTP can download it and work on it.

Dreamweaver handles the functionality of Check-In/Check-Out very efficiently. Whenever you establish an active FTP session between your local root folder and the host server, any files you get or put are displayed with a green check mark. If there are other people in your group also moving files back and forth, their transferred files are marked with a red check mark. This method provides a quickly recognized, visual representation of the status of files you and your teammates are handling. Files that do not have either a red or green check mark are not currently checked out by anyone and are available to work on.

If you want to see who is working on what, you can view user names in the Host Server window. (You may have to scroll the window horizontally to see the column.) The name shown is the user ID name that they use for logging on to the Host server. The Check Out name is entered through the Site Information dialog box.

Knowing who is working on what, and when, is a good control mechanism, but to really prevent duplication, site file control has to go one step further. Under

Dreamweaver's Check In/Check Out system, when you transfer a file from your local root folder to the host server, the file on your local folder becomes read-only. Making the file read-only allows others to see the Web page, but prevents anyone else from overwriting the file. The file must be checked in again before others can modify it.

Dreamweaver accomplishes Check In/Check Out by using a set of special files. When a file is checked out, a text file of the same filename but with the extension .lck is placed on the server. The .lck file contains the name of the user who checked out the file, as well as the date and the time that the file was checked out. The .lck files cannot be viewed in the Site Window display, but can be seen when a third-party FTP program is used.

Caution   Unfortunately, Dreamweaver is not able to make checked-out files in the host server read-only. This means someone in your group using a different FTP program other than Site FTP could very easily overwrite the checked-out file on the server.

Checking a file in and out

To check out a file, use any of these methods:

✦ Select the file(s) you want to transfer and then mark the Checked Out check box at the top of the Site Window. Then click the Get Button. All of the files will now be checked out in your name and denoted with a green check mark.

✦ Select files and choose File ➪ Check Out.

✦ Select files and use the keyboard shortcut, Ctl-Alt-Shift-D (Command-Option-Shift-D).

To check a file back in, do either of the following:

✦ Select the files and choose File ➪ Check In.

✦ Select the files and use the keyboard shortcut, Ctl-Alt-Shift-U (Command-Option-Shift-U).

To change the checked-out status of a file, use one of these methods:

✦ Select the file that's checked out, and then deselect the Checked Out check box at the top of the Site Window.

✦ Select the file and choose File ➪ Undo Check Out, or use the keyboard shortcut Ctrl-Shift-L (Command-Shift-L).

Checking Links

During a Web site's development, hundreds of different files and links are often referenced from within the HTML code. Unfortunately, it's not uncommon for a user to enthusiastically follow a link on a site only to encounter the dreaded Web server error 404: File Not Found. *Broken links* are one of a Webmaster's most persistent headaches, because a Web page may have not just internal links pointing to other pages on the Web site, but external links as well — over which the Webmaster has no control.

Orphaned files constitute a parallel nightmare for the working Web developer. An *orphaned file* is one that is included in the local or remote site but is no longer actively referenced by any Web page. Orphaned files take up valuable disk space and can erroneously be transferred from an old site to a new one.

Dreamweaver 1.2 has added a very useful feature to ease the labor in solving both of these problems for the Web designer: the Link Checker. The Link Checker command can be used to check a single page, selected pages, a subfolder, or an entire site. Once the Link Checker has completed its survey, you can view broken links, external files (links outside the site, such as absolute references and mailto's), and orphaned files. You can also repair broken links immediately or save the Link Checker results in a file for later viewing.

To check for links, follow these steps:

1. Be sure that the most current version of the file(s) have been saved.

2. To check a single document from within Dreamweaver, open the file and then choose File ➪ Check Links ➪ This Document, or use the keyboard shortcut, Ctrl-F7 (Command-F7).

3. To check for links on an entire site from within Dreamweaver, choose File ➪ Check Links ➪ Entire Site or use the keyboard shortcut, Ctrl-F8 (Command-F8).

When Dreamweaver has finished checking for all of the links on your page or site, it opens the Link Checker Window. The Link Checker Window, shown in Figure 27-4, provides a summary report of the broken links, external links and, when an entire site is reviewed, orphaned files. You can also use the Save button to store a report of the problems that the Link Checker has found, in a tab-delimited text file for future reference.

When you list broken links, you'll be able to observe any file that is included as a link, inserted as an image, or embedded in the page, and which cannot be located. If you want to fix the broken link, you can do so by double-clicking on the highlighted broken-link file. This will bring up the file in Dreamweaver and you can fix any problems with the Property Inspector.

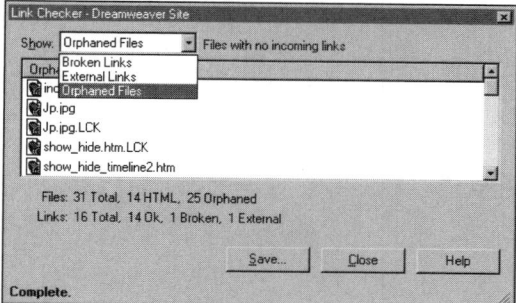

Figure 27-4: The Link Checker Window helps you see which files have broken links and then to fix the links directly.

You can also fix the link directly in the Link Checker window by following these steps:

1. Run the Link Checker command, either for the entire site or a single Web page.

2. In the Link Checker window, select the path and filename of the broken link you want to repair.

3. Enter the correct path for the missing file.

You can also open the page with the broken link and use the Property Inspector to locate the file in the Src attribute. To open the page from the Link Checker, double-click the Dreamweaver icon next to the broken link.

You can also access the Link Checker from the Site Window for both your local and remote folders. After you've selected your file(s) or folder(s), choose File ➪ Check Links to check either the selected files or the entire Web site. Or, you can right-click (Shift-click) any of the selected files to display the shortcut menu and choose the Check Link options from there.

Summary

With the Site Window and Dreamweaver's Site Management tools, a group or an individual Web designer can manage even large and diverse sites.

✦ Setting up a new site is an essential element in managing a Dreamweaver Web site. Without the root directory for the local files, Dreamweaver can not properly manage the Web pages and associated links.

✦ The Site Window allows you to drag and drop files from the host server to the local root folder.

✦ All file check-in and check-out functions for teams can be handled through the Site Window.

✦ Broken links can be quickly found and fixed with the Link Checker. You can also find orphaned files and identify external links.

In the next chapter, you see how to speed up your Web site production through the use of Dreamweaver templates.

✦   ✦   ✦

Using Dreamweaver Templates

Templates give you the advantages of consistency and speed. Let's face it: Web design is a combination of glory and grunt work. Creating the initial design for a Web site can be fun and exciting, but when you have to implement your wonderful new design on 200 or more pages, the excitement fades as you try to figure out the quickest way to finish the work. The proper use of templates can be a tremendous time-saver.

Dreamweaver makes it easy to access all kinds of templates — everything from the default blank page to your own creations. This chapter demonstrates the simple mechanism behind Dreamweaver templates and explores strategies for getting the most out of them.

Changing the Default Document

Each time you open a new document in Dreamweaver — or even just start Dreamweaver — a blank page is created. This blank page is based on an HTML file called Default.html that is stored in the Configuration\Templates folder.

The basic blank-page document is an HTML structure with only a few properties specified: a document type, a character set and a white background for the body:

```
<html>
<head>
<title>Untitled Document</title>
```

```
<meta http-equiv= Content-Type  content= text/html;
charset=iso-8859-1 >
</head>

<body bgcolor= #FFFFFF >

</body>
</html>
```

Naturally, you can change any of these elements — and add many, many more — once you've opened a page. But what if you want to have a `<meta>` tag with creator information in every page that comes out of your Web design company? Current Dreamweaver behaviors won't let you add anything to the `<head>` of a Web page except a JavaScript function. You can do it manually, but it's a bother; and chances are, sooner or later, you'll forget. Luckily, with Dreamweaver, you have a more efficient answer.

In keeping with its overall design philosophy of extensibility, Dreamweaver enables you to modify the Default.html file as you would any other file. In fact, Dreamweaver gives you a shortcut right into the default template, as well as any other templates you might want to use.

To access and modify the default template, follow these steps:

1. Choose Help ➪ Open Template.

2. When the Open Template dialog box appears, select the Default.html file and click OK.

Caution

If you are planning on extensive modifications to your Dreamweaver Default.html file, it's a good idea to save the original file under another name before you begin. To do this, choose Help ➪ Open Template and load Default.html. Immediately choose File ➪ Save As and enter a slightly different name for the file, like Default-Original.html, in the Filename text box.

When you look at Default.html, it appears to be exactly the same as a regular blank page. However, any alterations you make to this file are incorporated in any future new pages you construct. For example, let's return to our idea of entering a `<meta>` tag with page creator information.

3. With the Default.html file displayed, choose Window ➪ HTML or select the Show HTML Source. This opens the HTML Inspector.

4. In between the existing `<meta>` tag and the closing `</head>` tag, insert a line like this:

```
<meta http-equiv= Creator  content= JLowery Web Design >
```

5. After you've inserted whatever information you'd like, save the file with File ➪ Save or Ctrl-S (Command-S).

6. To test your changes, select File ➪ New and examine the code through the HTML Inspector. Your new information should be present.

Caution

Opening a template through Help ➪ Open Template replaces the current document, even if you have turned on the Open Files in New Window option in Dreamweaver's General Preferences (see Chapter 3, "Setting Your Preferences").

Naturally, you are not limited to just entering one or two <meta> tags in your new default document. For an extensive Web site that requires an elaborate template, you may want to replace the blank Web page temporarily with your more full-featured template. You can include layers, JavaScript functions — anything and everything. Just save your customized template as Default.html in the Configuration\Templates folder (after having saved the default blank page to another file, of course). Then you are ready to plug in your template and put in just the changing content on every new page you open.

Caution

When you access any of the Dreamweaver templates through the Help ➪ Open Template command, you notice an Open as Read Only option on the Open Template dialog box. Unfortunately, the Read Only switch is not functioning properly in the current version of Dreamweaver for Windows systems, although it works fine on the Macintosh.

Working with Existing Templates

If you're just starting out in Web design, templates are a good way to get a fast start. Aside from the Default.html template, Dreamweaver includes four different basic templates, each intended to offer a simple structure for you to build upon. You get the following templates with Dreamweaver:

✦ Basic Tables

✦ Company Profiles

✦ Story Column

✦ Basic Frames

All the templates include descriptive text describing how each area of the template can be used or modified.

Caution

Watch Out! Unlike the Default.html blank page, when you open one of the other working templates Dreamweaver does not create a new file based on that template. Instead, you must use the Save As command to save your new page under a different name before you do anything else. If you make any modifications to the templates and then save them in a normal fashion, the template is altered and the original template will be lost.

The Basic Tables template

The Basic Tables template reflects a popular, moderately backwards-compatible Web site design. Although it has the look and feel of a frame-based layout, it's actually just one page with a background image that splits the page into a navigation strip on the left and the main body of the document on the right. Take a look at Figure 28-1.

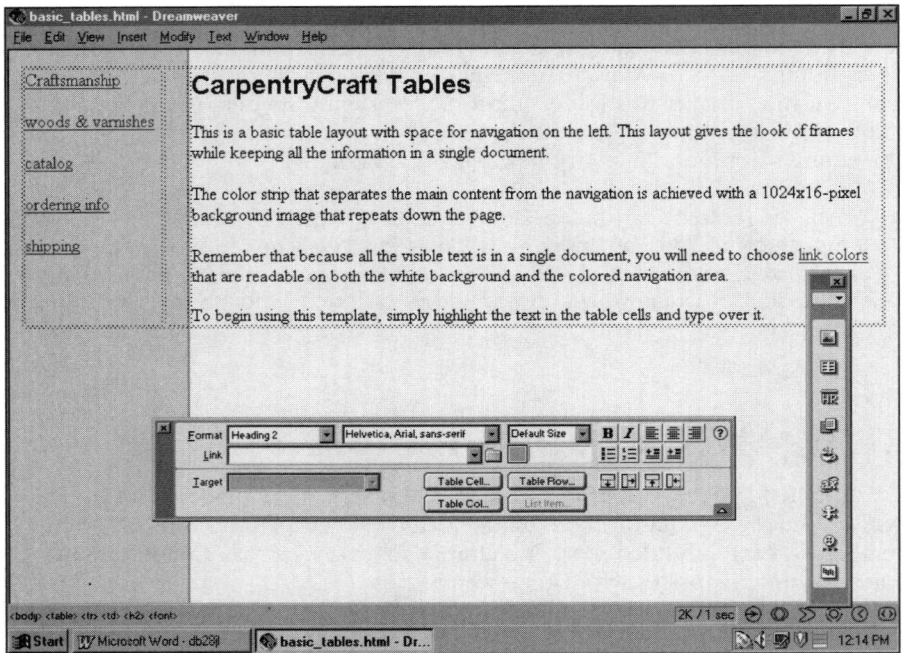

Figure 28-1: The Basic Tables template gives you room for a navigation bar on the left and information on the right.

To keep the navigation strip and main body consistently separate, a simple three-column table is used. The left-hand column contains the navigation links, and the right-hand column contains the main portion of the page. The middle column is used as a spacer.

Tip   As shipped, the leftmost column of the table is set to 130 pixels and doesn't quite cover the green color strip. In the graphic that is used for the background, sherbert.gif, the green strip is actually 160 pixels wide. To correct this, position your cursor in the first column of the table and, from the Property Inspector, select the Table Col button. In the Table Column Properties dialog box, change the value in the Column Width text box from 130 to 160 or greater.

Each of the links in the navigation strip is set to a dummy filename. You can change the links as usual in the Property Inspector. You can also add an additional element of structure by inserting a table within any or all of the table cells. This will maintain the overall layout while allowing you to align text and images.

The Company Profiles template

The Company Profiles template (Figure 28-2) provides a slightly more elaborate table structure than the Basic Tables template. This one introduces two graphic elements: the image used as the company logo, and the horizontal rule separating the logo from the main page.

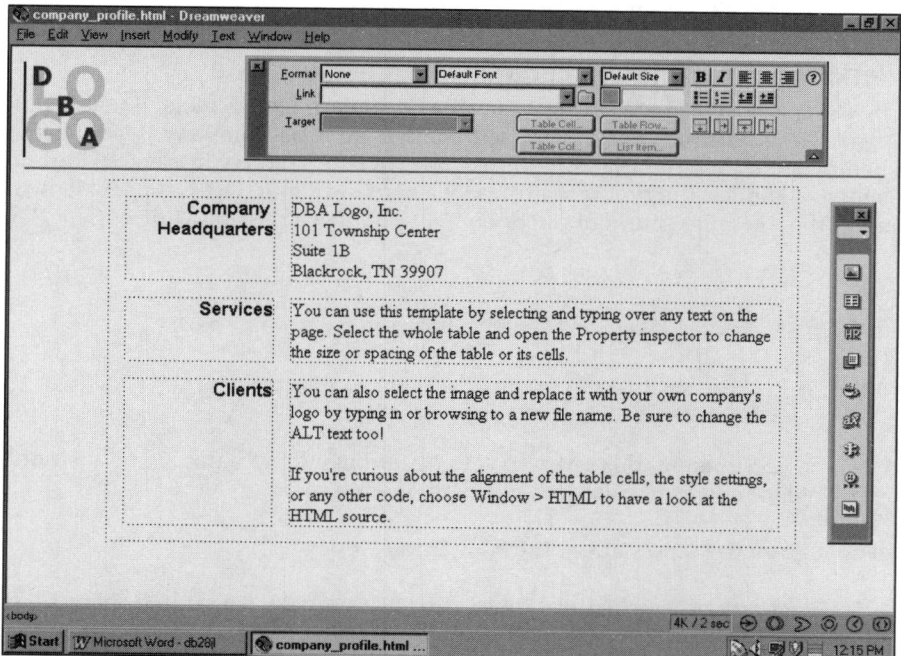

Figure 28-2: The Company Profiles template is good for a straightforward graphics and text layout.

To adapt the Company Profiles template, follow these steps:

1. First replace the graphic with your own logo. Double-click on the D.B.A. logo.

2. Dreamweaver opens the Select Image Source dialog box. Select your new image and click OK.

3. Generally, it's better to resize your graphics in a full-featured graphics program, but if necessary, you can adjust the size of the logo for placement, from within your template. Select the image and drag the sizing handles to a new position. If you hold down the Shift key while dragging, you'll maintain the graphic's aspect ratio.

5. Next, replace the existing text in the table with your own copy.

   • To erase the current text, highlight any cell and press Delete.

   • You can move the two columns closer together by selecting the table and then altering the CellSpace value in the Property Inspector.

   • To add an additional row in the same structure, position your cursor anywhere in the last cell in the final row and press Tab. A new row appears at the bottom of the table.

Working with CSS in the Company Profiles template

The Company Profiles template also uses Cascading Style Sheets. If you highlight any of the label information in the left column, such as Company Headquarters or Clients, you notice that the font information in the Property Inspector does not change—and yet the typeface is clearly a sans-serif font. Open the HTML Inspector, and in the <head> section of the document you'll see the following code:

```
<STYLE TYPE= text/css >
<!--
TD B {  font:700 12pt Arial, Helvetica, sans-serif; color:
black}
-->
</STYLE>
```

Here, the CSS command is given to set any text in a table data tag, <td>, that has been bolded, to a particular font, size, boldness and color.

To change all the labels at once, follow these steps:

1. Select any of the existing labels, such as Company Headquarters or Clients.

2. Open the Style Sheet Inspector by choosing Window ➪ Styles or selecting the Show Styles button from the Launcher.

3. In the Styles Palette, select the Style Sheet button.

4. In the Edit Style Sheet dialog box, highlight the TD B listing in the window and choose the Edit button.

5. Make any modifications you'd like in the Style Definition dialog box, and click OK when you are finished.

   You can view all of your changes in Dreamweaver.

6. If you'd like to continue making changes, select the Edit button again. If you're finished with styles, click the Done button in the Edit Style Sheet dialog box.

Tip Because you cannot currently select more than one cell at a time to make changes in a table, style sheets offer an excellent alternative to modifying an overall look in one step.

The Story Column Template

Although the Story Column template looks a little similar to the Company Profiles template, there is one major difference: no tables. Tables are widely supported in today's browsers, but there are still some that do not recognize tables in use. The Story Column template uses the `<blockquote>` tag—actually three of them—to achieve the indented look shown in Figure 28-3.

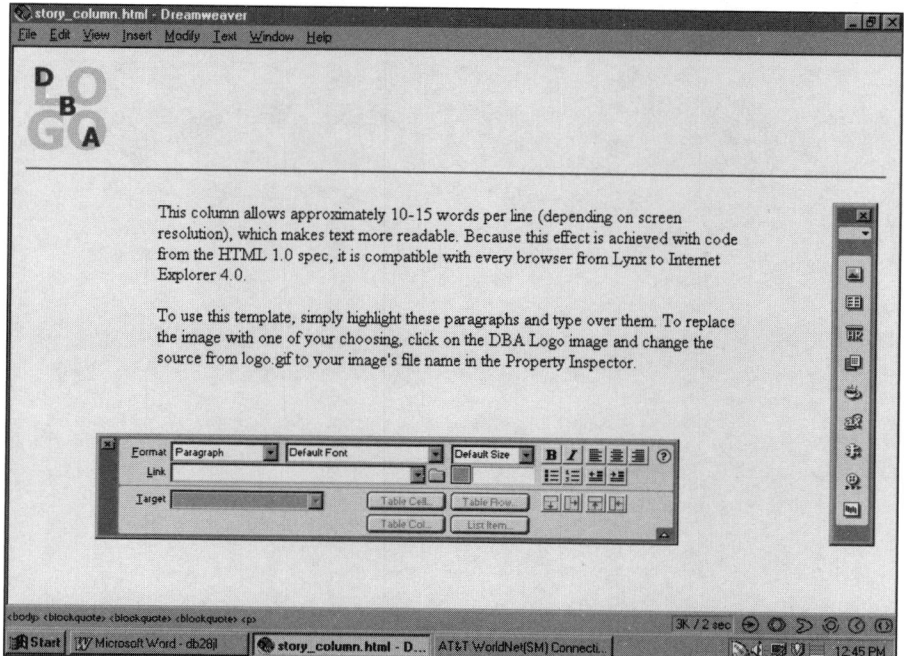

Figure 28-3: Compatible with even the oldest browsers, the Story Column template uses the `<blockquote>` tag inserted by the Indent command.

If you want to alter the indent, select the paragraphs and choose Text ➪ Indent or Text ➪ Outdent. You can also use the Text Indent and Text Outdent buttons on the Property Inspector.

The Basic Frames Template

Dreamweaver includes a very nice example of one of the more popular layout options, frames.

Note   Because frames use multiple files, you have to be sure to open the frameset and not one of the individual frame files.

To open the Basic Frames template, choose Help ➪ Open Template and double-click the Frames folder in the Open Template dialog box. Inside the Frames folder, select the basic_frames.html file and open it. When all the five files are read, you'll see a frameset with four separate frames as shown in Figure 28-4.

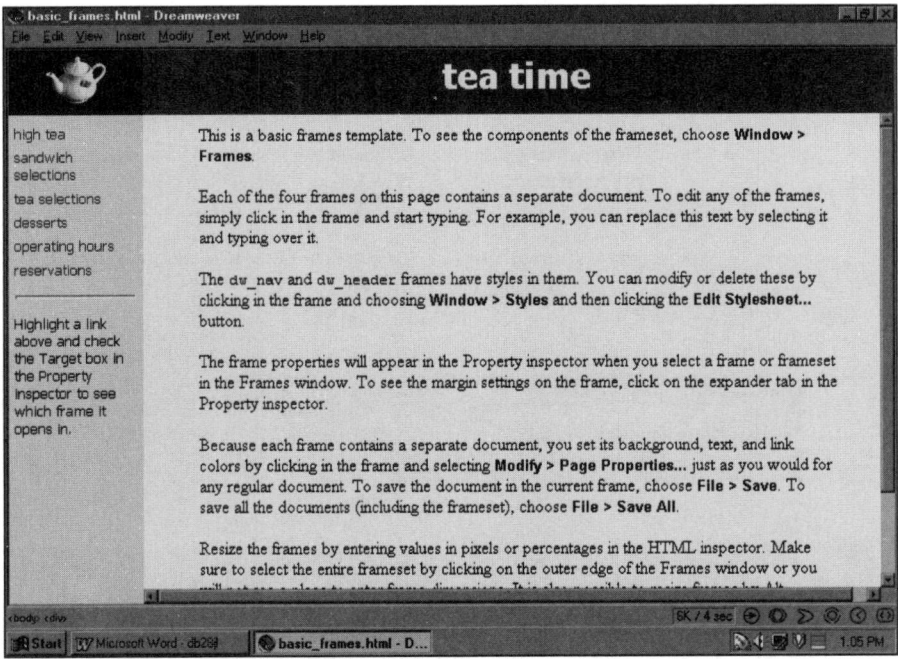

Figure 28-4: The Basic Frames template includes a navigation strip, logo, title bar, and main area for viewing documents.

This frame template has the frame borders set to zero for a seamless look. If you want to modify the frame size or select the frameset, choose View ⇨ Frame Borders. Now frames can be resized by clicking and dragging the borders. Or you can set the title for the entire frameset by selecting a border and choosing Modify ⇨ Page Properties.

Although the layout for Basic Frames is quite colorful, only one image is actually used. The other color effects are achieved through setting the background colors of the individual frames and using styles for the text. You'll notice that the navigation links are lacking the characteristic underline. This is achieved by setting the style for the `<a>` tag to `decoration:none`, through the Styles palette and Style Definition dialog box.

If, after working on a frameset, you want to open another template or example like the Basic Frames template, be sure to either close the entire frameset first or leave it in a selected state. If you don't, your newly opened file will not replace the entire frameset, but rather only appear in a single frame — because Dreamweaver loads a new template or example in the current frame.

You'll find additional templates on the CD-ROM. Just transfer the files from the Configuration\Templates folder on the CD-ROM to the same folder in your system. Feel free to use the templates and adapt them in any way that you see fit.

Creating Your Own Templates

You can use any design you like as your own template. For quick access, store your custom templates in the same folder where Dreamweaver stores its own: Configuration\Templates. You also can create your own subfolders within the Templates folder.

Remember, like all the other templates (aside from the Default.html file), you must use the Save As command to store each file you create from your template, or else the template will be overwritten.

Here are some points to consider when designing templates:

✦ **Use placeholders where you can.** Whether it's dummy text or an unspecified graphic, placeholders give shape to your page. They also make it easier to remember which elements to include. If you are using an image placeholder, set a temporary height and width through the Property Inspector or by dragging the image placeholder's sizing handles.

✦ **Finalize and incorporate as much as possible in the template.** If you find yourself repeatedly adding the same information or objects to a page, add them to your template. The more structured elements you can include, the faster your pages can be produced.

✦ **Use custom objects on the template.** Many times you have to enter the same basic object, such as a plug-in for a digital movie, on every page—and only the filenames change. Enter your repeating object with all the preset parameters possible on your template page, and you'll only have to select a new file for each page.

✦ **Include your <meta> information.** Search engines rely on <meta> tags to get the overview of a page and then scan the balance of the page to get the details. You can enter a <meta> tag with a keyword attribute on your template so that all your Web pages in a site have the same basic information for cataloging. In Dreamweaver, you need to enter the <meta> tags in the <head> section through the HTML Inspector or your favorite text editor.

Summary

Much of a Web designer's responsibility is related to document production, and Dreamweaver offers a variety of template options to reduce the workload. When planning your strategy for building an entire Web site, remember these advantages provided by templates:

✦ You can modify the default template that Dreamweaver uses, so that every time you select File ⇨ New a new version of your customized template will be created.

✦ Dreamweaver includes several basic templates to help get you started in Web page creation.

✦ You can include your own custom templates in the Template folder for easy access.

✦　　✦　　✦

Appendixes

BBEdit 4.5 Primer (For Macintosh Users)

◆   ◆   ◆   ◆

In This Appendix

BBEdit basics

Working with
Dreamweaver and
BBEdit together

Using BBEdit to
create and edit HTML
documents

Searching, marking,
syntax coloring, table
building, and other
handy features

BBEdit's FTP
capabilities

◆   ◆   ◆   ◆

Creating great-looking Web sites is easy thanks to
Dreamweaver's visual layout interface. Even so,
sometimes it's helpful to switch from Dreamweaver's visual
editor mode and edit the underlying HTML (Hypertext
Markup Language) source code — particularly when you're
troubleshooting HTML documents.

Dreamweaver has a basic built-in HTML editor: the HTML
Inspector. When a more advanced code editor is needed,
Macintosh users can use the BBEdit application from Bare
Bones Software (http://www.bbedit.com/). This stand-
alone editor is included on the CD-ROM that accompanies
this book.

BBEdit 4.5 is the most recent version of this popular, pre-Web,
Macintosh programmer's text editor. In recent years, the
program has evolved into a feature-packed text-based HTML
editor that elegantly exploits the ease-of-use capabilities of the
Mac OS. BBEdit is the choice of many Web professionals.

This appendix is written as a basic, beginner's guide to
BBEdit. The software has a myriad of features and capabilities;
some of BBEdit's more advanced features are not covered
here.

Getting Started

You can easily switch between Dreamweaver and BBEdit. A simple click on an icon toggles you from one application to the other. Elements selected in one application are automatically highlighted in the other. This capability makes it easy to find your place in the code, and modifications can happen quickly.

Key features

BBEdit is wonderfully full-featured and adaptable to your style of working. Just a few of BBEdit's many advantages follow:

- ✦ HTML syntax checking
- ✦ Multiple layers of Undo and Redo
- ✦ Spell checking
- ✦ Multiple-file search and replace
- ✦ Support for files up to 2GB
- ✦ A file comparison feature for locating differences among files
- ✦ HTML syntax coloring
- ✦ "Open from" and "Save to" FTP servers from the File menu
- ✦ Table builder
- ✦ Web-safe color palette
- ✦ One-click preview in any browser

BBEdit installation

BBEdit 4.5, like Dreamweaver, runs on Power Macintoshes and compatible computers. Install BBEdit by launching the Install BBEdit 4.5 application on the CD-ROM supplied with this book.

Choosing the Easy Install option automatically installs the software required to use BBEdit with your particular computer. You can also choose the Custom Install option to install additional software, or install a different version of BBEdit that runs on both 68K and Power Macintosh computers.

Special folders

BBEdit installs several special folders during the installation process that provide additional functionality. These folders can be removed if you don't need their features. The following items are installed within the BBEdit 4.5 folder.

Folder	Contents
BBEdit Plug-ins	Modules that offer additional BBEdit features written and contributed by BBEdit users.
BBEdit Scripts	AppleScripts ready for execution through the Scripts menu located on the right side of the main pull-down menu.
BBEdit Glossary	Text files that can be inserted into an active editing window. Simply add text files to the folder and then use the Glossary command in the Windows menu to insert the contents of a text file.
BBEdit Dictionaries	Dictionaries used by BBEdit's spell checker. The User Dictionary stores words you add to this personal dictionary. See the "Spell Checking" section for more information.

Working with Dreamweaver and BBEdit

Although Dreamweaver 1.2 and above enables you to assign any HTML editor as your external editor, Dreamweaver integrates optimally with BBEdit. Once you set up BBEdit as your default editor, switching between the two editors is just a button click or a keyboard shortcut away.

Setting up BBEdit as your default editor

Before Dreamweaver can access BBEdit, you must make BBEdit your default HTML editor. Dreamweaver for the Mac should ship with this feature enabled. A quick way to check is to look for a Launch BBEdit option under your Edit menu. If the option is not there, you can make this assignment through the Dreamweaver Preferences by following these steps:

1. In Dreamweaver, choose Edit ⇨ Preferences to open the Preferences dialog box.

2. From the Category list on the left, choose External Editors to display that panel.

3. In the External Editors panel, click in the box that says Enable BBEdit Integration and click OK. The Edit menu option that used to read Launch Text Editor should now be Launch BBEdit.

If this sequence doesn't work, Dreamweaver can't find where you've installed BBEdit. Go back to the External Editors preferences and use the Browse button to find BBEdit.

The External Editor options that control file synchronization between Dreamweaver and BBEdit are explained in Chapter 3, "Setting Your Preferences."

Switching between Dreamweaver and BBEdit

You have several ways to switch to BBEdit while in Dreamweaver:

✦ Click the External Editor button in the top-left corner of the HTML Inspector.

✦ Switch programs through the Finder.

✦ Choose Edit ⇨ External Editor.

✦ Use the keyboard shortcut, Command-E.

On the PC, you can also select the other program's button on the taskbar or use the Alt-Tab method to switch between applications, but the file integration does not work under these circumstances.

Depending on the synchronization options chosen in the External Editors preferences, Dreamweaver may ask if you want to save the file first before you switch to BBEdit. If you do not save your Dreamweaver file, your modifications do not appear in BBEdit, and vice versa. For this reason, you should set your synchronization option to Always.

After you've made your code modifications in BBEdit and you're ready to return to Dreamweaver, just click the Dreamweaver button near the bottom of BBEdit's HTML Tools Palette (see Figure A-1). The following "HTML Tools Palette" section in this appendix gives more information on this window.

You can switch from BBEdit to Dreamweaver's window by selecting the other's window, but the HTML file doesn't update properly. Use the Dreamweaver button or the Finder to switch programs.

Window list

Line numbers   Editing window   Pull-down menus   Status bar   HTML Tools Palette

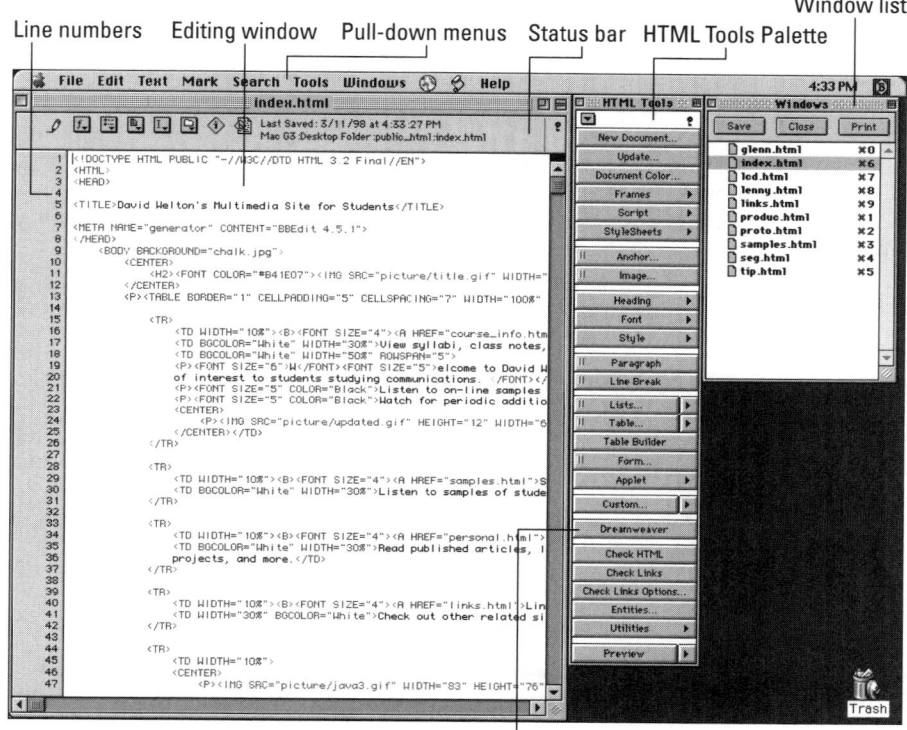

Switch to Dreamweaver button

Figure A-1: The BBEdit 4.5 workspace.

Disabling BBEdit integration

You may disable BBEdit integration if you prefer working with an older version of BBEdit or if you use a different HTML text editor.

1. Choose Edit ➪ Preferences.

2. Select General from the category list on the left.

3. Deselect the Enable BBEdit Integration option and click OK.

Note

Text selections are not tracked if integration is turned off.

BBEdit menus

Dynamic Menus: BBEdit uses an advanced menu system called dynamic menus. This system uses the Shift or Option keys to alter menu options while a menu is open.

Keyboard Shortcuts: Many of BBEdit's commands have keyboard equivalents. Pull-down menus show keyboard shortcuts. To see the keyboard equivalents for options in a dialog box, hold down the Command key. After a brief delay, the keyboard equivalents appear next to the buttons in the dialog box.

Info Link: Find a description of menu functions in the "Editing Documents" section.

BBEdit preferences

BBEdit offers a wealth of options for customizing the application to meet your needs. Use the Edit pull-down menu to select Preferences. A dialog box appears with several categories of options listed on the left side. When you select a category, a short description of the category is displayed at the top of the dialog box. Figure A-2 displays BBEdit's options for Editor preferences.

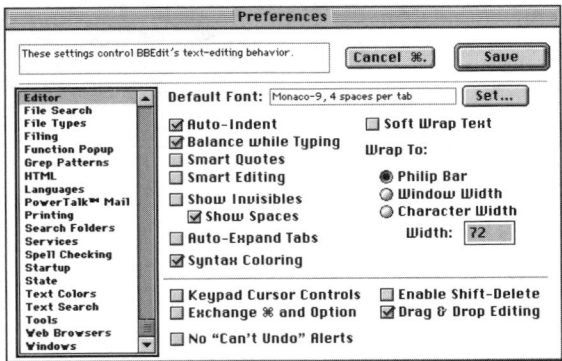

Figure A-2: BBEdit's Preferences dialog box showing Editor options.

Getting help

BBEdit provides assistance with its functions with the Help pull-down menu. You can choose the BBEdit Guide to show a window that offers help by topic, through an index, or via searching. This choice activates the Apple Guide-style interactive help in BBEdit. Use the Show Balloons option to display the functions of many buttons and features as you move the mouse over various parts of BBEdit windows. To open the manuals in the BBEdit Documentation folder, you need to have the Adobe Acrobat reader installed on your machine.

HTML Document Basics

Once the BBEdit software is installed, you're ready to author HTML documents destined to become great-looking Web pages. This section explains the basics of creating, saving, and opening BBEdit documents.

Creating and saving new documents

Use the File menu to select New, then follow the pointer to the submenu. The most common options are Text Document and HTML Document.

Text document

This command opens an empty text file with two suboptions:

✦ **With Selection.** Creates a new document containing text selected in another currently open BBEdit document. This is handy for quickly producing multiple pages that have common elements, such as a sitewide menu or background image.

✦ **With Clipboard.** Creates a new document containing text copied into the Mac OS Clipboard. The text could originate from any application.

HTML document

Choose HTML Document and you'll get a dialog box with options for creating a new HTML-formatted document. This option automatically places the HTML tags you need to begin building a page. This is the best option if you're starting a document from scratch.

Saving your work

When you're ready to save your newly created document, choose File ⇨ Save. Give the document a name and choose the location where you wish to save the document.

The Save As command opens a standard Mac OS dialog box. The Option button within this dialog box gives you control over how file attributes are saved. You have two choices:

✦ **Save As Stationery.** Saves the document as a Mac OS stationery document. Later when you open this document BBEdit uses it as a template for a new untitled document. This option is useful if you will be creating multiple Web pages with common elements, such as a sitewide menu or background image.

✦ **Save Selection Only.** Instructs BBEdit to only save the selected text.

Opening existing BBEdit files

You have three ways to open existing BBEdit documents:

✦ Drag a file's icon to the BBEdit application icon, or to an alias of the icon. You can place the alias on your desktop for easy access. This option takes advantage of the Mac OS drag-and-drop feature.

✦ Simply double-click a BBEdit file. You can identify BBEdit documents by the associated BBEdit icon.

✦ With BBEdit launched, use the Open, Open Several, or Open Recent commands from the File menu.

Let's take a look at these File ➪ Open commands

File ➪ Open

When you select Open from the File pull-down menu, a dialog box gives you the following options:

✦ **Open Read-Only.** This command opens the file so it can be viewed but not edited. To make a file editable, simply click the pencil icon in the status bar located at the top of each BBEdit document. (For a description of the status bar, see the "Editing Documents" section.)

✦ **Projector-Aware.** Use this option if collaboration on the document is ongoing with other users. This option is a safety feature; it assigns the file special notation that indicates the file is in use and should not be edited by another user. This is similar to Dreaweaver's Check-in/Check-out feature in the Site Window.

✦ **LF Translation.** Translates DOS or UNIX line breaks when you open a file. If this option is not selected, BBEdit leaves the original line breaks untranslated.

✦ **File Types.** A pop-up menu lets you select types of files to open. The default file type, All Available, lets BBEdit use its built-in translation system to open any files it can translate.

File ➪ Open Recent

The Open Recent menu contains a list of files recently opened. To open one of these files, simply choose it from the submenu.

File ➪ Open Several

This command lets you open multiple files simultaneously. This is particularly useful if you wish to open all the files in a folder — maybe all the HTML documents that make up your Web site. Here are the steps to open several files at once:

1. As you open the File menu, hold down the Option key to enable BBEdit's dynamic menu feature. You will see the Open Several command; select it and a dialog box appears (Figure A-3).

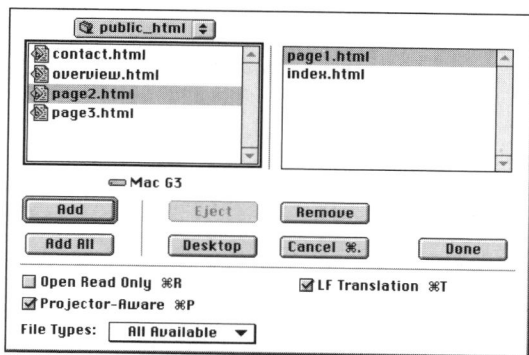

Figure A-3: Opening multiple files.

2. Choose a file you wish to open from the list on the left side of the dialog box.

3. Use Add to move the selected file to the list of files to be opened, on the right.

4. Use Add All to add all the files in the folder to the list of files to be opened.

5. Use the Add button to add any other files to the list on the right. Use Remove to eliminate unwanted files.

6. Choose any of the Open options you need (see File ➪ Open, described in the preceding section).

7. Press Done to have BBEdit open the files.

Using file groups

BBEdit enables you to group files in a way that makes managing your Web site easier. You may want to group all the files that make up your Web site, or divide them into logical subsections that make sense to you.

A *file group* is a special BBEdit file that references other files in the file group. Any type of file can be included in a file group.

To start a file group:

1. Select File ⇨ New ⇨ File Group.
2. The dialog box will ask you for a file group name (Figure A-4).
3. Click Create, and BBEdit opens a new empty file group.

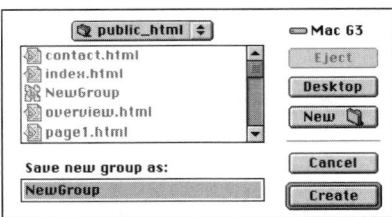

Figure A-4: Creating a new file group.

To add files to a file group, simply drag any file from the Finder into the file group window (see Figure A-5). Or you can click the Add button to open a dialog box that enables you to choose files.

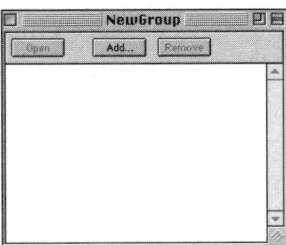

Figure A-5: An empty file group window.

To open files within a file group, double-click the file. Or you can select the file and click the Open button.

Note   If the file is a BBEdit file, then BBEdit will open it. If the file is not a BBEdit document, then the application that created the file will be launched.

Editing Documents

This section guides you through BBEdit's menus, windows, and functions.

Basic text manipulation

BBEdit handles text in a way similar to many Macintosh text editors and word processors. Characters typed in BBEdit appear at the blinking vertical insertion point. The insertion point is controlled by placing the mouse in the desired location and clicking.

Click and drag the mouse to select several characters or words. If you select some text and then type, the new entry replaces the selected text. Use the Delete key to remove selected text.

Moving text

To easily move text from one location to another, follow these steps:

Tip

1. With the mouse, select the text you want to move with the mouse.

   If you wish to select all the text within a document choose Edit ⇨ Select All (keyboard shortcut: Command-a).

2. Choose Edit ⇨ Cut (keyboard shortcut: Command-x) to remove the text from the window and store it in the Mac OS Clipboard.

3. Find the new place where you wish to move the text, and click your mouse at the insertion point.

4. Choose Edit ⇨ Paste (keyboard shortcut: Command-v) to place your text.

To copy text into the Clipboard without deleting it from its original location, select Copy from the Edit pull-down menu (keyboard shortcut: Command-C).

Dragging and dropping text

A fast and simple method to move text from one place to another takes advantage of the Mac OS drag-and-drop feature. Follow these steps:

1. Select the desired text.

2. Place the mouse pointer within the selected area.

3. Click and hold down the mouse button.

4. Drag the mouse pointer to the new position for the text.

5. Release the mouse button to drop in the text.

You can also use drag-and-drop to copy text to any other open BBEdit window.

 Tip   BBEdit enables you to drag and drop a text file from the Finder onto an editing window. Doing so inserts the file's contents where it's dropped.

Undo/Redo

The Edit ➪ Undo command (keyboard shortcut: Command-z) reverses changes — in chronological order — made to your file. The amount of available memory is the only limit to the number of edits that can be undone.

BBEdit also enables multiple Redos. Choose the Edit ➪ Redo command or use the keyboard shortcut Command-Shift-z.

Text wrapping

BBEdit wraps text in two ways, called *soft wrapping* and *hard wrapping.* You can choose the option that works best for you, and have it take effect globally or for just one document.

  ✦ **Soft Wrapping.** Soft wrapping handles text like most word-processing software. As the insertion point reaches the limit of the right margin, it automatically moves to the next line. You never need to type a "return" at the end of a line except when you begin a new paragraph.

  ✦ **Hard Wrapping.** Hard wrapping enables you to type as far as you wish on a single line. You have to enter a "return" to end each line in order to begin a new line of text.

To change the text wrapping in BBEdit, select Soft Wrap Text from the Window Options pop-up menu in the status bar (see "The Status Bar" section coming up). Or you can choose Window Options via the Edit menu and select (or deselect) the Soft Wrap Text option from the Window Options dialog box.

What's in the BBEdit windows

Basic operation of BBEdit windows follows the standard Mac OS format. BBEdit offers two extra features: the status bar and the split bar.

The status bar

The status bar (see Figure A-6) resides at the top of each editing window. This bar contains buttons and pop-up menus that help you work with the text in the window. Using the status bar you can save your work, show line numbers, display document information, and more.

Tip

Use the Show Balloons option under the Help pull-down menu to show the function of the icons in the status bar. Hide the status bar by clicking the Key icon on the right side of the status bar.

Figure A-6: BBEdit's status bar.

The split bar

Each editing window contains a *split bar* — it's a small black bar located just above the vertical scroll bar. The split bar divides the window into two panes, which is particularly helpful when you're editing a document in two places. Figure A-7 shows an editing window split into two panes.

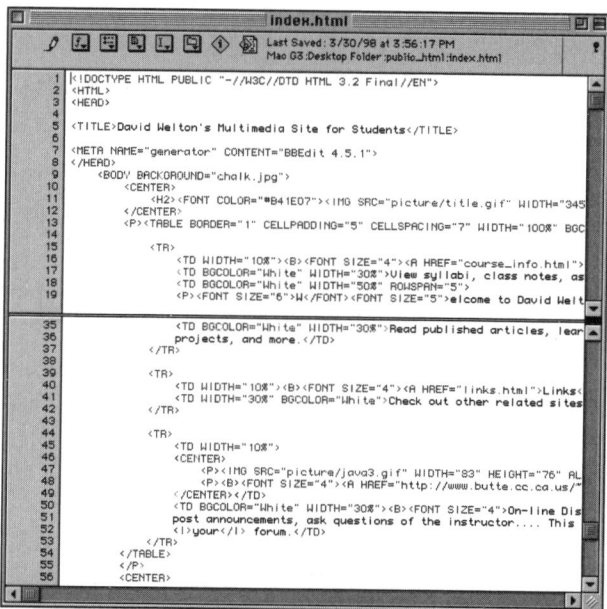

Figure A-7: Use the split bar to divide a window for editing a document in two places.

To split the window, drag the split bar from the top of the vertical scroll bar into the main window area. You can scroll both windows independently. Return to a full window by dragging the split bar to its original location.

Tip Double-clicking the split bar divides a window into two equal panes, or removes the division from a split window.

Window menu

It can get confusing when you have many BBEdit windows open simultaneously. The Windows menu helps you manage the clutter.

The Windows list

BBEdit's Windows list helps you gain quick access to the files that make up your Web site. A special floating window (see Figure A-8) lists the names of all the open files.

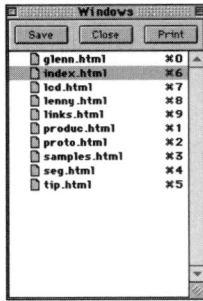

Figure A-8: BBEdit's Windows list.

To make a window active, simply double-click its name within the Windows list. In addition, you can open a file by dragging the file's icon into the Windows list. Buttons at the top of the window offer Save, Close, and Print options.

Tip Use the Option key to make the action of any button at the top of the window apply to all the files in the Windows list.

The Arrange command

BBEdit's Arrange command is a tool for organizing multiple windows in the editor. This is particularly helpful if you're using a small monitor to create your Web pages. When you select Window ⇨ Arrange, you get a dialog box from which to choose an arrangement for the windows.

Get Info

This command displays a dialog box that lists the number of characters, words, lines, and pages in any selected text as well as the document. (This same information is available by clicking the Info button in the status bar.)

Reveal in Finder

Reveal in Finder is a handy feature with which you can quickly find a particular file without leaving the BBEdit application. This command opens the Mac OS Finder window that contains the active file.

Select the text of a filename (for example, index.html) within a document and hold down the Option key while opening the File pull-down menu. Choose the Reveal Selection command to open the Finder folder that contains that file.

Send to Back

This command places the front window behind all other windows.

Exchange with Next

This command lets you switch your screen between the front two windows.

Synchro Scrolling

Synchro Scrolling enables multiple files to scroll in unison — the files in all open windows scroll when you scroll just one. This feature is great for comparing two versions of the same file.

Window names

All the open windows are listed at the bottom of the Windows pull-down menu. Simply select one to make it active.

Tools menu

The Tools pull-down menu and associated HTML Tools Palette together offer powerful assistance in designing the layout of your Web pages. In most respects the Tools menu and the HTML Tools Palette function similarly. Following are descriptions of some of the basic Tools menu functions.

Debugging menu

This set of commands helps you to find problems such as bad links and HTML coding errors in your Web documents. Errors are shown in a new window, complete with the line number of the offending HTML code. The Debugging menu contains the following commands:

◆ **Balance Tags.** Selects the pair of container tags nearest the cursor, highlighting the tags and all the HTML text in between. If you select Balance Tags again, the next pair of tags is selected.

◆ **Check Links.** Verifies that documents linked to a file actually exist, to help you identify bad links in your Web site. The command does not verify that these documents exist on your Web server, but rather that the documents exist in your site root folder (as defined in the HTML Preferences section of BBEdit's Preferences). See the "Internet Menu" section for information on checking external Web links.

◆ **Check HTML.** Checks the current document for HTML syntax errors. Faulty HTML may work fine when viewed in one browser but display incorrectly when viewed by another, and this command helps you avoid that problem.

One HTML error can result in the report of multiple subsequent errors. It's best to correct errors from the top of the document and then recheck the document after you correct each error.

◆ **Check Site Links.** Operates like the Check Links command, but it checks the validity of link references in every HTML file in the site root folder. No attempt is made to validate external links (such as sites on a remote Web server, for example). See the "Internet Menu" section for information on checking external Web links.

◆ **Format.** Reformats the structure and display of the HTML text. Choose from the following:

Hierarchical	Each set of tags is indented, and tag pairs appear on separate lines.
Gentle Hierarchical	Similar to Hierarchical, but anchors within other tags are not indented.
Document Skeleton	Hierarchical style but with everything removed that is not a tag or tag specification (such as all the text). Use this format to create a template.
Plain	Each tag appears on a separate line.
Compact	Deletes any unnecessary white space, including tabs, spaces, and carriage returns.

◆ **Index Site.** Creates an unordered list of all the links and images in every HTML page in the current site. Aside from the unordered list, there are four other predefined index styles available.

Document menu

Use the Document menu when you want to add a background image or color, calculate the file size, or update the page with all the placeholders and includes. The Document menu also enables you to include a `<div>` tag pair for alignment purposes.

- ✦ **Background Image.** Choose a background image for the current document.

- ✦ **Document Color.** Choose the color of the background, text, and links for the entire document. Double-click any of the 12 colors to alter it. Hold down the Option key while clicking a color to access a pop-up list of Web-safe colors.

- ✦ **Div (Division).** Inserts a `<div>` tag pair in the current cursor position and enables you to select left, right, or center alignment.

- ✦ **Document Size.** Returns the size of the current document.

- ✦ **Update.** Replaces all placeholders and includes in the current document (or the current site). See the BBEdit Help system for detailed information on using placeholders and includes.

Font menu

Set the size of your font — relatively or specifically — through the Font menu.

- ✦ **1 through 7.** Specify a particular font size for the selected text, corresponding to the HTML heading sizes `<h1>` through `<h7>`.

- ✦ **Font Color.** Specify a font color for the selected text. Double-click any of the colors to modify it.

- ✦ **Big.** Sets the current text to use the `<big>` tag pair.

- ✦ **Small.** Sets the current text to use the `<small>` tag pair.

- ✦ **Small Caps.** Uppercases all selected text and makes the first letter of each word two font sizes larger than the remainder of the text.

- ✦ **Options.** Opens a dialog box to specify any of the Font menu options except Small Caps; also enables you to set a `<base>` font for the page.

Heading menu

Use this menu to insert the HTML tags appropriate for the heading levels 1 through 6, to distinguish the various titles and subheadings within a page.

Links menu

Links are essential to Web pages. The Links menu is a handy way to add your hypertext links with all the necessary attributes.

- ✦ **Anchor.** Inserts an anchor tag with the associated attributes for creating a link or a base anchor.

- ✦ **Image.** Places a graphic image at the current insertion point. Size attributes are handled automatically for GIF, JPEG, and PNG files.

Lists menu

Lets you organize lists of textual items, with optional indentation and a choice of bullets. BBEdit supports these list types: Unordered, Ordered, Definition, Directory, and Menu.

Misc menu

The Misc menu holds a hodgepodge of special-purpose tools.

- ✦ **Index Document.** Creates an unordered list of all the links and images in every HTML page in the current page. The list appears at the current cursor position.

- ✦ **Placeholders.** Adds placeholders to templates.

- ✦ **NCSA to Client Imagemap.** Creates a client-side image map from an NCSA server-side image map.

- ✦ **Remove All Comments.** Deletes all commented material from the current page.

- ✦ **Tags to Lower Case.** Lowercases all HTML tags. Attribute values, such as filenames and functions, remain the same case.

- ✦ **Tags to Upper Case.** Uppercases all HTML tags. Attribute values, such as filenames and functions, remain the same case.

Preview menu

Loads the active document into the default Web browser defined in the Web Browser section of BBEdit's Preferences.

Table menu

This menu assists you in the creation of tables. Tables are a great way to organize your Web page layout.

- ✦ **Table.** Inserts a `<table>`...`</table>` tag pair or encloses selected text with the same tag pair.

✦ **Caption.** Inserts a `<caption>...</caption>` tag pair or encloses selected text with the same tag pair.

✦ **Cell.** Inserts a `<td>...</td>` tag pair or encloses selected text with the same tag pair.

✦ **Header.** Inserts a `<th>...</th>` tag pair or encloses selected text with the same tag pair.

✦ **Row.** Inserts a `<tr>...</tr>` tag pair or encloses selected text with the same tag pair.

✦ **Convert to Table.** Converts the currently selected text to a table format using the parameters set by the displayed dialog box.

✦ **Options.** Displays a dialog box to insert any of the preceding tags.

✦ **Tabulate.** Inserts a simple table to be used with monospaced font.

✦ **Table Builder.** Displays the Table Builder utility. If the cursor is currently positioned within a table, the table is first selected.

Utilities menu

The Utilities menu offers a variety of page-oriented tools especially useful for prepping a regular text document for publication on the Web.

✦ **Comment.** Surrounds selected text with HTML comment tags.

✦ **Uncomment.** Deletes comment tags from selected text.

✦ **Entities.** Displays the Entity dialog box that enables easy entry of HTML character entities.

✦ **Insert Hotlist.** Adds a list of links, also known as Bookmarks, usually stored in your Web browser.

✦ **PageMill Cleaner.** Fixes problems associated with Web pages created or edited in Adobe PageMill, including replacing multiple instances of the `<br>` tag with a single `<p>` tag. Removes the NATURALSIZE attribute from image tags and removes empty anchor tags.

✦ **Remove Tags.** Removes all HTML tags from the document or the selected area.

✦ **Translate.** Enables a variety of translation options, including conversions between the ISO Latin-1 and Macintosh character set, conversion of 8-bit characters to ASCII equivalents, and conversion of HTML standard characters such as < and > to character entities (and back). Adds or deletes `<p>` tags to paragraphs.

✦ **Web Color Palette.** Displays a palette of 216 browser-safe colors. Drag any color swatch from the palette to the document to insert a color value.

HTML Tools palette

The HTML Tools Palette (see Figure A-9) gives you a quick path to the most frequently used functions of BBEdit. You can place this floating palette anywhere on your desktop for easy access.

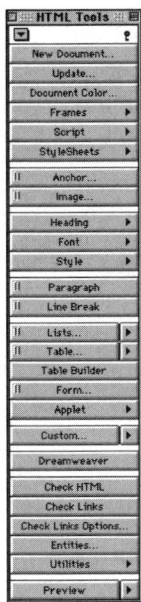

Figure A-9: The HTML Tools Palette.

Several buttons have submenus that appear when you click the button, presenting additional related options. Submenus are indicated by the right-pointing arrows on the right side of the button. For example, the Heading button enables the user to select the desired heading level.

A double vertical bar on the left side of some buttons (the *grip strip*) indicates that the button supports drag-and-drop. For example, you can drag the Form button into a document window to place a form at the insertion point. This action brings up the Form Tool dialog box.

Some of the buttons also accept drag-and-drop actions through the selection of a portion of your HTML document. For example, you can apply italic tags to text by selecting the text and dragging it onto the Style button. A dialog box appears, with choices of Italic, Bold, and other supported styles.

Internet menu

If your computer is connected to the Internet — and it undoubtedly is — BBEdit offers additional valuable features. The Internet menu is identified by a globe icon in the menu bar. Two helpful features of the Internet menu are Resolve URL and View HTML File.

Resolve URL

Follow these steps to check the validity of a URL:

1. Make sure you have an active connection to the Internet.

2. Place the insertion point anywhere within the URL.

3. Open the Internet menu and choose the Resolve URL command. BBEdit launches your default Web browser. (If the Web browser can't be found, an alert beep sounds.)

   Note that you can Command-click anywhere in a URL to resolve it.

4. If the URL is invalid, an alert beep sounds.

   If the URL is valid, you'll be able to view the site in your browser.

View HTML File

This command opens the active HTML file in your Web browser. You must save the file to see the changes in the Web browser. The HTML file must end with the suffix .html or .htm for this feature to work. To view an HTML file with this command, you need not have a connection to the Internet.

Printing

To print a document, select the Print command from the File menu. A standard Mac OS Print dialog box appears, with a few special BBEdit printing options. Each printer type presents its own options, of course; Figure A-10 shows the printer options associated with a LaserWriter 300.

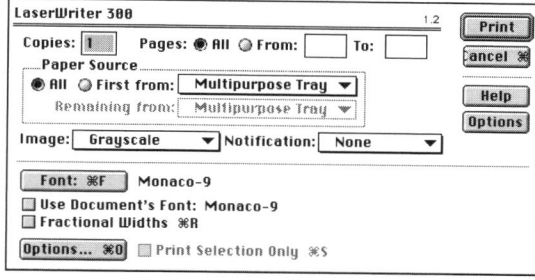

Figure A-10: The Print dialog box for a LaserWriter.

Click the Option button to see which options are available for your printer. Some of the commonly used options are outlined in the following table.

Print Option	Description
Print Page Headers	Prints page number, filename, time, and date from the header of each page.
Print Line Numbers	Displays line numbers along the left margin of the document. This is very useful when debugging a file because error reports point to actual line numbers within a file.
Print Two-Up	Use this option to save resources by printing two BBEdit pages on one sheet of paper.
1-Inch Gutter	Leaves a one-inch margin along the left side of the paper. Allows space for notes in the margin, for instance, or to accommodate placement in three-ring binders.
Print Full Pathname	Prints the full path name of the file, from the header.
Time Stamp: Date Last Saved Date of Printing	This option lets you decide whether the header date is the date the file was last modified or the date the file was printed.
Print Rubber Stamp	You can specify a message to be printed diagonally across the page in gray (or outline). This feature may not work on all printers.

Other Useful BBEdit Features

This section takes a look at some selected BBEdit features that you may find useful.

Spell checking

The Check Spelling command on the Text menu launches BBEdit's built-in spelling checker. The spelling checker compares each word in the document with words in the spelling checker's dictionaries. If a word can't be found in a dictionary, BBEdit attempts to offer a possible correction.

If the questioned word is actually spelled correctly, you can add the word to the User Dictionary or simply skip the word. BBEdit ignores HTML code and checks only the text that will actually appear in your Web page.

If you've used any spell checkers at all, these steps will be familiar to you:

1. Select Text ⇨ Check Spelling.

2. To limit spell checking to only selected text, choose the Selection Only option.

3. Click Start to begin spell checking.

4. If a Questioned Word is misspelled, choose the correct word from the Guesses list, or type a replacement word in the Replace With box.

   If a Questioned Word is not misspelled, choose a Skip command or use the Add command to enter the word into your personal user dictionary.

Altering the user dictionary

BBEdit's user dictionary is a simple editable text file that you can alter yourself. You can add and delete words quickly and easily.

Open the User Dictionary by double-clicking the file located inside the BBEdit Dictionaries folder within the main BBEdit 4.5. folder. Each dictionary word must be entered on a separate line. Edit the file just as you would any other BBEdit text file.

Caution

IMPORTANT: Do not alter the coded number that appears at the top of the file. This code lets BBEdit recognize the file as the user dictionary.

Comparing files

BBEdit's Search menu contains a Find Differences command for comparing two files. For example, you may want to compare a file you have been working on locally to a file you just retrieved from a server, to find differences between the two. Figure A-11 demonstrates this feature at work.

Follow these steps to use the comparison features of the Find Differences command:

1. Choose Search ⇨ Find Differences. The Find Differences dialog box appears.

2. Use the New and Old pop-up menus to choose the files you wish to compare. You can also drag file icons from the Finder into the New and Old portions of the dialog box.

3. Select the appropriate options — Case Insensitive or Ignore Leading Space — for your situation.

4. Click Compare to start the file-comparison operation.

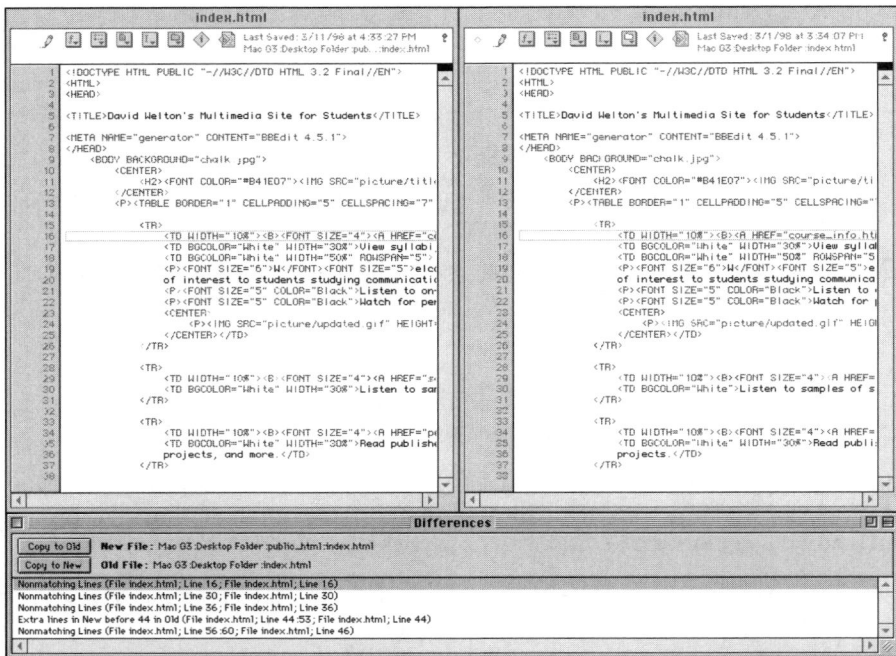

Figure A-11: Comparing differences in BBEdit files.

If BBEdit finds differences the two files will appear side by side. In addition, a Differences pane window detailing the found differences appears at the bottom of the screen (see Figure A-11). You can copy a line from one file to another by selecting the line and choosing either Copy to Old, or Copy to New. BBEdit italicizes the line in the Differences window to indicate the change has been applied.

Search menu

BBEdit's search and search-and-replace features work on a single file or multiple files. Follow these steps to search and/or replace text in the active window:

1. Select Search ⇨ Find.

2. Enter the text you wish to locate in the Search For box.

3. To enter a replacement string, do so in the Replace With box. Otherwise, leave this box empty.

4. Choose any options you wish to apply to the search, including the direction of the search (Start at Top, Wrap Around, or Backwards), the selection, and the case sensitivity.

5. Click any of the buttons along the right side of the dialog box to begin the search operation: Find, Find All, Replace, Replace All, Don't Find, or Cancel. Don't Find saves the settings of your search without actually performing the search.

One of the options in the Search command's dialog box lets you search and/or replace text in multiple files. A handy use for this feature is to update each occurrence of a revised filename in several related HTML documents.

Follow these steps to perform multifile searches:

1. Select Search ⇨ Find.

2. Enter the text you wish to locate in the Search For box.

3. To enter a replacement string, do so in the Replace With box. Otherwise, leave this box empty.

4. Find the Multi-File Search option and click the triangle to reveal the Multi-File Search options. (This portion of the dialog box may already be visible.)

5. Choose the files you wish to search, using the buttons and pop-up menus in the bottom part of the dialog box.

6. Select any other options you wish to apply to the search as in the single file search.

7. Click the appropriate button along the right side of the dialog box to begin the operation as in the single file search.

Go To Line command

It's easy to move the insertion point instantly to a specific line in your document. Use the Go To Line command under the Mark menu (see upcoming section). Enter the line number in the dialog box and click Go To. See Figure A-12.

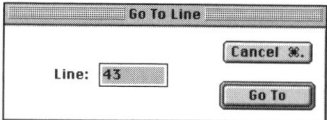

Figure A-12: The Go To Line dialog box.

Marker menu

BBEdit's *markers* enable you to quickly and easily move to a particular section of your file. You can give the marker a unique name that makes sense to you and helps you find it later. This feature helps you stay on track in a large HTML file.

To set markers:

1. First select the section of your document you wish to mark.
2. Choose Mark ⇨ Set Marker.
3. In the Set Marker dialog box enter a name for the marker and click the Set button.

   Once markers are established, the marker names appear at the bottom of the Mark pull-down menu. Simply select the marker name to take you to that location in your document.
4. When you need to clear markers you don't need anymore, select Mark ⇨ Clear Markers. In the Clear Markers dialog box, choose the marker you want to delete, and click the Clear button.

Syntax coloring

To make editing easier, BBEdit displays HTML tags in colored text. Be sure to save your HTML documents with the .html or .htm extensions to enable this feature. If you want to change the colors BBEdit uses for syntax coloring, you can do so in the Text Colors portion of the Preferences dialog box.

Working with servers

You will be placing your completed Web files on a public server that enables people to view your masterpiece worldwide. The public server uses the file transfer protocol (FTP) to send and receive files. Dreamweaver has built-in FTP capabilities that enable you to connect to a remote server to save (upload) and open (download) files; see Chapter 27 for more information on FTP publishing. In addition, BBEdit offers the following FTP capabilities.

Saving to a server (uploading)

Follow these steps to upload to a server:

1. With a document open in BBEdit, select File ⇨ Save to FTP Server.
2. To connect to a server, enter the name of the server. You can choose from previously used servers in the pop-up Server menu.

3. Enter your user name and password.

4. Click the Connect button to begin an FTP session.

5. Choose the destination directory on the server by using the standard Mac OS directory pop-up menu.

BBEdit will remember your password if you desire. Auto-Connect instructs BBEdit to automatically connect to a server using your saved password the next time you begin an FTP session.

Opening from a server (downloading)

If you wish to retrieve files from a server, use the File ➪ Open From FTP Server command. The steps are similar to those for Saving to an FTP Server in the preceding section. Figure A-13 is the dialog box used when opening files from a remote FTP server.

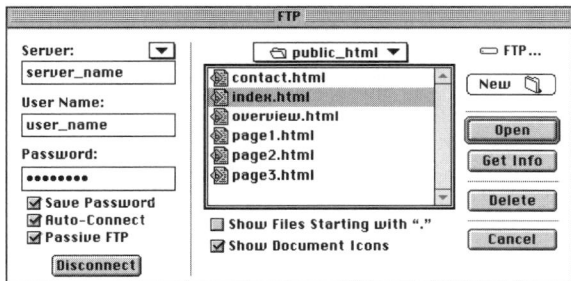

Figure A-13: The FTP Open dialog box.

Once the connection is made, you'll use a standard Mac OS directory pop-up menu to navigate through the directories — just as you would if the files were stored locally on your Mac. Once you have located the file you desire, choose Save to begin the downloading process. After the file is completely downloaded, BBEdit displays the file in a new text editing window.

✦　　✦　　✦

HomeSite 3.0 Primer (For Windows 95/NT Users)

✦ ✦ ✦ ✦

In This Appendix

A tour of the HomeSite workspace, menus, and toolbars

Getting HomeSite and Dreamweaver to work together

Making HTML files

Enhancing and editing Web pages with HomeSite

✦ ✦ ✦ ✦

Designing and creating Web sites is intuitive and easy with Dreamweaver's visual interface. Yet there may be times when you'll want to leave the visual editor and get your hands on the underlying HTML code. In some cases, the Dreamweaver's built-in HTML editor will be all you need. Whenever you need a more advanced HTML editor to add features or troubleshoot your page, the Windows 95 version of Dreamweaver includes a complete registered version of HomeSite 3.0. This standalone HTML editor package for Windows 95/NT works with Dreamweaver. HomeSite is one of the most popular HTML editors available today and enables you to produce HTML files without actually memorizing HTML tag commands.

This appendix provides instructions on how to access HomeSite's basic features. You can also access an Online User Manual and other invaluable help resources by clicking the Help tab in the Resources area of the HomeSite screen. (Remember that you can resize this frame by clicking and dragging the borders to make reading the help resources easier.) Also, you can visit Allaire's HomeSite 3.0 Web site at

```
http://www.allaire.com
```

Getting Started

It's easy to switch between Dreamweaver and HomeSite. A simple click on an icon toggles you from one application to the other. Elements selected in one application are automatically highlighted in the other, making it easy to keep your project organized.

Key features

"Full featured" just scratches the surface when it comes to describing HomeSite. Many of the tools are the perfect complement to Dreamweaver's visual editor; others serve to make straight coding as efficient as possible. Here are just a few of the HomeSite highlights:

✦ Multiple layers of Undo

✦ Spelling checker

✦ Site link validation

✦ Automatic color coding of HTML, CFML, and other scripts

✦ Extended search-and-replace capabilities for making global edits

✦ Tag Insight, offering a list of attributes and attribute values as you enter tag code

✦ Customization of main and tag toolbars

✦ Wizards for complex tasks, including incorporating dynamic HTML, RealAudio, and RealVideo

✦ Toggle among multiple documents

✦ Drag-and-drop from image libraries into the page

✦ Access to remote sites via built-in FTP

✦ Estimates of document sizes and download times

✦ Management for Cascading Style Sheets, CFML server-side tags, Netscape and Internet Explorer HTML extensions, embedded multimedia and plug-ins, and ActiveX and Java controls

✦ Web-safe color palette

✦ HTML syntax checking

✦ One-click preview in any browser

The HomeSite 3.0 interface

The HomeSite interface is simple and logical, making even the most demanding programming projects easier to accomplish. The workspace (see Figure B-1) has three primary areas: the Editor/Browser and Resource windows, and the command bars.

Resources window
Main toolbar   Editor toolbar (vertical)   Tag toolbar

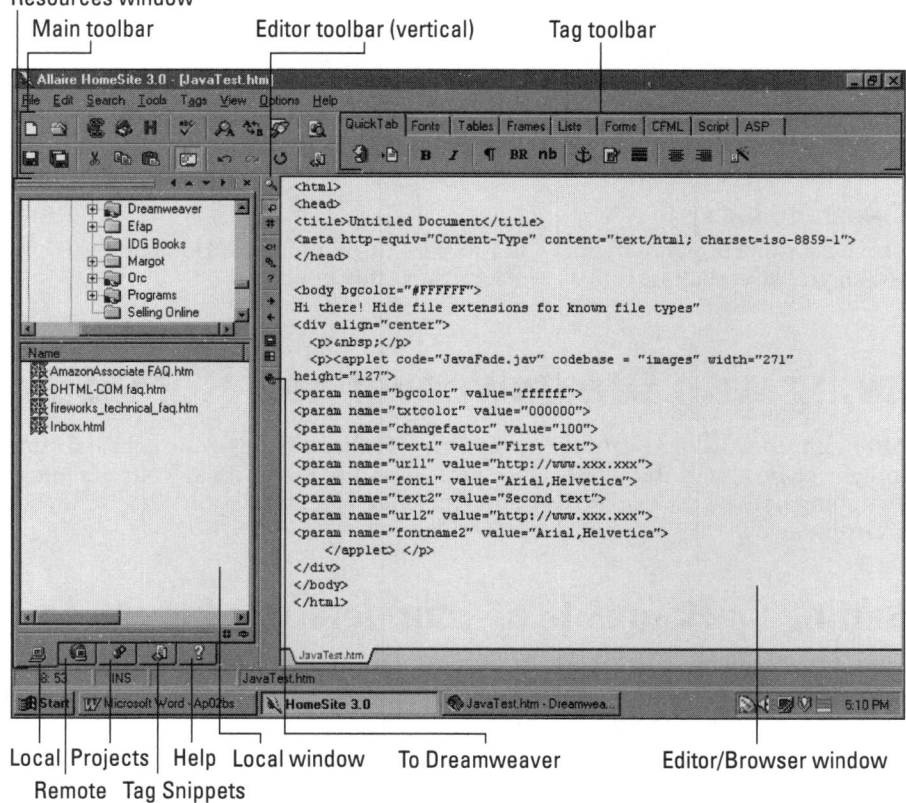

Local Projects Help Local window   To Dreamweaver   Editor/Browser window
Remote Tag Snippets

Figure B-1: The HomeSite 3.0 workspace.

Editor/Browser window

Toggle between these two screens with F12. The editor screen is where you enter HTML tags and place page content. The browser screen is where you render the current document in the browser you choose.

Resource window

Click the tab buttons at the bottom of the Resource window to access areas where you manage files, custom tags, and online help areas. From left to right, the tabs represent the following groups of resources:

+ **Local.** Use the Directory and File panes to access local and network drives.

+ **Remote.** Access remote servers with FTP.

+ **Projects.** Create and manage HomeSite projects.

+ **Tag Snippets.** Store code for later use; see the "Inserting Tags in a Document" section later in this chapter.

+ **Help.** Access help files, including User Manual, FAQ, HTML reference files, and more.

Command bars

There's a rich supply of menus and toolbars throughout the HomeSite workspace, which you'll read about as you work through this appendix.

Working with Dreamweaver and HomeSite

Although Dreamweaver lets you assign any HTML editor as your external editor, it integrates best with HomeSite. Once you've set up HomeSite as your default editor, switching between Dreamweaver and HomeSite is just a button click or keyboard shortcut away.

Setting up HomeSite as your default editor

Before Dreamweaver can access HomeSite, you must make HomeSite your default HTML editor. You can make this assignment through the Dreamweaver Preferences by following these steps:

1. In Dreamweaver, choose Edit ➪ Preferences to open the Preferences dialog box.

2. From the Category list on the left, choose External Editors to display that panel.

3. In the External Editor panel, enter the path to the HomeSite executable. The easiest way to do this is to select the Browse button and locate the file. If you installed HomeSite according to the defaults, this path should read c:\program files\allaire\homesite3.exe.

4. Click OK when you've finished.

Cross-
Reference

The External Editor options that control file synchronization between Dreamweaver and HomeSite are explained in detail in Chapter 3, "Setting Your Preferences."

Known Problem with HomeSite/Dreamweaver Integration

As of this writing, a known problem occurs with some Windows 95/NT systems that prevents the HTML file from transferring correctly to HomeSite from Dreamweaver. Allaire has posted an update program on its Web site (www.allaire.com) that you can download and install to take care of the problem. However, there's also another method you can use to establish the integration.

After you've followed the preceding steps for "Setting Up HomeSite as Your Default Editor," if your files do not display in HomeSite when you choose Launch External Editor or Ctrl-E, you may have encountered this problem. To verify and, more importantly, work around the problem, follow these steps:

1. Make sure that both Dreamweaver and HomeSite are closed.

2. From your desktop, open Windows Explorer, or choose Start ⇨ Programs ⇨ Windows Explorer.

3. From the Windows Explorer menu, select View ⇨ Options.

4. From the View tab of the Windows Explorer dialog box, make the following settings as appropriate for your system:

   • Windows 95: Deselect the option for "Hide MS-DOS file extensions for file types that are registered."

   • Windows NT: Deselect the option for "Hide file extensions for known file types."

5. Restart Dreamweaver and test the integration with HomeSite.

Switching between Dreamweaver and HomeSite

When you're in Dreamweaver, you have three ways to switch to HomeSite:

✦ Click the External Editor button in the top-left corner of the HTML Inspector.

✦ Choose Edit ⇨ Launch External Editor.

✦ Use the keyboard shortcut, Ctrl-E.

You can also select the other program's button on the taskbar or use the Alt-Tab method to switch between applications, but the file integration will not work under these circumstances.

Depending on the synchronization options chosen in the External Editor preferences, Dreamweaver may ask if you want to save the files first before you switch to HomeSite. If you do not save your Dreamweaver file first, your modifications will not appear in HomeSite (and vice versa). For this reason, I recommend setting your synchronization options to Always.

After you've made your code modifications in HomeSite and you're ready to return to Dreamweaver, you have three methods for switching back:

✦ Select the Dreamweaver button in HomeSite's Editor toolbar.

✦ Choose View ➪ Macromedia Dreamweaver.

✦ Use the keyboard shortcut, Ctrl-D.

If HomeSite doesn't switch to Dreamweaver using any of the methods just given, check your HomeSite settings. Choose Options ➪ Settings (or press F8) to open the HomeSite Settings dialog box and select the HomeSite reload options from this tab.

Disabling HomeSite integration

You may disable HomeSite integration if you prefer working with an older version of HomeSite or if you use a different HTML text editor. Here's how:

1. Choose Edit ➪ Preferences.

2. Select General from the category list on the left.

3. Turn off Enable HomeSite Integration and click OK.

Creating Pages: Making HTML Files

You have a couple of ways to work with HTML files. You can either create a new file or open an existing one and edit it. This section shows you how to create, open, apply tags to, and save Web pages in HomeSite. Remember, even if you create a Web page in another application, you can still edit the page with HomeSite.

If you're starting from scratch to create a new file, HomeSite offers the following ways to create a new document:

✦ Select File ➪ New (Ctrl-N) to open the New HTML Document dialog box. Select a blank document, one of the templates, or use any HTML file as a template. Customize the New HTML Document dialog box by adding or deleting it.

Template files are stored separately from the source documents, so you can modify the template files without worrying about changing the originals.

✦ Click the New button on the main toolbar to open a new document based on your default template. Change the default template by choosing Options ➪ Settings (F8) and selecting the Default Template tab.

✦ Use the Document wizard. Click the Quick Start button on the Quick Tab in the Tag toolbar (see Figure B-2), and follow the steps to design a new page or build your own template.

✦ Select File ➪ Convert Text File to convert an ASCII text file to an HTML file.

Quick Start button

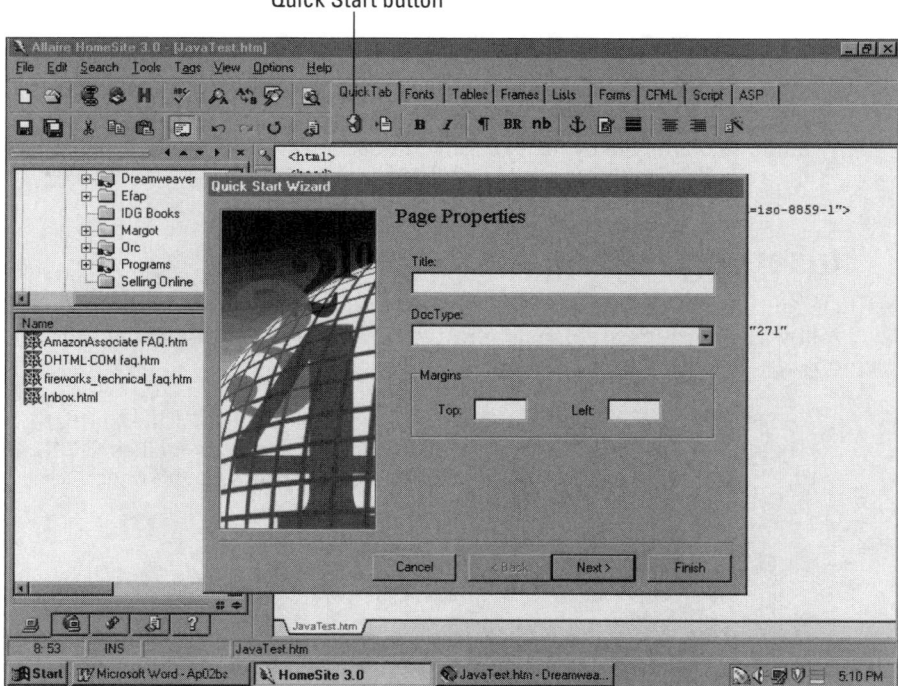

Figure B-2: Use the Quick Start wizard to build a new page or template.

Opening an existing Web page

Another way to create a new HTML document is to start with an existing Web page. Use any of the following methods to open files:

✦ Select File ➪ Open (Ctrl-O).

✦ Click the Open button on the main toolbar.

✦ In the Open HTML Document dialog box, double-click a file listed in the file list.

✦ To open Web files directly, select File ➪ Open from the Web. Type in a URL or select a URL from your Favorites or Bookmarks list.

✦ Select File ➪ Reopen to see a list of recently used files.

Note

HomeSite treats read-only files differently from other files. These files are marked with a small red dot in the Resource window file list, and a warning message pops up if you try to open one. You cannot edit read-only files, but you can change the attribute on the file by right-clicking it, selecting Properties in the shortcut menu, and then deselecting the read-only attribute.

Inserting tags in a document

Of course, you can type codes directly into the document in the Edit screen, but the following methods are usually more efficient. To have HomeSite add tags for you, choose among these commands:

✦ Select Tools ➪ Tag Chooser (Ctrl-E). Select from the Chooser list (see Figure B-3), which contains the complete HTML tag set as well as CFML, HDML, and Custom tag sets. Double-click a tag to insert it into the page.

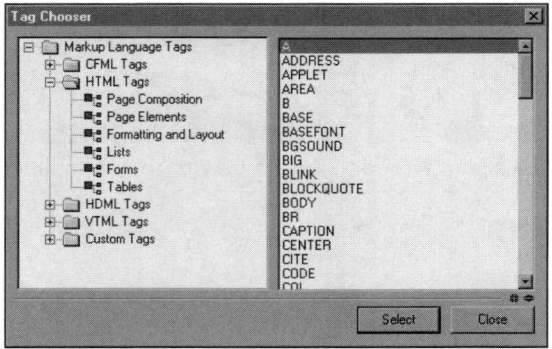

Figure B-3: Access any HTML tag — and many other varieties — through the Tag Chooser.

✦ From the Tags menu, choose from a basic set of formatting tags.

✦ Select Options ⇨ Settings (F8), and select the Tag Help tab to enable the display of options for Tag Tips, Tag Insight, and Tag Completion. The following paragraphs describe these three tools and their benefits.

✦ Select Options ⇨ Settings (F8), and open the HTML tab to set alignment and centering tags and to toggle the case of inserted tags.

✦ To repeat the previous tag, select Tags ⇨ Repeat Last Tag (Ctrl-Q).

Using tag tips

Tag Tips display basic syntax information in a floating rectangle for a tag when you place the cursor in the opening tag of a tag pair. To display Tag Tips:

✦ Click the Tag Tips button (the question mark) on the Editor Toolbar (between the Edit and Resources panels).

✦ Select Options ⇨ Settings and check the Tag Tips box in the Tag Help tab. Use the mouse to move the Delay slidebar to set the time interval for the display of Tag Tips.

✦ Leave the Tag Tips box unchecked in the Tag Help tab of the Settings dialog box and press F2 to toggle the Tag Tips display for the current tag.

Using tag insight

The Tag Insight tool is a valuable aid to all Web designers, even beginners. It's a quick way to develop a tag as you type it by displaying a drop-down list of attributes and values for each tag. Click the Tag Insight button on the Editor Toolbar to enable this feature. Or you can turn off Tag Insight in the Tag Help tab of the Settings dialog box (Options ⇨ Settings or F8). Finally, you can use it only when needed by pressing Shift-F2 when your cursor is in the first tag of a tag pair.

When Tag Insight is turned on, follow these steps to use this helpful feature:

1. Place the cursor in front of the start tag's end bracket (⇨). Press the Spacebar to open the attribute list.

2. To add an attribute to the tag, double-click the attribute in the list. The cursor then moves between the double quotes of the attribute's value.

3. A list of values appears if the attribute has a fixed set of allowed values. To select a value from the list, press the Spacebar. Once the value is inserted, the cursor moves in front of the closing bracket.

   If no allowed values appear, the attribute accepts programmer-specified values.

4. Continue selecting attributes until the tag code is complete.

Using tag completion

The Tag Completion feature automatically inserts the end tag after you type the start tag. Here are the steps to use this feature:

1. To enable Tag Completion, choose Options ⇨ Settings (F8), and in the Tag Help tab check the Tag Completion box.

2. In the Tag Completion section of the Tag Help tab, select Edit to change the syntax of a selected tag.

3. You can use the Add and Delete buttons in the Tag Completion section to manage the list.

Tag snippets

You can save portions of HTML code for easy recall in other files, using the valuable Tag Snippets feature. It's a lot easier than copying and pasting blocks of code from various files.

To save HTML code as a Tag Snippet, follow these steps:

1. Click the Tag Snippets tab at the bottom of the Resources panel to open the Tab Snippets window or right-click the Tag Snippets icon.

2. Select Create Folder.

3. Name the folder from which you want to save code, and press Enter.

4. From the Tag Snippets window, right-click the folder and select Add Snippet from the shortcut menu to open the Custom Tag dialog box.

5. Type the start and end tags or paste them from another file. Click OK to save the tag in the folder selected in Step 2.

To add additional snippets to a folder, right-click the snippet folder in the Tag Snippets window and select Add Snippet from the shortcut menu. You can delete or rename folders, as well, from the right-click shortcut menu.

To insert a Tag Snippet you've saved, follow these steps:

1. In the Editing window, place the cursor where you want to insert the tag.

2. Open the Tag Snippet window using one of the methods described previously.

3. Double-click the folder that holds the snippet you'd like to enter.

4. Double-click the snippet you wish to insert into your document.

Entering text in a document

In HomeSite's Editor window, you can type in page content and tags directly, or use the numerous shortcuts to speed up the process. To check your work, toggle to the Browse mode by pressing F12, clicking the Toggle Browser button in the Editor Toolbar, or by selecting Options ➪ Settings and opening the Internal Browser tab. Here are some examples:

✦ To change the default font, tag colors, and tag completion options, access the Editor tab by selecting Options ➪ Settings (F8).

✦ To change the defaults for text alignment, paragraph tags, and filename cases, access the HTML tab by selecting Options ➪ Settings (F8).

✦ To create a link, drag-and-drop a document file into the Editor window.

✦ To insert an image or other media file, drag-and-drop it into the Editor window to insert it.

✦ To insert an HTML, ASCII text, or Cascading Style Sheet file into a document, select File ➪ Insert.

✦ To display a menu of special and extended characters, select View ➪ Special Characters (Ctrl-Shift-X). In the Special Characters dialog box (see Figure B-4), double-click a character to insert it into your document.

✦ To insert text from any application to your document, use the standard Windows Copy, Cut, and Paste commands.

Figure B-4: Insert extended ASCII characters through the Special Characters dialog box.

Saving files

When you view an unsaved document in either the internal or external browser, HomeSite saves a temporary copy of the file in memory. Thus, you should always save documents with new links in them *before* viewing them in a browser, to ensure that the file paths are identified.

To set the default file format:

1. Select Options ⇨ Settings and open the General tab, shown in Figure B-5.

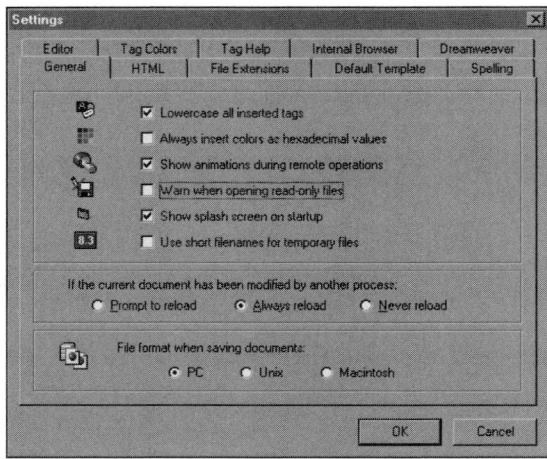

Figure B-5: HomeSite's Settings dialog box features many different options to customize your work environment.

2. Check a format box among the "File format when saving documents" choices.

3. Now select one of the four Save commands from the File pull-down menu:

Save (Ctrl-S)	Saves the current document
Save As (Ctrl-Shift-S)	Select a filename and location for the current document
Save All	Saves all open documents
Save Remote Copy	Select from the list of available servers (to set up a server, click the Remote tab at the bottom of the Resources window)

You can use any HTML file as a template. Template files have the .hst extension and are stored separately. Later changes to the source document do not affect the corresponding template file in any way.

To save file as a template:

1. Selecting Options ⇨ Settings and open the File Extensions.

2. Add .hst to the filename extensions list.

3. Select File ➪ Save As, and then save the file with an .hst extension to the HomeSite/Wizards/HTML/ folder.

4. To use the template, select File ➪ New (Ctrl-N) and choose the template file from the list.

Browsing pages

It's imperative that you view your HTML pages in more than just one browser. HomeSite provides many browser options so you can test your pages against the array of available browsers.

Internal browser

If HomeSite 3.0 detects Microsoft Internet Explorer on your system during installation, you have the option of selecting it as the default HTML browser (see Figure B-6). Netscape Navigator cannot be used as the internal browser in HomeSite.

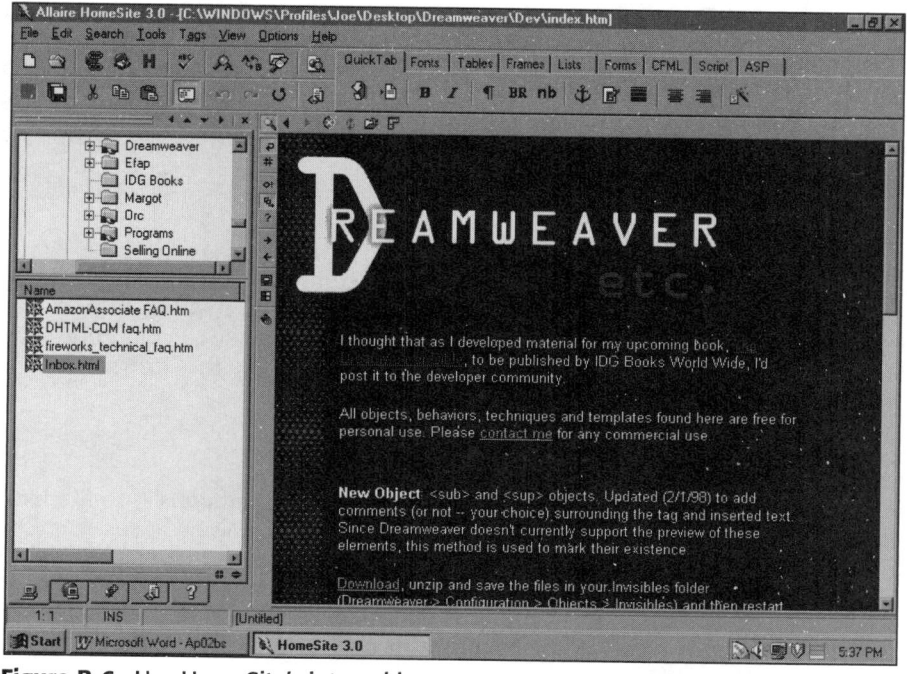

Figure B-6: Use HomeSite's internal browser to preview your Web pages.

Mapping Your Web Site

HomeSite's Default Mapping feature sends a document through the specified Web server. If you don't run your own Web server, leave the mappings settings blank. If you do run your own server, here's how to set a default mapping for your Web server:

1. Access the Internal Browser tab by selecting Options ⇨ Settings.

2. Check the Use Microsoft Internet Explorer box. Also, you can optionally check the box for Browse in Separate Pane to view your documents without having to toggle the Editor/Browser views.

3. Enter the local path of your HTML documents.

4. Enter a URL and click OK.

You also have the option to map any particular path to a file with a specific URL. This mapping capability enables you to use your remote server to preview server-side includes and other types of files. To define a separate mapping for a project:

1. In the Projects panel of the Resources window, right-click a project and select Properties.

2. In the Project Properties dialog box, access the Server Mapping tab. Enter the local path in the first text box, and the URL you want to use for that project in the second text box. Click OK.

Now, if you open this file from the project tree, the project mapping will override the default mapping.

If you don't want to have to toggle between the Editor and Browser windows (with F12 or the Toggle Browser button), you can enable a separate pane to view the Browser mode. That way, you can see the changes you make to your code without having to toggle the display. Remember that you can resize the Browser view by clicking and dragging the borders.

External browser

HomeSite makes it easy to add browsers — and browser versions — to the External Browser list. To add, delete, or reconfigure an external browser, access the External Browsers panel by selecting Options ⇨ External Browsers. When you add a new browser to your list, you have the following options in the External Browsers panel, shown in Figure B-7, that affect your current document when you launch an external browser. You can always change this option by accessing the External Browsers panel.

✦ Prompt to save changes to current document.

✦ Automatically save changes to the current document.

✦ Browse using a temporary copy (no need to save). This is the default setting; it enables you to view your current document without having to save the document itself. Thus, you can get a quick look at your current code without saving over the previous version of the file, in case you don't like what you see.

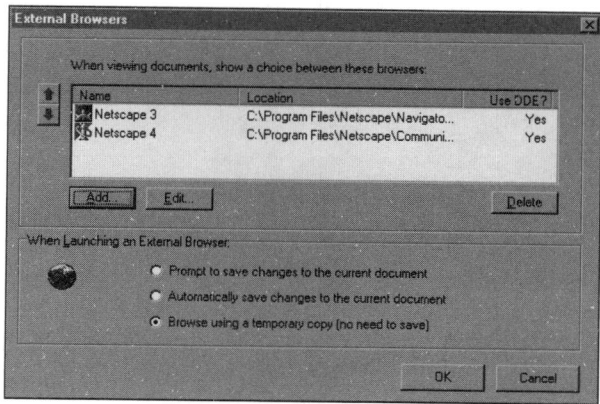

Figure B-7: Add more browsers for testing in the External Browsers dialog box.

Once you add at least one external browser to HomeSite, you can then choose a browser from the list when you click the Launch External Browser button on the main toolbar. Alternatively, pressing F11 loads the current document in the first listed browser. To place your preferred browser at the top of the list, open the External Browsers panel, click the browser, and click the blue arrow buttons to move it to the top. Then click OK to save the change.

Setting up an FTP server

To set up and access both remote and local (if any) servers, open the Remote tab in the Resources area. Right-click local host and select Connect to view the local drive directories. When you open a file from the Remote tab, the Remote URL setting tells HomeSite how to browse the file. When you toggle a browser, HomeSite determines if the server has a Remote URL specified and, if so, uses it to browse the file.

To establish an FTP server, follow these steps:

1. Right-click anywhere in the Remote tab panel, and select Add FTP Server to open the Configure FTP Server panel (see Figure B-8).

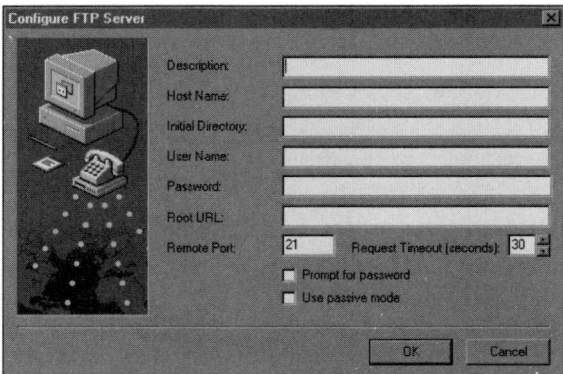

Figure B-8: Set up your FTP server so that you can publish direct to the Web from within HomeSite.

2. At a minimum, complete the following fields:

   Description   Name of server

   Host Name   The FTP address

   User Name   Your login name

   Password   Your password, if any

3. Change the default Remote Port entry as needed.

4. Check the Passive mode box if the FTP server requires a passive connection.

5. Click OK to close the dialog box. Right-click and select Refresh to update the server list.

6. Once you've established an FTP server, right-click the server name, and then select Connect. You'll see the server directory tree if you've connected correctly to the server.

To open a file on a server, you access the remote server's files directly. (To change server settings, right-click a server name, then select Properties to open the Properties panel.) Here are the steps for opening a file:

1. Click the Remote tab in the Resources window, and click a server name in the drop-down list to display the server's directory tree.

2. Double-click a folder to open it.

3. Double-click a file to open it in the Editor window.

Remote files have a small blue dot on their filename tab at the bottom of the Editor window. To save changes to a remote file, click the Save button on the Main Toolbar, or select File ➪ Save Remote Copy to upload the file to the server.

Editing and Enhancing Your Pages

HomeSite makes it easy to customize your working space, modify HTML code, and add bells and whistles to your pages.

Changing how the editor looks and works

You can customize the Editor window's appearance as well as its operation to your liking.

✦ To remove any of the three toolbars from the screen, toggle them off from the View menu.

✦ To switch between open documents, click the tabs at the bottom of the window. If more than five documents are open, use the scroll arrows to move through the tabs. If you've made changes to a document since the last time it was saved, the filename will be red.

✦ To adjust the size of the text line in the Editor, click the Toggle Word Wrap button on the Editor toolbar, or select Options ➪ Word Wrap.

✦ To change the default font and colors, select Options ➪ Settings and open the Editor tab.

✦ To view your document with an internal browser, press F12, or click the Toggle Browser button in the Editor toolbar. To change the internal browser to Microsoft Internet Explorer, select Options ➪ Settings and open the Internal Browser tab.

✦ To view your document with an external browser, press F11 to open the current document in the first browser in your External Browser list. Or click Launch External Browser on the main toolbar and select Browser from list.

✦ To have HomeSite insert ending tags automatically after you type in a start tag, toggle the Tag Completion button on the Editor toolbar.

✦ To find the paired tag to any tag in your document, place the cursor on a tag and press Ctrl-M, or select Tags ➪ Find Matching Tag. This feature works in nested tags.

Tag attribute values

Many HTML tags have attribute values that may enable you to define the tag's appearance or its usefulness. You can set attribute values as you create a tag, or later after you've previewed the page in a browser and you need to adjust the display. You can edit a tag in HomeSite using any of the following methods:

✦ Right-click any start tag and select Edit Tag.

✦ Place the cursor in a start tag and press F4.

✦ Select Tags ➪ Edit Current Tag.

To set or change attribute values with the Tag Editor, follow these steps:

1. Select a start tag or place the cursor inside it, right-click, and select the Tag Editor option.

2. Enter new values or edit the existing values in the Tag Editor panel, shown in Figure B-9.

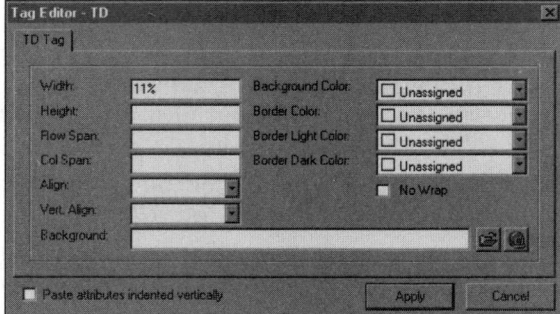

Figure B-9: The Tag Editor shows all of the options for any selected HTML tag.

3. Complex tags may have multiple tabs in their Tag Editor windows. Click the tab names at the top of the Tag Editor panel to access the other attributes.

4. Click the Apply button to close the Tag Editor and have the attribute changes appear in the document.

Using bookmarks

You can set up to ten bookmarks in a document — very handy for finding your spot in a large HTML file. To set and use bookmarks, follow these steps:

1. Select Edit ⇨ Set Bookmark (Ctrl-Shift-K) to open the bookmark list.

2. To insert a bookmark where the cursor is currently positioned in your document, select a number from the Set Bookmark dialog box (Figure B-10). HomeSite places a small numbered marker in the left margin of your code.

3. To go to a bookmark, select Edit ⇨ Go to Bookmark (Ctrl-K) to open the bookmark list, and pick a number to go to that bookmark.

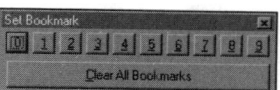

Figure B-10: You can set up to ten different bookmarks in your HTML file with the Set Bookmark dialog box.

Using search

HomeSite has two levels of search and replace. *Basic searches* scan only the current open document. *Extended searches* scan more than just the open document. Thus, it's easy to make global changes.

Performing basic searches

To search for a string in the current open document, select Search ⇨ Find (Ctrl-F). Then, if you want to replace a matching string in the current open document, select Search ⇨ Replace (Ctrl-R).

If the search panel is closed and you want to resume the previous search, select Search ⇨ Search Again (F3).

Performing extended searches

To search for a string among all open documents (or all HTML files in a particular directory, folder, or project), follow these steps:

1. Select Search ⇨ Extended Find and Replace (Ctrl-Shift-R).

2. Enter your selections in the Extended Find and Replace dialog box shown in Figure B-11.

3. You can see all of the matches in the Search Results tab. Double-click any match in the list to go directly to that file. Note that read-only files are not searched, and that you will not be prompted to confirm each replacement.

4. Right-click the Search Results tab for options.

5. If the search panel is closed and you want to resume the previous extended (or basic) search, select Search ⇨ Search Again (F3).

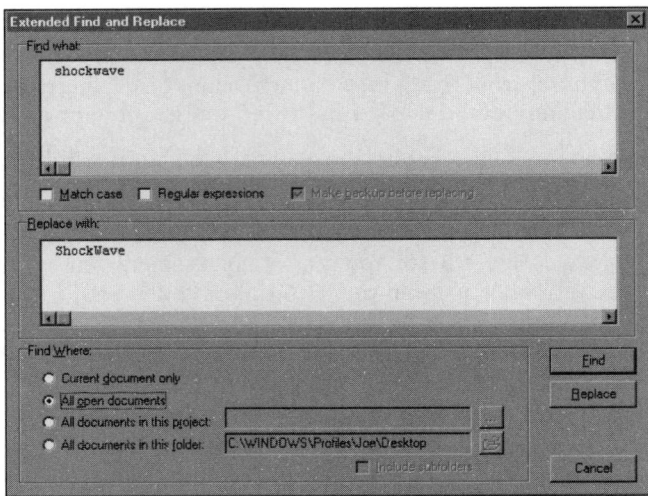

Figure B-11: HomeSite's Extended Find and Replace feature is extremely powerful and flexible.

Spell check

HomeSite takes the normal spell-checking operation to the next level by providing a multilanguage Spell Check feature. When you install HomeSite, you can select additional language dictionaries to use. To run Spell Check, use any of these methods:

✦ Select Tools ➪ Spell Check (F7) to scan your current document for spelling errors.

✦ Select Tools ➪ Spell Check All (Shift-F7) to check all open documents.

✦ To configure the spell checker to skip all text within HTML tags, select Options ➪ Settings and open the Spelling tab. In this tab you can also select the dictionaries you want the spell checker to use.

Using color-coded tags

To facilitate quick scanning of documents, HomeSite displays tags in distinct colors. This includes all HTML tags, quoted attributes, and script and object tags. You can change the default colors used, and create custom colors as well.

Changing colors

To change color coding, access the Tag Colors panel (see Figure B-12) by selecting Options ⇨ Settings. Choose your new colors from the drop-down lists.

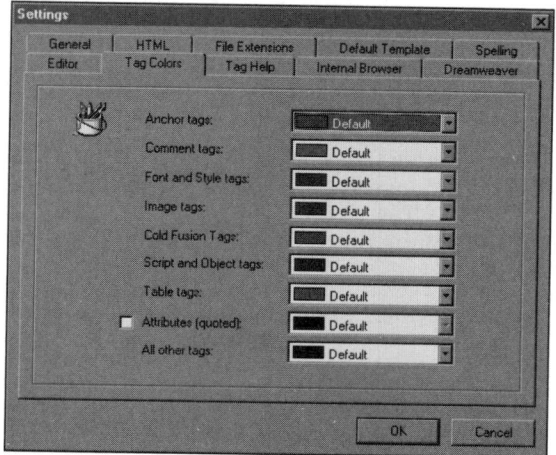

Figure B-12: Color-code your HTML to easily find specific or different kinds of tags.

You can also assign a color from the Basic Palette to any tag. Open the drop-down list for the tag you want to color, and choose Custom. This opens the color palette. Pick a basic color and click OK.

Creating new colors

To create a custom color for a tag, follow these steps:

1. Open the Tag Colors panel in the Settings dialog box.

2. Open the color palette by selecting Custom from the drop-down list for the tag.

3. Click the Define Custom Color button to expand the dialog box.

4. Drag the arrow on the brightness scale to set a level.

5. Drag the color pointer to define a color. The color values display as you move the pointer, and the color displays in the Preview box.

6. Click Add to Custom colors; then click OK to enter the color for the tag.

Adding colors

Wise use of color can make the difference between uninspired and exciting Web pages. HomeSite provides some easy ways to add and change colors in your pages. To insert a color tag using Tag Insight:

1. Open Tag Insight by placing the cursor in front of the start tag's closing bracket and pressing the spacebar.

2. Choose Color Values For Attributes from the pop-up list.

HomeSite provides a variety of color palettes (basic Web-supported colors, safety palette, and Windows default palettes). To insert a color from a palette:

1. To open a color palette, click the Palette button on the Editor toolbar. This opens the palette pane.

2. Position the cursor over any palette color to display its name or hexadecimal value.

3. Click a color to insert it into your document.

Working with palettes

To open a different palette from which to select colors, follow these steps:

1. Access the Open Palette dialog box, shown in Figure B-13, by clicking the Open Palette button on the left side of the palette pane.

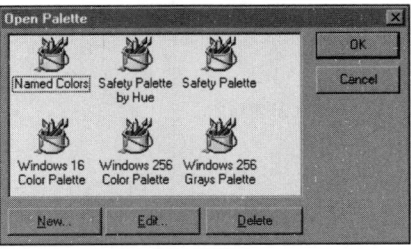

Figure B-13: Switch among any number of color sets through the Open Palette dialog box.

2. Double-click a palette to open it in the palette pane.

You can edit and delete existing palettes from the Open Palette dialog box. You can create a new palette, too. Follow these steps:

1. In the Open Palette dialog box, click the New button.

2. Select RGB values, or click the eye-dropper button and drag the dropper over the color spectrum to create a color.

3. Once you create a color you want to add to your palette, click the Add button.

4. When you are done creating a new palette, click the Save button and enter a name for the palette. The new file is saved with a default .pal extension in the Palettes subdirectory.

Adding a palette from Paint Shop Pro

Follow these steps to bring a Paint Shop Pro palette into HomeSite:

1. In Paint Shop Pro, select Colors ➪ Save Palette to open the Save Palette panel.

2. Enter a name for the palette.

3. Set the Save As type to PAL-JASC Palette.

4. Save the file in the HomeSite\Palettes directory.

Adding images

HomeSite supports the standard Web graphics formats: GIF, JPG, PNG graphics files, and BMP (Internet Explorer only). To see all of your image files, right-click in one of the file list resource tabs, select Filter, and then select Web Images to limit the file display to images only. If you want to view thumbnails of the image files, click one of the two Thumbnail buttons at the bottom of the file list to view the files one at a time, or all in a new window.

To add an image to the current document, follow these steps:

1. Select an image in the file list and drag it directly into your document. The default image width and height will appear in the tag code.

2. Place the cursor anywhere in the image tag, right-click, and select Edit Tag.

3. Change the image settings in the editor as needed. You can click the Clear button to delete the current entries.

To add a low-source image

To overcome the long load time for large image files, the `lowsrc` attribute lets you tell the browser to first load and display a smaller low-resolution image file. Then, when the whole page is finished loading, the browser can begin displaying a normal, high-resolution image.

1. In the Image Tag window, enter the final image filename in the Source box.

2. Complete the entries for attributes and values.

3. Click the Advanced tab and enter the name of the low-resolution image in the LowSrc box.

Caution The LowSrc extension only works for the Netscape Navigator browser.

Testing Your Pages

Before you launch your Web site, you should test your code. HomeSite has several key features — HTML Validation, Link Checking, and Document Weighing — to put your Web page through its paces.

HTML validation

Before you FTP your files up to the remote server, it's a good idea to verify that your HTML code is sound. HomeSite includes Alsoft's CSE 3310 HTML Validator 2.5, which is a powerful tool for checking and reporting on HTML syntax errors. Although it won't automatically correct errors, it will identify them and give you a list of errors and comments. Double-click an error message to highlight the offending code in your document.

To set the HTML Validator options:

1. Select Options ➪ Validator Settings and choose Program Options. Open the Validator tab shown in Figure B-14.

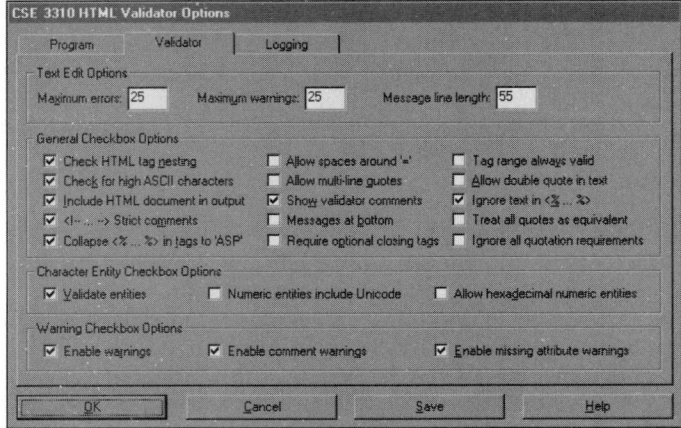

Figure B-14: Set up the HTML Validator to your specific parameters with the Validator options.

2. Complete the settings for Validator, and then do the same in the Program and Logging tabs. Save the settings.

3. Select Options ➪ Validator Settings and choose HTML Configuration. Set the options for closing tags and other settings.

4. Save your changes. Use the Save Config As option if you want to have multiple custom settings available to you.

When you have HTML Validator set up as desired, you're ready to use it to test code in your current document. Click the Validate Current Document button on the Main Toolbar, or select Tools ➪ Validate HTML. The results from the validation test appears in a new window below the current document. To find the code that corresponds to any error message, double-click it in the list.

Testing your links

Links change often, so it's important to do regular testing of your documents' links. HomeSite makes the task easier with its built-in Link Checker, shown in Figure B-15. Besides testing URLs, it also will check directory paths of images and other Web page elements specified in the current HTML document.

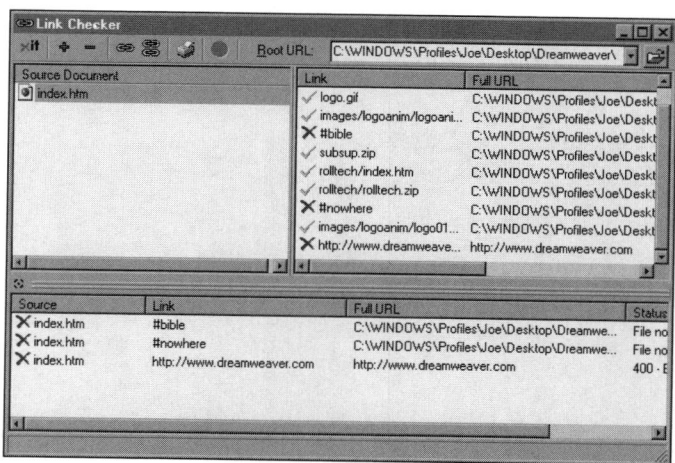

Figure B-15: Find orphan files and broken links through HomeSite's Link Checker.

Note that the Checker can't verify links to secure pages, FTP links, and mailto links. You need an active Internet connection to check remote URLs.

Follow these steps to use the Link Checker:

1. To start the Link Checker working on your current document, click the Verify Links button on the Main Toolbar, or select Tools ➪ Verify Links. A list is generated with each link's URL or path.

2. If you need to change the URL or the local directory, do this by selecting the path from the Root URL drop-down list. Use the Select Local Root browse button to set the root directory and drive against which local links should be tested.

3. Click the Verify Links button to begin the verification. The status of each link is updated as it is processed.

4. A check mark tells you that the link works. An X indicates that it's a failed link, which means that the document or file couldn't be located. Double-click an item in the Verifier List to find the code that refers to the failed link.

Document weight

This handy feature estimates the upload time of your current page. To find out how long it'll take you to upload a page, click the Document Weight button on the main toolbar or select Tools ➪ Document Weight. The Root URL setting in your FTP configuration is used to determine the relative path to files, and the results are displayed in the Document Weight dialog box (see Figure B-16).

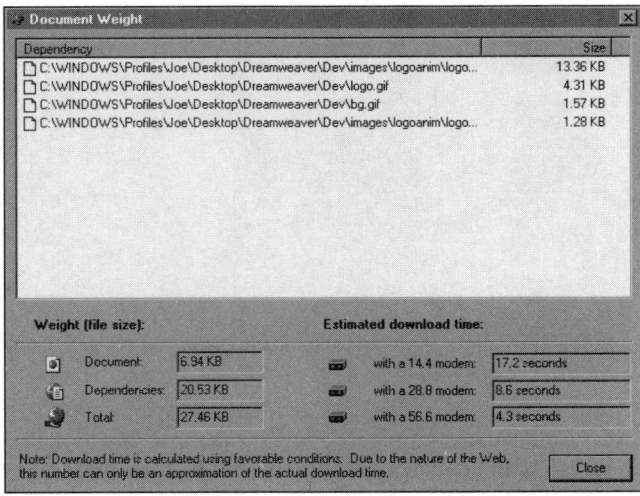

Figure B-16: It's a good idea to check on the probable download time for your Web page.

Creating Projects

If your Web site contains multiple files, you'll probably benefit by grouping the files as projects. HomeSite contains powerful project management features that help you organize your site or a collection of sites. Set up new projects using HomeSite's Project Wizard.

To create a new project, start by clicking the Projects tab at the bottom of the Resources window. From there, you have several alternatives. You can create a new project or import a project from an existing directory folder. There's a Project Wizard, as well, to help you out. To open the Project Wizard shown in Figure B-17, click the Create Project button in the Resources window. You can also start a new project by right-clicking in the Project folder area, or by selecting File ➪ New Project.

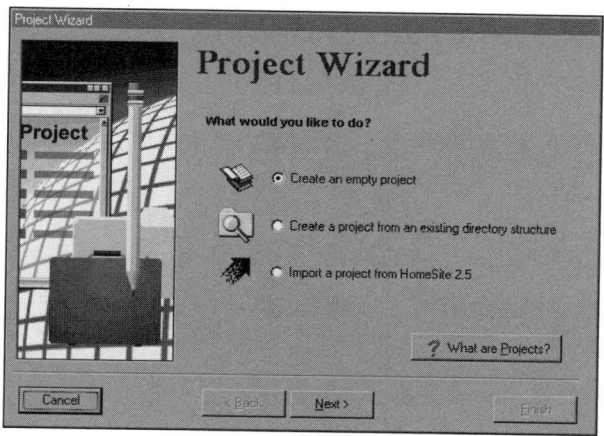

Figure B-17: Use the Project Wizard to start your new Web site.

The Project workspace gives you easy and organized access to related documents and files. The files in the project folders are pointers to your HTML documents. The documents are not physically moved or modified in any way.

Projects toolbar

When the Projects tab is open in the Resources window, you'll have access to the following tools:

Toggle Project List	Use the arrows to slide the Projects window open and closed.
Create Projects	Launches the Project Wizard.
Delete Project	Deletes the current project structure, but does not physically delete the project files from your hard drive or server. Just the project organization scheme is canceled.
Project Properties	Opens the Project Properties pane, where you can set the root URL and designate possible server maps for the project.
Create Folder	Creates new folders, at root level or inside a selected folder.
Delete Folder	Removes the current folder from the project. No files are physically deleted.
Upload Project	Launches the Upload Wizard.

Uploading a project to a server

Use the Upload Wizard to select and upload project files to a server. You can select from the list of server connections you have established in the Remote tab.

To upload a project, follow these steps:

1. First, launch the Upload Wizard by clicking the Upload Project button in the Project tab.

2. In the Upload Wizard, select a project in the Project Folder window, and then choose one of the file upload options: upload the entire site, or upload only the modified pages. Click Next.

3. Select the target server from the list in the Upload Wizard. (If the server you want is not on the list, close the Wizard and set up a protocol for an FTP connection.)

4. Enter the new name for your Root FTP Folder.

5. Select the necessary file and folder name options.

6. Click Next to start the upload. The uploaded files are displayed in the file list.

7. Click Finish to close the Upload Wizard.

Keyboard Shortcuts

As an alternative to using the pull-down menus, HomeSite 3.0 provides a full complement of keyboard commands, listed in Tables B-1 through B-4.

Table B-1 File Menu Keyboard Shortcuts	
File Command	*Keyboard Shortcut*
Open the New Document dialog box	Ctrl-N
Open an HTML document	Ctrl-O
Go to the next document	Ctrl-Tab
Go to previous document	Ctrl-Shift-Tab
Save current document	Ctrl-S
Save As	Ctrl-Shift-S
Print current document	Ctrl-P
Close current document	Ctrl-W
Exit from HomeSite	Ctrl-F4

Table B-2 Tag Selector Keyboard Shortcuts	
Tag	*Keyboard Shortcut*
Open the Tag Chooser	Ctrl-E
Open the Editor for the selected tag	F4
Open the Quick Start dialog box	Ctrl-Shift-Q
Open the Quick Anchor dialog box	Ctrl-Shift-A
Open the Table editor	Ctrl-Shift-T
Open the Frame wizard	Ctrl-Shift-W
Open the Quick Font dialog box	Ctrl-Shift-F

(continued)

Table B-2 (continued)

Tag	Keyboard Shortcut
Reduce font size by 1	Ctrl-Shift-- (hyphen)
Increase font size by 1	Ctrl-Shift-=
Open the Horizontal Rule editor	Ctrl-Shift-H
Open the Quick Image dialog box	Ctrl-Shift-I
Open the List editor	Ctrl-Shift-L
Convert selected text to an ordered list	Ctrl-Shift-O
Convert selected text to an unordered list	Ctrl-Shift-U
Insert a paragraph tab	Ctrl-Shift-P
Insert a break tag	Ctrl-Shift-B
Insert a break tag and line break	Ctrl-Enter
Insert a nonbreaking space	Ctrl-Shift-Spacebar
Insert a bold tag	Ctrl-B
Insert an italic tag	Ctrl-I
Insert an underline tag	Ctrl-U
Insert a center tag	Ctrl-Shift-C
Insert a comment tag	Ctrl-Shift-M
Insert heading levels 1–6	Ctrl-Shift-1 - 6
Insert empty ASP tags <% %>	Alt-%
Find matching tag	Ctrl-M
Repeat previous tag	Ctrl-Q
Go to the next tag	Ctrl-. (period)
Go to the previous tag	Ctrl-, (comma)
Special characters	Ctrl-Shift-E

Table B-3 Edit Menu Keyboard Shortcuts	
Edit Command	*Keyboard Shortcut*
Select all text in the current document	Ctrl-A
Copy selected text to the Clipboard	Ctrl-C
Cut the selection to the Clipboard	Ctrl-X
Paste selection from the Clipboard	Ctrl-V
Insert bookmark at the current line	Ctrl-Shift-K
Go to the bookmark	Ctrl-Shift-K (then select number)
Open the Find dialog box	Ctrl-F
Run the Find command again	F3
Open the Replace dialog box	Ctrl-R
Open the Extended Find and Replace dialog box	Ctrl-Shift-R
Open the Go To line number dialog box	Ctrl-G
Delete the current line	Ctrl-Y
Undo the previous edit	Ctrl-Z
Validate HTML in the current document	F6
Spell-check the current document	F7
Spell-check all open documents	Shift-F7
Open the special/extended character list	Ctrl-Shift-X
Indent the selected text block	Ctrl-Shift-. (period)
Unindent the selected text block	Ctrl-Shift-, (comma)

Table B-4
General Workspace Keyboard Shortcuts

Workspace Command	Keyboard Shortcut
Display the Tag toolbar	Ctrl-H
Display the Safety color palette	Ctrl-L
Display the Main toolbar	Ctrl-T
Display Help files	F1
Display HTML Help files	F2
Refresh the Resources file list	F5
Open the Options ⇨ Settings menu	F8
Toggle the Resources view	F9
Toggle Full Screen view	F10
View the current file in the external browser	F11
Toggle Editor/Browser views	F12

✦   ✦   ✦

Troubleshooting Dreamweaver

As with any complex software program, you run into difficulties with Dreamweaver from time to time. This appendix is intended to help you through some of those rough spots. You won't find answers to design problems here — the "How do I?" questions. Instead, this appendix helps with more fundamental questions about running Dreamweaver on your computer or network.

Because some of the issues here are platform-based, while others affect every implementation, this appendix is divided into a section each for Macintosh, Windows 95/NT, and General. If you can't find your answer here, investigate the following routes for seeking help:

✦ **Dreamweaver Support** — Macromedia runs an excellent help center on its Web site at

```
http://www.macromedia.com/support/
dreamweaver
```

Use the Search facility to examine the various Tech Notes at this site.

✦ **Dreamweaver Newsgroup** — For more specific feedback, join the Dreamweaver Newsgroup:

```
news://forums.macromedia.com/macromedia.
dreamweaver
```

Visited constantly by Macromedia support staff, Dreamweaver engineers, and informed professional developers, the newsgroup is a great place to get an answer for detailed problems or feedback on a new site. Highly recommended.

Macintosh

I'm having problems getting started. I turned off all the extensions, but nothing seems to help.

You may be experiencing some conflicts, but Dreamweaver needs certain extensions to work. Turn off all extensions but the following:

✦ Microsoft OLE Automation Version 2.06

✦ Microsoft OLE Extension Version 2.06

✦ Microsoft OLE Library Version 2.06

✦ WinSock Lib

What's the earliest Mac OS I can use to run Dreamweaver?

Although some Dreamweaver installers report that you need MacOS 7.5.5, Dreamweaver runs with 7.5.1 as well.

Why does the error message "Unable to create unnamed document" occur when I launch Dreamweaver?

This problem is due to an extensions conflict. Start with the extensions listed above and then, if necessary, add additional extensions one at a time to uncover the problem.

I just put a large image in my Dreamweaver page and now the screen is unreadable. What's the problem?

Very large images reduce the system resources. Allocating more RAM to Dreamweaver should help.

Keep in mind, in addition, that large images also mean substantially longer download times over the Web. Consider using a graphics program to reduce the size or number of colors in your image.

I've inserted an image that shows up fine in the browser preview, but I only get the placeholder in Dreamweaver. What's the cause?

Check to see if you entered the image source with a period and a slash, as in

```
./image.gif
```

Dreamweaver can't render this image correctly. Delete the period and slash, and the image should display in both the Document Window and the browser preview.

How can I stop my system from trying to go on line every time I launch Dreamweaver?

Chances are your PPP Control Panel is set to start up automatically whenever a TCP/IP connection is started by an application. Disable this optional feature to stop your system from trying to go on line.

When I preview my Web page with Netscape Navigator, why does it load into one of the frames instead of replacing the entire frameset?

Dreamweaver sends its previews to what is known as the top window. Normally this window replaces the entire frameset. A known problem with Netscape's browsers causes them to regard a selected window as the top window.

Two workarounds exist for this problem. First, close any open Navigator window before previewing your page. Second, if your previewed documents open in a frame, right-click (Shift-click) the frame to open the shortcut menu and select Open Frame in New Window.

Why can't I see my cursor when editing?

There is a conflict with the IXMicro Twin Turbo graphics card driver. You can download a new driver that corrects the problem at IXMicro's Web site:

```
www.ixmicro.com/download.htm
```

You also find instructions in their support area for proper installation.

Dreamweaver seems fairly sluggish — is there anything I can do to speed up response?

If you have many fonts active at one time, try reducing them for the project on which you're working. Some users have also reported that switching ATMs on their systems speeds up Dreamweaver's display considerably.

Windows 95/NT

My system crashes whenever I try to use the AfterShock utility. What's going on?

A crash occurs if you generate AfterShock outside of Dreamweaver and there are no object tags inside of the AfterShock comments. To avoid the crash, add the `<object> </object>` tags inside the Aftershock comments before cutting and pasting them.

I dragged and dropped a file on the Dreamweaver icon to start the program, and now all my links have a "../" in front of them. Why?

There's a known problem with using the drag-and-drop method for starting Dreamweaver. If the name of the folder containing the file is more than eight characters long, Dreamweaver misinterprets the name and adds the designation for a parent folder (../) to the front of the name. Files opened through the menu don't exhibit this behavior.

General

I'm constantly getting JavaScript errors when using layers, but I don't see anything wrong. What should I check?

Most of the problems that crop up with layers regard the layer's name. Each layer must have a unique name in the document — not just a unique name among the layers. Layer names must also be straight alphanumeric characters. No special characters, such as the underscore, hyphen, asterisk, and ampersand are allowed.

I've noticed that after working on a page for a while, Dreamweaver slows down noticeably. Can anything be done?

Dreamweaver keeps track of all your editing actions for its multiple Undo capability. If you haven't saved your document in a long time, the system resources can be affected. Saving your document clears the Undo stack and restores more memory to your system.

When using SiteFTP, I connect to my site but only see the root folder with no files or subfolders. What's wrong?

The Directory Listing Style of your Web server is set to DOS. Have your system administrator set the Directory Listing Style to UNIX. If appropriate, you can switch to Dreamweaver 1.2; this issue is strictly a Dreamweaver 1.0 problem.

When I select the Autoplay and Loop check boxes in a timeline, Dreamweaver says that the behaviors are not found. What can I do?

You can use two workarounds for this problem. First, on a Windows system, open Windows Explorer or any folder window, and then choose View ⇨ Options. Deselect the option for Hide MS-DOS File Extensions for File Types That Are Registered. Restart Dreamweaver.

Alternatively, rather than using the Autoplay setting, attach a Play Timeline behavior to frame 1 of your timeline. Likewise, to substitute for the Loop option, attach a Play Timeline behavior to frame 1 and add another behavior (a Go to Timeline Frame behavior) to the last frame of your timeline. Set the first frame as the one to "go to."

✦   ✦   ✦

What's On the CD-ROM

The CD-ROM that accompanies *Dreamweaver Bible* contains:

✦ A fully-functioning demo of Dreamweaver 1.2

✦ All the code examples used in the book

Also included are a wide range of Dreamweaver items designed to make your work more productive:

✦ Behaviors

✦ Objects

✦ Style Sheets

✦ Templates

✦ Browser Profiles

Using the CD-ROM

The CD-ROM is what is known as a *hybrid* CD-ROM, which means it contains files that run on more than one computer platform—in this case, both Windows 95 and Macintosh computers.

Only two files, the Dreamweaver trial program and the Beatnik player, are compressed. Double-click these files to begin the installation procedure. All other files on the CD-ROM are uncompressed and can be simply copied from the CD-ROM to your system by using your file manager.

The file structure of the CD-ROM replicates the structure that Dreamweaver sets up when it is installed. For example, objects found in the Dreamweaver\Configuration\Objects folder are located in both the CD-ROM and the installed program.

Files and Programs on the CD-ROM

Dreamweaver Bible contains a host of programs and auxiliary files to assist your exploration of Dreamweaver, as well as your Web page design work in general. Following is a description of the files and programs on the CD-ROM.

Dreamweaver demo

If you haven't had a chance to work with Dreamweaver, the CD-ROM offers a fully-functioning demonstration version of Dreamweaver 1.2 for both Macintosh and Windows 95/NT systems. The demo can be used for 30 days; it cannot be reinstalled for additional use time.

To install the demo, simply double-click the Dreamweaver icon in the Dreamweaver folder of the CD-ROM, and follow the installation instructions on your screen.

Trial versions of BBEdit and HomeSite, the external text editors supplied with the commercial version of Dreamweaver, are not included on the CD-ROM. You can download demos of both programs at the Web sites for these products, however.

Bare Bones Software for BBEdit:

    http://www.bbedit.com/

Allaire Software for HomeSite:

    http://www.allaire.com

Dreamweaver Behaviors

Dreamweaver Behaviors automate many functions that previously required extensive JavaScript programming. The Behaviors included on the CD-ROM are in addition to the standard set of behaviors included with Dreamweaver and discussed in Chapter 17, "Creating and Using Behaviors." The behaviors on the CD-ROM are stored in the Dreamweaver\Configuration\Behaviors\Actions folder. Copy the behaviors to a similarly named folder in your system installation of Dreamweaver, and restart Dreamweaver to access the new behaviors.

Table D-1 lists the Dreamweaver Behaviors available on the CD-ROM.

Table D-1
Behaviors on the CD-ROM

Behavior	Description
Add A Groovoid	Adds a Groovoid sound effect, playable with the Beatnik plug-in.
Center Layers	Allows layers to be centered automatically on any screen resolution.
Check Mime	Looks for a specific MIME type and redirects the user to a different URL if it is not found.
Conditional	Implements a form of If-Then-Else statements.
Execute Custom Code	Inserts any custom JavaScript code.
Filters-Transitions	Implements the Cascading Style Sheet filters and transitions.
Get Cookie	Allows you to retrieve a cookie previously set and assign it to a variable.
Persist Layer	Causes a layer to stay in the same relation to the browser window, regardless of how much the page scrolls.
Persist Layer Stop	Ends the Persist Layer Behavior.
Resize Layers Patch	Applies a workaround for the Navigator bug that causes layers to lose their position when the browser window is resized.
Set Cookie	Allows you to set a cookie and the number of days until it expires.
Show-Hide Layers for Objects	Allows layers to be displayed or hidden in objects and behaviors.
Watch	Implements a watch command that triggers programmable JavaScript if a particular property is changed.

Behavior Development Kit: The Behaviors folder on the CD-ROM contains a copy of Macromedia's Behavior Development Kit (BDK). The BDK contains detailed instructions on how to create your own Dreamweaver Behaviors. Much of the information can also be applied to creating your own Dreamweaver Objects.

Dreamweaver Bible code examples

Example code used in the Dreamweaver Bible can be found in the Code folder of the CD-ROM. Also included and of particular note are the Dreamweaver Techniques from various chapters throughout the book. Each Technique contains all the requisite example HTML files and graphics files within its own folder. You can easily view the files through Dreamweaver or your browser without transferring the files to your system. If you do wish to transfer the files, copy the entire folder over to your system.

Dreamweaver browser profiles

Dreamweaver recognizes the proliferation of browsers on the market today and makes it easy for you to check your Web page creations against specific browser types. The browser targeting capability is available through the use of Browser Profiles, covered in Chapter 25, "Maximizing Browser Targeting." In addition to the standard profiles that come with Dreamweaver 1.2, the CD-ROM contains several Browser Profiles for checking various implementations of HTML, including the following:

- ✦ HTML 2.0
- ✦ HTML 3.2
- ✦ HTML 4.0
- ✦ Opera 3.2
- ✦ Pocket Internet Explorer 1.0 (for Windows CE 1.0)
- ✦ Pocket Internet Explorer 1.1 (for Windows CE 1.0)
- ✦ Pocket Internet Explorer 2.0 (for Windows CE 2.0)

Each additional Browser Profile is contained in the Dreamweaver\Configuration\BrowserProfiles folder of the CD-ROM. To install the Browser profiles, the files must be copied to a similarly named folder in your system installation of Dreamweaver. Restart Dreamweaver to access the new Browser Profiles.

Dreamweaver Objects

Much of Dreamweaver's power derives from its extensibility. Each of the standard Dreamweaver Objects is based on an HTML file. The CD-ROM contains various Dreamweaver Objects designed to help you create your Web pages faster and more efficiently.

Each Dreamweaver Object consists of two files: an HTML file, and a GIF file with the same name that is used to create the button on the Object palette. For example, the Character Entities Object comprises the two files char_entities.htm and char_entities.gif.

Table D-2 lists the Dreamweaver Objects available on the CD-ROM.

Table D-2			
Dreamweaver Objects on the CD-ROM			
Object	*Filenames*	*Folder*	*Description*
ActiveMovie	amovie.htm amovie.gif	Media	Inserts an ActiveMovie/Audio file.
Beatnik	beatnik.htm beatnik.gif	Media	Inserts a Beatnik audio file.
Character Entities	char_entities.htm char_entities.gif	New	Inserts any Upper ASCII character.
DynSrc	dynsrc.htm dynsrc.gif	Media	Inserts a DynSrc tag and attributes for a Internet Explorer movie.
Enhanced Table	e_table.htm e_table.gif	Common	Allows additional table attributes (including attributes specific to Internet Explorer) to be inserted.
NewBreak	new_break.htm new_break.gif	Invisibles	Enhanced line break object.
QuickTime	qtime.htm qtime.gif	Media	Inserts QuickTime and QuickTimeVR movies.
Sub	sub.htm sub.htm	Invisibles	Inserts the $\langle sub \rangle$ tag for subscripted text.
Sup	sup.htm sup.htm	Invisibles	Inserts the $\langle sup \rangle$ tag for superscripted text.

To install the Dreamweaver Objects, go to Dreamweaver\Configuration\Objects\ and copy any pair of files from the subfolders Common, Forms, Invisibles, Media, and New to similarly named folders in your system installation of Dreamweaver. (The Media and New folders are not included in the standard release of Dreamweaver and must be created on your system.) Restart Dreamweaver to access the new Objects.

Dreamweaver style sheets

Dreamweaver makes using Cascading Style Sheets (CSS) a point-and-click affair. One of the great features of CSS is the ability to link your Web site to external style sheets. The CD-ROM contains several external style sheets that you can customize for your Web sites. Each external style sheet comes with an example HTML file that you can view in your browser.

To incorporate the external style sheets in your Web sites, copy the file with the .css extension into your local site root folder. Then follow the instructions in the "Linking to an External Style Sheet" section in Chapter 22.

Dreamweaver templates

One of the best ways to begin working in Web design is to customize another's designs. The CD-ROM includes several Web page templates aimed at giving you a running start in creating your own pages. Each template is found in its own subfolder in the Dreamweaver\Templates folder.

You can use these templates in two ways from within Dreamweaver:

+ Open them directly from the CD-ROM by using the File ➪ Open command.
+ Transfer the files to the Dreamweaver\Templates folder and use the Help ➪ Open Templates command after you've restarted Dreamweaver.

External programs

To extend their multimedia functionality, browsers use a fair number of plug-ins and external programs. The CD-ROM contains Beatnik Player, the plug-in from HeadSpace, Inc. To install the Beatnik Player, just double-click the icon in the External Programs folder and follow the instructions on your screen. The Beatnik® Player is © 1998 Headspace®, Inc.

The External Programs folder also contains an HTML file called the Beatnik Interactive Groovoid Page. Groovoids are small sound bytes that you can use to add audio feedback to your Web pages. Fifty samples are built into the Beatnik Player, and you can hear them by opening the Beatnik Interactive Groovoid Page and selecting a sound name.

Web resource directory

The World Wide Web is a vital resource for any Web designer, whether you're a seasoned professional or a beginner. The CD-ROM contains an HTML page with a series of links to resources on the Web; the series contains general as well as Dreamweaver-specific references.

✦   ✦   ✦

Index

(continued)

(continued)

(continued)

(continued)

Y

yellow highlights in Library items, 624

Z

Z-Index attribute, 531, 553, 558–559

IDG BOOKS WORLDWIDE, INC.
END-USER LICENSE AGREEMENT

<u>**READ THIS.**</u> You should carefully read these terms and conditions before opening the software packet(s) included with this book ("Book"). This is a license agreement ("Agreement") between you and IDG Books Worldwide, Inc. ("IDGB"). By opening the accompanying software packet(s), you acknowledge that you have read and accept the following terms and conditions. If you do not agree and do not want to be bound by such terms and conditions, promptly return the Book and the unopened software packet(s) to the place you obtained them for a full refund.

1. <u>**License Grant.**</u> IDGB grants to you (either an individual or entity) a nonexclusive license to use one copy of the enclosed software program(s) (collectively, the "Software") solely for your own personal or business purposes on a single computer (whether a standard computer or a workstation component of a multiuser network). The Software is in use on a computer when it is loaded into temporary memory (RAM) or installed into permanent memory (hard disk, CD-ROM, or other storage device). IDGB reserves all rights not expressly granted herein.

2. <u>**Ownership.**</u> IDGB is the owner of all right, title, and interest, including copyright, in and to the compilation of the Software recorded on the disk(s) or CD-ROM ("Software Media"). Copyright to the individual programs recorded on the Software Media is owned by the author or other authorized copyright owner of each program. Ownership of the Software and all proprietary rights relating thereto remain with IDGB and its licensers.

3. <u>**Restrictions On Use and Transfer.**</u>

    (a) You may only (i) make one copy of the Software for backup or archival purposes, or (ii) transfer the Software to a single hard disk, provided that you keep the original for backup or archival purposes. You may not (i) rent or lease the Software, (ii) copy or reproduce the Software through a LAN or other network system or through any computer subscriber system or bulletin-board system, or (iii) modify, adapt, or create derivative works based on the Software.

    (b) You may not reverse engineer, decompile, or disassemble the Software. You may transfer the Software and user documentation on a permanent basis, provided that the transferee agrees to accept the terms and conditions of this Agreement and you retain no copies. If the Software is an update or has been updated, any transfer must include the most recent update and all prior versions.

4. **Restrictions On Use of Individual Programs.** You must follow the individual requirements and restrictions detailed for each individual program in Appendix D of this Book. These limitations are also contained in the individual license agreements recorded on the Software Media. These limitations may include a requirement that after using the program for a specified period of time, the user must pay a registration fee or discontinue use. By opening the Software packet(s), you will be agreeing to abide by the licenses and restrictions for these individual programs that are detailed in Appendix D and on the Software Media. None of the material on this Software Media or listed in this Book may ever be redistributed, in original or modified form, for commercial purposes.

5. **Limited Warranty.**

   (a) IDGB warrants that the Software and Software Media are free from defects in materials and workmanship under normal use for a period of sixty (60) days from the date of purchase of this Book. If IDGB receives notification within the warranty period of defects in materials or workmanship, IDGB will replace the defective Software Media.

   (b) IDGB AND THE AUTHOR OF THE BOOK DISCLAIM ALL OTHER WARRANTIES, EXPRESS OR IMPLIED, INCLUDING WITHOUT LIMITATION IMPLIED WARRANTIES OF MERCHANTABILITY AND FITNESS FOR A PARTICULAR PURPOSE, WITH RESPECT TO THE SOFTWARE, THE PROGRAMS, THE SOURCE CODE CONTAINED THEREIN, AND/OR THE TECHNIQUES DESCRIBED IN THIS BOOK. IDGB DOES NOT WARRANT THAT THE FUNCTIONS CONTAINED IN THE SOFTWARE WILL MEET YOUR REQUIREMENTS OR THAT THE OPERATION OF THE SOFTWARE WILL BE ERROR FREE.

   (c) This limited warranty gives you specific legal rights, and you may have other rights that vary from jurisdiction to jurisdiction.

6. **Remedies.**

   (a) IDGB's entire liability and your exclusive remedy for defects in materials and workmanship shall be limited to replacement of the Software Media, which may be returned to IDGB with a copy of your receipt at the following address: Software Media Fulfillment Department, Attn.: *Dreamweaver Bible*, IDG Books Worldwide, Inc., 7260 Shadeland Station, Ste. 100, Indianapolis, IN 46256, or call 1-800-762-2974. Please allow three to four weeks for delivery. This Limited Warranty is void if failure of the Software Media has resulted from accident, abuse, or misapplication. Any replacement Software Media will be warranted for the remainder of the original warranty period or thirty (30) days, whichever is longer.

(b) In no event shall IDGB or the author be liable for any damages whatsoever (including without limitation damages for loss of business profits, business interruption, loss of business information, or any other pecuniary loss) arising from the use of or inability to use the Book or the Software, even if IDGB has been advised of the possibility of such damages.

(c) Because some jurisdictions do not allow the exclusion or limitation of liability for consequential or incidental damages, the above limitation or exclusion may not apply to you.

7. **<u>U.S. Government Restricted Rights.</u>** Use, duplication, or disclosure of the Software by the U.S. Government is subject to restrictions stated in paragraph (c)(1)(ii) of the Rights in Technical Data and Computer Software clause of DFARS 252.227-7013, and in subparagraphs (a) through (d) of the Commercial Computer — Restricted Rights clause at FAR 52.227-19, and in similar clauses in the NASA FAR supplement, when applicable.

8. **<u>General.</u>** This Agreement constitutes the entire understanding of the parties and revokes and supersedes all prior agreements, oral or written, between them and may not be modified or amended except in a writing signed by both parties hereto that specifically refers to this Agreement. This Agreement shall take precedence over any other documents that may be in conflict herewith. If any one or more provisions contained in this Agreement are held by any court or tribunal to be invalid, illegal, or otherwise unenforceable, each and every other provision shall remain in full force and effect.

my2cents.idgbooks.com

Register This Book — And Win!

Visit **http://my2cents.idgbooks.com** to register this book and we'll automatically enter you in our fantastic monthly prize giveaway. It's also your opportunity to give us feedback: let us know what you thought of this book and how you would like to see other topics covered.

Discover IDG Books Online!

The IDG Books Online Web site is your online resource for tackling technology — at home and at the office. Frequently updated, the IDG Books Online Web site features exclusive software, insider information, online books, and live events!

10 Productive & Career-Enhancing Things You Can Do at www.idgbooks.com

- Nab source code for your own programming projects.

- Download software.

- Read Web exclusives: special articles and book excerpts by IDG Books Worldwide authors.

- Take advantage of resources to help you advance your career as a Novell or Microsoft professional.

- Buy IDG Books Worldwide titles or find a convenient bookstore that carries them.

- Register your book and win a prize.

- Chat live online with authors.

- Sign up for regular e-mail updates about our latest books.

- Suggest a book you'd like to read or write.

- Give us your 2¢ about our books and about our Web site.

You say you're not on the Web yet? It's easy to get started with IDG Books' *Discover the Internet,* available at local retailers everywhere.

CD-ROM Installation Instructions

The *Dreamweaver Bible* CD-ROM contains a trial version of Dreamweaver as well as a full complement of auxiliary files such as Dreamweaver Objects and Behaviors.

Accessing the programs on the CD-ROM

Only two files, the Dreamweaver trial program and the Beatnik player, are compressed. Double-click these files to begin the installation procedure (Dreamweaver installation instructions are listed below). All other files on the CD-ROM are uncompressed and can be simply copied from the CD-ROM to your system by using your file manager.

The file structure of the CD-ROM replicates the structure that Dreamweaver sets up when it is installed. For example, objects found in the Dreamweaver\Configuration\Objects folder are located on both the CD-ROM and the installed program.

For a detailed synopsis of the CD-ROM contents, see Appendix D, "What's On the CD-ROM."

Installing Dreamweaver

To install Dreamweaver on your Windows system, follow these steps:

1. Insert the *Dreamweaver Bible* CD-ROM into your CD-ROM drive.
2. Double-click the dreamweaver.exe file to unpack it and begin the installation process.
3. Follow the onscreen instructions. Accept the default options for program location.

To install Dreamweaver on your Macintosh system, follow these steps:

1. Insert the *Dreamweaver Bible* CD-ROM into your CD-ROM drive.
2. Double-click the Dreamweaver program file; the filename depends on which version you've downloaded. This action unpacks Dreamweaver and begins the installation process.
3. Follow the onscreen instructions. Accept the default options for program location.